Christ Our Hope

Christ Our Hope

An Introduction to Eschatology

Paul O'Callaghan

The Catholic University of America Press • Washington, D.C.

Copyright © 2011
The Catholic University of America Press
All rights reserved
The paper used in this publication meets the minimum requirements of
American National Standards for Information Science—Permanence
of Paper for Printed Library Materials, ANSI Z39.48-1984.
∞

Library of Congress Cataloging-in-Publication Data
O'Callaghan, Paul.
Christ our hope : an introduction to eschatology / Paul O'Callaghan.
p. cm.
Includes bibliographical references and index.
ISBN 978-0-8132-1862-5 (pbk. : alk. paper)   1. Escatology.   2. Hope—
Religious aspects—Christianity.   3. Catholic Church—Doctrines.   I. Title.
BT821.3.O23 2011
236—dc22   2010050050

Contents

Preface vii
Principal Abbreviations xv

Part One. The Dynamic of Hope
    1. The Christian Virtue of Hope and the Epistemological Underpinnings of Christian Eschatology 3

Part Two. The Object of Christian Hope
    2. *Parousia:* The Future Coming of the Lord Jesus in Glory 39
    3. The Resurrection of the Dead 74
    4. The New Heavens and the New Earth 115
    5. Final Judgment 130
    6. Heaven: Eternal Life in the Glory of Christ 149
    7. Hell: The Perpetual Retribution of the Sinner 189

Part Three. The Stimulus of Hope in the World
    8. The Living Presence of the *Parousia* 225

Part Four. Honing and Purifying Christian Hope
    9. Death, the End of the Human Pilgrimage 253
    10. Purgatory: The Purification of the Elect 286
    11. The Implications of an "Intermediate Eschatology" 309

Part Five. The Power and Light of Hope
    12. The Central Role of Christian Eschatology in Theology 329

Selected Bibliography 339
General Index 341
Index of Names 349

Preface

Pope Benedict XVI named his 2007 Encyclical *Spe salvi*, "saved in hope," citing a text from Paul's letter to the Romans: "in hope we are saved" (Rom 8:24). The essence of Christian salvation is hope. The secret of Christian faith is hope. The most precious contribution Christianity makes to the world is hope. Christ, who speaks through his body, the Church, does not promise humans perfect happiness or fulfillment on earth. Christian faith does not claim to resolve and explain here and now the world's many problems and perplexities. Indeed, as we read in the letter to the Hebrews (13:14), "Here we have no lasting city." Rather, Christians believe primarily that through his Son Jesus Christ God has offered humanity *salvation:* salvation from sin, salvation leading toward eternal, loving communion with the Trinity. But salvation from sin is a gradual, laborious, lifelong process. And perfect, conscious union with God, though entirely dependent on grace, involves a drawn-out, arduous purification. That is why when as Christians we say "we are saved," we must add, *spe salvi*, we are saved in hope. We live off hope. And hope is what gives life surety, gaiety, lightness of touch; it serves as a living bond between the other two theological virtues that rule Christian life: faith and charity.[1] For the Christian Gospel, the saving power of Christ, is essentially eschatological.

The purpose of this text, *Christ Our Hope*, is twofold. First, to present the principal elements of Christian eschatology, that is, the *content or object of hope:* the coming of Jesus Christ in glory at the end of time, the resurrection of the dead, the renewal of the cosmos and judgment of humanity, followed by eternal life for those who have been faithful to God, or its perpetual loss for those who have not. And second, to consider the *stimulus of hope* on the present life, how it should and how it does influence human behavior and experience, how it shapes anthropology, ethics, spirituality. And all this in the context of the great challenge all religions strive to respond to: *death*, what Paul calls "the last enemy" (1 Cor 15:26).[2]

---

1. Charles Péguy compared hope with a small girl who confidingly holds the hand of her two older sisters, who represent faith and charity; see his work *Le porche du mystère de la deuxième vertu* (Paris: Gallimard, 1929).

2. See my study "Death," with F. Tiso, *Religions of the World: A Comprehensive Encyclopedia of Beliefs and Practices*, ed. J. G. Melton and M. Baumann, 2nd ed., 4 vols. (Santa Barbara, Calif.: ABC-CLIO, 2010), vol. 1.

In many ways the work is classic in its structure. But a lot of water has passed under the eschatological bridge over the last century and a half, and students of the last things, as Hans Urs von Balthasar once said, have of late been working extraordinary hours.³ In any case, I wish to draw attention to six salient features of the text.

First and foremost, the *Christological* underpinning of all eschatology. For Christ is our hope: he is the way to the Father, but also in person he is the truth, the ultimate object of faith and the living Reality humans will have to confront at the end of their lives, and the life, that life that derives from God for humans and is destined to become eternal, everlasting. Nobody can "come to the Father," either in this life or the next, Jesus tells us, "except through me" (Jn 14:6). Eschatology is entirely conditioned by Christology. It is its inner complement. As Jean Daniélou has cogently shown,⁴ should the Church forfeit its eschatology, it would be forced sooner or later to forfeit its redeemer and Savior, Jesus Christ, and as a result its ecclesiology, anthropology, ethics, and spirituality. Biblical studies over the last century or so have shown, beyond a shadow of doubt, that the identity, message, and saving work of Jesus Christ are profoundly eschatological. Christ is the One who provides the content and gives unity to the entire treatise of eschatology. Specifically, I will argue that New Testament eschatology offers a Christological reworking of traditional apocalyptic material, a thesis I have developed at length elsewhere.⁵ What this means should become clear as the text develops.

A second area of interest is the *pneumatological* side of eschatology. Christian faith situates eschatology in the third and final part of the Creed, dedicated to the Holy Spirit. It is true that Christ saves those who believe in him, communicating to them the gift of eternal life, explaining to them the content of the afterlife. But Jesus is the Christ, the Anointed One, the One who is filled with the Holy Spirit from the moment of his conception. As such, he saves us by sending—with the Father—the Holy Spirit, who is always the "Spirit of Christ." On this account, as we shall see, the Spirit is the "cause and power of hope," the gently insistent driving force behind hope, the one who introduces the paternal life, love, and truth of God into the hearts of believers, one by one, the one that makes hope concretely possible.

In the third place, of course, each topic will be addressed in the context and *horizon of hope*. The "last things" are not yet at our disposition, they have

---

3. See H. U. von Balthasar, "Eschatology," in *Theology Today*, vol. 1: *Renewal in Theology*, ed. J. Feiner, J. Trütsch, and F. Böckle (Milwaukee: Bruce Publishing, 1965), 222–44, here 222.

4. J. Daniélou, "Christologie et eschatologie," in *Das Konzil von Chalkedon. Geschichte und Gegenwart*, ed. A. Grillmeier and H. Bacht (Würzburg: Echter, 1954), vol. 3, 269–86.

5. See my work *The Christological Assimilation of the Apocalypse: An Essay on Fundamental Eschatology* (Dublin: Four Courts, 2004), abbreviated henceforth as *CAA*.

not yet been definitively revealed; that is, we still hope for them. Thus the epistemological key—the hermeneutic—for grasping the meaning of eschatological statements is hope. This principle should be clear enough when we are considering eternal life, perpetual union with God, for which we have been destined as creatures made "in the image and likeness of God" (Gn 1:27). It is somewhat more complex, however, though no less important, to appreciate when applied to other aspects of the eschatological promise, for example, resurrection of the dead and universal judgment.

A fourth area of considerable importance throughout the work may be termed *anthropological consistency*. Many of the hurdles experienced by believers in respect of Christian teaching on eschatology are of a practical, anthropological kind. Does it make sense to say that humans will live on forever? Will the vision of God truly satisfy the human heart? Or will it not absorb the human subject completely? Does the promise of communion with God distract humans from improving the world they now live in? Is it meaningful to claim that some humans, through their own fault, may be permanently excluded from the presence of their Creator? What destiny awaits the human body in the context of the eschatological promise? What kind of body will rise up? Will it retain its sexual character? Of the good things God created for us and gave us—our history, human society, the fruits of our work, the material world—how much will last and live on forever? And how much will have to be left behind? Is it possible in Christian eschatology to integrate the individual and collective sides of the human subject? As we shall see, the reply to these questions must be vouched for in strictly theological terms, for *eschatology is theology*, in that God is the one who creates man and promises the gift of eternal life. God is the one who responds (or should respond) to the questions and perplexities that arise in the human heart. Yet God's gifts are conditioned in an eschatological way, and so therefore is human response. We shall fully grasp what God wanted of us on earth, and what human identity consists of, only at the end of time. That is to say, our reflection on the last things is marked necessarily by what is called an "eschatological reserve."

Five, from the methodological point of view, the message of *the entire New Testament* is essential to eschatology, in that we stand totally in need of divine Revelation in order to know the content of the divine promise. By its very nature eschatology rests on "revelation" (the translation of the Greek term *apokalypsis*),[6] on

---

6. For the transliteration of Greek and Aramaic terms, I have followed the rules indicated in P. H. Alexander et al., eds., *The SBL Style Handbook. For Ancient Near Eastern, Biblical, and Early Christian Studies* (Peabody (MA): Hendrickson, 1999), 26–29. The titles of studies containing Greek terms, however, will be cited as in the original.

God's word of promise. It goes without saying, of course, that Scripture must be interpreted in a Christological way, for Christ in person is "the resurrection and the life" (Jn 11:25). Besides, special attention has been paid throughout the book to the works of the *Fathers of the Church*, whose theology is based substantially on sacred Scripture. We have been particularly attentive to Cyprian, Irenaeus, Origen, Tertullian, Hillary of Poitiers, Gregory of Nyssa, Jerome, Augustine, and Maximus the Confessor.[7]

In the sixth place, among the *theologians* that receive special attention, Thomas Aquinas figures highly. For Aquinas, the "last end" critically determines all aspects of anthropology, creation, and ethical life, and in turn is determined Christologically; this may be seen in the respective prologues of the *I-II* and the *III pars* of the *Summa theologiae*.[8] Among contemporary authors, I have frequently drawn on the writings of the Lutheran theologian Wolfhart Pannenberg, whose entire theology is structured from an eschatological standpoint.

Much has been written on eschatology over recent decades, and many excellent manuals are available in a variety of languages and from different theological backgrounds.[9] Contributions by American scholars, or influential works published in the United States by English or German authors, have been abundant in the area of eschatology. Textbooks of eschatology[10] are generally speaking based

---

7. I have made extensive use of B. E. Daley, *The Hope of the Early Church: A Handbook of Patristic Eschatology*, 3rd ed. (Cambridge: Cambridge University Press, 1995).

8. See M. L. Lamb, "The Eschatology of St Thomas Aquinas," in *Aquinas on Doctrine: A Critical Introduction*, ed. T. G. Weinandy, D. A. Keating, and J. Yocum (London: T. & T. Clark, 2004), 225–40.

9. Among others, see J. J. Alviar, *Escatología* (Pamplona: Eunsa, 2004); G. Ancona, *Escatologia cristiana* (Brescia: Queriniana, 2003); G. Biffi, *Linee di escatologia cristiana* (Milano: Jaca Book, 1984); M. Bordoni and N. Ciola, *Gesù nostra speranza. Saggio di escatologia in prospettiva trinitaria*, 2nd ed. (Bologna: Dehoniane, 2000); G. Colzani, *La vita eterna: inferno, purgatorio, paradiso* (Milano: A. Mondadori, 2001); G. Gozzelino, *Nell'attesa della beata speranza. Saggio di escatologia cristiana* (Leumann [Torino]: Elle di Ci, 1993); G. Greshake, *Stärker als der Tod. Zukunft, Tod, Auferstehung, Himmel, Hölle, Fegfeur* (Mainz: M. Grünewald, 1976); R. Guardini, *The Last Things* (orig. 1949; New York: Pantheon, 1954); R. Lavatori, *Il Signore verrà nella gloria* (Bologna: Dehoniane, 2007); W. Pannenberg, *Systematic Theology*, vol. 3 (Edinburgh: T. & T. Clark, 1998); the other two volumes of Pannenberg's *Systematic Theology* were published in English in 1991 and 1994; C. Pozo, *La teología del más allá*, 3rd ed. (Madrid: BAC, 1992); J. Ratzinger, *Eschatology: Death and Eternal Life* (Washington, D.C.: The Catholic University of America Press, 1988); J. L. Ruiz de la Peña, *La pascua de la creación* (Madrid: BAC, 1996); M. Schmaus, *Katholische Dogmatik*, vol. 4.2: *Von den letzten Dingen* (orig. 1948; München: Hüber, 1959); A. Ziegenaus, *Katholische Dogmatik*, vol. 8: *Die Zukunft der Schöpfung in Gott: Eschatologie* (Aachen: MM, 1996).

10. Recent American systematic texts on eschatology include (in chronological order): E. J. Fortman, *Everlasting Life after Death* (New York: Alba House, 1976); H. Schwarz, "Eschatology," in *Christian Dogmatics*, ed. C. E. Braaten and R. W. Jenson (Philadelphia: Fortress Press, 1984), vol. 2, 471–587; D. A. Lane, "Eschatology," in *The New Dictionary of Theology*, ed. J. A. Komonchak, M. Collins, and D. A. Lane (Wilmington, Del.: Glazier, 1987), 329–42; Z. Hayes, *Visions of a Future: A Study of Christian Eschatology* (Wilmington, Del.: Glazier, 1989); J. T. O'Connor, *Land of the Living: A Theology of the Last*

on Scripture; several of them are centered on the dynamics of the virtue of hope. Important, indeed essential, contributions have been made by American scholars in the area of biblical studies, especially in the field of apocalyptics.[11] Patristic and medieval studies are likewise frequent.[12]

Yet it is fair to say that the most significant American contributions relate to the influence of Christian eschatology on the life of society and individuals. Of particular interest are contributions made in the study of eschatology from the perspective of art and literature.[13] The anthropological implications of eschatology are commonly considered, often in tandem with works in Christian apologetics[14] and philosophy.[15] Special attention is paid to works dealing with: the dynamics of hope (in particular Ernst Bloch and Gabriel Marcel),[16] process theology (in dialogue with Alfred N. Whitehead and John B. Cobb),[17] and the question of the human soul and its immortality in the context of Scholastic philosophy.[18]

Things (New York: Catholic Books, 1992); R. Martin, *The Last Things: Death, Judgment, Heaven, Hell* (San Francisco: Ignatius Press, 1998); R. W. Jenson, "The Fulfillment," in *Systematic Theology*, vol. 2: *The Works of God* (New York: Oxford University Press, 1999), 307–69; H. Schwarz, *Eschatology* (Grand Rapids: W. B. Eerdmans, 2000); A. J. Kelly, *Eschatology and Hope* (Maryknoll, N.Y.: Orbis Books, 2006); N. T. Wright, *Surprised by Hope: Rethinking Heaven, the Resurrection, and the Mission of the Church* (New York: HarperOne, 2008).

11. See especially the bibliographical section of my work *CAA* 299–329, and chapter 2 of this text. Of special importance in the area of apocalyptics and eschatology must be included the writings (in alphabetical order) of D. C. Allison, R. J. Bauckham, G. R. Beasley-Murray, J. H. Charlesworth, J. J. Collins, P. Hanson, B. McGinn, G. W. E. Nickelsburg, M. E. Stone, and J. C. VanderKam, most of whom are Americans.

12. We have already mentioned B. E. Daley, *The Hope*. Many other studies on the Fathers written in English are cited throughout these pages.

13. See, for example, M. Himmelfarb, *Tours of Hell* (Philadelphia: Fortress, 1985); C. McDannell and B. Lang, *Heaven: A History* (New Haven, Conn.: Yale University Press, 1988); A. E. Bernstein, *The Formation of Hell: Death and Retribution in the Ancient and Early Christian Worlds* (London: UCL Press, 1993); J. B. Russell, *A History of Heaven: The Singing Silence* (Princeton, N.J.: Princeton University Press, 1997), with extensive bibliography. The study of C. W. Bynum, *The Resurrection of the Body in Western Christianity, 200–1336* (New York: Columbia University Press, 1995), is particularly interesting.

14. See P. Kreeft, *Heaven: The Heart's Deepest Longing*, 2nd ed. (San Francisco: Ignatius Press, 1990); idem., *Love Is Stronger than Death* (San Francisco: Ignatius Press, 1992); D. Aikman, *Hope: The Heart's Greatest Quest* (Ann Arbor, Mich.: Servant Publications, 1995).

15. See for example the monographic number "Eschatology" in the *Proceedings of the American Catholic Philosophical Association* 75 (2001). See also M. F. Rousseau, "The Natural Meaning of Death in the Summa Theologiae," in the *Proceedings of the American Catholic Philosophical Association* 52 (1978): 87–95.

16. See the works of Z. Hayes and E. Schwarz in n. 10.

17. On process theology, see pp. 43–44.

18. See A. C. Pegis, "Some Reflections on the Summa contra Gentiles II, 56," in *An Etienne Gilson Tribute*, ed. C. J. O'Neil (Milwaukee: Marquette University Press, 1959), 169–88; idem., "Between Immortality and Death in the Summa Contra Gentiles," *Monist* 58 (1974): 1–15; idem., "The Separated Soul and its Nature in St. Thomas," in *St Thomas Aquinas 1274–1974: Commemorative Studies*, ed. A. A. Maurer (Toronto: Pontifical Institute of Mediaeval Studies, 1974), 131–58.

Several important works have appeared in the context of Jewish studies.[19] Systematic elements of eschatology are for the most part developed in dialogue with twentieth-century European authors, especially Teilhard de Chardin, Karl Barth, Jürgen Moltmann,[20] Wolfhart Pannenberg,[21] Hans Küng, Karl Rahner,[22] and Hans Urs von Balthasar.[23] Particular interest has been taken of late in America in works relating eschatology and scientific cosmology. As we shall see presently,[24] modern physics seemed to have put the possibility of a cosmic consummation to the universe under considerable strain. Recent developments, however, indicate that eschatology and cosmology have more in common with one another than had been previously suspected.[25]

Another issue that has received more attention in America than in Europe is the relationship between the kingdom of God and society. In 1937 H. Richard Niebuhr published a work with a challenging title: *The Kingdom of God in America*.[26] Niebuhr of course was not concerned so much about writing on the doctrine of the "Kingdom of God" in American New Testament scholarship. The issue was a more important and complex one: the relationship between God's sovereign action in Christ on the one hand, and the political and social life of Americans on the other.[27] In the area of psychology and medicine, significant contributions have been made in two areas. First, in the therapeutics of death and dying, what is commonly known as "thanatology": the uncontested pioneer

---

19. For example, see N. Gillman, *The Death of Death: Resurrection and Immortality in Jewish Thought* (Woodstock, Vt.: Jewish Lights Publications, 1997); J. Neusner and A. J. Avery-Peck, eds., *Judaism in Late Antiquity*, vol. 4: *Death, Life-after-Death, Resurrection and the World-to-Come in the Judaisms of Antiquity* (Leiden: E. J. Brill, 2000); J. D. Levenson, *Resurrection and the Restoration of Israel: The Ultimate Victory of the God of Life* (New Haven, Conn.: Yale University Press, 2006). See also the recent work K. Madigan and J. D. Levenson, *Resurrection: The Power of God for Christians and Jews* (New Haven, Conn.: Yale University Press, 2009).

20. See the works of Hayes and Schwarz in n. 10.

21. See, for example, S. J. Grenz, *Reason for Hope: The Systematic Theology of W. Pannenberg* (Oxford: Oxford University Press, 1990).

22. On Rahner's eschatology, see, for example, P. C. Phan, *Eternity in Time: A Study of Karl Rahner's Eschatology* (Selinsgrove, Pa.: Susquehanna University Press, 1988).

23. See N. J. Healy, *The Eschatology of Hans Urs von Balthasar: Being as Communion* (Oxford: Oxford University Press, 2005).

24. See pp. 44–46.

25. See, for example, I. G. Barbour, *Religion in an Age of Science: Gifford Lectures 1989–1991* (San Francisco: Harper, 1990); C. R. Albright and J. Haugen, eds., *Beginning with the End: God, Science and Wolfhart Pannenberg* (Chicago: Open Court, 1997); G. F. R. Ellis, ed., *The Far-Future Universe: Eschatology from a Cosmic Perspective* (Philadelphia: Templeton Foundation Press, 2002). See also the works of F. J. Tipler, *The Physics of Immortality: God, Cosmology and the Resurrection of the Dead* (New York: Doubleday, 1994); J. C. Polkinghorne, *The God of Hope and the End of the World* (London: SPCK, 2002).

26. H. R. Niebuhr, *The Kingdom of God in America* (New York: Harper, 1957).

27. See, for example, the work of R. Wuthnow, *After Heaven: Spirituality in America since the 1950s* (Berkeley and Los Angeles: University of California Press, 1998).

in this area is Elizabeth Kübler-Ross.[28] And second, the parapsychological phenomenon of "near-death" experiences.[29] In a strictly religious context, New Age spirituality has obliged Christian thinkers to reflect on such issues as reincarnation.[30] Likewise the extraordinary abundance of popular works published before and after the turn of the millennium that deal with the end of time, dispensationalism, millennialism, "rapture," apocalyptics, and suchlike, has provided an important opportunity to deepen the true meaning of Christian eschatology.[31]

I have taught eschatology for many years, both at the University of Navarre in Pamplona (Spain) and at the Pontifical University of the Holy Cross in Rome. The text is the fruit of this teaching experience. I wish to express my gratitude to my students who over the years listened patiently to my lectures and enquired intelligently into obscurely explained points. I also thank friends and colleagues for the many indications and corrections they have given me in revising the text, especially Profs J. José Alviar, Giovanni Ancona, Nicola Ciola, Antonio Ducay, Justin Gillespie, and Juan Rego. In the revision of the text, I wish to thank Thomas Widmer and Francis Denis.

One final observation. I take it that in all likelihood the afterlife will turn out to be somewhat different from what I have attempted to depict in the coming pages. Human language is poor and awkward at the best of times, but even more so when it comes to giving expression to human love or to the divine mysteries. However, at least I will be in a position to fall back on Paul's words, drawn from the prophet Isaiah: "no eye has seen, nor ear heard, nor the heart of man conceived, what God has prepared for those who love him" (1 Cor 2:9; cf. Is 64:3).

---

28. Especially E. Kübler-Ross, *On Death and Dying* (New York: Macmillan, 1970); idem., *Death: The Final Stage of Growth* (Englewood Cliffs, N.J.: Prentice-Hall, 1975); idem., *Questions and Answers on Death and Dying* (New York: Collier, 1979), and also E. Becker, *The Denial of Death* (New York: Free Press, 1973); R. E. Neale, *The Art of Dying* (New York: Harper and Row, 1973); R. S. Anderson, *Theology of Death and Dying* (Oxford; New York: Blackwell, 1986).

29. See R. Moody, *Life after Life* (Harrisburg, Pa.: Stackpole Books, 1976); idem., *Reflections on Life after Life* (New York: Bantam Books, 1978). Other works on "near-death" experiences include A. N. Flew, *The Logic of Mortality* (Oxford: Clarendon Press, 1987); K. Kramer, *Death Dreams: Unveiling Mysteries of the Unconscious Mind* (New York: Paulist, 1993); C. Zaleski, *Otherworld Journeys: Accounts of Near-Death Experiences in Medieval and Modern Times* (New York: Oxford University Press, 1989).

30. On the question of reincarnation, for example, see J. Hick, *Death and Eternal Life* (London: Collins, 1976); J. Bjorling, *Reincarnation: A Bibliography* (New York: Garland, 1996).

31. Many of these works, thousands of which have been published over the last ten or twelve years, may be safely considered as fundamentalist and theologically shallow.

Principal Abbreviations

AAS: Acta Apostolicae Sedis (Città del Vaticano: 1929–2010).

CAA: my study *The Christological Assimilation of the Apocalypse: An Essay on Fundamental Eschatology* (Dublin: Four Courts, 2004).

CCC: Catechism of the Catholic Church (London: G. Chapman, 1994).

DS: J. Denzinger and A. Schönmetzer, *Enchiridion symbolorum, definitionum et declarationum de rebus fidei et morum,* 32nd ed. (Barcelona: Herder, 1963).

DTC: A. Vacant et al., eds., *Dictionnaire de théologie catholique,* 18 vols. (Paris: Letouzey et Ané, 1908–72).

GS: Vatican Council II, Const. *Gaudium et spes* (1965).

LG: Vatican Council II, Const. *Lumen gentium* (1964).

LThK: M. Buchberger and W. Kasper, eds., *Lexikon für Theologie und Kirche,* 3rd ed., 11 vols. (Freiburg i.B.: Herder, 1993–2001).

NIDNTT: L. Coenen, E. Beyreuther, H. Bietenhard, and C. Brown, eds., *The New International Dictionary of New Testament Theology,* 3 vols. (Exeter: Paternoster Press, 1978–86).

SS: Benedict XVI, Encyclical *Spe salvi* (2007).

TWNT: G. Kittel et al., eds., *Theologisches Wörterbuch zum Neuen Testament,* 11 vols. (Stuttgart: W. Kohlhammer, 1933–79).

WA: M. Luther, *Dr Martin Luthers Werke. Schriften,* 73 vols. (Weimar: H. Böhlaus Nachfolger, 1883–2000).

Part One. The Dynamic of Hope

1

The Christian Virtue of Hope and the Epistemological Underpinnings of Christian Eschatology

> Eschatology: a human problem without a human solution.
> —*Giacomo Biffi*[1]

> Hope is the breathing of the soul; Hope is a memory of the future; Hope is the very fabric out of which our soul is made.
> —*Gabriel Marcel*[2]

> The brain is not interested in reality; it is interested in survival.
> —*John J. Medina*[3]

> *Quoniam tu, Domine, singulariter in spe constituisti me.*
> —*Psalms 4:9*

Christianity, like Judaism, is the religion of God's promise. God, in creating the world and saving humanity, did not leave everything neatly and accurately arranged from the outset. His creating action marks the beginning of time. And time opens space for further progress: space for God, who continues to act, to create, to save, to provide, to perfect, to renew, to re-create; and space for humans, who are offered again and again the opportunity of freely responding to God's gifts. The incompleteness of the present moment belongs to the very essence of Christian revelation. The letter to the Hebrews reminds us that "here we have no lasting city" (13:14). Nonetheless, however transient and deficient the present situation may be, the ultimate horizon of Christian life may not be identified with incompleteness or transience, for according to Scripture God has promised "eternal life" to those who are faithful to him, "resurrection of the dead" for one and all, a "new heavens and a new earth in which righteousness dwells" (2 Pt 3:13).

---

1. G. Biffi, *Linee di escatologia cristiana* (Milano: Jaca Book, 1984), 7.
2. G. Marcel, *Homo viator* (Paris: Aubier-Montaigne, 1944), 79, 68; *Etre et avoir* (Paris: Aubier-Montaigne, 1935), 117.
3. J.J. Medina, "The Science of Thinking Smarter," *Harvard Business Review* (May 2008): 51–54, 54.

4 The Dynamic of Hope

The term "eschatology" derives from the Greek word *eschaton*, "that which comes last." Originally, the term refers to what is lowest in the hierarchy of being, to the very dregs of matter. From the Christian standpoint, however, what comes at the end is not decayed matter, the poorest, the lowest, and the weakest, but rather fullness, consummation, perfect fulfillment. Thus eschatology is the science of the "last things," the object of divine promise we hope for, because hope refers to the future and directs humans to gifts that are offered to them. Before considering the *object* of Christian promise (part 2), in this chapter we shall briefly consider some aspects of the dynamic of hope itself, as well as the epistemological and hermeneutical issues it gives rise to. The fundamental question being asked is the following: how can we ascertain the truth value of eschatological statements drawn from the New Testament, given that as yet they have not been verified? In other words, can the Church responsibly preach to humanity the promise of final resurrection and eternal life?

The Passion and Virtue of Hope

Hope as a Passion

Aristotle explains that the passion of hope arises from the perception of the *bonum futurum arduum possibile*, that is, the absent good that is difficult, though possible, to obtain.[4] Hope is occasioned in the first place by the *bonum futurum*, the absent good, the good that is perceived by the subject, but is not yet fully possessed. In this sense it may be said that hope is a form of desire, which, for Aristotle, is also a passion. However, hope and desire are not one and the same thing. Gabriel Marcel and other philosophers of hope have insisted on the point.[5] It is possible to desire something without ever really "hoping" to possess it, that is, without thinking that it is realistically possible to obtain. In effect, hope adds to desire the inner conviction that *it is possible* to obtain or possess the object desired, in spite of the difficulty in doing so. In other words, the good desired is *an arduous yet possible one*. Interestingly, according to Thomas Aquinas, who develops Aristotle's reflections on the passions, birds of prey and other animals also experience the passion of hope.[6] This should come as no surprise. Perception of its quarry awakens the bird's appetite, which turns into hope as it invests all its experience, resources, energy, agility, and ingenuity in an effort to capture its victim.

---

4. On the passions in Aristotle, *Metaph. IV*, 5, 1010 b33; *De mem. et rem.*, 450 a3; *De anima II*, 3, 427 b18. See also H. Bonitz, *Index Aristotelicus*, 2nd ed. (Graz: Akademische Druck- und Verlaganstalt, 1955), 555–57 (*pathos*), 239 (*elpis*).

5. On this point in Marcel, see my study "La metafísica de la esperanza y del deseo en Gabriel Marcel," *Anuario Filosófico* 22 (1989): 55–92, especially 55–57; 85; 89–92.

6. Thomas Aquinas, *S. Th. I-II*, q. 40, especially a. 3.

It may happen, of course, that the absent good, though perceived and desired, is considered as simply impossible to obtain. In this case one no longer experiences the passion of hope, but rather that of *despair*. This may occur either because the desired good is objectively unobtainable or because past experiences of a subjective kind produce the conviction that there is little or no hope of success in obtaining the object desired.[7] The passions of hope and despair, in other words, depend significantly on past experience. It is commonly held that the human faculty hope refers to most directly is that of *memory*,[8] which assimilates, calibrates, and retains past experiences, whether good or bad, and provides the basis for humans to react spontaneously in a hoping (or despairing) manner when confronted with novel situations. Those whose memory is largely dominated by negative experiences will tend toward the passion of despair rather than that of hope, especially if the experiences in question have taken place over an extended period of time. On the contrary, those whose experiences are for the most part positive and short-lived generally have a hopeful attitude toward the different situations they are confronted with. Thomas suggests for this reason that *in iuvenibus et in ebriosis abundat spes:* "both children and drunkards are strong in hope,"[9] because they are unaware of—or simply do not reflect upon—the obstacles that may arise in obtaining the arduous good they desire.

Is Hope a Virtue?

So far of course we have spoken of hope as a passion, as a dynamic factor that marks human (and animal) life in general, as something that happens to people, as it were. In other words, the experience of the passion of hope is, in principle, a pre-ethical one, anterior to moral virtue or vice.[10] We have not yet considered it as a *virtue*, that is, a stable, positive inclination of the will that prompts and facilitates good actions, binds humans ever more closely to their last end, and makes their self-realization possible.[11]

Many ancient philosophers, notably among the Stoics, considered hope-experiences as alienating, damaging to humans, and on no account virtuous.[12]

---

7. Aquinas speaks of an *existimatio possibilitatis*, "an appraisal of possibilities" ibid., a. 5, c.

8. On the notion of memory in Augustine, see *De Trinitate IX–XV* and especially the *Confessiones X–XI*. John of the Cross deals with the purification of memory in order to hope in his *Subida al Monte Carmelo*, especially books 2 and 3. For a presentation of their understanding of hope, see the somewhat dated but excellent work of P. Laín Entralgo, *La espera y la esperanza. Historia y teoría del esperar humano* (orig. 1956; Madrid: Alianza, 1984), 56–70 and 115–31 respectively.

9. Thomas Aquinas, *S. Th. I-II*, q. 40, a. 6, c.

10. Aquinas makes clear reference to the role of reason within the dynamic of human passions: *S. Th. I*, q. 76, a. 5. He concludes that the passions are *rationales per participationem: S. Th. I-II*, q. 56, a. 4 ad 1.

11. Aquinas also deals with hope as a virtue, a theological virtue, in *S. Th. II-II*, q. 17.

12. See P. Laín Entralgo, *La espera y la esperanza*, 26–33. In the interesting work of D. Konstan, *The*

6 The Dynamic of Hope

They looked upon hope as a perennial source of delusion, disappointment, and suffering for humanity. The aspiration of the wise man should be to live *nec metu nec spe*, without fear and without hope.[13] Paul likewise describes the pagans as "those who have no hope" (1 Thes 4:13; Eph 2:12). To live without hope, however, makes life meaningless. Friedrich Guntermann's studies of ancient tomb inscriptions has provided convincing evidence of the widespread presence of despair among pagans.[14] "Either they believed there was no survival after death," writes Paul Hoffmann, "or that the dead eked out a sad, dreary existence in the underworld."[15] In recent times the existentialist philosopher J.-P. Sartre gave expression to the senselessness of a life without hope when he said that man acts and lives as "a useless passion."[16] A similar attitude may be found among those who hold the doctrine of reincarnation, in its many and varied forms, both ancient and modern. In effect, reincarnation suggests that the next life will be an approximate replica of this one, and thus no longer the object of hope as such. We shall return to the topic presently.[17]

Nonetheless, in spite of the numerous, appalling tragedies that have marked modern times, perhaps indeed on account of them, the closing century of the last millennium has been, from the literary, philosophical, and theological standpoint, a century marked by reflection on hope.[18] Two particularly influential philosophies of hope are worth considering, those of Ernst Bloch and Gabriel Marcel.

Ernst Bloch's reflection on hope as the "principle" of human life has been very influential,[19] also among some theologians, such as Jürgen Moltmann. In an attempt to reread and "humanize" Karl Marx's anthropology on the basis of a reinterpretation of Aristotle, Bloch claims that hope is the source of human existence and action at all levels. Everything that exists is directed essentially toward the future (what he calls the "not yet") under the impulse of hope. Hope is written

---

Emotions of the Ancient Greeks. Studies in Aristotle and Classical Literature (Toronto: University of Toronto Press, 2007), many emotions and passions are considered: love, fear, gratitude, pity, jealousy, grief, envy, shame, but *not* hope.

13. Probably from the Stoic Cicero, *Post reditum in Senatu*, 7:9.

14. F. Guntermann, *Die Eschatologie des hlg. Paulus* (Münster: Aschendorff, 1932), 38.

15. P. Hoffmann, *Die Toten in Christus. Eine religionsgeschichtliche und exegetische Untersuchung zur paulinischen Eschatologie* (Münster: Aschendorff, 1966), 211.

16. J.-P. Sartre, *L'être e le néant* (Paris: Gallimard, 1946).

17. See chapter 3 on the resurrection.

18. Vols. 3–4 of C. Möller's five-volume work *Littérature du XXe siècle et christianisme* (Tournai: Casterman, 1954–) are of particular interest.

19. See especially Bloch's work *The Principle of Hope*, 3 vols. (Cambridge: MIT Press, 1986). The original was published as *Das Prinzip Hoffnung* (Frankfurt a. M.: Suhrkamp, 1954–59). On this work, see my study "Hope and Freedom in Gabriel Marcel and Ernst Bloch," *Irish Theological Quarterly* 55 (1989): 215–39.

Christian Eschatology 7

into the very constitution of matter, of the cosmos, of humankind. For Bloch, however, it is directed neither by nor toward any kind of transcendent, personal Deity. Hope does not draw on any divine promise. The forward-thrusting vitality of matter itself renders the existence and action of God redundant. Hope would be the exact expression of the living core of reality in evolution, in which humans play a critical role both as patients and as agents. In real terms, however, humans do not really hope in something (or in someone) other than themselves. They must simply allow themselves to be drawn along within a cosmic process, moving toward the future under the impulse of hope.

It may be observed, however, that although Bloch speaks extensively of the novelty of the future (what he calls the *Novum Ultimum*), in real terms the future holds no true novelty for humanity. What will take place later on is already at our disposal. It might be said that Bloch attempts to turn the passion of hope into a virtue, through a secularized reading of Jewish and Christian salvation history.[20] He tries, literally, to make virtue out of necessity.

Another interesting and influential understanding of hope is provided by the Christian personalist philosopher and playwright *Gabriel Marcel*.[21] Graphically, Marcel says that "hope is the very fabric out of which our soul is made."[22] Yet hope is not something that just "happens" to humans in an anonymous or collective fashion, nor may it be identified with the inner driving force of the evolutionary process. Rather, hope results from the opening of the human being to one who freely offers a gift.[23] Marcel limits his description of the dynamics of hope to the sphere of human sociality, but—differently from Bloch's understanding—his explanation easily opens out to the existence and hope-enabling activity of a supreme Divinity. He describes hope, however, in a somewhat dialectic way that pays scant attention to the spontaneous dynamic of human desire and corporeality.[24]

A reflection on these two very different authors is instructive on many counts,[25] because it demonstrates that a perennial and unresolved tension persists between hope as directed toward a transcendent Divinity on the one hand

---

20. See G. Gozzelino, *Nell'attesa*, 237.
21. See Marcel's works *Homo viator*, 37–86; "La Structure de l'Espérance," *Dieu Vivant* 19 (1951): 71–80; "Desire and Hope," in *Readings in Existential Phenomenology*, ed. N. Lawrence and D. O'Connor (New York: Prentice-Hall, 1967), 277–85. Also my study, already cited, "La metafísica de la esperanza y del deseo en Gabriel Marcel."
22. G. Marcel, "Desire and Hope," 283.
23. "At the root of hope, something is literally given to us," G. Marcel, *Homo viator*, 80.
24. See my critique of Marcel in "La metafísica de la esperanza y del deseo en Gabriel Marcel," 75–92.
25. See my study "Hope and Freedom in Marcel and Bloch."

and hope that fully involves the material world on the other—between a theologically and a humanly motivated hope.

Hope, as we saw, points to the future, to a good perceived or promised but not yet possessed. For hope to be possible and humanly meaningful, therefore, the future in question must be perceived as "superior" in content to the past, better than what one already possesses, and though "future," involving a greater good than the one now offered or available. Otherwise, there would be nothing to "hope" for.

Should it be demonstrated that the future promised or perceived will most likely be *inferior* to the past (as suggested for example by Sartre, Monod, and Leopardi, among others),[26] then hope can assume no meaningful role in human life, and despair is destined to occupy its place sooner or later.

In a similar vein, should it be shown that the future simply mirrors the past, that is to say, that it contains no more and no less than what the past offers, then there is no more space for hope than there is for despair, and neither passion can occupy a relevant place in human life. An example of the latter understanding is the so-called doctrine of eternal return,[27] typical of Greek antiquity. Here there is simply no place for hope as a virtue, that is, a stable inclination of the will through which humans may freely develop their true potential. *Elpis*, the Greek term commonly used for hope, is equivalent, at best, to "waiting."[28] In Hesiod's *The Works and the Days*, when Pandora opens the box sent by Zeus to Epimeteus, all the evils that afflict humans emerge: sickness, sorrow, and death. All that is left is hope, a vain consolation for mortals, and of no service to the gods.[29] Thus hope is said to be "the last thing we lose." It is of value only in that it distracts us from the present moment, giving us consolation and short-term, illusory respite from sorrow and pain. Besides, it belongs exclusively to the human sphere, not to the divine. It is uncertain and deceptive, because it is as unfaithful and fickle as man himself is. The Greeks attempted to overcome the ambivalence of hope

---

26. Those who do not believe in God (Sartre and Monod for example) coldly recognize the inherent metaphysical fragility of all existent things, and conclude that all that exists moves inexorably toward nothingness. For Sartre, "nothingness nests in the heart of being as a worm," *L'Être et le néant*, 57. His understanding is even clearer in a psychological context. He explains that human consciousness (*l'être-pour-soi*) manages to precariously overcome the dead and opaque quality of matter (*l'être-en-soi*), only to collapse back, at death, into complete oblivion and unconsciousness. According to Monod, the universe is gradually cooling off, and will eventually return to its true essence, which is nothingness: *Le hasard et la nécessité: essai sur la philosophie naturelle de la biologie moderne* (Paris: Seuil, 1970). On Leopardi, see G. Biffi, *Linee di escatologia*, 12–13.

27. See especially the classic work of M. Eliade, *Cosmos and History: the Myth of the Eternal Return* (New York: Harper and Row, 1959).

28. P. Laín Entralgo, *La espera y la esperanza*, 26–33.

29. Hesiod, *Works and Days*, 43–105.

and contribute toward the quality of their future destiny by having recourse to dreams, to rational forecasting, and to mystery cults.[30] But all in all, Paul's description of the pagans as those "who have no hope" (1 Thes 4:13) is justified.

Some Gnostics and Christian authors inspired by Origen and others tacitly accepted important aspects of the doctrine of eternal return.[31] But for the most part, it was decisively rejected by those who believed in Jesus Christ, the radical new beginning that is the Christian Gospel.[32] With the coming of Christ, his life, death, and resurrection, Augustine said, *circuitus illi iam explosi sunt*,[33] the eternal "cycles have been broken once and for all."

When a Passion Becomes a Virtue

So far we have spoken of hope from the standpoint of the individual, that is, as a passion. In effect, the passion of hope belongs to the structure of the individual who, on the basis of past experience and present capacity, becomes convinced that such and such a good may be obtained and possessed. This conviction impels persons to apply their energy and ingenuity in overcoming the difficulties (the *arduum*) involved in obtaining the good desired. However, it may happen that the *bonum futurum arduum* becomes *possibile* not just through the investment of one's *own* energies in overcoming the obstacles encountered. The *bonum futurum arduum* may also become *possibile* with the help of other persons.[34] The dynamic of the passion of hope is thus modified and amplified by this relationship with someone who contributes toward turning a simple desire into a real possibility. In fact, many things that seem to be impossible to obtain and possess through one's own efforts become accessible through the assistance of others. As a result, insofar as such people facilitate our obtaining a greater good, they become objects of love, albeit perhaps love of an "interested" kind. Insofar as we perceive that the love of those who help us is enduring, and their disposition to assist us is persevering, they may become, besides, objects of our trust and faith. In this way, hope ceases to be an individual experience, and becomes a personal—or better, an interpersonal—one, insofar as one person learns to hope in another who is in a position to help them turn their God-implanted desire into a God-willed reality.

---

30. P. Laín Entralgo, *La espera*, 29.
31. B. E. Daley, *The Hope*, 219.
32. J. L. Illanes, "Interpretaciones y figuras de la historia," *Analecta Cracoviensia* 25 (1993): 155–68, points out that whereas Christian thought distanced itself from a metaphysical reading of eternal return (the same cosmos and human life continually returning), it accepted tacitly an historiographical reading (the same kind of historical events tend to recur).
33. Augustine, *De Civ. Dei XII*, 20:4.
34. Thomas Aquinas, *S. Th. I-II*, q. 40, a. 7.

10 The Dynamic of Hope

But the question still remains: is hope of this kind truly a virtue, a stable inclination of the will that humans *should* foster with a view to developing themselves to the full, to obtaining their last end? On the one hand, the natural limitations of those who may assist us in obtaining our last end serve as a reminder that absolute trust and hope may not be placed in any human being. Indeed, humans are often undependable, incapable of acting in an entirely disinterested manner. On the other hand, they are capable of providing for others benefits of a limited, temporal kind. Yet experience tells us that humans do aspire after a good that goes far beyond their own limitations, well beyond the reach of what others can provide, and tends toward the Absolute. The finite seeks the Infinite,[35] the mortal immortality, the creature divinization.

For this reason, to hope unreservedly in other human beings would not be wholly virtuous, not only because humans are often unreliable, but principally because they are incapable of providing complete fulfillment or definitive realization for those who hope in them. That is to say, hope directed *exclusively* to other persons would not be a virtue, for it would not be ordered to the person's true good. Christian revelation unequivocally teaches that the human aspiration to infinite happiness may be satisfied by God alone, who created humans in the first place. To put it in technical terms, hope is a virtue only if it is a "theological virtue."[36] Paul, writing to the Corinthians, says: "If for this life only we have hoped in Christ, we are of all men most to be pitied" (1 Cor 15:19). And Pope Benedict XVI in *Spe salvi* says that "the great hope of believers can only be in God."[37]

Throughout history, some authors have taken it that hope, driven by the human desire for perfect happiness and fulfillment, constitutes a fundamental form of alienation.[38] Far from representing the true nature and destiny of humans, the desire for perfect, endless happiness would be a vain striving, a dangerous form of self-projection. By right, they say, it should be purged and eliminated.

But the key point, as we have just seen, is that hope is, in a strict sense, a theological virtue. *God* is the one who gives humans the gift of a stable, positive inclination toward their last end, that is, the virtue of hope. And God is considered to be (1) fully worthy of our trust, (2) altogether capable of fulfilling human desires for infinite and eternal happiness, and (3) fully determined to do so. Only if it can be demonstrated that such a Being exists does it become possible

---

35. The classic controversy on the so-called natural desire to see God deals with this question. See especially H. de Lubac, *Le mystère du surnaturel* (Paris: Aubier-Montaigne, 1965); L. Feingold, *The Natural Desire to See God according to St. Thomas Aquinas and His Interpreters* (Ave Maria, Fl.: Sapientia Press of Ave Maria University, 2009).

36. *CCC* 1817.   37. *SS* 31.

38. See pp. 153–55.

to consider hope as a virtue, and Christian eschatology as something real and tangible.[39] Pope Benedict XVI observes that "to come to know God—the true God—means to receive hope."[40] God, by infusing grace, provides believers with a stable, positive inclination of the will by which they hope to obtain their eternal happiness and fulfillment from him.

Christian eschatology deals with the divine promise of salvation, and the consequent self-realization for humans, that takes place through the power of God made manifest in Jesus Christ, and realized through the power of the Holy Spirit. The union with the Father that results from the infusion of divinizing grace won by Christ on the Cross is the only adequate object of the virtue of hope.

The treatise of eschatology attempts among other things to respond to the following questions: Are the claims of Christian believers, to the effect that God has promised humans an immortal destiny of perfect beatitude, justified? What does such a destiny consist of? Can it be forfeited? How should humans live for it to become possible? What implications do Christian eschatology and the dynamics of hope have for other aspects of theology: ethics and politics, anthropology, ecclesiology and sacraments, spirituality, the doctrine of the Trinity?

Eschatology as Theology: The Basis of Hope

As we have seen, hope may be considered a virtue only for strictly theological reasons: the God of Jesus Christ is fully worthy of our trust, is capable of fulfilling our desires for infinitude and immortality, and has actually undertaken to do so by sending his Son to be our Savior. Yet all humans, believers and nonbelievers alike, are aware that the virtue of hope does not produce the desired result of union with God immediately. God's action in saving humanity is not as apparent as we would wish it to be. As Wolfhart Pannenberg has shown,[41] Christian eschatology, although it involves the divine promise of grace and eternal glory, does not begin with them. The divine promise is based on the previous fact that God exists, that he is Lord of the universe, that he wishes to save humanity, and that he has revealed his will and power to do so. The demonstration of the validity of the divine promise—what Pannenberg terms the "justification of God"—will be fully realized only when, at the final consummation of the universe, all creatures

---

39. Benedict XVI in *SS* 7–8 analyzes Heb 11:1, which the Vulgate translates as *est autem fides sperandarum substantia rerum, argumentum non apparentium*. He explains that the object of Christian hope and faith is not a mere *conviction* in respect of God's fidelity or Love, as Protestants traditionally held (thus faith would be a "standing firm in what one hopes, being convinced of what one does not see"), but the very *substance* of God's life present in man through Christ: thus faith (and with it, hope), "is not merely a personal reaching out towards things to come that are still totally absent; it gives us something . . . a real presence," *SS* 8.

40. Ibid., n. 3.

41. W. Pannenberg, *Systematic Theology*, vol. 3, 540.

will clearly be able to see that the God of Jesus Christ is the loving and merciful Creator (and thus Savior) of the world that Christian faith proclaims him to be.[42] Once it reaches its scope, that is, definitive communion with God, hope in the strict sense will exist no longer. In the meantime, however, the dynamic of hope moves within the *chiaroscuro* of faith and trust. For hope is a profoundly human reality. Let us examine the latter statement more closely.

Eschatology as Anthropology: The Humanity of Hope

Even if it can be demonstrated that God has promised human beings eternal life and happiness in communion with him (and we intend to do just that in the coming chapters), it must still be shown that humans are constituted in such a way as to be able to receive this gift in a meaningful fashion. If humans are not structured for immortality, then to say they are destined for eternal communion with God is pointless, and the divine promise would be as useless to them as it would be to inferior created beings. In other words, humans must be in a position to recognize and desire the fulfillment of the divine promise *as a benefit for themselves*, as a true and definitive realization of their own being, nature, and potentialities, already structured for immortality. Pannenberg suggests that "a positive relation to the needs and wishes of the recipients of . . . [eschatological] statements is the criterion by which to distinguish promise and threat."[43] "Anthropology is the soil," he concludes, "on which we can argue for the universality of Christian eschatological hope."[44]

Peter's first letter invites Christians to "account for the hope that is in" them (1 Pt 3:15). Doubtless, the fundamental reason they must give for their hope is God's promise to reward those who believe in him with the prize of eternal life. This they do by pointing to Christ, in whom God's promises are fulfilled, and to the Church, which conveys these promises to believers. However, the promise is meaningful only if humans are in fact capable of receiving God's gift and are desirous to do so. But what does this capacity and desire involve? As we saw already, Marcel distinguishes carefully between hope and mere human desire,[45] considering the former as orientated toward God, the latter as alienating, closed to gift. Conversely, Bloch holds that hope begins and ends within the human sphere and constitutes the most powerful, pervasive, and enduring form of desire. In other words, he holds that hope is truly, fully, human. Bloch's position, although it excludes the promise of a transcendent Divinity as the ultimate basis for hope, at least raises the question of its humanity and realism.

Hope must be considered a virtue in that it corresponds, and corresponds

42. Ibid., 630–46.
44. Ibid.
43. Ibid., 541.
45. G. Marcel, "Desire and Hope," 278.

fully, to *the truth about God:* God alone can bring humans to fulfillment and efficaciously wishes to do so. Yet hope is a virtue also because it responds to *the truth about human nature.* In effect, eschatological fulfillment is not forced on humans, but presented to them by God indirectly, with a view to stimulating their generosity and free response, gently inclining their will toward their last end, bringing them to react to God's words, grace, and action with the same kind of self-effacing, munificent love with which God himself approached humanity in Christ by sending the Holy Spirit.[46] Hope involves taking a risk. It requires a conversion of heart, a launching out into the deep (Lk 5:4). It involves going beyond oneself and one's own resources and certainties. God does not directly reveal his face, his inner life, his triune processions. Rather he reveals himself in and through his works: through creation, through the prophets of the Old Testament, and especially in the words and works of his Incarnate Son, our Savior Jesus Christ. "Jesus ... brought ... an encounter with the Lord of Lords," Pope Benedict writes, "an encounter with the living God and thus an encounter with a hope stronger than the sufferings of slavery, a hope which therefore transformed life from within."[47]

Ultimate and Penultimate Hopes

The only sufficient object and motive for Christian hope is God, who is all-powerful, good, merciful, and faithful to his word. However, in immediate and subjective terms, the hope of humans is directed normally toward an inferior, more tangible, presence, that of creatures, in which God's love is manifested. Unsaved human beings may well be drawn toward God through those creatures in which he makes his presence felt (Mt 5:16), but, unweaned as they are from their impatient, sinful ways, they may likewise allow themselves be held back by such creatures from approaching their Creator. The created world should lead us to God, but it may not in fact do so (Rom 1:18–32). Christ came to save sinners (Mt 18:11), but many rejected his message and Person, the One in whom the fullness of the divinity lives bodily (Col 2:9), out of a disorderly love for creatures (Mt 19:22; Lk 12:19). Thus, unwittingly, human hopes can take the place of divine ones, idols ousting God. Dietrich Bonhöffer has spoken of the endemic tendency throughout history of confusing "penultimate" with "ultimate" hopes.[48] This phenomenon is particularly noticeable in Jürgen Moltmann's early theology of hope,[49] deeply inspired by Bloch's thought, which suggests that true Christian

---

46. On this, see my study "El testimonio de Cristo y de los cristianos. Una reflexión sobre el método teológico," *Scripta Theologica* 38 (2005): 501–68, here 548–56.

47. *SS* 4.

48. See J. L. Ruiz de la Peña, *La pascua de la creación*, 193; C. Pozo, *La teología del más allá*, 155.

49. According to Tödt, Moltmann, in his work *Theology of Hope*, attempts to transfer hope from the

hope, based on the fact of the resurrection of Christ, must be directed primarily toward resolving the world's social problems.[50]

Christian hope is based on God's promise yet lives within the world of human beings: it is both theology and anthropology. And it is clear that Christian hope is not a consolidated reality in believers, but gives rise, rather, to a process that involves the human being in its entirety: a dignifying, enriching, divinizing, though purifying, process, in which God's power and love become more and more manifest.

The Truth of Christian Hope

The object of Christian hope, as we have seen, is the divine promise of salvation made present to humanity through the life, death, and resurrection of Jesus Christ, the true Witness to the Father, and the sending of the Holy Spirit. But what is the *content* of this promise? A careful study of Scripture will be required to discover that. This will constitute the greater part of this treatise on Christian eschatology. But a further question must be asked: is the content of this promise *truthful;* does it correspond in fact to what God has intended for humanity? At the end of time, of course, the *content* and *truth* of eschatological revelation will coincide fully, in that the saints in glory shall see God "as he is" (1 Jn 3:2). What God has promised will be seen to be true: "Then you will know I am the Lord" (Ez 24:24). But at the present moment, our reflection on the content of the divine promise (what God has promised to those who love him) may be distinguished somewhat from our consideration of its truthfulness (that such a promise will be verified).[51] Let us consider the question more closely.

The Content of Biblical Eschatological Texts

As regards the content of New Testament eschatological texts, many interpretations have been given. Two extreme positions may be noted, the origins of which will be explained in greater detail in chapter 2.

On the one hand is a purely apocalyptic interpretation. According to the literal tenor of classical apocalyptic *corpus*, divine judgment is due to descend on

---

Ultimate to the penultimate: H. E. Tödt, "Aus einem Brief an Jürgen Moltmann," in *Diskussion über die 'Theologie der Hoffnung' von Jürgen Moltmann*, ed. W.-D. Marsch (München: Kaiser, 1967), 197–200. Tödt explains that Moltmann's position is unacceptable from a Lutheran standpoint in that it is based on the principle of the priority of "good works" and not on justification by faith. For a further discussion of Moltmann's theology of hope, see C. Pozo, *La teología del más allá*, 62–78, 150–161.

50. C. Pozo explains this well in his essay, "Teología de la esperanza," in *Iglesia y secularización*, ed. J. Daniélou and C. Pozo (Madrid: BAC, 1973), 87–119.

51. This theme is developed in my study "El testimonio de Cristo y de los cristianos."

the world in the very near future. The world as we know it will be destroyed, all humans will rise up and be judged in the power of God, the just will be gathered into God's kingdom and sinners delivered to eternal damnation.[52] The last things are already perfectly defined in God's mind and will shortly descend upon the world, establish the good once and for all, eliminate evil, and inaugurate the new and definitive age. Although many elements of the strict apocalyptic view are to be found in New Testament eschatology, the validity of this reading is substantially disproved by the simple fact that the end of the world has not in fact taken place.[53] Besides, Christ came primarily to open a space of salvation for all humans, before coming to judge humanity at the end of time. This is the key difference between apocalyptic and New Testament eschatology: the former is centered on judgment, the latter on salvation (and on that basis, on judgment). In addition, pure apocalyptic eschatology may be considered deficient from an anthropological viewpoint, in that it pays scant attention to the value and dignity of the individual, moral conscience, personal responsibility, and the like.[54] The position does have its proponents nowadays, for example in the so-called left behind literature, though much less so in the ambit of academic theology.[55]

On the other hand, an existential interpretation of New Testament eschatological texts has been common throughout history, but particularly so of late, mainly due to the writings of Rudolf Bultmann.[56] Biblical texts speaking of the end of time, of the afterlife, and so on, are seen as historicized expressions of present experiences of God's saving action, and thus as imperative though generic invitations to conversion. Eschatological texts call humans to a free, nonthematic decision of faith in God's total sovereignty over the universe. Though valuable from the anthropological point of view, the position is problematic from many standpoints,[57] principally because it neglects the future, historical, collective, and material side of eschatology. It tends rather toward a presentist, individualistic, and spiritual view of final consummation.

Taking our cue from the analytical philosopher John L. Austin, we may apply the term "performative" to Bultmann's understanding of eschatological language. Principally in his 1950s work *How to Do Things with Words*,[58] Austin explains that not all statements may be considered as simple assertions of truth or falsehood, of what is or what will be. Many utterances are made with a view to obtaining

---

52. For a detailed description of apocalyptic eschatology, see *CAA* 63–102.
53. See pp. 63–66. 54. *CAA* 232–56.
55. *CAA* 1–2. 56. *CAA* 38–43.
57. *CAA* 43–48.
58. See J. L. Austin, *How to Do Things with Words: The William James Lectures Delivered at Harvard University in 1955*, 2nd ed. (orig. 1962; Oxford: University Press, 1989).

specific effects from the listener (he terms them "performative" statements), and not so much to utter truth or falsehood (the latter are "assertive," or constative, statements). Performative statements are directed toward producing an effect or reaction on the hearer.

A case in point, it is sometimes suggested, is the New Testament doctrine of perpetual condemnation.[59] Some authors suggest that when the gospels tell us that the wicked will be condemned to eternal punishment for their sins, Scripture is primarily attempting to elicit from the hearer a salutary reaction in the context of their sinful life, and eventually a full Christian conversion.[60] In the third century Origen had already claimed that the purpose of Christian teaching on condemnation and hell is simply one of "inflicting terror among those who would not otherwise be restrained from an abundance of sin."[61] The theologian Karl Rahner adopts a similar position.[62] Likewise, some of the "existentialist" readings of New Testament apocalyptic texts we shall consider in chapter 2 fit into this category.[63]

The same issue is found among authors who have asked whether the key to Christian eschatology lies in the *eschaton* or in the *eschata*.[64] The *eschaton*, literally "the last thing," would refer to the final event, to eschatology as a whole, that is, to the Person of Christ, who comes to save and to judge. The plural *eschata* on the contrary refer to "the last things," that is, the different elements that go to make up the eschatological promise (judgment, resurrection, heaven, hell, purgatory, etc.). In the first case, eschatology would be understood in interpersonal, existential terms, as descriptions of the ultimate encounter between Christ and the believer; in the second, it would attempt to provide a more or less precise, objective description of the final state humans are destined for. In the first, a "per-

---

59. See pp. 189–222.
60. See the careful summary of positions in E. Castillo Pino, *Los argumentos teológicos sobre la posibilidad de la condenación eterna en la teología católica del siglo XX* (Rome: Pontificia Università della Santa Croce, 2000), passim.
61. Origen, *Contra Celsum*, 5,15; *De princip. II*, 10:6.
62. "What Scripture says about hell is to be interpreted in keeping with its literary character of 'threat-discourse.' . . . People are placed before a decision of which the consequences are irrevocable," K. Rahner, "Hell," in *Sacramentum Mundi*, vol. 3 (New York: Herder and Herder, 1970), 7–9, here 7.
63. See pp. 50–53.
64. See G. Moioli, *L'"Escatologico" cristiano. Proposta sistematica* (Milano: Glossa, 1994), 47. Protestant theology tends to concentrate on the *eschaton*, to some degree on account of its anthropological pessimism: see S. Hjelde, *Das Eschaton und die Eschata. Eine Studie über den Sprachgebrauch und die Sprachverwirrung in protestantischen Theologie, von der Orthodoxie bis zur Gegenwart* (München: Kaiser, 1987). Orthodox theology tends to move in the same direction, though not on account of a pessimistic account of man. A. Giudici puts it as follows: "il problema dell'escatologia si pone in un'alternativa essenziale: o *eschaton* o *eschata*," in "Escatologia," in *Nuovo Dizionario di Teologia*, ed. G. Barbaglio and S. Dianich (Milano: Paoline, 1988), 382–411, here 400.

formative" understanding of eschatology prevails; in the second, rather, what we called an "assertive" one.

It should be kept in mind, however, that—as Austin himself explained on repeated occasions—the performative and assertive aspects of language are simply inseparable from one another. He concludes that all statements do have a "performative" (or "illocutionary") aspect to them, though they cannot be reduced to it.[65] The performative aspect becomes meaningful only on the basis of the truth or mistruth of the statement in question. That is to say, the performative is deeply linked with the assertive. Only if a statement is true does it become reasonable for the listener to change his or her life or attitude on the basis of its utterance. To return to the example mentioned earlier on, the claim that "unrepentant sinners will be condemned forever" would constitute an act of gratuitous violence to the human intelligence should the statement prove to be simply untrue. As we shall see presently, the very credibility of Jesus' message depends on the seriousness given to his statements on such matters. It makes sense that in his teaching he would personally assume the principle he taught his followers, "Let your yes be yes, and your no, no" (Mt 5:37).

The foregoing discussion does go to demonstrate, among other things, the illegitimacy of applying a purely philosophical hermeneutic to a theological question such as the interpretation of eschatological texts. The hermeneutic applied must be a strictly theological one, or better, a Christological one, in which the Savior and Judge of the world, the *eschaton*, Christ our Hope, reveals to his disciples what he has seen in the glory of his Father, the *eschata*.[66] In effect, Jesus Christ in Person is the Truth (Jn 14:6). As we shall see presently, Christian eschatology excludes neither the apocalyptic nor the existential: it is built up on the basis of a critical sifting and assimilation of traditional apocalyptic materials undertaken by Christ himself, but may not be seen as a reductive rereading of such motifs in solely existential or apocalyptic terms. Indeed, eschatology is entirely centered on the Person of Christ, for it is the culmination of his saving work. Yet Christ did explain to his disciples the fundamental traits of the next life we hope for, beyond the reach of decay and death.[67]

The Truth of New Testament Eschatology

The content of Biblical eschatological statements is made known to us through the words and works and parables of Jesus. But the question of the in-

---

65. J. L. Austin, *How to Do Things with Words*, 133–64.
66. On the notion that Jesus "saw" what he lived and taught, see J. Ratzinger/Benedict XVI, *Jesus of Nazareth: From the Baptism in the Jordan to the Transfiguration* (New York: Doubleday, 2007), 1–8.
67. This is the principal thesis of my work *The Christological Assimilation of the Apocalypse* (*CAA*).

terpretation of these texts brings us to another, more fundamental, question, regarding their *truthfulness*. In effect, as we attempt to understand these statements, we come up against the simple question of whether they are true or not. Again, the point of reference can be only the words and works of Christ. He is the "true Witness" not only in that he teaches us what he has seen and heard from his Father, but because he actually gives us what he has received from the Father, what God has promised for us. In other words, Jesus not only teaches about eternal life, final resurrection, universal judgment. He actually presents himself as the source of all three: "I am the resurrection and the life" (Jn 11:25); he, in person, is the Judge of humanity (Jn 5:26–27). This point shall arise time and again in forthcoming chapters. As regards *eternal life*, Jesus communicated to the disciples the life he lived with the Father, the glory he received before the world was created (Jn 17:24); as regards *resurrection*, the disciples saw him die, and rise up again subsequently from the dead, "the first born among the dead" (Rom 8:29); in respect of *judgment*, his words and very presence established God's kingdom and judgment among the people. That is to say, not only the words of Jesus, but his whole life, death, and resurrection witnessed to the truth of his teaching.[68]

The truthfulness of New Testament eschatological statements may be sustained and presented in many different ways, four of which we shall now consider. Two of them are of an anthropological kind (coming under the umbrella of what may be called the *praeambula spei*, or "preambles of hope,"[69] rational preconditions for accepting the possibility and reasonableness of Christian hope), and two of a more spiritual kind. *First*, then, we shall examine to what degree is it possible to rationally affirm human immortality, specifically that of the human soul. *Second*, we shall consider different components of what might be called an integral immortality (that of "life" and that of "self"), as an anthropological testing ground for the validity of eschatological statements. *Third*, we shall attempt to address the perception many Christians presently experience to the effect that the price (death) to be paid for the fulfillment of the divine promise (eternal life, etc.), is simply excessive. God promises everything, it would seem, but also asks for all we have, for all he has given us, for our very lives. Is it possible to justify this extreme juxtaposition? *Fourth*, we shall briefly consider the firmness and consistency of Christian hope (that is, the perceived truthfulness of eschatological statements) in its ultimate source, that is, the action of the Holy Spirit. The four ways correspond more or less to different ways of approaching truth.[70]

---

68. See my study "El testimonio de Cristo y de los cristianos," 530–43.

69. I have used the term *praeambula spei*, "preambles of hope," in my study "La metafísica de la esperanza en Gabriel Marcel" (1989), 86.

70. I have presented them in my study "El testimonio de Cristo y de los cristianos," 513–17; 566–68.

The Rationality of Christian Eschatology and the Question of the Incorruptibility of the Human Soul

Traditionally, Christian anthropology and eschatology are based on the notion that humans are composed of body and soul, and that the soul, being spiritual, is incorruptible, and thus serves as an ontological basis both for human immortality and for continuity between this life and the next. This idea is well developed in the thought of Augustine and Aquinas, and was assumed by Christian theologians as a whole until quite recently.[71] It is fair to say that the existence of the soul, and even more so its spirituality and incorruptibility, though open to philosophical enquiry, is not susceptible to fully rigorous demonstration. Still Plato, when speaking of the soul, may have been on to something when he said that "it is worthwhile to take the risk of believing in the soul's immortality. It is a beautiful risk to take."[72] As we shall see, a certain knowledge of the soul's incorruptibility offers Christian eschatology a kind of *praeambulum spei*.

Protestantism and the Immortality of the Soul

The validity of the notion of an immortal separated soul has been questioned in recent centuries, principally in the ambit of Protestant theology. This is not to say, of course, that Protestants deny the afterlife in which believers will live forever in communion with the Divinity. Quite the contrary: Protestant theology is solidly centered on the eschatological moment.[73] Rather it is considered that the notion of the "immortal soul," borrowed—it is said—from Platonic thought, had, through a process of unwarranted "Hellenization," wrongfully taken the place of the central biblical doctrine of the resurrection of the dead.[74] To return to the purity of the Christian Gospel, therefore, the doctrine of the soul and its immortality must be purged.[75]

Historically, however, it should be kept in mind that Christians not only

---

The four ways to truth considered in the latter study are: coherency, consensus, pragmatism, and revelation.

71. The 1948 manual of M. Schmaus, *Katholische Dogmatik*, vol. 4.2: *Von den letzten Dingen*, marks a significant change. On the influence of Plato's theory of the soul in religions, see M. Elkaisy-Friemuth and J. M. Dillon, eds., *The Afterlife of the Platonic Soul: Reflections of Platonic Psychology in the Monotheistic Religions* (Leiden: Brill, 2009).

72. Plato, *Phaedo*, 63a. On the dynamics and importance of risk in human life, see P. Wust, *Ungewissheit und Wagnis* (Salzburg: A. Pustet, 1937).

73. See, for example, E. Kunz, *Protestantische Eschatologie: von der Reformation bis zur Aufklärung*, Handbuch der Dogmengeschichte, 4.7.3.1 (Freiburg i. B.: Herder, 1980).

74. Among the first authors to clearly defend this position is O. Cullmann, *Immortalité de l'âme ou résurrection des morts?* (Neuchâtel: Delachaux et Niestlé, 1957). See chapter 10.

75. The question is developed in greater detail in chapter 11.

avoided opposing immortality of the soul and resurrection of the dead, but integrated them quite successfully, and pacifically employed the category of the "soul" for the greater part of the history of Christian theology.[76]

It is interesting to note the suggestion of the Catholic theologian Ansgar Ahlbrecht to the effect that the doctrine of the "immortality of the soul" may have been understood by Protestants as equivalent to that of works-righteousness.[77] If the souls of humans are naturally immortal, believers might feel tempted to complacently present themselves before their Creator with an immortality "of their own," thus repudiating both their created status and divine sovereignty. This would be completely out of keeping with the Gospel of Christ centered on the divine saving power of grace. As a result, the doctrine of the immortality of the separated soul should be abandoned once and for all, it is said, as incompatible with the Christian Gospel of grace. The Calvinist Karl Barth made the same critique in slightly different terms: the soul cannot be immortal, he says, for the simple reason that, according to Scripture (1 Tm 6:16), God alone is immortal.[78]

Doubtless, the possibility of according a native (and potentially competitive and idolatrous) divinity to the human soul may have been present in Plato's analysis of human immortality and his understanding of the divinity.[79] The same danger should not by right be found in a Christian context, for it goes without saying that the soul, whether incorruptible or not, is always and only the product of God's creating action, and enjoys no metaphysical independence of its own. The soul is created by God "from nothing."[80] Both Clement of Alexandria and Theophilus of Antioch openly state that immortality is always a divine gift.[81] And

---

76. See my study "Anima," in *Dizionario Interdisciplinare di Scienza e Fede*, ed. G. Tanzella-Nitti and A. Strumìa, vol. 1 (Roma: Urbaniana University Press; Città Nuova, 2002), 84–101. An English translation may be found in www.disf.org/en/Voci/30.asp. On the impropriety of the process of "de-Hellenization" over the last century or so, see the last part of Benedict XVI's address at Regensburg, *Faith, Reason and the University* (12.9.2006).

77. See A. Ahlbrecht, *Tod und Unsterblichkeit in der evangelischen Theologie der Gegenwart* (Paderborn: Bonifatius, 1964), 112–20; C. Pozo, *La teología del más allá*, 191. Among Protestant authors, this position is held, for example, by H. Thielicke, *Tod und Leben. Studien zur christlichen Anthropologie*, 2nd ed. (Tübingen: Mohr, 1946), annex 4; E. Jüngel, *Tod* (Stuttgart: Kreuz, 1971), chap. 4.

78. In denying the immortality of the soul, Barth cites 1 Tm 6:15–16: God, "the King of kings and Lord of lords, who alone has immortality and dwells in unapproachable light, whom no man has ever seen or can see." From this he deduces that God alone is immortal, and the soul is not. See his work *Die Auferstehung der Toten* (Zürich: Zollikon, 1953).

79. Plato, *Laws*, 726a; my article, "Anima," 86.

80. In the words of Pope Leo IX, "Anima non esse partem Dei, sed e nihilio creatam . . . credo et praedico," Ep. *Congratulamur vehementer* (1053): *DS* 685. G. Gozzelino, *Nell'attesa*, 174 n. 18 explains that the Fathers of the Church deduce the soul's immortality for the most part from man's vocation to beatific vision, and not primarily from the soul's spiritual and indivisible nature.

81. Clement of Alexandria, *Paedagogus*, 2, 19:4–20; Theophilus, *Ad Autolycum*, 1:4. On the notion of immortality by grace in recent Orthodox authors, see the study of B. Petrà, "Immortalità dell'anima:

Irenaeus of Lyons: "the soul itself is not life, but partakes in that life bestowed upon it by God."[82] Thus the immortality of the soul in the Christian context may be termed "dialogical,"[83] in that humans belong to that part of the created realm that is capable of seeing God.[84] Besides, Scripture does not avoid the topic of human immortality.[85]

Historically speaking, it is probably correct to say that when recent Protestant authors reject the notion of the "immortality of the soul," in real terms they intended to repudiate a peculiar rationalistic and Romantic understanding of the category.[86] Karl Barth in particular openly opposed authors who saw in the spiritual, immortal human soul the foundation of a rationally based ethical autonomy in which God had no substantial place.[87] Dieter Hattrup observes that for Protestants the "immortality of the soul" was perceived as a clear manifestation of "religion within the bounds of reason alone," to quote the title of one of Kant's most influential works.[88] However, in recent times, several Protestant scholars have come to recognize the Christian value of the soul and its immortality, and its relevance at a metaphysical level.[89]

---

per natura o per grazia? Un dibattito greco-ortodosso nel secolo ventesimo," *Vivens Homo* 19 (2008): 299–308.

82. Irenaeus, *Adv. Haer. II*, 34:4.

83. J. Ratzinger explains that the immortality of the soul is "dialogical" in character: *Eschatology*, 150–53; on this, see G. Nachtwei, *Dialogische Unsterblichkeit. Eine Untersuchung zu Joseph Ratzingers Eschatologie und Theologie* (Leipzig: St. Benno, 1986), and the comments on this work by Ratzinger, *Eschatology*, 267–68.

84. See J. Ratzinger, *Eschatology*, 154–55.

85. On the use of the term "soul" in Mt 10:28, see C. Pozo, *La teología del más allá*, 246–47. On immortality in the Old Testament, R. J. Taylor, "The Eschatological Meaning of Life and Death in the Book of Wisdom I–V," *Ephemerides theologicae Lovanienses* 42 (1966): 72–137; M. Kolarcik, *The Ambiguity of Death in the Book of Wisdom 1–6: A Study of Literary Structure and Interpretation* (Roma: Pontificio Istituto Biblico, 1991). Recently, P. Sacchi, "L'immortalità dell'anima negli apocrifi dell'Antico Testamento e a Qumran," *Vivens Homo* 19 (2008): 219–38.

86. See I. Escribano-Alberca, *Eschatologie: von der Aufklärung bis zur Gegenwart*, Handbuch der Dogmengeschichte, 4.4.7.4 (Freiburg i. B.: Herder, 1987), 138–41. On this period, see especially J. Pieper, *Tod und Unsterblichkeit* (München: Kösel, 1968), 150–68. Spinoza states that *mens nostra aeterna est*, "our mind is eternal": *Ethica V*, 31, schol. The natural quality of the soul's immortality was commonly held by the Romantics, among them Mendelssohn, Robespierre, and others. C. Stange called it "the central dogma of the *Aufklärung*" in his work *Die Unsterblichkeit der Seele* (Gütersloh: Bertelsmann, 1925), 105. It is particularly clear in J.-G. Fichte, *Einige Vorlesungen über die Bestimmung des Gelehrten*, Vorl. 3 (1794), in *Sämtliche Werke* (Berlin: De Gruyter, 1965), vol. 6, 313–23.

87. For example, that of J. A. L. Wegscheider, who considers the immortality of the soul as the basis of the ethical norm. Karl Barth looks upon his position as entirely rationalistic. See the latter's *Protestant Theology in the Nineteenth Century* (orig. 1947; Grand Rapids: W. B. Eerdmans, 2002), 460–67, especially 466.

88. See D. Hattrup, *Eschatologie* (Paderborn: Bonifatius, 1992), 309–16 and G. Gozzelino, *Nell'attesa*, 341.

89. See W. Pannenberg, *Systematic Theology*, vol. 3, 570–75; C. Hermann, *Unsterblichkeit der Seele*

The Knowableness of the Soul's Immortality

It may be noted that the difficulties many Protestant scholars encounter with the doctrine of the soul and its immortality lie more in the direction of whether or not such immortality is natural and, as a result, philosophically knowable.[90] In effect, classical Protestant thought, inspired by late medieval philosophy and spirituality and strongly influenced by Nominalism, did not deny the existence and immortality of the soul as such, but considered it an article of faith, and therefore unknowable by unaided reason.[91] Thus, the existence of the soul and its immortality can be perceived only by faith, that is, in submission to God's word of promise, but not by the power of the mind: in humility, one might say, not in arrogance; in gratefulness, not in dominion. The divine promise of eternal reward should enjoy absolute precedence over any knowledge we may have of the existence and immortality of the soul. Similar positions may be found in the writings of Duns Scotus, William of Ockham, Thomas de Vio Caetanus (usually called Cajetan, a contemporary of Luther) and others.[92]

It may be noted that the positions just described tend to revert to a Platonic (indeed, somewhat dualistic) view of the relationship between body and soul, frequently held by modern philosophers from Descartes onward. Besides, they easily give rise to a fideistic approach to eschatology and the afterlife, compatible not only with certain tenets of Protestant theology but also with postmodern pessimism in respect of the power of reason.[93] But Christians are asked to "give an account for their hope" (1 Pt 3:15). Indeed, as we have seen above, Christian eschatology makes sense not only because of the divine promise of eternal life to believers, but also because such a promise is seen to be anthropologically and rationally meaningful to humans.[94] And if we say that the soul's spirituality (and immortality) is rationally knowable, that can be only because the soul is naturally spiritual, and therefore incorruptible. If it cannot be shown that immortality is structurally rooted in the human constitution, then faith may well become fideistic, and hope utopian.

---

durch Auferstehung. Studien zu den anthropologischen Implikationen der Eschatologie (Göttingen: Vandenhoeck and Ruprecht, 1997).

90. If the soul is naturally immortal, in principle it should be possible for reason to deduce such immortality. On the knowability of the soul's immortality, see John Paul II, Enc. *Fides et ratio* (1998), n. 39.

91. See my study "Anima," 92–93.

92. According to Duns Scotus, philosophy can demonstrate at best that the soul is possibly not mortal; the reason for this is that the soul does not communicate being to the body, in that the body is a reality in its own right (*Op. Oxon IV*, D. 48, q. 2, n. 16). Ockham argues that people just imagine that the soul, as the form of the body, is immortal, whereas if the soul is truly the form of the body, it must be perishable (*Quodl. I*, 10).

93. See the work of J. Derrida, *La dissémination* (Paris: Seuil, 1972).

94. See pp. 11–13 above.

Christian Eschatology 23

Leaving aside for the moment the content of the biblical promise of eschatological fulfillment, which we shall consider presently, it is interesting to note that many philosophers throughout history have consistently offered a wide variety of more or less plausible explanations for the natural character of human immortality, thus making it knowable by means of human reason.

Philosophical Reasons in Favor of Personal Immortality

Many if not most of the Church Fathers held that the soul was immortal.[95] They often did so on the basis of Plato's conception of the soul. The reasons Plato gives for the soul's immortality, therefore, are of some interest.

Plato was convinced of the immortality of the soul, the *psychē*, for four reasons.[96] *First*, he says, what comes into being originates from its contrary (for example, a thing that is cold becomes warm). In this way, according to the principle of cyclical return, death must be the beginning of life.[97] And so the soul survives death. *Second*, Plato bases his conviction of the soul's immortality on his theory of knowledge. To know, for Plato, is to remember. Before being born humans have contemplated the Ideal World.[98] At present, we know universal concepts such as the good and the beautiful, even though the things to which we apply these categories are always limited. This shows that the soul belongs to a world different from that characterized by becoming and change. It is therefore

---

95. From Tertullian onward, most Greek and Latin Fathers accept a more or less Platonic view of the soul, as indestructible, conscious, and self-determining, anticipating eternal life and personal judgment: see B. E. Daley, *The Hope*, 220. On the soul's immortality in Origen and Clement of Alexandria, see G. Ancona, *Escatologia cristiana*, 146–49. Origen's position is very clear: the soul's immortality is like that of the angels: *De princip. IV*, 4:9. Lactantius finds the proof of the soul's immortality in divine goodness, in the soul's yearning for the highest good and its right to receive a reward for virtue: *Div. Instit. VII*, 9. Athanasius uses Plato's arguments to explain the soul's immortality: the soul is immortal because in its very essence it is a source of movement (*Or. C. Gentes*, 33), and because it yearns for happiness (ibid., 32). According to Gregory of Nyssa the soul must be considered immortal because since God predestined man to share in all spiritual goods, he must give him a nature corresponding to that goal. Eternity is one of these goods; therefore man must be immortal (*Orat. Catech.*, 5). Gregory also insists on the simplicity of the soul (*De anima et res.*, 44). For Augustine, the soul knows what is eternal and immutable, and because of its intimate relationship with truth, it cannot perish (*De immort. animae; Soliloquia II*, 2–4). The soul is better than the body, Augustine continues, because it gives life to it; besides, it is independent of the body and eternal, although God creates it and keeps it in being (*Ep. 3 ad Nebridium*). Substantially the same position may be found in Claudius Mamertius's *De statu animae* (469); Cassiodorus's *De anima;* in Maximus the Confessor's *Opusc. de anima;* in Anselm's *Monologion*, 68–69, and in Alcuin's *De animae ratione*. The latter holds that on account of sin, part of the soul has become mortal, although its deepest core is immortal by virtue of its divine vocation.

96. At the origin of Plato's thought, the role of unwritten sources (myths, etc.) should not be neglected. See my study "Is Christianity a Religion? The Role of Violence, Myth and Witness in Religion," *Fellowship of Catholic Scholars Quarterly* 29 (2006): 13–28, especially 20–21 and n. 72.

97. Plato, *Phaedo*, 72b.

98. Ibid., 75c.

incorruptible and endures forever. *Third,* he explains that the equal, the good, and so on, are always the same, although concrete things change.[99] Hence there are two kinds of things, the invisible and the visible. The invisible keeps its own identity, whereas the visible does not. Since the soul is akin to the invisible, it will not change, it will not cease to exist.[100] *Fourth* and last, Plato explains that the purpose of the soul is to give life. But life by its very nature cannot turn into its opposite, death. The soul therefore lasts forever. He adds that this implies that it is our duty to take care of our soul.[101]

Understandably, several earlier Fathers of the Church were less than convinced of the solidity of the Platonic proofs, among other reasons because Plato takes it for granted that humans are divine in their innermost constitution, whereas the soul cannot but be a creature, with an entirely received existence. Thus both Justin Martyr and Irenaeus openly rejected the Greek notion of the soul being immortal by nature, affirming that humans live on after death in a state of shadowy existence, by God's grace.[102] In effect, to demonstrate the immortality of the created soul is not as easy as it may appear to be. This is especially so when one attempts to approach the problem from an Aristotelian angle, that is, including the mortal body as an essential element of the human composite.[103]

Thomas Aquinas, drawing on elements of both Platonism and Aristotelianism, offers three principal reasons for the immortality—or more precisely, the "incorruptibility"—of the human soul.[104] *First,* the soul is said to be incorruptible because it is in a position to know all material things. As a result it must be immaterial itself, that is, spiritual; were it not, then it would be incapable of knowing certain material things. And since the intellect is spiritual, it cannot decompose, it is incorruptible.[105] *Second,* Aquinas explains that corruption and perishing are

---

99. Ibid., 78d.
100. Ibid., 79c–d.
101. Ibid., 105b; see also *Phaedrus,* 245c ff.
102. Justin, *Dial. cum Tryph.,* 6:2; Tatian, *Or. ad graecos,* 9:4; Irenaeus, *Adv. Haer. II,* 43; Tertullian, *De anima,* 14.
103. See my study "Anima," 86–87.
104. Aquinas studies the incorruptibility of the soul in *II Sent.,* D. 19, q. 1, a. 1; *II C. Gent.,* 49–55; 79–81; *Quodl. X,* q. 3, a. 2; *De Anima,* a. 14; *S. Th. I,* q. 75, a. 2 and 6; *Comp. Theol.,* 74, 79, 84. Other studies on the question include: E. Bertola, "Il problema dell'immortalità dell'anima nelle opere di Tommaso d'Aquino," *Rivista di filosofia neo-scolastica* 65 (1973): 248–302; A. C. Pegis, "Between Immortality and Death in the *Summa Contra Gentiles,*" *Monist* 58 (1974): 1–15; J. A. Novak, "Aquinas and the Incorruptibility of the Soul," *History of Philosophy Quarterly* (1987): 405–21; L. Scheffczyk, *Unsterblichkeit bei Thomas von Aquin auf dem Hintergrund der neuren Diskussion* (München: Bayerische Akademie der Wissenschaften, 1989); L. Iammarrone, "L'affermazione razionale dell'immortalità dell'anima umana nel pensiero di S. Tommaso," in Pontificia Accademia di san Tommaso, *Antropologia Tomista* (Città del Vaticano: Vaticana, 1991), 7–21; J. Cruz Cruz, *¿Inmortalidad del alma o inmortalidad del hombre?: introducción a la antropología de Tomás de Aquino* (Pamplona: Eunsa, 2006).
105. Thomas Aquinas, *S. Th. I,* q. 75, a. 6. See D. R. Foster, "Aquinas on the Immateriality of the Intellect," *Thomist* 55 (1991): 415–38.

the result of contrary conditions. However, thought conceives all contraries together, and so cannot be subject to their decomposing influence. Since the soul is the seat of thought, therefore, likewise it is incorruptible. *Third*, Thomas observes that all humans desire to live forever; this desire would be in vain should the soul be corruptible. It is true that this argument is somewhat lacking in rigor in that it involves a move from the subjective to the objective realm. Yet Aquinas accepts its validity in that it is based on universal human experience.[106]

Aquinas's arguments in favor of the incorruptibility of the human soul just presented are consistent and coherent as far as they go, although they are not by any means as watertight as one might wish. They are certainly incapable of "proving" the Christian doctrine of immortality in the fullest sense of the word, that of the divine promise of eternal life and perfect communion with the Triune God. They are not in a position of providing either complete philosophical certitude or definitive religious conviction. Nonetheless, as we have seen, philosophical inquiry affords useful pointers regarding the demonstrability of the incorruptible character of the human soul, and makes the risk of accepting the divine promise of eschatological salvation, humanly speaking, reasonable and responsible. That is, these demonstrations provide what we have called *praeambula spei*. To accept the divine promise of eternal life may involve taking a risk, the risk of faith and hope, but as Plato says when speaking of this very topic, "it is a beautiful risk to take."[107]

The Anthropological Coherence of Christian Eschatology: Integrating the Immortality of Life and of Self

At an empirical level, it is not difficult to show that all humans, whether consciously or unconsciously, aspire to some kind of immortality.[108] Whether in the memory of the people they know, in their children or colleagues or friends, in the noble deeds they carried out, in continued life after death (immortality of the soul, resurrection, eternal life), in reincarnation, or whatever other way, sane persons of all cultures, philosophies, and religions have desired to continue existing. Immortality constitutes an instinctive need for human beings. We already saw that, according to Thomas Aquinas, the soul's immortality may be indicated by the simple fact that all humans desire it.[109]

---

106. Thomas Aquinas, *S. Th. I*, q. 75, a. 6.   107. Plato, *Phaedo*, 63a.

108. The bibliography is vast; as an introduction, see J. Gevaert, "L'affermazione filosofica dell'immortalità," *Salesianum* 28 (1966): 95–129; also R. W. K. Paterson, *Philosophy and the Belief in a Life after Death* (New York: St. Martin's Press, 1995), 103–30; F. Kerr, *Immortal Longings: Versions of Transcending Humanity* (Notre Dame: University of Notre Dame Press, 1997).

109. Thomas Aquinas, *II C. Gent.* 55 (ed. Marietti, 1309); *II C. Gent.* 79 (n. 1602); *De Anima*, a. 14; *S. Th. I*, q. 75, a. 6. See J. F. Jolif, "Affirmation rationelle de l'immortalité de l'âme chez Saint Thomas,"

26 The Dynamic of Hope

The novelist and philosopher Miguel de Unamuno expresses, in no uncertain terms, his disdain for those who propose a resigned acceptance of human mortality, and insists that the desire for a full-blooded immortality at which death seems to mock is no sign of self-delusion or improper self-love. In this desire, he writes in a letter to a friend:

> I see no pride . . . neither healthy nor unhealthy. I'm not saying that I deserve an afterlife, nor that its existence may be proven. I'm saying that I need it, whether I deserve it or not, and that's enough! I am saying that passing things do not satisfy me, that I thirst for eternity, and that without eternity nothing is of importance for me. I need it, I ne-ed it! And without it, there is no joy in life; or the joys of life have no meaning whatsoever. It is too easy to say "we must live, we must be content with life as it is!" And for those of us who are not content, what then?[110]

Yet it must be asked: what does the human aspiration toward immortality draw on? Could it be the result of some kind of cultural alienation? Perhaps the result of an overheated imagination? Emmanuel Kant looks on immortality at best as a postulate of practical reason.[111] So could it be, as Ludwig Feuerbach and others have suggested,[112] that humans systematically project their desires beyond their objective, finite situation, conjuring up worlds that do not exist, unwittingly shifting their attention from the finite real to the infinite unreal, imagining the existence of divine worlds beyond their immediate experience, deluding themselves that they are made for greater things, and acting in consequence, "as if" they were meant to be immortal? Friedrich Nietzsche for example speaks of "the great lie of personal immortality."[113] "Be faithful to the earth," he wrote, "and do not believe in those who speak of ethereal hopes; they are venomous, whether they know it or not."[114] Marxist thought in fact has consistently held that authentic, honest, human life involves renouncing personal immortality for the sake of the immortality of humanity as a whole,[115] and that an excessive attachment to

---

Lumière et Vie 4 (1955): 755–74, especially 769–71. G. St. Hilaire, "Does St. Thomas Really Prove the Soul's Immortality?" *New Scholasticism* 34 (1960): 340–56, claims that Aquinas's argument by desire provides the only valid proof of the soul's immortality.

110. M. de Unamuno, *Revista de la Universidad de Buenos Aires* 9 (1951): 135.

111. I. Kant, *Critique of Practical Reason*, n. 220; see F. Copleston, *History of Philosophy VI: Wolff to Kant* (New York: Image Books, 1985), 338–50.

112. L. Feuerbach, *Das Wesen des Christentums* (Stuttgart: F. Frommann, 1903), the section entitled "Christian heaven or personal immortality"; see also his *Gedanken über Tod und Unsterblichkeit*, ed. F. Jodl (Stuttgart: F. Frommann, 1903). On this aspect of Feuerbach's thought, see J. L. Ruiz de la Peña, *La pascua de la creación*, 220–23.

113. F. Nietzsche, "Der Antichrist," n. 43, in *Nietzsche Werke*, vol. 6/3 (Berlin: De Gruyter, 1969), 215.

114. F. Nietzsche, "Also sprach Zarathustra," Vorrede 3, in *Nietzsche Werke*, vol. 6/1 (Berlin: De Gruyter, 1968), 9.

115. See K. Marx, *Theses on Feuerbach* (1845).

Christian Eschatology 27

oneself, or one's own life project, is most certainly detrimental to the progress of humanity, and thus a source of profound alienation.

Although the basic thrust for immortality is well-nigh universal in the history of humankind, philosophers and writers have pictured human immortality in a myriad of different ways. Two basic forms may be considered: the immortality of human life, and the immortality of human selfhood.[116]

The Immortality of Human Life

Humans instinctively seek recognition, appreciation, acceptance, admiration, fame, love. They wish to be remembered, if possible forever, by the people they lived with and loved, and even by those whom they never knew or met. Humans wish to be known and appreciated; they wish to be famous, albeit on a limited scale, although some are happy enough with being infamous, perhaps on a larger one. But nobody is willingly prepared to be neglected or forgotten. People wish to leave a mark in the memory of gods or humans for the greater or lesser deeds and noble accomplishments they were responsible for. Their *lives and actions* reach out toward immortality, seeking permanence. History itself is nothing other than an attempt to recount the process of this striving. The Czech novelist Milan Kundera, reflecting on the Romantic-idealist period, considers fame as the true essence of immortality.[117]

Greek literature from the time of Homer onward was also focused in this way. Homer's epic poetry has preserved for humanity the heroic deeds of Patroclus, Ajax, Ulysses, and others at the battle of Troy. Herodotus wrote his *Histories* with the express intention of ensuring that the deeds of the heroes would not be forgotten by mortal humans.[118] The tragic drama of the Greeks (Euripides, Sophocles, Aeschylus) confirms the same thing in the opposite direction: humans constantly seek fame, permanence, and glory, they strive after immortality, but usually do so in vain, for no explanation is given for their suffering, no justification is provided for the sacrifices they make.[119]

Cicero summed up this kind of immortality by saying that "death is terrible

---

116. See H. Arendt, *The Human Condition*, 2nd ed. (Chicago: University of Chicago Press, 1959); A. Ruiz-Retegui, "La teleología humana y las articulaciones de la sociabilidad," in T. López et al., eds., *Doctrina social de la Iglesia y realidad socio-económico en el centenario de la "Rerum Novarum"* (Pamplona: Eunsa, 1991), 823–47.

117. M. Kundera, *Immortality* (London: Faber and Faber, 1991). Kundera describes immortality as the "unbearable lightness of being."

118. Herodotus wrote his *Histories* "to preserve the memory of the past by putting on record the astonishing achievements both of our own and other peoples," *Histories I*, 1 (London: Penguin, 1972), 41.

119. On the confrontation between Greek tragedy and Christian faith, see A.-J. Festugière, *De l'essence de la tragédie grecque* (Paris: 1969), 11–28; C. Möller, *Sagesse grecque et paradoxe chrétien* (Paris: Casterman, 1948), 162–233.

for those for whom life extinguishes everything. But not so for those who do not die in the esteem of the people."[120] Humans fervently wish that everything they lived for on earth, everything that filled their hearts with deep satisfaction, should last forever in the memory of their family, their friends, their people, their race. For this reason, according to the Greeks, the city (*polis*) is considered as a sacred place, for it is meant to conserve for future generations the memory of previous ones. To destroy a city does not involve merely making its inhabitants homeless until they manage to rebuild it; it is to destroy the identity of a people, to rob them of their memory and, in a sense, of their immortality. The organ of collective memory is the city, and its agent is the poet, the historian, the artist, and the sculptor. They are the ones who ensure that racial identity and memory are conserved, and if possible enhanced, with the passing of time; they are the guarantors of immortality. Thucydides, in his *Peloponnesian Wars*, memorably recounts the address of Pericles, governor of Athens, to the people after the victorious battle of Marathon,[121] describing the city as the place of the memory of the gods and immortality of the people.[122]

According to this understanding of human immortality, however, death marks the end of *individual* human existence, the extinction of the person, for the simple reason that human life, such as it is, is directly linked with the earth, with matter, with the body, with the senses, with time, with other people, with history, with the joys and sorrows of a world that passes.

The philosopher Epicurus expresses this experience in a graphic and drastic way in saying that "death means nothing for us; for when we exist, death does not exist, but when death comes, we no longer exist."[123] The Stoic Solon had it that we should "not call any man happy until he dies; at best, he is fortunate."[124] The same position is to be found in recent centuries, for example, among Marxist humanists, who attribute immortality only to a generalized "humanity," but not to individual humans, whose selfish striving for individual immortality is considered to be the root of all alienation.[125] Still, it is not unfair to say that Marx's utopian philosophy has been responsible for the destruction of millions of indi-

---

120. "Mors est terribilis iis, quorum cum vita omnia extinguuntur, non iis quorum laus emori non potest," Cicero, *Paradoxa*, 18.

121. Thucydides, *History of the Peloponnesian War II*, 41–48.

122. "The Greek *polis* is the only adequate basis for the immortality of the people. . . . One's own history is conserved in memory; memory is the organ of identity," A. Ruiz-Retegui, "Teleología humana," 832. "The fall of the *polis* occasioned the fall of what was thought to be the only basis for immortality," ibid., 834.

123. Epicurus, *Letter to Menoceum*, 125, cit. by Diogenes Laertius, *Vitae phil.*, 10:125.

124. Solon, in Herodotus, *Histories I*, 32.

125. See note 115 above on Marx. On this topic, J. L. Ruiz de la Peña, *El hombre y su muerte* (Burgos: Aldecoa, 1971), and my study "Hope and Freedom in Gabriel Marcel and Ernst Bloch."

Christian Eschatology 29

vidual human lives in the name of collective humanity.[126] Nihilistic existentialists such as Sartre and Camus go even further, focusing on death in terms of the annihilation of human existence,[127] and, as a result, on life itself as something absurd.

Modern scientific *thanatology*, a branch of medicine that deals with the process of dying, is frequently based on the notion that death involves the elimination of the individual.[128] Thanatology requires not belief in a life after death, but rather a coming to grips with and acceptance of the idea that dying is a process at the end of which the individual disappears forever, a process all humans must learn to cope with and, if possible, welcome.

Strange though it may seem, important elements of the anthropology of the Old Testament move in the same direction: death virtually eliminates the individual, who endures only in family, in fame, in moral reputation, and also, in some vague way, in the mind of God. God in fact establishes a covenant with his People, not primarily with individual human beings, taken one by one.[129] And God's People lives on, the Covenant endures, through human generation.[130] The glory of Abraham is in his children, as abundant as the sand on the sea shore. The identity of Israel is in its memory of the great deeds God worked for it: "Bless the Lord, my soul," the Psalmist proclaims, "and forget not all his benefits" (Ps 103:2).

The Immortality of Human Selfhood

The second kind of immortality is more typical of the philosopher than the poet, of the intellectual than the soldier, of the sage than the politician. It considers humans to be immortal in their ontological and spiritual constitution. At heart, the human being is considered as a spiritual soul. As a result, the self, the individual spirit, surviving death, living on forever, is immortal.[131] What will

---

126. See S. Courtois, R. Kauffer, et al., *The Black Book of Communism: Crimes, Terror, Repression* (Cambridge, Mass.: Harvard University Press, 1999).

127. Earlier on we considered the positions of Heidegger, Sartre, and Monod. Albert Camus also insisted that we should not seek any consolation in the illusory hope of salvation after death. The fact that there is no hope turns life into something absurd. Thus his work *Le mythe de Sisyphe. Essai sur l'absurde* (Paris: Gallimard, 1943).

128. On the contemporary notion of the disappearance of man after death, see A. N. Flew, "Death," in *New Essays in Philosophical Theology*, ed. A. N. Flew and A. MacIntyre (London: SCM, 1955), 267–72. E. Kübler-Ross and others have contributed substantially to the notion of a therapeutic "acceptance" of death, what is often called "thanatology": see preface, n. 28. For a critique of these positions, see B. Collopy, "Theology and the Darkness of Death," *Theological Studies* 39 (1978): 22–54.

129. On the question of death in Sacred Scripture, see ch. 9, n. 48.

130. On immortality and memory in Judaism, see C. F. Burney, *Israel's Hope of Immortality: Four Lectures* (Oxford: Clarendon Press, 1909); B. B. Schmidt, "Memory as Immortality," in *Judaism in Late Antiquity*, vol. 4, ed. J. Neusner and A. J. Avery-Peck (Leiden: E. J. Brill, 2000).

131. On the human soul, see my study "Anima."

not attain immortality, however, is what is perceived as perishable, corruptible, ephemeral: life as it is lived out day by day, impassioned dedication and hard work, military or political success, fame, material riches, historical memory, the human body. What remains is the immortal soul, and alongside this, at best, the virtues acquired and consolidated in this life through a systematic detachment from everything that on its own is not in a position to partake of eternity and permanence.[132]

This "immortality of self" is clearly different from the "immortality of life," explained above. Death no longer involves the annihilation of the individual, but rather the continuance forever of the better, spiritual, part of man, the soul, as soon as the bonds of the flesh, of the world, of this temporal, blase, life, have been shaken off for good. The position is typical of the Pythagoreans, especially of Plato, the Neoplatonists, and the Gnostics, and is perennial in the history of religions and anthropology.[133]

However, this understanding of human immortality has important drawbacks. It tends to turn the death of humans into something banal, involving neither improvement nor impoverishment of the human being at a substantial level, but simply continuity between this life and the next for the central core of the human being, the spiritual, immortal soul. As a result, it tends to trivialize life on earth, and in the process, matter, human corporeality, human society and history, all of which are simply forfeited and rendered superfluous by the entrance of the individual into eternity.

Immortality of Life and Immortality of Self: Are They Compatible with One Another?

It is obvious that the two understandings of human immortality just presented are different from one another—indeed, opposed to one another. For the first, what endures is the fruit of human life and endeavor. Though more tangible, it is, nonetheless, a precarious kind of immortality, since it endures for humanity (not for the individual) and as the result of human effort (producing the memory of great deeds carried out in the past). In the second case, immortality is less tangible though metaphysically more robust, at least on the face of things, for what

---

132. J. Ratzinger points out that the Platonic understanding of the soul does not necessarily involve an individualistic understanding of man, because to enjoy immortality humans must consolidate those virtues that contribute toward public life, especially justice: *Eschatology: Death and Eternal Life*, 79; 142–43.

133. See the classic work of F. V. Cumont, *Lux perpetua* (Paris: Librairie P. Geunthuer, 1949). See also W. Jaeger, "The Greek Ideas of Immortality," in *Immortality and Resurrection*, ed. K. Stendhal (New York: Macmillan, 1965), 96–114, and my study "Anima," 84–87. See the recently published work of A. Millán-Puelles, *La inmortalidad del alma humana* (Madrid: Rialp, 2008). See also pp. 19–25 above.

endures is what has always existed: the spiritual and incorruptible souls of individuals.[134] It may be said that classical thought establishes "an insoluble alternative: either my life endures but I do not; or I endure and my life does not. . . . In other words, either immortality or eternity."[135] In another sense, however, the two positions are not entirely unrelated, in that they share a common (somewhat dualistic) metaphysical structure, that may be summed up in the following terms: what is perishable and changeable (matter, the cosmos, the body, human life, and history) is unrelated to and independent of what is permanent and spiritual (the soul).

It should be remembered, however, that these explanations of immortality account for the two basic modes of the thrust toward permanence and survival present in the hearts of all humans: the search for a meaningful life, lived fully and freely in active solidarity with the rest of humanity in the midst of the world, and the drive for autonomy, freedom, and individual existence. And the question must be asked: is it possible to overcome the dilemma between them and speak *at once* of the immortality of human life and the immortality of human selfhood?

We hope to show, principally in chapters 3 (on the resurrection of the dead), 5 (on final judgment), and 11 (on intermediate eschatology),[136] that the two "immortalities" coalesce and merge successfully in the light of Christian revelation, becoming fully compatible with one another. In this way it should be clear that Christian eschatology provides the keystone for an ample, all-integrating, coherent anthropology.

The Spiritual Consistency of Christian Eschatology: The Prize and the Price of Heaven

Despite the insistence of the New Testament on the promise of life after death, the fact is that many people do not believe in any form of afterlife. Those who accept it often do so in a minimalist way, for example in terms of the doctrine of reincarnation.[137] Many others simply do not accept a "happy ever after" solution to life and death, as Christian faith explains it, or believe that the next life will involve definitive fulfillment and happiness. It is one thing to accept the existence of an afterlife, as a more or less perfect replica of the present life, quite another—given the poverty and misery of human life on earth—to believe in an eternity of perfect bliss in unsullied communion with God and humanity. On this point, the moral and spiritual issues involved in Christian hope come to the

---

134. According to Socrates, what will last forever existed from all eternity: Plato, *Phaedo*, 70d–72e.
135. A. Ruiz-Retegui, "La teleología humana," 834.
136. See pp. 309–26.   137. See pp. 76–78.

fore. In his encyclical *Spe salvi*, Pope Benedict XVI candidly asks the question, "Do we really want this—to live eternally?" And he suggests that "perhaps many people reject the faith today simply because they do not find the prospect of eternal life attractive. What they desire is not eternal life at all, but this present life, for which faith in eternal life seems something of an impediment."[138]

Earlier on, we saw that hope may be considered as a virtue insofar as it involves complete trust in (and love for) a person who is in a position to offer what one is unable to obtain for oneself, with a view to perfect self-realization.[139] It should be clear that if hope demands trustful love, it also requires a spirit of openness and humility. Content-wise, the gift in question derives entirely from the Giver, yet the receiver is invited to receive and accept it in humility and trust. Those who place hope in another person may eventually be enriched beyond their wildest dreams. Yet this takes place at the price of establishing an ever-growing dependency on the one in whom they hope. And the fact is that humans for the most part tend to prefer depending on their own resources, however limited they may be, rather than accepting the gifts others offer them, fearing they may develop an excessive dependence on the giver. Achilles, the hero of Greek mythology, said he would rather remain forever a beggar in this life than a king of shadows in the next. Likewise, the poet John Milton in his epic *Paradise Lost* spoke of those who would prefer to "reign in hell than to serve in heaven."[140] Obviously, this reluctance and closed attitude is a sign of an original sinfulness, of broken mediation, of a deeply rooted spirit of mistrust in God, whose goodness and total sovereignty is not recognized, of excessive attachment to material creatures. All we have has been received from God sooner or later. Hence there is no way we can obtain perfect fulfillment on the basis of our own resources, even should we wish to do so. In fact the anguish experienced at death frequently derives from a disorderly attachment to this life, which humans attempt to grasp and hold on to on their own terms.[141]

However, Jesus in redeeming humanity from sin entered into this very dynamic, freely taking on death, "losing" his life out of obedience to his Father, and then, in the power of God, who is the only source of all life, rising up to a new, glorious, immortal existence. This dynamic of gaining and losing, or better, gaining while losing, goes to the very heart of the Christian Gospel. Jesus said that "he who finds his life will lose it, and he who loses his life for my sake will find it" (Mt 10:39). In effect, according to Christian revelation, not only does God promise believers more than they could ever reasonably expect—eternal communion

---

138. *SS* 10.   139. See pp. 7–11.
140. J. Milton, *Paradise Lost*, I, 262.
141. This theme is further developed on pp. 274–75.

Christian Eschatology 33

with the Trinity—but he does so freely and magnanimously, for "God is love" (1 Jn 4:8). However, this requires a deep conversion of heart on the part of the believer, an unreserved and unconditional trust in God (Mt 18:3), to the point of being prepared to "leave all things" and follow Christ (Mt 19:27), even to the point of death. That is to say, openness to the divine gift of eternal life involves taking a risk, the risk of sacrificing one's life, the risk of losing everything, the risk of faith in God. Theresa of Lisieux, who looked on heaven as a pouring out of divine love on the whole earth, put this conviction in very personal terms: "I told Jesus I was prepared to shed the last drop of my blood to confess that there is a heaven."[142]

In brief, the grace of eternal life is true grace, yet "costly" grace, to use the expression of Dietrich Bonhöffer: God requires from those who believe in him and wish to receive eternal life, the willing sacrifice of their earthly lives as a definitive token of their faith in God. At first sight this may seem to be a contradiction in terms. However, in the light of the theology of the Cross (1 Cor 1), it is fully coherent with Christ's own life, death, and resurrection, and therefore with the Christian spiritual message.

The Interior Revelation of the Truth of Christian Eschatology: The Action of the Holy Spirit, Cause and Power of Hope

Frequently throughout the New Testament, the Holy Spirit is presented as the second witness, alongside Christ (Jn 14:26; 16:14), alongside the Church (Rv 22:17), alongside Christians (Jn 15:26–27; Acts 5:32). Whereas the Gospel proclaims Christ as "the life" (Jn 14:6), the Creed of Nicea-Constantinople calls the Spirit the "Lord who gives life." Thus it is clear that the action of the Spirit is not simply appended to that of Christ, of the Church, of the individual believer. Rather, the eschatological consummation of the Church (Christ's Body) and of each Christian is the work of the Holy Spirit, the Spirit of Christ.[143] That is to say, in every single (exterior) action of Christ, of the Church, of the Christian believer, the action of the Holy Spirit may be considered as the (interior) empowering complement. The action of the Holy Spirit is not so much one of describing, revealing, or teaching to Christians the content of eternal life and the *Parousia*. As we have seen, the content of eschatological hope is clearly Christological in character, in

---

142. Theresa of Lisieux, *The Story of a Soul*, MS C 7r, in *Œuvres complètes* (Paris: Cerf, 1992), 243.
143. See *CAA* 257–94, with ample bibliography in n. 1. See also M. Bordoni, "Risurrezione, Parusia, Pneumatologia," in *Servire Ecclesiae. Miscellanea in onore di Mons. Pino Scabini*, ed. N. Ciola (Bologna: EDB, 1998), 229–40; N. Ciola, "Intorno al rapporto pneumatologia-escatologia," in *Spirito, eschaton e storia* (Roma: Mursia; Pontificia Università Lateranense, 1998), 7–16; J. J. Alviar, "La dirección pneumatológica de la escatología," in *El tiempo del Espíritu: hacia una teología pneumatológica*, ed. J. J. Alviar (Pamplona: Eunsa, 2006), 211–34.

that it is meant to be "read off" the life and words and works of Jesus Christ,[144] handed on to humanity from generation to generation through the Church and through Christians. However, the Spirit is the One who makes the reality behind the words *present and operative* in the mind and heart of humans as a divine gift, and who therefore communicates or implants at the deepest possible level the truthfulness of the revealed message in the human heart. In technical terms it might be said that the Spirit is the One who concretely establishes the *adaequatio* between revealed reality and the human mind and heart.

Paul speaks to the Corinthians of "what no eye has seen, nor ear heard, nor the heart of man conceived, what God has prepared for those who love him" (1 Cor 2:9; cf. Is 64:3).[145] These words intend neither to obscure the message of salvation nor to discourage believers in their hope. Quite the contrary. The eschatological promise becomes for them a source of unspeakable light and joy through the Spirit, who "explains" what God has prepared for those who love him, making this reality present in the life and heart of each believer. In fact, the Pauline text just mentioned goes on to speak of the "words of eternal life," that "God has revealed to us *through the Spirit*" (1 Cor 2:10).

The Holy Spirit is the One who vivifies the divine eschatological promise, making it concretely present—credible, loveable, worthy of hope—in the heart of the Christian believer. The Spirit accomplishes this by awakening in the heart of the believer an *affectus*, a deep, almost infantile, conviction, to the effect that the reception of the infinite gift of eternal life is a real possibility. It might be said that the Spirit infects the Christian with something of his own "élan de tendresse,"[146] that paternal-filial enthusiasm and tenderness which constitutes his very being, the hypostatic Gift expressing both the love of the Father who gives all things unreservedly to the Son, and the ardent love of the Son who obeys and glorifies the Father in all he does. In the words of Jean Giblet, the Spirit may be considered as "the cause and power of hope."[147] Likewise the Easter liturgy in the Latin rite speaks of the *gustus spei*,[148] "the taste of hope," fruit of divine grace. Ac-

---

144. See notes 66 and 67 above.

145. The entire text reads as follows: "As it is written, 'What no eye has seen, nor ear heard, nor the heart of man conceived, what God has prepared for those who love him,' God has revealed to us through the Spirit. For the Spirit searches everything, even the depths of God. For what person knows a man's thoughts except the spirit of the man which is in him? So also no one comprehends the thoughts of God except the Spirit of God," 1 Cor 2:9–12.

146. M.-J. Le Guillou, "Le développement de la doctrine sur l'Esprit Saint dans les écrits du Nouveau Testament," in *Credo in Spiritum Sanctum*, ed. J. Saraiva Martins, vol. 1 (Città del Vaticano: Vaticana, 1982), 729–39, here 731.

147. J. Giblet, "Pneumatologie et Eschatologie," in *Credo in Spiritum Sanctum*, vol. 2, 895–901, here 899.

148. *Ad Officium lectionis temp. pasch., Hymnum in feriis post octavam Paschae.*

cording to Paul, the primary reason why "hope does not disappoint us," in spite of the tribulations and difficulties that may arise, lies in the fact that "the love of God has been poured into our hearts *through the Holy Spirit* which has been given to us" (Rom 5:5).

Yet the action of the Spirit is not a power or influence that humans experience in a passing or fleeting way, as in moments of unexpected or overwhelming fervor. According to Augustine, the Spirit reveals God as love in continuity and fidelity.[149] His action points rather to what is eternal and permanent, where true love will abide. Thus it would be mistaken to identify the action of the Spirit with what is unforeseen, spectacular, or improvised, because the work of the Spirit always tends to "create an abode," to bring about "a love that unites in abiding," hiding itself, not speaking in its own name, not creating divisions, but rather reminding and uniting.[150]

When the Spirit brings the Christian believer to cry out "Abbà, Father" (Rom 8:15; Gal 4:6), this does not refer to a kind of Gnostic revelation of what humans already were by nature (sons or daughters of God, brothers or sisters of Christ), such as might give rise perhaps to a sense of sterile self-complacency. The Spirit acts always in the context of adoptive sonship (Rom 8:33; Gal 4:5; Eph 1:5), that is, for those who become children of God by grace, and are destined to receive the family inheritance, eternal life, in the modality of an infinite and undeserved gift of the Father. The Spirit does so as the One who expresses hypostatically within the Trinity the overflowing and unreserved mutual donation of the Father and the Son that constitutes the life of the Trinity.[151] The role of the Spirit in hope is precisely one of making present in the believer something of the relationship between the Father and the Son, which is perceived by the believer as an ineffable presence of divine life as gift. Entering the human heart with the infinite refinement of divine love,[152] the Spirit makes the Person of Christ be known and

---

149. See J. Ratzinger, "Der Heilige Geist als communio. Zum Verhältnis von Pneumatologie und Spiritualität bei Augustinus," in *Erfahrung und Theologie des Heiligen Geistes*, ed. C. Heitmann and H. von Mühlen (München: Kösel, 1974), 223–38.

150. Ibid., 228–31.

151. S. N. Bulgàkov expresses this well: "the Spirit announces what is not his own, but what belongs to the Son and the Father. He is the transparent ambience, he is imperceptible in his transparency. He does not exist for himself, because he is everything in others, in the Father and in the Son. His own being is like non-being. But in this sacrificial annihilation takes place the happiness of love, the self-consolation of the Consoler, joy on its own, beauty, self-love, the peak of love. In this way the love which is the most holy Trinity, the Third Hypostasis is Love itself, who brings about in himself, hypostatically, all the fullness of love," *Utesitel* [The Paraclete] (Paris: YMCA Press, 1936), 98.

152. "If the fullness of divine life in Christ is determined by the measure of divine nature, the measure of the receptivity of the Holy Spirit is determined by the level of this receptivity. Human liberty intervenes as a primordial element of this receptivity. Grace does not do violence to freedom: nonethe-

loved, and in him, the eternal Father. Objectively speaking, therefore, the Spirit is the most direct and real "protagonist" of the dynamic of hope in the life of Christians.

In brief, it may be said that the Holy Spirit convinces believers in the depths of their being that the *bonum futurum arduum* (eternal life) is *possibile*.[153] He implants in the heart of believers the certitude that what God has revealed in Christ through the Church will come true.

The Divinity and Humanity of Hope

In part 2 (chapters 2–7) we shall consider different aspects of the object of Christian hope, its content, what earlier on we called the *eschata*, that derive from the Person and work of Christ, the *eschaton*. In the foregoing paragraphs we have attempted to establish the fundamental coordinates for a theologically and anthropologically responsible reflection on what Christian revelation tells us of a future that has not yet made its presence fully felt. We have paid special attention to the fact that Christian eschatology should attempt to justify its pretension of proclaiming the truth. We have attempted to do this in four ways: showing that the incorruptibility of the human soul may be rationally affirmed with a fair degree of certainty; showing how Christian eschatology is in a position to integrate the two fundamental thrusts for human immortality, that of "life" and that of "self," thus offering a basis for an integral anthropology; showing that the apparent disproportion between the price (death) and prize (eternal life) of eschatological fulfillment is reasonable and acceptable in the context of the spirituality that derives from the Gospel of the life, death, and resurrection of Jesus Christ; and lastly, that the truth of eschatological hope is imprinted on the human heart directly by the Holy Spirit, power and cause of hope.

---

less, it convinces it and submits it. . . . The correlation between grace and freedom in the creature is the particular characteristic of the action of the third hypostasis in *kenosis* in the world," ibid., 273–74.

153. See pp. 9–11.

Part Two. The Object of Christian Hope

The Apostles' Creed openly proclaims that Jesus Christ "will return to judge the living and the dead."[1] And the Nicea-Constantinople Creed says more or less the same thing: "he will come again in glory to judge the living and the dead, and his kingdom will have no end."[2] Vatican II's constitution on divine revelation, *Dei Verbum*, speaks likewise of the "the glorious manifestation of Our Lord Jesus Christ."[3] Pope Paul VI's *Creed of the People of God* says: "he ascended into heaven and will come again, in glory, to judge the living and the dead."[4] Finally, in the *Catechism of the Catholic Church* we read: "The resurrection of all the dead . . . will precede the Last Judgment. . . . Then Christ will 'come in his glory, and all the angels with him.'"[5]

According to the doctrine of faith, God's Incarnate Word, Jesus Christ, who lived and died among us some two thousand years ago, and after his resurrection from the dead ascended into heaven for the purpose of sending the Holy Spirit, will surely come to the earth again in his risen glory after the elapse of a period of time that God alone knows, in order to definitively judge the whole of humanity. This event is normally called the *Parousia*, or final "manifestation" of Christ. The Christ will come to judge not only those who have died before his coming, but also those who are still alive when he returns, the Church teaches.

The Church likewise holds that Christ's return to judge humanity will follow on from the universal resurrection of the dead, which in turn will involve the destruction and renewal of the cosmos as we now know it. As we shall see presently, these four elements—Christ's coming or

1. *DS* 30. 2. *DS* 150.
3. Vatican Council II, Const. *Dei verbum*, n. 4.
4. Paul VI, *Creed of the People of God* (1968), n. 12.
5. *CCC* 1038.

Parousia, universal resurrection, the destruction and renewal of the cosmos, and final judgment—are closely linked with one another. In effect, at the end of time the power of the risen Christ will be definitively communicated to humanity and the entire created order, thus bringing about the resurrection of all, living and dead, just and unjust, in a fully cosmic context.

Let us examine these aspects of the mystery of Christ's definitive presence one by one.

2

Parousia: The Future Coming of the Lord Jesus in Glory

> The return of Christ will be neither a terrifying act of power, nor a compensation for a long, drawn-out frustration, but the fulfillment of a gift guaranteed from the beginning and already secretly present.
> —*B. Sesboüé*[1]
>
> The universe will end in a whisper.
> —*T. S. Eliot*

The future coming of Jesus Christ in glory is generally called the *Parousia* (a Greek term derived from the verb *pareimi*, "to be present").[2] The term *Parousia* is to be found in many books of the New Testament that refer explicitly to the future coming of Christ at the end of time.[3] In Greek and Roman literature *Parousia* often refers to the solemn entrance of a king or emperor into a province or city, as a conqueror proclaiming victory, or as a quasi-divine savior-figure inaugurating a new age.[4] The term *epiphaneia*, used for example in Matthew's Gospel to designate the manifestation of the newborn Jesus to the Kings (2:1–12), has a similar meaning. The Greek term *apokalypsis*, usually translated as "revelation," is similar, besides being the title given to the last book of the New Testament. However, *Parousia*, as it is used in Scripture and Christian theology, evokes something more definitive, public, universal, victorious, and incontrovertible than the other terms mentioned. Some authors have suggested that to translate *Parousia* as "return of Christ" is not quite correct,[5] in the sense that the risen Christ has

---

1. B. Sesboüé, "Le retour du Christ dans l'économie de la foi chrétienne," in *Le retour du Christ*, ed. C. Perrot (Bruxelles: Facultés universitaires Saint-Louis, 1983), 121–66, here 149.

2. On the New Testament doctrine of the *Parousia*, see the studies of A. Feuillet, "Le sens du mot Parousie dans l'évangile de Matthieu. Comparaison entre Matth. xxiv et Jac. v, i–xi," in *Background of the New Testament and Its Eschatology*, ed. D. Daube and W. D. Davies (Cambridge: Cambridge University Press, 1956), 261–80; "Parousie," in *Dictionnaire de la Bible, Supplément* 6 (1960): 1331–419; A. Oepke, "παρουσία," in *TWNT* 5, 856–69.

3. See Mt 24:3,27,37,39; Acts 7:52; 13:24; 1 Cor 15:23; 1 Thes 2:19; 3:13; 4:15; 5:23; 2 Thes 2:1,8,9; Jas 3:7,8; 2 Pt 1:16; 3:4,12. Paul also uses the term to speak of the coming of Titus (2 Cor 7:6–7) and himself (Phil 1:26).

4. See A. Oepke, "παρουσία," 858.

5. Thus W. Kasper, "Hope in the Final Coming of Jesus Christ in Glory," *Communio* (English ed.) 12

never strictly speaking "left" the world he redeemed, with a view to "returning" to it later on, for he remains fully present, though hidden, in his Body, the Church. With the *Parousia*, or "second coming," however, the presence and action of Christ will no longer be discrete, hidden, patient, and silent, as it was for the first coming, when the Word became incarnate and lived among humans, and as it is some degree in respect of his actual presence in and through the Church. When Christ comes in glory, his presence will become decisive, public, and definitive for humanity as a whole.

Before attempting to understand what the glorious, definitive coming of Jesus Christ at the end of time involves, we wish to note that this central affirmation of Christian faith and hope—that Christ will return in glory to judge the living and the dead—has itself been called into question, especially in recent centuries. And this in spite of the critical role it plays in theology, liturgy, ethics, and spirituality.

Will the *Parousia* Ever Take Place?

Hope in the *Parousia* as a certain, albeit future, event has been contested in recent times in four areas: cultural anthropology, philosophy, science, and biblical exegesis. Let us examine them one by one.

The Anthropological Issue: Fear of the Parousia

For many centuries Christians have associated the return of the Lord Jesus at the end of time with fear rather than with joy, with anguish rather than with hope. And understandably so. For many believers the notion of the resurrection of the body[6] is considered at best uninspiring, at worst as a return to the prison of the body.[7] It may even be perceived as the very opposite of salvation, at least for the more Platonically minded. The destruction and renewal of the cosmos, accompanied with spectacular signs of tumult, chaos, and devastation of our natural habitat, likewise produces little assurance. Worst of all, perhaps, is the *Parousia* itself, for Christ will return, we are told, not as Savior, but as Judge, as the Lord of heaven and earth, to judge everything humans have ever done, and pronounce a definitive sentence on the lives of individuals and of humanity as

---

(1985): 376. The fact is that the New Testament does not speak as such of the *return* of Christ, but rather of the "Coming," or of the "One who comes": I. Biffi, *Linee di escatologia*, 25. Thus, in Mk 11:9: "blessed is he who comes."

6. For a religious and sociological overview of resurrection belief in the Middle Ages, see C. W. Bynum, *The Resurrection of the Body in Western Christianity*.

7. This was the critique Neoplatonist authors directed against belief in final resurrection, drawing on Plato's play on words between *sōma* (body) and *sēma* (tomb) in *Cratylus*, 400bc. "For the soul the body is a prison and a tomb," said Plotinus: *Enneadas IV*, 8:3.

a whole. Indeed it is difficult to imagine that the *Parousia* should be an object, much less the prime object, of Christian hope. Traditionally Christians have designated the return of the Lord Jesus in a variety of different ways that inspire neither enthusiasm nor tenderness: the "second coming," "the end of time," "the end of the world," "the end of history," "judgment day," "Doomsday," and the like. *Dies irae, dies illae,* the medieval hymn sang, drawing on the book of the prophet Zephaniah (1:14–18), a "day of wrath, that day"; *dies magna et amara valde,* "a day of wonder and spectacle, though bitter to the core."[8]

It is of little surprise therefore that Christians throughout history should have looked upon the return of the Lord Jesus to judge humanity with a certain dose of fear and trepidation. Artistic representations of final judgment, with a glorious, often severe, Christ occupying center stage surrounded by the angels and the saints, meting out justice to the just and the unjust, are well known.[9] The fact that some persons have perpetrated, at different stages in human history, unspeakable and manifold crimes, often unavenged, hardly serves as a consolation for the rest of humanity. In the sixteenth century Martin Luther records his own experiences of fear and anguish upon hearing the very name "Jesus."[10] Jean Delumeau, in his influential studies *Fear in the West* and *Sin and Fear*[11] covering a period that extends from the fourteenth to the eighteenth centuries, documents the cultural phenomenon of fear, theologically based fear, also among Christians, often related to end-time events. He traces the influence of the doctrine of final judgment, alongside social factors such as the plague, in bringing about a generalized attitude of fear throughout Western society during the late Middle Ages and up to modern times. However valid this analysis may be, it should come as no surprise that the collective side of Christian hope (centered on the *Parousia*) received less and less attention in the systematic study of eschatology, whereas the individual aspect (personal salvation) came to occupy center stage.[12] In the sphere of theo-

---

8. On the hymn *Dies irae,* see B. Capelle, "Le 'Dies irae', chant d'espérance?" in *Questions liturgiques et paroissiales* 18 (1937): 217–24; F. Rädle, "Dies irae," in *Im Angesicht des Todes. Ein interdisziplinäres Kompendium,* ed. H. Becker et al., vol. 1 (St. Ottilien: EOS, 1987), 331–340; P. Stefani, *Dies irae. Immagini della fine* (Bologna: Il Mulino, 2001).

9. See A. M. Cocagnac, *Le jugement dernier dans l'art* (Paris: Cerf, 1955).

10. Luther recounts his sense of terror when the name of Jesus was simply mentioned, and especially his sense of vertigo when pronouncing the first words of the Roman Canon during his first Mass: "Te igitur clementissime Pater, per Iesum Christum Filium tuum Dominum nostrum." See for example his work *In Gen.,* 25:21: WA 43:382.

11. See J. Delumeau, *La peur en Occident, XIVe–XVIIIe siècles. Une cité assiégée* (Paris: Fayard, 1978), especially chapter 6; *Le péché et le peur. La culpabilisation en Occident, XIIIe–XVIIIe s.* (Paris: Fayard, 1983). See also C. Carozzi and H. Taviani-Carozzi, *La fin des temps. Terreurs et prophéties au Moyen Age* (Paris: Stock, 1982).

12. This may be seen in many classic manuals of eschatology. *Pars pro toto,* see L. Billot, *Quaestiones*

logical anthropology and spirituality, the neglect of end-time eschatology showed up in terms of a special emphasis on the interior, intimist union of the individual with God by grace, and on individualized ascetical struggle, untempered by the social aspect of the life of grace, that is, of belongingness to the Church and apostolic commitment.

In sum, fear of the end of the world has quite possibly contributed to a waning of appreciation among Christians of the decisive theological weight of the *Parousia*. Theologically speaking, of course, fear is not a reliable parameter, for "he who fears," Scripture tells us, "is not perfected in love" (1 Jn 4:18). However, other important factors, reacting perhaps against such fear, have also contributed to calling the *Parousia* into question.

Philosophical Implications of the Parousia

Of particular interest is the contribution made by George W. F. Hegel to our understanding of the *Parousia* and the end of time. In his *Philosophy of History* he views the course of time as a kind of theodicy, the historical working out of the confrontation between a good, all-powerful God and the presence of evil in a world he created and governs.[13] The thinking Spirit will gradually and definitively overcome the negativity and reluctance present in the world, Hegel says, thus bringing about, in time, a total reconciliation (*Versöhnung*) of reality. This involves principally the reconciliation of the finite spirit (man) with the Absolute Spirit (God) by means of the renunciation of the former's autonomy and distinctness from the Divinity, the incorporation of the finite into the eternal, the union of human nature with the divine. In an exceptional and paradigmatic way this synthesis has already been achieved, Hegel tells us, in the Incarnation, death, and resurrection of God's Word in Jesus Christ.

However, since the death (and ultimately, elimination) of the individual is a necessary part of the process of the "coming about of the Absolute Spirit," no future end-time consummation beyond this world will be required, such as would involve the resurrection of the dead and final judgment above and beyond the world as we know it. The process of ultimate "reconciliation" will take place, rather, within the world as it stands. In the words of Wolfhart Pannenberg summing up the position of Hegel, "the presence of the *eschaton* in the Christian religion *needed only its actualizing in the world* that Hegel believed had been achieved

---

de Novissimis, 7th ed. (Roma: Pont. Univ. Gregoriana, 1938), which follows the following chapter order: death, particular judgment, hell, purgatory, paradise, resurrection, final judgment.

13. On the relation between Hegel and Christian eschatology, see P. Cornehl, *Die Zukunft der Versöhnung. Eschatologie und Emanzipation in der Aufklärung, bei Hegel und in der Hegelschen Schule* (Göttingen: Vandenhoeck & Ruprecht, 1971); I. Escribano-Alberca, *Eschatologie*, 122–29; D. Hattrup, *Eschatologie*, 124–38; W. Pannenberg, *Systematic Theology*, vol. 3, 635–36.

by the secular actualizing of Christian freedom that resulted from the Protestant Reformation."[14] In other words, Hegel's theodicy—the reconciliation of God's action with the presence of finitude and evil in the world—takes place within the world as it is, and will reach its consummation without going beyond the world's present framework. No transcendent *Parousia* need be added.

Evaluating Hegel's View In defending this position Hegel wished to correct the somewhat individualistic and private approach to eschatological salvation we referred to earlier on. He fully intended to recuperate the historical, collective, public, earth-centered, and global dimension of the reconciling action of God in Christ in the world.

The price paid by Hegel, however, would be a high one, for in any "this-worldly" eschatology the actualization or reconciliation of the collectivity (of "humanity" as a whole) may be obtained only at the expense of the individual. This principle becomes especially apparent in Marxist thought, in which the fundamental Christian eschatological principle of transcendent salvation beyond death is decisively eliminated. On the contrary, as Rudolf Otto pointed out, it is essential to apocalyptic literature that both "beatitude and justification, as being-justified, are simply not possible in the worldly state of affairs, but only within a totally diverse way of being that God will give; besides, they cannot be present in 'this age' but only in the 'new age'; they cannot come about in 'this world' but only 'in heaven' and in 'the kingdom of heaven.'"[15] Hegel's view, therefore, as it gradually left its mark on Christian theology, put the "other-worldly" emphasis of apocalyptic texts under considerable strain.

"Process Philosophy" and the Denial of the Parousia Twentieth-century process philosophers and theologians, taking their cue from Hegel's writings, came to render the *Parousia* irrelevant in quite another direction.[16] Authors such as Alfred Whitehead and John Cobb held that the world, in the inner development of which God is the prime protagonist, will continue to develop forever, in that the world is as eternal as God is. As a result, just as the Divinity will never reach its culmination or end, but will continue developing indefinitely, there will be no common or collective end to the world, for "the creative action of God will never come to an

---

14. W. Pannenberg, *Systematic Theology*, vol. 3, 635.
15. R. Otto, *The Kingdom of God and the Son of Man* (London: Lutterworth Press, 1938), 32.
16. See especially A. N. Whitehead, *Process and Reality* (New York: Harper, 1960), and also J. B. Cobb and D. R. Griffin, *Process Theology: An Introductory Exposition* (Philadelphia: Westminster, 1976). For a critique, see R. C. Neville, *Creativity and God* (New York: Seabury Press, 1980), 3–20; W. Temple, *Nature, Man and God* (London: Macmillan, 1949), 257–63; L. Gilkey, *Maker of Heaven and Earth: The Christian Doctrine of Creation in the Light of Modern Knowledge*, 2nd ed. (Lanham, Md.: University Press of America, 1985), 48–55; W. Pannenberg, *Systematic Theology*, vol. 2, 14–17.

end."[17] According to Whitehead, the future is undetermined, "for there will be no end to the new occasions that arise, no definitive meaning to the occasion."[18]

It should be clear, however, that this position, which seriously understates the transcendence of the Creator in respect of the creature, eliminates history in a global sense by eliminating the end of history, excluding besides any kind of meaningful finality. Something of a kind had been developing on the scientific front for some time.

The Parousia and Scientific Cosmologies

Traditionally, both Catholic and Protestant theology, on the basis of well-known New Testament texts such as 2 Peter (3:10-13) and Revelation (21:1), took it for granted that the *Parousia* would involve the definitive and total destruction of the entire universe by fire, and its posterior renewal through the power of God.[19]

As the study of astronomy and physics developed, some theologians came to limit this understanding to our solar system, and even restrict it to planet Earth.[20] It seemed to make little sense to claim that the whole of creation, the immeasurable reaches of time-space, should be linked with the dynamic of Christian faith, or could in any way depend on "spiritual" events taking place on an apparently insignificant planet and extending therefrom to the rest of the universe. Such promises should be limited at best—it was said—to the final resurrection of human beings. In fact, the popular conviction among believers to the effect that widespread natural cosmic convulsions would mark the end of time[21] gradually came to be considered as naive and even fundamentalist. Precipitated claims by some Christians in respect of the imminence of the end of time merely served to accentuate this impression.[22] Followers of the biblical scholar Albrecht Ritschl went so far as to claim that what the Bible says about the end of the world finds its true meaning not in a series of cosmic catastrophes affecting the whole of humanity and the rest of the universe, but simply in the death of individuals.[23] This is as much as to say that the "world" ends with the death of each person, not

---

17. D. D. Williams, "Response to Pannenberg," in *Hope and the Future of Man*, ed. E. W. Cousins (Philadelphia: Fortress, 1972), 86-87.

18. J. B. Cobb, "Pannenberg and Process Theology," in *The Theology of Wolfhart Pannenberg*, ed. C. E. Braaten and P. Clayton (Minneapolis: Augsburg, 1988), 54-74, here 60.

19. See the bibliography in n. 2 above.

20. See W. Pannenberg, *Systematic Theology*, vol. 3, 588-95.

21. We shall consider them later on: pp. 117-18.

22. The twentieth century has been marked by a considerable growth of interest in the possibility of the world coming to an end: see, for example, T. Daniels, *Millennialism: An International Bibliography* (London: Garland, 1992); R. A. Landes, ed., *Encyclopedia of Millennialism and Millennial Movements* (New York: Routledge, 2000).

23. See for example, the works of H. H. Wendt, W. Hermann, and E. Hirsch.

Parousia 45

when the universe is destroyed by fire and reconstituted by the power of God.

As a result, developments in the area of physics brought Christian thinkers not only to think twice before linking the Christian *Parousia* with possible mutations in the physical universe, but even to doubt whether end-time events could in any way be related to chronological time, physical matter, and its possible "eternalization." Matter and cosmos, it was said, have their own laws, distinct from those of soul and spirit, and the saving work of Christ should relate by right principally to the spiritual sphere. In approximate terms, it might be said that this approach is consonant with the idea that Christ is Savior of humans but not the Creator of the universe, the Word through whom all things were made (Jn 1:3).

Recent Scientific Developments On the scientific front, however, things have changed somewhat over recent decades, as Newtonian and mechanistic understandings of the physical universe—impervious to the spirit—were gradually improved upon, and eventually discarded.[24] Physicists became convinced that the universe may no longer be considered as a fixed, indefinitely extended space, but rather should be seen as a process of expansion and even of growth. In this sense, the future consummation or completion of the entire cosmos may not be excluded a priori on scientific grounds, at least at a hypothetical level, whether this be explained in terms of the principle of entropy or as the swallowing up of matter in black holes.[25]

It is interesting to note, besides, that apocalyptic ideas centered on a full-blown destruction and renewal of our earthly environment have become popular of late, perhaps excessively so, and not only with the aid of Scripture-based speculation, but often with the apparent support of scientific findings.[26] By a strange quirk of fate, at the same time as Hegelian metaphysics was being discredited and scientific thought became less and less closed to the possibility of a meaningful final consummation to the entire universe, non-cosmic and even anti-cosmic interpretations of Scripture were becoming more and more common among theologians and biblical exegetes, who, understandably, looked upon popular apocalyptics with systematic suspicion and disdain.

In any case, as a result of scientific and philosophical developments, some of which have already been mentioned, two ideas came to prevail in eschatological thought throughout the first half of the twentieth century, particularly among

---

24. See G. F. R. Ellis, ed., *The Far-Future Universe: Eschatology from a Cosmic Perspective* (Philadelphia: Templeton Foundation Press, 2002).

25. See my study "Risurrezione," in *Dizionario Interdisciplinare di Scienza e Fede*, vol. 2, 1218–31. An English translation of the article may be found in www.disf.org/en/Voci/103.asp.

26. See the suggestive work of F. J. Tipler, *The Physics of Immortality: God, Cosmology and the Resurrection of the Dead* (New York: Doubleday, 1994).

Protestant authors: first, that the eschatological texts of the New Testament refer primarily to the ultimacy of the present moment and not to a chronologically displaced future; second, that the Christian *eschaton* impinges neither on matter nor on the cosmos, but rather on human interiority, spirit, and personhood.[27]

Does the New Testament Teach the Final Coming of Christ in Glory?

The doctrine of the final coming of Jesus Christ in glory, the *Parousia*, has been challenged on several occasions throughout the twentieth century on strictly biblical grounds. Two positions deserve a special mention: the so-called thoroughgoing eschatology of Weiss, Schweitzer, and others, on the one hand, and the "realized eschatology" of Dodd, alongside the "supra-temporal eschatology" of Bultmann, on the other. Let us consider them briefly.

The "Thoroughgoing Eschatology" School The theory of "thoroughgoing eschatology" was explained for the first time in the works of Johannes Weiss, particularly in his 1892 study *Jesus' Proclamation of the Kingdom of God*,[28] subsequently by Albert Schweitzer, in his 1906 work *The Quest for the Historical Jesus*,[29] and later on by Martin Werner in his *The Formation of Christian Dogma*, published in 1941.[30] Many other Protestant and some Catholic theologians have developed their own reflections on the basis of this theory,[31] with the intention, as Schweitzer once said, "of preserving the imaginative intensity of the apocalyptic without its illusory fanaticism."[32]

According to Weiss and Schweitzer, the key to understanding the preaching of Jesus Christ lies in the doctrine of the eschatological kingdom of God, which

---

27. The classical position is that of J. Wellhausen (nineteenth century), who gave an essentially psychological perspective to apocalyptic texts, seeing them as original literary creations giving new meaning to the present situation; see *CAA* 122.

28. See J. Weiss, *Die Predigt Jesu vom Reiche Gottes*, 2nd ed. (orig. 1892; Göttingen: Vandenhoeck & Ruprecht, 1900). English translation: R. H. Hiers and D. Larrimore, eds., *Jesus' Proclamation of the Kingdom of God* (Philadelphia: Fortress, 1971). For precedents and studies of Weiss, see *CAA* 23–24, n. 12.

29. See A. Schweitzer, *Geschichte der Leben-Jesu-Forschung*, 9th ed. (Tübingen: J. C. B. Mohr, 1984). The work was first published in 1906 and was entitled *Von Reimarus zu Wrede. Eine Geschichte der Leben-Jesu-Forschung*. English translation: *The Quest for the Historical Jesus* (New York: Macmillan, 1910). On this work of Schweitzer, see *CAA* 24, n. 13.

30. See M. Werner, *Die Entstehung des christlichen Dogmas* (Bern: P. Haupt, 1941). English translation, *The Formation of Christian Dogma: An Historical Study of its Problem* (London: Adam, 1957); *Der protestantische Weg des Glaubens* (Bern: P. Haupt, 1955), vol. 1.

31. Among Protestant authors, see especially the works E. Grässer, F. Buri, G. Bornkamm, W. Marxsen, E. Käsemann, W. Schmithals, E. P. Sanders, D. C. Allison, detailed in *CAA* 24–25, nn. 16–24. Among Catholics, the first to defend this position was Alfred Loisy. See also the positions of E. Castellucci, J. P. Meier, R. H. Hiers, C. Sullivan, detailed in *CAA* 25, nn. 25–27.

32. Cit. in W. D. Davies, "From Schweitzer to Scholem: Reflections on the Sabbatai Svi," *Journal of Biblical Literature* 95 (1976): 529–58, here 558.

should be understood strictly in terms of the distinction and opposition between two different ages: the old and the new, the earthly and the heavenly, the natural and the supernatural, the demonic and the divine, the temporal and the heavenly.[33] This position is to be found in the so-called apocalyptic literature.[34] The two ages or worlds, according to the Gospels, are simply opposed to and incompatible with each other. The preaching of Jesus about tribulations, distress, the coming of the Son of man, final judgment and resurrection, new creation, and the rest, they say, is all about the coming of the definitive age. Since the coming of the kingdom is considered by Jesus as an entirely future event, they say that the New Testament message is totally, or "thoroughly," eschatological (hence the term "thoroughgoing" eschatology, or *Konsequenteschatologie* in German).

Jesus, in addition to considering the coming of the kingdom as a future event, looked on it besides as an imminent one. Both Matthew (4:17) and Mark (1:15) speak of the "closeness" or "presence" of the kingdom, employing the Greek term *engiken*, which may be understood in either spatial or temporal terms, much like the English term "nearness." The "thoroughgoing" eschatologists argue that these texts indicate that the kingdom is chronologically "near at hand," that it is about to appear at any moment. This imminent expectation gives the key to understanding Jesus' mind, mission, and public ministry, they insist: he urgently attempted to prepare the people for the imminent breaking in of the kingdom, through radical conversion and penance, "before the Son of man comes" (Mt 10:23). For this purpose Jesus sent his followers to preach in the towns and villages, saying that "the kingdom of heaven is at hand" (Mt 10:7). In somber tones he warned that those who did not convert would be judged more severely than the inhabitants of Sodom and Gomorra (Mt 10:15), who had been harshly punished in their day (Gn 19:24–25). The ethical demands Jesus places on his followers (contained mainly in the Sermon on the Mount) are particularly exacting, these authors suggest, and would be virtually impossible to fulfill except in the end-of-time emergency situation the disciples were living in. Jesus' ethics, in other words, were strictly of an interim kind.[35]

However, according to these authors, it was at this point that a major crisis arose in the life of Jesus. The disciples returned from their mission (Lk 10:17–20) clearly aware that the expected kingdom had not in fact arrived, though Jesus had said it would. As a result, no longer would Jesus consider himself as the

33. See M. Werner, *Der protestantische Weg des Glaubens*, vol. 1, 106–12. The summary given by J. L. Ruiz de la Peña, *La otra dimensión* (Madrid: Eapsa, 1975), 107–11, has been used.

34. See *CAA* 63–136.

35. For the use of the term "interim ethics," see T. Söding, "Interimsethik," in *LThK* 5:559–60; E. Grässer, "Zum Stichwort 'Interimsethik,'" in *Neues Testament und Ethik. Für Rudolf Schnackenburg*, ed. H. Merklein (Freiburg: Herder), 16–30.

prophet destined to usher in the kingdom of heaven, but as the *promised Messiah*, destined to become the *"Son of man,"* the one who, according to the book of Daniel, was meant to inaugurate the definitive kingdom of God. This conviction would not be verified until he had risen from the dead. Jesus' Messianic secret, however, was revealed by the apostle Judas, and Jesus was arrested and put on trial on the charge of wrongfully claiming to be the Messiah. Before being put to death, Jesus openly claimed to be the Messiah, and confirmed that his true identity would be revealed at the resurrection (Mt 26:24). This would ratify his Messiahship and inaugurate the definitive advent of the kingdom of God.

After the death of Jesus the disciples certainly encountered the risen Lord, the "thoroughgoing" eschatologists tell us. They had to learn to cope, however, with a new crisis occasioned by the fact that the resurrection appearances of Jesus were not of the ultimate or definitive kind they had expected, for the "Son of man" did not return in majesty and power, surrounded by his angels, separating the just from the unjust as the wheat is separated from the chaff. The apostles discovered that, instead of sitting on thrones to judge the twelve tribes of Israel, they were sent forth to continue preparing for the definitive *Parousia* by an extensive ministry of preaching, baptizing, and giving witness to the Lord Jesus until his return in glory (Acts 1:11). In preparation for this, the sacrament of baptism, which confers an anticipation of the riches of the kingdom (the forgiveness of sins and the gift of the Spirit), is administered. However, as time went by and the possibility of a final coming of the Son of man became more and more remote, Christians made adjustments and corrective additions to Jesus' original message according to the needs of the developing faith communities. The process has continued unabated up to the present day, say Weiss, Schweitzer, and Werner.

In sum, all the teachings of Jesus, of his disciples, and of Paul had been based on, verified by, and determined by the expectancy of an imminent and definitive inbreaking of God's kingdom. But since the promised kingdom did not in fact arrive, these authors claim, Jesus' teachings must be considered at best conditioned and misleading, at worst, tendentious or even false.[36] Jesus himself was a well-intentioned though mistaken prophet, inspiring perhaps in his own way. Of course this position places the very substance of Christianity, its ethics, spirituality, and message of salvation, under considerable strain. "The longer the non-fulfillment of the *Parousia* of Christ and the final events connected therewith con-

---

36. Werner attempts to respond to the following question: if Jesus' teaching is entirely an illusion, what does it mean to be a Christian? He says that the Christian message can be maintained by saying "yes" to God, in spite of a history in which no divine design can be detected. See M. Werner, "Der Gedanke der Heilsgeschichte und die Sinnfrage der menschlichen Existenz," *Schweizerische Theologische Umschau* 3 (1962): 129–40. This can hardly be considered a fully satisfactory reply.

tinued," Werner concludes, "the weaker became the conviction that the End of the world would come in the Apostolic Age and that the death and resurrection of Jesus had, correspondingly, a fundamentally eschatological significance."[37]

Difficulties Posed by the Doctrine of "Thoroughgoing" Eschatology The position of the "thoroughgoing" eschatologists is problematic from many points of view, most of them quite obvious, above all because it takes it for granted that Jesus Christ was substantially unaware of his identity and mission, and in spite of his upright life and admirable intentions, is unworthy of any kind of definitive trust or faith.[38] If Christ was mistaken in central aspects of his mission and teaching, those who follow him would be like "the blind leading the blind" (Mt 15:14). As Thomas Aquinas cryptically puts it when speaking of the knowledge Christ had of his person and saving mission, *ignorantia per ignorantiam non tollitur*, "ignorance cannot be removed by ignorance":[39] Christ could not have saved us unless he knew us and understood the mission the Father commended to him.

However, the studies of Weiss, Schweitzer, Werner, and others have had the merit of showing that, at least according to the witness of the New Testament, Christian life, spirituality, ethics, and missionary activity are deeply eschatological in character. They are driven from within by the prospect of an inbreaking of the future promise of eschatological consummation into the world and of the provisional quality of the world's present situation that results from this. Perhaps this was why the Lutheran exegete Ernst Käsemann suggested that the apocalyptic, situated at the core of Jesus' teaching, was the "mother of all Christian theology."[40] It will still have to be seen, however, whether the reading these theologians made of the New Testament, though cogent to some degree, is substantially correct.[41] Many authors now consider it at best one-sided.[42]

---

37. M. Werner, *The Formation of Christian Dogma*, 30.

38. O. Cullmann criticizes Schweitzer's position unequivocally. "With his extremely consistent, but purely hypothetical, exegetical account of Jesus' teachings and his flagrant inconsistency in his practical conclusions, Schweitzer's imposing theological work left behind burning and unanswered questions and therefore has determined the debate of the present to an extent which the parties in dialogue today hardly recognize" *Salvation in History* (London: SCM, 1967), 32. For further critiques, see also D. Flusser, "Salvation Present and Future," in *Types of Redemption*, ed. R. J. Z. Werblowsky and C. J. Bleeker (Leiden: E. J. Brill, 1970), 46-61; D. E. Aune, "The Significance of the Delay of the Parousia for Early Christianity," in *Current Issues in Biblical and Patristic Interpretation (FS M. C. Tenney)*, ed. G. F. Hawthorne (Grand Rapids: W. B. Eerdmans, 1975), 87-109.

39. Thomas Aquinas, *S. Th. III*, q. 15, a. 3, *s. c.*

40. E. Käsemann, "Die Anfänge christlicher Theologie." See my study "La Biblia en la configuración de la teología," *Scripta Theologica* 36 (2004): 855-75.

41. See pp. 53-66 below.

42. See the critique of O. Cullmann in n. 38 above. C. Duquoc points out that if the *Parousia* is a manifestation of Christ's death and resurrection, then the denial of the *Parousia* would involve the denial of the Paschal mystery: *Christologie: essai dogmatique*, vol. 2: *Le Messie* (Paris: Cerf, 1972), 281-317. Emil

50　The Object of Christian Hope

It should be noted, however, that whereas Weiss and Schweitzer claimed that Christ's teaching was based on and conditioned by his conviction of the imminent inbreaking of the kingdom of God, other exegetes suggested the very opposite position: that Jesus' own life and teaching brought about the fullness of God's kingdom on earth. That is to say, Christian salvation deals with the present, not with the future; the end event has already taken place. The latter position is frequently called "realized eschatology."

The "Realized Eschatology" of Charles Dodd The best-known exponent of the so-called doctrine of "realized eschatology" is the Congregational exegete Charles Harold Dodd. His first work on the question, entitled *The Parables of the Kingdom*, was published in 1935,[43] and his position has had an ample following.[44] Dodd attempts to counter Schweitzer's "discovery" of Jesus as a false prophet,[45] a discovery highly humiliating for Christian believers, and interprets Christianity as a religion that fully recognizes and incorporates within itself both temporal and historical reality, decisively avoids the doctrine of eternal return, and defends a clearly teleological approach to human life.

On the one hand, Dodd claims that the "eschatological" kingdom of God is already fully present among believers in the life, words, miracles, death, and resurrection of Jesus Christ.[46] The latter do not constitute a prelude to a definitive coming of the kingdom, but are to be simply identified with its coming. In other words, the kingdom of God is already complete, active, or "realized"; nothing substantially new is to be expected in the future. This position is to be found, Dodd says, in many New Testament writings, but particularly in John's Gospel, centered on the following proclamation of Jesus: "he who believes [now] *has* eternal life."[47]

Brunner points out that "a faith in Christ which does not await the *Parousia* is like a staircase that ends up nowhere," *Das Ewige als Zukunft und Gegenwart* (Zürich: Zwingli, 1953), 219.

43. See C. H. Dodd, *The Parables of the Kingdom*, 6th ed. (London, 1960), and also later works such as *The Apostolic Preaching and Its Developments*, 2nd ed. (London, 1944); *History and the Gospel* (London: Nisbet, 1938); *The Interpretation of the Fourth Gospel* (orig. 1950; London: Cambridge University Press, 1965). On Dodd's theory, see *CAA* 31, n. 45.

44. For other authors who hold Dodd's position, see *CAA* 31, n. 46. Among the most prominent defenders of a "non-eschatological" Jesus today must be included J. D. Crossan. See his works "The Servant Parables of Jesus," in *Society of Biblical Literature 1973 Seminar Papers*, ed. G. W. MacRae (Cambridge, Mass.: Society of Biblical Literature, 1973), vol. 2, 94–119; *The Historical Jesus: The Life of a Mediterranean Jewish Peasant* (San Francisco: Harper, 1991); *The Birth of Christianity: Discovering What Happened in the Years Immediately after the Execution of Jesus* (San Francisco: Harper, 1998). For a critique, see *CAA* 31–32, n. 47.

45. In the preface to a 1960 edition of *The Parables of the Kingdom*, Dodd stated: "my work began by being orientated to the problem as Schweitzer had stated it."

46. The idea may be found to some degree in G. Florovsky's "inaugurated eschatology," and J. Jeremias's term *sich realisierende Eschatologie*, translated as "an eschatology in process of realization": *The Parables of Jesus* (London: SCM, 1963), 230. It may be noted that this was really a way of criticizing Dodd's theory.

47. See C. H. Dodd, *The Parables of the Kingdom*, 82–83; *The Apostolic Preaching and Its Developments*, 80–81.

On the other hand, scriptural texts unequivocally referring to an eschatological future are interpreted by Dodd either as apocalyptic motifs inserted by the evangelists for contingent purposes or as literary devices intending to express the transcendence of the kingdom within the present historical situation. However, they should not be considered as referring literally to future events. It is not that Dodd denies outright that certain "eschatological" events may take place in the future, but he insists that, such as they are, they will have no special theological relevance.[48] Unlike Schweitzer, Dodd claims that Jesus was not mistaken in his teachings; fault lay perhaps, rather, with the early Church, in that it reinterpreted Jesus' "apocalyptic" predictions in terms of its own developing eschatology.[49]

Nonetheless, the validity of many elements of Dodd's critique of Schweitzer does not serve to justify his own position. It stretches credibility to claim, as he seems to do, that the early Church first "eschatologized" Jesus' doctrine of the kingdom, and in the space of a few short years, seeing that the expected *Parousia* had not in fact arrived, proceeded to de-eschatologize it once more. Besides, although Jesus did not accept the apocalyptic worldview in its entirety, it is difficult to argue that certain apocalyptic elements were not present in and essential to his own teaching.[50]

Bultmann's Supra-temporalism The Lutheran exegete Rudolf Bultmann has left a lasting mark on contemporary biblical exegesis. His position has in common with Dodd's the fact that he links eschatological fullness unequivocally with the present moment: the kingdom of God is already as fully active in believers as it will ever be; it is fully present and open to them. Yet he differs from Dodd in that he pays no attention to when the kingdom of God as such was established among us. In other words, for Bultmann the past has as little weight as the future; only the present counts. The historical particulars of salvation (the *historia salutis*), and especially the concrete life of Jesus Christ, contain no specific theological message. Bultmann holds that the person's encounter with the preached word does not as such bring them into contact with historically revealed realities to be shared with other potential or actual believers, but rather offers the pos-

---

48. See O. Cullmann, *Salvation in History*, 204, who writes: "C. H. Dodd brings about a reinterpretation of eschatology in another way, particularly in an appendix to his book, *The Apostolic Preaching and Its Development*, entitled 'Eschatology and History.' He can see no essential feature in a temporal event of the future because, as he understands it, the expectation of the kingdom of God is already fulfilled for Jesus. Whatever remains to take place in a future event . . . he interprets philosophically. His philosophy is, however, not Heidegger's, as in Bultmann, but Platonism. Hence he speaks of eternity, for which the temporal images of the future are only symbols, and of the Absolute, of timeless reality, of the 'Wholly Other' that has broken into history (Rudolph Otto influenced Dodd in this respect)," ibid., 204.

49. Ibid., 102.

50. See V. Balabanski, *Eschatology in the Making: Mark, Matthew and the Didache* (Oxford: Oxford University Press, 1997), 9.

sibility, in a free personal decision of faith, of opening one's inauthentic existence to an authentic human existence based on the Christ-event (*Christusereignis*). The historical events recounted by the Gospels are theologically irrelevant, he says, for they are unconnected with the reality of faith, more or less in the same way as the "Jesus of history" is unrelated to the "Christ of faith."[51] "History is swallowed up by eschatology,"[52] Bultmann states. "Mythical eschatology [the term he gives the apocalyptic] is untenable for the simple reason that the *Parousia* of Christ never took place as the New Testament expected. History did not come to an end, and, as every sane person knows, it will continue to run its course."[53]

According to Bultmann, Jesus' conviction regarding the imminence of the coming of the kingdom is an expression of the key notion of the sovereignty of God, before whom the world is as nothing. In other words, the substance of Jesus' eschatological preaching does not refer to any possible "end of time" coming eventually into view, but rather to the fact that God transcends history, while placing humans before their last end, and bringing them to submit themselves to the divine majesty.[54] The fact that Jesus' expectancy as regards the end of time has not been verified to the full does not mean that the content of his message is empty or false. Rather its true meaning is now clarified: humans are being called urgently to respond to the word of God in the present moment. The kingdom does not come from the outside, as it were, in a cosmic context, in association with material mediations. Rather it comes from within, in the existential context of a radical decision of faith.

Bultmann admits that not only the Synoptics but also Paul speak openly of a forthcoming *Parousia*. Yet he observes that, whatever of earlier epistles (1 and 2 Thes; 1 Cor), in later ones Paul speaks more of the saving weight of the decision of faith in the present moment rather than a final drama of destruction, renewal, and salvation. World history, history on a global scale, is of little import; all that matters is the individual's free decision of faith. At best, Bultmann would concede—somewhat individualistically—that "the 'Last Day' is a mythological concept, which must be replaced by the language of *thanatos*, or death of the individual."[55] This suggestion he made not improbably under the influence of Mar-

---

51. See especially Bultmann's *Theology of the New Testament*, 2 vols. (New York: Scribner, 1951–56); "The Christian Hope and the Problem of Demythologizing," *Expository Times* 65 (1954): 228–30 and 276–8; *History and Eschatology: the Presence of Eternity* (Edinburgh: T. & T. Clark, 1957). On the eschatology of Bultmann, see *CAA* 39, n. 73.

52. R. Bultmann, "History and Eschatology in the New Testament," *New Testament Studies* 1 (1954): 6.

53. R. Bultmann, "New Testament and Mythology," in *Kerygma and Myth*, ed. H.-W. Bartsch (New York: Harper and Row, 1961), 1–44, here 5.

54. See R. Bultmann, "New Testament and Mythology," 17–20.

55. R. Bultmann, "A Reply to the Theses of J. Schniewind," in *Kerygma and Myth*, 114. In the words

tin Heidegger's understanding of the human being as "a being marked out for death."[56] "In every moment slumbers the possibility of the eschatological instant," he writes. "You must awaken it."[57] "The meaning of history lies in the present," says Bultmann, "and when the present moment is conceived as the eschatological present by Christian faith, the meaning in history is realized."[58]

To support his position, understandably, Bultmann draws mainly on John's Gospel, but little on the Synoptics, which speak openly of eschatological consummation in the future. He argues that the latter texts should be interpreted in the light of the former. However, even if his interpretation is legitimate, Bultmann has to force things considerably to suggest an "ecclesiastical redaction" for many Johannine texts that also speak of future consummation.[59] As is well known, Bultmann's work, though exegetical, depends to a considerable degree on a series of philosophical and theological presuppositions that draw deeply on the liberal Protestant tradition and on the existentialist philosophy of Martin Heidegger.[60]

The respective positions of "thoroughgoing" and "realized" eschatologists are clearly different from one another. Both coincide, however, in denying the *Parousia* as a doctrine of faith (and hope), an end of the world and of time. It still has to be seen, however, whether this is the only legitimate reading of New Testament texts.

The Realism of the *Parousia:* Evidence from Scripture

From the strictly eschatological point of view, the principal defect of both schools of thought just examined—thoroughgoing and realized eschatology—lies in their all-or-nothing approach: either the kingdom of God appears to the full—now or in the near future—or it does not appear at all. Neither position envisages the possibility of God's kingdom appearing in a *real yet gradual or hidden way*. "The thought of Jesus was eschatological or non-eschatological, but not both at the same time," Schweitzer stated significantly.[61] Putting it in slightly

---

of J. Weiss: "The world will further endure but we, as individuals, will soon leave it. Thereby, we will at least approximate to Jesus' attitude in a different sense, if we make the basis of our life the precept 'live as if you were dying,'" *Jesus' Proclamation of the Kingdom of God*, 135–36.

56. See M. Schmaus, *Katholische Dogmatik*, vol. 4.2: *Von den letzten Dingen*, 32–35; R. Jolivet, *Le problème de la mort chez M. Heidegger et J.-P. Sartre* (Abbaye Saint Wandrille: Editions de Fontenelle, 1950).

57. R. Bultmann, *History and Eschatology*, 155.

58. Ibid.

59. For example, see Jn 5:28–29; 6:39,40,44,54; 12:48. See R. Schnackenburg, "Kirche und Parusie," in *Gott in Welt: für Karl Rahner*, ed. J. B. Metz et al. (Freiburg i. B.: Herder, 1964).

60. For a further critique of Bultmann, see my study *Fides Christi: The Justification Debate* (Dublin: Four Courts, 1997), 155–58.

61. From A. Schweitzer, *Das Messianitäts- und Leidensgeheimnis. Eine Skizze des Lebens Jesu*, 3rd

different terms, Paul Feine, paraphrasing the teaching of Weiss, said that Jesus preached the apocalyptic end of time, or founded the Christian Church, but not both.[62] Something of a kind may be said of Dodd and Bultmann: if the kingdom of God is now as present and active as it will ever be, then no theologically relevant future consummation is to be expected. This approach has been quite typical of a number of Protestant scholars, although the Reformed theologian Oscar Cullmann famously opposed it in arguing that Christian eschatology is characterized principally by an "already but not yet" approach.[63]

In any case, it may be helpful to examine some texts from the Synoptic gospels that speak of an imminent end expectation for the present age, which has not yet taken place. At first sight they seem to give support to the position defended by Weiss, Schweitzer, and Werner, but it should become clear that if taken alongside other texts from the same gospels, they assume a wider, richer meaning. Later on, we shall examine texts from both Paul and John that, in spite of their "presentism," unequivocally speak of the future coming of the Lord Jesus.[64]

Predictions of an Imminent Parousia

The following three texts from Matthew's Gospel that predict an imminent *Parousia* should be sufficiently illustrative of New Testament teaching. Similar ones may be found in Mark and Luke, and elsewhere in the New Testament.

Matthew 10:23 Speaking of the persecutions in store for the twelve sent out on mission, Jesus says: "When they persecute you in one town, flee to the next; for truly, I say to you, you will not have gone through all the towns of Israel, *before the Son of man comes*" (Mt 10:23). Some authors have suggested that the text may be taken to mean that final judgment will not take place until the whole of Israel has been evangelized.[65] However, this motif, though also present in Paul (Rom 11:12, 25–26), is applied by Matthew not to Israel but rather to the Gentiles (24:14). Others have suggested that the text is applicable to the destruction of

---

ed. (orig. 1901; Tübingen: J. C. B. Mohr, 1956), praef., cit. by W. G. Kümmel, "L'eschatologie conséquent d'Albert Schweitzer jugée par ses contemporains," 61. And in his work on the history of Pauline research, he attempted to dissociate Paul from the Judaism of his time by suggesting that between a fantastic apocalyptic and a soulless Rabbinism *tertium non dabatur:* A. Schweitzer, *Geschichte der paulinischen Forschung* (Tübingen: J. C. B. Mohr, 1911), 36.

62. P. Feine, *Theologisches Literaturblatt* 24 (1903): 440.
63. See nn. 38 and 48 above.
64. See pp. 61–63.
65. See W. D. Davies and D. C. Allison, *A Critical and Exegetical Commentary on the Gospel according to Saint Matthew* (Edinburgh: T. & T. Clark, 1988–97), vol. 2, 189–90; J. Gnilka, *Das Matthäusevangelium* (Freiburg i. B.: Herder, 1988), vol. 1, 378–79.

Jerusalem and the Temple, a key theme in Matthew's Gospel.[66] As it stands, however, the text seems to be saying simply that the "coming of the Son of man" (which the evangelist associates invariably and directly with universal judgment and the *Parousia*)[67] will take place within a limited period of time, before the Apostles get around to preaching the Good News throughout the towns of Israel.[68] In other words, that the final end is imminent.

Matthew 16:28 Something of a kind may be found in Matthew 16. After prophesying that he would be put to death and subsequently rise again, Jesus insisted that the disciples must be prepared to follow him to the end, taking up their own cross, losing their life in order to save it (Mt 16:21–26). He concludes by promising eschatological salvation through judgment, "for the Son of man is to come with his angels in the glory of his Father, and he will repay every man for what he has done" (Mt 16:27). But then he adds: "truly, I say to you, there are some standing here *who will not taste death* before they see the Son of man coming in his kingdom" (Mt 16:28). The text is followed in all three Synoptics by the episode of Jesus' transfiguration.[69] It is understandable therefore that Matthew 16:28 has traditionally been applied to the glorious appearance of Jesus in the company of Moses and Elijah to Peter, James, and John, on a high mountain, some days after the prophecy.[70] Against this argument, however, it may be noted that during the intervening six days, the three apostles who witnessed the transfiguration could hardly be said to have experienced the predicted fatigue and persecution of following the Lord to the point of giving their lives for him. As a result, many authors are content to apply the text to the coming of the Son of man at the *Parousia* and final judgment.[71] However, if this is so, the text likewise indicates that the end of the world is near at hand.

---

66. See n. 96 below.
67. See Mt 13:41; 16:27; 24:27–44; 25:31.
68. This is the position of M. Künzi, *Das Naherwartungslogion Markus 9,1 par: Geschichte seiner Auslegung: mit einem Nachwort zur Auslegungsgeschichte von Markus 13,30 par.* (Tübingen: J. C. B. Mohr [Paul Siebeck], 1977); P. E. Bonnard, *L'Évangile selon Saint Matthieu*, 2nd ed. (Neuchâtel: Delachaux et Niestlé, 1970), on Mt 10:23; R. H. Gundry, *Matthew: A Commentary on His Literary and Theological Art* (Grand Rapids, Mich.: W. B. Eerdmans, 1983), 194–95; D. A. Hagner, *Matthew*, 2 vols. (Dallas, Tex.: Word Books, 1993–95), 279.
69. The link-up between the end-time prediction and the transfiguration is particularly noticeable in Mark. See G. H. Boobyer, *St. Mark and the Transfiguration Story* (Edinburgh: T. & T. Clark, 1942); W. D. Davies and D. C. Allison, *Matthew*, vol. 2, 677–78.
70. Mt 16:28 is referred to the Transfiguration by Clement of Alexandria, Ephrem the Syrian, Hillary of Poitiers, Cyril of Jerusalem, John Chrysostom, Augustine, Cyril of Alexandria, detailed in *CAA* 142–43, n. 29. For further references, see U. Luz, *Matthew 8–20: A Commentary* (Minneapolis: Fortress, 2001), 387.
71. See A. Plummer, *An Exegetical Commentary on the Gospel according to St. Matthew*, 236; W. D. Da-

56 The Object of Christian Hope

Matthew 24:34 After explaining to the disciples the meaning of the fig tree putting forth its leaves as a sign that the end-time is approaching, Jesus adds: "Truly, I say to you, this generation will not pass away *till all these things take place*" (Mt 24:34). A similar text is found shortly before the eschatological discourse: "For I tell you, you will not see me again until you say 'Blessed is he who comes in the name of the Lord'" (Mt 23:39). The entire context of chapters 23–25 would seem to indicate that the principal object of Matthew 23:39 and 24:34 is the *Parousia* and final judgment that is about to take place at the "close of the age" (Mt 24:3).[72] Again, Jesus predicts that the end of the world is about to come.

Interpreting Texts That Refer to the Parousia

If the three predictions just mentioned refer unequivocally to the *Parousia*, it would seem that for Jesus the definitive end of time was close at hand. And if this was the case, then either he was mistaken in his predictions or the gospel writers interpolated the texts for their own purposes. The first option would give support to "thoroughgoing eschatology"; the second would lean toward "realized eschatology." Either interpretation, however, would amount to a simplistic reading of the Gospel texts. The following five observations may be made.

Parousia, Church, and Evangelization Whereas the texts mentioned indicate the imminence of the end of time, other texts of Matthew's Gospel seem to exclude such imminence.[73] At a wider level, it is clear that Matthew had a developed idea of the "Church" as an institution (Mt 16:18–19; 28:19–20), with clearly defined organizational and disciplinary structures (Mt 18:15–35). Such structures, which indicate stability and permanence, would seem unnecessary should the end of the world be at hand.[74] Besides, the Church for Matthew is essentially missionary in character, being directed first to Israel, and then to the Gentiles (Mt 9:47–10:42; 28:16–20).[75] Jesus urges his followers, "until the close of the age" (Mt 28:20), to "go and make disciples of all nations" (Mt 28:19). If the

---

vies and D. C. Allison, *Matthew*, vol. 2, 678–79; L. Sabourin, "Matthieu 10.23 et 16.28 dans la perspective apocalyptique," *Science et Esprit* 37 (1985): 353–64; J. Gnilka, *Matthäusevangelium*, vol. 2, 89; W. Grundmann, *Das Evangelium nach Matthäus;* R. H. Gundry, *Matthew;* U. Luz, *Matthew 8–20*, 386–88.

72. See W. D. Davies and D. C. Allison, *Matthew*, vol. 3, 367; C. L. Blomberg, *Matthew* (Nashville: Broadman Press, 1992).

73. See *CAA* 143–50.

74. See G. Strecker, *Der Weg der Gerechtigkeit: Untersuchung zur Theologie des Matthäus*, 3rd ed. (Göttingen: Vandenhoeck & Ruprecht, 1971), 43–44; H. C. Kee, *Christian Origins in Sociological Perspective* (London: SCM, 1980), 143; S. Schulz, *Die Stunde der Botschaft. Einführung in die Theologie der vier Evangelisten* (Hamburg: Furche, 1967), 229.

75. On Matthew's community and particularly on the universality of its sense of mission, see B. Maggioni, "Alcune comunità cristiane del Nuovo Testamento: coscienza di sé, tensioni e comunione," *Scuola Cattolica* 113 (1985): 404–31, especially 417–24.

Church's mission is meant to be universal, it makes sense to think that the end of time is not close at hand.[76] It is worthwhile noting, however, that early Christian writings such as the *Shepherd of Hermas* (second century) take a different view of the matter: although the Church and its mission constitute "the central eschatological sign,"[77] nonetheless the end is considered to be close at hand.[78]

Parables of Growth and Waiting At a strictly exegetical level, several parables situated within Matthew's eschatological discourse seem to indicate that the end of time is by no means imminent. In the parable of the faithful and unfaithful servants (Mt 24:45–51), the wicked servant thinks in his heart that "my master is delayed" (v. 48), only to find that "the master . . . will come on a day when he does not expect him and at an hour he does not know" (v. 50). Likewise, in the parable of the ten virgins (Mt 25:1–13), the "bridegroom was delayed, [and] they all slumbered and slept" (v. 5) before his arrival. In the parable of the talents (Mt 25:14–30), the servants were entrusted with the master's property and had sufficient time to trade with it, for "*after a long time* the master of those servants came and settled accounts with them" (v. 19). Other parables from Matthew's Gospel seem to indicate that the definitive consolidation of the kingdom at the end of time is a drawn-out affair, for example that of the grain of mustard seed (Mt 13:31–32),[79] the

---

76. See G. Strecker, *Der Weg,* 44; S. Schulz, *Die Stunde,* 229; T. L. Donaldson, *Jesus on the Mountain: A Study in Matthean Theology* (Sheffield: JSOT Press, 1985), 166–67. "The end of the present age, concerning which the disciples inquire in the question of v. 3, cannot come immediately but must be preceded by a period of universal evangelization. The parousia must therefore be delayed," D. A. Hagner, *Matthew,* 696.

77. B. E. Daley, *The Hope,* 17.

78. The angelic visitor, speaking of the Church being built as a tower, says: "Foolish man! Do you not see the tower yet building? When the tower is finished and built, then comes the end; and I assure you it will be soon finished. Ask me no more questions. Let you and all the saints be content . . . with my renewal of your spirits," Hermas, *Vis.,* 3:8:9.

79. W. D. Davies and D. C. Allison, *Matthew,* vol. 2, 417, has the following to say on the parable of the mustard seed: "Most modern scholars would argue that the theme is not growth but contrast—the contrast between the veiled kingdom in the present and its glorious future." J. Jeremias, *The Parables of Jesus,* 148–49, takes the same line: "In the Talmud (*b. Sanh.* 90b), in Paul (1 Co 15:35–38), in John (12:24), in *1 Clement* (24:4–5), the seed is the image of the resurrection, the symbol of mystery of life out of death. The oriental mind sees two wholly different situations: on the one hand the dead seed, on the other, the waving corn-field, here death, there, through the divine creative power, life. . . . The modern man, passing through the ploughed field, thinks of what is going on beneath the soil, and envisages a biological development. The people of the Bible, passing through the same plough-land, look up and see miracle upon miracle, nothing less than resurrection from the dead. Thus did Jesus' audience understand the parables of the Mustard seed and the Leaven as parables of contrast." However, N. A. Dahl can hardly be mistaken when he comments: "The growth of seed and the regularity of life in nature have been known to peasants as long as the earth has been cultivated . . . the idea of organic growth was far from foreign to men of antiquity; to Jews and Christians organic growth was but the other side of the creative work of God who alone gives growth," *Jesus the Christ: The Historical Origins of Christological Doctrine* (Minneapolis: Augsburg, 1991), 149–50. According to R. Otto, the kingdom is "an eschatologi-

leaven (Mt 13:33),[80] the wheat and the tares (Mt 13:24–30).[81] All in all, the return of the Lord, according to Matthew's parables, seems to be deferred indefinitely, and its timing is simply unknown to humans (Mt 24:36,39,42,44,50; 25:13).[82] The fact that considerable space is dedicated in the first Gospel to the primacy of ethical endeavor also suggests a relatively extended interim period in order for the righteousness of God's kingdom to be manifested.[83] Likewise the promises made by Jesus seem to presuppose an extended time of waiting.[84] Clement of Rome, speaking about the end of time in his letter to the Corinthians, teaches that things take time to come to ripeness, also in the Church.[85]

The Gradual Unfolding of the Parousia Many authors hold that the final event prophesied by Jesus in Mt 10:23, 16:28, 24:34, and other texts does not refer to the *Parousia* as such, that is, the definitive coming of the Son of man in power to judge the living and the dead, but rather to some other critical moment of fulfillment in Christ's mission that is previous to the *Parousia* and prepares for it.[86] This in fact has been the common position among the Fathers, Scholastics, and Reformation authors, until the eighteenth century, when the Protestant Samuel Reimarus attempted to explain for the first time the difficult biblical texts just mentioned by suggesting that they were not pronounced by Jesus, but had been invented after him by his followers and interpolated by the Church.[87] As we saw

---

cal sphere of salvation, which breaks in, makes a small, unpretentious beginning, miraculously swells, and increases; as a divine 'field of energy' it extends and expands further and farther," *The Kingdom of God and the Son of Man*, 124.

80. See M. J. Lagrange, *Évangile selon saint Matthieu*, 5th ed. (Paris: Lecoffre; Gabalda, 1941), 187–90.

81. This parable is clearly meant as a reaction to those who attempt to judge now instead of leaving judgment up to God. Apart from the paraenetic content, however, the eschatological imagery used is quite clear content-wise: God's kingdom will come in God's good time.

82. See D. A. Hagner, "Imminence and Parousia in the Gospel of Matthew," in *Texts and Contexts: Biblical Texts in Their Textual and Situational Contexts: Essays in Honor of Lars Hartman*, ed. T. Fornberg and D. Hellholm (Oslo: Scandinavian University Press, 1995), 77–92; Excursus "Imminence, Delay and Matthew's εὐθέως," in *Matthew*, 711–13.

83. See D. A. Hagner, "Matthew's Eschatology," 60–61. See especially Mt 5–7; 9:15; 12:33–37; 16:21–27; 18:21–22; 22:15–21; 23:8–11.

84. D. A. Hagner, "Matthew's Eschatology," 61. See also Mt 18:20; 28:20; 6:33; 7:11; 17:20; 21:21–22.

85. See Clement of Rome, *Ep. in Cor.*, 23:3–4. See O. B. Knoch, *Eigenart und Bedeutung der Eschatologie im theologischen Aufriss des ersten Klemensbriefes: eine auslegungsgeschichtliche Untersuchung* (Bonn: P. Hanstein, 1964).

86. On this question, see P. Gaechter, *Das Matthäusevangelium: ein Kommentar* (Innsbruck: Tyrolia, 1964).

87. Samuel Reimarus said that Mt 16:28 refers to a near *parousia*, such as would involve an error on the part of Jesus or the early Church: see C. H. Talbot, ed., *Reimarus: Fragments*, II, § 38 (Philadelphia: Fortress, 1970), 215–18. Later Protestant liberal authors, such as F. C. Baur, H. A. W. Meyer, C. H. Weisse, O. Pfleiderer, and H. J. Holtzmann took it that this was not a genuine statement of Jesus. On the history of the use of this text, see M. Künzi, *Das Naherwartungslogion Matthäus 10,23*, 105–12; U. Luz, *Matthew 8–20*, 387.

earlier on, the fact that eschatology tends to be an all-or-nothing affair for many Protestant thinkers easily lends itself to this kind of interpretation.

Conversely, the Fathers of the Church and other theologians refer the texts in question to a wide variety of moments that mark the history of salvation: the pre-Easter reunion of Jesus with his disciples after their return from their missionary assignment,[88] the transfiguration,[89] death,[90] or resurrection[91] of Jesus, or perhaps the coming of the Holy Spirit at Pentecost.[92] Traditionally it has also been common to apply Jesus' words to the consolidation of the Christian mission and Church,[93] to different stages of the active presence of the kingdom of God on earth. As we shall see presently, the sacraments, especially the Eucharist, represent a special inbreaking of the power and love of God into our present age.[94] Authors such as Origen have interpreted the texts in a spiritual fashion, speaking of the timeless presence of God's kingdom in the hearts of Christians in the absence of external manifestations.[95] In recent centuries it has been commonly suggested that Jesus' predictions relate directly to the desecration of the Temple and the destruction of Jerusalem in AD 70.[96]

Those who espouse "thoroughgoing" eschatology argue that since the coming of the Kingdom did not leave as tangible a mark on history as the apocalyptic texts said it would, then it should not be considered worthy of trust and acceptance. It seems, however, that in doing so they are "seeking a sign" (Mt 12:38).[97] Their quest would undo both the logic of the Incarnation as the "self-emptying" of God in taking on a common, historical humanity,[98] the need for faith in order to be saved, and the inevitable *chiaroscuro* of the Christian pilgrimage on earth,

88. See for example, John Chrysostom, *Hom. in Matth.*, 34:1 (on Mt 10:23).

89. See *CAA* 142, n. 28.

90. See R. Clark, "Eschatology and Matthew 10:23," *Restoration Quarterly* 7 (1963): 73–81.

91. The position is relatively recent, probably posterior to the Protestant Reformation. For details, see *CAA* 147, n. 52.

92. This is also typical of Protestant theologians; see *CAA* 147, n. 53.

93. It is quite typical among some of the Fathers to identify the kingdom of God, purely and simply, with the Church. See for example, Gregory the Great, *Hom.* 32:7; Bede the Venerable, *In Marci Evangelii Expositio III*, 8. For recent authors, see *CAA* 147, n. 54. Mt 24:34 has also been understood in this sense by John Chrysostom, *Hom. in Matth.*, 17:1; Eusebius, *Fram. in Luc.*, on Lk 21:32.

94. See Benedict XVI, Apost. Exh. *Sacramentum caritatis* (2007), n. 31.

95. This is typical of Origen. In his *Comm. in Joh.*, 12:33, for example, he says that Mt 16:28 refers to the spiritual person's vision of the glorious and all-surpassing word of God. The apocryphal (and possibly Gnostic) *Gospel of Thomas*, log. 1, speaks in a like fashion, saying that those who understand the words of the living Jesus will not taste death, an idea suggested, it may be said, in Jn 8:51.

96. Mainly among Protestant authors. For details, see *CAA* 148–49, n. 57.

97. See *CAA* 150–54.

98. See my study "Il mistero dell'incarnazione e la giustificazione. Una riflessione sul rapporto antropologia-cristologia alla luce della *Gaudium et spes* 22," in *Il mistero dell'incarnazione e il mistero dell'uomo*, ed. M. Gagliardi (Città del Vaticano: Vaticana, 2009), 87–97.

presided over by the Cross of Christ. The eschatological kingdom of God is powerfully present and active, alive although hidden, awaiting the final revelation of the children of God (Rom 8:19).[99]

In any case, whatever way the texts are to be understood, it is clear that their gradual or partial fulfillment throughout the history of salvation always constitutes a kind of "typological foreshadowing"[100] of the final, glorious, *Parousia*. The exegete Donald Hagner concludes, therefore, that "although Jesus taught the imminent fall of Jerusalem, he did not teach the imminence of the *Parousia*, leaving the latter to the undetermined future."[101] He suggests, however, that "the disciples, upon hearing the prophecy of the destruction of the temple, thought immediately of the *Parousia* and the end of the age. Knowing that Jesus had taught the imminence of the fall of the temple, they naturally assumed the imminence of the *Parousia*. In their mind, the two were inseparable."[102] The position was probably not untypical among Christians of the first hour (1 Thes 4:13–17).

Human Involvement in the Parousia Commenting on Matthew 23:39 ("For I tell you, you will not see me again until you say 'Blessed is he who comes in the name of the Lord'"), several authors[103] have suggested that Matthew's imminent end texts constitute a kind of *conditional prophecy*.[104] Dale Allison interprets Matthew 23:39 as follows:

---

99. See pp. 228–35 below on the "Kingdom of God."

100. M. Künzi, *Das Naherwartungslogion Markus 9,1 par*, 188–89.

101. D. A. Hagner, *Matthew*, 711. For all the similarities Mt 24–25 has "to apocalyptic writings, there are at the same time some striking differences. Most important, the discourse does not attempt to provide a timetable for the end time. Information concerning the time of the parousia is conspicuously absent, denied even to Matthew's central figure, the Son of man himself (24:36). The text does not intend to inflame the expectation of an imminent end, or even a predictable end. If anything, it cools such ideas. Tribulations that might have been thought to indicate an imminent end are described as 'but the beginning of the birth pangs' (24:8). All that is assured in the discourse is the *fact* of the end. The time is deliberately left indeterminate. Consequently, the discourse retains its relevance in every Christian generation," ibid., 684.

102. Ibid., 711. This would explain, Hagner says, why "*immediately* after the tribulation of those days . . . the sign of the Son of man will appear in heaven . . . and [the tribes of the earth] . . . will see the Son of man coming on the clouds of heaven with power and great glory" (Mt 24:29–30). On the term "immediately," what E. Grässer, in *Das Problem der Parusieverzögerung in den synoptischen Evangelien und in der Apostelgeschichte* (Berlin: Töpelmann, 1957), 218, calls the "puzzle of Matthew," see F. C. Burkitt, "On *Immediately* in Mt 24.29," *Journal of Theological Studies* 12 (1911): 460–61.

103. Such as H. van der Kwaak, "Die Klage über Jerusalem (Matth. xxiii 37–39)," *Novum Testamentum* 8 (1966): 156–70, and especially D. C. Allison, in a widely accepted article, "Matt. 23:39 = Luke 12:35b as a Conditional Prophecy," *Journal for the Study of the New Testament* 18 (1983): 75–84. See also *CAA* 149, n. 62.

104. The position is not a recent one, for Ronald Knox once described Mt 16:28 as a "conditional prophecy, depending for its fulfillment on the realization of certain human conditions," R. A. Knox, *Off the Record* (London: Sheed and Ward, 1953), 36. For a further analysis, see *CAA* 150, n. 63.

The text means not: "When the Messiah comes, his people will bless him"; but rather, "When his people bless him, the Messiah will come." In other words, the date of the redemption is contingent upon Israel's acceptance of the person and work of Jesus. . . . He affirms that, if she will, Jerusalem can, in the end, bless in the name of the Lord the one who will come, and her doing so, that is, her repentance, will lead to deliverance.[105]

The end of time depends, therefore, not only on the divine predetermination of history, but also on the response of humans to God's offer of salvation. Since the new heavens and the new earth are bound to appear, Peter says in his second letter, "what sort of persons ought you to be in lives of holiness and godliness, waiting for *and hastening* the coming of the day of God" (3:11–12). The term "hastening" is a translation of the Greek *speudotas*, which means "to speed" or "urge on." Perhaps a Lutheran view of Scripture that rejects works-righteousness might find such a synthesis between divine action and human response less than acceptable.[106] Yet if human involvement is critical in the context of *individual* salvation, as Scripture clearly teaches, why should ethical endeavor not play some part in the coming about of the *Parousia*, that is, in the salvation *of the whole*? We shall return to this issue presently.[107]

The Parousia in Paul and John For both Paul and John the articulation between the future and present aspects of the *Parousia* is complex and deeply rooted.

Paul openly speaks of the futurity of the *Parousia* in the context of the doctrine of final resurrection. In his earlier epistles,[108] for example 1 and 2 Thessalonians and 1 Corinthians, Paul expresses definitive eschatological salvation in openly future terms. In the former, Paul exclaims: "for the Lord himself will descend from heaven with a cry of command, with the archangel's call" (1 Thes 4:16). In 1 Corinthians 15 he addresses Christians who, because they either were excessively attached to charismatic and apocalyptic experiences or had come under the influence of Greek thought-forms, inimical to the human body,[109] interpreted the doctrine of final resurrection in spiritual terms, or as something

---

105. C. F. Allison, "Matt. 23:39 = Luke 12:35b as a Conditional Prophecy," 77, 80. Allison bolsters this opinion in four ways: *first*, belief in the contingency of the time of the final redemption is well attested to in Jewish sources of the second century and later; *second*, the term "until" (*heōs*) can indicate a contingent state in Greek sentences in which the realization of the apodosis is dependent on the realization of the protasis—thus the term is perhaps closer to "unless" than to "until"; *third*, the structure of Mt 23:39 indicates a conditional interpretation according to the Rabbinic traditions; *fourth*, the context does not seem to involve either an unqualified announcement of salvation or its utter rejection, but rather a middle ground between the two.

106. See my work *Fides Christi*, 161–69.

107. See pp. 109–12 below.

108. On Pauline eschatology in general, see S. Zedda, *L'escatologia biblica*, vol. 2: *Nuovo Testamento* (Brescia: Paideia, 1975), 9–256.

109. See B. Maggioni, "Alcune comunità cristiane del Nuovo Testamento."

already achieved through baptism (a kind of realized eschatology). Paul teaches that even though the new life of the baptized constitutes a real anticipation of the resurrection, final transformation still has to come. "For this perishable nature must put on the imperishable, and this mortal nature must put on immortality. When the perishable puts on the imperishable, and the mortal puts on immortality, then shall come to pass the saying that is written 'Death is swallowed up in victory'" (1 Cor 15:53–54).

Later Pauline epistles concentrate more on the present moment of believing in Christ.[110] Less attention is paid to the end of time and to future salvation, although the latter are never called into question. The "Day of Yahweh" that the prophets of the Old Testament spoke of, called the "Day of the Lord" in 1 Thessalonians and 1 Corinthians, becomes the "day of judgment" in later Pauline writings,[111] the day of the resurrection of the dead (Rom 8:11; Phil 3:21), of the manifestation of glory (Rom 8:18; Col 3:4), of the end of the present age (Eph 1:21; 2:7; 4:30).

Besides, Pauline exhortations to believers constantly refer to the essentially fleeting character of "the flesh" and of all human endeavor, "for the form of this world is passing away" (1 Cor 7:31). In fact Christians are saved only in hope (Rom 8:24),[112] for they live "awaiting their blessed hope, the appearing of the glory of our great God and Savior Jesus Christ" (Ti 2:13). Celebrating the Eucharist "until he [Christ] comes" (1 Cor 11:26), they must live upright lives consisting of patience, perseverance in good works, detachment, vigilant prayer, fraternal charity, and joy.

It is well known that the *Gospel of John* gives particular emphasis to the "presentist" character of Christian salvation, as Dodd and other exegetes have correctly pointed out. However, the future aspect of salvation is by no means neglected.[113] It is probably true to say that, far from *denying* the eschatological side of Christian salvation, the fourth Gospel gives expression to a movement that goes from the future to the present. Doubtless, "eternal life"—a key term in this Gospel—is already present and active within believers in the present moment, for the one who believes is said to already enter into, or have, eternal life (Jn 3:36; 5:24; 6:47). However, the promise of final resurrection clearly refers to a future event (Jn 6:55), that will take place "on the last day" (Jn 6:39,40,44,54), along

---

110. See S. Zedda, *L'escatologia biblica*, vol. 2, 195–200.

111. See Rom 2:5–11; 14:10–13; 2 Cor 4:5; Eph 5:5; Col 4:24; Heb 10:27–29.

112. See H. Schlier, "Das, worauf alles wartet. Eine Auslegung von Römer 8, 18–30," in *Das Ende der Zeit. Exegetische Aufsätze und Vorträge* (Freiburg i. B.: Herder, 1971), 250–71.

113. It is not uncommonly held that older parts of the Johannine corpus may be traced to the Synoptic tradition: M.-É. Boismard, "L'évolution du thème eschatologique dans les traditions johanniques," *Revue Biblique* 68 (1961): 507–24.

with judgment (Jn 12:48). The first letter of John speaks likewise of the great day of judgment (1 Jn 4:17) as the final manifestation of the Lord (1 Jn 2:28). Besides, the book of Revelation, which belongs to the Johannine corpus, is fully directed toward the definitive return of the Lord Jesus in glory.[114]

How Christians Perceived the Promise of the Lord's Return

Did Early Christians Expect Jesus to Return in a Short Space of Time? It is probable that some early Christians sincerely expected their beloved Savior to return to the earth in glory within their own lifetimes. After all, he had promised he would come back to be with the Apostles (Lk 17:22; Jn 13:36; 14:3; 18:28). In the first letter to the Thessalonians, probably the first text of the New Testament, Paul addresses an acute problem experienced by Christians anxious for the salvation of their loved ones who had died before the return of the Lord Jesus.[115] He makes it quite clear that although Christ had not yet returned, his future coming was assured. "But we would not have you ignorant, brothers, concerning those who are asleep, that you may not grieve as others do who have not hope. . . . For this we declare to you by the word of the Lord, that we who are alive, who are left until the coming of the Lord, shall not precede those who have fallen asleep. For the Lord himself will descend from heaven with a cry of command, with the archangel's call. . . . And the dead in Christ will rise first; then *we who are alive, who are left,* shall be caught up together with them in the clouds to meet the Lord in the air" (1 Thes 4:13,15–17).[116] The second letter to the Thessalonians speaks of the moment when "the Lord Jesus is revealed from heaven with his mighty angels in flaming fire" (2 Thes 1:7), even though Paul also notes that the return of the Lord is not imminent (2 Thes 2:1–3).

As we have seen, some authors claim that the phenomenon described by Paul may have been due to a conscious falsification on the part of Jesus or his disciples. It is more likely, however, that the harried, persecuted Christian community experienced a profound nostalgia for their beloved Savior who had

---

114. See S. Zedda, *L'escatologia biblica*, vol. 2, 427–515; U. Vanni, "Dalla venuta dell' 'ora' alla venuta di Cristo. La dimensione storico-cristologica dell'escatologia nell'apocalisse," in *L'Apocalisse: ermeneutica, esegesi, teologia* (Bologna: EDB, 1988), 305–32.

115. See J. Dupont, *ΣΥΝ ΧΡΙΣΤΩΙ. L'union avec le Christ suivant saint Paul* (Bruges: Abbaye de Saint-André, 1952), 40–41, 43; B. Maggioni, "L'escatologia nelle lettere ai Tessalonicesi," *Rivista di Pastorale Liturgica* 9 (1972): 308–13.

116. The Thessalonians, it would seem, believed the *Parousia* would certainly come, but were concerned about the departed, fearing the latter would not share in the joy of the Lord's coming because of the excessive time that would elapse between *Parousia* and resurrection/judgment. The point Paul makes, however, is an important one: that *Parousia* and resurrection/judgment coincide. As a result, those who are still alive when Jesus returns will enjoy the company of those who were dead and now rise. For this reason those alive now will have no advantage over the dead.

promised to be with them always, and hoped indeed that he would come to them again as soon as possible, pronouncing the ineffable words "peace be with you" (Lk 24:36; Jn 20:19) that he had uttered upon appearing to them after the resurrection, thus convincing them they had been pardoned their sins and sent to evangelize the whole world.

The philosopher Maurice Blondel, criticizing Weiss's theory of "thoroughgoing" eschatology in a 1904 work, observed that the latter did not take real Christian life, faith, and martyrdom sufficiently seriously. "If the work of Jesus survived beyond his death, if it has overcome all delusions, this is not only because the *Parousia* that inflamed Jewish hopes was firmly expected to take place, but because Christians kept in their hearts what is essential to every spiritual movement, an invincible love, devotion to the adored person of the Good Teacher."[117]

The Fathers of the Church, Parousia, and the Millennium It would seem that several of the Apostolic Fathers understood the Synoptic texts (and others) announcing the *Parousia* as referring to the imminent end of time.[118] Ignatius of Antioch openly said that "the last days are here."[119] So did Justin Martyr,[120] although he added that the end will not come until the number of the just has reached completion.[121] Likewise Irenaeus was of the opinion that the end-time is near at hand. Given that, according to the commonly held opinion, the end of the world was due to occur six thousand years after its creation,[122] he took it that the Incarnation of the Word has taken place "at the evening of history."[123] Cyprian often expresses his conviction that human history has reached its sundown.[124] He says: "the world is failing, passing away, and it witnesses to its ruin not now by its age, but by the end of all things."[125] Lactantius (third–fourth century) also said that the earth would come to an end after six thousand years, and that in the present moment we are witnessing the "extreme old age of a tired and crumbling world."[126]

---

117. M. Blondel, "Histoire et dogme. Les lacunes philosophiques de l'exégèse moderne," in *Les premiers écrits de Maurice Blondel* (Paris: PUF, 1956), 149–228; here 179–80. In this text of 1904, Blondel analyzes and criticizes historicist exegesis of Scripture.

118. On the Fathers of Church, see B. E. Daley, *The Hope*, 3–4; J. Timmermann, *Nachapostolisches Parusiedenken untersucht im Hinblick auf seine Bedeutung für einen Parusiebegriff christlichen Philosophierens* (München: Max Hueber, 1968), 38–91.

119. Ignatius of Antioch, *Ad Eph.*, 11:1; *Ad Mag.*, 5:1.

120. Justin, *Dial. cum Tryph.*, 28, 32:40.   121. Justin, *1 Apol.*, 28, 45; *Dial. cum Tryph.*, 39.

122. Irenaeus, *Adv. Haer.* V, 28:3.

123. Ibid., *V*, 15:4. On this aspect of the eschatology of Irenaeus, see W. C. Van Unnik, "Der Ausdruck 'In den letzen Zeiten,'" in *Neotestamentica et Patristica. Festschrift O. Cullmann*, ed. W. C. Van Unnik (Leiden: E. J. Brill, 1962), 293–304.

124. Cyprian, *Ep.* 63:16.

125. Cyprian, *De mort.*, 25 (= *Ep.* 56); *Ep.* 61:4; 67:7.

126. Lactantius, *Div. Instit.* VII, 14.

According to Eusebius of Caesarea,[127] popular expectation of an immediate end of the world seems to have reached fever pitch in several parts of Western Christendom during the third century, especially in times of persecution. It was commonly held that the world was already old and was coming to its end, what the Stoics called the *senectus mundi*, the world's senescence.[128] John Chrysostom takes it that Matthew's prophecy concerning universal evangelization has already been fulfilled and that the end is close at hand.[129] Augustine has the following to say:

> You are surprised that the world is losing its grip? That the world is grown old? Think of a man: he is born, he grows up, he become old. Old age has its many complaints: coughing, shaking, failing eyesight, anxious, terrible tiredness. A man grows old; he is full of complaints. The world is old; it is full of pressing tribulations. . . . Do not hold on to the old man, the world; do not refuse to regain your youth in Christ, who says to you: "The world is passing away, the world is losing its grip, the world is short of breath. Do not fear, Thy youth shall be renewed as an eagle." (Augustine, *Sermo* 81, 8)

Pope Gregory the Great, in the midst of the tribulations occasioned by the fall of the Roman Empire, was convinced that the end was imminent.[130] In the *Life* of St. Gregory written by John the Deacon, we read that "in all his words and acts Gregory considered that the final day and the coming judgment were imminent; the closer he felt the end of the world to be, with its numerous disasters and calamities, the more carefully he pondered all human affairs."[131] "The world is not merely announcing its end," Gregory says, "but pointing directly to it."[132] The reason for the social ills that abound, he added, lies in the fact that the world has grown old[133] and is now in its final agony.[134]

Nonetheless, it is important to point out that the Fathers on the whole consider that the coming of the Son of God in the flesh constitutes a first stage in the *Parousia*.[135] For this reason, Chrysostom argues that our interest in the when and wherefore of the end of the world constitutes a form of idle curiosity, and he asks: "Is not the consummation of the world, for each of us, the end of his own

---

127. Eusebius of Caesarea, *Hist. Eccl.*, 6:7.
128. On the Stoic notion of the *senectus mundi*, see M. Spanneut, *Le stoïcisme des Pères de l'Église: De Clément de Rome à Clément d'Alexandrie* (Paris: Seuil, 1957), 258; B. E. Daley, *The Hope*, 33–43.
129. John Chrysostom, *Hom. in Matth.*, 10:5–6; *In Hebr. Hom.*, 21:3.
130. See C. Dagens, "La fin des temps et l'Église selon Saint Grégoire le Grand," *Recherches de science religieuse* 58 (1970): 273–88.
131. John the Deacon, *Vita Greg.*, 4:65.   132. Gregory the Great, *Dial.*, 3:38:3.
133. Gregory the Great, *Hom. in Ev.*, 1,1:1.   134. Ibid., 5.
135. To an important degree, Ignatius of Antioch taught a realized eschatology (*Ad Eph.*, 19:3), and called Jesus' coming the "parousia" (*Ad Philad.*, 9:2). On this issue, see the work of D. E. Aune, *The Cultic Setting of Realized Eschatology in Early Christianity* (Leiden: E. J. Brill, 1972).

life? Why are you concerned and worried about the common end? . . . The time of consummation took its beginning with Adam, and the end of each of our lives is an image of the consummation. One would not be wrong, then, in calling it the end of the world."[136]

Still, we may ask: what did the Fathers of the Church and early Christian writers have to say about the fact that the promised *Parousia* did not, in fact, take place immediately, as Scripture seemed to indicate it should? The fact that they reacted pacifically may be taken as a sign that such a delay occasioned no particular crisis among believers. A spiritual reading was commonly given to the delay in the *Parousia*. Augustine commented that "this last hour is long in coming; but it is the last."[137] Cándido Pozo concludes that in the writings of Church Fathers "there is no historical indication whatever of a crisis. Christians lived in the most natural way possible their experience of the delay in the *Parousia*."[138]

What is worthy of note, however, during the first three centuries of Christendom, is the phenomenon of *millennialism*, the prediction of a more or less imminent thousand-year reign of peace on earth (referred to by Rv 20:2–7) before the *Parousia* takes place. We shall return to this question later on.[139]

The *Parousia*, the Hope of the Church

After having attempted to clarify some of the theological and exegetical issues involved in New Testament eschatological texts, we can now turn our attention to the principal object of this chapter: the content and meaning of the hope of Christians, the hope of the Church, the *Parousia* or final coming of Jesus Christ in glory, "the theme that dominates all others" in the New Testament.[140] First we shall consider the doctrine of the *Parousia* in Scripture and some liturgical texts. Then we shall consider some of its properties as God's final, public victory in Christ over the power of evil, as the consummation of history.

The Parousia in Scripture and the Liturgy

In Scripture and in the liturgical tradition of the Church, the *Parousia* occupies a central role.

Joyfully Hoping for the Coming of the Lord The New Testament makes it clear not only that Christians expected Jesus to come again in glory, but that his return was an object of joyful hope. "Now when these things begin to take place," Jesus said, speaking of the eschatological signs, "look up and raise your heads, because

---

136. John Chrysostom, *In Ep. 1 ad Thess.*, 9:1.
138. C. Pozo, *La teología del más allá*, 114–15.
140. Thus E. Brunner, *Das Ewige*, 149.
137. Augustine, *In I Ep. Jo. tr.*, 3:3, on 1 Jn 2:18.
139. See pp. 242–51.

your redemption is drawing near" (Lk 21:28). The desire of Christians that God's power would be made manifest to the whole world is contained in the vibrant petition of the Lord's Prayer, "your kingdom come."[141]

Paul exhorts Titus and Christian believers alike to "live sober, upright, and godly lives in this world, awaiting our blessed hope, the appearing of the glory of our great God and Savior Jesus Christ" (Ti 2:12–14). Other Pauline texts speak in the same way. "But our fatherland is in heaven, and from it we await a Savior, the Lord Jesus Christ" (Phil 3:20). To Timothy he says: "I charge you to keep the commandment unstained and free from reproach until the appearing (*epiphaneia*) of our Lord Jesus Christ" (1 Tm 6:14). While in the second letter we read: "Henceforth there is laid up for me the crown of righteousness, which the Lord, the righteous judge, will award to me on that Day, and not only to me but also to all who have loved [*egapekosi*] his appearing" (2 Tm 4:8). Likewise in both James (5:7–8) and Peter (1 Pt; 2 Pt 3:1–9) it is clear that hope in the return of the Lord Jesus constitutes for Christians an invitation to vigilance and perseverance in the faith.

The end of the book of Revelation offers a *crescendo* of joyful hope in the final coming of the Lord Jesus: "The Spirit and the Bride say, 'Come.' And let him who hears say, 'Come.' And let him who is thirsty come, let him who desires to take the water of life without price. . . . He who testifies to these things says, 'Sure I am coming soon.' Amen. Come, Lord Jesus!" (Rv 22:17,20).

The Place of the Parousia in the Church's Liturgy Writing to the Corinthians Paul speaks of the celebration of the Eucharist of the Lord Jesus *"until he comes"* (1 Cor 11:26). In effect, the Eucharistic celebration, the mystery of faith, gives believers a foretaste of the Lord's future coming.[142] "Christian hope of ancient times is above all a liturgical hope," observes Henri Bourgeois.[143] A case in point is the early Christian prayer called the *Didachē*, or the "Doctrine of the Twelve Apostles," which contains the following liturgical intercession: "May grace come and may this world be scattered. *Maranatha*, come, Lord Jesus [alternatively: the Lord Jesus has come]."[144]

---

141. On the close relationship between eschatology and the "Our Father," see *CCC* 2818 and J. Jeremias, *Paroles de Jésus: le Sermon sur la montagne, le Notre-Père* (Paris: Cerf, 1969), 70.

142. On the relationship between eschatology and the Eucharist, see *inter alia*, P. de Haes, "Eucaristia e escatologia," in *Eucaristia. Aspetti e problemi dopo il Vaticano II* (Assisi: Cittadella, 1968), 158–78; J. Ntedika, *L'évocation de l'au-delà dans la prière pour les morts: étude de patristique et de liturgie latines (IVe–VIIIe s.)* (Louvain: Nauwelaerts, 1971); F.-X. Durrwell, "Eucharistie et Parousie," *Lumen Vitae* 26 (1971): 89–128; E. Martínez y Martínez, *La escatología en la liturgia romana antigua* (Salamanca: Instituto Superior de Pastoral, 1976); G. Wainwright, *Eucharist and Eschatology;* N. Conte, *Benedetto Colui che viene. L'eucaristia e l'escatologia* (Napoli: EDB, 1987).

143. H. Bourgeois, *L'espérance maintenant et toujours* (Paris: Desclée, 1985), 90.

144. Anon., *Didachē*, 10:6. C. Pozo, *La teología del más allá*, 122–23, argues that the normal form

68 The Object of Christian Hope

The early liturgy of the Roman Church[145] was clearly directed in hope toward the *Parousia*, the coming of the Lord Jesus in glory. This liturgy is focused on Christ as our Mediator. The prayer of the Church is directed to God the Father, through Christ, who is our intercessor; he is situated "on our side," as it were. Christ acts as the prolongation upwards of the Church and of Christians. Hence, all the prayers of the celebration are directed to God, *per Christum Dominum nostrum*, "through Christ Our Lord."

In later Carolingian liturgy, which developed in the wake of the condemnation of Arianism, in a context closer to monophysitism, prayer is directed to the Trinity, Father, Son, and Holy Spirit. Christ is now represented as "belonging," as it were, to the Godhead, and no longer as the one who presents us to the Father. The reason for this change of emphasis, which influenced not only Western and Eastern liturgies in general, but the Roman liturgy itself, was the attempt to avoid any kind of subordinationism in Christology in the wake of the Arian crisis. The Carolingian liturgy tends to express the "descendent" side of Christ's mediation and presents Christ in his divinity.

The following examples of this phenomenon in the modern Latin liturgy, not common in earlier Roman liturgy, may be of interest. *First*, in the prayer after the embolism of the "Our Father" during the Communion Rite, we hear: "Lord Jesus Christ . . . *look not on our sins* but on the faith of your Church and grant us the peace and unity of your kingdom where you live and reign for ever and ever." Here the prayer requesting forgiveness and assistance is directed to Christ as God. *Second*, in the prayer that directly precedes the Communion Rite we read: "Lord Jesus Christ, *Son of the living God*, your death brought life to the world." Again a divine action on the part of Christ is invoked and a descendent mediation is involved. *Thirdly*, the Latin liturgy terminates its most solemn prayers with the invocation: "through Our Lord Jesus Christ your Son, who lives and reigns with you in the unity of the Holy Spirit." Here Christ is clearly situated "within" the Trinity, along with the Father and the Holy Spirit.

Of course no fundamental opposition need be found between the two liturgical traditions. Neither one questions the divinity or the humanity of Jesus Christ. It is a question of emphasis. The Carolingian liturgical style, however, which undoubtedly became prevalent in both East and West, better accounts for the

---

is the future one, not the present. 1 Cor 16:22 also uses the term *maranatha;* see R. B. Brown, *Broadman Bible Commentary: 1 Corinthians* (Nashville: Broadman Press, 1970), 397; F. F. Bruce, *1 and 2 Corinthians* (London: Oliphants, 1971), 162; H. D. Wendland, *Die Briefe und die Korinther*, 7th ed. (Göttingen: Vandenhoeck & Ruprecht, 1954), 143.

145. See C. Pozo, *La teología del más allá*, 125–28. Pozo draws on the 1925 work of the liturgist J. A. Jungmann, *The Place of Christ in Liturgical Prayer* (Collegeville: Liturgical Press, 1989), and K. Adam, *Christus unser Bruder*, 8th ed. (Regensburg: J. Habbel, 1950), 46–80.

sense of eschatological pessimism in respect of the *Parousia* that we have referred to above.[146] Still, the Church has never lost that sense of serene and expectant joy that is meant to mark the return of her Lord and Savior in glory. In the *Catechism of the Council of Trent* (1567) we read: "Just as from the very beginning of the world the desire of humankind turned toward that day when the Lord would come as man to free humanity, so also after the death and ascension of the Son of God we should look forward with the same ardent desire to that second day of the Lord in which, in accord with our holy hope, will come the manifestation of the glory of our great God."[147]

The liturgical reform inaugurated by Vatican Council II wished to renew the Church's liturgical emphasis on the final coming of Christ in glory. "In the earthly liturgy . . . we eagerly await the Savior, Our Lord Jesus Christ," we read in *Sacrosanctum Concilium*, "until he our life appears and we too will appear with him in glory. . . . In the course of the year . . . [the Church] unfolds the whole mystery of Christ from the incarnation and nativity to the ascension, to Pentecost and the expectation of the blessed hope of the coming of the Lord."[148]

After the Eucharistic consecration, the proclamation of the mystery of faith consistently makes reference to the past (cross and resurrection), to the present (liberation from sin), and to the future: "Christ will come again," "Lord Jesus, come in glory," ". . . until you come in glory." Whereas the first and second Eucharistic Prayers do not refer to the *Parousia* in the *anamnesis* pronounced just after the consecration, all the others make an explicit mention of it. In the third we read: "Father, calling to mind the death your Son endured for our salvation, his glorious resurrection and ascension into heaven, and *ready to greet him when he comes again*, we offer you in thanksgiving this holy and living sacrifice." In the fourth: "Father, we now celebrate this memorial of our redemption. We recall Christ's death, his descent among the dead, his resurrection, and his ascension to your right hand; and, *looking forward to his coming in glory*, we offer you his body and blood." To the embolism of the "Our Father," "Deliver us, Lord, from every evil. . . . In your mercy keep us free from sin and protect us from all anxiety," is added: "as we wait in joyful hope for the coming of our Savior, Jesus Christ."

Likewise Vatican II insisted that the liturgy of Advent should not only refer to the birth of the Savior, and the joyful recurrence of that feast, but also bring Christians to look forward to the future coming of Christ in glory, the *Parousia*, in remembrance of the patient and prayerful awaiting of Simeon and Anna (Lk 2:21–40). It may be noted, besides, that many ancient liturgies made an ex-

---

146. See pp. 40–42.
147. *Roman Catechism I*, 7:2.
148. Vatican Council II, Const. *Sacrosanctum Concilium*, nn. 8, 102.

plicit mention of the *Parousia*.¹⁴⁹ The so-called *Liturgy of James*¹⁵⁰ speaks of the "second glorious and terrifying return of Christ." The *Liturgy of the Stowe Missal*, of Celtic origin, contains the following *anamnesis:* "Do this, every time, in memory of me. You will announce my Passion and give witness to my Resurrection. *You will hope for my return until I come to you again from heaven.*"¹⁵¹

In the pre-anaphora of the Syro-Malabarese liturgy we read the following description of the Eucharistic sacrifice: "You have ordered us, Lord, our God, to prepare and place on the holy altar these mysteries, glorious and holy, vivifying and divine, *until the second glorious coming of Christ from heaven,* to whom is glory and praise, adoration and honor, for ever and ever."¹⁵²

The common practice of the priest facing the east during the celebration of the Eucharist is also indicative, for it is from there that Christ, the Sun of Justice, will come.¹⁵³ Conversely, baptism, in which Satan is repudiated, may be celebrated facing the west, the location of clouds and darkness.¹⁵⁴ The white garment worn by infants at baptism is a sign of the Kingdom of God already present.¹⁵⁵ In the words of Sesboüé, "just as the Eucharist is a kind of 'sacramental Parousia,' so also the life of the Church is a 'sacrament of the future.' The definitive reality of the last times progresses by means of an encounter with the Lord Jesus that is always present and incessantly new."¹⁵⁶

John Paul II in his 2003 encyclical *Ecclesia de Eucharistia* says:

The acclamation of the assembly following the consecration appropriately ends by expressing the eschatological thrust which marks the celebration of the Eucharist (1 Co 11:26): "until you come in glory." The Eucharist is a straining toward the goal, a foretaste

---

149. E. Keller, *Eucharistie und Parusie: Liturgie- und theologiegeschichtliche Untersuchungen zur eschatologischen Dimension der Eucharistie anhand ausgewählter Zeugnisse aus frühchristlicher und patristischer Zeit* (Fribourg [Suisse]: Universitätsverlag, 1989).

150. See J. Leclercq, "Jacques (Liturgie de Saint)," in *Dictionnaire d'Archéologie chrétienne et de liturgie*, vol. 7/2, cols. 2116–21.

151. See L. Gougand, *Celtiques (Liturgies)*, in ibid., vol. 2, cols. 2973–75. The same may be said of the liturgies of Mark, John Chrysostom, and Basil, as well as the Ambrosian and Mozarabic rites: see J. J. Alviar, *Escatología*, 74–75.

152. From the Syro-Malabar liturgical celebration of the Eucharist.

153. See the classic work of F. J. Dölger, *Sol Salutis. Gebet und Gesang im christlichen Altertum: mit besonderer Rücksicht auf die Ostung in Gebet und Liturgie*, 2nd ed. (Münster: Aschendorff, 1920). See also J. M.-R. Tillard, "L'Eucharistie, sacrement de l'espérance ecclésiale," *Nouvelle Revue Théologique* 83 (1961): 561–92; J. Ratzinger, *The Spirit of the Liturgy* (San Francisco: Ignatius Press, 2000), 74–84; U. M. Lang, *Turning Towards the Lord: Orientation in Liturgical Prayer* (San Francisco: Ignatius Press, 2004).

154. See D. E. Aune, *The Cultic Setting of Realized Eschatology;* W. Rordorf, "Liturgie et eschatologie," *Augustinianum* 18 (1978): 153–61.

155. See V. Pavan, "La veste bianca battesimale, indicium escatologico nella Chiesa dei primi secoli," *Augustinianum* 18 (1978): 257–71.

156. B. Sesboüé, *Le retour du Christ*, 155.

of the fullness of joy promised by Christ (Jn 15:11); it is in some way the anticipation of heaven, the "pledge of future glory." In the Eucharist, everything speaks of confident waiting "in joyful hope for the coming of our Savior, Jesus Christ." Those who feed on Christ in the Eucharist need not wait until the hereafter to receive eternal life: *they already possess it on earth*, as the first-fruits of a future fullness which will embrace man in his totality. For in the Eucharist we also receive the pledge of our bodily resurrection at the end of time: "He who eats my flesh and drinks my blood has eternal life, and I will raise him up at the last day" (Jn 6:54). This pledge of the future resurrection comes from the fact that the flesh of the Son of Man, given as food, is his body in its glorious state after the resurrection. With the Eucharist we digest, as it were, the "secret" of the resurrection.[157]

Characteristics of the Parousia

The Parousia as God's Final, Public Victory The *Parousia* is often described by Paul as the moment of God's definitive victory over sin, death, and the devil. The prophets of the Old Testament looked forward to the "Day of the Lord," when God would intercede with power in favor of his people, destroying their enemies once and for all. It is especially present in the writings of Zephaniah,[158] and also in Zechariah, Isaiah, Jeremiah, and Amos. The latter writes: "Alas for you who desire the Day of the Lord! Why do you want the day of the Lord? It is darkness, not light . . . and gloom with no brightness in it" (Am 5:18,20). Jeremiah speaks of the "day of the Lord" as the beginning of a new epoch (46:10).[159]

In the New Testament, however, the "day of the Lord" becomes the "day of Christ."[160] Since the *Parousia* involves the definitive victory of good over evil, it is clearly a public event, as the very term *Parousia* indicates. The *Parousia* will contrast vividly with the first coming of the Savior, in which Jesus knocked gently at the hearts of humans, seeking their free response (Rv 3:20). At the *Parousia* he will come in power and glory, to judge the living and the dead. And his judgment will be definitive and without appeal. Nobody will be able to avoid encountering

---

157. John Paul II, Enc. *Ecclesia de Eucharistia* (2003), n. 18. See Benedict XVI, Ap. Exh. *Sacramentum caritatis* (2007), nn. 30–32.

158. See H. Irsigler, *Gottesgericht und Jahwetag. Die Komposition Zef 1,2–2,3, untersucht auf der Grundlage der Literarkritik des Zefanjabuches* (St. Ottilien: EOS, 1977).

159. See also Is 13:6–9; 22:5; 34:8; 63:4.

160. There are many examples throughout the New Testament. Mt 24:36 uses the expression "that day," Rom 2:5, the "day of wrath . . . and judgment." 1 Cor 3:13 states: "the Day will disclose . . . each man's work." 1 Thes 5:2: "the Day of the Lord will come like a thief in the night"; 2 Tm 1:12 speaks of Paul guarding "until that Day what has been entrusted" to him. In 2 Tm 4:8 he says that "the righteous Lord will reward me on that Day." Jas 5:3, "You have laid up treasures for the last days." 2 Pt 3:12 speaks of the Christian "waiting for and hastening the coming of the day of God." Rv 16:14 speaks of kings and demons who will "assemble for battle on the great day of God the Almighty." On the equivalence between the Old Testament "day of the Lord" and the New Testament *Parousia*, see C. Pozo, *La teología del más allá*, 104–10.

the Son of man who comes, for the *Parousia* will be evident and undeniable for one and all. Matthew explains that news of the Lord's coming will not be communicated by one person to the next, but to the whole of humanity directly.

> Then if any one says to you, "Lo, here is the Christ!" or "There he is!" do not believe it. For false Christs and false prophets will arise and show great signs and wonders . . . So, if they say to you, "Lo, he is in the wilderness," do not go out; if they say, "Lo, he is in the inner rooms," do not believe it. *For as the lightning comes from the east and shines as far as the west, so will be the coming of the Son of man.* . . . Immediately after the tribulation of those days the sun will be darkened . . . and the powers of the heavens will be shaken. Then will appear the sign of the Son of man in heaven, and then all the tribes of the earth will mourn, and they will see the Son of man coming on the clouds of heaven with power and great glory; and he will send out his angels with a loud trumpet call, and they will gather his elect from the four winds, from one end of heaven to the other. (Mt 24:23,26–27,29–31)

The delay in the final coming is meant to induce people to reflect on the mercy of God. "Do you presume upon the riches of his kindness and forbearance and patience? Do you not know that God's kindness is meant to lead you to repentance?" (Rom 2:4–6; cf. 2 Pt 3:9).

What Will the Parousia Consist of? At the best of times, it is risky to attempt to describe in detail God's way of acting with creatures; more so, to attempt a description of the *Parousia*.[161] Nevertheless, Scripture does give some indications that may be of help in imagining what the coming of Jesus in glory will consist of. The apostles, gazing up to heaven after the ascension of the Lord, heard the following words from the angel: "Men of Galilee, why do you stand looking up into heaven? This Jesus, who was taken up from you into heaven, *will come in the same way as you saw him go into heaven*" (Acts 1:11). The point of reference for the *Parousia*, therefore, will be the risen and glorious humanity of Jesus. Nonetheless, in a sense this just puts off the problem of describing the *Parousia*, for Scripture tells us little about the risen, spiritualized body (1 Cor 15:44), that of Christ and that of humans. However, the text just cited from the Acts of the Apostles does indicate that the *Parousia* will involve the coming of Christ, whose glory will be visible to all. His manifestation will no longer be restricted to believers, as occurred in the apparitions that took place after the resurrection, but will be seen by the whole of humanity, also by those who are far from God.

Besides, it should be said that the *Parousia* will not consist so much of a movement of Christ toward humanity, from the heavens to the earth, although such a way of speaking may be helpful from a metaphorical standpoint. The post-

---

161. A. Feuillet considers the theme of the *Parousia* among the most difficult in the New Testament: "Parousie," col. 1141.

resurrection appearances of Jesus to Mary Magdalene or to the apostles may facilitate our understanding; perhaps the encounter of Paul with Jesus on the road to Damascus is indicative. Theologically speaking, it is more accurate to say the following. Since the whole world was created through him (Jn 1:3), in him, and for him (Col 1:16), and since, besides, Jesus through his resurrection became the Lord of heaven and earth (Phil 2:9–11), then the *Parousia* may be said to consist of a new, deeper relationship of the entire cosmos with Christ, a definitive one, on the basis of the fundamental relationship between him and the cosmos established by creation and renewed by redemption. Perhaps it may be said that the *Parousia* consists of the definitive actualization of the fundamental relationship between Christ and creation. At that moment Christ will "deliver the kingdom to God the Father after destroying every rule and every authority and power. For he must reign until he has put all his enemies under his feet. The last enemy to be destroyed is death. . . . When all things are subjected to him, then the Son himself will also be subjected to him who put all things under him, that God may be everything in everything" (1 Cor 15:24–28).

3

The Resurrection of the Dead

> The promise of resurrection is the soul of history.
> —*Gabriel Marcel*[1]

> The resurrection of the body means the resurrection of the life that has been lived.
> —*Romano Guardini*[2]

> I don't want to achieve immortality through my work. I want to achieve immortality through not dying.
> —*Woody Allen*

Belief in the resurrection of the dead by the power of God is deeply rooted in the Old Testament and is central to Christian faith.[3] Tertullian went so far as to say that "the hope of Christians is the resurrection of the dead."[4] And this is so for the simple reason that the final resurrection of humanity is the ultimate fruit of the resurrection of Christ (which is the basis of our hope), and of his glorious *Parousia* (the definitive manifestation of our hope). Indeed it may be said that the prime and immediate effect of the coming of Jesus Christ in glory will be that of the resurrection of the dead.

The Church has taught this doctrine from the earliest times. The Apostles' Creed speaks consistently of the "resurrection of the flesh,"[5] whereas the Creed of Nicea-Constantinople says: "we look forward to the resurrection of the dead."[6] The *Quicumque*, or Ps.-Athanasian Creed, has: "and at his coming all will rise up, each one with their own body, to give an account of their deeds."[7] Paul VI in the *Creed of the People of God* says: "Death will be destroyed on the day of the resur-

---

1. G. Marcel, "Structure de l'espérance," 79.
2. R. Guardini, *The Last Things*, 69.
3. See especially my study "Risurrezione," which is closely followed in the coming pages.
4. Tertullian, *De res.*, 1.
5. On this expression, see especially my study "La fórmula 'Resurrección de la carne' y su significado para la moral cristiana," *Scripta Theologica* 21 (1989): 777–803.
6. DS 150.
7. DS 76.

rection, when these souls will be united with their bodies."[8] Likewise, the *Catechism of the Catholic Church* gives ample expression to this fundamental belief and hope of Christians.[9]

In this chapter we shall first consider the doctrine of final resurrection in Scripture and throughout history, under four headings: (1) the originally Jewish and Christian character of resurrection belief; (2) resurrection in the Old Testament; (3) resurrection in the New Testament; and (4) Christian witness to resurrection belief: early Christian anthropology and ethics. Later on, we shall examine some questions relating to the theology of resurrection and its implications.

Resurrection Belief in Scripture, Theology, and Church Life

The Originally Jewish and Christian Character of Resurrection Belief

Ancient Sources Although ancient authors such as Aesculapius refer sporadically to the possibility of the dead rising up, for the most part such a notion was considered unthinkable by Greek philosophers and poets such as Homer, Aeschylus, and Sophocles. Certainly the possibility of universal resurrection was excluded.[10] Still, significant traces of resurrection belief are to be found in ancient Egyptian fertility rites,[11] although the explanation is far removed from Jewish thought. For the Egyptians, resurrection is understood as a purely natural process, reserved in any case to those whose bodies had in some way been preserved, for example, through mummification. In the Indian *Rig-Veda* (before 2000 BC) the soul of the deceased is said to be taken by the fire-god and "receives a new, more 'subtle' body, and its life is a replica of human life on earth, though freed from all the imperfections that are inseparable from it here."[12] Some authors have suggested that the doctrine of resurrection derives from Persian salvation theology, which, in effect, employs resurrection language.[13] Jewish and Persian understandings of resurrection, however, are clearly distinct from one

---

8. Paul VI, *Creed of the People of God*, n. 28.
9. See *CCC* 992–1004.
10. See M. Hengel, *Judaism and Hellenism: Studies in their Encounter in Palestine during the Early Hellenistic Period* (London: SCM, 1981), vol. 1, 196, nn. 574–75, on the non-revealed aspects of resurrection doctrine.
11. See H.H. Rowley, *The Faith of Israel: Aspects of Old Testament Thought* (London: SCM, 1956), 161–68; H. Wissmann, "Auferstehung der Toten I/1: Religionsgeschichtlich," in *Theologische Realenzyklopädie*, ed. G. Krause and G. Müller, vol. 4 (Berlin: De Gruyter, 1979), 442–43; J.H. Charlesworth, "The Origin and Development of Resurrection Beliefs," in J.H. Charlesworth, with C.D. Elledge et al., *Resurrection: The Origin and Future of a Biblical Doctrine* (New York: T. & T. Clark, 2006), 218–31.
12. R.C. Zähner, *Hinduism* (London: Oxford University Press, 1962), 75.
13. See A. Bertholet, "The Pre-Christian Belief in the Resurrection of the Body," *American Journal of Theology* 20 (1916): 1–30.

another. For the Jews, resurrection involves the awakening of buried corpses through the power of God. For the Persians, who exposed corpses to dissolution by the elements, resurrection is understood as a restitution to life through the agency of the selfsame elements of nature, and a selective restitution at that.[14] That is to say, the special intervention of divine power is considered unnecessary, as is universal resurrection. In sum, some continuity at a linguistic level may be detected between Jewish and Persian teaching in respect of life after death, but not as regards its mode (resurrection), cause (the power of God), and extension (universal).[15]

Resurrection and Reincarnation Some authors,[16] taking up a suggestion of Tertullian,[17] have detected something similar to resurrection belief in the Orphic and Pythagorean doctrine of the "transmigration" (or *metempsychosis*) of souls, which has led to the popular and recurrent doctrine of "reincarnation."[18] The ancient doctrine of transmigration envisages the eventual liberation of the soul after repeated purifying incarnations in diverse bodies, human and animal. It is to be found in the Hindu and Buddhist concepts of *samsāra*, the cycle of birth and death, and *karma*, the accumulated ethical consequences of one's actions;[19] in the

14. See W. F. Albright, *From the Stone Age to Christianity*, 2nd ed. (Baltimore: John Hopkins Press, 1957), 358; R. H. Charles, *A Critical History of the Doctrine of a Future Life in Israel, in Judaism, and in Christianity*, 2nd ed. (London: Black, Adam & Charles, 1913), 139–41.

15. See W. F. Albright, *From the Stone Age*, 361; R. C. Zähner, *The Dawn and Twilight of Zoroastrianism* (London: Weidenfeld and Nicolson, 1961), 57.

16. I. Lévy, *La légende de Pythagore de Grèce en Palestine* (Paris: Leroux, 1927), 255; T. F. Glasson, *Greek Influence in Jewish Eschatology, with Special Reference to the Apocalypses and Pseudepigraphs* (London: SPCK, 1961), 29.

17. Tertullian, *De res.*, 1:5.

18. *Pars pro toto*, see L. Bukovski, "La réincarnation selon les Pères de l'Église," *Gregorianum* 9 (1928): 65–91; A. de Georges, *La réincarnation des âmes selon les traditions orientales et occidentales* (Paris: Michel, 1966); J. L. Ruiz de la Peña, "¿Resurrección o reencarnación?" *Communio* (Ed. española) 2 (1980): 287–99; L. Scheffczyk, "Die Reinkarnationslehre und die Geschichtlichkeit," *Münchener Theologische Zeitschrift* 31 (1980): 122–29; A. Couture, "Réincarnation ou résurrection? Revue d'un débat et amorce d'une recherche," *Sciences Ecclésiastiques* 36 (1984): 351–74; 37 (1985): 75–96; H. Waldenfels, "Auferstehung, Reinkarnation, Nichts? Der Mensch auf der Suche nach seiner Zukunft," *Lebendiges Zeugnis* 41 (1986): 39–50; P. Thomas, *La Réincarnation, oui ou non?* (Paris: Centurion, 1987); H. Beck, *Reinkarnation oder Auferstehung: Ein Widerspruch?* (Innsbruck: Resch, 1988); M. Kehl, "Wiedergeburt—Häresie oder Hoffnung?" *Geist und Leben* 63 (1990): 445–57; C. Schönborn, *La vie éternelle. Réincarnation. Résurrection. Divinisation* (Paris: Mame, 1992); S. Del Cura Elena, "Escatología contemporánea. La reencarnación como tema ineludible," in Aa. vv, *Teología en el tiempo. Veinticinco años de quehacer teológico* (Burgos: Facultad de Teología del Norte de España, 1994), 309–58; B. Kloppenburg, *Reincarnação* (Petrópolis: Vozes, 2003).

19. The doctrine of reincarnation is to be found in association with the Hindu notion of *karma* (the accumulation of good and bad behavior in a person's life), which must be expiated. On the complex relationship between *karma* and reincarnation, see B. Pandit, "Karma and Reincarnation," *The Hindu Mind* (New Delhi: New Age Books, 2001), 117–26. According to Buddhism the Bodhissattva refuses to

teachings of Pythagoras, Plato, and the Orphics in Greece, and by Gnostics. Recent understandings of reincarnation (developed by theosophists, anthroposophists, and spiritualists), however, take it that the soul will continue forever to occupy different human bodies. This position has become quite popular in some quarters of late, particularly in the context of "New Age" spiritualities.[20]

Indeed, both resurrection and reincarnation underline the fact that the immortal destiny of the human being is related in a significant way to the body. However, although some scriptural texts seem to support the doctrine of reincarnation,[21] in real terms it is far removed from Christian and Jewish belief.[22] Church Fathers and later theologians have repeatedly said so.[23] Resurrection is acceptable, Tatian (second century) says, "but not in the way in which the Stoics dogmatize, for according to them the same things are born and die in periodic cycles."[24]

Resurrection is not comparable with reincarnation in the *first* place because the purpose of transmigration is the perfect purification of the soul by means of its eventual separation from matter, whereas that of resurrection involves the perpetual reunification of soul and body, of spirit and matter. The anthropologies involved are different, indeed opposed, for the nature of the human being is defined by the union of body and soul (resurrection), not by their eventual perpetual separation (reincarnation). *Second,* resurrection differs from transmigration in that the latter may take place many times with a particular soul (until purification is complete), or indefinitely, whereas resurrection (and human life for that matter) takes place only once. As a result, belief in final resurrection implies that humans may live this life only once (just as Christ lived, died, and rose from the dead *ephapax,* "once only," as we read in the letter to the Hebrews).[25]

---

become immersed in the *nirvāna* as long as there is only one person in hell. "Behind this impressive notion of Asian religiosity," J. Ratzinger comments, "the Christian sees the true Bodhissattva, Christ, in whom Asia's dream became true," *Eschatology,* 188.

20. See A. Feder, *Reinkarnationshypothese in der New-Age-Bewegung* (Nettetal: Steyler, 1991); M. Introvigne, *La sfida della reincarnazione* (Milano: Effedieffe, 1993).

21. It is common to cite texts such as Mt 16:14; Jn 1:21; Mt 14:1–2; Jn 9:2; Mt 17:12; 2 Cor 5:10; Gal 6:7 in support of reincarnation. See the classic refutation of A. Orbe, "Textos y pasajes de la Escritura interesados en la teoría de la reincorporación," *Estudios Eclesiásticos* 33 (1959): 77–92.

22. See L. Scheffczyk, "Die Reinkarnationslehre"; C. Schönborn, *La vie éternelle.*

23. See H. Cornélis et al., *La résurrection de la chair* (Paris: Cerf, 1962), 165–262; H. J. Weber, *Die Lehre von der Auferstehung der Toten in den Haupttraktaten der scholastischen Theologie* (Freiburg i. B.: Herder, 1973), 83–85.

24. Tatian, *Or. ad graecos,* 6.

25. On the uniqueness and unrepeatable character of Christ's death and resurrection as a basis for rejecting reincarnation, see C. Schönborn, *La vie éternelle,* 141–43. Commenting on John Hick's extensive study of the doctrine of reincarnation, *Death and Eternal Life* (London: Collins, 1976), 297–396, W. Pannenberg notes: "Astonishingly, Hick in his discussion of the relation between Christianity and the concept

78 The Object of Christian Hope

Modern reincarnation belief, which envisages the repetition of the human life cycle, tends to consecrate the provisional, undermine fidelity, and trivialize everyday life.[26] Besides, *third*, whereas transmigration is applied to the individual's destiny and purification, resurrection refers to humanity as a whole, since it will take place simultaneously for all humans at the end of time. *Fourth*, whereas reincarnation can provide a justification for social inequalities, resurrection develops in Scripture as a divine means of ensuring definitive justice.[27] *Fifth* and last, whereas transmigration is normally considered a natural process, in that souls spontaneously pass from one body to the next, resurrection depends entirely on the re-creating power of God. The latter is what makes resurrection belief strictly theological and characteristically Judeo-Christian.[28]

Resurrection in the Old Testament

The doctrine of the resurrection of the dead is not to be found as a clearly developed doctrine in the early stages of the Old Testament. In fact, the first books of Scripture make hardly any reference to the possibility of meaningful human life after death.[29] The reason for this probably lies in the possibility that a cult of the dead might occasion idolatrous practices, opposed to the adoration meant for God alone.[30]

Life after Death in the Old Testament Still, the acceptance of the immortality of humans is expressed in several ways in the Old Testament, three of which are worthy of note.

First, human immortality is understood fundamentally in terms of the immortality of *God's People*. According to the faith of Israel, the People of God will remain forever, being founded on the covenant God established with them and

---

of reincarnation [*Death and Eternal Life*, 365–73] does . . . mention Christian interest in the uniqueness of redemption by the death of Jesus Christ [372] but not the anthropological correlate of this belief, i. e., interest in the uniqueness of earthly life," *Systematic Theology*, vol. 3, 565, n. 128.

26. G. Colzani says that reincarnation provides "a kind of happy permanent vacation which allows one elude the dramatic choices of everyday life," G. Colzani, *La vita eterna*, 15. Maximus the Confessor calls reincarnation "death going on forever."

27. See my study *La muerte y la esperanza* (Madrid: Palabra, 2004), 97–109.

28. G. Gozzelino, *Nell'attesa*, 426, suggests the following objections to reincarnation belief: the nullification of the personal human subject; the debasement of the human body, considered as a mere receptacle for the spirit; the removal of a sense of responsibility from personal life; the provision of an ideological justification for social inequalities.

29. See L. Wächter, *Der Tod im Alten Testament* (Stuttgart: Calwer, 1967); J. Ratzinger, *Eschatology*, 80–92.

30. See for example Lv 19:31: 20:6; Is 8:19. The Old Testament encountered in ancestor worship a form of competition with faith in God as the only one with power over the future. On this topic, see L. Wächter, *Der Tod*, 187–88; J. Ratzinger, *Eschatology*, 84–85, as well as the classical work of A. Lods, *La croyance à la vie future et le culte des morts dans l'antiquité israélite* (Paris: Fischbacher, 1906).

The Resurrection of the Dead 79

on the promise He made to Abraham. For this reason, for married people not to have children was considered as the ultimate sign of disgrace, for children are seen as a sign of God's blessing, a sure guarantee of belonging to his People, of contributing to its immortality (Gn 24:60; Ex 1:21; 23:26), of preparing the way of the Messiah. In the context of the covenant, the most positive thing that is said of individual members of God's people is that they will "die old and full of days" (Gn 25:7–8).

In the *second* place, the Old Testament speaks frequently of the survival in the underworld, or *she'ol*,[31] of "the dead," called *refa'im*.

She'ol, the underworld, is the dark abode of the dead, a place of impurity, in which no cult is offered to God. It serves as a sign of the absence of God's presence, and is similar to the Greek *hadēs* inhabited by the shades.[32] Job describes it as follows: "The days of my life are few enough: turn your eyes away, leave me a little joy, before I go to the place of no return, to the land of darkness and shadow, dark as death, where dimness and disorder hold sway, and light itself is like dead of night" (Jb 10:20–22).

She'ol is inhabited by the *refa'im*, the dead. The root of the term *refa'im* is *râfa*, that which is weak or languid. Hence the *refa'im* are represented as a kind of replica of human beings, a poor but real shadow of their earthly existence, a personal nucleus that is semi-conscious, lethargic, and on the whole inactive.[33] The *refa'im* are generally spoken of in a collective way, living without individuality or personal consciousness. They cannot praise God[34] and are barely conscious of existing (1 Sm 28:8–19). However, it is also true that just as *she'ol* does not coincide with the burial place or tomb, the *refa'im* may not be identified with human corpses. That is to say, the Old Testament teaches that a kind of spiritual remnant of humans remains after death that goes beyond the immortality of collective memory.[35] Wisdom literature on the whole takes a more positive attitude

---

31. On *she'ol* and the *refa'im*, see R. Martin-Achard, *De la mort à la résurrection d'après l'ancien Testament* (Neuchâtel: Delachaux et Niestlé, 1956); L. Wächter, *Der Tod*, 181–98; C. Pozo, *La teología del más allá*, 200–20.

32. The term *she'ol* is very close to the Greek *hadēs*, or world of shades, according to the classic work of E. Rohde, *Psyche: The Cult of Souls and Belief in Immortality among the Greeks* (orig. 1891; New York: Harcourt Brace, 1925), 236–40; see also G. Deiana, "L'inferno. She'ol, Geenna, Ade: il castigo dell'inferno," in *I novissimi nella Bibbia*, ed. G. Bortone (L'Aquila: ISSRA, 1999), 93–113; L. Moraldi, *L'aldilà dell'uomo*, 2nd ed. (Milano: A. Mondadori, 2000), 123–49. For a detailed analysis, see P. S. Johnson, *Shades of Sheol: Death and Afterlife in the Old Testament* (Downers Grove, Ill.: Inter-Varsity, 2002). See also G. L. Prestige, "Hades in the Greek Fathers," *Journal of Theological Studies* 24 (1923): 476–85.

33. See Jb 3:13,17–18; Na 3:18. R. Martin-Achard, *De la mort à la résurrection*, finds the origins of the idea of *refa'im* in underground fertility divinities. Among other things, this would account for fear of the dead.

34. See Is 38:18; Ps 88:11–14; 30:10; Sir 17:22.

35. This is the explanation given by C. Pozo, *La teología del más allá*, 200–10.

80 The Object of Christian Hope

toward the existence of the dead (Ws 3). Yet for the most part, death is not seen as a liberation, nor *she'ol* as a place of hope.

Christian revelation certainly speaks of the afterlife in more positive terms. Nonetheless, it is fair to say that Christian doctrine derives from the Old Testament notion of the dead (*refa'im*) inhabiting *she'ol*, though Christologically corrected.[36]

Third, the term "immortality" (*athanasia*) first appears in the Old Testament in the book of Wisdom.[37] Even though immortality understood as remembrance and fame is not excluded (Ws 8:13), this book associates immortality principally with the upright life of the human soul. "For the souls of the just are in the hands of God, and no torment will ever touch them" (Ws 3:1); "For God created man for immortality, and made him in the image of his own eternity" (Ws 2:23); "for righteousness is immortal" (Ws 1:15); "But the just live forever, and their reward is with the Lord; the Most High takes care of them" (Ws 5:15).

The doctrine of individual resurrection of the body makes an explicit appearance only in later books of the Old Testament, from 200 BC onward, especially those of an apocalyptic kind. That is to say, at an explicit level it may not be considered a primitive doctrine, although its roots may be found at the earliest stages of Scripture, as Jesus himself teaches.[38] The doctrine may be seen to develop in three stages:[39] theological and literary foundations; Old Testament teaching on personal resurrection; finally, New Testament doctrine on resurrection.

Literary and Theological Foundations for the Doctrine of Resurrection In the Old Testament the groundwork for the doctrine of resurrection is prepared in a variety of ways, both literary and theological, over an extended period of time. The following six may be mentioned.

In the *first* place, awareness of human fate after death provoked a painful di-

---

36. See J. Ratzinger, *Eschatology*, 146.
37. See P. Grelot, *De la mort à la vie éternelle: études de théologie biblique* (Paris: Cerf, 1971), 105, holds the doctrine of immortality is proper to the Old Testament. See C. Pozo, *La teología del más allá*, 227–37.
38. See pp. 86–87.
39. On resurrection theology in the Old Testament, see J. Becker, *Auferstehung der Toten im Urchristentum* (Stuttgart: Katholisches Bibelwerk, 1976); P. Hoffmann, *Die Toten in Christus*; U. Kellermann, "Überwindung des Todesgeschicks in der alttestamentlichen Frömmigkeit vor und neben dem Auferstehungsglauben," *Zeitschrift für Theologie und Kirche* 73 (1976): 259–82; G. Greshake and J. Kremer, *Resurrectio Mortuorum. Zum theologischen Verständnis der leiblichen Auferstehung* (Darmstadt: Wissenschaftliche Buchgesellschaft, 1992); C. Pozo, *La teología del más allá*, 324–41; É. Puech, *La croyance des Esseniens en la vie future: immortalité, résurrection, vie éternelle?: histoire d'une croyance dans le judaïsme ancient*, 2 vols. (Paris: Gabalda, 1993); J. D. Levenson, *Resurrection and the Restoration of Israel: The Ultimate Victory of the God of Life* (New Haven, Conn.: Yale University Press, 2006); K. Madigan and J. D. Levenson, *Resurrection*; J. Gillespie, *The Development of Belief in the Resurrection within the Old Testament* (Rome: Edusc, 2009).

lemma for those attempting to live an upright life:[40] while the just man strove to serve God but frequently suffered disgrace and tragedy, sinners often enjoyed the good things of life in a way apparently out of proportion to their merits.[41] This may be observed especially in the so-called mystical Psalms (16, 49, and 73).[42] In some cases the Psalmist comes to the conclusion that the just man will triumph in the end, even during his earthly pilgrimage. But the awareness that justice would not be done after death moved people to despair of God and of others, falling into a triple spiral first of rebellion and blasphemy, then of violent remonstrance (temporal Messianisms),[43] and finally of idolatry and paganism (seeking protection from other divinities in aspects of life apparently neglected by Yahweh). In any case, the dilemma was particularly painful for the just in the Old Testament, and their perception of the matter was clear: either justice is obtained here on earth or it will never come about.[44]

In brief terms, the human quest for definitive personal justice sets the scene for the doctrine of final resurrection.[45] Final resurrection is not only for the just, but is, rather, a prerequisite for justice being done.[46] Something of a kind may be found in some Eastern religions: the *nirvāna* will come about once justice has been fully established.[47]

Second, the Old Testament teaches that the supreme, liberating power of Yahweh is present everywhere, even in *she'ol*, the resting place of the dead.[48] That is to say, no one will escape divine justice.[49] "Therefore my heart is glad and my soul rejoices; my body also rests secure. For you do not give up to *she'ol*, or

---

40. See R. Martin-Achard, *De la mort*, 57–84; D. Cox, "'As Water Spilt on the Ground': Death in the Old Testament," *Studia Missionalia* 31 (1982): 1–17; C. Marucci, "Teologia della morte nell'a. T.," in G. Bortone, *I novissimi nella Bibbia*, 3–30.

41. See C. Pozo, *La teología del más allá*, 327–30; G. Colzani, *La vita eterna*, 99–100.

42. See R. J. Tournay, "L'eschatologie individuelle dans les Psaumes," *Revue Biblique* 57 (1949): 481–506; M. Dahood, *Psalms: Introduction, Translation, and Notes*, Anchor Bible, vols. 16, 17, and 17.1 (Garden City, N.Y.: Doubleday, 1981–82); C. Pozo, *La teología del más allá*, 214–20.

43. On the topic of temporal Messianism and its perennial propensity toward revolution, see G. Scholem, *Sabbatai Tsevi. Le Messie mystique, 1626–1676* (Paris: Verdier, 1985).

44. In Psalm 73:23–26,28 we read: "Nevertheless I am continually with you; you hold my right hand. You guide me with your counsel, and afterward you will receive me to glory. Whom have I in heaven but you? And there is nothing upon earth that I desire besides you. My flesh and my heart may fail, but God is the strength of my heart and my portion forever. . . . For me it is good to be near God; I have the Lord God my refuge, that I may tell of all your works."

45. W. Pannenberg says that "the object of hope became a future life of individuals after death only where this involved expectation of a better life and especially of fellowship with the deity. This is the second and deeper root of the biblical belief in resurrection," *Systematic Theology*, vol. 3, 566.

46. Among apocalyptic texts see, for example, Syr. Bar. 50:2–4. Also Jn 5:29; Acts 24:15.

47. See n. 19 above.

48. See 1 Sm 2:6; Am 9:1–2; Ps 16:9–10; Ws 16:13–14.

49. See Ps 88:11; 139:8–12; Jb 14:13–14.

let your faithful one see the pit" (Ps 16:9–10). "For you have power over life and death; you lead mortals down to the gates of Hades and back again" (Ws 16:13). The same doctrine is to be found in Jesus' teaching on the "bosom of Abraham" (Lk 16:22), which may be considered as a part of the underworld in which God's saving power is active.[50]

In the *third* place, Yahweh may be distinguished from the pagan gods (who jealously grasp at life and attempt to dominate it) in that He is the "God of the living" (1 Sm 17:26,36; Ps 18:47), the fountain (Ps 36:10; Jer 2:13) from whom life springs incessantly and without measure (Dn 14:25). A clear continuity may be detected between the doctrine of creation and that of resurrection as manifestations of God's giving of life.[51] This motif is present consistently throughout the whole of Scripture.

Fourth, as a conclusion of the above, death and definitive corruption do not belong to God's original plan, for he has created everything for life. Historically speaking, in fact, death came into the world through human sin.[52] "Do not invite death by the error of your life, or bring on destruction by the work of your hands; because God did not make death, and he does not delight in the death of the living" (Ws 1:12–13). We shall deal with the question of the relationship between sin and death later on.[53] Suffice it to say for the present, however, that the overcoming of sin (redemption) is closely linked with the overcoming of death, that is, resurrection, which becomes an important manifestation of God's saving power. Scripture often states, besides, that those who live in union with God will be freed from death.[54]

In the *fifth* place, literary material to describe the resurrection is provided in the book of Kings, which explains how the holy prophets Elijah and Elisha performed resurrection miracles.[55] Likewise, the "assumption" into heaven of Enoch[56] and Elijah[57] provides a clear indication of a generalized acceptance of the possibility of full bodily life being restored after death, albeit in a transitory and earthly context, especially for those who are specially favored by God.[58]

In the *last* place, many prophetic texts—particularly belonging to the post-exilic period—speak of the falling away and rising up of Israel in terms of a pro-

---

50. On the image of "Abraham's bosom," see the different interpretations presented by J. Nolland, *Luke 9:21–18:34*, Word Biblical Commentary 38 (Dallas: Word Books, 1993), 829.
51. See N. T. Wright, *The Resurrection of the Son of God* (Minneapolis: Fortress, 2003), 123.
52. See Gn 3:17–19; Ws 1:13–14; 2:23–24; Rom 5:21; 6:23; Jas 1:15.
53. See pp. 262–67.   54. Jb 14:10–21; Sir 14:16.
55. 1 Kgs 17:17–24; 2 Kgs 2:9–10; 4:31–7; Sir 48:5,14.
56. Gn 5:24; Sir 44:16, 49:14.   57. 1 Kgs 2:1–11; Sir 48:9.
58. Thus Irenaeus, *Adv. Haer.* V, 5. See also H. C. C. Cavallin, *Life after Death: Paul's Argument for the Resurrection of the Dead in I Cor 15*, vol. 1: *An Enquiry into the Jewish Background* (Lund: Gleerup, 1974), 23.

The Resurrection of the Dead 83

cess of bodily death and resurrection. The idea is to be found in Is 25:8, a text Paul later applies to bodily resurrection (1 Cor 15:54 f.), as well as in Is 26:19: "Your dead shall live, their corpses shall rise. O dwellers in the dust, awake and sing for joy! For your dew is a radiant dew, and the earth will give birth to those long dead [*refa'im*]." The same idea is to be found in Hosea 6:1–3. The best example of this motif is in Ezekiel 37:1–14, which speaks of the people of Israel rising up from prostration in terms of the raising up and enlivening of a field of dry bones. Moved by God, the prophet pronounces these words: "O dry bones, hear the word of the Lord. . . . I will cause breath to enter you, and you shall live. I will lay sinews on you, and will cause flesh to come upon you, and cover you with skin, and put breath into you, and you shall live; and you shall know that I am the Lord" (Ez 37:4–6). "I prophesied as he commanded me," says Ezekiel, "and the breath came into them, and they lived, and stood on their feet, a vast multitude" (Ez 37:10).

Several observations may be made on the text.[59] *First*, resurrection, such as it is, is the fruit of the power of God's Spirit, although God inspired the prophet to become an instrument in the process of raising the dead. *Second*, speaking as it does about "flesh" and "breath," Ezekiel's text serves as a gloss of the Yahveist account of creation (Gn 2–3, esp. Gn 2:7). Thus resurrection belief may not be considered an unpredictable manifestation of divine power, for it stands in continuity with the work of creation, of God who gives life. *Third*, Ezekiel does not openly teach personal resurrection, for the text clearly refers to the resurrection of the fallen people of Israel: "These bones are the whole house of Israel" (Ez 37:11). It is clear that these texts principally envisage the collective, world-based return of God's people to its former glory, rather than individual resurrection after death. The "new Exodus" of the people of Israel is expressed in terms of bodily resurrection. However, and this is the *fourth* point, the fact that the image used to speak of the rising up of Israel is precisely one of bodily resurrection is highly relevant, given the relation of both to creation and Exodus.[60] Besides, the metaphor of the field of dry bones coming back to life has been used frequently in a liturgical and artistic setting to express the doctrine of final resurrection.[61]

---

59. See E. Haag, "Ez 37 und der Glaube an die Auferstehung der Toten," *Trierer theologische Zeitschrift* 82 (1973): 78–92. See the commentaries of W. Zimmerli, *Ezekiel: A Commentary on the Book of the Prophet Ezekiel*, vol. 2 (Philadelphia: Fortress, 1983), chaps. 25–48; J. Blenkinsopp, *Ezekiel. Interpretation: A Bible Commentary for Teaching and Preaching* (Louisville, Ky.: John Knox Press, 1990); C. J. H. Wright, *The Message of Ezekiel: A New Heart and a New Spirit* (Leicester: Inter-Varsity, 2001); L. C. Allen, *Ezekiel 20–48* (Dallas: Word Books, 1990); D. I. Block, *The Book of Ezekiel*, 2 vols. (Grand Rapids, Mich.: W. B. Eerdmans, 1997–98); M. Greenberg, *Ezekiel 21–37: A New Translation with Introduction and Commentary* (New York: Doubleday, 1997).

60. See J. D. Levenson, *Resurrection and the Restoration of Israel*, 163.

61. See E. Dassmann, *Sündenvergebung durch Taufe, Busse und Martyrerfürbitte in den Zeugnissen*

84 The Object of Christian Hope

Personal Resurrection of the Dead in the Old Testament Personal resurrection in the Old Testament[62] is proclaimed tacitly in Job 19:25, and quite openly in the book of Daniel. This canonical work, belonging to the corpus of apocalyptic literature and written about 165 BC,[63] situates the doctrine of final resurrection in the context of the persecution of the Jews by Antiochus Epiphanes and the "king of the south" (Dn 11). The prophet Daniel describes first the trial Jews underwent and then the divine "solution" communicated by God through the prophet. We read: "there shall be a time of anguish, such as has never occurred since nations first came into existence. But at that time your people shall be delivered, everyone who is found written in the book. *Many of those who sleep in the dust of the earth shall awake,* some to everlasting life, and some to shame and everlasting contempt" (Dn 12:1–2).

This text was occasioned by the martyrdom of some of the just of Israel, and serves as an explanation of how they will be vindicated. The prophet tells us that God will ensure justice is done, even after death, by raising to life both the traitors who persecuted the just (to everlasting contempt) and those who suffered persecution (to everlasting life).[64] Theologically speaking, the novelty of Daniel 12 is worthwhile noting: resurrection is no longer earth-bound and collective, reserved to God's people as such, but rather transcends death and is applicable to individuals, Jews or pagans, on the basis of their actions, whether good or bad. In brief terms, it may be said that in Daniel the ethical displaces the ethnical. Resurrection no longer is a synonym for the salvation of the people, but is deeply linked with providing justice for humanity as a whole.[65]

It should also be noted that according to Daniel, resurrection does not seem

---

frühchristlicher Frömmigkeit und Kunst (Münster: Aschendorff, 1973), 60, 70, 220–21. See R.M. Jensen, "Born Again: The Resurrection of the Body and the Restoration of Eden," in *Understanding Early Christian Art* (London: Routledge, 2000), 156–82, especially 167–70.

62. See G.F. Hasel, "Resurrection in the Theology of the Old Testament Apocalyptic," *Zeitschrift für die alttestamentliche Wissenschaft* 92 (1980): 267–84; L.J. Greenspoon, "The Origins of the Idea of Resurrection," in *Traditions in Transformation,* ed. B. Halpern and J.D. Levenson (Winona Lake, Ind.: Eisenbrauns, 1981), 247–321; M.S. Moore, "Resurrection and Immortality: Two Motifs Navigating Confluent Theological Streams in the Old Testament (Dan 12:1–4)," *Theologische Zeitschrift* 39 (1983): 17–34. Martin-Achard considers both Is 26 and Ez 37 as referring to personal resurrection, as do G.F. Hasel and L.J. Greenspoon.

63. See B.J. Alfrink, "L'idée de résurrection d'après Dn 12,1–2," *Biblica* 40 (1959): 355–71; *CAA* 89–92.

64. Some authors hold that the text speaks only of resurrection "for life"; for the rest there will be eternal death, not resurrection; thus J.L. Ruiz de la Peña, *La pascua de la creación,* 82; P. Grelot, *De la mort à la vie éternelle,* 184, n. 4. This is not the most common position, however.

65. According to R.H. Charles, resurrection is "a kind of eschatological property, a means through which the members of the nation present themselves before God to receive their definitive retribution," "Eschatology," in *Encyclopedia Biblica* 2 (1901): 1355.

to be everybody's lot, for he speaks of *"many* of those who sleep in the dust." It would seem that God vindicates only some graver crimes and certain heroic lifestyles. Other noncanonical apocalyptic texts, however, do speak of resurrection for all.[66] Besides, many authors argue that in the overall context of apocalyptic literature, which is clearly universalistic in character, "many" is, in fact, equivalent to "all."[67]

A similar message is to be found in the second book of Maccabees (7:1–29), which is roughly contemporaneous with Daniel and develops his teaching.[68] This book presents resurrection in terms of a reward for heroic obedience to the law of God, of faith in him even to the point of martyrdom. One of the young men threatened by the king with death cries out: "I got these [members] from Heaven, and because of his [God's] laws I disdain them, and from him I hope to get them back again" (2 Mc 7:11). Likewise his brother proclaimed: "One cannot but choose to die at the hands of mortals and to cherish the hope God gives of being raised again by him" (2 Mc 7:14). And he adds, addressing the king: "But for you there will be no resurrection to life." It is made clear that God's saving and vivifying power, God's doing definitive justice, is no longer to be experienced or expected in a world-bound, collective context, as earlier prophets had taught, but beyond death and—in principle—for the whole of humanity, for both saints and sinners.

As in Isaiah and Ezekiel, the doctrine of resurrection in Daniel and Maccabees is in line with that of creation, for the God who gives life and existence in the first place will give it back in fullness to those who are faithful to him. In fact the passage from Maccabees concludes with the exhortation of the young man's mother, who says: "I beg you, my child, to look at the heavens and the earth and see everything that is in them, and recognize that God *did not make them out of things that existed* [a surprisingly explicit allusion to the doctrine of creation]. And in the same way the human race came into being. . . . Accept death, so that in God's mercy I may get you back again along with your brothers" (2 Mc 7:28–29); it is interesting to note that in this text, resurrection involves the reconstitution of human society.

It should be added that *Wisdom literature*, though dealing extensively with immortality in general, pays less attention to resurrection as such.[69] Besides,

---

66. See *CAA* 91–92.

67. According to R. Martin-Achard, *De la mort à la résurrection*, 453, the expression refers literally to "the many"; for other authors, it refers to "one and all": E. F. Sutcliffe, *The Old Testament and the Future Life*, 2nd ed. (London: Burns, Oates and Washbourne, 1947), 138–40; J. Jeremias, *The Eucharistic Words of Jesus* (London: SCM, 1966).

68. See U. Kellermann, *Auferstanden in den Himmel. 2 Makkabäer 7 und die Auferstehung der Märtyrer* (Stuttgart: Katholisches Bibelwerk, 1979), who argues the text is closely linked with Dn 12.

69. See H. Bückers, *Die Unsterblichkeitslehre des Weisheitsbuches* (Münster: Aschendorff, 1938);

whereas apocalyptic texts of the intertestamentary period generally accept the doctrine of resurrection,[70] the authors of the *Dead Sea Scrolls* were clearly hesitant about it.[71] All three, however, do accept the notion of the immortality of soul.[72]

Resurrection of the Dead in the New Testament

The doctrine of resurrection as developed throughout the Old Testament seems to have been pacifically accepted by many if not most Jews in the time of Our Lord.[73] When Martha complained to Jesus for having allowed her brother Lazarus to die, and Jesus replied to the effect that he will rise again, she exclaimed: "I know that he will rise again in the resurrection at the last day" (Jn 11:24). Resurrection seems to have been a commonplace belief. However, several new aspects of resurrection doctrine are to be found in the New Testament.[74] Five may be mentioned.

The Nature of Final Resurrection In the time of the New Testament, the Sadducee party, who accepted only the first five books of Scripture (the Pentateuch), denied the doctrine of the resurrection, and any kind of afterlife for that matter. On the contrary, the Pharisees openly taught these doctrines.[75] "For the Sadducees say that there is no resurrection, nor angel, nor spirit; but the Pharisees acknowledge them all," Paul tells us (Acts 23:8). Although Daniel understood that resurrection takes place beyond death, as we just saw, the Pharisee party understood resurrection in more materialistic and worldly terms (perhaps as something not unlike reincarnation).[76] Their view was closer to the prophetic vision of Isaiah and Ezekiel, in which God is said to intervene directly in the workings of

---

P. Beauchamp, "La salut corporel des justes et la conclusion du Livre de la Sagesse," *Biblica* 45 (1964): 491–526; G. Dautzenberg, *Sein Leben bewahren. Ψυχ in den Herrenworten der Evangelien* (München: Kösel, 1966), 42–46; P. Grelot, "L'eschatologie de la Sagesse et les Apocalyptiques juives," in *De la mort*, 187–99; C. Larcher, *Études sur le Livre de la sagesse* (Paris: Gabalda; Lecoffre, 1969); C. Pozo, *La teología del más allá*, 227–37; M. V. Fabbri, *Creazione e salvezza nel libro della Sapienza: esegesi di Sapienza 1,13–15* (Roma: Armando, 1998).

70. See G. W. E. Nickelsburg, *Resurrection, Immortality and Eternal Life in Intertestamental Literature* (Cambridge, Mass.: Harvard University Press, 1972); *CAA* 86–92.

71. See J. Pryke, "Eschatology in the Dead Sea Scrolls," in *The Scrolls and Christianity*, ed. M. Black (London: SPCK, 1969), 45–57; *CAA* 87, n. 119.

72. See *CAA* 87, n. 120; 92–93.

73. See K. Schubert, "Die Entwicklung der Auferstehungslehre von der nachexilischen bis zur frührabbinischen Zeit," *Biblische Zeitschrift* 6 (1962): 177–214; E. Schürer, *The History of the Jewish People in the Age of Jesus Christ (175 B.C.–A.D. 135)*, vol. 2 (Edinburgh: T. & T. Clark, 1979), 462–500; G. Stemberger, *Der Leib der Auferstehung. Studien zur Anthropologie und Eschatologie des palästinischen Judentums im neutestamentlichen Zeitalter (ca. 170 v. Chr.–100 n. Chr.)* (Roma: Biblical Institute Press, 1972).

74. See L. Coenen and C. Brown, "Resurrection," in *NIDNTT* 3, 259–79.

75. On the Sadducees and Pharisees, see *CAA* 88, nn. 123–24; recently, see J. Neusner and B. Chilton, eds., *In Quest of the Historical Pharisees* (Waco, Tex.: Baylor University, 2007).

76. See *CAA* 164, n. 143.

The Resurrection of the Dead 87

the world in favor of Israel.[77] When requested by the Sadducees to explain what kind of resurrection would be obtained by a woman who had been successively married to seven brothers (Mt 22:23–33; cf. Dt 25:5), Jesus replied: "You are wrong, because you know neither the Scriptures nor the power of God. For in the resurrection they neither marry nor are given in marriage, but are like angels in heaven. And as for the resurrection of the dead, have you not read what was said to you by God: 'I am the God of Abraham, and the God of Isaac, and the God of Jacob'? He is not God of the dead, but of the living" (Mt 22:29–32).[78]

Against the denial of final resurrection by the Sadducees, Jesus taught that it will take place, through the power of God, the God of the living, that is, "the God of Abraham, the God of Isaac and the God of Jacob" (Mt 22:32 = Ex 3:6). In doing so, significantly, he traced the theological roots of resurrection belief, which involves the power and sovereignty of God over the entire created order, to the book of Exodus, which the Sadducees claimed to accept. Against the teaching of the Pharisees, however, Jesus taught that the resurrection would signal a return not to the earthly, corruptible state, but to a transformed, glorified, and permanent one: "for in the resurrection they neither marry nor are given in marriage, but are like angels in heaven" (Mt 22:30).[79] In this way Jesus gives full expression to the teaching of Daniel and 2 Maccabees.[80]

Universal Resurrection The New Testament confirms what had already been suggested in the Old: that since the power of God over creation is unlimited and the salvation won by Christ is destined for all, resurrection will be universal. In John 5:28–29, which is clearly referring to Daniel 12:2 and developing it, we read: "The hour is coming when *all who are in the tombs* will hear his voice and come forth, those who have done good, to the resurrection of life, and those who have done evil, to the resurrection of judgment." Paul, speaking before the pagans, taught the same thing: "there will be a resurrection of both the just and the unjust" (Acts 24:15).[81]

---

77. Thus the classic work of L. Finkelstein, *The Pharisees: The Social Background of their Faith* (Philadelphia: Fortress, 1938), 145–59.

78. On this text in the Marcan version, see F.-G. Dreyfus, "L'argument scripturaire de Jésus en faveur de la résurrection des morts (Mc 12,26–27)," *Revue Biblique* 66 (1959): 213–24; B. Rigaux, *Dieu l'a ressuscité. Exégèse et théologie biblique* (Gembloux: Duculot, 1973), 30–60; G. Greshake and J. Kremer, *Resurrectio Mortuorum*, 53–56.

79. On the meaning of "angels" in this text, see *CAA* 164.

80. The same teaching may be found in Paul, who in 1 Cor 15 rejects the Jewish idea that the risen body is identical with the earthly one: F. Mussner, *Die Auferstehung Jesu* (München: Kösel, 1969), 101–5.

81. This universality is in keeping with Paul's Pharisaic background: see P. Volz, *Die Eschatologie der jüdischen Gemeinde im neutestamentlichen Zeitalter nach den Quellen der rabbinischen, apokalyptischen und apokryphen Literatur*, 2nd ed. (Tübingen: Mohr, 1934), 229–71; J. Bonsirven, *Le judaïsme palestinien au temps de Jésus-Christ: sa théologie*, 2nd ed. (Paris: Beauchesne, 1935), vol. 1, 468–85.

However, the view that resurrection is reserved to the saints alone may be found among some early Christian writers.[82] This was probably inevitable, since special attention is paid in the New Testament to the "resurrection of the living" as a doctrine addressed to Christian believers, baptismally bonded to the death and resurrection of Jesus, and not to pagans. In fact, when both John (Jn 6:55,57) and Paul (1 Cor 15:14–19) speak of resurrection of the living, they are clearly addressing believers.

The Resurrection of Christ and the Resurrection of Humanity The most characteristic element of New Testament teaching regarding resurrection is that it will take place not only through God's enlivening power, but in virtue of the resurrection of Jesus Christ from the dead by the pouring out of the Holy Spirit.[83] The *Catechism of the Catholic Church* puts it as follows: "Jesus links faith in the resurrection with his own person. . . . It is Jesus himself who on the last day will raise up those who have believed in him."[84] Jesus' rising from the dead provides the promise, guarantee, exemplar, and foretaste of universal resurrection, which may be considered an "extension of Christ's own resurrection to humans."[85]

More specifically, according to John, Jesus in person claims to be "the resurrection and the life" (Jn 11:25), for he is "the Son of the living God" (Jn 11:27), the One in whom "life was made manifest" (1 Jn 1:2). And he explains: "for my Father, who is the source of life, has made the Son the source of life. . . . The hour is coming when the dead will leave their graves at the sound of his voice: those who did good will rise again to life, and those who did evil, to condemnation" (Jn 5:26, 28–29).

Likewise Paul forcefully insists on the doctrine of final resurrection in Christological terms.[86] Christ is "the first-born among many brothers" (Rom 8:29; cf.

---

82. See for example the *Didachē*, 16:4–5. Polycarp (*Phil.*, 2:2) says that resurrection is destined for those who "do [God's] will and follow his commandments and love what he loved." On Polycarp, see A. Bovon-Thurneyson, "Ethik und Eschatologie im Philipperbrief des Polycarp von Smyrna," *Theologische Zeitschrift* 29 (1973): 241–56. See also Ignatius of Antioch, *Trall.*, 9:2; *Ad Smyrn.*, 5:3. According to *Ad Smyrn.*, 2:1, the condemned are destined to a bodiless existence. On the issue in apocalyptic and Rabbinic literature, see *CAA* 88–89; H. L. Strack and P. Billerbeck, *Kommentar zum Neuen Testament aus Talmud und Midrasch*, 4th ed. (München: C. H. Beck, 1965), vol. 4, 799–976. On the whole issue, E. Lohse, *Märtyrer und Gottesknecht: Untersuchungen zur urchristlichen Verkündigung vom Sühnetod Jesu Christi*, 2nd ed. (Göttingen: Vandenhoeck & Ruprecht, 1963), 50–51.

83. See my study *Muerte y esperanza*, 55–74.

84. *CCC* 994.

85. Congregation for the Doctrine of the Faith, Doc. *Recentiores episcoporum Synodi* (1979), n. 2. From the biblical standpoint, see B. M. Ahern, "The Risen Christ in the Light of the Pauline Doctrine of the Risen Christian (1 Co 15:35–37)," in *Resurrexit. Actes du Symposium international sur la résurrection de Jésus*, ed. E. Dhanis (Città del Vaticano: Vaticana, 1974), 423–39.

86. Acts 24:14–15; 1 Thes 4:14–17; Eph 2:5–6; 3:1–4; Phil 3:10–11; 1 Cor 15.

Col 1:18). The Apostle pays particular attention to final resurrection in 1 Cor 15,[87] and explains that it depends entirely on the power of the risen Christ. He places this belief at the very center of Christian faith: "if there is no resurrection of the dead," he says, "Christ has not been raised, and if Christ has not been raised then our preaching is in vain and your faith is in vain" (1 Cor 15:13–14). Yet "Christ has been raised from the dead," he adds, "the first fruits of those who have fallen asleep" (1 Cor 15:20). Hence, "just as we have borne the image of the man of dust, we shall also bear the image of the man of heaven" (1 Cor 15:49). Had Christ not risen, there would be no resurrection of the dead, for his resurrection will bring about that of humans. In that sense Christ is not one more case of the general rule, but in the fullest sense of the term is the "first fruits" of those who have died.[88]

Paul also explains that resurrection is anticipated in the present life for those who partake in the death and resurrection of Christ by baptism.[89] In that sense it may be said that to some degree resurrection has already taken place, although Paul principally associates resurrection with the *Parousia* that will occur at the end of time.[90]

The Social and Corporal Aspect of Resurrection Another consequence to be drawn from Christ's resurrection is that ours will be both corporative and corporeal.[91] This brings us to consider the risen humanity of Christ, in all its objectivity and realism, as the critical point of reference for the truth and tangible quality of final resurrection, as witnessed by the apostles and handed on in the Church to all believers. Four elements attest to the historical and objective value of their

---

87. On the purpose of 1 Cor 15, whether it was destined for those who say resurrection has already taken place or for those who simply denied it, see W. Schmithals, *Die Gnosis in Korinth. Eine Untersuchung zu den Korintherbriefen* (Göttingen: Vandenhoeck & Ruprecht, 1956); H. Rusche, "Die Leugner der Auferstehung von den Toten in der korinthischen Gemeinde," *Münchener Theologische Zeitschrift* 10 (1959): 149–51; G. Sellin, *Der Streit um die Auferstehung der Toten* (Göttingen: Vandenhoeck & Ruprecht, 1986).

88. In this sense Christ's resurrection involves that of humans, but not the other way around: see G. Bucher, "Auferstehung Christi und Auferstehung der Toten," *Münchener Theologische Zeitschrift* 25 (1976): 1–32; J. L. Ruiz de la Peña, *La pascua de la creación*, 155.

89. Rom 6:3–11; Eph 2:6; Col 3:1–17.

90. This point is well documented by P. Lengsfeld, *Adam et le Christ: la typologie Adam-Christ dans le Nouveau Testament et son utilisation dogmatique par M. J. Scheeben et K. Barth* (Paris: Aubier-Montaigne, 1970), 56–57; G. Greshake and J. Kremer, *Resurrectio Mortuorum*, 112–14.

91. 1 Cor 6:14–15. J. L. Ruiz de la Peña, *La pascua de la creación*, 156, insists on the point: resurrection cannot be atomized, for it is corporative and corporal. See also J. A. T. Robinson, *The Body: A Study in Pauline Theology* (London: SCM, 1961), 88–89: "It would be a mistake to consider Pauline texts with the modern idea that bodily resurrection is in some ways related to the moment of death. . . . No part of the New Testament establishes an essential relationship between resurrection and the moment of death. The key moments . . . are Baptism and the Parousia."

testimony,[92] and thus to the meaningfulness and tangible quality of belief in final resurrection.

1. *The empty tomb.* The historical reality of "the empty tomb of Jesus indicates the corporeal identity between the one that was crucified and the one that rose up."[93] In fact both 1 Corinthians 15:3–4 and Acts 2:31 refer to one and the same human subject before and after resurrection.[94] Conversely, the possibility of a miraculously accelerated decomposition of the buried body of Christ before the third day, suggested by some,[95] or the idea that the body might have been consumed by wild animals,[96] are hardly plausible explanations.[97]

2. *Apparition terminology.* Jesus' apparitions are expressed most frequently in terms of Jesus "showing himself" (*ophthē*),[98] or "making himself seen."[99] Since the term is presented in aorist, passive form, the text seems to favor a real sight-encounter with the physical body of Christ, as distinct from a subjective vision.

3. *Recognition.* In spite of the apostles' fear, apprehension, and incredulity, Jesus brought them to recognize him by inviting them to "touch and see" (Lk 24:39), and by eating a piece of fried fish in their company.[100] Specifically, he invited them not to look at his face but rather at his "hands and feet, it is myself" (Lk 24:39). This was because his hands and feet carried the marks of crucifixion and proved his identity as the one who had been crucified.[101]

4. *Jesus' glorious resurrection.* The difficulties the apostles experienced in recognizing Jesus (he appeared *en hetera morphē*, "in another form," Mark tells us, 16:12) stemmed from the fact that Our Lord rose not in a temporal and worldly way as did Lazarus, but with a glorious body (Phil 3:21) that will die no more (Rom 6:9). Although at first the apostles did not recognize him as one and the same human subject, later on they did.[102] Though still living in space and acting

---

92. See F. Mussner, *Die Auferstehung Jesu;* R. H. Gundry, *Sōma in Biblical Theology with Emphasis on Pauline Anthropology* (Cambridge: Cambridge University Press, 1976); S. T. Davis, "Christian Belief in the Resurrection of the Body," *New Scholasticism* 62 (1988): 72–97; C. Pozo, *La venida del Señor,* 34–39.

93. F. Mussner, *Die Auferstehung Jesu,* 134.

94. Ibid., 133–34; see A. Schmitt, "Ps 16, 8–11 als Zeugnis der Auferstehung in Apg," *Biblische Zeitschrift* 17 (1973): 229–48.

95. For example X. Léon-Dufour, *Résurrection de Jésus et message pascal* (Paris: Seuil, 1971), 204.

96. This position is suggested by J. D. Crossan, *The Historical Jesus: The Life of a Mediterranean Jewish Peasant* (San Francisco: Harper, 1991), who in turn is critiqued by W. L. Craig, "John Dominic Crossan on the Resurrection of Jesus," in *The Resurrection: An Interdisciplinary Symposium on the Resurrection of Jesus,* ed. S. T. Davis, D. Kendall, and G. O'Collins (Oxford: Oxford University Press, 1997), 249–71.

97. See C. Pozo, *La teología del más allá,* 272–79, with bibliography.

98. 1 Cor 15:3–8; 1 Tm 3:16; Lk 24:34; Acts 9:17; 13:31; 26:16.

99. See F. Zorell, *Lexicon Graecum Novi Testamenti* (Paris: P. Lethielleux, 1931), 928.

100. Lk 24:42–43; C. M. Martini, "L'apparizione agli Apostoli in Lc 24, 36–43 nel complesso dell'opera lucana," in *Resurrexit,* 230–45.

101. Jn 20:20,25,27; F. Mussner, *Die Auferstehung Jesu,* 102–6.

102. Lk 24:16,31; Jn 20:15–16.

within the world, the risen Christ no longer belongs to or depends on this world. To an important degree his redemptive *kenosis* (or self-emptying, Phil 2:7) has been left behind. From now on, "at the name of Jesus every knee should bow, in heaven and on earth and under the earth, and every tongue confess that Jesus Christ is Lord, to the glory of God the Father" (ibid., 10–11).

Besides, Christians instinctively perceived two important elements in Christ's resurrection. *First*, it provided an incontrovertible sign of God's faithful love for humanity, in spite of the fact that humans had openly rejected that love by putting Jesus to death on the Cross and should, by right, have incurred God's eternal wrath (Mt 21:40–41). *Second*, Christ's resurrection constituted an important benefit for humans themselves, a sure promise for the whole of humanity. Christ had risen, the "first born" (Rom 8:29), and as a result all those who belonged to him must also rise up (1 Cor 15:12; 2 Cor 4:14). Resurrection became a catalyst not only for the Church's mission, but also for the Church's thought, and especially for its anthropology and ethics, as we shall see presently.

Resurrection, Holy Spirit, and the Eucharist The New Testament likewise attributes eschatological resurrection to the action of the Holy Spirit[103] and to the Eucharist.[104]

It should come as no surprise that the *Holy Spirit* is the agent, as it were, of the "extension" of Christ's resurrection to believers. This is so in the first place because he is "the Spirit of Christ."[105] Hence we read in the letter to the Romans: "If the Spirit of him who raised Jesus from the dead dwells in you, he [the Father] who raised Christ Jesus from the dead will give life to your mortal bodies also *through his Spirit* which dwells in you" (Rom 8:11). As we have shown elsewhere, "the Spirit . . . is the One who applies, communicates and makes present the content of revelation and the saving power that derives entirely from the words and works of Jesus Christ, God's anointed One."[106] And in the second place, Scripture tells us that the Spirit dwells in our body as in a temple; hence the body is marked out for resurrection, for becoming a "spiritual body" (1 Cor 15:44). To the Corinthians Paul wrote: "Do you not know that your body is a temple of the Holy Spirit within you, which you have from God?" (1 Cor 6:19; cf. 1 Cor 3:16).

Hillary of Poitiers says that resurrection is the fruit of the marriage of human flesh with the Spirit, its eternal spouse.[107] Irenaeus speaks openly of the work of

---

103. See "The Pneumatological Interpretation of New Testament Apocalyptic," in *CAA* 257–94.
104. See G. Martelet, *Résurrection, eucharistie et genèse de l'homme. Chemins théologiques d'un renouveau chrétien* (Paris: Desclée de Brouwer, 1972); G. Wainwright, *Eucharist and Eschatology*.
105. Acts 10:38; Rom 8:9; 2 Cor 3:17.
106. *CAA* 273.
107. Hillary of Poitiers, *In Matth.*, 27:4.

the Holy Spirit in bringing about final resurrection: "The Spirit of Christ is the one who will gather the scattered members of the dead that are dispersed on the earth, and bring them to the kingdom of heaven."[108] One author who paraphrases the final articles of the Apostles' Creed says that Christians believe "in the Holy Spirit, in the holy Church for the resurrection of the flesh."[109]

In the same direction Christ's resurrection will be extended to those who are nourished on his risen body, the Eucharist: "Anyone who eats my flesh and drinks my blood has eternal life, and I shall raise him up on the last day" (Jn 6:54). Again Irenaeus, following the Gospel of John, insists on the role of the Eucharist in a cosmic context as a guarantee and preparation for resurrection. Specifically, he says that the Holy Spirit acts principally through the Eucharist.[110] "Just as the bread which is the fruit of the earth, once the divine blessing has been invoked over it, is no longer common bread, but Eucharist, composed of two realities, one earthly, the other heavenly, so also our bodies that receive the Eucharist are no longer corruptible, from the moment they carry within the seed of resurrection."[111] Ignatius of Antioch, on his way to Rome to receive the crown of martyrdom, termed the Eucharist the "medicine of immortality."[112]

In this context, however, it may be asked how the condemned, those who are not united with Christ, in whom the Holy Spirit does not dwell, will rise from the dead, given that resurrection seems to be virtually synonymous with salvation.[113] Cyril of Alexandria insists on the universality of resurrection, that all will rise, and explains that "the grace of resurrection has been given to the whole of [human] nature."[114] Likewise Paul Althaus has it that the resurrection of sinners will take place not by the action of Spirit of Christ, but by the "common creative action of God."[115] Above we referred to the relationship between God's creating action and his raising of the dead.

Still, neither the role of Holy Spirit nor that of the Eucharist need be entirely excluded in the resurrection of the condemned. For the Spirit is the *creator Spiritus*, the one who created the whole universe, both spiritual and material, and must bring it to completion and perfection at the end of time. And as regards

---

108. Irenaeus, *Adv. Haer.* V, 9:4.

109. See P. Nautin, *Je crois à l'esprit Saint dans la sainte Église pour la résurrection de la chair* (Paris: Cerf, 1947).

110. Irenaeus, *Adv. Haer.* V, 2:2–3.   111. Ibid., *IV*, 18:4–5.

112. Ignatius of Antioch, *Ad Eph.*, 20:2.

113. See A. Winklhofer, *Das Kommen seines Reiches: von den Letzten Dingen*, 2nd ed. (Frankfurt a. M.: Josef Knecht, 1962), 272; J. L. Ruiz de la Peña, *La pascua de la creación*, 157, 167. The latter defends the idea of resurrection simply as salvation.

114. Cyril of Alexandria, *In Joann.*, 6, on Jn 10:10.

115. See P. Althaus, *Die letzten Dinge*, 9th ed. (Gütersloh: Bertelsmann, 1964), 116, 122.

The Resurrection of the Dead 93

the Eucharist, Paul explains that condemnation is not unlinked with Eucharistic communion, for "whoever eats the bread or drinks the cup of the Lord in an unworthy manner will be guilty of profaning the body and blood of the Lord" (1 Cor 11:29).

Christian Witness to Resurrection Belief: Early Christian Anthropology and Ethics

The doctrine of final resurrection was taught openly by Christians from the very inception of the Church's mission.[116] Justin Martyr stated that it was a hallmark of Christian orthodoxy.[117] In fact, no aspect of Christian eschatology was dealt with in greater detail by Fathers of the Church and ecclesiastical writers than the resurrection of the dead. Ps.-Justin,[118] Athenagoras (second century),[119] Irenaeus,[120] Tertullian,[121] Origen,[122] Methodius,[123] Cyril of Jerusalem,[124] Gregory

---

116. On the development of the doctrine of the "resurrection of the flesh" in the early centuries of Christianity, see H. B. Swete, "The Resurrection of the Flesh," *Journal of Theological Studies* 18 (1917): 135–41; L. E. Boliek, *The Resurrection of the Flesh: A Study of a Confessional Phrase* (Amsterdam: Jacob van Campen, 1962); G. Kretschmar, "Auferstehung des Fleisches. Zur Frühgeschichte einer theologischen Lehrformel," in *Leben angesichts des Todes. Beiträge zum theologischen Problem des Todes. Helmut Thielicke zum 60. Geburtstag*, ed. M.-L. Henry (Tübingen: J. C. B. Mohr [Paul Siebeck], 1968), 101–37; A. Fierro, "Las controversias sobre la resurrección en los siglos II–V," *Revista Española de Teología* 28 (1968): 3–21; T. H. C. von Eijk, *La résurrection des morts chez les pères apostoliques* (Paris: Beauchesne, 1974); C. W. Bynum, *The Resurrection of the Body*; G. Greshake and J. Kremer, *Resurrectio Mortuorum*; my study "La fórmula 'Resurrección de la carne.'"

117. Justin, *Dial. cum Tryph.*, 80:4.

118. Ps.-Justin, *De resurrectione*. Most authors do not accept Justin's authorship of this text: see B. E. Daley, *The Hope*, 230, n. 1. Some, however, do consider the text authentic, for example, P. Prigent, *Justin et l'Ancien Testament* (Paris: Cerf, 1964), 50–61.

119. Athenagoras, *De resurrectione mortuorum*. On this text, see M. Marcovich, "On the Text of Athenagoras, De resurrectione," *Vigiliae Christianae* 33 (1979): 375–82; G. Filoramo, *L'escatologia e la retribuzione negli scritti dei Padri* (Roma: Borla, 1997), 218–21; B. E. Daley, *The Hope*, 23–24, 230, n. 4.

120. Irenaeus, *Adv. Haer.* V. On his eschatology, see A. S. Wood, "The Eschatology of Irenaeus," *Evangelical Quarterly* 41 (1969): 30–41; P.-J. Carle, "Irénée de Lyon et les fins dernières," *Divinitas* 34 (1990): 57–72; 151–71; A. Orbe, "Gloria Dei vivens homo," *Gregorianum* 73 (1992): 205–68; J. J. Ayán Calvo, "Escatología cósmica y Sagrada Escritura en Ireneo de Lyon," *Annali di Storia dell'esegesi* 16 (1999): 197–233.

121. Tertullian, *De resurrectione carnis*. See P. Siniscalco, "L'escatologia di Tertulliano: tra rivelazione scritturale e dati razionali, 'psicologici', naturali," *Annali di Storia dell'esegesi* 17 (2000): 73–89.

122. There is no extant work of Origen on resurrection, although he wrote extensively on the subject. Still, see *C. Cels.*, 1:5 and 8. On his teaching, see W. L. Knox, "Origen's Conception of the Resurrection Body," *Journal of Theological Studies* 39 (1938): 247–53; H. Chadwick, "Origen, Celsus and the Resurrection of the Body," *Harvard Theological Review* 41 (1948): 83–102; H. Crouzel, "Les critiques adressées par Méthode et ses contemporains à la doctrine origénienne du corps ressuscité," *Gregorianum* 53 (1972): 679–714.

123. Methodius, *De resurrectione*. See the classic work of G. N. Bonwetsch, *Die Theologie des Methodius von Olympus* (Berlin: Weidmannsche Buchhandlung, 1903); H. Crouzel, "Les critiques adressées par Méthode."

124. Cyril of Jerusalem, *Catech. Myst.*, 18.

of Nyssa,[125] Augustine,[126] John Chrysostom[127] and others, keenly aware of the novelty of the doctrine, all wrote *ex professo* works on final resurrection. Daley says that "Christian writers stressed the need to take the biblical promise of resurrection literally, and went to extraordinary lengths to argue that such a hope is neither impossible nor unworthy of human dignity."[128] The reason for this was simple. Not only did the Fathers perceive that the resurrection of Jesus Christ was the living center of Christian faith and mission (Acts 4:33, etc.) and that the promise of final resurrection was its necessary complement, but also they realized that this teaching came into sharp conflict with the prevailing (Neoplatonic and Gnostic) anthropologies, cosmologies, and ethical systems of their time.

Some Implications of Resurrection Belief: Liturgy, Cremation From the very outset, as we have seen, Christians gave exceptional importance to the event of Christ's resurrection and the teaching of universal resurrection that derives from it. Christians decorated their tombs with epitaphs representing the resurrection of Lazarus, Ezekiel's field of dry bones coming to life, the prophet Jonah coming out of the mouth of the whale after three days (a prefigurement of Christ's resurrection: Mt 12:40).[129] Whereas pagans termed the place of burial the *nekropolis* or *nekrotaphiōn*, which means the place or city of the dead, the common term assumed by Christians was *koimētērion*, transliterated into Latin as *coemeterium*,[130] cemetery, which refers to a place of sleep,[131] whence the dead would eventually awaken to a new life. Quite possibly the term arose in the context of Christ's words to the young girl whom he rose from the dead: "the girl is not dead but

---

125. Gregory of Nyssa, *De anima et resurrectione dialogus*. On this work, see J. Daniélou, "La résurrection des corps chez Grégorie de Nysse," *Vigiliae Christianae* 2 (1953): 154–70; L. F. Mateo-Seco, "La muerte y su más allá en el 'Diálogo sobre el alma y la resurrección' de Gregorio de Nisa," *Scripta Theologica* 3 (1971): 75–107; A. Le Boulluec, "Corporéité ou individualité? La condition finale des ressuscités selon Grégoire de Nysse," *Augustinianum* 35 (1995): 307–26; L. F. Mateo-Seco, "Resurrezione," in *Gregorio di Nissa. Dizionario*, ed. L. F. Mateo-Seco and G. Maspero (Roma: Città Nuova, 2007), 488–91.

126. See principally Augustine, *De Civ. Dei XXII*. See P. Goñi, *La resurrección de la carne según San Agustín* (Washington, D.C.: The Catholic University of America Press, 1961); K. E. Börresen, "Augustin, interprète du dogme de la résurrection," *Studia Theologica* 23 (1969), 143–55; M. Alfeche, "The Rising of the Dead in the Works of Augustine (1 Co. 15:35–57)," *Augustiniana* 39 (1989): 54–98; P. A. Ferrisi, "La risurrezione della carne nel 'De fide et symbolo' di S. Agostino," *Augustinianum* 33 (1993): 213–32.

127. John Chrysostom, *De resurrectione mortuorum homilia*. See A. Miranda, "La resurrezione dei corpi nel Cristostomo (In 1 Co 15). Una nuova percezione della realtà 'corporea' tra IV e V secolo," *Aquinas* 78 (2001): 387–404.

128. B. E. Daley, *The Hope*, 220.

129. See R. M. Jensen, "Born Again: The Resurrection of the Body and the Restoration of Eden," 156–82. On the resurrection of Lazarus, see E. Mâle, "La résurrection de Lazarus dans l'art," *Revue des arts* 1 (1951): 44–52.

130. The Latin transliteration *coemeterium* was probably first used by Tertullian in *De anima*, 51.

131. On the Greek terms *koimētērion* and *nekrotaphiōn*, see G. W. H. Lampe, *A Greek Patristic Lexicon*, 5th ed. (Oxford: Clarendon Press, 1978), 760, 902.

The Resurrection of the Dead 95

sleeping" (Mt 9:24), and his description of his friend Lazarus who had died: "I go to wake him out of sleep" (Jn 11:11).

The Church has traditionally dissuaded believers from the practice of cremation, that is, the intentional destruction by fire of the body after death. As long as scandal is avoided, however, cremation is considered licit.[132] In the *Code of Canon Law* we read: "The Church earnestly recommends that the pious custom of burial be retained; but it does not forbid cremation, unless this is chosen for reasons which are contrary to Christian teaching. . . . Church funeral rites are to be denied to . . . those who for anti-Christian motives chose that their bodies be cremated . . . unless they gave some signs of repentance before death."[133] Some centuries ago, in fact, it was quite common for apostates to request cremation, with a view to publicly confirming their denial of Christian faith.[134]

It is interesting to note that, by contrast, in Eastern funeral rites (especially those associated with the Hindu religion) the body is completely consumed by fire with resinous firewood, and the ashes are scattered on rivers or the sea. In this way, it is hoped that the spirit will be completely and definitively separated from the mortal body.[135]

From the point of view of God's power, of course, resurrection is equally possible for the cremated as for those who are buried. However, should someone opt for cremation in order to profess their belief in the perishable character of matter, to deny life after death or the power of God over matter, then the practice would be illicit. "If those who do not believe in the resurrection of the flesh bury the bodies of the dead," Augustine said, "even more so should believers do so, because the dead body will rise up and remain forever, and this becomes a public witness to this very faith."[136] All in all, therefore, burial is to be recommended over cremation,[137] which can be seen as an attempt to eliminate Christian burial places and prayer for the dead, as well as to trivialize death.[138]

---

132. See International Theological Commission, *Problems of Eschatology* (1992), n. 6.4; Congregation for the Doctrine of the Faith, "The Cremation of Cadavers" (1963). On the history of cremation, see J. L. Angué, "Incinération et rituel des funérailles," *Études* (1985): 663–76, and Z. Suchecki, *La cremazione dei cadaveri nel Diritto Canonico* (Roma: Pontificia Università Lateranense, 1990).

133. *Code of Canon Law* (1983), n. 1176, § 3; 1184, § 1, 2.

134. See P. Palazzini, "Cremazione," in *Enciclopedia cattolica*, vol. 4 (Città del Vaticano: Vaticana, 1950), cols. 838–42.

135. On the significance of cremation for pagan religions, see F. Cumont, *Lux perpetua*, 390.

136. Augustine, *De cura pro mortuis gerenda*, 18:22.

137. On the notion of burial being preferable to cremation, see I. Lotzika, "Incinération: malaise pour un dernier adieu," *Études* (1985): 657–62; G. Gozzelino, *Nell'attesa*, 446–47; V. Croce, "La sepoltura, nuovo e ultimo battesimo," in *Cristo nel tempo della Chiesa: teologia dell'azione liturgica, dei sacramenti e dei sacramentali* (Leumann: LDC, 1992), 454–55.

138. See J. L. Schlegel, "Logiques de l'incinération," *Études* n. 363 (1985): 677–80.

The Theological and Philosophical Challenge of Resurrection From the very outset of Christian preaching, the perplexity of pagans[139] and of Christians themselves,[140] in the face of this new teaching, was palpable. When preaching at the Areopagus of Athens, Paul found a good hearing when he spoke of divinities, rituals, and ethical practice. But "when they heard of the resurrection of the dead, some mocked, but others said: 'We will hear you again about this'" (Acts 17:32). When brought before Festus and Agrippa at Caesarea, Paul again spoke of the resurrection, while Festus called out to him: "Paul, you are mad; your great learning is turning you mad" (Acts 26:24). The Apostle warned Timothy of two individuals, Hyrmenaeus and Philetus, "who have swerved from the truth by holding that the resurrection is past already. They are upsetting the faith of some" (2 Tm 2:17–18). Likewise, among Corinthian believers there was considerable doubt as regards the resurrection.[141] This explains Paul's insistence to the effect that "if Christ is preached as raised from the dead, how can some of you say that there is no resurrection of the dead?" (1 Cor 15:12). And he replies categorically: "If there is no resurrection of the dead, then Christ has not been raised; if Christ has not been raised, then our preaching is in vain and your faith is in vain" (1 Cor 15:13–14).

Early Christian writers were keenly aware of the difficulties resurrection belief involved. Origen said that "the mystery of the resurrection is also on the lips of the infidels, but it is a cause of ridicule for them because they do not understand it."[142] Tertullian wrote that "we also laughed about these things."[143] "No article of Christian faith is more repudiated than the resurrection of the flesh," Augustine noted.[144] And Gregory the Great had it that "many doubt the resurrection, as we did in our time."[145] Two principal difficulties were suggested by pagan opponents.[146]

First, the doctrine of final resurrection was questioned because it seemed to go against common sense and the laws of nature. Matter and the cosmos, according to the Greek worldview, marked by cosmic determinism and dualism, are invariably linked with time and corruption, and can on no account share in the glory and immortality that belongs only to the gods. The pagan Porphyry cites the hypothetical case of a drowned man's corpse eaten by fish, and the fish eaten subsequently by a fisherman, and the latter by dogs, and the dogs by vultures. Understandably, he poses the question: with what body will humans rise?

---

139. Acts 17:16–34; 26:25.
140. 1 Cor 15:12; 2 Tm 2:17.
141. See nn. 80 and 87 above.
142. Origen, *C. Cels.*, 1:7.
143. Tertullian, *Apol.*, 18:4.
144. Augustine, *Enn. in Ps.*, 88:2.
145. Gregory the Great, *Hom. in Ev. II*, 26, n. 12.
146. Here we follow C. Pozo, *La teología del más allá*, 353–58.

In contesting the Christian doctrine of resurrection, he spares neither satire nor cynicism.[147]

Second, on a more philosophical plane, the doctrine of resurrection was commonly rejected in the context of the Neoplatonic cosmology and anthropology then in vogue. In Greek cosmology, matter was considered as inherently impervious or extraneous to spirit. As a result, the human soul could be considered only as a prisoner of the body, or at best, its pilot, bound to it externally.[148] For the Platonic mindset, resurrection would constitute a shameful return to the prison of the body, which is considered to be the source of all evil, disgrace, and limitation, the epitome of non-salvation; after all, man is his soul, and the body is a mere accidental adjunct.[149]

Christian authors replied in a variety of ways to the challenge of the pagan philosophers. The main argument they offered, however, was a strictly theological one: God is the sovereign, all-powerful and faithful Creator of the earth and of humankind; therefore he is capable of raising up humans from the dead, and has promised to do so by the miracles he worked through Christ, and in particular by raising him up from the dead; this same power will be applied to all humans at the end of time through the Spirit of Christ. Justin Martyr, for example, says that "we will receive again our own bodies, though they be dead and cast into the earth, for we hold that for God nothing is impossible."[150]

Besides, by referring to semblances taken from nature—the rising and setting of the sun, the blossoming of seeds and flowers,[151] the Phoenix rising from its own ashes[152] (an image first used by Clement of Rome)[153]—Christians explained that the doctrine of resurrection does not contradict the dynamic of nature and the cosmos. The power of God who raises from the dead is not opposed to the laws of nature, but rather brings them to fullness, and gives them a new, definitive lease on life. In that sense, as C. S. Lewis puts it, the miracle of resurrection is what gives meaning to nature, and not the other way round.[154] Purely cosmological and anthropological arguments against resurrection are challenged by

---

147. Porphyry, *Contra christianos*, fr. 94.   148. See pp. 23–24 above.
149. See pp. 19–22 above.
150. Justin, *1 Apol.*, 18–19. Likewise Athenagoras speaks of God's power involved in the resurrection: *De res.*, 9. On the same issue, see also Tertullian, *De res.*, 11:3,10; Augustine, *De cura pro mortuis gerenda*, 2:4; Gregory the Great, *Hom. in Ev. II*, 26.
151. Minucius Felix, *Octavius*, 34.
152. Clement of Rome, *Ep. in Cor.*, 24–26; Tertullian, *De res.*, 13; Cyril of Jerusalem, *Catech. Myst.*, 18:8; Eusebius, *Vita Const.*, 4:72; Lactantius, *De ave Phoenice*. See R. Van den Brock, *The Myth of the Phoenix according to Classical and Early Christian Tradition* (Leiden: E. J. Brill, 1972); B. R. Reichenbach, *Is Man the Phoenix? A Study of Immortality* (Washington, D.C.: Christian University Press, 1978).
153. Clement of Rome, *Ep. in Cor.*, 24–25.
154. See C. S. Lewis, *Miracles* (London: Sheed and Ward, 1947), 112–14, 147–50.

the divine promise of resurrection. In the light of God's eternal design, expressed in the doctrine of the Incarnation, death, and resurrection of the Eternal Word, matter and the human body are dignified beyond all expectations. In the light of final resurrection, matter, though created and corruptible, is seen to have a true vocation to eternity. Besides, it is fair to say that the doctrine of eschatological resurrection was instrumental in bringing about a new, unitary, and highly flexible anthropology.[155]

In the face of the Platonizing tendency that reemerged during the early Middle Ages, Thomas Aquinas, taking his cue from Aristotle's theory of the substantial unity of the human composite (*anima forma corporis*),[156] insisted on the centrality of the doctrine of resurrection of the dead not only as a doctrine of faith but as one that is open to philosophical reflection.[157] He taught that the soul separated from the body is in a state "contrary to nature,"[158] for the human soul by nature is meant to inform the body. However, the separated soul retains what Aquinas calls a *commensuratio* toward its own body,[159] with which it will be united anew at the end of time through the power of God. As a result, he says, "resurrection is natural as to its end, inasmuch as it is natural for the soul to be the form of the body; whereas its active principle is not natural, but is caused solely by divine power."[160] In other words it may be said that "the final cause of resurrection is human nature, but the efficient cause is God."[161] Likewise, Gregory of Nyssa graphically describes the soul (*eidos*) recognizing its own body, drawing it to itself, "attracting again to itself that which is its own."[162] And the reason why this is possible is that the soul remains united in some way with the body: "there is no force that can tear [the soul] away from its cohesion with [its members]."[163]

The Growing Irrelevance of Resurrection Belief It is interesting to note that the doctrine of resurrection, that both of Christ and of humans, though not generally denied throughout the later Middle Ages, by the Protestant Reformers, and in modern times, gradually came to lose its capacity to challenge and catalyze scientific, philosophical, and theological reflection. One reason for this lies

---

155. See my studies *Cristocentrismo y antropocentrismo en el horizonte de la teología. Una reflexión en torno a la epistemología teológica*, in *Cristo y el Dios de los cristianos*, ed. J. Morales et al. (Pamplona: Servicio de Publicaciones de la Universidad de Navarra, 1998), 367–98; and "Resurrezione."

156. See my study "Anima," 86–87, 91–92.

157. See M. Brown, "Aquinas on the Resurrection of the Body," *Thomist* 56 (1992): 165–207; M. L. Lamb, "The Eschatology of St Thomas Aquinas," 229–34. The same thing may be said of Athenagoras, according to M. Marcovich, "On the Text of Athenagoras, *De resurrectione.*"

158. Thomas Aquinas, *IV C. Gent.*, 79. 159. Ibid., 80.

160. Ibid., 81; *S. Th. III, Suppl.*, q. 75, a. 3.

161. M. Brown, "Aquinas on the Resurrection," 186.

162. Gregory of Nyssa, *De hom. opif.*, 27,5:2.   163. Gregory of Nyssa, *De anima et res.*

The Resurrection of the Dead 99

in a pervasive return to the basic tenets and terminology of Platonic thought, in anthropology and eschatology.[164] As a result, philosophy and spirituality came to turn their attention more and more, in the name of biblical interiority, to the human spirit and subjectivity, the *res cogitans*, and away from the body, *res extensa*, to use Descartes's terminology. Philosophers came to accord resurrection less and less value. Emmanuel Kant, for example, declared that he saw "no reason whatever to drag about a body for the rest of eternity, a body which, however purified it may be, will nonetheless always be made up of matter."[165]

The result was that final judgment and eschatological salvation came to be linked principally with the ethical behavior and the individual immortal soul, and no longer with final resurrection, which of its very nature would involve the manifestation of the true state of the individual, not only before God, but also in its bodily integrity before the rest of humanity. We have considered this question in chapter 1.[166] Final judgment divorced from the corporeal easily lends itself to an ethical and spiritual vision that is individualistic, interior, spiritualistic, subjective, and unheeding of society and nature, both human and cosmic. This approach, coupled with a somewhat Platonic view of the human subject typical of the modern period, led in practice to a reductionist, symbolic understanding of resurrection (of Christ and of humanity) that became quite common throughout the twentieth century. The Good News of the Resurrection of Christ and (in him) of humanity would refer only to personal or interior life, to the novelty of conversion, but would have little or nothing to say in the realm of the material world, of political action, or of human corporality. Matter with its laws and properties would, as a result, become and remain the exclusive domain of science. Marxist philosophers such as Ernst Bloch developed theories about the origin and development of matter, life, and cosmos that with time came to be completely divorced from transcendence.[167] Of particular importance and influence in this regard is the thought of the Lutheran biblical exegete Rudolf Bultmann.[168]

As we saw already, Bultmann interpreted New Testament and early Christian texts speaking of resurrection (that of Christ and of humanity) in terms of a personal faith decision of an individualistic and existentialist kind: Christ's resurrection can be considered an event, a true event, he said, for the Christian. Through their faith in him, Bultmann would say, Christians have already risen

164. See pp. 22–24 above.
165. I. Kant, *Religion within the Bounds of Pure Reason*, n. 119.
166. See pp. 25–31.
167. See my study "Hope and Freedom in Gabriel Marcel and Ernst Bloch," 216–22.
168. See pp. 51–53 above. Bultmann's position has been repeated of late, for example, by A. Torres Queiruga, *Repensar la resurrección: la diferencia cristiana en la continuidad de las religiones y de la cultura*, 3rd ed. (Madrid: Trotta, 2005).

from the dead; believers are already saved. However, according to Bultmann, the physical universe as such is impermeable to the power of grace: "Faith in spirits and demons has been liquidated by the knowledge of the forces and the laws of nature.... It is simply impossible to use electric light and the radio, use modern medical instruments and chemicals for the sick, and at the same time believe in a world of spirits and miracles of the New Testament."[169] Thus New Testament miracles, and especially resurrection accounts, should not be considered as literal explanations or real events. The term "resurrection of the flesh" would constitute a kind of Hellenization of true Hebrew theology that is personal and not substantial (or objective) in character.[170]

As we have seen earlier, Bultmann's position undoes the realism and catalytic quality of resurrection doctrine and has influenced theological reflection in many ways, principally by according material things merely symbolic value in the religious order.[171] His teaching has, however, been sharply challenged by both Protestant and Catholic authors over recent decades.[172]

Some Theological Implications of Resurrection

Two specific aspects of the Christian doctrine of final resurrection should be considered: the *novelty* of the risen, glorified body, and its *identity* with the earthly body.[173] Needless to say, both aspects relate directly to the dynamic of Christ's own resurrection and its application in the power of the Holy Spirit to humanity: the historical Jesus Christ who lived in Palestine and died in Jerusalem is identical with the one who rose from the dead to a state of glory, and now sits "on the right hand of the Father." Throughout the forthcoming discussion it should become clear how resurrection belief critically determines central aspects of Christian ethics, anthropology, spirituality, and dialogue with the sciences.

The Glory and Novelty of the Risen Body

The risen body is clearly distinct in form from the earthly body in that it will be glorified, incorruptible, impassable, and immortal.[174] Jesus said that the risen will be "like angels in heaven" (Mk 12:25), a text interpreted almost literally by Origen (who says that the risen body will no longer be crass and earthly,

---

169. R. Bultmann, *Kerygma und Mythos*, 17–18.
170. Thus W. Beider, "Auferstehung des Fleisches oder des Leibes? Eine biblischtheologische und dogmengeschichtliche Studie," *Theologische Zeitschrift* 1 (1945): 105–20.
171. See J. Ratzinger, *Eschatology*, 57–58.
172. See pp. 318–25.
173. On the issue, see A. Fierro, "Las controversias sobre la resurrección."
174. See especially Thomas Aquinas, *IV C. Gent.*, 84–88.

but heavenly, subtle, ethereal, luminous, and spiritual, that is angelic),[175] but more figuratively by Tertullian[176] and the great majority of early Christian theologians.[177]

Paul in his extended reflection on resurrection in 1 Corinthians 15 states openly that the risen will have "a spiritual body" (*sōma pneumatikon:* 1 Cor 15:44). This conviction is clearly based on the experiences Christians had of Jesus risen from the dead in the power of the Holy Spirit. "Our homeland is in heaven, and from it we await a Savior, the Lord Jesus Christ, *who will change our lowly body to be like his glorious body*, by the power which enables him even to subject all things to himself" (Phil 3:20–21; cf. Rom 6:5). In the Apostles' Creed the article "and life everlasting" was added to "resurrection of the flesh" in order to ensure that the latter would not be understood in terms of a temporary, earthbound resurrection like that of Lazarus, but a truly eternal one.[178] *Resurgit non aliud corpus, quamvis in aliud,* Hillary of Poitiers says,[179] "not another body rises up, but the body rises in another way." And Cyril of Jerusalem: "the same body rises up, but it is no longer the same."[180] John Chrysostom holds the same doctrine.[181] Augustine says: "We speak of the resurrection of the flesh, not like the resurrection of some who die later on, but for eternal life (*resurrectio carnis in aeternam vitam*), just as the flesh of Christ rose up."[182]

Caution is certainly advisable when attempting to provide a description of the risen state of humans, of the "spiritual body."[183] The *Catechism of the Catholic Church* says that the "how" of final resurrection "exceeds our imagination and understanding; it is accessible only in faith. Yet, our participation in the Eucharist already gives us a foretaste of Christ's transfiguration of our bodies."[184] The first letter to the Corinthians (15:35–54), in fact, does offer some indications to help us appreciate how Paul "had seen" the Risen Jesus (2 Cor 12:2–4). Keeping in mind the corporal realism of the risen Christ, already referred to,[185] and following the reflections of Thomas Aquinas on the risen state (who in turn is inspired

---

175. Origen, *Comm. in Matth.*, 17:2. 176. Tertullian, *De res.*, 62:1–4.

177. See B. E. Daley, *The Hope*, 54, on different interpretations among the Fathers. Methodius of Olympus was openly opposed to Origen (ibid., 62–64), as was Epiphanius of Salamis, in his work *Ancoratus*.

178. Thus Tertullian, *De res.*, 38:7; Augustine, *Enchirid.*, 84; *Serm. ad catech.*, 9; John Chrysostom, *Hom.* 40:2.

179. Hillary of Poitiers, *Tract. Ps.*, 2:41. 180. Cyril of Jerusalem, *Catech. Myst.*, 18.

181. John Chrysostom, *Hom.* 40:2.

182. Augustine, *Enchirid.*, 84. See also *Ep.* 102 *ad Deogratias*.

183. Understandably, contemporary authors sensibly avoid going into excessive detail as regards the nature of final resurrection: J. L. Ruiz de la Peña, *La pascua de la creación*, 166–68; M. Bordoni and N. Ciola, *Gesù nostra speranza*, 248–49.

184. *CCC* 1000. 185. See pp. 89–91. above.

by Augustine and other Church Fathers)[186] and M.-J. Scheeben,[187] the following suggestions may be usefully made.[188]

Characteristics of the Risen Body Thomas says that the properties of the risen body are three: spiritualization, immortality, and incorruptibility.[189]

In the first place, *spiritualization*, for "it is sown a physical body, it is raised a spiritual body" (1 Cor 15:44). Of course the human being does not become a spirit (an "angel"); rather the human body takes on to some degree the properties of the soul. With the resurrection, Aquinas says, the soul (which is the *forma corporis*) becomes perfectly united with the body, and so "the body becomes totally subject to the soul, not only in respect of its being, but also in respect of its actions and passions and movements."[190] John Paul II in his catechesis on the human body takes up this idea and says that "'spiritualization' does not only mean that the spirit dominates the body, but also that it thoroughly permeates the body: the energies of the spirit fully permeate the energies of the body."[191] Likewise Tertullian said that our risen bodies *spiritalem subeant dispositionem*, "take on a spiritual disposition."[192]

As a result of spiritualization, *immortality:* "For this perishable nature must put on the imperishable, and this mortal nature must put on immortality. When the perishable puts on the imperishable, and the mortal puts on immortality, then shall come to pass the saying that is written: 'Death is swallowed up in victory'" (1 Cor 15:53–54). Explaining the doctrine of resurrection to the Sadducees, Je-

---

186. Augustine, *De Civ. Dei XXII*, 12–21; *Sermo* 242–43; *Enchirid.*, 23:84–93. Jerome, *Ad Pammachium*, who opposes Origen's teaching and draws on Tertullian; see Y.-M. Duval, "Tertullien contre Origène sur la résurrection de la chair." Gregory of Nyssa, in his work *De anima et res.* speaks of the body restored to its original state, incapable of weakness, corruption, or suffering, suffused with honor, grace, and glory: see M. Alexandre and T. J. Dennis, "Gregory on the Resurrection of the Body," in *The Easter Sermons of Gregory of Nyssa*, ed. A. Spira and C. Klock (Cambridge, Mass.: Philadelphia Patristic Foundation, 1981), 55–80. See also Hugh of St. Victor, *De sacramentis II*, 17:14–18; Peter Lombard, *IV Sent.*, D. 44.

187. See M.-J. Scheeben, *The Mysteries of Christianity* (London: Herder, 1946), § 95.

188. Pannenberg has the following to say: "The future does not meet the present reality of individual or social life as a totally different reality because present life itself is to be seen as a form of manifestation and a process of becoming for the essential form that will be revealed eschatologically," *Systematic Theology*, vol. 3, 605–6. In the risen state, man will be "purged of all heterogeneous admixtures . . . traces and consequences of evil in the achieving of independence from God by his creatures," ibid., 606. See also L. Audet, "Avec quel corps les justes ressuscitent-ils? Analyse de 1Cor 15,44," *Studies in Religion* 1 (1971): 165–77.

189. Thomas Aquinas, *S. Th. III, Suppl.*, q. 79–86; *IV C. Gent.*, 84–86.

190. Thomas Aquinas, *IV C. Gent.*, 86.

191. John Paul II, Audience "Resurrection will Bring the Person to Perfection" (9.12.1981), in *Insegnamenti Giovanni Paolo II*, 4/2 (Città del Vaticano: Vaticana, 1982), 880–83.

192. Tertullian, *De res.*, 62. In his Montanist period Tertullian says that risen human beings will be like angels in that "we shall be changed in a moment into the substance of angels," *Ad Marc.*, 3:24.

sus himself says, in Luke's gospel, that "they cannot die any more" (20:36). Even should they wish to, humans can no longer die, for their immortal soul permanently informs their entire being.[193] Their immortality will not be of a prelapsarian kind (a *posse non mori*, as Augustine called it),[194] but a *non posse mori:* the risen can no longer die; they become definitively immortal.

And finally, according to Aquinas, the risen body is *incorruptible*. "What is sown is corruptible, what is raised is incorruptible" (1 Cor 15:42). That is to say, in the risen state there is no longer generation, nor physical growth, nor organic renewal. "Neither eating, nor drinking, nor sleeping, nor generating belong to the risen state," Aquinas says, "for all these relate to corporal life."[195]

The fact that Jesus contrasts the risen angelic state with the married state indicates that human procreation will have no place in heaven: "For in the resurrection they neither marry nor are given in marriage" (Mt 22:30). On account of this teaching, some Christian writers have suggested that no sexual distinction will obtain among humans in the risen state. This position was held for example by Origen, although it was rejected by the Synod of Constantinople in AD 543.[196] According to Cassiodorus the same idea was taught by Pope Vigilius I.[197] Likewise, both Basil and Gregory of Nyssa held that the human body would be sexless at resurrection.[198]

The majority of Church Fathers, however, took it that men and women will remain as such in the risen state, because the sexual distinction belongs, according to the book of Genesis (1:27), to human nature itself, and may not be considered a result of the primitive fall, to be redeemed by Christ. "He who established both sexes will restore both. . . . Nothing of the body will be lost, in such a way that in it everything will be according to rule," said Augustine.[199] At first Jerome followed the Origenist position,[200] but later on rectified his teaching, saying that risen humans will have the same sex they had while on earth.[201] Likewise Theodoret of Cyrus teaches that the sexual difference remains, in the absence of procreation.[202] C. S. Lewis explains, besides, that sexual union as such will be superfluous in heaven on account of the intense joy of being definitively

---

193. Thomas Aquinas, *S. Th. III, Suppl.*, q. 80, a. 1.
194. Augustine, *De Gen. ad litt.*, 6:36.
195. Thomas Aquinas, *S. Th. III, Suppl.*, q. 81, a. 4c.
196. *DS* 407.
197. Cassiodorus, *De institutione div. litt.*
198. This is the position, for example, of Gregory of Nyssa, *De mortuis or.*
199. Augustine, *De Civ. Dei XXII*, 17 and 19,1. See the nuanced study of T. J. Van Bavel, "Augustine's View on Women," *Augustiniana* 39 (1989): 1–53.
200. Jerome, *In Eph.*, 5:29; *Adv. Jovinianum*, 1:36.
201. Jerome, *Ep.* 108:23–24.
202. Theodoret of Cyrus (attrib.), *Quaest. et respons.*, 60:53.

united with God.²⁰³ It is quite clear that the purpose of Jesus' comparison of the risen state to the angelic life was one of helping believers avoid an excessively materialistic and worldly view of final resurrection, insisting rather on its glory and permanence.²⁰⁴

The Glory of the Just Besides the general characteristics of the risen body—spiritualization, immortality, and incorruptibility—Thomas also explains that the just will be glorified in the risen state in a singular way.²⁰⁵ In the first place there will be *no suffering:* "they will wipe every tear from their eyes, and death shall be no more, neither shall there be mourning nor crying nor pain any more, for the former things have passed away" (Rv 7:16–17). The risen state will be one of complete harmony, in which the perfect penetration of body and soul will permit the glory of the latter to redound fully in the former. Aquinas also speaks of the quality of *subtlety*.²⁰⁶ Again, Jesus' own apparitions as the risen One give us the cue: he became present among the disciples in spite of the doors being closed (Jn 20:19). This does not mean, however, that Jesus' glorified body was completely ethereal: "See my hands and my feet, that it is I myself; touch me and see; for a spirit has not flesh and bones as you see that I have" (Lk 24:39). Gregory the Great says that "in the glory of the resurrection, our body will surely be subtle, as a result of its spiritual power, but it will be palpable because of its true nature."²⁰⁷ Thomas explains this as follows: "According to its own nature the glorified body is palpable, but by a supernatural power it is capable, when it so wishes, of not being perceived by a non-glorious body."²⁰⁸

Besides, Thomas claims that the risen body of the just will be both *agile and active*.²⁰⁹ The body, Paul says, "is sown in weakness, it is raised in power" (1 Cor 15:43). The risen human being, filled with God's Spirit, in some way shares in God's own power, dynamism, and omnipresence. "Those who hope in the Lord," says the prophet Isaiah, "shall renew their strength, they shall run and not be weary, they shall walk and not faint" (Is 40:31). And in the book of Wisdom: "In the time of their visitation [the souls of the just] will shine forth, and will run like

---

203. On the absence of sexual activity in heaven, see C. S. Lewis, *Miracles*, 165–66. Lewis holds that the question "will there be sexual union in heaven" is like the child's question "will it be possible to eat candy during sexual union."

204. See above pp. 86–87.

205. Thomas Aquinas, *S. Th. III, Suppl.*, qq. 81–85. In this he is followed by M.-J. Scheeben, *The Mysteries of Christianity*, 673–82; in respect of subtlety, incorruptibility, and agility.

206. Thomas Aquinas, *S. Th. III, Suppl.*, q. 83, a. 1.

207. Gregory the Great, *Mor. in Job*, 14:72. See Y.-M. Duval, "La discussion entre l'apocrisiaire Grégoire et le patriarche Eutychios au sujet de la résurrection de la chair," in *Grégoire le Grand*, ed. J. Fontaine, R. Gillet, and S. Pellistrandi (Paris: Éditions du CNRS, 1986), 347–65.

208. Thomas Aquinas, *S. Th. III, Suppl.*, q. 83, a. 6c.; *IV C. Gent.*, 84.

209. Thomas Aquinas, *S. Th. III, Suppl.*, q. 84.

sparks through the stubble. They will govern nations and rule over peoples" (Ws 3:7–8). Augustine said that the risen body will have "a wondrous ease of movement, a wondrous lightness."[210] He went so far as to say that the perfect integration between the inner and the outer is such that each person will know everyone else perfectly, even their innermost thoughts.[211] Of course no sin may remain in this state, since it would be the cause of unsupportable shame and grief. Julian Pomerius argues that perception and movement will be as swift as willing itself, since none of the conditions slowing down the body's response will remain.[212]

Lastly, Thomas argues that the just who rise up will be filled with *beauty* (*claritas*). "This beauty is caused by the reflection of the glory of the soul in the glorious body, in the same way as the color of a body enclosed in a glass vessel is shown through the glass."[213] Some idea of the glorious beauty of the risen may be found in the description the book of Exodus gives of the face of Moses when he descended from Mount Sinai: "Moses did not know that the skin of his face shone because he had been talking with God . . . they were afraid to come near him" (Ex 34:29–30). Likewise, at the transfiguration, Jesus' "face shone like the sun, and his garments became white as light" (Mt 17:2). In the parable of the separation of the wheat and the weeds, Jesus concludes: "Then the righteous will shine like the sun in the kingdom of their Father" (Mt 13:43). Of course this beauty is none other than the communication of Christ's own beauty to those who believe in him and become his followers by doing the will of the Father in all: "you are the most beautiful of men; grace is poured upon your lips," the Psalmist writes (Ps 45:2) in a clearly Christological context. Irenaeus likewise speaks of the "unimaginable beauty" of the risen state.[214] Gregory of Nyssa speaks of risen humanity "with a brighter, more entrancing beauty."[215]

The medieval author Honorius of Autun summed up the characteristics of the risen body as follows: "They will have seven special glories of the body, and seven of the soul: in the body, beauty, swiftness, strength, freedom, delight (*voluptas*), health, immortality; in the soul, wisdom, friendship, harmony, power, honor, security, joy."[216]

By contrast with the just, Thomas concludes, the condemned in the risen state will be marked with the opposite qualities:[217] suffering, awkwardness, heaviness, ugliness.[218]

---

210. Augustine, *Sermo* 242:8.
211. Augustine, *Sermo* 243:5–6.
212. Julian Pomerius, *De vita contemplativa*, 1:11.
213. Thomas Aquinas, *S. Th. III, Suppl.*, q. 85, a. 1c.
214. Irenaeus, *Adv. Haer. IV*, 33:11; 39,2.
215. Gregory of Nyssa, *De anima et res.*
216. Honorius of Autun, *Elucidarium II*, 17. Theresa of Avila speaks of her vision of risen body in the *Libro de la vida*, 28:2–3.
217. Thomas Aquinas, *S. Th. III, Suppl.*, q. 86.
218. The same notion is to be found in Hillary of Poitiers, *In Matth.*, 5:8.

The Identity of the Risen and Earthly Body: The Implications of Resurrection Belief for Ethics and Spirituality

In spite of being immortal and glorious, the risen body will be identical to the earthly body, in that the same human person will rise from the dead. This basic truth is contained in the apostles' joyful exclamation in the presence of the risen Jesus, "It is the Lord!" (Jn 21:7), and the Church has insistently taught not only the resurrection of the dead in general, but the resurrection "of *this* body (or flesh)."[219] Indeed the very term "resurrection" (rising up) suggests this, referring as it does to a previous, fallen reality that takes on a new, definitive life. This gives a strongly realistic tone to patristic statements about final resurrection. Hillary of Poitiers explains this as follows: "The bodies of all who will rise will not be formed from extraneous material, nor will natural qualities of strange origin and extrinsic sources be used; the same body will emerge, fit now for eternal beauty, and what is new in it will come about by change, not by creation."[220] Jerome has it that *resurrectionis veritas sine carne et ossibus, sine sanguine et membris, intelligi non potest,*[221] that "the truth about the resurrection without flesh and bones, without blood and members, is simply incomprehensible." Also Gregory of Nyssa insists that there will be an obvious identity and continuity between the earthly and the risen body.[222]

Material or Formal Identity? Affirmation of the identity of the risen body with the earthly one, however, does not require a strict *material identity* between the physical elements of our earthly condition and those of the risen state, as Theophilus of Antioch, Tatian, Athenagoras, and Hillary of Poitiers seem to suggest.[223] In effect, as Origen explained in his commentary on Jeremiah's image of the potter,[224] the matter of our risen bodies is not numerically identical to that of our earthly body.[225] In any case, as we have already seen, resurrection takes place by the power of God. Besides, it is now well known that the human metabolism is such that the physical and chemical elements of the human composite are cyclically replaced over a limited span of years.

---

219. See my study "La fórmula 'Resurrección de la carne.'"
220. Hillary of Poitiers, *In Ps.*, 2:41. See G. Blasich, "La risurezione dei corpi nell'opera esegetica di S. Ilario di Poitiers," *Divus Thomas* (Piacenza) 69 (1966): 72–90.
221. Jerome, *C. Joh.*, 31.
222. Gregory of Nyssa, *De mortuis or.*
223. Theophilus of Antioch, *Autol.*, 2:26; Tatian, *Or. ad graecos*, 6; Athenagoras, *De res.*, 2:4–6; Hillary of Poitiers, *Tract. Ps.*, 2:41. The classic restatement of this position is to be found in F. Segarra, *De identitate corporis mortalis et corporis resurgentis* (Madrid: Razón y fe, 1929).
224. Origen, *Hom. in Jer.*, 18:4.
225. On the philosophical implications of risen identity, see G. Gillet, "Identity and Resurrection," *Heythrop Journal* 49 (2008): 254–68.

Some authors, conversely, have suggested that *formal identity*, involving merely the identity of the human soul (which the "only form of the body"),[226] would be sufficient to ensure human identity at resurrection. In other words, the same soul that informs matter would ensure the identity of the same person, independently of the physical matter people had in this life. This theory was put forward during the Middle Ages by Durandus,[227] and has been followed in recent times by several neo-Thomists.[228] In the same direction, Origen, who takes up Paul's representation of resurrection in terms of a sprouting seed (1 Cor 15:35), spoke of a spiritual *eidos* (image) in humans that remains unchanged throughout all the mutations of life and after glorification.[229] Likewise John Philoponus, an Alexandrian philosopher and Monophysite Christian, holds that resurrection involves the complete re-creation of the human body, just as Jesus' risen body is different in species (*eidos*) from the mortal body that died.[230]

It should be noted that in patristic times Origen's somewhat spiritualist understanding of resurrection was openly opposed by several authors, among them Methodius of Olympus (fourth century) and Gregory of Nyssa.[231] It would seem that the position does not give sufficient weight to the realism and objectivity of Jesus' resurrection,[232] which by no means excludes the earthly and bodily existence of Jesus. Neither does it take sufficiently into account the eschatological implications of the liturgical praxis of venerating bodily relics of the saints (every liturgy is celebrated in prevision of the *Parousia*),[233] and the dogma of the assumption of Our Lady into heaven.[234] In fact, Durandus's explanation of identity in formal terms could be read as an equivalent to the doctrine of transmigration of souls, or reincarnation.[235]

Resurrection, Human Identity, and Ethics   Of particular interest in the patristic period is the attention paid to the expression "resurrection *of the flesh*."[236] It

226. See C. Pozo, *La teología del más allá*, 370–72; J. Ratzinger, *Eschatology*, 180–81.
227. Durandus of St. Porcianus, *In Sent.* L. 4, D. 44, q. 1, n. 6.
228. He has been followed in recent times by neo-Thomists such as F. Hettinger, H. Schell, L. Billot, A. Michel, and D. Feuling; see J. Ratzinger, *Eschatology*, 181; M.-J. Nicolas, "Le corps humain et sa résurrection," *Revue Thomiste* 87 (1979): 533–45.
229. Origen, *Sel. Ps.*, 1; *Comm. in Ps.*, 1, 5:22. See the studies cited in n. 122 above.
230. See B. E. Daley, *The Hope*, 195–96. See especially John's lost work *De resurrectione*.
231. See nn. 123 and 125 above, respectively.
232. See pp. 88–89 above.
233. See J. Ratzinger, "Auferstehungsleib," in *Lexikon für Theologie und Kirche*, vol. 1 (1957): 1052–53; DS 1822. See also G. Gozzelino, *Nell'attesa*, 447–48.
234. See J. Ratzinger, *Eschatology*, 107. See Congregation for the Doctrine of the Faith, Doc. *Recentiores episcoporum Synodi* (1979), n. 6.
235. See G. Colzani, *La vita eterna*, 122.
236. See my study "La fórmula 'Resurrección de la carne.'" Clement of Rome uses the expression "resurrection of the flesh [*sarx*]": *Ep. in Cor.*, 24–25.

is fundamentally anti-Gnostic in character,[237] providing a theological basis for affirming the inherent value of matter and the human body.[238] The Church has insisted on the propriety of using the expression literally in the liturgy.[239] However, "resurrection of the flesh" may also be understood in terms of the Aramaic expression *kol-basar* ("all flesh," an expression often found in the Old Testament: Ps 65:3; 136:25; Jer 25:31), thus indicating the *universality* of final resurrection.[240] Indeed the Valentinian Gnostics wished to restrict the number of those destined for resurrection, because, in making resurrection synonymous with salvation, they took it that only the chosen or spiritual ones (*pneumatakoi*), who are already saved, are eligible for it.[241] But as we saw earlier on, resurrection is destined for all[242] and may not therefore be considered ipso facto synonymous with salvation.

Specifically, the formula "resurrection of *this* body" arose principally as an attempt to express the ethical continuity that exists between this life and the next, and hence the eternal projection and value of historical human actions carried out in a limited, temporal, material context.[243] Tertullian succinctly summed up the position of the Gnostics by saying that "nobody lives so much according to the flesh as those who deny the resurrection of the flesh."[244] Tyranius Ruffinus in his commentary on the Symbol of faith said that "the Church teaches us the resurrection of the flesh, though qualifying it with the term *huius*, 'this.' 'This,' doubtless, so that the faithful know that their flesh, if it has been conserved free from sin, will in future be a vessel of honor, useful to the Lord for all good works; if however it is contaminated by sin, in future it will be a vessel of anger for destruction."[245] This position is taken up by many other Christian writers[246] and is

---

237. Thus H. B. Swete, "The Resurrection of the Flesh," T. H. C. von Eijk, *La résurrection des morts*. On eschatology during the Gnostic period, see B. E. Daley, *The Hope*, 25–28.

238. Justin, *Dial. cum Tryph.*, 80; Hermas, *Simil.*, 5,7:2; Irenaeus, *Adv. Haer. I*, 27:3; *II*, 31:2; Tertullian, *De res.*, 19:2.

239. It is interesting to note that the Congregation for the Doctrine of the Faith insisted in a 1983 document on the need to provide literal translations of the expression *resurrectio carnis* in liturgical texts, thus: "resurrection of the flesh": "The Article 'Carnis Resurrectionem'" (1983), *Notitiae* 20 (1984): 180–81.

240. Thus G. Kretschmar, "Auferstehung des Fleisches," 108–11.

241. See, for example, the *Ep. ad Rheginos;* and *Evang. Philippi*, sent. 23. On the question, see F.-M.-M. Sagnard, *La gnose valentinienne et le témoignage de saint Irénée* (Paris: Vrin, 1947); A. Orbe, "La mediación entre los valentinianos," *Studia Missionalia* 21 (1972): 265–301; D. Devoti, "Temi escatologici nello gnosticismo valentiniano," *Augustinianum* 18 (1978): 75–88; A. Magris, "L'escatologia valentiniana," *Annali di Storia dell'esegesi* 16 (1999): 133–39; B. E. Daley, *The Hope*, 231, n. 6.

242. See pp. 87–88.

243. This is the thesis of my study "La fórmula 'Resurrección de la carne.'"

244. Tertullian, *De res.*, 11:1.

245. Tyranius Ruffinus, *Comm. in Symb. Apost.*, n. 46.

246. For example, Minucius Felix, *Octavius*, 34:12; Ps.-Justin, *De res.*, 2; Irenaeus, *Demonstr.*, 41; *Adv. Haer. V*, 11; Tertullian, *De res.*, 14; Gregory of Elvira, *Tract. Orig. XVII*, 6:19–32.

summed up in the following declaration of Lateran Council IV, convened in 1215 to counter medieval neo-Gnostic teachings: "All [the living and the dead] . . . will rise again with their own bodies which they now bear, to receive according to their works, whether these have been good or evil."[247]

This explanation makes it clear that final resurrection is distinct neither from the return of the risen Lord Jesus in glory (the *Parousia*) nor from general judgment, but is both the first fruit of the *Parousia* and a precondition to final judgment.

From what we have just seen it should be clear that resurrection cannot be considered, as Valentinian Gnostics thought, as simply synonymous with salvation (the New Testament teaches that whereas salvation is not necessarily universal, resurrection will be strictly so), but responds to God's fidelity to his decision to create humans, in body and soul, as immortal beings.

Resurrection of a Life That Has Once Been Lived

Emphasis on the ethical relevance of final resurrection brings us to the remarkable conclusion that the risen state to which humans are elevated by the power of God consists of *the manifestation and perpetuation of the personal life history of each person*. Everything people do and are during their lifetimes, even the smallest, most apparently hidden actions, will remain forever impressed on their risen body, will seal their eternal identity. Gregory of Nyssa said that through our actions we become "parents of ourselves."[248] Anscar Vonier said that "resurrection from the dead is the act of God by which He gives back to us . . . the whole realm of sense activity, which had ceased to be."[249] We shall consider the dynamic of final resurrection in three stages: in respect of the life one has already lived, in respect of one's relationship to other people, and—in the next chapter—in respect of one's relationship with the cosmos.

Resurrection of a Life Once Lived That the *Parousia* will bring about the resurrection of the life one has lived is a common position among many recent theologians, both Protestant and Catholic.[250] Henri Rondet, commenting on the

---

247. *DS* 801.
248. Gregory of Nyssa, *De vita Moysi II*, 2–3.
249. A. Vonier, *The Life of the World to Come* (London: Burns and Oates, 1935), 150.
250. See for example K. Barth, *Church Dogmatics*, III/2 (Edinburgh: T. & T. Clark, 1960), 624–25. E. Jüngel writes: "God is my identity beyond. At resurrection, our person will be . . . our history manifested," *Tod*, 156–57. Jüngel does not accept the idea of resurrection as a dissolution and overcoming of all limits. Resurrection is promised so that human life as such be saved, because salvation is not possible beyond life as it is lived, in that it is hidden in the risen life of Christ. On Jüngel, see my study *La muerte y la esperanza*, 72, n. 42. Likewise in W. Pannenberg, the history and life of each person is, as it were, "codified" or recorded in God, in view of future resurrection, which is "the act by which God through his Spirit restores to the creatures existence that is preserved in his eternity the form of being-

110 The Object of Christian Hope

Vatican II constitution *Gaudium et spes*, says: "What would the risen Gutenberg be with a body which is identical with his earthly body of flesh, but without any relation to the discovery for which he is famous? What would a Christian painter be without his work, a musician without his symphonies, a poet without his poems? And is nothing to remain of the tremendous efforts of modern industry, of engineers and workmen? Do we have to continue to say with the medieval dictum: *solvet saeculum in favilla?*"[251] In his encyclical *Sollocitudo rei socialis* (1987) Pope John Paul II clearly said of human endeavor that "nothing will be lost or will have been in vain."[252] Theodor Bovet sums up the same idea as follows: "The face of the human person contains in a stenographic way his or her biography."[253]

Two authors in particular are worthwhile mentioning, the poet Gerard Manley Hopkins and the theologian Romano Guardini.

for-themselves," *Systematic Theology*, vol. 3, 606. It should be noted, however, that in the explanation of Pannenberg (and of Jüngel) the metaphysical identity of the human subject, as distinct from its historical identity, is not fully accounted for (*CAA* 56). A. Ruiz Retegui explains the same idea in the following terms: "La inocencia de la infancia, la generosidad de la juventud pujante, las brillantes realizaciones de la madurez . . . todo esto que la vida va envejeciendo sin piedad, nos será entregado de nuevo, si nos resistimos a la tentación de conservarlos únicamente en cintas magnetoscópicos, o fotografías, o poemas gloriosos, o diarios íntimos, y los confiamos a Dios, al Dios eterno que se entrega en Cristo," "La teleología humana," 838–39. And he concludes: "El problema clave de la Resurrección de los muertos no es únicamente el problema de la nueva unión del alma con el cuerpo, la identidad de éste, etc. sino el problema de la recepción de la vida que es la que configura la identidad personal. Quizá la recepción del cuerpo en la resurrección se identifique con la recepción de la vida que se ha vivido," ibid., 837. The Catholic theologian W. Breuning expresses this as follows: "The resurrection of the flesh means that nothing is lost for God, because he loves mankind. All the tears will be gathered up, no smile is lost on him. The resurrection of the flesh means that in God man will find anew not only his last moment on earth but his entire history," *Mysterium salutis. Grundriss heilsgeschichtlicher Dogmatik*, ed. J. Feiner and M. Löhrer, vol. 5 (Zürich: Benzinger, 1976), 882–83. To some degree von Balthasar explains the same idea in the following terms: "Our life as we lived it on earth remains in heaven not only as a memory but as something which is perennial presence. This is based on the reciprocity of heaven and earth: heaven is the ultimate depth of the fragmentary and incomplete life we live on earth. No earthly instant can disappear completely (this is the problem of Goethe's *Faust*); what it hides in itself as eternal content is placed for us in heaven: there we live . . . the entire and eternal content of what on earth we obtained in the form of an unsuppressed and transcendent nostalgia," *Theodramatik 4/2: Das Endspiel* (Einsiedeln: Johannes, 1983), 379. The same idea may be found in J. T. O'Connor, *Land of the Living*, 258–60, and G. Ancona, *Escatología cristiana*, 354–55, who cites B. Sesboüé. Teilhard de Chardin, glossing Rv 14:13, expresses the idea as follows: "If we love God, nothing of our inner activity, of our *operatio*, will ever be lost. But will not the work itself of our minds, of our hearts, and of our hands—that is to say, our achievements, what we bring into being, our *opus*—will not this, too, in some sense be 'eternalized' and saved? . . . Show all your faithful, Lord, in what a full and true sense 'their work follows them' into your kingdom—*opera sequuntur illos*," *The Divine Milieu* (New York: Harper and Row, 1960), 55–56.

251. H. Rondet, "The Theology of Work," in *Commentary on the Documents of Vatican II*, ed. H. Vorgrimler, vol. 5 (New York: Herder and Herder, 1969), 197, on *GS* 39. *Solvet saeculum in favilla:* "the world will dissolve into embers."

252. John Paul II, Enc. *Sollicitudo rei socialis* (1987), n. 48.

253. The author reflects on the wrinkles of his wife's face: *Die Ehe*, 3rd ed. (Tübingen: P. Haupt 1972), 139.

Hopkins in his poem *The Leaden Echo and the Golden Echo* encourages his reader to give everything to God, the very best things, holding nothing for oneself, for God will give it back in return, purified and eternalized, at the end of time. "Give beauty back, beauty, beauty, beauty, back to God, beauty's self and beauty's giver. See, not a hair is, not an eyelash, not the least lash lost; every hair is, hair of the head, numbered . . . O why are we so haggard at the heart, so care-coiled, care-killed, so fagged, so fashed, so cogged, so cumbered, when the thing we so freely forfeit is kept with fonder a care, fonder a care kept than we could have kept it . . . Where kept? Do but tell us where kept, where.—Yonder.—What high as that!"[254] Hopkins's verses powerfully evoke Jesus' exhortation for his followers to "accumulate treasures in heaven" (Mt 6:20). Peter Chrysologus (fifth century) stated: *quod tu alteri non reliqueris, non habebis:* "what you do not give to others, you will lose it yourself."[255] When all is said and done, as Charles Péguy put it, "all that is not given is lost."

Romano Guardini asks the following question regarding the nature of the risen body. "From its origin to its decay [the body] goes through an endless number of forms. Which of these is properly its own? Is it the child's, the mature man's, the elderly man's?" And he replies:

The answer can only be: All are essential. The individual form does not exist only that the next should take its place, and so on, one after the other, in order that the last one, death, might appear. Each phase is the man, and each is indispensable to his life as a whole. That endless series of configurations which is the human body must be included in the resurrected body. It must have a new dimension, that of time, but time raised to the power of eternity, with the result that its history is included in the present, and all the successive moments of its past exist in an absolute now. . . . There must also be present his joys, sorrows, frustrations, liberations, victories, defeats, his love and his hatred. All the unending experiences of the soul were expressed in and by the body and have become part of it, contributing either to its development or to its crippling and destruction—all are present and retained in the risen body. The pattern of life is there with all that befell man, for the resurrection of the body means the resurrection of the life that has been lived, with all its good and all its evil. . . . In the resurrection, form, substance, life, all will rise. Nothing that has been is annihilated. Man's deeds and his destiny are part of him, and, set free from the restrictions of history, will remain for all eternity, not by any power of his own, not as a final phase of an inner development, but at the summons of the Almighty, and in the strength of his Spirit.[256]

---

254. G. M. Hopkins, "The Leaden Echo and the Golden Echo," in *The Poetical Works of Gerald Manley Hopkins*, ed. N. H. Mackenzie (Oxford: Clarendon Press, 1992), 170–71.
255. Peter Chrysologus, *Sermo* 43.
256. R. Guardini, *The Last Things*, 68–69.

Resurrection and Society In a special way final resurrection involves the reconstitution of human society, which death and sin have broken up. Gabriel Marcel understood immortality and the drama of death in a strictly interpersonal way; thus human life is not complete until all broken relationships are healed and reconstituted. "To be in love means saying to a person: you should never die."[257] Immortality without human love would be meaningless.[258] The poet John Donne said the same thing in a memorable passage: "Any man's death diminishes me, because I am involved in Mankind; and therefore never send to know for whom the bell tolls; it tolls for thee."[259] To put it the other way around, human life is never complete, is never fully "risen," if it does not include that part of me that is other people, that is my personal history lived with them and in them.

The explanation just given provides a reasonably cogent explanation for the integration, spoken of in chapter 1, between the "immortality of life" and the "immortality of selfhood."[260] It provides a basis for explaining the dignity of each and every human being, not only in respect of their metaphysical individuality, but in respect of the eternal value of the concrete life that they have lived.[261]

Resurrection of the Dead as an Object of Hope

"The resurrection of the dead is the hope of Christians," Tertullian said.[262] It is the hope of Christians in the *first* place because of its content, for in rising from the dead human beings will reach the plenitude God made them for. Ignatius of Antioch wrote to the Christians of Rome of his fervent desire for martyrdom, and concluded: "When I reach it, then I will be fully human."[263] Augustine said that at the end of time, *nos ipsi erimus*, "we will truly be ourselves."[264] *Second*, resurrection is an object of hope in the strict (theological) sense of the word, because one hopes in the power and goodness of God alone, for only he is capable of raising us from the dead and destroying all corruption. That is to say, no human agency is in a position to bring about the resurrection of humans, to establish true and

---

257. This phrase is of Arnaud Chartrain in Marcel's play *La soif*.

258. See pp. 27–29.

259. John Donne, "Devotion upon Emergent Occasions, 17," in *Complete Poetry and Selected Prose*, ed. J. Hayward (London: Nonsuch Press, 1949), 538.

260. See pp. 25–31.

261. See M. L. Lamb, "The Eschatology of St Thomas Aquinas," 233–34. Aquinas explains that "the resurrection is not ordered to the perpetuity of the species, for this could be safeguarded by generation. It must, then, be ordered to the perpetuity of the individual: but not to the soul alone, for the soul already had perpetuity before the resurrection. Therefore it regards the perpetuity of the composite," *IV C. Gent.*, 82.

262. Tertullian, *De res.*, 1.

263. Ignatius of Antioch, *Ad Rom.*, 6:2–3.

264. Augustine, *De Civ. Dei XXII*, 30:4.

definitive justice on earth. And *third*, the resurrection of the dead is the object of hope because it serves as a stimulus to live an upright moral and Christian life that will be fully and eternally manifested before God and humanity in and through the resurrection.

Resurrection, Relationships, and Matter

Perhaps the principal challenge to Christian eschatology in recent centuries has come from Hegel and Marx. Hegel famously accused Christians of "wasting in heaven treasures destined to life." Marx of course considered religion as the "opium of the people" because, being centered on another world, it distracts humans from the present life and from the struggle for justice and equality.[265] According to both Hegel and Marx, humanity reaches fullness either in this life, within the world as we know it, or not at all. However, although their view of history and progress centers everything on life in the world, in doing so it trivializes this life as well, for nothing humans do or achieve can endure forever, can assume eternal value. It is not surprising that some authors with Marxist leanings, such as Theodor Adorno, said that there was a need for the resurrection of the flesh for definitive justice to be done.[266]

This is where the explanation just given to final resurrection comes into its own. Final resurrection is not a new creation in the strict sense of the word; it is not a completely new life. Rather, it is the rising up of the flesh in the power of God, the eternalization of life once lived on earth. Resurrection thus gives meaning and depth and value to the humblest and most material things, and actions and events of life. Hope in final resurrection is what makes it possible to live each and every moment "in resonance with eternity," to use a phrase of St. Josemaría Escrivá.[267]

Some authors are prepared to accept that final resurrection consists indeed in the reestablishment of our relationships with others and with the world, but hold that this does not involve the eternity of matter, but rather a kind of spiritual communion and sharing between humans under Christ.[268] However, a risen life completely unlinked with matter, besides being at odds with several aspects of the doctrine of the faith, especially the resurrection of Christ, does not take

---

265. See the reflections of Pope Benedict XVI, in *SS* 20–21.
266. See T. W. Adorno, *Negative Dialektik* (Frankfurt a. M.: Suhrkamp, 1966), 205, 393. This text is also mentioned in *SS* 42.
267. The Spanish original, "vibración de eternidad," is difficult to translate: see Josemaría Escrivá, *Friends of God*, n. 239b, *Forge*, n. 917, where the phrase is translated into English—inadequately—as "lively awareness" and "dynamic echo."
268. See A. Schmemann, *O Death, Where Is Thy Sting?* (Crestwood, N.Y.: St. Vladimir's Seminary Press, 2003).

human life, as it is lived on earth, in all its seriousness. There is such a thing as an authentic "Christian materialism."[269] If matter is excluded from the risen state, Marx would indeed have reason to doubt the good intentions of Christians who argue that eschatology is a force of empowerment for those intending to establish justice in the world. This brings us to consider the cosmic framework inhabited by the risen, what Scripture calls "the new heavens and the new earth."

269. St. Josemaría wrote: "Authentic Christianity, which professes the resurrection of all flesh, has always quite logically opposed 'dis-incarnation', without fear of being judged materialistic. We can, therefore, rightfully speak of a 'Christian materialism', which is boldly opposed to that materialism which is blind to the spirit" *Conversations with Msgr Escrivá de Balaguer* (Dublin: Scepter, 1968), § 115.

4

The New Heavens and the New Earth

> Dans ma ciel, il y aura des choses.
> —*Charles Péguy*[1]

> While the Truth which You are was present, we wondered what the future, eternal life of the saints would be like.
> —*Augustine*[2]

In direct continuity with the doctrine of final resurrection, the return of the risen Lord Jesus Christ in glory (what is called the *Parousia*) will involve not only the universal resurrection and judgment of humans, but also the destruction, purification, and renewal of the material cosmos, what Scripture calls the new creation (Mt 19:28; Rom 8:18–25; Gal 6:15). Doubtless, humans are destined to govern the world as God's images or envoys (Gn 1:26–28).[3] But it is no less true that humans belong to the world in the fullest possible sense on account of their corporal condition. In other words, the human process of death and resurrection, in all its realism, requires a kind of parallel death and resurrection process on the part of the entire cosmos, the ruin and renewal of the material world. Among other authors, Julian of Toledo addressed this issue; he summed up Western patristic thought in the following terms: "The world, having been renewed for the better, will be suitably accommodated to humans who will also have been renewed for the better in the flesh."[4] Likewise Hugh of St. Victor established a clear connection between final resurrection and the renewal of the world.[5] In the life to come, Thomas Aquinas writes, "the whole of bodily creation will be appropriately changed to be in harmony with the state of those who will then be living."[6]

---

1. C. Péguy, *Le Mystère des Saints-Innocents*.
2. Augustine, *Conf.* IX, 10.
3. See M. Bordoni, *Gesù di Nazaret Signore e Cristo* (Roma: Herder; Pontificia Università Lateranense, 1986), vol. 3, 611–12.
4. Julian of Toledo, *Prognosticon futuri saeculi*, 2:46.
5. Hugh of St. Victor, *De sacramentis II*, 18:1. He explains that the world will be transformed according to the model of the resurrection.
6. Thomas Aquinas, *IV C. Gent.*, 97.

The Cosmos and the End of the World

Vatican Council II documents pay special attention to the cosmic side of the end of the world. The Church, we read in *Lumen Gentium*, "will receive perfection only in the glory of heaven, when will come the time of the renewal of all things (Acts 3:21). At that time, together with the human race, the universe itself, which is so closely related to man and which attains its destiny in him, will be perfectly re-established in Christ (Eph 1:10; Col 1:20; 2 Pt 3:10–13)."[7] This will not take place, the same document continues, "until there be realized new heavens and a new earth where justice dwells (2 Pt 3:13)."[8] In the constitution of the Church in the world, *Gaudium et spes*, the message is repeated:

> The form of the world, distorted by sin, is passing away (1 Cor 7:31; Irenaeus, *Adv. Haer.* V, 36:1) and we are taught that God is preparing a new dwelling and a new earth in which righteousness dwells (2 Cor 5:2; 2 Pt 3:13), whose happiness will fill and surpass all the desires of peace arising in the hearts of men (1 Cor 2:9; Rv 21:4–5). Then with death conquered the sons of God will be raised in Christ. . . . Charity and its works will remain (1 Cor 13:8) and all of creation (Rom 8:19–21), which God made for man, will be set free from its bondage to decay.[9]

Lastly, the *Catechism of the Catholic Church* deals with the topic at length.[10] "The visible universe is itself destined to be transformed," it says, "'so that the world itself, restored to its original state, facing no further obstacles, should be at the service of the just' showing their glorification in the risen Jesus Christ."[11]

Renewal and Matter

This doctrine serves to express fully the realism of the doctrine of final resurrection. In doing so the Church distances its teaching from Origenism (and Bultmann), which suggests that the material and corporal world as we know it will be destroyed, and only spiritual realities, of which material reality is considered but a symbol, will remain.[12]

The notion of the material re-creation of the world was common in the sub-apostolic age, although it waned somewhat among the apostolic Fathers.[13] Among the Apologists it was commonly taught, though often in association with the doc-

---

7. *LG* 48a.
8. Ibid., 48c.
9. *GS* 39a.
10. *CCC* 1042–50.
11. *CCC* 1047; which includes a citation of Irenaeus, *Adv. Haer.* V, 32:1.
12. Council of Constantinople (553), can. 10, in J.D. Mansi, *Sacrorum Conciliorum nova collectio* (Graz: Akademische Druck- und Verlaganstalt Graz, 1901), vol. 9, col. 399; see also *DS* 1361. On Bultmann, see *CAA* 38–44.
13. See A. O'Hagan, *Material Re-Creation in the Apostolic Fathers* (Berlin: Academie, 1968), 141.

trine of millennialism.[14] Citing the central text of Romans 8:21 ("creation will be set free from its bondage to decay and obtain the glorious freedom of the children of God"), Thomas Aquinas states that this refers to material creation as well.[15] The fact is that human fulfillment cannot but involve materiality. The poet William Wordsworth wrote that our happiness in this world is:

> Not in Utopia—subterranean fields,—
> Or some secreted island, Heaven knows where!
> But in the very world, which is the world
> Of all of us,—the place where, in the end,
> We find our happiness, or not at all![16]

Walter Kasper explains this in the following terms: "God's faithfulness not only concerns the history of salvation, but also the steadfast existence of the orders of nature, which again and again draw amazement from the observer and praise of the Creator from the pious. Both aspects, historical contingency and enduring orders, were connected with one another in late Old Testament and early Jewish apocalyptic. The Apocalypse includes nature and its orders in God's historical saving plan."[17] And Leo Scheffczyk: "In the transformation of the cosmos humans will recognize the secret of conformity with Christ present in the material world, and in everything that goes to make it up."[18]

The Destruction of the Universe Scripture does speak indeed of a wide variety of destructive signs and portents that will serve as a prelude to the end of the world.[19] "For then there will be great tribulation, such as has not been from the beginning of the world until now, no, and will never be" (Mt 24:21–22). Several such signs are mentioned throughout the New Testament: the breaking up of human society; the triumph of idolatry and irreligion; the spreading of war; various cosmic calamities. Among the latter we read in Matthew's Gospel: "Immediately after the tribulation of these days the sun will be darkened, and the moon will not give its light, and the stars will fall from heaven, and the powers of the heavens will be shaken" (24:29); "And there will be famines and earthquakes in various places" (24:7).

---

14. The idea of material re-creation is clear in Irenaeus, *Adv. Haer.* V, 32, though his teaching is linked with millennialism (see p. 243, n. 87).
15. Thomas Aquinas, *In Rom. 8*, l. 4 (ed. Marietti, n. 660).
16. W. Wordsworth, *The Prelude*, X–XI, lines 724–29.
17. W. Kasper, "The Logos Character of Reality," *Communio* (English ed.) 15, no. 3 (1988): 282.
18. See L. Scheffczyk, "Die Wiederkunft Christi in ihrer Heilsbedeutung für die Menschheit und den Kosmos," in *Weltverständnis im Glauben*, ed. J. B. Metz, 2nd ed. (Mainz: Matthias-Grünewald, 1966), 161–83, here 180. See also J. H. Wright, "The Consummation of the Universe in Christ," *Gregorianum* 39 (1958): 285–94.
19. *CAA* 150–54.

Scripture speaks openly of the discontinuity between the present cosmos and the future glorified world,[20] but not of the former's total elimination, for there will also be a true continuity between the two. While highlighting the continuity between creation and salvation in the face of the Gnosticism of Marcion, Tertullian acutely observes that "God is judge because he is Lord, and Lord because he is Creator, and Creator because he is God."[21] Judgment could hardly be considered as fully just should resurrection be understood in terms of a violent, completely novel, and unpredictable intrusion into the existing, created order. After all, the God who judges is at one and the same time the only Creator and Lord of the universe and of everything it contains, the One who is faithful to the Covenant.

The "New World" in Scripture However, the fact that the world as we know it is under the threat of destruction does not mean it will be utterly destroyed or annihilated, for God, Scripture tells us, has promised he will bring about a "new world," a "new heavens and new earth," a "new creation."

The notion of a renewed cosmos is present in the Old Testament. In Isaiah, for example, we read: "For behold, I create new heavens and a new earth; and the former things shall not be remembered or come to mind. But be glad and rejoice forever in that which I create; for behold, I create Jerusalem a rejoicing, and her people a joy" (Is 65:17–18). The renewal is often presented in terms of a return to paradise (Is 11:6–9). But the cycle of destruction, novelty, and re-creation comes to the fore principally in apocalyptic texts.[22]

In the New Testament the same doctrine is to be found, on several occasions. Matthew refers to the collapse of the present cosmic order as a sign of the coming of the Son of man (24:29), but also of the new creation (19:28: *paliggenesia*) that coincides with his coming.[23] The letter to the Romans speaks openly of the new world that God has promised, and the present situation of creation in terms of a new birth. "For the creation awaits with eager longing for the revealing of the sons of God; for the creation was subjected to futility, not of its own will but by the will of him who subjected it in hope; because the creation itself will be set free from its bondage to decay and obtain the glorious liberty of the children of God" (Rom 8:19–21).[24]

Likewise the book of Revelation speaks of the renewal of the cosmos through the merciful power of God, in a clear paraphrase of Isaiah 65:17–18.

Then I saw a new heaven and a new earth; for the first heaven and the first earth had passed away, and the sea was no more. And I saw the holy city, the new Jerusalem, com-

---

20. Rom 8:19–21; 2 Pt 3:10–13; Rv 21:1–2.
21. Tertullian, *De res.*, 14:6.
22. *CAA* 79–81.
23. For an analysis of this text, *CAA* 167–69.
24. See J. L. Ruiz de la Peña, *La pascua de la creación*, 182–85, mainly in respect of Rom 8:19–21.

ing down out of heaven from God, prepared as a bride adorned for her husband; and I heard a loud voice from the throne saying, "Behold, the dwelling of God is with men. He will dwell with them, and they shall be his people, and God himself will be with them; he will wipe away every tear from their eyes, and death shall be no more, neither shall there be mourning nor crying nor pain any more, for the former things have passed away." (Rv 21:1–4)

Perhaps the clearest text is to be found in the second letter of Peter (3:10–13), which describes the destruction of the world and its replacement with a new creation. "The day of the Lord will come like a thief, and then the heavens will pass away with a loud noise, and the elements will be dissolved with fire, and the earth and the works that are upon it will be burned up. . . . The heavens will be kindled and dissolved, and the elements will melt with fire!" (vv. 10, 12). Believers are exhorted, therefore, to be vigilant: "Since all these things are thus to be dissolved, what sort of persons ought you to be in lives of holiness and godliness, waiting for and hastening the coming of the day of God" (vv. 11–12). However, the text continues, "according to his promise we wait for new heavens and a new earth in which righteousness dwells" (v. 13). The letter continues to exhort believers: "Therefore, beloved, since you wait for these, be zealous to be found by him without spot or blemish, and at peace" (v. 14).

The text teaches that the world as we know it will be destroyed and recreated again through the power of God. For this reason believers are encouraged to live in virtue and vigilance in order to enter the kingdom of God when it arrives in fullness.

A Profile of Paradise It makes a lot of sense to avoid simplistic representations or detailed descriptions of the eschatological paradise Scripture speaks of, the "new heavens and the new earth."[25] Some opinions are worth noting, however. According to Thomas Aquinas, not only will eating, sleeping, and generating be absent in the risen state; neither will there be animals, nor plants, nor minerals. However, taking it from Aristotle that stars are immobile and incorrupt (in fact they are divine), Aquinas accepts that the heavenly firmament will occupy a permanent place in the next life.[26] Other authors are more optimistic, however. Inspired perhaps by the writings of the ancients, many early Christian works speak of an eternal paradise with pastures, springs, and rivers.[27] In the second-century *Passion of Perpetua and Felicity*, for example, we read that paradise will consist of "a vast space, a garden of pleasure, having trees and roses, as well as

---

25. On the need for sober reflection on the matter, see G. Ancona, *Escatologia cristiana*, 359.
26. Thomas Aquinas, *S. Th. III, Suppl.*, q. 91, a. 5; *Comp. Theol.* 170.
27. Virgil, *Aeneid VI*, 640–59, which speaks of pastures, springs, and rivers.

every other kind of flowers, the height of the trees being like that of a cypress."[28] Jerome was convinced of the continuance of animal and vegetative life in heaven,[29] as was C. S. Lewis, who held there will be animals in paradise, especially domestic ones such as dogs and cats.[30] The medieval author Arnold of Bonneval suggested the following characteristics of the eschatological paradise: intimacy with God, trees and flowers delighting touch and smell, nothing to harm and all that will enchant, work involving effortless creativity.[31] Both Chrysostom[32] and Augustine, however, took a more allegorical and spiritual approach to scriptural references to an eschatological paradise. The latter spoke, for example, of the new world that would exist for the sake of beauty.[33]

Cosmic Renewal, Science, and the Eternal Value of Human Activity

We shall now consider two aspects of the promise of the new heavens and the new earth, with all that it implies in respect of novelty and continuity, topics that have been considered already in chapter 3 on final resurrection. *First*, the implications resurrection and cosmic renewal have for scientific cosmology, and *second*, the significance and value of human activity in the light of faith in a world that will eventually be destroyed and recreated by God.

Cosmic Renewal, Science, and Matter

Classical cosmology (that of Aristotle and Plato, and up as far as Isaac Newton) considered the world in ultimately fixed or mechanical terms. The gods, in keeping with their immortal, immobile nature, leave the infinite cosmos more or less as it has been made, with its permanent, unchangeable laws, and gradual though regular fluctuations and modulations.[34] Likewise, in classic thought human souls were considered to interact with their bodies in a somewhat extrinsic fashion. The problem areas that link science and religion generally involved describing the diverse mediations between the world of spirit and that of matter. As a result, special divine action over the cosmos, such as it is, was envisaged as "interventionist," or even as catastrophic and destructive. Indeed, divine intervention of a physical kind was excluded by many authors of a Deistic bent.[35] Such would be the case, for example, of miracles that impinge on the cosmos,

---

28. *Passio Perpetuae et Felicitatis*, 4:11–12.   29. Jerome, *In Is.*, 18:17–18.
30. C. S. Lewis, *Miracles*, 166–67; *The Problem of Pain* (New York: Macmillan, 1948), 117–31. Interestingly, Lewis speaks here of domestic animals, not wild ones. That is to say, the presence of animals in the afterlife is qualified anthropologically.
31. Arnold of Bonneval, *De operibus sex dierum*.   32. John Chrysostom, *In Ep. ad Rom.*, 14.
33. Augustine, *De Civ. Dei XXII*, 30.
34. See W. G. Stoeger, "Cosmologia," in *Dizionario Interdisciplinare di Scienza e Fede*, vol. 1, 285–89.
35. For a classic history of Deism, see J. Forget, "Déisme," in *DTC* 4 (1918): cols. 232–43.

worked by Christ directly or through the intercession of the saints; the same may be said of resurrection belief and cosmic re-creation, both of which originate in the context of apocalyptic literature.[36]

Resurrection, Science, and Cosmos The following alternative may be considered. Should the promise of resurrection and cosmic renewal be looked upon as a phenomenon belonging to the potentiality of nature, already written into its established laws and evolutionary process, as Egyptian fertility rites, for example, understood it?[37] Or alternatively, will resurrection be the result of a divine intervention that must ignore, bypass, or substantially alter the laws of nature, a kind of second creation riding roughshod over the existing world and reflecting a two-tier or even dualistic vision of reality?

It is clear that any ethical or spiritual system, no matter how much it attempts to confer dignity on human beings and action, if it remains unconnected with the reality and dynamism of the universe, with matter and human corporality, runs the risk of becoming meaningless, impracticable, or escapist. In addition, progress in the field of physics has brought about a general awareness that matter and its laws do not come under the exclusive sway of implacable, predictable rules.[38] The physical world is commonly perceived to involve a dynamic process that moves between *increasing entropy* (that produces an ever-increasing destructuring or dissolution of beings) on the one hand, and on the other, an *ever-higher structuring*, in that physical processes take place in open rather than closed systems.[39] Such processes in fact may not be impermeable to factors of a personal or spiritual kind.[40] Likewise, developments in contemporary philosophical anthropology are based, to a significant degree, on studies concerning the phenomenology of the human body;[41] this runs contrary to the predominance enjoyed by spirit-centered anthropologies and psychologies in recent centuries.

An awareness of these factors brought many twentieth-century authors to attempt a recovery of the strictly cosmological and anthropological implications of Christian salvation, and specifically of the doctrine of resurrection and cosmic renewal. Indeed Christ's work of salvation involves not only the negative aspect of overcoming the disharmony of sin and death that stems from the primordial disobedience of humans, but also the positive one, in which the cosmos created

---

36. *CAA* 86–92.   37. See pp. 75–76.
38. See pp. 44–46.
39. On this question, see H. Wehrt, "Über Irreversibilität, Naturprozesse und Zeitstruktur," in *Offene Systeme*, ed. E. U. von Weizsäcker, vol. 1 (Stuttgart: Klett, 1974), 114–99.
40. See my study "Whose Future."
41. See C. Bruaire, *Philosophie du corps* (Paris: Seuil, 1968); M. Merleau-Ponty, *L'union de l'âme et du corps chez Malebranche, Biran et Bergson* (Paris: Vrin, 1978); M. Henry, *Une philosophie de la chair* (Paris: Seuil, 2000).

by God advances under divine power toward definitive, glorious fullness. In this sense Christ's resurrection from the dead (and our promised resurrection in him) is not only the tangible sign of the Father's joyful love toward his Son for having been "obedient to death, death on the Cross" (Phil 2:7) and of the promise of divine pardon for humans. It also constitutes God's supreme and perpetual affirmation of the value of the created universe, of his wish to express his sovereignty over creation not by destroying or humiliating it, but by adopting and confirming its inner, filial reality, and by raising it in Christ to the fullness of glory and splendor.

Science and the "Cosmic Christ" One of the authors who spoke most forcefully of the continuity between human evolution and the progress of the Kingdom of God was Pierre Teilhard de Chardin in his doctrine of the "Cosmic Christ."[42] From the scientific standpoint, Teilhard considered the process of evolution of the universe as one of convergence of all phenomena toward an "Omega Point" of ultimate perfection. Theologically speaking, he says, this coincides with the eschatological "Christification" of the universe. When the process of the "incarnation" of the Word comes to completion, he notes, Christ will become, in the words of the Apostle, the *plērōma*, or fullness of creation.[43]

Teilhard's reflections on the cosmic Christ have provided a valuable expression of a central aspect of the Christian understanding of the world that had been somewhat neglected in previous centuries. Several authors have followed through on his intuitions,[44] some with more success than others.

It has been asked, however, whether Teilhard's "Cosmic Christ"—whom he speaks of as a mysterious super-human "third" personage in Christ—refers to the humanity of Christ hypostatically united to the Father, or to his divinity, consubstantial with the Father.[45] In the first case, Teilhard would seem to be extending the hypostatic union to the entire cosmos, and not only to the historical humanity of Jesus of Nazareth. Clearly, the possible dissolution of the concrete humanity of Jesus this involves may be somewhat out of place. In the second case, his understanding of things may place the real distinction between God and the created universe in jeopardy. In either case, a certain "panchristic" vision

---

42. See C. F. Mooney, *Teilhard de Chardin and the Mystery of Christ* (London: W. Collins, 1966); J. A. Lyons, *The Cosmic Christ in Origen and Teilhard de Chardin* (Oxford: Oxford University Press, 1982).

43. See L. Galleni, "Teilhard de Chardin, Pierre," in *Dizionario Interdisciplinare di Scienza e Fede*, vol. 2, 2111–24.

44. See É. Mersch, *Le Christ, l'homme et l'univers* (Paris: Desclée de Brouwer, 1962); G. Martelet, *Résurrection, eucharistie et genèse de l'homme* (Paris: Desclée de Brouwer, 1972); J.-M. Maldamé, *Le Christ et le cosmos* (Paris: Desclée, 1993); and also the Orthodox theologian O. Clément, *Le Christ, terre des vivants: le "Corps spirituel," le "Sens de la terre"* (Bégrolles-en-Mauges: Abbaye de Bellefontaine, 1976).

45. J.-M. Maldamé, *Le Christ et le cosmos*, 183–84.

of the universe may be detected in Teilhard's thought, a possibility Pope Pius XII made reference to in his 1943 encyclical *Mystici corporis*.[46]

It should be noted besides that the scriptural texts cited by Teilhard in reference to the strictly cosmic aspect of Christology (for example Col 1:17; 2:10; 3:11) pay attention only to the eschatological side of Christ's cosmic role (Christ as the "Omega Point" of creation), and neglect somewhat the strictly *protological* role played by God's Eternal Word in the creation of the world (Christ as the "Alpha Point" of creation).[47] The exclusively eschatological understanding of cosmic "christification" suggested by Teilhard may lend itself to either (1) an *extrinsic* understanding of God's intervention over nature that can be rectified only by strong affirmations of a panchristic or even pantheistic kind, or (2) a confusion between evil on the one hand, and simple cosmic limitation that derives from God's act of creation on the other. In fact, a truly Christian understanding of the universe and of matter in the light of eschatological resurrection can be founded only on a fully Christological vision of creation.[48]

Christ between Creation and Consummation The Lutheran theologian Wolfhart Pannenberg gives expression to the needed balance of emphasis between the eschatological and the protological while reflecting on the resurrection of Christ. Speaking of the scriptural texts that refer to the action of Christ over the cosmos, he says:

In *Jesus—God and man* [his 1964 Christology] . . . I linked these sayings to another group of New Testament Christological statements, those pertaining to the election or predestination of Jesus Christ to be the Head of a new humanity. . . . What is said here about the Son as Mediator of creation has primarily a "final" sense. It is to the effect that creation will be consummated only in Jesus Christ. . . . Yet true though this is in the light of the New Testament statements, it is not the only aspect of the Son's mediation of creation. The final ordering of creatures to the manifestation of Jesus Christ presupposes *that creatures already have the origin of their existence and nature in the Son*. Otherwise the final summing up of all things in the Son would be external to the things themselves, so that it would not be the definitive fulfillment *of* their own distinctive being.[49]

Indeed, according to Platonic and Neoplatonic thought, God is said to have created (or formed) the universe, once and for all, in a static and unchangeable way, through the external and temporary agency of a Demiurge or *Logos* serving as an intermediary between the eternity and transcendence of the Divine on the one hand, and the intractable corruptibility of matter on the other. For

46. *DS* 3816.
47. For example in Teilhard's 1924 work *Mon Univers* (Paris: Seuil, 1965).
48. See my study, "Il realismo e la teologia della creazione," *Per la filosofia* 12 (1995): 98–110.
49. W. Pannenberg, *Systematic Theology*, vol. 2, 24–25.

Platonists the *Logos* was brought into existence for the express purpose of placing order (*kosmos*) in the universe. Expressions of a similar kind may be found throughout the New Testament: God creates the world through the Word (Jn 1:3), or through Christ (1 Cor 8:6; Col 1:16). But the New Testament goes further, in employing two other ways of considering the relationship between the Word (Christ) and the world: the world is made *for* Christ and *in* Christ.

The World Made "for" Christ The letter to the Colossians (1:16) makes it clear that the universe was created not only through Christ, but also for him. Hence Christ, the Word incarnate, is not simply a means or instrument for the creation and perfection of the world, a means that might well be subordinated to a distinct ultimate end (such as the goodness or embellishment of the universe), and therefore ultimately expendable. That is to say, should the creating "Word" be considered as ultimately subordinate to the final perfection of creation, it would be contingent and not fully divine, as Arius in his Neoplatonic reading of the New Testament held. But according to Christian faith, Christ—God's Word destined to become incarnate—is himself (and no other) the end and supreme purpose of the universe. In the words of Tertullian, "Everything that was impressed on the earth was the thought of Christ, the man to come, the Word made flesh, even though it was then but mere mud and earth."[50] In other words, the universe from its very inception strains toward nothing else but its ultimate perfection, Jesus Christ, God's Eternal Word made flesh, the risen Lord of all creation, who will "unite all things in Him" (Eph 1:10), so that God may be "everything to every one" (1 Cor 15:28). In other words, the finalistic role of Christ further specifies and intensifies his mediating role: the expression "for him" qualifies the expression "through him." It is clear besides that whereas in Neoplatonic thought the Word is produced on account of the world, for Christian belief the very opposite is the case, for the world is made on account of the Word. For the former, therefore, the Word is contingent and produced, thus depending on both God and the world; for the latter, the Word is as necessary as God is, and depends totally and exclusively on the Father in being generated, but to no degree on the world.[51]

The World Made "in" Christ Paul often states that we are not only saved by Christ and live "in" him, but also that we have been created *in* Christ: "in him all things subsist" (Col 1:16); "He [the Son] . . . upholds the universe by his word of power" (Heb 1:3).[52] Christ, in other words, is not a mere instrumental cause of

---

50. Tertullian, *De res.*, 6.
51. This is the reason why the Council of Nicea (325) declared the "consubstantial" divinity of the Word with the Father: *DS* 125.
52. On the Pauline "in Christ" motif, see my study "The Inseparability of Holiness and Apostolate:

creation in the sense of giving shape to the world once and for all when it was formed long ago, nor just its final cause in the sense that all creation points to him as a faraway goal. That is to say, Christ is not the mere extrinsic cause of a creation that aspires to a perfection beyond its own capacities. Rather, as a full-fledged creating divinity, Christ is continually present to creation, keeping it in existence (conservation), moving all beings to act according to their nature (concourse), bringing them to their ultimate end (providence), for "in him we live and move and have our being" (Acts 17:28). Just as in the Old Testament Yahweh is looked upon as the fountain of life, so also in the New Jesus is the one who gives life (Jn 4:10). This he can do because "as the Father has life in himself, so he has granted the Son also to have life in himself" (Jn 5:26). It can be said therefore that all created things receive existence, subsistence, vitality, intelligibility, and consistency from the inexhaustible source of vitality that is the Word. The universe as a whole may be considered as a kind of living, filial being, created, enlivened, conserved, and eventually brought to eschatological perfection from within through the agency of God's own Word-Son made man. The culmination of this process, in the human and cosmic sphere, consists of final resurrection and cosmic recreation, carried out through the power of the One who, in person, is "the resurrection and the life" (Jn 11:25).

Summing Up Belief in final resurrection by the power of God (based on the witness of the apostles who had "seen" the risen Lord Jesus Christ) has acted as a powerful catalyst throughout history for the development and consolidation of Christian anthropology, cosmology, and ethics. Besides, it taught something the ancient world never dared to suggest: that corruptible matter had been created by God with a vocation to eternity. However, classical cosmology, by considering the universe in a rigid and mechanical way, made it difficult for the doctrine of the resurrection to be understood in anything but discontinuous and interventionist terms of an apocalyptic kind, or even in purely symbolic or spiritual ones. On account of this, resurrection belief in modern times tended to become both meaningless and superfluous for scientists and even for Christian philosophers. However, a renewed theology of creation "through" Christ, "for" Christ, and "in" Christ, as well as a more dynamic and open understanding of the laws of the physical universe, has made it possible to clarify and recuperate the fully cosmological side of resurrection belief, which of course had never been absent from Church life, spirituality, liturgy, art, and Eucharistic devotion.

The Christian 'alter Christus, ipse Christus' in the Writings of Blessed Josemaría Escrivá," *Annales Theologici* 16 (2002): 135–64, here 139–46.

The Perpetual Value of Work and Human Activity

We have seen that the world as we know it, infected by sin, will be destroyed, and renewed (or re-created) anew in the power of God, as the "new heavens and the new earth." Just as the risen state of humans involves the novelty of eternal glory, there will be a clear discontinuity between the earth as we know it now and the renewed world, from a cosmic and anthropological standpoint. But there will also be continuity and identity between the two stages. The biblical texts we have seen above situate this continuity principally at an ethical level: the virtues exercised during our earthly pilgrimage will remain forever, especially charity (1 Cor 13:8). Through God's power the new world will be filled with justice and peace. Those who wish to belong to it must live these virtues.

However, above and beyond the virtues and attitudes Christians acquire during their earthly sojourn, will anything remain in "the new heavens and the new earth" of the fruits of human work and endeavor? If humans are made "in the image of God" with a view to dominating the earth and subduing it (Gn 1:26–27), is it not thinkable that in the new world they will be accompanied, as it were, by the fruits of their labors, at least those in which God was glorified and obeyed, and other humans were loved and served? On this issue, two contrasting positions emerged during the 1950s and 60s, one called "eschatologism," the other "incarnationism."[53] The issue became popular in the period following Vatican Council II in the context of the dialogue some Christians attempted to establish with Marxist authors.

Eschatologists tend to emphasize the discontinuity between this world and the next, holding that the only continuity worth talking about consists of the virtues that Christians acquire as they "store up treasures in heaven" (Mt 6:20; 19:21), especially the virtue of charity. The position tends to be somewhat pessimistic in respect of the world and human activity. Incarnationists, on the contrary, consider that the realism of the Incarnation of the Word requires us to speak of a clear continuity between this world and the next, just as there was between the life of Jesus on earth and his present glorious identity at the right hand of the Father.

One of the earlier attempts at developing the incarnationist position was that of Teilhard de Chardin, whom we have considered earlier on.[54] Later on, some authors argued that comparisons could fairly be made between incarnationism and some forms of Marxist humanism, especially that of Ernst Bloch. The latter,

---

53. On the debate, see L. Malevez, "Deux théologies catholiques de l'histoire," *Bijdragen* 10 (1949): 224–40; J. L. Illanes, *Cristianismo, historia, mundo* (Pamplona: Eunsa, 1973); C. Pozo, *La teología del más allá*, 128–37.

54. See pp. 122–23.

as we already saw,[55] considered that "hope," rooted in the dynamism of matter and not in divine action, was the motor of history, and that through hope-driven work we will be in a position to establish on earth the humanity we all dream of.

That Christians would attempt to dialogue with Marxist thought, given the latter's Christian roots, is comprehensible to some degree. At heart, however, differences between the two are profound and insurmountable, especially as regards the doctrine of God and the dignity of the human person. For Marxism, the progressive humanization of the world, such as it is, is the direct result or product of human effort. Conversely, the advent of the Kingdom of God on earth—whether this be apparent and visible as incarnationists think, or hidden and invisible as eschatologists suggest—is always the result of God's action through Christ in the Spirit. And until the Christ returns in glory, his saving work will always be present in the world under the sign of the Cross, that is, under the sign of weakness, ambivalence, and apparent failure. For the Marxist, man (who has taken God's place) constructs the future; for the Christian, God brings the future into being, counting of course on intelligent human collaboration. In a sense humans do not "cooperate" in this process, for the action of the creature is incommensurable with that of the Creator; perhaps it would be more correct to say that they employ their God-given talents to joyfully receive and act upon the gifts—of nature and of grace—that God has abundantly supplied them with.[56] "Seek first his kingdom and his righteousness," Jesus says, "and all these things [food, clothes, etc.] shall be yours as well" (Mt 6:33).

Preparing the "New Cosmos": Some Recent Church Documents The discussion between incarnationists and eschatologists also found an echo in Vatican Council II discussions. Some Council Fathers requested the inclusion of a clear reference to the discontinuity between this world and the next—citing 2 Peter 3:10–13, already examined—in order to avoid "favoring the opinion of those who said that this world must pass on to glory just as it has been constituted by humans."[57] The suggestion was accepted and the Petrine text was included in *Lumen gentium*.[58]

The constitution *Gaudium et spes*, which also deals with the problem, insists on the distinction between this world and the next, yet unequivocally mentions the relevance of temporal progress for the Kingdom of God.

We have been warned, of course, that it profits man nothing if he gains the whole world and loses or forfeits himself (Lk 9:25). Far from diminishing our concern to develop this

---

55. See pp. 6–7.
56. My study "Hope and Freedom in Gabriel Marcel and Ernst Bloch," 232.
57. *Acta Concilii Vaticani*, III, 3, 8, 140; See C. Pozo, *La teología del más allá*, 141–44.
58. *LG* 48c.

earth, the expectancy of a new earth should spur us on, for it is here that the body of a new human family grows, foreshadowing in some way the age which is to come. That is why, although we must be careful to distinguish earthly progress clearly from the increase of the Kingdom of Christ, such progress is of vital concern to the Kingdom of God, insofar as it can contribute to the better ordering of human society.[59]

Perhaps on account of overly optimistic interpretations given to this carefully worded conciliar statement (for example in the ambit of liberation theology), a 1979 Letter of the Congregation for the Doctrine of the Faith on eschatology had the following to say:

> Christians . . . must believe, on the one hand, in the fundamental continuity that exists, by the power of the Holy Spirit, between the present life in Christ and future life; in effect, charity is the law of the Kingdom of God, and the charity we live on earth is the exact measure of our participation in the glory of heaven. On the other hand, Christians must discern the radical fracture that exists between the present and the future on the basis of the fact that the condition of faith will be substituted by one of full light.[60]

John Paul II in his 1981 encyclical *Laborem exercens*, when speaking of the spirituality of work, takes up the question once again, and points to the need to take into account the place of the Cross in the dynamic of progress and in the preparation of the "new heavens and the new earth." "In work, thanks to the light that penetrates us from the Resurrection of Christ, we always find a glimmer of new life, of the new good, as if it were an announcement of 'the new heavens and the new earth' (2 Pt 3:13) in which man and the world participate precisely through the toil that goes with work. Through toil, and never without it."[61]

Finally, in the Holy See's *Instruction on Christian Freedom and Liberation* (1986), we read that Christian

> hope does not weaken commitment to the progress of the earthly city, but rather gives it meaning and strength. . . . [The] distinction between earthly progress and the growth of the Kingdom . . . is not a separation; for man's vocation to eternal life does not suppress but confirms his task of using the energies and means which he has received from the Creator for developing his temporal life. . . . Enlightened by the Lord's Spirit, Christ's Church can discern in the signs of the times the ones which advance liberation and those that are deceptive and illusory. . . . She knows that we shall rediscover all these good things—human dignity, fraternal union and freedom—which are the result of efforts in harmony with God's will, "washed clean of all stain, illumined and transfigured when Christ will hand over to the Father the eternal and universal kingdom" which is a Kingdom of freedom. The vigilant and active expectation of the coming of the Kingdom is also the ex-

---

59. *GS* 39b, citing Pope Pius XI, Enc. *Quadragesimo anno* (1931).
60. Doc. *Recentiores episcoporum Synodi*, n. 7.
61. John Paul II, Enc. *Laborem exercens* (1981), n. 27e.

pectation of a finally perfect justice for the living and the dead, for people of all times and places, a justice which Jesus Christ, installed as supreme Judge, will establish.... This promise, which surpasses all human possibilities, directly concerns our life in this world. For true justice must include everyone; it must bring the answer to the immense load of suffering borne by all the generations. In fact, without the resurrection of the dead and the Lord's judgment, there is no justice in the full sense of the term. The promise of the resurrection is freely made to meet the desire for true justice dwelling in the human heart.[62]

Concluding Reflection It is understandable that Christians might look upon the promised destruction and purification of the cosmos with fear and trepidation, rather than with hope and joy. Following the logic of the Cross and Resurrection of Christ, however, it is clear that beyond the destruction comes the promise of renewal, the return to paradise, the glorious beauty of God's finished work. Taking into account what was said above on the resurrection of a life once lived and the social dimension of this mystery, it makes sense to hold that much of what humans have accomplished on earth, along with their fellow human beings, employing the best of their God-given energies and intelligence—in works of art and architecture, of legislation and literature, works of training and education, and so on—will live on forever. The doctrine of final judgment, which we shall now consider, only goes to confirm this.

---

62. Congregation for the Doctrine of the Faith, *Instruction on Christian Freedom and Liberation* (1986), n. 60, citing *GS* 39c.

5

Final Judgment

> Then you will know I am the Lord.
> —*Ezekiel 24:24*

> In the evening of our life, we will be judged by love.
> —*John of the Cross*[1]

> A world which has to create its own justice is a world without hope.
> —*Benedict XVI*[2]

Christian faith openly proclaims that when Jesus comes in glory at the end of time, not only will the dead rise up by the power of God in the likeness of the risen Christ, not only will the cosmos be renewed, but the whole of humanity will be judged by the Lord of heaven and earth. The Symbols of the faith are virtually unanimous in proclaiming final judgment as the primary motive of Christ's glorious coming: he "will come again in glory to judge the living and the dead."[3] Pope Benedict's encyclical *Spe salvi* pays special attention to the doctrine of judgment. In it we read: "The prospect of Judgment has influenced Christians in their daily living as a criterion by which to order their present life, as a summons to their conscience, and at the same time as hope in God's justice."[4]

The Church teaches that judgment takes place in two stages: at death, humans are judged by God for the life they have lived; at the end of time, humanity as a whole will be judged by the Lord Jesus who comes in glory. The latter is usually termed "final, or universal, judgment," the former "particular judgment,"[5] which we shall consider later on.

---

1. "En la tarde de nuestra vida, seremos juzgados por el amor," John of the Cross, *Palabras de luz y de amor*, n. 57.
2. *SS* 42.
3. *DS* 150.
4. *SS* 41–48, here n. 41.
5. Thomas Aquinas, *Comp. Theol.*, 242; *IV C. Gent.*, 91; *Catechismus Romanus*, I, art. 7, *CCC* 1022. See pp. 280–85.

Judgment in Scripture

The Old Testament provides a constant testimony of the judgment of God over humanity, especially over the People of the Covenant.[6] Through the prophets God taught his people to do his will and live as "his people" through a pedagogy of reward and punishment. In a myriad of different ways he showed them whether or not they were being faithful to the covenant. All the successes, failures, catastrophes, triumphs, all favorable or adverse happenings, were seen to come from God, who protected, instructed, consoled, corrected, and punished his people. However, judgment, such as it was, was depicted principally as referring to the people as a whole. It was taken for granted that the sins of parents would be visited on their children (Jer 31:29).[7] Besides, God's judgment and punishment were limited in the main to this life, to the world as it is (Jb 42:7–17). The doctrine of eschatological (*post mortem*) judgment, reward, and punishment remained somewhat undeveloped.[8]

At a deeper level, however, the affirmation of divine judgment is strictly theological in character, in the sense that it is equivalent to (or is a consequence of) Yahweh's total sovereignty over the universe.[9] "Then you will know I am the Lord" (Ez 24:24). At heart, the affirmation of divine judgment is anti-idolatrous in character: God alone is judge over the universe, because God alone is Lord. It is interesting to note that both Tertullian and Aquinas derive the doctrine of judgment from that of creation: everything that exists, without exception, comes directly from God; hence, at the final reckoning each person and every single thing will receive what is its due.[10]

The Transition from the Prophetic to the Apocalyptic

According to the prophets, the People of the Covenant, in the midst of the desolation that characterized the post-exilic period, were tempted to think that God no longer cared for them, that no new prophets would arise, that the Spirit had been "put out," to use an expression of Paul (1 Thes 5:19). Some began to take it for granted that God's people would no longer triumph on earth, that full justice would never be achieved.[11] At best, justice would be only obtained after

---

6. On judgment in Scripture, see W. Schneider, "Judgment," in *NIDNTT* 1, 362–67; *CAA* 96–99; 159–62.

7. On the Old Testament notion of corporate personality, *CAA* 72–73.

8. See J. J. Alviar, *Escatología*, 195.

9. On the fundamental notion of God as Lord, at the very heart of Scripture, see W. Pannenberg, *Systematic Theology*, vol. 3, 527–32.

10. Tertullian, *De res.*, 14:6; Thomas Aquinas, *S. Th. III, Suppl.*, q. 88, a. 1.

11. The prophet Habakkuk seems to accuse God: "Why do you look on the treacherous, and are

132 The Object of Christian Hope

death, in a transcendent sphere, through God's power and in his own good time.

The latter position finds expression in some prophetic works,[12] particularly those of Amos, Zephaniah, and Joel. The prophet Zephaniah[13] is notable not only for his severe and definitive rendering of the doctrine of divine judgment, but also for his claims that judgment will be applied to the nations and not only to Judah.

> I will utterly sweep away everything from the face of the earth, says the Lord. . . . I will cut off humanity from the face of the earth, says the Lord . . . those who have turned back from following the Lord, who have not sought the Lord or inquired of him. Be silent before the Lord God! For the day of the Lord is at hand. . . . On that day I will punish all who leap over the threshold, who fill their master's house with violence and fraud. . . . At that time I will search Jerusalem with lamps, and I will punish the people who rest complacently on their dregs, those who say in their hearts, "the Lord will not do good, nor will he do harm." . . . That day will be a day of wrath, a day of distress and anguish, a day of ruin and devastation, a day of darkness and gloom, a day of clouds and thick darkness. (Zep 1:2–3,6–7,9,12,15)

And for the prophet Joel, the "Day of Yahweh"[14] is the day of definitive judgment of the nations and the vindication of Judah. Speaking of the "day of the Lord" (Jl 1:15; 2:1–2; 10–11), he says: "For then, in those days and at that time, when I restore the fortunes of Judah and Jerusalem, I will gather all the nations and bring them down to the valley of Jehoshaphat, I will enter into judgment with them there. . . . Let the nations rouse themselves, and come up to the valley of Jehoshaphat; for there I will sit to judge all the neighboring nations. . . . Multitudes, multitudes in the valley of decision!" (Jl 4:1–2,12,14).

These texts (and many others besides) prepared the way for the so-called apocalyptic movement, which began to consolidate some 250 years before the coming of Christ.[15] For the apocalyptics, judgment is no longer considered in terms of a gradual process taking place within the world as we know it. Rather it is seen as a definitive, future, public, and universal event, probably an imminent one, by which God will triumph directly over all evil and determine the entire

---

silent when the wicked swallow those more righteous than they?" (Hb 1:13). On the dynamic of injustice and oppression in the Old Testament, Qo 4:1–3.

12. See Y. Hoffmann, "The Day of the Lord as a Concept and a Term in the Prophetic Literature," *Zeitschrift für allgemeine Wissenschaftstheorie* 93 (1981): 37–50; M. Cimosa, "Il giorno del Signore e l'escatologia nell'antico Testamento," in *Dizionario di spiritualità biblico-patristica*, 16: *Escatologia* (Roma: Borla, 1997), 20–45; G. de Carlo, "Il giudizio di Dio nell'a. T. Il giorno di JHWH," in *I novissimi nella Bibbia*, ed. G. Bortone, 33–78 (L'Aquila: ISSRA, 1999).

13. See H. Irsigler, *Gottesgericht und Jahwetag. Die Komposition Zef 1,2–2,3, untersucht auf der Grundlage der Literarkritik des Zefanjabuches* (St. Ottilien: EOS, 1977).

14. See J. Bourke, "Le jour de Jahvé dans Joël," *Revue Biblique* 66 (1959): 5–31; 192–212.

15. *CAA* 63–136.

course of human history. "When the Most High made the world . . . the first thing he prepared was judgment, and everything that relates to it," we read in 4 Ezra (7:70), an important Jewish apocalyptic text dating from the first century AD.

The principal development in the doctrine of judgment within the Old Testament lies in the fact that whereas in earlier works (particularly of a prophetic kind) an ethnical and restrictive judgment was applied by God to the Jewish people through the agency of the prophets, in apocalyptic works, an ethical criterion came to be applied by God in person (or through the agency of the Son of man) to the whole of humanity.[16] That is to say, each and every person will be judged on their own merits, by God himself, not on the simple basis of whether or not they belonged exteriorly to God's people. The beginnings of this turnabout are to be found, for example, in writings of the prophet Ezekiel, who states clearly that "the one who has sinned is the one to die" (Ez 18:4).[17] A fresh, universalistic panorama is opened, where individual responsibility before God comes to prevail over collective responsibility.

Judgment in the New Testament

John the Baptist, in his preaching, openly takes up the imminent apocalyptic motif in respect of final judgment.[18] "When he saw many of the Pharisees and Sadducees coming for baptism, he said to them, 'You brood of vipers! Who warned you to flee from the wrath to come? . . . Even now the axe is laid to the root of the trees; every tree therefore that does not bear good fruit is cut down and thrown into the fire'" (Mt 3:7,10). Of the one who is to come, he said, "his winnowing fork is in his hand, and he will clear his threshing floor and gather his wheat into the granary, but the chaff he will burn with unquenchable fire" (Mt 3:12).[19]

In the Synoptic gospels Jesus, freely using apocalyptic language, proclaims not only the doctrine of final judgment, but, more importantly, that he himself, as the Son of man, will be the Judge.[20] This is especially clear in Matthew's Gospel, which culminates in the famous judgment scene (Mt 25:31–46).[21] "For the Son of man will come with his angels in the glory of his Father, and then he will repay every man for what he has done" (Mt 16:27). "When the Son of man

---

16. *CAA* 96–9.
17. In the early books of the Old Testament, solidarity in guilt is the most common feature: Ex 20:5–6; Jer 31:29; Ez 18:2. Later on, personal retribution came to the fore: Jer 17:10; 31:30–4; Ez 18:20–30; 28:24–6; 33:12–20,25–9, as well as Job and Qoheleth.
18. *CAA* 193–200.
19. On judgment in the Gospel of Matthew, see D. L. Marguerat, *Le jugement dans l'évangile de Matthieu*, 2nd ed. (Geneva: Labor et fides, 1995); *CAA* 158–62.
20. See n. 55 below.
21. *CAA* 158–62.

comes in his glory and all the angels with him," Matthew continues, "then he will sit on his glorious throne. Before him will be gathered all the nations, and he will separate them one from another as a shepherd separates the sheep from the goats, and he will place the sheep at his right hand, but the goats at the left" (Mt 25:31–33).

The principal elements of the doctrine of final judgment are summed up in Paul's second letter to the Corinthians: "For we must all appear before the judgment seat of Christ, so that each one may receive good or evil, according to what he has done in the body" (2 Cor 5:10). The same idea is present throughout the book of Revelation. For example: "Then I looked, and lo, a white cloud, and seated on the cloud one like a son of man, with a golden crown on his head, and a sharp sickle in his hand. And another angel came out of the temple calling with a loud voice to him who sat upon the cloud, 'Put in your sickle, and reap, for the hour to reap has come, for the harvest of the earth is fully ripe.' So he who sat upon the cloud swung his sickle on the earth, and the earth was reaped" (Rv 14:14–16).

Among the Fathers of the Church, the doctrine of judgment is accepted generally. Basil in a special way insists on this teaching, while rejecting the Origenist doctrine of universal reconciliation (*apokatastasis*), which, he argues, would amount to a denial of final judgment.[22]

Judgment and Salvation: The Role of Christ

It should be noted, however, that New Testament teaching on judgment[23] marks a distance from the strict apocalyptic genre, in that it is tempered and contextualized by the doctrine of salvation won by Christ.[24] This is an important novelty. Jesus is primarily the Savior of humanity, the one who carried the weight of sinfulness to the point of dying for the human race, who offered us redemption and divine pardon of our sins. Only on the basis of his being our Savior can we speak about him being our Judge.[25] It may be said that he will judge those whom he has saved, or more precisely, he will judge those to whom he has offered salvation.[26]

---

22. On Basil, see M. Girardi, "Il giudizio finale nella omeletica di Basilio di Cesarea," *Augustinianum* 18 (1978): 183–90; B. E. Daley, *The Hope*, 81–82. In the prologue to the *Moralia* "on the judgment of God," Basil rejects Origen's idea of *apokatastasis*. See also his *Regulae brevius tractatae*, resp. 267.

23. Whereas judgment is central for Matthew, neither Mark nor Luke pays particular attention to it; *CAA* 159, n. 109.

24. This is the fundamental thesis of my work *CAA*; especially 232–56.

25. "God now reveals his true face in the figure of the sufferer who shares man's God-forsaken condition by taking it upon himself," *SS* 43.

26. "Whereas the classical apocalyptic envisaged the prompt coming of God in power in terms of divine wrath being unleashed upon impenitent sinners, and as deserved consolation for the just who

And salvation is expressed in two forms in the New Testament: as resurrection and as personal redemption.

Judgment, Resurrection, and Truth

The doctrine of eschatological judgment develops side by side with that of final resurrection. In this, New Testament teaching draws on the book of Daniel and other apocalyptic sources.[27] We have already seen that the quest for definitive justice is what sets the scene for the doctrine of final resurrection.[28] And justice is achieved, once and for all, of course, through universal judgment. Tertullian was candid about the matter when he said that judgment "is the very reality which makes resurrection entirely necessary."[29] In the *Epistle of Barnabas* (second century) we read that there is certainty of judgment and retribution for both just and sinners, and then the epistle adds: "for this reason there will be a resurrection."[30] Aristides (second century) said that the righteousness of the Christian may be attributed to their hope in the resurrection, which is followed by judgment and eternal recompense.[31] In the *Adversus haereses* Irenaeus says that there will be resurrection for both just and unjust,[32] although in the *Demonstratio* he speaks of resurrection only for believers,[33] that is, for those who possess the Holy Spirit.[34] And Cyril of Jerusalem writes: "We shall be raised, therefore, all with our bodies eternal . . . the just in order to hold converse with the angels, and the sinner in order to burn eternally in fire."[35]

The promise of resurrection gives the key to judgment, insofar as it makes the latter possible. "There can be no justice without a resurrection of the dead," Pope Benedict writes.[36] And at the same time, judgment gives full meaning to resurrection, in that it constitutes the definitive, total manifestation before God

---

are already saved, according to Matthew Jesus came as God's Messiah in the first place *to save sinners*. Because he gave his whole life to this mission, that is, because he was our *Savior*, he would be in a position to later *judge* the world in perfect justice, since humans will have been given every possible opportunity of responding fully to saving grace. He carried out the work of salvation, according to the first evangelist, by carrying the weight of a sinful, downtrodden world on his shoulders, by taking the place of sinners, by going so far as to endure in his person the punishments apocalyptic texts seem to have reserved for the reprobate," *CAA* 297.

27. *CAA* 165–69.
28. See pp. 80–85. On the relationship between resurrection and justice, J. L. Ruiz de la Peña, *La pascua de la creación*, 178–80.
29. Tertullian, *De res.*, 14:8.   30. *Ep. Barn.*, 21:1; 5:6–7.
31. Aristides, *Apol.*, 15–16.   32. Irenaeus, *Adv. Haer. II*, 33:5.
33. Irenaeus, *Demonstratio*, 42.
34. On this see J. Arroniz, "La salvación de la carne en S. Ireneo," *Scriptorium Victoriense* 12 (1965): 7–29.
35. Cyril of Jerusalem, *Catech. Myst.*, 18,1:19. On Cyril's eschatology, see G. Hellemo, *Adventus Domini. Eschatological Thought in 4th-Century Apses and Catecheses* (Leiden: E. J. Brill, 1989), 146–98.
36. *SS* 42. "Yes, there is a resurrection of the flesh. There is justice," ibid., n. 43.

and creatures of the true identity of each and every person. What was hidden or unknown on earth, whether good or bad, will then be fully revealed. Final judgment will be, simply, *the decisive and supreme moment of truth*, the moment in which the extraordinarily complex mystery of God's Providence and human response will be revealed, once and for all.

Judgment and Personal Salvation

Since judgment is closely associated with resurrection, which is necessarily universal, it is clear that judgment may be considered as a form of salvation only in the sense that God intervenes to raise up the living and the dead, thus bringing human nature to its fullness, for judgment refers principally to personal salvation. This does not mean, however, that judgment is an alternative form of personal salvation, as is sometimes held.[37] In fact, salvation and not judgment occupies center stage in Christian revelation, God's action in Christ. Jesus "did not come to judge the world, but to save the world" (Jn 12:47). In that sense it may be said that with judgment salvation reaches its culmination. In Ratzinger's words, "the truth that judges man has appeared to save him."[38] Still, judgment is judgment, and salvation is salvation. At the end of time man will be judged, not justified. In fact the verb "to judge" used by John in the above text (12:47), *krinō*, actually means "to condemn." Thus judgment may be considered as the definitive and universal revelation of the gift of salvation, whether received or rejected, that has consolidated in each human life lived historically, the very manifestation of the meaning of history.[39] Salvation is offered to humans, but the offer will not last indefinitely. Judgment marks the end to God's concrete offer of mercy. After that, repentance will no longer be possible, for the just will remain perpetually separated from the unjust.

The Scale, Measure, and Scope of Eschatological Judgment

According to the New Testament, judgment may be characterized in three ways: it will be universal, based on charity, and definitive.[40]

---

37. F.J. Nocke does not accept the idea that Jesus who once was our Savior will later on be our Remunerator, because this involves a shift from the present experience to the future. Yet we do experience Christ as judge, he says: *Eschatologie*, 3rd ed. (Düsseldorf: Patmos, 1988), 71–72, 75, 139–43. Scripture, he concludes, does not teach judgment but reconciliation. Likewise W. Pannenberg is of the opinion that Christ comes only to save, and that the "message of Jesus is the standard of judgment," *Systematic Theology*, vol. 3, 615. Thus he speaks of the "redemptive transformation of judgment" ibid., 617, drawing, he claims, on J. Ratzinger, *Eschatology*, 206. On the linkup between judgment and purification, see W. Pannenberg, *Systematic Theology*, vol. 3, 616–20. On this topic, see also J.J. Alviar, *Escatología*, 203–4.

38. J. Ratzinger, *Eschatology*, 206.

39. Theodoret of Cyrus explains that judgment and salvation are not equivalent, "for all people will put on the garment of incorruption, but not all will share in divine glory," *In II Cor.* 5:3.

40. *CAA* 161–62.

First, eschatological judgment will be universal, for "before him will be gathered all the nations" (Mt 25:32). On the one hand, this is in keeping with the apocalyptic character of New Testament eschatology: judgment draws on an ethical, not an ethnical, criterion. In order to obtain entrance into "the joy of your Master" (Mt 25:21,23), it is not sufficient to passively "belong" to Israel or to the Church. John the Baptist had already warned some Pharisees and Sadducees that they should "bear fruit that befits repentance," not presuming "to say to yourselves: 'We have Abraham as our Father'" (Mt 3:8–9).[41] During the Sermon on the Mount, Jesus repeats: "Not everyone who says to me 'Lord, Lord', shall enter the kingdom of heaven, but he who does the will of my Father who is in heaven" (Mt 7:21). "They made the mistake of thinking that physical descent from Abraham granted them an automatic immunity from God's eschatological wrath," Hagner notes.[42] It is clear that belonging exteriorly to God's people will be of little use if upright personal behavior is lacking. On the other hand, the universality of judgment is also in keeping with the missionary and ecclesial character of New Testament eschatology. "This gospel of the kingdom will be preached throughout the whole world, as a testimony to all nations; and then the end will come" (Mt 24:14).

It might seem that this shift from an ethnical to an ethical criterion of judgment, typical of apocalyptic works, might give rise to the idea of an abstract and highly objective judgment standard, in which an "exact correspondence between the quality of the sin and that of the punishment is mapped."[43] This tends to be the case in classical apocalyptic works.[44] However, this would introduce a predominantly impersonal element into judgment and, as a result, into Christian ethics as a whole, hardly in keeping with the moral teaching of the New Testament in general and the spirit of the Beatitudes in particular.

This brings us to the *second* characteristic of judgment in the New Testament: what might be termed its "interpersonal" character, based on the fact that charity occupies center stage in Christian life. Matthew's judgment discourse leaves no doubt as regards the final verdict. No appeal is possible. Yet both the saved and the condemned seem surprised by the decision made, Matthew tells us (25:37,44). And the reasons given in each case are of a personal, or better, "interpersonal," kind. Jesus does not offer a detailed and rigorous transgressions list, but rather a single criterion, which explains the inner meaning of the trans-

---

41. "Visible Israel and the people of God are no longer identical," comment W. D. Davies and D. C. Allison on this text: *Matthew*, vol. 1, 308. On the process of Old Testament Judaism moving beyond a collective view of salvation, see Is 55:7; Ez 18:21–22; 33:11. Later on, see especially Philo of Alexandria, *De praemiis et poenis*, 152.

42. D. A. Hagner, *Matthew*, 50.   43. *CAA* 97.

44. *CAA* 96–98.

gressions committed. "As you did it to one of the least of these my brothers," he says, "you did it to me" (Mt 25:40,45). That is to say, sinful transgressions that grievously offend God refer in the main to a refusal to serve and assist Christ by not recognizing him in the practical needs of "the least ones." This connects with the first observation (the universality of judgment), because among the "least ones" are to be included not only the poor but also those sent to evangelize in the name of Jesus (Mt 10:1–15,33; 11:20–4). Salvation no longer depends as such on a passive, exterior belonging to God's people, or on a merely outward fulfillment of the law, but on an interior union through charity with Christ and with those who belong to him, those for whom he has given his life, that is, the whole of humanity. Charity, which according to Paul will last forever (1 Cor 13:13), will be the measure of judgment. Of special value will be those good actions that only God can see, for "God who sees in secret will reward you" (Mt 6:4,6). "In the evening of our life," as John of the Cross wrote, "we will be judged on love."[45]

"Belonging to Christ" through faith and charity, being conformed to him, requires of course both moral rectitude (openness to God's law, which Christ revealed to his disciples, and to which he exacted obedience)[46] and truly belonging to the Church, insofar as it is Christ's own body. But it is clear that the ultimate criterion for judgment is that of belonging to Christ, conformity with him, through faith and charity.

Third and last, universal judgment is characterized by the fact that it is public and definitive. According to the gospel parable (Mt 13:24–30), the wheat and the weeds are often not separated from one another in this life. Indeed it may be difficult to distinguish them apart.[47] But at judgment, the separation will be made. The householder will say: "Let both grow together until the harvest; and at harvest time I will tell the reapers, 'Gather the weeds first and bind them in bundles to be burned, but gather the wheat into my barn'" (Mt 13:30). At the end of time, says Augustine, there will be only two possibilities, *aut vitis, aut ignis*:[48] either life, that is, eternal union with Christ, the vine (Jn 15:1), or fire, perpetual separation from him. To the fact that God's mercy has temporal limits we shall return later on.[49]

God as the One Who Judges

From the anthropological standpoint, end-time judgment should be considered an absolute and all-encompassing event: (1) as definitive, it speaks of the

---

45. John of the Cross, *Palabras de luz y de amor*, n. 57.
46. Jn 14:15,21,23; 15:10; 1 Jn 2:5.   47. See D. A. Hagner, *Matthew*, 381–84; 391–95.
48. Augustine, *In Io. Ev. tr.*, 15:6.
49. On the moment of the *Parousia*, see pp. 225–27.

immortal destiny of humans; (2) in association with resurrection, it involves human corporality; (3) as "interpersonal," it links directly with the personal and social character of the human being. That is to say, judgment occasions, or better, manifests, the ultimate and eternal "definition" or identity of each human person, and of humanity as a whole, in the eyes of the Creator, Redeemer, and Judge. Judgment is the supreme and definitive anthropological moment. And of course it is quite clear that none other than God, the Creator of all things, is in a position to pronounce such a judgment, to reveal the hidden name of humans (Rv 2:17), to fathom their innermost thoughts (Sir 42:18), their true intention. Tertullian put it as follows in a text we have already cited: God is "judge because he is Lord, he is Lord because he is Creator, he is Creator because he is God."[50]

In the Old Testament, in fact, it is clear that God, and God alone, is the one who judges.[51] Only God can create, reward, punish, console, strengthen, and forgive. "Who can forgive sins but God alone?" we read on the lips and in the hearts of Jesus' listeners (Mk 2:7). But what does it mean to say that God judges man? When we say that God is just, or that God judges, or that justice is a divine attribute, does this mean simply that God measures human action to ensure that it conforms to a preestablished standard, and rewards or punishes in consequence?

Three points should be kept in mind. *First*, as we have seen already, judgment is posterior to justification (or salvation) and contingent upon the human response to the divine grace of conversion; to put it slightly differently, God's justice must be primarily considered as an active attribute (in the sense that God justifies sinners, offering them the gift of saving grace), and only on that basis is it a passive one (that God rewards or punishes according to humans' concrete response to grace).[52] Awareness of this brings the Psalmist to cry out: "Do not enter into judgment with your servant, for no one living is righteous before you" (Ps 143:2). And in the New Testament, the same awareness may be found: "We are unworthy servants; we have only done what was our duty" (Lk 17:10). And Peter: "Depart from me, for I am a sinful man, O Lord" (Lk 5:8). *Second*, since God is Creator of the universe, he is the only one who fully knows and comprehends the human heart, and thus the only one truly capable of judging humans. For this reason, on repeated occasions Jesus exhorted his followers not to judge others (Mt 7:1–5). Human wisdom and judgment counts little, for Paul says that "the wisdom of this world is folly with God" (1 Cor 3:19). As a result, no created thing,

---

50. Tertullian, *De res.*, 14:6.
51. Ezra 7:33–36.
52. On this, see my study *Fides Christi*, 186–94.

no aspect of human life, "is excluded from or eliminated in God's judgment."[53] *Third*, God alone, in creating the world and revealing the mystery of divine life, is the only one who can decide what the "standard" of judgment should be, and has revealed it through created nature (Rom 1:18–23) and (definitively) in the life, death, and resurrection of his Word-Son, Jesus Christ.[54]

Further light may be shed on the matter by the fact that, according to the New Testament, the supreme judge of the living and the dead will be none other than Jesus Christ, God's only Son made man.[55]

Christ Receives the Power to Judge from His Father

The coming of the Son of God made man to the earth was marked by simplicity, defenselessness, openness, and apparent weakness. He came knocking on the door of the human heart (Rv 3:20); he came "to seek and to save the lost" (Lk 19:10). Jesus was and is our merciful Savior. But he was and is our Lord as well, and for this reason Christians called the risen Jesus *Kyrios*, "Lord," from the very beginning. He spoke as one having authority (Lk 4:32). His presence imposed respect and even fear (Lk 4:30; 8:37; Jn 18:6). His miracles were powerful and undeniable (Jn 2:22–23), his power over Satan evident (Lk 8:32–33). He spoke with God as did Moses, the legislator and judge (Lk 9:29). Of Jesus Peter proclaimed: "You are the Christ, the Son of the living God" (Mt 16:16). His presence, words, and actions enkindled enthusiasm and love, as well as anger and rejection. While not being "divisive" in the common sense of this word, he nonetheless divided the spirits of those whom he encountered (Jn 6:66). "Do not think that I have come to bring peace on earth," he said; "I have not come to bring peace, but a sword" (Mt 10:34). Demons openly resisted his presence and action (Mt 12:28; 13:25,28,39; Jn 8:43–44; 12:31). Presenting himself as "the way, the truth and the life" (Jn 14:6), it was impossible to remain indifferent before him. If we keep in mind that for John "judgment" is equivalent to "condemnation," the following words are impressive: "Who does not believe [now] is already judged" (Jn 3:18).[56]

---

53. *CAA* 135.

54. The same message may be found in Sermon on Mount: Mt 6:4,6,15,18; 10:28 and par. See also 1 Pt 4:5; Rv 20:11; in Paul, Rom 2:3–11; 3:6; 14:10; 1 Cor 5:13; 2 Thes 1:5.

55. Mt 7:22–23; 13:41–3; 16:27; 25:31–46; Lk 13:25–27; 1 Thes 4:6; 1 Cor 4:4–5; 11:32; 2 Cor 5:10, and especially Jn 5:22–30. "And he [Christ] commanded us to preach to the people, and to testify that he is the one ordained by God to be judge of the living and the dead" (Acts 10:42). See *CAA* 154–58, on the meaning of the coming of the "Son of Man." Some authors hold that the idea of Jesus as Judge is not particularly important in the New Testament: see H. Merkel, "Gericht Gottes IV," *Theologische Realenzyklopädie*, vol. 12 (Berlin: W. De Gruyter, 1984), 484–92; W. Pannenberg, *Systematic Theology*, vol. 3, 613–14.

56. G. R. Beasley-Murray, *John*, Word Biblical Commentary (Waco: Word Books, 1987), 51, holds that the term "judgment" in John may be understood either as "separation" or as "condemnation."

When the infant Jesus was presented in the temple, Simeon prophesied to his mother that "this child is set for the fall and rise of many in Israel and for a sign that is spoken against (and a sword will pierce through your own soul also), *that thoughts out of many hearts may be revealed*" (Lk 2:34–35). Jesus on his earthly pilgrimage, though human, vulnerable, and apparently weak, was already the Lord and Judge of humanity.

It is quite clear, however, that Jesus' actions and words, which already on earth revealed and separated saints from sinners (or better, repentant sinners from unrepentant ones), were primarily acts of salvation, not of judgment. He had come to save humankind, and would do so in the most powerful and effective way possible, appealing to the human heart even to the point of willingly allowing himself be judged and condemned by sinners.[57] When Jesus was brought before the Roman authorities, Pilate asked him: "Are you the King of the Jews?" (Jn 18:33). To which Jesus replied: "My kingship is not of [*ek*] this world. If my kingship were of [*ek*] this world, my servants would fight, and I might not be handed over to the Jews; but," Jesus insists, "my kingdom is not from here [*enteuthen*]" (Jn 18:36). Nonetheless, Jesus let Pilate know in no uncertain terms that he was a king, explaining that this constituted his very identity and mission: "For this I was born, and for this I have come into the world, to bear witness to the truth. Every one who is of the truth hears my voice" (Jn 18:37).

Three elements emerge from these texts. *First*, that Jesus is a king, yet that his kingdom does not have its origin (*ek*) in any kind of human authority (what he calls "this world"). In saying that his "kingdom is not of this world," Jesus does not claim he has no authority of his own. Quite the contrary. He has authority, real authority, that finds its origin exclusively in the Father, not in humans. Thus in real terms he is subject to no one on earth. "Do you not believe that I am in the Father and the Father is in me? The words that I say to you I do not speak on my own authority, but the Father who dwells in me does these works" (Jn 14:10). Those who listened to Jesus were overwhelmed, "for he taught them as one who had authority [*exousia*], and not as their scribes" (Mt 7:29). This is why Jesus must be considered as Judge, as is made particularly clear in chapter 5 of John's Gospel.

The Father judges no one, but *has given all judgment to the Son*. . . . Truly, truly, I say to you, he who hears my word and believes him who sent me has eternal life; he does not come into judgment, but has passed from death to life. Truly, truly, I say to you, the hour is coming, and now is, when the dead will hear the voice of the Son of God, and those

---

57. *CAA* 187–231, especially 226–30, on the notion that Christ gave his life as a ransom for many (Mt 20:28).

who hear will live. For as the Father has life in himself, so he has granted the Son also to have life in himself, and *has given him authority to execute judgment,* because he is the Son of man. Do not marvel at this; for the hour is coming when all who are in the tombs will hear his voice and come forth, those who have done good, to the resurrection of life, and those who have done evil, to the resurrection of judgment. I can do nothing on my own authority, as I hear, I judge; and my judgment is just, *because I seek not to do my own will but the will of him who sent me.* (Jn 5:22,24–30).

Jesus' power to judge derives ultimately from his divinity, from his union with the Father. However, this text also provides the key to understanding why Jesus was constituted Judge in his human condition, in that he does the will of his Father in all things, for "my food is to do the will of him who sent me" (Jn 4:34).

Secondly, the corollary that Jesus himself draws from the fact that his authority does not derive "from this world" is that, paradoxically, he seeks no form of human defense, violent or otherwise, to escape from the dramatic situation he finds himself in of his own will (Jn 10:17). In the presence of Pilate sinners unjustly accuse the One who will come publicly, in all justice, to judge them and the rest of humanity at the end of time.[58] This does not mean, of course, that his authority lacks force or relevance in human affairs. Quite the contrary. "The earth is the Lord's and all that is in it" (Ps 24:1). Jesus' Father could have sent twelve legions in his defense (Mt 26:53). His is an authority that is not "from" the world, but is certainly "over" the world. But he does not exercise it.

This brings us to the *third* point. Jesus' kingdom, received from the Father, we are told, is a kingdom of truth.[59] His whole life was a witness to truth, and those who are open to God (who are "of the truth," Jn 18:37) listen to the voice of Jesus, they recognize the good shepherd (Jn 10:4,8,14). By implication, those who are not prepared to repent, those who are not "of the truth" and do not pay attention to him, attempt, rather, to get rid of him, to judge him, that is, to condemn him, eventually to kill him (Jn 7:19), numbering him "with the transgressors" (Is 53:12). "Truth" is the standard according to which Jesus, having received all authority from his Father, will judge.[60]

Trinity, Judgment, and the Revelation of Truth

"Revelation" is the term commonly used to translate the Greek word *apokalypsis*. It is fair to say, therefore, that the apocalyptic *Parousia,* the glorious coming of Christ that brings about the resurrection of the dead and leads to the

---

58. Augustine, *De Civ. Dei XXII,* 27.
59. *Roman Missal,* preface of Christ the King.
60. Benedict XVI (*SS* 44) notes that Plato in the *Gorgias,* 525a–526c speaks in a like way.

final judgment of humanity, is none other than the moment of supreme and definitive revelation. The term *apokalypsis*, though etymologically not eschatological, in real terms refers to the end-time. Christ is God's own Word, the One in whom the Father expresses himself perfectly and entirely, the One through whom he made the universe (Jn 1:3). And the Word incarnate constitutes God's definitive revelation to the created world, in particular to humans, although this will not be revealed until the end of time. First, saving revelation . . . and then eschatological revelation. First, Jesus as Savior . . . and then as Judge.

In effect, divine revelation becomes definitive when the glorious Christ openly confronts and judges the world he created and redeemed. The Father seeks the likeness to the risen Christ that each and every creature was meant to assume during its earthly pilgrimage. In this sense, rather than as a divine verdict extrinsic to humanity, it is probably more correct to consider final judgment as a definitive manifestation of humanity itself by the power of God.[61] This does not mean, as Peter Lombard suggested, that judgment will reveal all the sins of humanity, even those already forgiven.[62] Given the tenor of scriptural texts ("come, o blessed of my Father," "depart from me, you cursed," Mt 25:34,41), perhaps it may be said that judgment is the definitive manifestation of the truth of creation before its Creator, from which a perfectly just and unappealable verdict spontaneously arises.[63]

It should be noted, of course, that at the *Parousia* divine revelation will be communicated by the Word in the power of the Holy Spirit, who "searches everything, even the depths of God" (1 Cor 2:10).[64] "The Spirit is the One who applies, communicates and makes present the content of revelation and the saving power that derives entirely from the words and works of Jesus."[65] Jesus, himself the Way, the Truth, and the Life (Jn 14:6), tells us in John's Gospel that "When the Spirit of truth comes, *he will guide you into the whole truth*. He will glorify me, for he will take what is mine and declare it to you" (Jn 16:13–14). In the words of Gregory of Nyssa, the Spirit of God is the one who "accompanies the Word and reveals its efficacy."[66] Thomas Aquinas said it as follows: "The Son gave us doc-

---

61. Thus J. Ratzinger: "Judgment lies in the fall of the mask that death involves. Judgment is simply truth itself, its revelation. This truth of course is not something neutral. The truth that judges man has appeared to save him," *Eschatology*, 206.

62. Peter Lombard, *IV Sent.*, D. 43, a. 2.

63. J. J. Alviar describes scriptural judgment motifs in three stages: retribution, discrimination, and revelation: *Escatología*, 198–201.

64. Pannenberg explains that judgment is the work of the Holy Spirit, as is the glorification of God by humans, and of humans by God: *Systematic Theology*, vol. 3, 622–26. On the Holy Spirit and eschatology, *CAA* 257–98.

65. *CAA* 273.   66. Gregory of Nyssa, *Orat. Catech.*, 5:29.

trine, since he is the Word; but the Holy Spirit has made us capable of receiving his doctrine."[67] And for M.-J. Le Guillou, "the Spirit is the one who interiorizes in Christians the knowledge of the mystery of Christ."[68] That is to say, judgment is a Trinitarian event: God judges by the Word in the power of the Holy Spirit.[69]

"Nothing is covered up that will not be revealed," says Luke's Gospel, "or hidden that will not be known. Therefore whatever you have said in the dark shall be heard in the light, and what you have whispered in private rooms shall be proclaimed upon the housetops" (Lk 12:2–3). And in the *Catechism of the Catholic Church*, we read:

> The Last Judgment will come when Christ returns in glory. Only the Father knows the day and hour; only he determines the moment of its coming. Then, through his Son Jesus Christ, he will pronounce the final word on all history. We shall know the ultimate meaning of the whole work of creation and of the entire economy of salvation, and understand the marvelous ways by which his Providence led everything towards its final end. The Last Judgment will reveal that God's justice triumphs over all the injustices committed by his creatures and that God's love is stronger than death.[70]

"The question of justice constitutes the essential argument, or in any case the strongest argument, in favor of faith in eternal life," Benedict XVI concludes when speaking of final judgment.[71]

The Humanity of Christ's Judgment

The fact that God has given all power of judgment to his Son Jesus Christ is a simple consequence of the fact that Jesus is God's own Word-Son incarnate, whose Lordship over creation was manifested at the resurrection and will shine forth once and for all when he comes in glory. That Christ would be the judge is appropriate for many reasons, among them three that refer—for want of a better word—to the "humanity" of final judgment. They correspond to the three aspects of God's role as Judge mentioned above: God who justifies and acts justly; God who knows the human heart; God who sets the standard for judgment.[72]

The *first* reason why it is fitting for Christ to be Judge is that the One who will judge humanity is the one who at the cost of his own life offered humanity, in the most human way possible, the precious gift of salvation, which some may accept and others reject.[73] The One who justifies will eventually impart judgment. The

---

67. Thomas Aquinas, *In Ioann. Ev.* 14, l. 6 (on Jn 14:26).
68. M.-J. Le Guillou, "Le développement de la doctrine sur l'Esprit Saint," 734.
69. See G. Gozzelino, *Nell'attesa*, 319.
70. *CCC* 1040. Robert Bellarmine in his work *De arte bene moriendi* offers a wide variety reasons for universal judgment: see G. Ancona, *Escatologia cristiana*, 213.
71. *SS* 43. 72. See pp. 138–40.
73. *CAA* 227–31.

One who offered mercy, will then establish justice: the purpose of mercy is to bring about justice, just as the purpose of justice is to ensure that mercy is not meaningless or squandered.

In the *second* place, Jesus knows the human condition perfectly well. He was One "like us in all things but sin" (Heb 4:15); John tells us that Jesus "himself knew what was in man" (Jn 2:25). Not only does Jesus know humans, what is to be found in the mind and heart of each one. Above all, he loves them with an impassioned, merciful, and patient love that brings him to do everything he possibly can to save them, for "he will *not break a bruised reed or quench a smoldering wick*, till he brings justice to victory, and in his name will the Gentiles hope" (Mt 12:20–21).

And *thirdly*, if judgment is understood as the definitive manifestation of the entire created world (and in particular of humanity) before God, then it might be said that resurrection, which is as it were the extension of Christ's resurrection to humanity, may virtually be identified with judgment. Risen humanity will show forth, in all its richness and variety, the ethical and spiritual history of each and every human person, the influence of their actions on others, the unrepeatable character of their lives.[74] God indeed is the one who establishes the standard according to which humans are judged; but that standard, the concrete, living standard, is Jesus Christ in person. Yet Jesus' own standard is that of being the perfect Son; for this reason he exhorts his followers to live holy lives as children of God, that is to "be perfect, as your heavenly Father is perfect" (Mt 5:48). Even more: judgment will constitute the final revelation of God's wisdom before the whole of creation.[75]

The Presence and Role of Angels and Saints in Judgment

On several occasions, Scripture speaks of the angels and saints who will accompany Christ when he returns in glory. "When the Son of man comes in his glory, and *all the angels with him*, then he will sit on his glorious throne" (Mt 25:31). And earlier: "Truly, I say to you, in the new world, when the Son of man shall sit on his glorious throne, *you who have followed me* will also sit on twelve thrones, judging the twelve tribes of Israel" (Mt 19:28). Paul, when writing to Corinthian believers and warning them not to denounce one another before the secular courts, states categorically: "Do you not know that *the saints will judge* the world? And if the world is to be judged by you, are you incompetent to try trivial cases?

---

74. See pp. 109–12.

75. On the notion of "wisdom eschatology," especially in Augustine and Aquinas, see M. L. Lamb, "The Eschatology of St. Thomas Aquinas," and "Wisdom Eschatology in Augustine and Aquinas," in *Aquinas the Augustinian*, ed. M. Dauphinais, B. David, and M. W. Levering (Washington, D.C.: The Catholic University of America Press, 2007), 258–75.

Do you not know that we are to judge angels?" (1 Cor 6:2–3). And elsewhere: "The spiritual man judges all things, but is himself judged by no one" (1 Cor 2:15).

If Christ is the only Judge, as God's Son-Word made man, what kind of supplementary role could be played by the angels and the saints? In what way can it be said that they judge humans? If it is kept in mind that judgment is primarily manifestation rather than verdict, it should be clear that the angels and saints, redeemed by Christ, and perfectly conformed to him according to the personal vocation of each one, do not judge as such, but serve as divine standards, living points of reference to what it means to give glory to God, to do the will of the Father, to be like Christ. Since Christ himself lives and acts in his followers (Gal 2:20) they are meant to be and to live as "other Christs," as "Christ himself," to use the terminology of St. Josemaría Escrivá.[76] The living presence of the angels and saints with Christ will constitute a silent and powerful judgment on a world that did not glorify the Father, that did not accept the word of God and do his will, a world in which truth was not to be found. Their lives ipso facto serve both to accuse sinners of not achieving the conformity to Christ they could have obtained and to confirm their verdict. Partaking in the holiness and justice of Christ, therefore, they partake, albeit indirectly, in his role as judge.

Besides, judgment constitutes a moment of glorification of the Father through Christ in the Spirit. "When grace has united men and angels," Gregory of Nyssa says, "they will all sing out the same hymn of praise."[77] Likewise Hillary of Poitiers: "The reason why the angels await is the beatitude of humans. . . . They desire to see the Gospel promises fulfilled: and once this promise has been effected, they are called to give glory with us for the gift of beatitude."[78] Again Gregory: "the joy of the angels will be great when they see the unity of spiritual creation reconstituted anew."[79]

Scripture refers on some occasions to the location of judgment. The book of Joel, in a text already cited, speaks for example of "the valley of Jehoshaphat," where God "will gather all the nations . . . and . . . enter into judgment with them there. . . . Let the nations arouse themselves, and come up to the valley of Jehoshaphat; for there I will sit to judge all the neighboring nations" (Jl 4:2,12).

That interest in the physical location of final judgment would arise is understandable given the realism of the doctrine of resurrection and cosmic renewal as Scripture presents it, as well as the universality of judgment. In fact many Moslems and Jews as well as some Christians believe that final judgment will

---

76. See my study "The Inseparability of Holiness and Apostolate."
77. Gregory of Nyssa, *Hom. in Ps.*, 9.
78. Cit. by J. Daniélou, *Les anges et leur mission d'après les Pères de l'Église* (Paris: Desclée, 1951), 152.
79. Ibid., 153.

truly take place in "the valley of Jehoshaphat." However, the term "Jehoshaphat" literally means "God judges." Elsewhere, the prophet Joel calls it the "valley of decision" (Jl 4:14). Only in the fourth century AD did the so-called valley of Jehoshaphat come to be identified with the valley of Kidron, to the south-east of the Temple esplanade in Jerusalem.[80] Besides, if we keep in mind that the *Parousia* involves principally a new, deeper relationship of Christ with the entire cosmos, on the basis both of the original creative relationship between him and the universe and of his work of redemption,[81] then there is no danger of denying the realism of judgment by not speaking of a physical place of judgment.

Judgment and Hope

The last question: may final judgment be considered an object of Christian hope? Clearly, it may. Traditionally, however, such an affirmation might seem hazardous, for the promise of judgment is normally looked upon as a source of fear, not of hope.[82] Yet Pope Benedict XVI in his encyclical *Spe salvi* explains that "faith in the Last Judgment is first and foremost hope."[83]

It is probably true to say that Christians for the most part do not pray for the coming of judgment. Nonetheless, crying out to Christ for definitive judgment is no different than crying out to God for perfect justice, a justice that humanity seems unable to provide for itself, at least in a lasting way. The desire for justice (Mt 5:6) and the desire for judgment have much in common. In fact, the book of Revelation speaks of the desire Christians have for judgment, because it will mark the definitive triumph of justice, the final defeat of the devil.

This can be seen *first* in the prayer of Christian martyrs for justice. "When he [the Lamb] opened the fifth seal," we read in the book of Revelation, "I saw under the altar the souls of those who had been slain for the word of God and for the witness they had borne. They cried with a loud voice, 'O Sovereign Lord, holy and true, how long before you will judge and avenge our blood on those who dwell upon the earth?'" (Rv 6:9–10). *Second*, judgment may be seen as the definitive defeat of the devil. "And I heard a loud voice in heaven saying, 'Now the salvation and the power and the kingdom of our God and the authority of his Christ have come, for the accuser of our brothers [the "accuser," *satanas*, is John's way of designating the devil, Rv 12:9] has been thrown down, who accuses them day and night before our God'" (Rv 12:10).

---

80. Thus in the *Onomasticon* of Eusebius and in Jerome's *Commentary on Joel*.
81. See pp. 72–73.
82. On judgment as an object of fear or hope, see A. M. Sicari, "Il giudizio e il suo esito," *Communio* (Ed. italiana) 13 (1985): 8–13. On judgment in the history of art, see A. M. Cocagnac, *Le jugement dernier dans l'art*.
83. *SS* 43.

As we saw above, final judgment in real terms is the final manifestation, the definitive unveiling of the whole truth. For the just it will constitute a moment of intense expectation, joy, and wonderment, "for there is nothing hid, except to be made manifest; nor is anything secret, except to come to light" (Mk 4:22). And the just do not fear this moment of truth, for as John says, "he who believes in him [Christ] is not judged; he who does not believe is judged [*krinetai*, "condemned"] already" (Jn 3:18). In the words of Gozzelino, divine judgment must be "hoped for, desired, invoked and then received . . . with a joy and recognition due to the appreciation of the absolute value of the absolute future."[84]

"The resurrection of the body will take place at the end of time," Augustine says, "and, through final judgment, will introduce some into the second death, others into that life where there is no death."[85] Resurrection of the dead and renewal of the cosmos; then final judgment; and then the definitive separation of just and unjust. We shall examine the latter in the coming two chapters.

84. G. Gozzelino, *Nell'attesa*, 369.
85. Augustine, *De Civ. Dei XXII*, 6:2.

6

Heaven: Eternal Life in the Glory of Christ

Deus . . . : duae istae syllabae sunt totum quod expectamus.
—*Augustine*[1]

Something friendly from afar must be close to me.
—*Friedrich Hölderlin*[2]

My hopes touch upon the infinite.
—*Theresa of Lisieux*[3]

The outcome of final judgment is unequivocal: eternal life or eternal perdition. The promise made by God through his Son is equally clear: those who follow and believe in him receive the promise of eternal communion with the Trinity; those who do not believe will forfeit the divine promise. And the very cause of Christianity holds or falls on the hope provided by this promise.

In the Christian lexicon, several equivalent terms may be used to designate the same reality of the afterlife.[4] Perhaps the most popular term is simply "heaven" (Greek, *ouranos*), which indicates intuitively the transcendence and divinity of the final state, the contrast between sun (which provides heat, light, life, divinity) and earth (suggesting cold, darkness, dust, death), between justice and guilt, between light and darkness, between infinitude and finitude, between openness and constraint, between activity and passivity. "Heaven," besides, is where Christ lives (Jn 17:5), and has gone to prepare a place for his disciples (Jn 14:2–3; 2 Cor 5:1). There the angels contemplate God (Mt 18:10); heaven is the treasure-house of the just (Mk 10:21).

Another term is "beatific vision," which speaks of the inner reality of heaven

---

1. Augustine, *In Ep. I Jo.*, 4:6. 2. F. Hölderlin, *Menon's Lament for Diotima*.
3. Theresa of Lisieux, *Œuvres complètes*, 224.
4. On different images and descriptions of eternal paradise, see for example F. J. Nocke, *Eschatologie*, 135–41. Several recent works have dealt with the reality of heaven and paradise in art, literature, history, for example: C. McDannell and B. Lang, *Heaven: A History* (New Haven: Yale University Press, 1988); J. B. Russell, *A History of Heaven: The Singing Silence* (Princeton, N.J.: Princeton University Press, 1997); J. Delumeau, *Une histoire du paradis*, 2nd ed., 3 vols. (Paris: Hachette Littératures, 2002–3); A. E. McGrath, *A Brief History of Heaven* (Oxford: Blackwell, 2003).

as a contemplation of God that produces definitive fulfillment for humans (1 Cor 13:12; 1 Jn 3:1–2); for some authors the vision of God constitutes the true essence of eternal life.[5] In the third place, there is "communion" with God, which expresses the loving bond with the Divinity, the One and Triune God, a union that does not eliminate the human subject but brings it to ultimate fulfillment. Then, "perpetual happiness," which indicates in an anthropological way the fullness and permanence that derives for man from union with God.[6] Fifth, "paradise" (in Greek *paradeisos*, from the Persian term *pairidaēza*, meaning "closed garden"), which evokes the more material and bodily aspect of human fulfillment (Gn 2:10–14; Is 65:17–25; Rv 2:7; 22:2–5).[7]

In addition, Scripture often refers to the afterlife with the term "glory" (in Greek, *doxa*), an expression that denotes honor, riches, power, influence. Of course, glory is principally a divine attribute that God shares with no other (Is 42:8; 48:11). It is God's very name (Ps 66:2; 79:9). God's glory, besides, is revealed in natural phenomena (Ex 24:15–18; 33:18–19; Ez 1:4). In that sense to "give God glory" is simply to recognize his majesty (Acts 12:23; Rom 4:20). But God's glory is present and has been revealed in Christ (Jn 1:14; 11:4,40). Believers are promised the eschatological contemplation of this glory (1 Cor 13:12) and a direct partaking in the glory of Christ (Jn 17:22; Rom 8:17–18; Phil 3:21).

Finally, the term "eternal life" (Greek, *zōē aiōnia*) provides perhaps the most accurate and complete definition of the afterlife from the biblical and theological standpoint, being especially frequent in John's Gospel and letters.[8] The God of the Bible is the God "of the living" (Mk 12:27), the God who gives life through his Son (Jn 5:21,26), bringing believers to share in this life. At one level the term "life" suggests dynamism, activity, fullness, interiority, autonomy, permanence, happiness, and so on. But at another, deeper level, it involves a sharing in God's intimate life, for God is the only source of life, and God alone is eternal. In that sense the gift of "eternal life" is equivalent simply to the fullness of life that comes from God, the gift of God himself. "Eternal life" is the root, cause, and summary expression of all the rewards that God has destined for those who believe in him: of heaven, of vision, of communion, of happiness, of paradise, of glory.

Alongside the doctrine of final resurrection, the Nicea-Constantinople Creed

---

5. This is particularly so in Thomas Aquinas, who situates his study of beatific vision at the beginning of his treatise on moral law and grace: *S. Th. I-II*, q. 3, a. 8.

6. See G. Gozzelino, *Nell'attesa*, 348–49.

7. See pp. 119–20.

8. It also may be found in New Testament books besides John: Mt 19:16,29; 25:46 and par.; Lk 18:30; Acts 13:46,48; Rom 2:7; 5:21; 6:22–23; Gal 6:8; 1 Tm 1:16; 6:12; Ti 1:2; 3:7; Jude 1:21. On "life" in the New Testament, see H.-G. Link, "Life," in *NIDNTT* 2, 476–83, especially 482–83.

proclaims that we "await the life of the world to come."[9] The same creed professes that the kingdom of Christ "will have no end."[10] The Apostles' Creed simply professes belief "in eternal life."[11] The Bangor Antiphonary Creed (eighth century) contains the following rich profession of faith, which provides the title for this chapter: "I believe in life after death and eternal life in the glory of Christ."[12] Finally, in Benedict XII's constitution *Benedictus Deus* (1336), we read that the just in heaven "are truly blessed and have eternal life and rest."[13] It is worthwhile noting that in all cases the doctrine on eternal life is set in the context of the third part of the creed, dealing with the Person and action of the Holy Spirit. Above, on several occasions, we have referred to the pneumatological side of eschatology. The question will also arise in this chapter.

Lumen gentium sums up Christian doctrine on eternal life in the following terms: "Christ lifted up from the earth, has drawn all men to himself.... Rising from the dead he sent his life-giving Spirit upon the disciples and through him set up his Body which is the Church as the universal sacrament of salvation. Sitting at the right hand of the Father he is continually active in the world.... By nourishing them with his own Body and Blood, he makes them [believers] partakers of his glorious life."[14] "United with Christ in the Church and marked with the Holy Spirit ... we are truly called and indeed are children of God ... though we have not yet appeared with Christ in glory ... in which we will be like God, for we shall see him as he is."[15] In heaven, the same document continues, the just will be "in glory, contemplating 'in full light, God himself triune and one, exactly as he is.'"[16]

We shall study the topic of eternal life as follows. First, we shall consider eternal life in Scripture. Then we shall examine the patristic understanding of eternal life in terms of the definitive "divinization" of the Christian. This will be followed by a consideration of the relationship between eternal life and beatific vision, which was well developed by medieval authors. After this, we shall consider some of the anthropological outworkings of eternal life: the perpetual character of "eternal life" and its consequences for a proper understanding of human freedom; the social and interpersonal quality of eternal life; the place of progress, temporality, and resurrection within eternal life. The last section of the chapter

---

9. *DS* 150.   10. Ibid.
11. *DS* 10.
12. *DS* 29. The Bangor Antiphonary Creed is a well-developed form of the Apostles' Creed dating from the late eighth century in Ireland. On this document, see my study "The Bangor Antiphonary Creed: Origins and Theology," *Annales Theologici* 6 (1992): 255–87, especially 282–83.
13. *DS* 1000.   14. *LG* 48b.
15. Ibid., 48d.
16. Ibid., 49a, citing the Council of Florence, *Decretum pro Graecis*, *DS* 1305.

will deal with, among other issues, the grades of eternal life and glory, and the role played in them by Christ and the Spirit.

Eternal Life in Scripture

We have already seen that Scripture presents Yahweh as the *God of the living*, the God who gives life.[17] In comparison with the dead and impotent gods of the pagans (1 Kgs 18:20–39)—the same could be said with idols of all kinds, past and present—*God imparts life* to the whole of creation, he renews it constantly, and he brings his gift to fullness by offering humanity the opportunity of sharing in his very own life.

Whereas in the Old Testament God is said to give "life" in general, the New speaks specifically of the gift of "eternal" life. This constitutes a significant novelty from the theological standpoint, for the term "eternal" (*aionios*), strictly speaking, may be attributed to God alone.[18] If life in general is always a gift of God, "eternal life" is a singular one, for it involves a gift that brings those who receive it to share permanently in God's own life, living as sons and not as slaves.

The notion of eternal life is developed especially in John's Gospel,[19] where Jesus describes it as a mysterious reality that already exists and acts and lives within the believer, yet that is open to eternal consummation. The following aspects of John's doctrine may be noted.

First, if God is the source and fountain of life in the Old Testament, for "the Father has life in himself" (Jn 5:26), in the New "he has granted the Son also to have life in himself" (ibid.). "God gave us eternal life, and this life is in his Son" (1 Jn 5:11). In the Word "was life and that life was the light of men" (Jn 1:4). Through faith (Jn 1:12) and baptism (Jn 3:5) we become children of God in Christ and partake in this new life. In other words, eternal life is linked directly to our union with Jesus Christ in faith.

In the *second* place, perhaps the most remarkable feature of John's doctrine on eternal life is that it is obtained by those who in the present moment believe. Jesus teaches this solemnly and on repeated occasions. "Truly, truly, I say to you, he who hears my word and believes him who sent me *has eternal life;* he does not come to judgment but has passed from death to life" (Jn 5:24). "Truly, truly, I say to you, he who believes *has* eternal life" (Jn 6:47). And in the negative: "anyone who hates his brother is a murderer, and you know that no murderer has eternal

---

17. See pp. 82–83.
18. See J. Schneider, "God," in *NIDNTT* 2, 70–82, especially 77–78.
19. See F. Mussner, *"Zōe." Die Anschauung vom "Leben" im vierten Evangelium unter Berücksichtigung der Johannesbriefe. Ein Beitrag zur biblischen Theologie* (München: K. Zink, 1952); C. Pozo, *La teología del más allá*, 382–84.

life abiding in him" (1 Jn 3:15). "He who has the Son has life; he who has not the Son has not life" (1 Jn 5:12).[20] This new life is real in the believer, though hidden like a seed, growing gradually until it reaches fullness (1 Jn 3:9).

Third, John distinguishes two ways in which God gives life in an eschatological context: as eternal life for those who believe in the present moment, and as resurrection of all that will take place at the end of time. "He who eats my flesh and drinks my blood *has* eternal life, and *I will raise him up* on the last day" (Jn 6:54). In other words, though deriving from the oneness of the Divine Source of life, eternal life and resurrection are yet distinct from one another, the one belonging to the invisible presence of faith, the other to the tangible future of corporal fullness.

What Does Eternal Life and Glory Consist of?

Given that eternal life involves a mysterious participation in divine life, believers often experience difficulty in imagining what it will actually consist of. Scripture confirms this, telling us that "no eye has seen, nor ear heard, nor the heart of man conceived, what God has prepared for those who love him" (1 Cor 2:9; cf. Is 64:3). Still, the following reflection may be helpful.

The Apparent Futility of Human Desire for Plenitude

All humans desire a fullness of happiness and satisfaction. Their hope points toward the infinite, toward the eternal.[21] However, many people doubt whether or not the "eternal life" promised by God to those who believe in his Son is capable of providing such happiness and fulfillment. And the point is a critical one. On the basis of this promise of perfect happiness and total fulfillment, Christ required of his followers a real capacity for sacrifice, an all-embracing missionary spirit, a sincere disposition to give one's life even to the point of accepting martyrdom. "And every one who has left houses or brothers or sisters or mother or children or lands, for my name's sake," Matthew tells us, "will receive a hundredfold, *and inherit eternal life*" (Mt 19:29). It cannot be denied that the hope of eternal life has consistently been the true motor of the lives of the saints.[22] Still, many people nowadays spontaneously call into question the fact of its existence and the validity of its motivating power.

Pope Benedict XVI in his encyclical *Spe salvi* openly asks the following question: "Do we really want this—to live eternally? Perhaps many people reject the

---

20. Other texts include: Jn 3:36; 6:54; 1 Jn 2:25; 5:20.
21. See pp. 11–13.
22. We have already cited the text of Ignatius of Antioch, *Ad Rom.*, 6:2–3.

faith today simply because they do not find the prospect of eternal life attractive. What they desire is not eternal life at all, but this present life, for which faith in eternal life seems something of an impediment. To continue living for ever—endlessly—appears more like a curse than a gift. . . . To live always, without end—this, all things considered, can only be monotonous and ultimately unbearable."[23]

It is not uncommon for authors to think that the prospect of "eternal life" would involve a kind of perpetual and uninterrupted boredom.[24] Such a life would hold little attraction for humans, and can hardly be the object of impassioned desire or the source of indefatigable apostolic zeal, as was the case for example with Theresa of Avila.[25] The possibility that eternal life might turn out to be a life of perpetual boredom has been described in a graphic though somewhat irreverent manner by the existentialist author Miguel de Unamuno:

> A beatific vision, a loving contemplation in which the soul is absorbed in God, and lost, as it were, in him, is perceived either as a real annihilation, or as a prolonged form of boredom for our usual way of feeling. This conviction occasions that sentiment we have often heard expressed, with satire, irreverence or impiety, to the effect that a heaven of eternal glory will be an abode of eternal boredom. And there is no point in despising these sentiments, so spontaneous and natural, or of ridiculing them.[26]

Some classical figures even seem to prefer the (imagined) mobility and excitement of hell, populated by a multitude of interesting personalities.[27] How meaningful can hope be when the future prospect of human life is of this kind?

The term "life" suggests activity, movement, dynamism, whereas "eternity" evokes the notion of rest, peace, tranquility, permanence, that is, inactivity. During our earthly pilgrimage both activity and rest, movement and permanence, are woven inextricably into every aspect of existence. On the one hand, activity

---

23. *SS* 10.
24. On the possible boredom associated with "eternal life," see M.-J. Le Guillou, *Qui ose encore parler de bonheur?* (Paris: Mame, 1998), who refers to R. Le Senne, A. Gide, S. de Beauvoir, H. de Montherlant. See also A. Frossard, *Dieu en questions* (Paris: Desclée de Brouwer, 1990), 195–96, who speaks of the fear Descartes had of getting bored contemplating God for 10,000 years. Frossard comments cryptically that Descartes "did not have the clear and distinct idea that perhaps God might get bored much more quickly of contemplating Descartes," ibid., 196. The same objections may be found in M. Vernet, *L'ateismo moderno* (Roma: Ed. Riuniti, 1963), 197. The Spanish agnostic E. Tierno Galván stated: "There is nothing that more contradicts the human being and his essential finitude than the afterlife or another life" ¿*Qué es ser agnóstico?* 4th ed. (Madrid: Tecnos, 1986), 85.
25. Theresa of Avila, *Libro de la Vida I*, 1:5.
26. M. de Unamuno, *El sentimiento trágico de la vida*, § 10, in *Ensayos*, vol. 2 (Madrid: Aguilar, 1945), 915.
27. See the French medieval romance *Aucassin et Nicolette*, in C. McDannell and B. Lang, *Heaven: A History*, 100–101.

easily occasions tiredness and exhaustion, and moves one to seek peace and repose. On the other, rest induces boredom and weakness, which one seeks to overcome through activity and movement. Common human experience shows us that full activity and complete repose are difficult to reconcile with one another; at best they relate to each other in a dialectical way. The woman Jesus encountered at Jacob's well in Samaria expressed this when she asked the Lord to give her the water he had spoken of, "that I may not thirst, nor come here to draw" (Jn 4:15). Jesus was fully aware, of course, that all those who drink of the water of the well "will thirst again" (Jn 4:13).

Possible Solutions to the Dilemma

Throughout the history of philosophy and religion, different solutions have been devised to account for the human desire for perfect happiness and fulfillment, in which both human activity and rest are harmonized and integrated.

Eastern religious forms commonly consider that after death humans will encounter perfect tranquility and peace, as long as all forms of autonomous consciousness and activity cease.[28] In a sense, humans must disappear in order to be happy; the price to pay for happiness is that of individual existence and autonomy. From the Hindu teaching contained in the so-called *Upanishad*, the human soul is said to be destined for dissolution, to be fused with the Brahman. "Just as a grain of salt cast into water dissolves and cannot be found again, but rather the water becomes salted and the salt is present everywhere, so also the One, the Infinite, the Limitless, the All-spiritual."[29] In Buddhist thought, which does not as such speak of an afterlife, individual striving and activity is considered the true cause of pain and suffering, of alienation in general. Growth is achieved when the passions are eliminated; fulfillment, when life is quenched (this is usually called the *Nirvāna*). In simplistic terms, it may be said that salvation in Eastern religions involves the elimination of activity and individual consciousness, and the perpetuation of rest and immobility. It may be eternal or permanent, it may even be better than worldly existence, but it can hardly be described as "life."

At the opposite extreme is to be found the position, typical of some Enlightenment philosophers, especially Johann G. Fichte, affirming that human happiness consists exclusively of movement, activity, full individual awareness, since, they argue, "life" is not the capacity for movement, but is movement itself.[30]

28. See W. Rahula, *What the Buddha Taught* (London: G. Fraser, 1978).
29. *Brihad-Aranyaka-Upanishad* 2:4,12–13. "Truly the Brahman is happiness and the one who admits it becomes the happy Brahman," ibid., 4:4,25.
30. J. Fichte, "Anweisung zum seligen Leben, 6. Vorlesung," in *Sämtliche Werke II* (Berlin: W. de Gruyter, 1965), 299.

Both understandings, despite their obvious differences, have one thing in common: humans are responsible for making themselves happy with their own resources and activities, whether through the accumulation of good works (*karma*), or through their autonomous and creative activity. Friedrich Nietzsche had a similar view of human fulfillment and happiness, which he expressed with his customary incisiveness and clarity. "Only one thing is necessary," he said in *Gay Science*, and it is that "man would acquire fulfillment on his own and with himself, whether by poetry, or by art . . ."[31] In brief, humans are entirely responsible for their own self-realization and happiness. Yet Christian faith focuses eternal happiness in a very different way.

Eternal Life and Divinization

The Fathers of the Church, especially in the East, explained the life of Christ in Christians in terms of "divinization," *theosis*, that is, humans being transformed into gods.[32] It may be held that the two terms—eternal life and divinization—are coextensive, if not equivalent, in that the former refers to the life of Christ in believers, whereas the latter is the fruit of the Incarnation of the Word in the created sphere. As we saw above, "eternal life" can mean only belonging to the life of God himself, who is eternal and glorious. Indeed eternal life, John tells us, is the fruit of a new birth (Jn 3:3), the birth of God in man. Irenaeus explains eternal life in terms of companionship with God and participation in his life. For him not only does vision derive from divinization, but participation in God's life comes from vision. "For God is the one who is yet to be seen, and the beholding of God produces immortality, but immortality renders one close to God."[33]

The gift of divinization, in all its realism, may help us understand the dynamics of eternal life. To say that believers are divinized does not simply mean they find themselves in the divine presence, a heavenly climate, a spiritual paradise, a peaceful haven. The happiness of heaven does not consist merely of being with God, "in the presence" of God, "in the company of" the Divinity. Rather, those

---

31. F. Nietzsche, "Fröhliche Wissenschaft," n. 290, in *Nietzsche Werke*, vol. 5/2 (Berlin: De Gruyter, 1973), 210–11. Emphasis added.

32. The question of divinization is considered in the context of eschatology by G. Ancona, *Escatologia cristiana*, 220–21. On divinization in general, see J. Gross, *La divinisation du chrétien d'après les pères grecs. Contribution historique à la doctrine de la grâce* (Paris: Lecoffre, 1938); G. Bardy, I. H. Dalmais, and E. Des Places, "Divinisation, I–III," in *Dictionnaire de Spiritualité*, vol. 3 (Paris: Beauchesne, 1957), cols. 1370–98; the introduction to J.-C. Larchet, *La divinisation de l'homme selon saint Maxime le Confesseur* (Paris: Cerf, 1996), 20–59.

33. Irenaeus, *Adv. Haer. IV*, 38:3. On beatific vision and divinization in Irenaeus, see M. Aubineau, "Incorruptibilité et divinisation selon saint Irénée," *Recherches de science religieuse* 44 (1956): 25–52; E. Lanne, "La vision de Dieu dans l'œuvre de saint Irénéee," *Irénikon* 33 (1960): 311–20; J. Arroniz, "La inmortalidad como deificación en S. Ireneo," *Scriptorium Victoriense* 8 (1961): 262–87.

who have received eternal life are fulfilled in heaven because God fulfills them, because God fills them with something of his own life, glory, and beatitude. To put it differently, should heaven not produce fulfillment and happiness, the fault would lie not so much with humans, but with God. By faith we know that God is *in se et ex se beatissimus*,[34] "in himself and of himself most blessed." Through faith and hope Christians trust in God's goodness and power, in his determination to communicate something of his own beatitude to humans. Those in love do not simply profess their conviction to the effect that "you will be happy with me"; their determination, rather, is that "I will make you happy." Thus it may be said that eternal life consists of "partaking in the limitless dynamism of the divine relations."[35] As we shall see later on, this does not mean that the saved forfeit their liberty in heaven.[36]

Scripture itself suggests this understanding of eternal life. Believers will not be disappointed in their hope, Paul tells us when writing to the Romans, "because God's love has been poured into our hearts through the Holy Spirit which has been given to us" (Rom 5:5). The Neo-Vulgate translates Jesus' words to the just in Matthew's Gospel as follows: *Intra in gaudium Domini tui:* "Well done, good and faithful servant; you have been faithful over a little, I will set you over much; *enter into the joy of your master*" (Mt 25:23). This is what eternal life entails: an eternal participation in God's own life, glory, and beatitude by grace.

Besides, as Benedict XVI points out in his encyclical on hope, the "eternity" of eternal life does not involve so much "an unending succession of days in the calendar," such as might sooner or later produce boredom, "but something more like the supreme moment of satisfaction, in which totality embraces us and we embrace totality. . . . It would be like plunging into the ocean of infinite love, a moment in which time—the before and the after—no longer exists. . . . A plunging ever new into the vastness of being, in which we are simply overwhelmed with joy."[37]

Heaven as Divine Praise, Activity, and Repose

What does the doctrine of divinization offer in understanding the dialectic mentioned above between life and rest, between activity and permanence? In the encounter of Jesus with the woman at the well of Jacob, already referred to, we read: "If you knew the gift of God, and who it is that is saying to you, 'give me a drink', you would have asked him, and he would have given you living water" (Jn 4:10). And Jesus goes on to explain: "Every one who drinks of this water

---

34. *DS* 3025.
35. B. Forte, *Teologia della storia* (Cinisello Balsamo: Paoline, 1991), 358.
36. See pp. 171–74.
37. *SS* 12.

will thirst again, but whoever drinks of the water that I shall give him will never thirst; the water that I shall give him will become in him a spring of water welling up to eternal life" (Jn 4:14–15). That is to say, the gift of divinizing grace produces in the blessed an eternal outpouring of praise and adoration, and as a result, a faultless integration between activity and repose in the human subject.

Ephrem the Syrian describes heaven as a "Paradise": the "tents" in which the just will dwell are the trees of the garden, each one offering shelter, fruit, and perfume, regaling each of the senses.[38] But at the center of the garden, Christ stands as the tree of life, illuminating Paradise with his radiance; all the other trees bow to him in homage.[39] The round of seasons will disappear, and the whole year will be blessed with flowers and fruit, refreshing breezes and delicious fragrances.[40]

Augustine pictures eternal life as "a holy and perpetual rest free of all fatigue and weight; yet it does not involve an inactive indolence, but an ineffable peace full of delightful activity. . . . It involves the praise of God, without effort of the members, without anxiety and concern; hence there is no succession of rest and work, and it cannot be said that activity begins as soon as rest ceases."[41] In heaven, he says, all our desires will be fulfilled, for "life, well-being, food, riches, glory, honor, peace and all good" will be found there.[42] He explains besides that our activity in heaven will not be impeded by the contemplation of God: "then we shall see best because we shall be supremely at leisure. When, after all, are we fully at leisure, except when these times of labor, these times of the hardships in which we are now ensnared, have passed? . . . We will be at leisure, then, and we will see God as he is, and when we see him we shall praise him. And this will be the life of the saints, the activity of those at rest: we shall praise without ceasing."[43] In heaven, he says, "all our activity will be 'Amen' and 'Alleluia.'"[44] According to many authors, divine praise will be the main activity of the blessed in glory.

Cyprian says that "as Christians we shall live with Christ in glory, we shall be blessed in God the Father, living in eternal joy before the face of God, full of continual joy and giving thanks to God forever. Because only the one who has fallen at death but has been lifted above all concerns to immortality, can be grateful forever."[45] Quodvultdeus of Carthage, a contemporary of Augustine, included among the promises God makes to the risen just "the perpetual singing of *Alleluia* by the saints."[46] Likewise the Monophysite Severus of Antioch says: "And this

---

38. Ephrem, *Hymns on Paradise*, 9:3–6; 7:16,18. See B. E. Daley, *The Hope*, 75–76.
39. Ephrem, *Hymns on Paradise*, 3:2,15.   40. Ibid., 9:7–17; 10:2–4,6–9; 11:9–15.
41. Augustine, *Ep. 55 ad Iannerion*, 9:17.   42. Augustine, *De Civ. Dei XXII*, 30:1.
43. Augustine, *Sermo 362*, 30–31.   44. Ibid., 28–29.
45. Cyprian, *Ad Demetr.*, 26.
46. Quodvultdeus, *Liber de Promissionibus*, 31. This work has traditionally been attributed to Prosper of Aquitaine, but almost certainly belongs to Quodvultdeus. See R. Braun in *Sources chrétiennes*, n. 101 (Paris: Cerf, 1964), 88–103.

... is the food of those who are about to live the awaited life: continual songs of praise and the sublime contemplation on which the angels also feed, and joy and inexplicable exaltation, in a life that does not end."[47] According to Caesarius of Arles, in heaven there will be no need for food or sleep, there will be no envy (despite the different grades of glory of each one), no further possibility of committing sin. The just will be perfectly happy, and will "never tire of giving thanks" for their eternal inheritance.[48] Commenting on the book of Revelations, Andrew, a sixth-century bishop of Caesarea, says the just will be like the angels, joining in their praise of the Triune God, although this sharing in angelic life "exceeds all understanding."[49]

In the Assyrian-Babylonian myth of *Gilgamesh* (third millennium BC) we read: "Gilgamesh, where are you going, where do you wander? The life you seek you will never find it! For when the gods created man they gave him death, but life they kept for themselves."[50] This vision is quite in keeping with revealed doctrine: in the created order, humans are simply incapable of providing fulfillment, life, and perpetual peace for themselves. Only "the gods" are in a position to do so. And humans can obtain this life only by the divinizing gift of eternal life, for which they are freely moved to praise God eternally. Thus the prayer of Augustine, deeply rooted in the classical tradition and in Christian faith: "Our hearts will not rest until they rest in you."[51] Eternal life, he argues, gives humans a vitality far in excess of anything possible on earth, with perfect self-possession, without distraction, or ponderousness of spirit, or reluctance of will, without hesitation or laziness.[52]

Praising God and Being Praised by God, the Joy of the Blessed

"Overwhelmed with joy," Benedict XVI says in the text cited above from *Spe salvi*. Likewise, C. S. Lewis argues that Matthew's "well done, good and faithful servant, enter into the joy of your Lord" (Mt 25:23) perfectly expresses the essence of the joy of heaven. He says that the just, upon hearing these words being pronounced for them in person by God himself, will be filled with the kind of exquisite joy a child experiences when being praised by its superiors.[53] And of

---

47. Severus of Antioch, *Epist.* 96.
48. Caesarius of Arles, *Sermo 58*, 4. See B. E. Daley, *The Hope*, 208–9.
49. Andrew of Caesarea, *Comm. in Apoc.*, 203:11–12; 205:18.
50. On this epic, see S. N. Kraner, *Ancient Near Eastern Texts Relating to the Old Testament* (Princeton, N.J.: Princeton University Press, 1950), 106–8. See also L. Moraldi, *L'alidlà dell'uomo*, 18–20.
51. Augustine, *Conf. I*, 1:1.
52. See M. Schmaus, *Katholische Dogmatik*, vol. 4.2: *Von den letzten Dingen*, 675–81. See Ambrose, *In Luc.*, 10:121.
53. C. S. Lewis in his essay "The Weight of Glory," in *Screwtape Proposes a Toast and Other Pieces* (London: Collins, 1965), 94–110, expresses the essence of heaven as follows: "'Well done, good and faith-

course all true believers are meant to be childlike in spirit; for otherwise they will "not enter into the kingdom of heaven" (Mt 18:3). The just will rejoice in a special way at God being definitively glorified and "justified" in the eyes of creation.[54]

Tertullian suggested that the joy of the blessed will also be motivated by the spectacle of divine retribution of the unjust.[55] Likewise Peter Lombard speaks of the joy and satisfaction the just experience at the condemnation of sinners.[56] Some authors have suggested that the just rejoice at seeing God's justice being carried out, also in respect of the condemnation of their own friends and relatives.[57] However, this affirmation is not easily justifiable, because the charity that fills their hearts is incompatible with any kind of envy or vindictiveness. Thomas Aquinas holds simply that the just, being perfectly identified with the divine will, are not saddened by the punishments divine justice inflicts on the condemned.[58]

The "Eternity" of Heaven

As we have seen above, eschatological communion with God is presented throughout Scripture as perpetual, truly without end. Since this communion is with God, and is the fruit of God's divinizing grace, the term "eternal" is more exact than "perpetual," insofar as the just not only will enjoy divine life forever, but will directly partake in God's own life and eternity. The liturgy of the Church uses an equivalent, reduplicative, term in many of its prayers when speaking of divine life and the eternal reward that lasts "for ever and ever."[59] Other scriptural texts speak clearly besides of the permanence of God's gift. Matthew describes the eschatological reward in terms of "eternal life" (Mt 19:16,29; 25:46); Luke refers to

---

ful servant.' With that, a good deal of what I had been thinking all my life fell down like a house of cards. I suddenly remembered that no one can enter heaven except as a child; and nothing is so obvious in a child ... as its great and undisguised pleasure in being praised.... It is the most creaturely of pleasures, nay, the specific pleasure of the inferior: the pleasure of a beast before men, a child before its father, a pupil before his teacher, a creature before its Creator. I am not forgetting how horribly this most innocent desire is parodied in our human ambitions, or how very quickly, in my own experience, the lawful pleasure of praise from those whom it was my duty to please turns into the deadly poison of self-admiration. But I thought I could detect a moment—a very, very short moment—before this happened, during which the satisfaction of having pleased those whom I rightly loved and rightly feared was pure," 102–3.

54. See W. Pannenberg, *Systematic Theology*, vol. 3, 630–46, on the eschatological "justification of God by the Spirit."

55. Tertullian, *De Spect.*, 30.

56. Peter Lombard, *In IV Sent.*, D. 50, q. 2.

57. See A. Royo-Marín, *¿Se salvan todos?: estudio teológico sobre la voluntad salvífica universal de Dios* (Madrid: BAC, 1995), who puts forward an optimistic solution to the question of the salvation of humanity.

58. Thomas Aquinas, *S. Th. I*, q. 89, a. 8.

59. The formula is very common in the New Testament: Rom 11:36; 16:27; Gal 1:5; Eph 3:21; Phil 4:20; 1 Tm 1:17; 2 Tm 4:18; Heb 13:21; 1 Pt 4:11; Rv 1:6; 4:9,10; 5:13; 7:12; 10:6; 11:15; 14:11; 15:7; 19:3; 20:10; 22:5.

the "eternal habitations" (Lk 16:9); Paul, to the "imperishable crown" (1 Cor 9:25), the "eternal weight of glory" (2 Cor 4:17), and the "eternal home" (2 Cor 5:1); Peter, to the "unfading crown of glory" (1 Pt 5:4).

Of course in John's Gospel the eternity of the Christian's union with God takes center stage, as we have seen above.[60] Eternity is something more than mere permanence and continuation, because it involves a real participation in the eternity of God himself, in whom the (created) past, present, and future merge with one another.[61] "Whoever drinks of the water that I shall give him will never thirst; the water that I shall give him will become in him a spring of water welling up to eternal life" (Jn 4:13–14). In the Eucharistic discourse of John 6, we read that Jesus tells his disciples that "I am the bread of life; he who comes to me shall not hunger and he who believes in me shall never thirst" (Jn 6:35). When Christ returns to bring his own to heaven, their "joy will be full" (Jn 16:24).

It is worthwhile noting in this context the definition of "eternity" given by the Christian philosopher Boethius: *aeternitas est interminabilis vitae tota simul et perfecta possessio*.[62] In objective terms, eternity involves a life that never ends (*interminabilis vita*), but at a personal level it consists properly speaking of a *possessio*, a "simulataneous and perfect possession of the life that never ends." Those who are divinized partake to some degree in God's own eternity, his very timelessness, his inner life. The blessed, Augustine tells us, "will know all totally and simultaneously without any succession of time."[63] The philosopher and doctor of the Church Edith Stein (Theresa Benedicta of the Cross) said the same thing in slightly different terms: "My being thirsts not only to continue forever, but also for a full possession of that being."[64] Eternal life, we read in *Spe salvi*, will "be like plunging into the ocean of infinite love, a moment in which time—the before and after—no longer exists."[65]

Eternal Life and the Vision of God

Life and light (Greek, *phōs*) are complementary qualities in John's Gospel. On the one hand, as we have already seen, John tells us that "he who believes in the Son *has eternal life*." On the other hand, according to the same text, "he who does not obey the Son *shall not see life*, but the wrath of God rests upon him"

---

60. See pp. 152–53.
61. This is especially so in Augustine. See M. L. Lamb, "Eternity Creates and Redeems Time: A Key to Augustine's *Confessions* within a Theology of History," *Divine Creation in Ancient, Medieval, and Early Modern Thought: Essays Presented to the Re'vd Dr. Robert D. Crouse*, ed. M. Treschow, W. Otten, and W. Hannam (Leiden: Brill, 2007), 117–40.
62. Boethius, *De consol. phil.*, 5, pr. 6:4.   63. Augustine, *Conf. XII*, 15.
64. E. Stein, *L'Etre fini et l'être éternel* (Louvain: Nauwelaerts, 1972), 60–61.
65. *SS* 12.

(Jn 3:36). That is to say, "to have life" is merged with, or made equivalent to, "to see life." To have eternal life, to be divinized, in other words, does not mean that the Christian comes to be in any way fused with the divine substance, thus forfeiting its autonomous, created existence. The person is divinized, suffused with divine life, but at the same time is made capable of seeing God. But if God is seen, then there is no fusion of subjects, for the seer and the seen by definition must be distinct from one another. Augustine briefly summed up the unity that exists between union and vision, between divinization and distinction, when he said of God: "To see you is to possess you."[66]

The foregoing explanation gives expression to a particularly essential element of Christian anthropology and eschatology: God and the human subject never ontologically merge with one another, neither by grace on earth nor by glory in heaven. God is the one who divinizes, who imparts divine life, yet this action unites humans with himself without destroying either human nature or human personhood, that is, the distinctiveness and singularity of the human person in respect of the Divinity. In fact, in heaven believers will fully encounter their "personhood"; they will fully become themselves. This apparently elementary but critical aspect of Christian anthropology was at the center of the controversy over the correct interpretation of Aristotle's writings during the Middle Ages.[67] Authors such as Averroes and Maimonides claimed that the human intellect (or an important part of it) belonged to the Divinity. The dispersion presently to be found in human thought, now expressed in individual existence, will be overcome at death, they held, and all will be absorbed back into the divine origin of thought and life.

This position is unacceptable, Thomas Aquinas and others insisted, also from a strictly philosophical standpoint.[68] Pope Leo the Great had already said as much: "Just as God does not change in the exercise of his mercy, so also humans are not consumed in their dignity."[69] And in the *Catechism of the Catholic Church* we read: "To live in heaven is 'to be with Christ.' The elect live 'in Christ', but they retain, or rather find, their true identity, their own name."[70]

That the divinized "see" God forever is an expression of the real distinction between God and the created world at the deepest possible level, an affirmation of God's transcendence on the one hand and of creation's autonomy on the other. Of course the doctrine of the vision of God is well developed in Scripture

---

66. Augustine, *Soliloquia I*, 1:3. And P. Teilhard de Chardin draws the conclusion: "either we see or we perish," *The Phenomenon of Man* (New York: Harper, 1959), 31.

67. The bibliography is ample on the subject. See, for example, R. McInerny, *Aquinas against the Averroists: On There Being Only One Intellect* (West Lafayette, Ind.: Purdue University Press, 1993).

68. See pp. 24–25.   69. Leo the Great, *Ep. 28 ad Flav.*, 4.

70. *CCC* 1025.

Heaven: Eternal Life 163

and in the history of theology. That such vision be termed "beatific" is a simple corollary of fact that the saints contemplate the One who is all Goodness, Beauty, Harmony, and Power. This necessarily makes them fully blessed.

Eschatological Vision of God in Scripture

Three principal New Testament texts speak about the vision of God: 1 Corinthians 13:12, 1 John 3:1–2, and Matthew 5:8.

At the end of the hymn of charity in his first letter to the Corinthians, Paul writes: "for now we see in a mirror dimly, but then face to face. Now I know in part, then I shall understand fully, even as I have been fully understood" (1 Cor 13:12).[71] Several observations may be made about this text. *First*, a clear eschatological tension may be detected between the "now" and the "then," faith being reserved for the present, vision for the future. *Second*, the vision of God spoken of is open and clear, "face to face," Paul tells us. The expression is to be found in the Old Testament, where it expresses friendship and intimacy with God.[72] However, it would not be correct to say that the just "see" God face to face in the sense that their visual capacities are simply amplified, as if God was a kind of supreme creature that only those especially equipped are capable of knowing by means of a supreme concept. It should be said that the just see God in that God makes himself seen; hence the Pauline adjunct: "even as I have been [by God] fully understood."[73] Humans come to know God (and in all likelihood other things in God, who created them) insofar as they partake in God's knowledge of himself and his creatures. *Third*, the text closely associates the vision of God and the virtue of charity. We shall come back to this question presently.[74]

Another important text is found in the *first letter of John* (3:1–2). The text deals with the characteristics and consequences of divine sonship, an important Pauline and Johannine expression of the Christian's participation in divine life, of being "divinized." "Beloved, we are God's children now [this "now" evokes John's teaching of having eternal life by faith], it does not appear what we shall be, but we know that when he appears we shall be like him, for we shall see him as he is" (1 Jn 3:2). Like Paul's words to the Corinthians, the text is structured eschatologically, and clearly points toward the future from the present, like the doctrine of final resurrection (Jn 6:54): "what we shall be," "we shall be like him,"

---

71. On this text, see A. Robertson and A. Plummer, *The First Epistle of St. Paul to the Corinthians* (orig. 1911; Edinburgh: T. & T. Clark, 1994), 298–99.

72. Ex 33:11–12; Nm 12:8; Jn 16:29.

73. The text is in the "passive as a periphrasis of the divine subject," W. F. Orr and J. A. Walther, 1 *Corinthians*, Anchor Bible 32 (Garden City, N.Y.: Doubleday, 1976). R. Bultmann distinguishes clearly in this text between Paul's notion of the knowledge of God and that typical of Gnostics: R. Bultmann, "γινώσκω," in *TWNT* 1, 680–719, here 710.

74. See pp. 174–75.

"we shall see him." As previously mentioned, John's affirmation is based on the Christian's divinization through faith, "we are God's children . . . we shall be like him." It may be noticed that not only is divinization the cause of vision ("we are children of God now"), but to an important degree it is also caused by vision: "we shall be like him, *for* we shall see him . . ." Divinization, in other words, makes vision possible, and vision in turn gives full expression to divinization. Later, we shall return to this text to consider the object of vision, that is, who or what is actually seen, whether God or Christ.[75]

The practical consequence of John's teaching is clear. "And every one who thus hopes in him purifies himself as he is pure" (1 Jn 3:3). The hope of seeing God moves one to sanctify one's entire existence, to prepare for the moment of ultimate encounter. This is a clear repetition of what Jesus had said in the Sermon on the Mount: "Blessed are the pure of heart for they shall see God" (Mt 5:8), a text that serves to further express the eschatological vision of God.[76]

The Understanding of the "Vision of God" throughout History

The Fathers of the Church, especially those of the Alexandrian tradition, spoke extensively of the contemplation of God and of eternal vision. Cyprian is among the first to explain that the vision of God is necessarily a source of happiness for the saved; thus the qualifier "beatific vision": "How great will your glory and happiness be," he says, "to be allowed to see God, to be honored with sharing the joy of salvation and eternal light with Christ your Lord and God, . . . to delight in the joy of immortality in the Kingdom of heaven with the righteous and God's friends."[77] The vision of God was particularly central for Origen: "There shall be one activity for those who have come to be with God through the Word who is with him: to apprehend God."[78] Likewise, the Cappadocians,[79] Augustine,[80] and John Chrysostom[81] speak frequently of the beatific vision. For Augustine, the vision of God is the very core of eternal beatitude.[82] "In a certain way, the human mind dies and becomes divine, and is inebriated with the riches of God's house."[83] Chrysostom expresses this as follows: "For why do we live,

---

75. See pp. 184–88.
76. The same notion is found in Rv 22:4, which says that the elect "will see his [the Lamb's] face, and his name shall be on their foreheads."
77. Cyprian, *Ep.* 58, 10:1.   78. Origen, *Comm. In Jo.*, 1, 16:92.
79. For example, Gregory of Nazianzen, *Or. 8*, 23.   80. Augustine, *Conf. IV*, 10–13; *IX*, 10.
81. John Chrysostom, *Ad Theod. lapsum tract.*, 11.
82. Augustine, *Enn. in Ps. 26*, 2:9 and 43:5; *Sermo 362*, 29:30–30:31; *Ep. 130*, 14:27. On philosophical aspects of vision in Augustine, see L. Cilleruelo, "*Deum videre* en San Agustín," *Salmanticensis* 12 (1965): 1–31; B. E. Daley, *The Hope*, 145–46. Augustine states that the vision of God is the very basis of our union with him: *Ep.* 147, 37.
83. Augustine, *Enn. in Ps.*, 35:14.

why do we breathe, what are we, if we do not receive a share in that vision? . . . O blessed, thrice blessed, many times blessed are those who will be worthy to look on that glory!"[84]

In the fourth century Eunomius, a follower of Arius, taught that the knowledge all beings can have of God is of the same kind, and strictly limited.[85] This principle is applicable, he said, to humans, to angels, and to Christ himself, the Word, whom the Arians looked upon as the prime creature, derived from God and subordinated to him. As a consequence, God cannot be seen directly by the creature, yet all creatures would perceive the divinity in substantially the same way. Some Fathers of the Church, notably John Chrysostom, reacted energetically against this doctrine. They did so, however, by going to the other extreme, teaching that whereas Christ does see the divine substance (for he is consubstantial with the Father), angels and humans do not. That is to say, according to Chrysostom, the Father is seen only by the Son and by the Spirit.[86] At best, creatures may be said to see God indirectly; they see his glory but not his substance.

Faced with the Arian challenge, which seemed to gainsay Paul's teaching regarding face-to-face vision,[87] Chrysostom's reaction was understandable. The latter's position was shared by Theodoret of Cyrus,[88] who argued that when in the Old Testament it was said that humans "saw" God—Moses is the best-known case—they did not see the divine essence (*ousia*) as such, but only a kind of glorious splendor (*doxa*), because they were creatures. A similar position was held in the Byzantine Church in the late Middle Ages by Gregory Palamas.[89] Palamas insisted on the absolute invisibility of the Divinity, and claimed that humans are in a position to contemplate only the glory that irradiates from the divine essence. This glory is eternal and uncreated (Palamas speaks of the "divine energies"), but may not be identified with the divine essence, which belongs to the ambit of divine transcendence, but rather with divine operations, grace, glory,

---

84. John Chrysostom, *In Io. Hom.*, 12:3.
85. According to the historian Socrates, *Hist. Eccl.*, 4:7, Eunomius held that "God knows of his own being no more than we do. His being is not clearer for him than it is for us. Everything we know about him he knows it in the same way, and everything that he knows about himself we find it easily and without diversity in ourselves."
86. John Chrysostom, *De Incomprehens. Dei natura*, 1:6; *In Io. Hom.*, 15:1.
87. Basil, *Ep.* 8:7, on direct vision in 1 Cor 13:12.
88. See C. Pozo, *La teología del más allá*, 375–7. The principal work of Theodoret is the *Eranistes seu Polymorphus*, dial. I.
89. On Palamas's theory of divinization much has been written, for example, the classic work of M. Jugie, "Palamas," in *DTC* 11 (1930): cols. 1735–76. Against this study, see V. Lossky, *Théologie mystique de l'Église d'Orient* (Paris: Cerf, 1944), and J. Meyendorff, *St. Gregory Palamas and Orthodox Spirituality* (Crestwood, N.Y.: St. Vladimir's Seminary Press, 1974). Recently, see A. N. Williams, *The Ground of Union: Deification in Aquinas and Palamas* (Oxford: Clarendon Press, 1999).

and splendor. This divine glory was manifested, for example, during the transfiguration of Jesus on Mount Thabor, and was, he said, the basis of the apostles' vision of God, and the beginning of the mystical divine knowledge experienced by many saints.[90]

In the context of Theodoret's distinction between divine essence and divine glory, Gregory the Great detected in the doctrine of the divine energies the danger of compromising divine simplicity. "In that most simple and unchangeable essence," he said, "it is not possible to distinguish between the clarity/glory and the essence; for in God the nature is clarity; the clarity is nature."[91] In his own day Palamas was accused, unjustly as it transpired, of duo-theism.[92] But the fact is that whereas his doctrine was accepted officially at the Synod of the Byzantine Church in 1352, the Council of Florence in 1439 did not accept it. Convoked with a view to bringing about union between Latins and Greeks, the council proclaimed that "the souls of those who . . . have been cleansed . . . see clearly God himself, one and three, as He is."[93] Palamas's doctrine was discussed, however, during the council, and in its decrees no mention is made of the vision of the "divine glory." However, the council did insist on the gradualism of vision, a doctrine held by many Eastern authors, such as Origen, Ps.-Denis the Areopagite (fifth century), and Maximus the Confessor. "They see God himself," the Council of Florence decreed, "one in three, as he is, though some more perfectly than others, according to the diversity of merits."[94] A century earlier, Pope Benedict XII, in a somewhat different context,[95] taught the same doctrine: the souls of those purified "see the divine essence with an intuitive vision and even face to face, without the mediation of any creature by way of object of vision; rather the divine essence immediately manifests itself [*divina essentia immediate se . . . ostendente*] to them, plainly, clearly and openly, and in this vision they enjoy the divine essence."[96] The same doctrine is to be found in the *Catechism of the Catholic Church*.[97]

Theological Issues Involving the Direct Vision of God

It should be kept in mind that when Eastern theology spoke of the indirect vision the just have of God, they were attempting to defend a particularly central aspect of Christian faith, that of divine transcendence. How could humans and angels be said to see the face of God in the same way as did Christ, God's own Son and Word?

90. Gregory Palamas, *Triads I*, 3; *II*, 3: *III*.   91. Gregory the Great, *Mor. in Iob*, 18, 54:90.
92. This was done by his adversary Barlaam of Calabria. See J. Jugie, "Palamas," col. 1754.
93. *DS* 1305 (the *Decretum pro graecis*).
94. *DS* 1305. On this see G. Moioli, *L' "Escatologico" cristiano*, 130–31.
95. See pp. 278–80.   96. *DS* 1000.
97. *CCC* 1028.

It is interesting to note that in many versions of the first article of the Apostles' Creed a specific mention is made of God not only as all-powerful, but also as invisible.[98] Scripture itself is insistent on the point. When Moses requested to contemplate the glory of God, he received the following reply: "I will make all my goodness pass before you, and will proclaim before you the name 'the Lord'; and I will be gracious to whom I will be gracious, and will show mercy on whom I will show mercy. But *you cannot see my face;* for *no one shall see me and live*" (Ex 33:19–20). In fact, many Old Testament texts speak of those who desire to see God,[99] but they are aware that it is impossible and that such a vision would occasion their death.[100]

The New Testament confirms this doctrine. In the prologue of John's Gospel we read that "no one has ever seen God" (Jn 1:18). Paul, speaking about the divine attributes, says that God is "the blessed and only Sovereign, the King of kings and Lord of lords, who alone has immortality and dwells in approachable light, *whom no man has ever seen or can see*" (1 Tm 6:15–16).

However, as several Fathers of the Church point out,[101] God is said to be invisible in a specific sense: that creatures are unable to contemplate the Divinity by their own powers. This does not mean of course that God is not able to make himself seen by creatures should he wish to do so. Rather than a limit on the Divinity, or an expression of divine incapacity, invisibility is an attribute that expresses divine transcendence and otherness, that is, God's complete metaphysical independence in respect of creation. To be visible, in a sense, would be a sign of weakness or deficiency on God's part, a kind of passivity or vulnerability, a power the creature could conceivably have over the Creator. In fact the text just mentioned from John's prologue, "no one has ever seen God," goes on to proclaim that "the only Son, who is in the bosom of the Father, he has made him known" (Jn 1:18). In a strict sense this text does not speak of actually seeing God face to face. However, it is clear that God's own Word can reveal to humans what they are completely incapable of seeing for themselves by their own powers. "The light shines in the darkness, and the darkness has not overcome it," we read elsewhere in John's prologue. "The true light that enlightens every man was coming into the world.... And the Word became flesh ... we have beheld his glory, glory as of the only Son from the Father" (Jn 1:5,9,14).

Augustine says that "God is invisible by nature, but may be seen when he

---

98. See *DS* 16, 21, 22, 29.
100. Ex 19,21; Lv 16,2; Nb 4,20.
99. Jb 19:26; 42:5; Ps 16:5.
101. Some Fathers of the Church who speak of the impossibility of seeing God "face to face" simply intend to exclude the possibility of seeing God with one's own strength; see Basil, *Adv. Eunomium*, 1:14; Didymus the Blind, *De Trin.*, 3:16.

wishes, as he wishes."[102] He adds that we do not see God by physical sight: "God is not seen in a place, but by a clear heart; nor may he be sought by the eyes of the body, nor can be grasped by sight, nor held by touch, nor heard by sound, nor felt by invasion."[103] In brief terms the *Catechism of the Catholic Church* sums up this teaching as follows: "Because of his transcendence, God cannot be seen as he is, unless he himself opens up his mystery to man's immediate contemplation and gives him the capacity for it."[104] Let us consider now what this "capacity" consists of.

The "Capacity to See God" and the "Lumen Gloriae"

The Council of Vienne (1312) took a stance against neo-Gnostic authors who held that the divine substance could be seen by the elect by their own powers, given that in real terms they belonged to the Divinity in the first place.[105] The council made it clear that the close union between God and the soul, and the direct vision that results from it, is due not to the powers of nature, but to God's supernatural gift. "The soul stands in need of the light of glory [*lumen gloriae*] to be elevated and indeed to see God and rejoice in him," the Council teaches.[106] The notion of a special "light" that is infused into the just so that they can see God is suggested in several biblical texts. For example in Psalm 36:9 we read: "for with you is the fountain of life; *in your light* we see the light." And in the book of Revelation, "The throne of God and of the Lamb shall be in it [the New Jerusalem], and his servants shall worship him; and they shall see his face, and his name shall be on their foreheads. And night shall be no more; they need no light of lamp or sun, for *the Lord God will be their light*, and they shall reign for ever and ever" (22:3–5).

According to the classical theory, human knowledge of created beings takes place by means of intelligible species (or forms), abstracted by the mind from different objects, or obtained by way of illumination. Obviously the vision of God requires a further explanation, for God is not a simple created object. Thomas Aquinas explains it in the following terms: "When the created intellect sees the divine essence, that same divine essence *becomes the intelligible form* of the intellect."[107] Indeed, since "the natural power of the created intellect is insufficient to

---

102. Augustine, *Ep.* 147, 37: "Deum . . . invisibilem esse natura, videtur autem cum vult, sicut vult."

103. God is not seen by human sight, Augustine says: "Nec in loco Deus videtur, sed mundo corde; nec corporalibus oculis quaeritur, nec circumscributur visu, nec tactu tenetur, nec auditur effatu, nec sentitur incessu," *De Civ. Dei XXII*, 29.

104. *CCC* 1028.

105. The Church condemned, for example, the position of the Beguins, who claimed that all contemplation is *contemplatio beatorum*: *DS* 895.

106. *DS* 895; see also Pius XII, Enc. *Mystici Corporis Christi* (1943): *DS* 3815.

107. Thomas Aquinas, *S. Th. I*, q. 12, a. 5c.

see the essence of God, one's power of knowing must be expanded [*superaccrescere*] by divine grace."[108] Elsewhere Aquinas says that for this vision to take place, humans must be divinized: "by means of this light, the blessed are deified."[109] In a brief formula, he says, the divine essence is *quod videtur et quo videtur*,[110] "that which is seen [God as object of vision] and that *by which* God is seen [what is called the formal object *quo*]."

However, if it was necessary to avoid the Gnostic position, which denied the gratuitousness of the beatific vision and with it the transcendence of God in respect of humans, another difficulty arose during the Middle Ages, typified in the writings of Henry of Gand (also called Gandavius). Gandavius held that the reception of the *lumen gloriae* was a gift indeed, but that it occasioned an assimilation of the substance of the soul with that of God.[111] His challenge is an important one: if the divine essence itself is that by which we see God (*quo videtur Deum*), how can we avoid God becoming substantially identified with our own intellect? Or at a more practical level: what does it mean to be fully human when one is completely absorbed—at a psychological and ontological level—by God's own life? Cajetan attempts to clarify the issue by saying that in the beatific vision the human intellect is drawn into God's very being, not physically of course, but on the level of intention or representation.[112] As Aquinas says in the text cited above, the divine essence "becomes the *intelligible form* of the intellect."

Listening to the Word of God

Although eschatological union with the Divinity certainly involves vision, the definitive revelation of God's glory, it should be kept in mind that divine communication with man throughout the greater part of Scripture is centered principally on the Word.[113] Thus Master Eckhart was fully to the point, though

---

108. Ibid.
109. Ibid.
110. Thomas Aquinas, *III C. Gent.*, 51.
111. Gandavius, *Quodl. 13*, q. 12. Other authors such as Scotus Eriugena spoke of union with God without any medium: "Non ipsum Deum per semetipsum videmus, quia neque angeli vident; hoc enim creaturae impossibile est . . . sed quasdam factas ab eo in nobis theophanias contemplabimur," *De divisione naturae I*, 1:10. The same position may be found in Alexander of Hales, Hugh of Saint-Cher, and Hugh of St. Victor: see G. Moioli, *L'"Escatologico" cristiano*, 126–27. Almaricus of Bène said: "creator non videtur nisi tamquam sub operimento universi," whereas according to Aristotelian authors, the divine is known through created effects. Both positions, one leading to pantheism, the other to materialism, were rejected by the University of Paris in 1241: "quod divina essentia in se nec ab homine nec ab angelo videbitur." On the question, see H.-F. Dondeine, "L'objet et le 'medium' de la vision béatifique chez les théologiens du XIIIe siècle," *Recherches de théologie ancienne et médiévale* 19 (1952): 60–99.
112. Cajetan, *In S. Th. I*, q. 12, a. 2.
113. See my study "Alcune implicazioni giuridiche e antropologiche della comunicazione della parola di Dio," in *Parola di Dio e missione della Chiesa. Aspetti giuridici*, ed. C. J. Errázuriz and F. Puig (Roma: Edusc, 2009), 27–57.

somewhat imprecise, in saying: "in eternal life we will be much more blessed on account of hearing than of seeing. This is because the act of hearing the Eternal Word is within me, whereas the act of seeing goes out of me."[114] Hans Urs von Balthasar notes that the theology of the *visio* has neglected that of the *auditio*, and insists with Eckhart that "the Son of God remains forever the Word of the Father."[115] Within eternity we are destined to "receive the Word of God in the Holy Spirit of the Father,"[116] to which we respond in wonderment and praise.

This observation brings us once more to consider some of the principal anthropological implications of the doctrine of eternal life, divinization, and beatific vision. They relate respectively to the *freedom, sociality, and temporality* of those who enjoy the vision of God (which we shall deal with in the following sections). From the outset it must be stated that face-to-face vision of God not only does not destroy the freedom, sociality, and temporality of the human condition, but, to the contrary, enhances them and gives them their full meaning. In the absence of their eschatological complement, we would be unable to fully understand these fundamental elements that characterize the present human condition.

The "Never-Ending Character" of Heaven: Eternity and Freedom

In the following sections we shall consider some anthropological aspects of the life of the blessed on the basis of a simple yet perfectly legitimate Christian intuition: that the gift of eternal life (which ultimately includes that of final resurrection) constitutes the fullest realization of the human person, the point of reference for understanding what it means to be human in the present situation, and that nothing truly good in human life and nature will be absent in heaven.[117]

Origen's Denial of Heaven's Eternity

To appreciate the anthropological implications of the eternity of heaven, it is worthwhile to examine some aspects of Origen's eschatology.[118]

According to Origen's work *De principiis*, God, all-powerful and supremely good, cannot be inactive, and so has created things from all eternity.[119] At first

---

114. Master Eckhart, *Sermo* 58, in *Deutsche Predigten und Traktate*, ed. J. Quint, 3rd ed. (München: C. Hanser, 1969), 430–31.

115. See H. U. von Balthasar, *Theodramatik 4/2: Das Endspiel*, 372–73. Emphasis added.

116. Ibid.

117. See my studies *La muerte y la esperanza*, 64–74; "Cristo revela el hombre al propio hombre," *Scripta Theologica* 41 (2009): 85–111.

118. Origen, *De princip. I*, 5.

119. "Just as nobody can be a father without having a child, nor a master without owning a slave, neither can God be called all-powerful if there are no other beings over whom he can exercise his power. Hence, so that God may show himself as all-powerful, created beings must necessarily exist. If by chance

all spiritual beings created by God were characterized by perfect equality, as they contemplated the Word of God. However, being free spirits, many of them sinned.[120] And the material world was created on account of this sin, principally as a means of punishment and purification. The variety that exists between different spiritual beings derives from the greater or lesser intensity of the sin of each one. The spirits who sinned most grievously became the devil and his angels, and are punished under the earth. Those who sinned to a greater or lesser degree are human beings, who live on the earth, clothed in human bodies. The spirits who did not sin at all are the angels, who were perfectly faithful to God and remained purely spiritual. Origen accepts the doctrine of the preexistence of souls, and considers the material world as an agent for the purification of sinners. After the purification obtained during life on earth or after death, one and all will return to the original state they were in before sinning. This process will come to completion at the end of time, and Origen designated it with the Greek term *apokatastasis*, used in Scripture (Acts 3:21) to mean universal reconciliation.[121] However, even when this reconciliation/restoration takes place, humans will retain their freedom, and in principle there is no reason why they should not be in a position to separate themselves from God again through sin, even though on the basis of biblical revelation, Origen does not accept that this will be the case.

Whatever the merits or demerits of the Origenist reading of Christian anthropology and soteriology, what he has certainly clarified is that human freedom and eternal life seem to be at loggerheads. If humans are free, sooner or later some of them are bound to reject the gift of communion with God, and so forgo its possible eternity. Or the other way round, if heaven is eternal, if it lasts forever, then we lose our freedom. Putting it differently, the eternity of heaven is correlative with the sinlessness of humans. Yet how can the latter be explained without denying human freedom?

Human Freedom and Eternal Life

Two principal solutions have been offered to explain the eternity of beatific vision. On the one hand authors taking a *Scotist* approach claim that the vision of God imposes no absolute necessity on humans to love God and avoid sin, in such a way that the will retains its freedom "of exercise" and "of specification," not only in respect of the created world, but also in respect of the Supreme Good,

---

there were a time when God was not all-powerful, things must have existed so that he could receive this title," Origen, *De princip. I*, 2:10.

120. According to Origen in *De princip. II*, 3, man is always free. In that way he can maintain a continuous dynamism toward and from God. His freedom is never definitively fixed.

121. Ibid., *III*, 6:6. See H. Crouzel, "L'hadès et la géhenne selon Origène," *Gregorianum* 59 (1978): 291–329; J. R. Sachs, "Apocatastasis in Patristic Theology," *Theological Studies* 54 (1993): 617–40.

which is God. The sinlessness of the blessed is due therefore to an extraordinary providential grace that prevents the blessed from deviating from the fulfillment of the will of God. That is, heaven will be eternal to some extent by divine decree.[122]

This solution is not without its difficulties, in that it seems to suggest that God is obliged to undo his own work of creating (in making humans free) in order to concede them the definitive reward. Human freedom seems to be the problem, not the solution. Besides, freedom is considered in a restrictive way, in terms of pure indifference and arbitrariness in respect of the good.

The other solution is offered by *Thomas Aquinas*, who attempts to explain the eternity (and thus sinlessness) of the heavenly state without having recourse to a special divine decree.[123] The human will remains free, certainly in the sense that it is capable of choosing different created objects. However, the proper object of the human will is not choice, but the good. While on earth, the good associated with particular choices is made present to humans with a greater or lesser intensity, and for the most part does not impose itself. For this reason, humans are in a position to choose, and, given their fallen and limited condition, may do so mistakenly. But the object of the will is always and only the good. Thus, when someone contemplates God face to face they become simply incapable of choosing something that excludes the Divinity. And this because God, who is directly perceived by the blessed, is a greater good than all the other partial goods. Besides, creatures, although they may be in a position to offer earth-bound humans the temptation of putting aside the God they do not see, have in fact received through God's creation the very goodness they possess. Perceiving the very source of goodness makes it impossible for the blessed to offend God in heaven, to reject the Creator in the name of the creature. Aquinas states: "Since God in himself is Goodness by essence, he cannot be displeasing to any will. Whoever sees him in his essence cannot hate him,"[124] that is, cannot sin.

In other words, by means of an immanent psychological process in full consonance with human nature, it is simply impossible for humans to abandon the vision of God once they have obtained it. In a sense they have lost their freedom, in that they can no longer sin (Aquinas has it that to sin is not a part of human freedom, but rather a sign of fallen freedom),[125] but in the truest sense of the word they freely do not want to sin. Humans who contemplate God are simply incapable of forfeiting the Source of all goodness for the sake of a lesser good.

---

122. Duns Scotus, *Oxon. IV*, D. 49, q. 4. On this, see H. Lennerz, *De novissimis*, 5th ed. (Roma: Gregoriana, 1950), 30–33.

123. Thomas Aquinas, *IV C. Gent.*, 92. See S. Gaine, *Will There Be Free Will in Heaven? Freedom, Impeccability, and Beatitude* (London: T. & T. Clark, 2003).

124. Thomas Aquinas, *S. Th. III, Suppl.*, q. 98, a. 5c.

125. Thomas Aquinas, *S. Th. I*, q. 62, a. 8 ad 3.

Aquinas notes: "For the blessed are satisfied with the One in whom true happiness is to be found; other things would never fill up their desire."[126] On earth sinning remains a possibility, for God is not perceived directly, but only through his words and works. His presence and goodness, therefore, do not impose themselves on humans during their earthly sojourn, for God intends to obtain a free, generous response from creatures who must strive with his help to overcome the disorderly pull of creatures toward sin while indirectly and less tangibly perceiving divine action and love.[127]

The Ultimate Meaning of Human Freedom

Following Paul and Augustine, it should be said that freedom in a Christian sense is above all a liberation, the freedom Christ has won for us (Gal 5:1). More than an act or a capacity ("free will"), freedom is a state. The freedom acquired by a Christian through baptism and in eternal life involves in the first place a complete exclusion of enslavement, what Paul calls the "glorious freedom of the children of God" (Rom 8:21). Paradoxically, enslavement on earth is frequently encountered by those who wish to enjoy their freedom fully by leaving all their options open, by refusing to commit themselves, thus identifying freedom with the simple possibility of choice. In heaven, however, humans encounter perfect identification with themselves and with their own aspirations, a complete absence of agitation, dissatisfaction, and nostalgia, fulfillment of all they were searching for—perhaps without fully realizing it—during the earthly sojourn, the joy of having obtained the Absolute Good forever, the fullness of freedom. The freedom characteristic of eternal life is what gives full meaning to the exercise of freedom on earth (where the Good illustrates the choice and gently moves the will), and not the other way around (that the choice would dictate or create the good). Reflecting on eternal life, Augustine speaks of "a freedom that is beyond the power of human nature alone but given to those who are *participes Dei*, freedom so great even as to exclude the possibility of sinning." He continues saying that the saints "do not lack free will because they are unable to delight in sin. On the contrary, their will is so fully freed from delight in sinning that it is liberated to an unswerving delight in not sinning."[128]

126. Thomas Aquinas, *IV C. Gent.*, 96.

127. It is interesting to note that, in all probability, Origen considered the Word contemplated by created spirits in a subordinationist fashion: J. Daniélou, *Origène* (Paris: Cerf, 1948), 249–51; Origen, *De princip. IV*, 4:1. Spirits therefore do not see God, but only the Word, inferior to God, and therefore are not "obliged" by vision to avoid sinning. That is to say, Origen's possible subordinationism and his denial of the eternity of reward and punishment go hand in hand. This also explains why the idea of an indirect perception of God would not be sufficient to account for the eternity and fullness of eschatological communion with God, as Theodoret of Cyrus, Palamas, and others suggested.

128. Augustine, *De Civ. Dei XXII*, 30.

But it may be asked: does the vision of God exclude the possibility of free action in the created sphere? Or are the blessed in heaven capable of making real choices regarding their everyday lives? Thomas Aquinas would seem to deny it. For the resurrected, he says, "it can be seen that all the occupations of the active life will cease. . . . Only the occupation of the contemplative life will remain."[129] Authors such as Gregory of Nyssa, however, seem to hold the contrary: the human being, while contemplating God, will be in a position to choose freely within the created order.[130]

The Social Aspect of Eternal Life and the Role of Christian Charity

If the vision of God does not exclude freedom, but brings freedom to fullness, it is logical that the supreme act of human freedom, which consists in the love of God and of neighbor, would also reach its culmination in heaven.

Vision of God and Charity

As we saw above, Paul in 1 Corinthians 13 associates the vision of God with charity. Seeing God may not be considered as a kind of cold, purely intellectual contemplation. Rather vision is the final act, the supreme act of charity. Faith will be substituted by vision (knowledge), hope by presence (joy), but charity will always accompany vision, for "love never ends" (1 Cor 13:8). "Charity is immortal and does not change nature essentially when it is transformed into glory."[131] The law of charity, says Augustine, will come to fulfillment only "in that life when we see God face to face."[132] And Hugh of St. Victor wrote that God in heaven "will be seen without faith, will be loved without aversion, will be praised without fatigue."[133]

The controversy between Thomas Aquinas and Bonaventure on the question of the respective priority of knowledge and charity in Christian life and beatific vision is worth noting.[134] Thomas takes up the classical Augustinian maxim to the effect that *nihil amatur nisi cognitum*, "nothing is loved or wanted if it is not previously known."[135] That is to say, knowledge—and therefore vision—is prior to love, in that it makes love possible. Heaven in the first place would consist

---

129. Thomas Aquinas, *IV C. Gent.*, 83.
130. Life is understood as a changeover between two free agents, neither of which can dispose of the other. Hence, according to Gregory, human life under freedom will go on forever: see G. Maspero, *La Trinità e l'uomo. L'Ad Ablabium di Gregorio di Nissa* (Roma: Città Nuova, 2004).
131. F. Prat, *La théologie de Saint Paul*, vol. 2 (Paris: Beauchesne, 1930), 405.
132. Augustine, *De spir. et litt.*, 36:64.
133. "Sine fide videbitur, sine fastidio amabitur, sine fatigatio laudabitur," Hugh of St. Victor, *De sacramentis II*,18:20.
134. Thomas Aquinas, *S. Th. I-II*, q. 3, a. 4; Bonaventure, *In III Sent.*, D. 31, a. 3, q. 1.
135. For example, in Thomas Aquinas, *S. Th. I*, q. 60, a. 1, s. c., from Augustine *X de Trin.*

of an act of knowledge through vision, from which love arises. Bonaventure, conversely, insists on the priority of love over vision, of will over knowledge.[136] Eternal life consists in the first place of the love of God that is poured into the human heart, bringing it to respond with a love of correspondence. It is an act mainly of the will, superior to mere knowledge. This position finds expression in the famous phrase of Blaise Pascal: "The heart has its reasons which reason does not understand."[137]

It is clear of course that love is made possible by knowledge, but it is also true that the act of knowledge is stimulated and conserved by love of what is known. It is interesting to note that in Hebrew the terms "to love" and "to know" are virtually equivalent.[138] Perhaps it is not all that necessary to distinguish between these two aspects of eternal life, for the one humans possess is God, in whom the Truth and the Good coincide absolutely, and in whose Life the blessed participate. In any case, it should also be kept in mind that eternal life is in the first place a divine gift that produces a participation of the Christian in Trinitarian life, that is, at one and the same time, it involves the knowledge and love of the divine Persons.

The Role of Other Creatures in Eternal Life

Throughout history the doctrine of eternal life has been understood principally in terms of the vision and love of God. God is the One who makes eternal life possible through grace, and is the direct object of vision. Humans always move in the sphere of God, often without knowing it, even sometimes purposefully ignoring it. In heaven such ignorance will be impossible, for God will necessarily receive man's full attention. Understandably, spiritual authors sometimes insist that the prospect of seeing God and living in communion with him forever should move believers to consciously disregard creatures as so many distractions on their way to perfect union with God. On an objective level, however, this does not mean that the knowledge and charity that unites the blessed to God will not unite them also with other creatures, especially those with whom they have shared their earthly pilgrimage. At heart this doctrine is present in the notion of the "communion of saints."[139] In eternal life humans are united not only with God in Christ, but also with the rest of humanity. This idea is expressed in Vatican II teaching on the eschatological vocation of the whole Church.[140]

136. Bonaventure, *In III Sent.*, D. 31, a. 3, q. 1.
137. B. Pascal, *Pensées* (ed. Brunschvig), n. 277.
138. E. D. Schmitz, "To Know," in *NIDNTT* 2, 392–406, especially 395.
139. See my study "Comunión de los santos," in C. Izquierdo, J. Burggraf, and F. M. Arocena, eds., *Diccionario de Teología* (Pamplona: Eunsa, 2006), 142–46.
140. *LG* 48.

Specifically, *Gaudium et spes* says that faith brings people "to be united in Christ with their loved ones who have already died, and gives hope that they have found true life with God."[141] If this is the case for communion with the Church in its present state, much more so will it be so among the blessed themselves in heaven. In the chapter on the pilgrim Church, *Lumen gentium* speaks of three states in the Church—the pilgrim, the purifying, and the heavenly—and indicates Christ and the Spirit he sends as the basis of their unity. "All of us . . . in varying degrees and in different ways share in the same charity towards God and our neighbors, and we all sing the one hymn of glory to our God. All, indeed, who are of Christ and who have his Spirit form one Church and in Christ are united with one another."[142] The text continues: "Being more closely united to Christ, those who dwell in heaven fix the whole Church more firmly in holiness, add to the nobility of the worship that the Church offers to God here on earth, and in many ways help in a broader building up of the Church."[143]

Many Fathers of the Church and theologians hold that in heaven we will encounter the fullness of the mystery of creation. Augustine says that "wherever we turn our eyes we shall, with absolute accuracy, see God present everywhere and controlling all things, even material ones, through the bodies we shall have and through those we shall see."[144] Gregory the Great says that in contemplating God the blessed shall see all things.[145] And Hugh of St. Victor explains that the blessed will see all that takes place in the universe.[146]

Communion between the Saved in Heaven

Communion with the elect forms an essential part of the joy of heaven. This doctrine is clearly present, albeit implicitly, in Scripture when it speaks of heaven in terms of a sumptuous banquet (Mt 22:1–14), with abundance of food (Mt 22:4), drink (Jn 2:1–11), and light (Mt 22:13), a banquet that God himself has prepared for the delight of the elect—even to the point of serving them at table (Lk 12:37)—while insisting that they are bound to partake of it (Mt 22:3–4,7–10).[147]

Likewise several Fathers of the Church pay especial attention to the eschatological communion between the saints in heaven. Cyprian wrote to the faithful on one occasion in the following terms: "What glory, what a pleasure it will be when you are admitted to see God, when you are considered worthy of the honor of rejoicing with Christ, your Lord and God, the joy of salvation and of

---

141. *GS* 18b.
142. *LG* 49.
143. Ibid.
144. Augustine, *De Civ. Dei XXII*, 29.
145. According to Gregory the Great, in contemplating God the just know all things: *Mor. in Job* 12, 21:26.
146. Hugh of St. Victor, *De sacramentis II*, 18:16–20.
147. See P. Rouillard, "Aspect communautaire de la béatitude," *Vie spirituelle* 44 (1962): 217–21.

eternal light, the joy of greeting Abraham, Isaac, Jacob and all the Patriarchs, the Apostles, the prophets and martyrs, to rejoice with the just and the friends of God in the kingdom of heaven."[148] And elsewhere: "There await for us the multitude of our loved ones, our parents, brothers and sisters, children, who are sure of their safety, yet solicitous for our salvation. To reach their presence, their embrace, what a great joy it will be for us and for them!"[149] Gregory of Nyssa speaks of beatitude, of the fullness of joy and happiness that the just, as children of God, illuminated by the Sun of divine grace, communicate to one another.[150] According to Ambrose an essential aspect of life in heaven is the union of the blessed with one another in the love that unites them, as witnessed in the many funeral orations he delivered.[151]

In his work *De Civitate Dei*, Augustine describes eternal life as "a perfectly ordered and harmonious common life [*societas*] of those who enjoy God and one another in God."[152] And elsewhere: "Who does not long for that city where no friend leaves and no enemy enters, where no one tries or disturbs us, no one divides the people of God, no one wearies God's Church in the service of the devil? . . . We will have God as our common sight [*spectaculum*], we will have God as our common possession, we will have God as our common peace."[153] Even though there will be many differences between the just, there will be no discontent or envy among the citizens of heaven,[154] for all will be joined in the peace that marks the heavenly city. Besides, Augustine frequently teaches that the just will enjoy the company of the angels, the *societas angelorum*.[155] "With the angels [the blessed] will possess in common the holy and sweet communion of the city of God."[156]

Likewise Bede the Venerable says that beatitude consists in "the joy of a fraternal society."[157] Thomas Aquinas, as we saw, emphasized in a particular way the contemplative side of eternal life, and rated the material aspects of risen humanity more soberly, the reason being that eating, drinking, sleeping, and the like would serve no purpose in heaven.[158]

The theologian Karl Adam, when speaking of those who are united in charity, spoke of the "respiration of the blessed." And the philosopher Gabriel Marcel

---

148. Cyprian, *Ep.* 58:27.
149. Cyprian, *De mort.*, 26. For other texts, see J. T. O'Connor, *The Land of the Living*, 264.
150. Gregory of Nyssa, *De vita Moys.*, 2.
151. Ambrose, *De obitu Theodos. or.*, 29:32; *De obitu Valentiniani consolatio*, 71:77; *De bono mortis*, 11.
152. Augustine, *De Civ. Dei XIX*, 13:17.   153. Augustine, *Enn. in Ps.*, 84:10.
154. Augustine, *De Civ. Dei XXII*, 30.
155. Augustine, *Sermo* 19, 5. For similar texts, see B. E. Daley, *The Hope*, 146–47.
156. Augustine, *De Civ. Dei XXII*, 29.
157. Bede the Venerable, *De Tabernac. et vasis eius*, 2:13.
158. Thomas Aquinas, *S. Th. III, Suppl.*, q. 81, a. 4c.

spoke of the presence of the dead as a "throbbing vault" surrounding and reassuring the whole of creation.

Love of God and Love of Others

Christian spirituality has always argued that to love God with a total, radical love ("leaving all things," Mt 19:27), may be, but is not necessarily, an obstacle to loving other people, as long as that love is properly ordered. It might seem, however, that if the love of God in heaven becomes an all-consuming passion, love for others should by right be eliminated or severely diminished. This anthropomorphic view of the love of God in competitive terms does not take into account the fact that the love with which we love God merges with the love of neighbor, that is, charity, which finds a twofold expression: praising and thanking God and doing his will, on the one hand, and unstintingly giving to others what one has received from God for them, on the other. Within the dynamic of charity, Christians take part in the current of love that is the very life of the Blessed Trinity, which God wished to communicate to humanity not only directly to the person of the believer, but also indirectly through other people. When we love other people, we may say that God is loving them through us. "No matter how much you may love, you will never love enough," writes Josemaría Escrivá. "The human heart is endowed with an enormous coefficient of expansion. When it loves, it opens out in a crescendo of affection that overcomes all barriers. If you love Our Lord, there will not be a single creature that does not find a place in your heart."[159] The more one loves God, the more one will love neighbor, intensively and extensively. When the love of God comes to perfection in eternal life, love of others will grow not only in intensity and extension, but, perhaps above all, in constancy. No longer will the love between humans be fickle and erratic.

Thomas Aquinas says that in the beatific vision, one "sees God in his essence and other things in God [*et alia videt in Deo*], just as God himself, by knowing himself, knows all other things."[160] That is, the blessed contemplate not only God, but others as well, in God. It may be deduced, therefore, that they love God, and others as well, in God. True human love will not be impeded or eliminated by the vision of God; it will be purified, perhaps, and intimately associated with the love of God. Thus the love of God will include a true and orderly love for Our Lady, for the angels and saints, for all those saved, especially those who are close to us, for those who were our "neighbor." Josemaría Escrivá writes: "Do not ever

---

159. Josemaría Escrivá, *Via crucis*, 8:5.
160. "Hominis autem Christi est duplex cognitio. Una quidem deiformis, secundum quod Deum per essentiam videt, et alia videt in Deo, sicut et ipse Deus intelligendo seipsum, intelligit omnia alia, per quam visionem et ipse Deus beatus est, et omnis creatura rationalis perfecte Deo fruens," Thomas Aquinas, *Comp. Theol.*, n. 216.

forget that after death you will be welcomed by Love itself. And in the love of God you will find as well all the noble loves which you had on earth."[161]

The Role of Progress, Temporality, and Resurrection within Eternal Life

Is it legitimate to speak of human progress and development in heaven? Substantially speaking, no, insofar as the prize of heaven, eternal life, has been obtained once and for all, and can never be lost. However, in the sense that the life of the blessed is human in the fullest sense of the word, it is not unthinkable that humans will be enriched more and more in eternal life. Irenaeus, for example, said that in heaven the Son will recount ever new things about the Father.[162] Likewise Gregory of Nyssa held that eternal life will involve never-ending growth.[163] Bernard was of a like mind.[164]

Time and Eternity

It should be asked, however, how meaningful it is to speak of time or succession within the category of eternal life, for if life is eternal, then it is timeless. And if it is timeless, then there will be no change, there will be no progress.[165] Yet, how can humans who participate in God's eternity remain within time? Clearly, this is a complex issue, and an important one. As one author puts it, "the relation between time and eternity is the crucial problem in eschatology."[166]

It is clear that the blessed do not experience the perfect and ineffable coming together of past, present, and future that characterizes the eternity of God, for they are creatures whose actions take place necessarily one after another, in succession, in such a way that each action is incapable of expressing the entirety of their being. Nonetheless, they do participate in God's eternity, and do not experience time as earthly wayfarers do. Time on earth is the characteristic of the pilgrim state: a space for growth and conversion, the opportunity God gives them to demonstrate their fidelity and love. In this sense time as opportunity will no longer be found in heaven.[167] But since humans will remain creatures always, their actions will be multiple and noncoincident, perpetually succeeding

---

161. Josemaría Escrivá, *Friends of God*, n. 221b.
162. Irenaeus, *Adv. Haer. IV*, 20:5–7; *II*, 28:3.
163. Gregory of Nyssa, *In cant. Hom.*, 9; on this see H. U. von Balthasar, *Présence et pensée. Essai sur la philosophie religieuse de Grégoire de Nysse* (Paris: Beauchesne, 1942), 67–80.
164. Bernard, *Tractatus de vita sol.; Ep.* 253.
165. In *SS* 12, Pope Benedict XVI says eternal life is "like plunging into the ocean of infinite love, a moment in which time—the before and after—no longer exists."
166. W. Pannenberg, *Systematic Theology*, vol. 3, 595.
167. According to Aquinas, there will be no succession in heaven: *III C. Gent.*, 61. The same idea is expressed by M.-J. Scheeben, *The Mysteries of Christianity*, 664.

one another. Their lives will never be absorbed, as it were, into God, but will be characterized always by some form of succession,[168] similar perhaps to the *aevum* that characterizes angelic existence.[169] It may be said that as creatures the blessed in heaven partake of "eternity as an inner possession of the totality of life," to use the expression of Karl Barth.[170] Another recent author has it that "if life is meaningful now because our time is filled with the activity of God, there seems to be no reason why a temporal process after death should not acquire a similar or greater meaningfulness because the same God is active in it."[171]

Resurrection and Eternal Life

Final resurrection is not the same thing as eternal life, not only because eternal life really starts on earth in faith,[172] but also in the sense that—according to a unanimous and ancient Christian tradition—the martyrs and those who are perfectly purified will be able to see God before resurrection takes place.[173] Nonetheless, the human subject cannot be said to be perfectly constituted as human in the absence of the corporeal complement resurrection provides.[174] Hence, though they are distinguishable from one another, the Christian creed has always associated eternal life and bodily resurrection. Jesus himself promises that "he who eats my flesh and drinks my blood has eternal life, and I will raise him up on the last day" (Jn 6:54). Only when resurrection takes place, when human society and corporality is fully reconstituted, when God's sovereignty is definitively manifested, can it be said that eternal life has reached its culmination and ultimate purpose.

As we saw already, Gregory of Nyssa speaks of eternal life as a process of gradual assimilation to God, beginning with death and culminating only when God is "all in all."[175] At resurrection, he says, humans, freed from aging and de-

---

168. Pannenberg says this in the following terms: "The finitude of the perfected . . . will no longer have the form of a sequence of separated moments of time but will represent the *totality* of our earthly existence," *Systematic Theology*, vol. 3, 561.

169. Speaking of the *aevum*, Aquinas says: "aevum differt a tempore et ab aeternitate. . . . Aeternitas non habet prius et posterius; tempus autem habet prius et posterius cum innovatione et veteratione; aevum habet prius et posterius sine innovatione et veteratione. . . . Aevum habet principium, sed non finem," *S. Th. I*, q. 10, a. 5c.

170. K. Barth, *Church Dogmatics* II/1 (Edinburgh: T. & T. Clark, 1957), 610–11. Barth changed from a dualistic opposition of eternity and time, and moved toward a view closer to Boethius, and at heart Plotinus.

171. R. F. Aldwinckle, *Death in the Secular City* (Grand Rapids, Mich.: W. B. Eerdmans, 1974), 160. According to Ruiz de la Peña, the dynamic view of eternal life is now a majority position: *La pascua de la creación*, 216, n. 58.

172. See pp. 152–53.   173. See pp. 276, n. 136.

174. See M. Brown, "Aquinas on the Resurrection of the Body."

175. See G. Filoramo, *L'escatologia e la retribuzione negli scritti dei Padri*, 272.

cay, will be consumed with an ever-increasing desire for God that transcends their own limitations constantly in a "beautiful passion of insatiability."[176] "This is really what seeing God means," Gregory concludes, "never to be satiated in one's desire; one must look always through what is possible to move towards the desire of seeing more, and be further inflamed."[177] John Chrysostom says that even Abraham and Paul "are waiting until you have reached fulfillment, that they then may receive their reward. For unless we too are present, the Savior has said that he will not give it to them, just as a kind and gentle father might tell his children, who have worked hard and deserved well, that he will not give them anything to eat until their brothers and sisters come."[178]

Augustine says: "When resurrection takes place, then the joy of the good will be greater, and the torments of the wicked worse, as they are tortured [or rewarded] along with their bodies."[179] For the interim state, between death and resurrection, he notes, is only a "small portion of the promise."[180] "For the day of retribution is coming when, our bodies having been returned to us, the whole man will receive what he has deserved."[181] In the Easter Liturgy of the *Roman Breviary* the following prayer is proclaimed: "Fill up the hope of the dead, so that they may obtain resurrection in the coming of Christ."[182]

Concluding Reflection: Eternal Life as Communion with the Trinity

When considering beatific vision above, we came across the possibility and danger of positing a quasi-substantial presence of God in the one who contemplates him directly, "without the mediation of any creature by way of object of vision."[183] We have also seen that the specific characteristic of Christian salvation lies in the notion that the divinizing union with God requires, as its inner complement, the human being's personal distinction from the Divinity. Pantheism, whether of an ontological or an existentialistic kind, would result should this distinction not be maintained. In this last section we shall consider two related issues: the so-called grades and relative infinity of eternal life in Christians, and the mediating role of Christ and the Spirit within eternal life.

The Grades and Relative Infinity of Eternal Life

The gift of divinization provides believers with a dignity quasi-divine. Becoming children of God, Christians obtain the inheritance of entering their

---

176. Gregory of Nyssa, *De mortuis or.*
177. Gregory of Nyssa, *Vita Moys.*, 2:239.
178. John Chrysostom, *In Hebr. Hom.* 28:1.
179. Augustine, *In Io. Ev. tr.*, 49:10.
180. Augustine, *Sermo* 280, 5.
181. Ibid.
182. "Spem defunctorum adimple, ut in adventu Christi resurrectionem assequantur," *Preces, ad II Vesp., Fer. VI, Haeb. VII Paschae.* See also Bernard, *Sermo 3*, on the feast of all the saints.
183. *DS* 1000. See pp. 168–69.

Father's house and praising him forever. However, this does not mean that participation in divine life involves complete identification with God, for humans are divinized, certainly, but do not become of one substance with the Divinity.[184] The human intellect, though united directly with God, is incapable of embracing the infinitely rich perfection of God without losing itself. As the book of Exodus says, "you cannot see my face; for no one shall see me and live" (33:20). The Scholastics described the phenomenon by saying that the blessed shall see God *totus sed non totaliter*;[185] they see "all" of God, in that God cannot be seen in parts on account of his simplicity; yet the depth of their knowledge depends on their personal capacity and situation. In other words the limits of the knowledge (and love) of the blessed derive not from God, but from themselves. It might be said that in heaven God gives people all the love and knowledge they are capable of receiving. In other words, there are grades in heaven.

The notion that heaven provides different rewards for different persons is common among the Fathers of the Church. According to Cyprian, the longer the martyr or confessor suffers, "the loftier will be his crown."[186] Those who consecrate themselves to God in virginity, he says, will receive "a double glory," the hundredfold fruit.[187]

The Council of Florence (1439) states clearly that the intensity of vision depends on the merit of each one; the blessed see "clearly God Himself, one and three, as He is, though some more perfectly than others, according to the diversity of their merits."[188] Like bottles filled with wine, each soul will be filled to the brim, even though each bottle may be very different in size from the rest.[189] Giovanni Moioli says that "the different ways of participating in the charity of Christ, that is different 'charisms,' different 'vocations,' etc. will not be leveled out even in heaven."[190] And Giacomo Biffi: "Each one of the blessed will have a beauty of his own, which is an expression not only of the different grade of love of God each one has, but also of the different way it has loved while on earth."[191]

The idea that there are different grades in eternal life and beatific vision was called into question by Luther, who argued that since salvation depends exclusively on God's grace and not on human works and merits, each one will receive simply what God gives. Humans may refuse the gift of eternal life, but whatev-

---

184. Thomas Aquinas, *De Ver.*, q. 8, a. 2 ad 3; *III C. Gent.*, 55; *S. Th. I*, q. 12, a. 7.
185. Thomas Aquinas, *S. Th. I*, q. 2, a. 7 ad 3; q. 12, a. 7 ad 3.
186. Cyprian, *Ep.* 37:3.   187. Cyprian, *Ep.* 76:6.
188. *DS* 1305.
189. This explanation is to be found in the Catechism of the German Episcopal Conference: Deutsche Bischofskonferenz, *Katholischer Erwachsenen-Katechismus: das Glaubensbekenntnis der Kirche*, 2nd ed. (Kevelaer: Butzon und Bercker, 1985), vol. 2, 421–22. See also Theresa of Avila, *Libro de la vida*, 37:2.
190. G. Moioli, *L'"Escatologico" cristiano*, 106.   191. G. Biffi, *L'al di là* (Roma: Paoline, 1960), 76.

er variety there may be among the blessed depends entirely on God's grace.[192]

Paul considers the eternal reward in connection with personal fidelity and dedication. "Henceforth there is laid up for me the crown of righteousness," he says, "which the Lord, the righteous Judge, will award me on that Day, but not only to me but also to all who have loved his appearing" (2 Tm 4:8). Doubtless, the Apostle gives priority to the gift of God, but the effort and correspondence of the believer is by no means excluded: "Neither he who plants nor he who waters is anything, but only God who gives the growth. He who plants and he who waters are equal, and each shall receive his wages according to his labor" (1 Cor 3:7–8). Elsewhere Paul speaks figuratively of the variety of God's gifts: "There is one glory of the sun, and another glory of the moon, and another of the stars; for star differs from star in glory" (1 Cor 15:41). In John's Gospel, Jesus tells us that "in my Father's house there are many rooms" (Jn 14:2).

However, in the parable of the workers in the public square (Mt 20:1–16), Jesus seems to be teaching that the wage given is the same for all, in spite of difference in effort and number of hours worked by each one. Understanding the parable in an eschatological sense, it would seem that the eternal reward is the same for each laborer, no matter how he worked or responded to God's gifts.[193] This would seem to lend support to Luther's position. However, the Fathers of the Church interpreted the parable in a variety of different ways.[194] Thomas Aquinas explains it as follows. "The oneness of the wage means the similar situation among the blessed in respect of the object [God]. But the diversity of places [Jn 14:2] refers to the diversity of beatitude according to the different grades of rejoicing."[195] The gift is substantially the same, but the quality of reception may vary a lot. Aquinas specifies that "the one who has *more charity* will participate more in the light of glory; the one who loves more will see God more perfectly and will be more blessed."[196]

However, Thomas also teaches that the grade of glory depends fundamentally on the grace of God, insofar as human response to grace is itself the fruit of grace.[197]

---

192. On the grades of glory in Protestant theology, see E. Disley, "Degrees of Glory: Protestant Doctrine and the Concept of Rewards Hereafter," *Journal of Theological Studies* 42 (1991): 77–105.

193. See D. A. Hagner, *Matthew*, 573–74.

194. Gregory of Nazianzen, *Or.*, 40:20; Gregory the Great, *Hom. in Ev.*, 10.

195. "Unitas denarii significat unitatem beatitudinis ex parte obiecti. Sed diversitas mansionum significat diversitatem beatitudinis secundum diversum gradum fruitionis," Thomas Aquinas, *S. Th. I-II*, q. 5, a. 2 ad 1.

196. "Plus autem participabit de lumine gloriae, qui plus habet de caritate, quia ubi est maior caritas, ibi est maius desiderium; et desiderium quodammodo facit desiderantem aptum et paratum ad susceptionem desiderati. Unde qui plus habebit de caritate, perfectius Deum videbit, et beatior erit," Thomas Aquinas, *S. Th. I*, q. 12, a. 6c.

197. Thomas Aquinas, *S. Th. I-II*, q. 112, a. 4c.

The Role of Christ in Eternal Life

This chapter is entitled "Eternal Life in the Glory of Christ." Heaven is, indeed, as the *Catechism of the Catholic Church* says, that "blessed community of all who are perfectly incorporated into Christ."[198] It is clear from Scripture that the situation of the blessed (as well as that of the condemned) depends directly on the person and saving action of the risen Lord. "Come, o blessed of my Father," Christ says to the just (Mt 25:34). And to the reprobate: "Depart *from me*, you cursed, into the eternal fire" (Mt 25:41). And to the repentant thief on the Cross, "Truly, I say to you, today you will be *with me* in paradise" (Lk 23:43).

It made sense that the deacon Stephen would cry out to Jesus, just before dying, "Lord Jesus, receive my spirit" (Acts 7:59). Among others, Saul—later Paul—was among those who witnessed and consented to his death (Acts 8:1). Paul expressed his own appreciation of the mystery and presence of Christ in dying, and in "eternal life in Christ Jesus our Lord" (Rom 6:23) in the following terms: "I am hard pressed between the two," he says. "My desire is to depart and be with Christ, for that is far better. But to remain in the flesh is more necessary on your account" (Phil 1:23–24). To the Philippians he also confided: "And my God will supply every need of yours according to his riches in glory in Christ Jesus" (Phil 4:19).

Thus, being with God in eternal life means being with Christ. The doctrine is clearly enunciated in John's Gospel. "In my Father's house there are many rooms; if it were not so, would I have told you that *I go to prepare a place for you?* And when I go and prepare a place for you, I will come again and *will take you to myself*, that *where I am you may be also*" (Jn 14:2–3). After the apostle Thomas asked him, "How can we know the way?" (Jn 14:5), Jesus summed up his identity in the following terms: "I am the way, and the truth, and the life; no one comes to the Father, but by me" (Jn 14:6).

We may ask, however, what the presence of Christ involves? Does he simply accompany believers in heaven, like the saints and angels, or does he actually unite the blessed with the Father? Is his role merely existential, or is it also ontological; is it decorative or metaphysical? The clarity of the New Testament texts just mentioned would seem to suggest the latter position. Yet we may ask a further question: once Jesus has united believers with God, is his task over, or does he give perpetual continuity to this union? As we saw above, the vision of God in heaven is considered to be direct, "without the mediation of any creature by way of object of vision."[199] So it would seem that once Christ has established the saved in communion with the Father, once he has redeemed us from our sins, his

---

198. *CCC* 1026.
199. *DS* 1000.

Heaven: Eternal Life 185

work is done, for the creature sees God "face to face." The question, however, is somewhat more complex. Three observations may be made.

First, Christ is the only mediator of Christian salvation,[200] of which eternal life is an integral part. "All things have been delivered to me by my Father, and no one knows the Father except the Son and any one to whom the Son chooses to reveal him" (Mt 11:27). Following the imagery of the heavenly banquet, Christ not only invites, admits, and accompanies the guests, but also serves them at table (Mt 20:28; Lk 12:37).

In the *second* place, it is correct to consider Christ's saving mediation eternal.[201] In contrast with the Levitical priesthood, Christ "holds his priesthood permanently, because he continues for ever. Consequently he is able for all time to save those who draw near to God through him, since he always lives to make intercession for them" (Heb 7:24–25). The same principle is to be found in the Church's creed: "his kingdom will have no end."[202] This formulation was added at the Council of Constantinople (381) to the Creed of Nicea (325) to avoid the position of some authors, who held that the Incarnation of the Word would come to a close at the end of time,[203] as soon as the work of "redemption" (that is, the forgiveness of sins in the strict sense, and liberation from the bondage of sin) is done, that is, once Christ delivers the kingdom to his Father (1 Cor 15:28).

Third, the permanence of Christ's priesthood is linked directly with the eternal glory of the saints. Thomas Aquinas has two interesting observations to make. *First*, he says, the fundamental reason why Christ is said to have possessed the immediate vision of God on earth is because he would eventually have to communicate it to the saved.[204] *Second*, Aquinas holds that the glory of the saved depends on Christ. While commenting on the text from the letter to the Hebrews cited above ("he always lives to make intercession for them"), Aquinas states: "The saints in heaven will have no need of expiation for their own sins, for, once they have been expiated, they must be consumed by Christ himself, on whom their glory depends [*a quo gloria eorum dependet*]."[205] It is clear of course

---

200. Jn 14:6; 1 Tm 2:5.
201. See the study of J. Alfaro, "Cristo glorioso, Revelador del Padre," *Gregorianum* 39 (1958): 222–70.
202. Creed of Nicea-Constantinople, *DS* 150.
203. The idea is inspired by Origen and is found, for example, in Marcellus of Ancyra and Evagrius Ponticus, as well as some Protestant authors following Calvin. For a good overview, see J. F. Jansen, "I Cor 15:24–28 and the Future of Jesus Christ," *Scottish Journal of Theology* 40 (1987): 543–70.
204. On the beatific vision of Christ, see the recent studies of R. Wielockx, "Incarnation et vision béatifique. Aperçus théologiques," *Revue des sciences philosophiques et théologiques* 86 (2002): 601–39; T. J. White, "The Voluntary Action of the Earthly Christ and the Necessity of the Beatific Vision," *Thomist* 69 (2005): 497–534; M. Hauke, "La visione beatifica di Cristo durante la Passione. La dottrina di San Tommaso d'Aquino e la teologia contemporanea," *Annales Theologici* 21 (2007): 381–98.
205. Thomas Aquinas, *S. Th. III*, q. 22, a. 5 ad 1.

that Christ's *humanity* is not as such the object of beatific vision. If it were, then no longer would there be a direct vision of the Father. However, in the order of what Aquinas calls the *medium sub quo* of knowledge (that does not determine the content of knowledge yet makes it possible),[206] or what elsewhere he calls the *vim cognoscendi*,[207] "the power to know," it is reasonable to suppose that the instrumental action of the humanity of Christ is in some way involved in the reception and maintenance of the perpetual vision of God.[208]

Seeing and Glorifying the Father and the Son in the Holy Spirit

Above we considered the text of John's first letter speaking of beatific vision. "Beloved, *we are God's children now;* it does not appear what we shall be, but we know that when he appears *we shall be like him,* for *we shall see him as he is*" (1 Jn 3:2). From an exegetical standpoint, it is not completely clear from the text who the object of vision is meant to be, whether God or Christ. Given that God is the subject of the phrase, God, simply, should be the object of vision. This is the most common and traditional interpretation,[209] which Vatican Council II and recent liturgical texts have adopted.[210] However, the use of the term "appear" (*phanerōthe:* "when he appears"), would seem to indicate that the subject of the sentence is Christ, for at the *Parousia* he, not the Father, is the One who will appear and be made manifest.[211] Instead of speaking of the vision of God, therefore, by right the text should be understood as referring to our vision of Christ.

Alternatively, it might be said that the vision of God should in fact exclude Christ, since, as we read in 1 Corinthians 15:28, at the end of time Christ will deliver the Kingdom to the Father, and God will be "all in all." So it would seem that two possible readings may be made: beatific vision is directed either to Christ or to the Father.

---

206. Thomas Aquinas, *In IV Sent.*, D. 49, q. 2, a. 1 ad 15, and *S. Th. I*, q. 12, a. 5 ad 2.

207. Thomas Aquinas, *In IV Sent.*, D. 49, q. 2, a. 1 ad 15.

208. See J. A. Riestra, *Cristo y la plenitud del cuerpo místico* (Pamplona: Eunsa, 1985), 170–76.

209. Thus Augustine, *In Io. Ev. Tr.*, 4; *De Civ. Dei XXII*, 29:1; Thomas Aquinas, *S. Th. I*, q. 12, a. 5 c. The same idea may be found in C. Spicq, *Agapé dans le Nouveau Testament*, vol. 2 (Paris: Lecoffre, 1959), 101, n. 3. Spicq concludes that "God in person is the object of vision," ibid.

210. In *LG* 48d, we read: "we have not yet appeared with Christ in glory (cf. Col 3:4) in which we will be like to God, for we will see him as he is (cf. 1 Jn 3:2)." In the 1979 document of the Congregation for the Doctrine of the Faith on eschatology, we read: "we shall be with Christ and 'we will see God' (cf. 1 Jn 3:2)," in *Enchiridion Vaticanum*, vol. 6, n. 1545. Toward the end of the III Eucharistic Prayer, the text of John is paraphrased as follows: "Welcome into your kingdom our departed brothers and sisters, and all who have left this world in your friendship. There we hope to share in your glory when every tear will be wiped away. On that day *we shall see you, our God, as you are.* We shall become like you and praise you for ever through Christ our Lord, from whom all good things come."

211. 1 Jn 2:28 and 1 Jn 3:5, situated immediately before and after the text we are considering, both apply the term "appear" to Christ.

Heaven: Eternal Life 187

Perhaps there is no real need to contrast excessively the two readings. After all, to see Christ "as He is" (*auton kathōs estin:* 1 Jn 3:2) is to perceive his divinity, which is always consubstantial to and inseparable from that of the Father. The text, in other words, may be indicating simply that to see God is to see the Father and the Son in their distinction and mutual love. During the Last Supper, Philip asks Jesus, "'Lord, show us the Father, and we shall be satisfied.' Jesus said to him, 'Have I been with you so long, and yet you do not know me, Philip? *He who has seen me has seen the Father. . . .* Do you not believe that *I am in the Father and the Father is in me?*'" (Jn 14:8–10). Later on, during the priestly prayer, Jesus says: "And this is eternal life, that they know you, the only true God, and Jesus Christ whom you have sent. . . . And now, Father, glorify me in your own presence with the glory which I had with you before the world was made. . . . Father, I desire that they also, whom you have given me, may be with me where I am, to behold my glory which you have given me in your love for me before the foundation of the world" (Jn 17:3,5,24). In seeing Christ as he is, as the only Word-Son of the Father, the blessed will ipso facto see the Father.[212] Besides, as regards the Son who delivers the Kingdom to the Father (1 Cor 15:28), Hillary of Poitiers says, "he shall deliver the Kingdom to the Father, not in the sense that he resigns his power by the delivering, but that we, being conformed to the glory of his body, shall form the Kingdom of God."[213]

In following the basic thrust of the New Testament it is clear that Christ is the one who reveals the Father (Jn 1:18, etc.). Yet given that our union with Christ is the fruit of grace, of God's self-giving, it is also clear that our knowledge of the Son, and of the Father in the Son, takes place in the Holy Spirit, "who interiorizes in Christians the knowledge of the mystery of Christ."[214] As we saw above, the Spirit is not only the One who communicates God's grace, but also the one who perennially reminds believers of the gift-quality of such graces.[215] The Holy Spirit is "the One who expresses hypostatically within the Trinity the overflowing and unreserved mutual donation of the Father and the Son which constitutes the

---

212. See A. Fernández, *La escatología en el siglo II* (Burgos: Aldecoa, 1979), 271–80; R. Winling, "Une façon de dire le salut: la formule 'être avec Dieu-être avec Jésus Christ' dans les écrits de l'ère dite des Pères Apostoliques," *Revue des sciences religieuses* 54 (1980): 97–108. According to Irenaeus, "God will be seen in the kingdom of heaven; the Son will lead us to the Father," *Adv. Haer IV,* 20:5. Origen says: "Then, one will see the Father and the things of the Father for oneself, just as the Son does, no longer merely recognizing in the image the reality of the one whose image it is. And I think this will be the end, when the Son hands over the Kingdom of God to his Father, and when God becomes all in all," *Comm. in Io.,* 20,7:47–48.

213. Hillary of Poitiers, *De Trin.,* 11:39. On the doctrine of Hillary, see M.-J. Rondeau, "Remarques sur l'anthropologie de saint Hilaire," *Studia patristica* 6 (1962): 197–210.

214. M.-J. Le Guillou, "Le développement de la doctrine sur l'Esprit Saint," 734.

215. See pp. 33–36.

life of the Trinity." The Spirit makes "present in the believer the fullness of the relationship between the Father and the Son, which is perceived as an ineffable presence of divine life in the perpetual modality of donation."[216]

Pannenberg speaks of the work of the Spirit as that of achieving in creatures the glorification and praise of God. The notion of glorification

> links the new life of the resurrection to the moment of judgment that carries with it the transfiguration of this earthly life by means of the relation to God the Father and to the praise of God. The glorifying of God in this comprehensive sense is the proper and final work of the Spirit, who is also the Creator of life, the source of all knowledge, as also of faith and hope and love, and therewith, too, of freedom and peace, and hence of the common life of creatures in mutual recognition that is perfected in the kingdom of God and that finds expression already in sign in the fellowship of the church. In all these areas the work of the Spirit always aims already at the glorifying of God in his creation, and in his eschatological work this aspect will come to the fore in an overwhelming way, gathering together and transforming all else.[217]

Speaking of the Holy Spirit, Louis Bouyer likewise writes that

> the more that contemplatives, the friends of God, experience personally "how good the Lord is," the more they have held, without a shadow of doubt, that the One [the Spirit] they have known will remain unknown until the final day, until the day of the Parousia, when finally we will know how we are known from all eternity. But it is also true, as Gregory of Nyssa said, that we will never be capable of absorbing, of completely interiorizing this knowledge: rather, this knowledge will absorb us; "by surpassings that never end, it will immerse us in an abyss of light, from which then and ever more will we know to what degree it is ineffable."[218]

---

216. *CAA* 291.
217. W. Pannenberg, *Systematic Theology*, vol. 3, 623–24. He explains that in the New Testament, the Spirit and the glory of God stand for the same thing: see ibid., 624.
218. L. Bouyer, *Le Consolateur: Esprit-Saint et vie de grâce* (Paris: Cerf, 1980), 452.

7

Hell: The Perpetual Retribution of the Sinner

Hell is not to love any more.
—*Georges Bernanos*[1]

The possibility of perpetual condemnation of the unrepentant sinner is a nonnegotiable element of the doctrinal patrimony of Christian faith. This does not mean of course that Christians "believe" as such in hell. Much less are they obliged to believe that some specific individuals have actually been condemned, or that a certain percentage of believers have forfeited, or will have to forfeit, eternal life forever. Rather they believe in a God who has created humans in such a way that they are capable of freely losing the reward of communion with the Trinity promised to those who are faithful, if they do so in such a clear-minded, responsible, and irrevocable way, that their alienation from God becomes insuperable. Acceptance of the doctrine of eternal condemnation (commonly termed "hell") has important anthropological implications, and more important theological ones. Anthropological implications, in that human freedom is considered such that humans are truly to blame for their perdition; theological ones, because eternal perdition is no less than the loss of God, and God created all humans with a capacity for rejecting a love he is not prepared to impose on them. Paradoxically, the existence of hell—or more precisely the real possibility of eternal condemnation or "eternal death"[2]—is based on two of the most sublime and liberating truths of the Christian faith: that God is a faithful, loving God, and that humans are truly free.

The Church has consistently taught this doctrine throughout history.[3] As re-

---

1. G. Bernanos, *Diary of a Country Priest* (London: Catholic Book Club, 1937), 177.
2. On terminological questions, see J. J. Alviar, *Escatología*, 245–46.
3. The *Quicumque* Symbol professes that "those who do good will go to eternal life; those who do evil, to eternal fire," DS 76. Pope Vigil at the Synod of Constantinople (543) condemned Origen's position in respect of the temporality of punishment: can. 9, DS 411. Pope Innocent III in his *Profession of Faith* at Lateran Council IV (1215) proclaimed the eternity of condemnation: DS 801. He also taught that "the punishment for original sin is the exclusion from the vision of God, while that for actual sin is the perpetual torment in Gehenna," DS 780. Other medieval Church documents speak in similar terms: DS 858 and 1306. Paul VI in his 1968 *Profession of Faith* taught that "those who have opposed God to the end

gards recent Church declarations, the following ones from Vatican Council II and the *Catechism of the Catholic Church* should suffice. *Lumen gentium* speaks of the vigilance Christians should have, "so that, when the single course of our earthly life is completed, we may merit to enter with [the Lord] into the marriage feast and be numbered among the blessed and not, like the wicked and slothful servants (Mt 25:26), be ordered to depart into the eternal life (Mt 25:41), into the outer darkness where 'men will weep and gnash their teeth' (Mt 22:13 & 25:30)."[4] And in the *Catechism:* "The teaching of the Church affirms the existence of hell and its eternity. Immediately after death the souls of those who die in a state of mortal sin descend into hell, where they suffer the punishments of hell, 'eternal fire.'"[5]

In this chapter on eternal punishment we shall consider the following five questions: the development of the doctrine of perpetual condemnation in Scripture and the Fathers of the Church; the nature of hell from a theological standpoint; its relationship with the justice and mercy of God; how real the possibility of some being condemned is; and the question of the hope of universal salvation.

Perpetual Condemnation in Scripture and the Fathers

The notion of some form of retribution after death was assumed generally by many, if not most, religious visions with which the people of Israel had contact.[6] This should not come as a surprise given the perennial human desire for both immortality and justice. Humanity has never been able to live with the thought of grave crimes remaining unredressed. The consolidation of the doctrine of hell is the natural consequence of this desire for justice: humans must pay, before or after death, for their crimes, unless they are prepared to repent and make amends beforehand.

It may come as a surprise, however, to find that among the Jews the idea of *postmortem* retribution for sinners was uncommon, or more accurately, that it consolidated gradually as a later doctrinal development. Elsewhere we have briefly considered the question.[7] On the one hand, the Israelites feared that a doctrine of punishment after death could facilitate the development of cult toward the dead,

---

will go to eternal fire," n. 12. The 1979 document on eschatology of the Congregation for the Doctrine of the Faith taught that "the Church, in fidelity to the New Testament and Tradition, believes in the happiness of the just . . . and that a perpetual punishment awaits the sinner, who will be deprived of divine vision; the Church also believes that this punishment will affect the entire being of the sinner," *Recentiores episcoporum Synodi*, n. 7.

4. *LG* 48d. 5. *CCC* 1035.
6. See indications in L. Moraldi, *L'alidlà dell'uomo*, passim.
7. See pp. 78–80.

and they wished to avoid this on account of the danger of idolatry.[8] On the other hand, the prophets for the most part were convinced that God would bring about justice here on earth, as he had done on other occasions.[9] In any case the doctrine of perpetual other-worldly punishment did not consolidate till later on.

The Old Testament

Several moments in the development of the doctrine may be noted.[10] *First*, the dilemma of the punishment of sinners, already considered when examining the origin of the doctrine of final resurrection.[11] The same predicament may be found in the book of Job. At the outset Job was unable to understand why he had been afflicted and punished, and he rebelled against God's apparent arbitrariness and harshness. Later on, however, he discovered that he had no right to contest divine providence (Jb 38–42). It gradually became clear to him that God will vindicate the just and punish sinners, but not necessarily in this life, but rather, after death. In the *second* place, a kind of evolution may be observed in the Old Testament teaching about the "underworld," or *she'ol*. In effect, *she'ol*, which has many elements in common with the Greek *hadēs*, is considered in earlier biblical texts as being identical for all the dead, whether just or unjust. Gradually, however, different "levels" emerged within *she'ol*. This is especially noticeable in the prophets (Ez 32:22–32; Is 14:15) and the Psalms. Because of this, it is said that the just may be saved from the depths of *she'ol* (Ps 15; 48; 72). The book of Wisdom contrasts the situation of sinners in *she'ol* (Ws 4:19) with that of the just (Ws 5:3–13) who live in the "bosom of Abraham" (Lk 16:22).

Third, the book of Isaiah speaks of a place near Jerusalem where sinners would be tormented forever. The prophet describes the future restoration of Israel, especially the triumph of Jerusalem, where the elect will go to contemplate the glory of God and make their offering (Is 66:18–20). Then the prophet tells us that, on leaving the city, pilgrims "shall look at the dead bodies of the people who have rebelled against [the Lord]; for their worm shall not die, their fire shall not be quenched, and they shall be an abhorrence to all flesh" (Is 66:24). The text is of particular interest on account of the fact that it is employed by John the Baptist and Jesus himself to speak of eternal punishment. In fact, the very term used in the New Testament to designate hell, *gēnna* or Gehenna (Mt 5:30; 10:28; etc.),[12] seems to be derived from the term *Ge-hinnòm*, the same place where corpses were cremated, probably in the valley of Hinnom, close to Jerusalem (Jr 7:31–34; 19:4–7), where the abomination of offering human sacrifices to Moloch had been committed.

---

8. See p. 78, n. 30.
9. See pp. 80–82 above.
10. See C. Pozo, *La teología del más allá*, 424–31.
11. See pp. 80–81.
12. *CAA* 100.

The New Testament

References to eternal punishment in the New Testament are conspicuously abundant and consistent. There is considerable continuity with Old Testament texts. John the Baptist, from the beginning of his preaching, speaks of the punishment of those who will not convert. "Every tree that does not bear good fruit is cut down and thrown into the fire" (Mt 3:10). When the Messiah comes at harvest time, he adds, "the chaff he will burn with unquenchable fire" (Mt 3:12).

All in all, five doctrinal elements may be noted in Jesus' teaching and that of the apostles.

First the existence of an unpardonable sin, usually related to the rejection of the Holy Spirit and refusal to open oneself to God's pardon. "And whoever says a word against the Son of man will be forgiven; but whoever speaks against the Holy Spirit will not be forgiven, either in this age or in the age to come" (Mt 12:32). In John's Gospel the unpardonable sin is related to the lack of belief in Jesus, for he said to the scribes and Pharisees that "you will die in your sins unless you believe that I am He" (Jn 8:24). In this he repeats what was said earlier on in the Gospel: "He who does not believe is condemned already, because he has not believed in the name of the only Son of God" (Jn 3:18).

In the *second* place, Jesus establishes a clear distinction between the good and the evil, the saved and the condemned, even though the distinction between them will be revealed only at the end of time. "So it will be at the close of the age. The angels will come out and separate the evil from the righteous" (Mt 13:49). The idea is repeated often throughout the gospels (Mt 24:31; 25:31–32; etc.). For example, the *locus classicus:* "When the Son of man comes in his glory, and all the angels with him . . . he will separate them one from the other as the shepherd separates the sheep from the goats" (Mt 25:31–32).

Third, Paul speaks frequently of the exclusion of the sinner from "eternal life" or from the kingdom. "Do you not know that the unrighteous will not inherit the kingdom of God? Do not be deceived: neither the immoral, nor idolaters, nor adulterers, nor sexual perverts, nor thieves, nor the greedy, nor drunkards, nor revilers, nor robbers will inherit the kingdom of God" (1 Cor 6:9–10). When speaking about certain kinds of sin, the same idea arises (Gal 5:19–26; Eph 5:5). This is Paul's equivalent to Jesus' way of explaining condemnation in terms of a definitive distancing from God: "Depart from me you cursed" (Mt 25:41); "And then I will declare to them: 'I never knew you; depart from me, you evildoers'" (Mt 7:23). To the unwise virgins, the Spouse announced: "Truly I say to you, I do not know you" (Mt 25:12). In other words, hell is presented in the New Testament not simply as a neutral "lack" or absence of eternal life, but rather as a true privation of what man was destined for, a divine condemnation.

Fourth, the New Testament goes into quite some detail in explaining the nature of eternal punishment, particularly of the "fire of *gēnna*." "If your eye causes you to sin," Mark writes, "pluck it out; it is better for you to enter the kingdom of God with one eye than with two eyes to be thrown in *gēnna*, where their worm does not die, and the fire is not quenched" (Mk 9:47–48; cf. Mt 5:29), a virtual repetition of Isaiah 66:24, already cited. As we saw above, the expression *"gēnna"* seems equivalent to "furnace of fire" (Mt 13:42,50). In this furnace, Matthew tells us, "men will weep [*Ge-hinnòn*, translated as the "valley of groanings"] and gnash their teeth" (Mt 13:50). The three most common expressions in the New Testament are therefore: "furnace of fire," the "worm that does not die," and the "gnashing of teeth." According to the Psalms (37:12; 112:10) the latter expression probably refers to the dismay, frustration, and envy of the wicked upon seeing the virtuous rewarded.

Fifth and last, the New Testament speaks clearly of the perpetual character of eschatological punishment. Hell involves, as we have seen, an unpardonable sin, an exclusion from the kingdom, a fire that is not quenched. Permanence and impenitence are essential. Of course the term "eternal" is more properly applied to heaven than to hell, in that the former involves a partaking in God's own (eternal) life, and the latter, more than anything else, involves a separation from God. Still, Matthew speaks of "eternal fire" (Mt 25:41) and "eternal punishment" (Mt 25:46). To the Thessalonians Paul speaks of "eternal destruction" (2 Thes 1:9). The book of Revelation applies the liturgical formula "forever and ever"—equivalent to "eternal"—to hell: "And the smoke of their torment goes up forever and ever; and they have no rest, day or night, these worshipers of the beast and its image" (Rv 14:11).

Interpreting New Testament Texts That Speak of Hell

The openness with which the New Testament speaks of eternal punishment is undeniable. Given the harshness and insistence of these texts, some of which we have just cited, it is understandable that many authors have considered them open to alternative interpretations, perhaps of an existentialist or performative kind.[13] As we saw earlier on, this position was put forward, for example, by Origen and by Rahner.[14] It is commonly held that the purpose of these texts is that of provoking a salutary reaction among Christians or potential converts, with a view to ensuring that they take the revelation of the love of God in Jesus Christ in all its seriousness. By implication, this means that there is no need to take the

---

13. *CAA* 46.
14. Origen, *C. Cels.*, 5:15; *De princip. II*, 10:6. The same position may be found in K. Rahner: see p. 16 above, n. 62.

texts literally, as predictions about the future, but rather they should be seen as expressions of the power and transcendence of God who will tolerate no rivals. Two observations may be made.

In the *first* place, the language used in Scripture to speak of matters eschatological is openly metaphorical. The reason for this is simple: the reality of reward and punishment goes beyond any experience we have or can have on earth. Hence metaphors have to be used. As Pannenberg observes, however, "the matter itself is not metaphor, only the way of stating it. We must not infer the unreality of the matter from the metaphorical form of statement."[15] Expressions such as the "furnace of fire," the "worm that does not die," and the "weeping and gnashing of teeth" are clearly open to different forms of interpretation. Yet expressions that refer openly, for example, to the perpetual character of condemnation can hardly be metaphorical. If these expressions did not correspond to what they seem to be saying, they would be flagrantly misleading in a matter of enormous significance, and cannot be considered as belonging to the inspired text.

Second, the apparent injustice and harshness that typifies the classical apocalyptic should not be taken as a measure for interpreting the New Testament affirmations about the existence and nature of hell. It should rather be taken the other way around. According to the former texts, God would suddenly punish the wicked, without giving them a chance to repent, and reward the just who are lucky enough to be on the right side when the Son of man makes his appearance.[16] According to Scripture, however, neither reward nor punishment will be unjust or improper, because salvation has already been extended to humanity, offered, besides, in the most human and accessible possible way. "Whereas the classical apocalyptic envisaged the prompt coming of God in power in terms of divine wrath being unleashed upon impenitent sinners, and as deserved consolation for the just who are already saved," according to the New Testament,

> Jesus came as God's Messiah in the first place *to save sinners*. Because he gave his whole life to this mission, that is, because he was our *Savior*, he would be in a position to later *judge* the world in perfect justice, since humans will have been given every possible opportunity of responding fully to saving grace. . . . The One who would mete out eschatological punishment was one and the same as he who in the first place had suffered it. As a result, humans are not merely the objects of arbitrary punishment for their sinfulness, or of preordained reward for their goodness. All humans are placed in a position to react freely *and responsibly* to the saving power that Christ makes available to them, and at the same time are invited to communicate the saving message of Christ to the rest of humankind.[17]

---

15. W. Pannenberg, *Systematic Theology*, vol. 3, 621.
16. *CAA* 79–81, 99–100, 253.
17. *CAA* 297.

Thus there is no reason not to take the New Testament affirmations on face value, in a substantially literal way.

Perpetual Condemnation among the Fathers of the Church

Three principal positions may be found among the Fathers of the Church in respect of eternal punishment.

First, the early Fathers repeat for the most part New Testament statements in respect of eternal punishment, just as they are. This is so with Ignatius of Antioch, the *Martyrdom* of Polycarp, Clement's *Letter to the Corinthians*, and so on. The Apologists—Justin, for example—attempt to come to grips with the doctrine and explain it in greater depth. Likewise, Irenaeus distinguishes between eternal and temporal punishment.[18] The *Letter to Diognetus* reflects on the gravity of hell.[19] However, the principal thrust of Christian teaching in the first two or three centuries is that Christ brought the good news of salvation and that those condemned would not necessarily be a majority.[20]

In the *second* place, particular attention should be paid to the position adopted by Origen.[21] The latter considered the pains of hell as temporary and medicinal. Eventually all sinners will be purified of the sins they freely committed, he said, and will be saved: this is usually called the doctrine of the *apokatastasis*, or universal reconciliation.[22] For Origen, the reason why the Church should preach about eternal condemnation is to inflict "terror on those who would not otherwise be held back from sinning abundantly."[23] The ignorant masses must be instructed with harshness, although true Christian believers are aware that the doctrine of eternal punishment constitutes a mere verbal threat. "To communicate these things (speculations about the *gēnna*) openly and at length, by ink and pen and parchment, seems to me incautious," Origen observes.[24] The medicinal

18. Irenaeus, *Adv. Haer. IV*, 28:2.
19. Anon., *Letter to Diognetus*, 10:7–8.
20. See A. Michel, "Elus, (Nombre des)," in *DTC* 4, cols. 2350–78, here, cols. 2364–65.
21. On the deterrence argument, see Origen, *Hom. in Jer.*, 12:4. See also B. E. Daley, *The Hope*, 56–57; P. Nemeshegyi, *La paternité de Dieu chez Origène* (Paris; Tournai: 1960), 203–24; J. Rius-Camps, "La hipótesis origeniana sobre el fin último (*peri telous*). Intento de valoración," in *Arché e telos: l'antropologia di Origene e di Gregorio di Nissa: analisi storico-religiosa*, ed. U. Bianchi and H. Crouzel (Milano: Vita e pensiero, 1981), 58–117.
22. See pp. 170–71. Origen doubted this doctrine in earlier writings, for example in his *Letter to Friends in Alexandria* (231), recorded by Jerome, *Apol. adv. Ruf.*, 2:18–19. According to C. C. Richardson, "The Condemnation of Origen," in *Church History* 6 (1937): 50–64, and H. Crouzel, "A Letter from Origen 'to Friends in Alexandria,'" in *The Heritage of the Early Church: Essays in Honor of the Very Reverend Georges Vasilievich Florovsky*, ed. D. Neiman and M. Schatkin (Roma: Pontificium Istitutum Studiorum Orientalium, 1973), 135–50, Origen strongly rejects the devil's redemption. Later on, however, at least according to Ruffinus's translation of *De principiis*, the question is left open to the reader.
23. Origen, *C. Cels.*, 5:15.
24. Origen, *Comm. Serm. in Matth.*, 16.

character of punishment in "hell," he says, has to be concealed from "those who are still 'little ones' with respect to their spiritual age."[25] He insists, nonetheless, that the punishment of hell, though temporal, is terrifyingly painful.

Origen's teaching exercised a significant influence over Christian believers, especially those of a Gnostic or spiritualistic bent, and was accepted by other ecclesiastical writers such as Evagrius Ponticus and Didymus the Blind.[26] Some Fathers of the Church, the so-called merciful Fathers,[27] Gregory of Nyssa,[28] Ambrose,[29] and Jerome,[30] accepted it for a time.

25. Origen, *Hom. I in Ezek.*, 3. Origen cites 1 Cor 3:11–15 to justify his theory of medicinal purification: see H. Crouzel, "L'exégèse origénienne de 1 Co 3,11–25 et la purification eschatologique," in *Epektasis. Mélanges patristiques offerts au cardinal Jean Daniélou* (Paris: Beauchesne, 1972), 273–83. All are sent, Origen says, to what he calls a "school for souls," *De princip.* II, 11:6, what Scripture calls paradise or the heavenly Jerusalem. Salvation for all, he says, is part of Paul's promise in 1 Cor 15:24–8, and will constitute the end of all evil.

26. See B. E. Daley, *The Hope*, 90–91.

27. Ambrose, Ambrosiaster, and Jerome are generally considered as "merciful fathers," and hold that humans for the most part will be saved through purification. Against Novatianus it was said that the faithful will be saved, because, though sinners, they are still part of the Church, unless they leave it by apostasy or heresy. See H. De Lavalette, "L'interprétation du Psaume 1,5 chez les Pères 'miséricordieux,'" *Recherches de science religieuse* 48 (1960): 544–63.

28. On Gregory of Nyssa, see B. E. Daley, *The Hope*, 85–89; J. Daniélou, "L'apocatastase chez Saint Grégoire de Nysse," *Revue des sciences religieuses* 30 (1940): 328–47; B. Salmona, "Origene e Gregorio di Nissa sulla resurrezione dei corpi e l'apocatastasi," *Augustinianum* 18 (1978): 383–88. Gregory openly rejects Origen's doctrine of the preexistence of souls, because even a life of heavenly contemplation is not secure from sin. In fact it could involve an endless cycle of falls and restorations: *De An. et Res.* In some texts Gregory seems to share Origen's hope for universal salvation, although others do exclude sinners from the kingdom of God, for example: *In Inscr. Psal.*, 2:16; *De Paup. Amand.* On the question, see C. N. Tsirpanlis, *Greek Patristic Theology: Basic Doctrines in Eastern Church Fathers* (New York: EO Press, 1979), 41–56. The reason Gregory gives for this is that evil cannot endure forever, not being a substance in its own right. Only the good can assume the character of permanence: *De An. et res.; De hom. opif.* 21:1; *De Tridui Spatio.* On this issue, see J. Daniélou, "Le comble du mal et l'eschatologie de S. Grégoire de Nysse," in *Festgabe Joseph Lortz*, ed. E. Iserloh and P. Manns, vol. 2 (Baden-Baden: Grimm, 1958), 27–45. Evil and death, on the contrary, are the creation of humans (*De Virg.*, 12), whereas every life will move toward the good, especially by means of resurrection: see J. Daniélou, "La résurrection des corps chez Grégoire de Nysse," *Vigiliae Christianae* 2 (1953): 154–70. However, as Maspero points out, universal reconciliation in Gregory is applied to human nature as a whole, but not to each and every individual: G. Maspero, *La Trinità e l'uomo*, 176–200.

29. Likewise, Ambrose (*In Ps.*, 1) holds that punishment is entirely medicinal and therefore temporary: see B. E. Daley, *The Hope*, 98–99. He repeats Gregory's idea to the effect that evil is not a substance and thus cannot endure forever. Daley sums up his position as follows: "God constrains us to repentance through suffering, so that the evil accident we know as wickedness is burned and consumed by repentance, and disappears. Then that region of the soul, which was possessed by the accident of wickedness, will be laid open to receive virtue and grace," *The Hope*, 98–99. The times of purification are linked with first and second resurrection, and "so Ambrose transforms the millennial tradition . . . into an allegory of the 'interim' state between death and general resurrection," ibid., 99. On Ambrose, see J. Deramburre, "Le millénarisme de S. Ambroise," *Revue des études anciennes* 17 (1910): 545–56. He insists on God's mercy to all (*In Ps.*, 39:17; 118,20,29), but bliss is reserved only for those who are "joined to the holy Church" (*De Exc. Frat.*, 116).

30. Jerome held a position similar to Origen's in his early works. He said that "all rational creatures

Hell: Perpetual Retribution   197

Others, such as John Chrysostom, were openly critical of Origen's pedagogical argument.[31] "It is impossible that punishment and *gēnna* should not exist," he said.[32] "If God takes such care that we should not sin, and goes to such trouble to correct us, it is clear that he punishes sinners and crowns the upright."[33] Punishments are now "for our correction," certainly, "but later they will be for vindication."[34] Likewise Augustine openly rejected Origen's allegorical interpretation of scriptural teaching on the eternity of hell.[35] The permanence of hell and the eternity of heaven, he argued, are two sides of the same coin.[36]

The doctrine of the *apokatastasis* was not eventually accepted by the Church, the following Origenist position being rejected at the Synod of Constantinople in 543: "The punishment of the demons and of impious men is temporary, and that it will come to an end at some time, or that there will be a complete restoration [*apokatastasis*] of demons and impious men."[37]

Third, most of the Fathers of the Church from the third and fourth centuries onward not only held to the eternal character of hell, but also that the greater part of humanity was destined to condemnation. This position was assumed, besides, by the majority of the principal theologians and spiritual authors up to the modern period, as well as by many Eastern and Protestant theologians.[38] Thomas Aquinas's position, though couched in positive terms, is not untypical:

---

will see the glory of God in ages to come," all will be restored, even the "renegade angels," *In Eph.*, 1,2:7. Yet in other early works, he says that sinners will have no chance of repentance and purification: *In Eccl.*, 7:16. In later works, however, eternal punishment is clearly reserved for the devil and the enemies of Christ: *Comm. in Matth.*, 1,10,28; 2,22,11–12; 4,25,46.

31. E. Michaud, "St. Jean Chrysostome et l'apokatastase," *Revue internationale de théologie* 18 (1910): 672–796, attempts to show John's eschatology is Origenist. However, S. Schiewietz, "Die Eschatologie des hl. Johannes Chrysostomus und ihr Verhältnis zu der Origenistischen," *Der Katholik* (Strasbourg) 4, no. 12 (1913–1914), 445–55; 4, no. 13 (1914): 45–63, 200–16, 271–81, 370–79, 436–48, convincingly shows the contrary.

32. John Chrysostom, *In I Thess.*, 8:4.

33. John Chrysostom, *In Rom. Hom.*, 31:4. "He says that he has prepared Gehenna that he might not cast into Gehenna," *In Ps.*, 7:12.

34. John Chrysostom, *In Rom. Hom.*, 3:1.   35. Augustine, *De Civ. Dei XXII*, 23.

36. Augustine explains it as follows: "Christ in the very same passage included both punishment and life in one and the same sentence when he said, 'So those people will go into eternal punishment, while the righteous will go into eternal life' (Mt 25:46). If both are 'eternal,' it follows necessarily that either both are to be taken as long-lasting but finite, or both as endless and perpetual. The phrases 'eternal punishment' and 'eternal life' are parallel and it would be absurd to use them in one and the same sentence to mean 'Eternal life will be infinite, while eternal punishment will have an end,'" *De Civ. Dei XXI*: 23. See also his *Ad Orosium*, 6,7.

37. Origen's position was condemned by the Synod of Constantinople (543): *DS* 411.

38. A. Michel, in his study "Elus," claims that according to many Fathers of the Church, *maior pars hominum damnatur*, the greater part of humanity will be condemned: thus Basil, John Chrysostom, Gregory of Nazianzen, Hillary, Ambrose, Jerome, Augustine, Leo the Great; during the Middle Ages and later, Bernard, Thomas Aquinas, Molina, Suárez, Alphonsus de Liguori, etc.

pauciores sunt qui salvantur:[39] "those who are saved are fewer in number." Later on, we shall return to this disconcerting affirmation.[40]

Everlasting Punishment as the Fruit of Unrepentant Sin

What does eternal condemnation actually consist of? On the one hand, the affirmations of Scripture, though metaphorical in many cases, offer useful indications as regards the nature of hell. On the other hand, given that eternal condemnation is the final product and definitive outcome of sin, it makes sense to seek understanding by considering the theological nature of sin and its consequences, not just its psychological or anthropological traits. We should keep in mind, however, that hell reveals the depths of sin, and not the other way around. We can best comprehend sin when we contemplate what sin—grave sin—has brought about: the death of God's Son on the Cross and the perpetual condemnation of the sinner. The reality of unrepentant sin is perceived and experienced only when it blossoms, as it were, in its final product, which is perpetual condemnation. "Hell in its deepest reality is a mystery," Schmaus says, "the mystery of sin, because it is the effect and experience of mortal sin, just as heaven is the fullness of union with God, so also hell is the fullness of sin."[41]

Sin and Its Issue

Thomas Aquinas explains that just as there are two stages in grave sin, so also two stages or aspects may be attributed to hell: the pain of loss and the pain of sense. "There are two elements in sin," he writes. "One is the turning away from the unchangeable Good [usually called the *aversio a Deo*], and in this sin is infinite. The other is the inordinate turning toward the changeable good [*conversio ad creaturas*], and in this sin is finite. The pain of damnation corresponds to the turning away from God, the loss of an infinite good. Whereas the pain of the senses corresponds to the inordinate turning toward creatures."[42] Instead of

---

39. Thomas Aquinas, *S. Th. I*, q. 23, a. 7 ad 3.
40. See pp. 215–16.
41. M. Schmaus, *Katholische Dogmatik*, vol. 4.2: *Von den letzten Dingen*, 467. In the words of G. Minois, hell "is the mirror of the failed attempts of each civilization to resolve its social problems; it is a mark of the ambiguity of the human condition," *Histoire des enfers* (Paris: Fayard, 1991), 7.
42. "Poena proportionatur peccato. In peccato autem duo sunt. Quorum unum est aversio ab incommutabili bono, quod est infinitum, unde ex hac parte peccatum est infinitum. Aliud quod est in peccato, est inordinata conversio ad commutabile bonum. Et ex hac parte peccatum est finitum, tum quia ipsum bonum commutabile est finitum; tum quia ipsa conversio est finita, non enim possunt esse actus creaturae infiniti. Ex parte igitur aversionis, respondet peccato poena damni, quae etiam est infinita, est enim amissio infiniti boni, scilicet Dei. Ex parte autem inordinatae conversionis, respondet ei poena sensus, quae etiam est finita," Thomas Aquinas, *S. Th. I-II*, q. 87, a. 4c.

submitting himself to God, the creature who sins turns away from the Divinity and becomes attached in a disorderly way to creatures. Let us examine these two aspects of hell: pain of loss and pain of sense.

The Pain of Loss

"The principal pain of hell," the *Catechism of the Catholic Church* says, "is eternal separation from God."[43] Sin brings about separation from the Divinity; unrepented sin perpetuates this situation forever. We have already seen different expressions of this aspect of sin and hell, for example, when Jesus said to sinners: "Depart from me, you cursed" (Mt 25:41), and "I never knew you, depart from me, you evildoers" (Mt 7:23). It is clear that hell is not simply the continuation of the situation of sin; rather it is presented as an act of God who banishes forever the creature who has rejected him. Hell is not merely a lack or an absence of God, but "the privation of the vision of God," as a recent Church document states.[44] In other words, God refuses his communion with those who have rejected his friendship: "Truly I say to you, I do not know you" (Mt 25:12). To hear these words from Jesus, says John Chrysostom, "to see his meek face moving away, to see his serene gaze distance itself from us, not allowing us watch him any longer, will be worse than being burnt up by a thousand bolts of lightning."[45] Basil has the same thing to say: what is most to be feared is being eternally reproved by God; man suffers unbearable interior sorrow on account of his eternal shame and the perpetual vision of his guilt.[46] Tertullian says that everlasting fire kills "without annihilating either of those substances [the soul and the flesh]: it brings about a 'never-ending death', and is more formidable than a merely human murder."[47]

On earth the sinner may not fully realize the appalling implications of what it means to be separated from its Creator, even to the point of being surprised by the divine verdict of condemnation (Mt 25:44). In this world both saints and sinners benefit from and are comforted by God's gifts: "For your Father in heaven makes his sun rise on the evil and on the good, and sends rain on the just and on the unjust" (Mt 5:45). "Both bad and good" (Mt 22:10) were invited to the marriage feast. The grain remains alongside the tares until the time of judgment (Mt 13:30). Yet the rich man buried in *gēnna*, full of anguish, contrasts the good things he enjoyed on earth with the unbearable torment of hell (Lk 16:19–31). The depth of his sin is revealed only in the next life, in which he no longer experiences the apparent irrelevance of his sinful actions, nor the numbing comfort

---

43. *CCC* 1035.
44. Congregation for the Doctrine of the Faith, *Recentiores episcoporum Synodi*, n. 7.
45. John Chrysostom, *Hom. in Matth.*, 23:8.   46. Basil, *Hom. in Ps.*, 33.
47. Tertullian, *De res.*, 35:6.

afforded by God's created gifts, which he did not recognize as such by thanksgiving, praise, and active charity. Just as heaven constitutes in the Spirit the fullness of divine praise, so also condemnation represents the rejection of God by the creature.

Alongside the indications provided by Revelation, the personal experience of those who have attempted to live as if God did not exist may be of interest to record. Many novelists, poets, and philosophers of the twentieth century—and other periods—have provided useful insights into what it may mean to be separated from God forever. Three specific aspects may be noted: frustration, despair, and solitude.

Frustration Humans are made in the image and likeness of God (Gn 1:26) and are destined to live in eternal communion with him. They are structured therefore in native openness to the Divinity, with the "capacity to know and love their own Creator"[48] and to praise him forever. In hell this capacity will remain but will be eternally frustrated, through the personal fault of the sinner. Without the cocoon-like reassurance provided by created consolations, the contradiction and frustration will be especially acute and unavoidable. Nietzsche, speaking of the banishment of God from society, writes: "God is dead: God is dead! *And we have killed him!* Can we ever be consoled, assassins of all assassins? The Most Holy and the Most Powerful One that the world has known until now is bleeding to death under our knives. And so, who can absolve us from his blood?"[49] Hell is not simply an undesired side effect of egoism, of sickness, of bad luck; it is a true and definitive metaphysical frustration. Instead of joyfully praising God, the condemned are filled with hate[50] and sadness.[51]

Despair "Lose all hope, all you who enter here"; so reads the inscription that Dante Alighieri, in his *Divine Comedy*,[52] placed on the lintel of the entrance into hell. Despair as it is experienced on earth derives from the impossibility of reaching objectives one has set for oneself: establishing a friendship, finding a job, finishing a project, and the like. But some degree of hope always remains, because one may lose hope in certain objectives, but others may be individuated and obtained. Hope, classical authors have told us, is the last thing we lose. In hell this is no longer the case, for the true and only object of hope, the basis of all hope, is lost irremediably, and the entire dynamism of hope simply collapses. No

---

48. *GS* 12c.
49. F. Nietzsche, *Fröhliche Wissenschaft*, n. 125:15–19, in *Nietzsche Werke*, vol. 5/2, 159.
50. Thomas Aquinas, Suppl., q. 98, a. 5, c.
51. Ibid., a. 8. Isidore of Seville says that "in hell, fire burns the body but *tristitia* burns the mind," *Sent. I*, 28:1.
52. Dante Alighieri, *Divina Commedia III*, 9.

hope, no distraction,[53] no escape, no love, no life, no pleasure, can enter the domain of eternal damnation. In such a situation, writes Benedict XVI, "all would be beyond remedy and the destruction of good would be irrevocable."[54]

Solitude The gospels speak openly of the solitude of those who have lost Christ, who is the only way to the Father. After the promise of the Eucharist some of Jesus' hearers abandoned him, and he asked the others: "Will you too go away?" (Jn 6:67). To this Peter replied: "Lord, to whom should we go? You have words of eternal life" (Jn 6:68). Sin primarily involves separation, the destruction of communion: separation from God, from others, and from oneself. The profoundly social nature of humans—the need to share their lives with other people—will remain forever frustrated. The English word "sin," in fact, may well be related to the German "Sünde," separation, and in turn to the term "sunder," separate. In hell the condemned will have no other "god" they can turn to; the idols they invented and whose precarious existence they lived off will be perceived in their true nothingness. They will be left with themselves and their vain fantasies, all alone, forever. Jean-Paul Sartre said it well, though in an inverted way, by saying that "hell is other people."[55] C. S. Lewis expressed the same idea in his fantasy novel *The Great Divorce*, which represents the total separation between heaven and hell, attributing to the inhabitants of the latter a singular power: that of creating at will a new home in a vast grey, almost uninhabited city, should the presence of other people become minimally unsavory.[56]

The Pain of Sense

As we have seen, Scripture speaks of eternal punishment in terms of physical torments inflicted by God on the human body. Leaving aside for the moment the question of how a spiritual soul can suffer physical torture,[57] would it not be correct from the outset to consider such pains in a purely metaphorical way, as graphic expressions of the subjective repercussions on the human spirit of the pain deriving from the loss of God? The latter position was defended, for example, by Origen.[58] He said that "every sinner himself lights the flames of his own fire, and is not immersed in some fire that was lit by another or existed before him."[59] This pain is a

53. On the role and importance of distraction in human life, see B. Pascal, *Pensées* (ed. Brunschvig), nn. 210–15.
54. *SS* 45.
55. This is the central message of J.-P. Sartre's drama *Huis-clos*.
56. See C. S. Lewis, *The Great Divorce*, 46th ed. (New York: Macmillan, 1946).
57. See pp. 24–25.
58. *Inter alia*, see H.-J. Horn, "Ignis aeternus: une interprétation morale du feu éternel chez Origène," *Revue des études grecques* 82 (1969): 76–88; B. E. Daley, *The Hope*, 274–75.
59. Origen, *De princip. II*, 10:4.

fever within, he said, coming from a deeply troubled conscience.[60] It is entirely of the sinner's own making.[61]

On the whole, however, the Fathers of the Church did not consider hellfire as a mere metaphor.[62] Jerome found Origen's position especially disturbing.[63] Gregory of Nazianzen, commenting on Jesus' words "I came to cast fire upon the earth" (Lk 12:49), said: "I know also of a fire that is not cleansing, but avenging . . . the unquenchable fire that is associated with the worm that does not die, eternal fire for the wicked. For they all belong to the destructive power—though some may prefer, even on this point, to take a more merciful view of this fire, one more worthy of the one who chastises."[64]

Doubtless, the "pain of loss" is easier to understand than that of the senses, for in principle it is the direct result of unrepentant grave sin freely committed by the human person: God dismisses from his presence those who have openly rejected his love. But how could it be that God—albeit indirectly, through created agencies—actually comes to inflict punishment on condemned creatures? After all, one thing is justice, but the other, cruel vengeance.

God and Fire in Scripture

In the Old Testament,[65] fire is commonly considered as a symbol of the presence of God, of his glory, grace, and love, and also of his ire and judgment, of punishments and trials. "Mount Sinai was wrapped in smoke, because the Lord had descended upon it in fire" (Ex 19:18). For the punishment of the idolatry of Nadab and Abiu, "fire came out from the presence of the Lord and consumed them, and they died before the Lord." And Moses explained: "This is what the Lord meant when he said: 'Through those who are near me I will show myself holy, and before all the people I will be glorified'" (Lv 10:2–3). In brief terms, even though "fire" in the Old Testament is sometimes used as a metaphor (for example, in Is 47:17; Sir 21:9), it is presented generally as an instrument of God's action, specifically of his punishment.

In the New Testament, the fire of hell is frequently referred to in highly realistic terms, especially in the Synoptics: *first*, as the explanation of a metaphor (Mt 13:40) and therefore not as the metaphor itself; and *second*, as a reality that exists in precedence to those who suffer it, for it is said that the fire has been

---

60. Ibid., 5–6.
61. Origen, *Hom. 3 in Ezek.*, 7; *Hom. in Lev.*, 8:8.
62. See A. Michel, "Feu de l'enfer," in *DTC* 5, cols. 2208–16; A. Piolanti, *La communione dei santi e la vita eterna* (Città del Vaticano: Vaticana, 1992), 435–37; C. Pozo, *La teología del más allá*, 448–53, 458.
63. Jerome, *Ep. 124 ad Avitum*, 7; *In Eph.*, 3 (on Eph 5:6); *Apol. adv. Ruf.*, 2:7.
64. Gregory of Nazianzen, *Or.*, 40:36, on holy baptism.
65. See H. Bietenhard, "Fire," in *NIDNTT* 1, 652–58.

Hell: Perpetual Retribution 203

"*prepared* for the devil and his angels" (Mt 25:41). It would seem therefore that the fire already "exists" in order to inflict punishment on those who behave like the devil and his angels. Schmaus concludes: "From the frequency and precision with which Christ speaks of the fire of hell, may be deduced that it is a real fire."[66] This, as we saw, seems to be the majority position among the Fathers of the Church, in opposition to Origen's teaching. Likewise, several Church documents have spoken in realistic terms of the fire of hell, in the context of affirming the double punishment, that of loss and that of the senses.[67] From the scriptural point of view, however, several authors have noted that "fire is everything in hell,"[68] in the sense that fire, which is opposed to the Kingdom of God (Mt 25:34,41), expresses the entirety of infernal punishment.

What Kind of Fire?

Over recent centuries theologians have wisely abandoned the popular idea that the condemned and those being purified share a punishment of fire located somewhere under the earth's surface.[69] Nonetheless, it should be asked why the distinction between the pain of loss (the privation from God) and the pain of sense (punishment by God through created agencies) developed and consolidated in the first place. Perhaps the following explanation, suggested in different ways by Gregory the Great,[70] by Thomas Aquinas,[71] and, more recently, by Alois Winklhofer and others,[72] may be of interest.

Already we saw how separation from God (the pain of loss) corresponds to the *aversio a Deo* in sin, becoming an *aversio Dei ab homine* as it were, in that God distances himself from the sinner who willingly rejects his saving love. But sin is occasioned in the first place by a *conversio ad creaturas*, when sinners allow themselves to be drawn in a disorderly fashion by the attraction of created be-

---

66. M. Schmaus, *Katholische Dogmatik*, vol. 4.2: *Von den letzten Dingen*, 492.
67. *DS* 76, 409, 411, 801, 1002, 1351, 858, 1306; Paul VI, *Creed of People of God*, n. 12; *CCC* 1034–36.
68. See J. L. Ruiz de la Peña, *La pascua de la creación*, 230. See also Mt 13:43,50; 18:9. On this question, see F.-X. Remberger, "Zum Problem des Höllenfeuers," in Aa. vv., *Christus vor uns. Studien zur christlichen Eschatologie* (Frankfurt a. M.: Gerhard Kaffke, 1966), 75–83, especially 78–80.
69. According to Aquinas, hell is situated under the earth's surface: *S. Th.* III, *Suppl.*, q. 97, a. 7. More recently, see J.-M. Hervé, *Manuale Theologiae Dogmaticae IV: De Novissimis* (Paris: Berché et Pagis, 1929), 617.
70. Gregory the Great, *Dial.* 4:29,32.
71. Thomas Aquinas, *S. Th.* III, *Suppl.*, q. 70, a. 3: fire acts on the condemned "alio modo, secundum quod est instrumentum divinae iustitiae vindicantis: hoc enim divinae iustitiae ordo exigit, ut anima quae peccando se rebus corporalibus subdidit, eis etiam in poenam subdatur."
72. A. Winklhofer, *Das Kommen seines Reiches*, 99. See also C. Journet, *Le mal. Essai théologique* (Paris: Desclée, 1961), 224; F.-X. Remberger, "Zum Problem des Höllenfeuers," 80–81; J. Ratzinger, "Hölle" in *Lexikon für Theologie und Kirche* 5 (1960): 449; G. Moioli, *L'"Escatologico" cristiano*, 150–53.

ings, which to some degree come to occupy God's rightful place in their lives.[73] The pain of sense, therefore, may be considered as a kind of *conversio creaturarum in hominem:* that creatures would in some way turn against the one who, though made in God's image and likeness and destined to establish divine rule over them (Gn 1:26–27), attempted sinfully to exercise an improper, destructive dominion over creatures. For sin offends not only the Creator, but also the creature that is maltreated, whose purpose, inner truth, and dignity, is thwarted. Sin, Paul insists, not only distances humans from God, but enslaves them inordinately to creatures. And the whole of creation, he says, "subjected to futility" (Rom 8:19), will eventually avenge this disorder introduced by sin, being "set free from its bondage to decay" (Rom 8:21).

"The one who sins divinizes the world, and becomes its slave," writes Schmaus. "Now he must discover what it means when the world treats man as its slave. Man experiences a presentiment of slavery in which creation chains him as soon as he divinizes it, and thus tributes to him the honor due only to the living God, while creation descends upon him to annihilate him, while fire and water and punishment destroy his very life."[74] The condemned "will experience the world not as a welcoming ambience but as an inhospitable abode which assails and oppresses them ceaselessly and from which there is no escape, because they are linked to it by their very belongingness to the world."[75] Moioli suggests that hell may be understood in terms of the "materialization of the rational being by a kind of inversion of the relationship between spirit and matter."[76] Likewise, Gozzelino refers to "the created world allowing itself to be manipulated by a false absolutizating of values,"[77] for "fire" is not only a symbol of divine transcendence, but above all an application of divine punishment.[78]

Just as sin is committed for the most part through the disorderly treatment of

73. Thus Thomas Aquinas, in *S. Th. I-II*, q. 84, a. 1, commenting on 1 Tm 6:10: "the love of money [*cupiditas*] is the root of all evil." Aquinas distinguishes between sins directly involving God and those related to creatures. "In quolibet peccato mortali est quodammodo aversio a bono incommutabili et conversio ad bonum commutabile, sed aliter et aliter. Nam principaliter consistunt in aversione a bono incommutabili peccata quae opponuntur virtutibus theologicis, ut odium Dei, desperatio et infidelitas, quia virtutes theologicae habent Deum pro obiecto, ex consequenti autem important conversionem ad bonum commutabile, inquantum anima deserens Deum consequenter necesse est quod ad alia convertatur. Peccata vero alia *principaliter consistunt in conversione ad commutabile bonum*, ex consequenti vero in aversione ab incommutabili bono, non enim qui fornicatur intendit a Deo recedere, sed carnali delectatione frui, ex quo sequitur quod a Deo recedat," *S. Th. II-II*, q. 20, a 1 ad 1.

74. M. Schmaus, *Katholische Dogmatik*, vol. 4.2: *Von den letzten Dingen*, 485–86.

75. J. L. Ruiz de la Peña, *La pascua de la creación*, 240.

76. G. Moioli, *L'"Escatologico" cristiano*, 152.

77. G. Gozzelino, *Nell'attesa*, 414.

78. Besides the authors mentioned above (n. 72), other texts of H. Rondet, K. Rahner, H. U. von Balthasar, J. A. Robillard, J. Guitton, and A. M. Sicari, may be found in G. Gozzelino, *Nell'attesa*, 415–16.

creatures, from which derives an essential distancing or separation from God,[79] so also the punishment for sin is immediately referred to the created world, which will eternally enslave and oppress the condemned, making it impossible for them to live according to "the glorious freedom of the children of God" (Rom 8:21). Thomas Aquinas notes that the immediate effect of fire on living bodies is one of *alligatio*, of binding, constricting, restraining, enclosing.[80]

Hell as Punishment for Sin

It is not uncommon nowadays to hold that hell is simply a continuation of the sinful state man finds himself in on earth. Authors as diverse as Scotus Eriugena, Friedrich Nietzsche, and George B. Shaw[81] attempted to explain that hell is not a penal estate, but rather one chosen by the subject for reasons of intimate affinity. Nietzsche suggested that man could be happy and fulfilled without any God. In this line of thought it may be said that humans design and construct their own future. Some theologians have also suggested a similar doctrine. "Hell is not something that simply happens from the outside," writes Ladislao Boros.

> It is not something that God imposes on us afterwards for our misdeeds. . . . It is no more and no less than the human being who is totally identified with what he is, with what he can forcibly acquire and accomplish for himself. Hell is not a threat; it is the ontological projection of our own pettiness. . . . The state of our heart is all there is. Everything lives in heaven, because God created the world in view of heaven. And heaven is experienced through the state of the heart. Those who have become poor can appreciate its beauty. Those who have remained rich must be content with their own wealth.[82]

This position is correct from many points of view, as we have seen above. Humans responsibly create their own destiny. God is not to blame for their condemnation. However, the position does not take the inner nature of sin sufficiently into account. Sin is not a mere error in one's own life project, though it be a major one. Sin above all occasions a break, a separation from God, from other people, from the cosmos to which we belong, from our very selves. It involves a substantial shift in our spiritual position within the created and uncreated world. Sin occasions offense to God, breakup in society, alienation within the cosmos, and eventually death. For this reason, it must be said that hell is not just the continuation of the self, alienated from God, but truly a punishment, in that the whole of reality—and God in the first place—must resituate itself with

---

79. See n. 73 above.
80. Thomas Aquinas, *IV C. Gent.*, 90. The same notion is found in F. Suárez, *De Angelis*, 8,14:9.
81. See especially Eriugena, *Periphyseon*, 2:593b. Nietzsche speaks in the same way in *Man and Superman*.
82. L. Boros, *We Are Future* (New York: Herder and Herder, 1970), 172.

respect to the sinner. In sum, to say that hell simply involves a continuance of the sinful state would suggest an individualistic and spiritualistic (at least anti-corporal) anthropology. Humans do not just construct themselves, as Fichte, Nietzsche, Sartre, and others would say. They develop their identity and their future in living dialogue with everything and everyone that surrounds them, whether they intend to or not. Hence their immoral actions introduce an objective disorder within the cosmos that demands the reestablishment and resituating of the whole of reality. Hell is precisely the crystallization and final expression of the unrepentant sinner's innermost conviction: that of wishing to exist and act as if nothing else existed and acted, or better, as if everything else that existed fell under his exclusive, despotic dominion.

The Perpetual Character of Condemnation

Scripture speaks openly, as we have seen, of the perpetual nature of hell. It is clear, however, as Aquinas says, that "in hell there is no real eternity, but rather the kind of time suggested by Psalm 81:16: 'those who hate the Lord would cringe before him, and their doom would last forever.'"[83] Besides, as we have seen, the Church never accepted Origen's teaching on the *apokatastasis*, or universal reconciliation. The French writer Georges Bernanos, in his *Diary of a Country Priest*, says that "hell is not to love any more."[84] C. S. Lewis explains this in greater detail:

> To love at all is to be vulnerable. Love anything, and your heart will certainly be wrung and possibly broken. If you want to make sure of keeping it intact, you must give your heart to no one, not even to an animal. Wrap it carefully around with hobbies and little luxuries. Avoid all entanglements: lock it up in the safe casket or coffin of your selfishness. But in that casket—safe, dark, motionless, airless—it will change. It will not be broken. It will become unbreakable, impenetrable, irredeemable. The alternative to tragedy, or at least the risk of tragedy, is damnation. The only place outside heaven where you can be perfectly safe from the dangers and perturbations of love is hell.[85]

However, the notion of the permanence of condemnation occasions two serious difficulties. Lessius, understandably, stated that the four most difficult mysteries of our faith are the Trinity, the Incarnation, the Eucharist, and the eternity of the pains of hell.[86] First, why should someone who has not managed to repent of their sins in this life be unable to do so in the next? How does their will come

---

83. Thomas Aquinas, *S. Th. I*, q. 10, a. 3 ad 2.
84. G. Bernanos, *Diary of a Country Priest*, 177. In this he reflects the expression of the Russian novelist Fydor Dostoevskij, who likewise said that hell means "to love no longer," *The Brothers Karamazov*, VI, 3:1.
85. C. S. Lewis, *The Four Loves* (London: Bles, 1960), 138–39.
86. See L. Lessius, *Tractatus de beatitudine, actibus humanis et legibus*, in *Opera 3/1*, ed. I. Neubaur (Paris: Lanier, 1852), 395.

to be hardened and fixed forever? Second, why should a finite act, or a finite series of finite acts, give rise to a situation that will endure perpetually, a situation that—at least on an accumulative basis—will become infinite? In other words, how can we respond to the impression that eternal punishment for sin seems to be disproportionate and unjust?

How Can the Will of the Damned Be Fixed Forever?

Obviously one could solve the problem of the perpetual obstinacy of the unrepentant sinner with the aid of what might be called a "decree theology"—God in some way forcing the will of the sinner into immobility. While this is always possible, it does not seem to take into account the realism of human nature as God has foreseen it. Thomas Aquinas has suggested two possible alternatives to explain why hell lasts forever.

One is that God simply does not save those who die in mortal sin.[87] No one can oblige God to offer his grace and friendship forever, and with death and judgment God's magnanimity comes to a close, for he no longer offers the grace that would make conversion possible. This explanation has the drawback of not seeming to take divine mercy—which takes no satisfaction in the loss of the sinner (Ws 1:13)—sufficiently seriously.

The other possibility is that the human being after death survives as a "separated soul," a spirit that has committed itself irrevocably to God or against him, as angels and demons do.[88] For purely anthropological reasons, it is suggested, the unrepentant sinner is no longer able to change its will, which remains forever fixed against God. This position was adopted by John Chrysostom.[89] Bonaventure likewise suggests that the condemned are embittered by their punishment but do not regret their sin: "The will to sin lives on in them, even though on account of the pain induced by their punishment they are impeded from actually sinning."[90] Giacomo Biffi suggests that "the true reason is that in the state that awaits us after death beyond the world and beyond time, humans do not experience succession and therefore are incapable of changing."[91]

---

87. Thomas Aquinas, *IV C. Gent.*, 93. See also M. Premm, *Katholische Glaubenskunde*, vol. 4, 4th ed. (Wien: Herder, 1961), 656. On the issue, see G. Moioli, *L'"Escatologico" cristiano*, 154–55, and M. Bordoni, *Dimensioni antropologiche della morte* (Roma: Herder, 1969), 263–69.

88. Thomas Aquinas, *IV C. Gent.*, 95; *De Ver.*, q. 24, a. 11; C. Journet, *Le mal*, 210–24; H. Rondet, "Les peines de l'enfer," *Nouvelle Revue Théologique* 67 (1940): 397–427; F.-X. Remberger, "Zum Problem des Höllenfeuers."

89. Chrysostom says there will be no repentance after death. Once the soul is separated from the body we are no longer "masters of our own conversion" because we lack the freedom to change our fundamental orientation: *De Laz. Conc.*, 2:3. The condemned will experience some regrets, he adds, but all in vain: *In II Cor.*, 9:4.

90. Cit. by G. Biffi, *Linee*, 59.   91. Ibid.

In principle, the latter solution respects divine justice to a greater degree, in that humans are seen to determine their own future. Yet it is also a problematic one on several accounts. *First*, humans are not angels and do not act like them; in fact, according to Scripture what distinguishes angels from humans is the former's incapacity to repent, and the latter's capacity to do so (Lk 15:10).[92] *Second*, as distinct from those who contemplate the divine essence and whose will is fixed on God, it is not clear why the condemned should ratify after death, forever, the decisions they have taken when alive, and not rather repent of them (Lk 16:19-31). *Third* and last, even if a certain similarity may be said to exist between the angel and the separated soul, this would not be the case once final resurrection has taken place, after which it should not be impossible for the person, fully reconstituted as human, to change their will again.

Augustine admits that the notion of perpetual punishment seemed contradictory to his pagan adversaries, since classical anthropology generally associated suffering with corruption, and assumed that the former must come to an end at some stage.[93] Nonetheless, he explains that the root of suffering is not the intra-animic situation of the condemned person, but is in their tormented relationship with God; they will be "tortured by fruitless repentance," he said.[94] To the different positions envisaging universal divine pardon, Augustine offers the same response: "Scripture, infallible Scripture": the Bible tells us that all sinners will be consigned to everlasting punishment.[95]

All in all, no easy solution, theological or anthropological, may be found to explain how condemnation can become perpetual.

The Possibility of Annihilation

Several authors, keenly aware of the gravity of the New Testament message of eternal condemnation, have suggested, on the basis of some biblical texts[96] and other authorities,[97] that unrepentant sinners will, in all probability, be sim-

---

92. See pp. 170-71.

93. Augustine, *De Civ. Dei XXII*, 2. See A. Lehaut, *L'éternité des peines de l'enfer dans S. Augustin* (Paris: 1912); B. E. Daley, *The Hope*, 148-49.

94. Augustine, *De Civ. Dei XXI*, 9.   95. Ibid., 23.

96. See the 1988 study of B. J. Korosak in n. 98 below. See, for example, Mt 10:28; Lk 20:36.

97. The position has arisen not infrequently throughout history, for example, among the Socinians: see G. Moioli, *L'"Escatologico" cristiano*, 67. On Socinianism, see G. Pioli, *Fausto Socino: vita, opere, fortuna. Contributo alla storia del liberalismo religioso moderno* (Modena: U. Guanda, 1952); M. Martini, *Fausto Socino et la pensée socinienne: un maitre de la pensée religieuse (1539-1604)* (Paris: Klincksieck, 1967). The same position was taken up by liberal Protestants with a view to overcoming the apparent unreasonableness of eternal condemnation. To some degree this led to Barth's optimistic understanding of predestination involving salvation of all. In recent times, Berdiaev spoke of the impossibility of the simultaneous eternal existence of good and evil.

Hell: Perpetual Retribution 209

ply annihilated after death.[98] The text of Bernanos cited above suggests that if condemned humans are not actually annihilated, in any case they will be greatly diminished in their natural powers; he speaks of the condemned as "those charred stones that once were human beings."[99]

However true it may be that the condemned must be considered as failed and severely diminished human beings, and thus "less" human than those who are saved, this explanation does not take into account the fact that God constituted humans as immortal beings[100] and that if he annihilated hardened sinners, he would be going against his original design.[101] The idea does not fit in well with the obvious meaning of scriptural texts.[102] "You love everything that exists," we read in the book of Wisdom, "and reject nothing you have made. If you had hated something, you would not have made it. And how could a thing subsist, had you not willed it? Or how be preserved, if not called forth by you?" (Ws 11:24–25).

Besides, the possibility of annihilation would involve an unwarranted confusion between the order of grace/salvation and that of human nature/creation.[103] Death and nothingness do of course derive in some way from sin.[104] But humans do not enjoy complete control over their own lives, and are incapable of total meta-

---

98. The position is defended especially by, B. J. Korosak, *Credo nella vita eterna. Compendio di escatologia* (Roma: Pontificia Università Urbaniana, 1983), 74; "L'eternità dell'inferno," *Euntes Docete* 41 (1988): 483–94; "Pensare l'oltre: l'inferno esiste? E quale inferno?," in Aa. vv., *Sulle cose prime e ultime* (Palermo: Augustinus, 1991), 71–84, drawing on elements of the theology of von Balthasar, Bouillard, Brunner, and Malevez. The position is also held by T. Sartory and G. Sartory, *In der Hölle brennt kein Feuer* (München: Deutsches Taschenbuch, 1968), 61–248; A. Schmied, "Ewige Strafe oder endgültiges Zunichtewerden?" *Theologie der Gegenwart* 18 (1975): 178–83; M. F. Lacan, "Le mystère de l'enfer," *Communio* (Éd. fr.) (July–August 1979): 76–81; J.-M. Perrin, "À travers la mort l'esprit nous recrée pour la vie sans fin," *Nouvelle Revue Théologique* 103 (1981): 58–75; J. Delumeau, *Ce que je crois* (Paris: Grasset, 1985), 80–82; E. Schillebeeckx, *Umanità: la storia di Dio* (Brescia: Queriniana, 1992), 180–85; A. Rizzi, "L'inferno: dogma da cancellare o da ripensare?" *Servitium* 24 (1990): 42–49; J. R. Sachs, "Current Eschatology: Universal Salvation and the Problem of Hell," *Theological Studies* 52 (1991): 227–54; A. Tornos, *Escatología*, vol. 2 (Madrid: Publicaciones de la Università Pontificia Comillas, 1991), 226–31; J. L. Kvanvig, *The Problem of Hell* (New York: Oxford University Press, 1993); M.-É. Boismard, *Faut-il encore parler de 'résurrection'?: les données scripturaires* (Paris: Cerf, 1995), 164–68. E. Jüngel, *Tod*, 117–20 speaks of the possibility of self-annihilation. The position is rejected by Protestant authors such as F. Heidler, *Die biblische Lehre von der Unsterblichkeit der Seele, Sterben, Tod, ewiges Leben im Aspekt lutherischer Anthropologie* (Göttingen: Vandenhoeck & Ruprecht, 1983), 122–39.

99. "The error common to us all is to invest these damned with something still inherently alive, something of our own inherent mobility, whereas in truth time and movement have ceased for them; they are fixed for ever. . . . The sorrow, the unutterable loss of those charred stones which once were human beings, is that they have nothing more to be shared," G. Bernanos, *Diary of a Country Priest*, 177.

100. See pp. 19–31 above.

101. See J. L. Ruiz de la Peña, *La pascua de la creación*, 244–45.

102. See G. Colzani, *La vita eterna*, 160–61.

103. On the survival of the human soul between death and resurrection, see pp. 325–26 below.

104. See pp. 260–65 below.

physical suicide. Even in hell divine dominion and Lordship will be respected. Though severely diminished, the condemned will remain as human beings forever.

Divine Justice and Mercy in Understanding the Mystery of Hell

Temporal punishment has a purpose: it is meant to purify and correct the sinner. Perpetual punishment, however, belongs to another order, in that it seems to achieve nothing for the person condemned. The lives of the condemned become useless, irrelevant, sterile, and eternally so. Now, how is it that an all-powerful and omniscient God could create a human being who would eventually fall into this situation? The tragedy written into this question is expressed in Jesus' own words: "The Son of man goes, as it is written of him, but woe to that man by whom the Son of man is betrayed! It would have been better for that man if he had not been born" (Mt 26:24). Better never to have been born than to be condemned forever. Then why did an omniscient God create beings who could eventually be condemned? On God's part, eternal condemnation seems to be, at least to some degree, if not unjust, certainly unmerciful. Understandably, authors such as Gregory of Nyssa come to the conclusion that in God there is no such thing as vindictive punishment: God acts only to "separate good from evil and to draw it into the communion of blessedness."[105] Kierkegaard puts it in the following way: "That God can create free creatures in his sight is the cross that philosophy is incapable of carrying, but which it has to shoulder."[106]

Still, some preliminary questions could usefully be considered.

On Justice and Mercy

In strict terms eternal condemnation does not involve injustice on God's part, for God gives to each one according to his or her merits. The sinner, by attempting to exercise despotic dominion over God's creatures, proudly seeks out his own self-sufficient solitude. This goes against the very nature and destiny God had planned for him. Personal communion with God becomes simply impossible. Humans are condemned through their own fault. They can cast the blame on no one else but themselves. According to the doctrine of faith, God offers humans through Christ and the Spirit all the opportunities they need to repent of their sins.[107] Their refusal to do so is as much a sad reminder of God's merciful and patient insistence in saving them as it is of his justice.

Yet, if for the sake of argument it may be said that condemnation does not

---

105. Gregory of Nyssa, *De anima et Res.*
106. S. Kierkegaard, *Diary II*, A, 752.
107. This is a consequence of the doctrine of God's universal saving will: 1 Tm 2:4; *DS* 624; *CCC* 605.

involve injustice on God's part, it seems certainly to involve a lack of mercy, the "attribute" God brings to bear especially in the presence of the sinner.[108] On the one hand, it should be noted that God does exercise mercy to some extent toward condemned sinners in that, according to many authors, he punishes them less than they deserve.[109] At a more substantial level, however, it is easy to share Catherine of Siena's confiding protests to the effect that she will never be happy as long as even one of those united to her in nature or in grace has been condemned. She implores God that, if at all possible, hell should be simply destroyed.[110] Her sentiment has been and is shared by very many.

It should be kept in mind, however, that God's mercy does not invalidate the consistency and realism of human action. A merciful God is very different from an indifferent God. And in Christ God has committed himself totally to the task of redeeming humankind, to the extent of accepting the death of his only Son on the Cross.[111] If the sinful actions of humans were of little relevance in their relationship with God, something of a kind could be said of their good actions, which merit salvation. The greatness of the Love of God is manifested by the seriousness with which he takes our actions, both good and bad. Mercy has little to do with careless tolerance, with disinterest in the real, true situation of humans. Thomas Aquinas said in fact that "mercy does not render justice superfluous, but is, as it were, the fullness of justice [*quaedam iustitiae plenitudo*]."[112] The contrast we perceive between justice and mercy derives from the imperfection with which human beings live these virtues. But in God justice is merciful, for God knows the frailty of the one he made in his image and likeness, and treats him accordingly. Moreover, mercy is completely just, because God lovingly gives to each one more than they truly need and deserve. Besides, it should be kept in mind that the situation of condemnation is different for each one. "They descend into hell," the Second Council of Lyons says in 1274, "to be punished with different pains."[113] All those condemned numerically share the same *aversio a Deo*,

---

108. John Paul II, Enc. *Dives in misericordia* (1980), passim.

109. God's mercy extends even to the most hardened sinners, Augustine says, in "that he will let them suffer less horrible punishments than those they deserve" *De Civ. Dei XXII*, 24. Likewise, Thomas Aquinas, *S. Th. III, Suppl.*, q. 99, a. 2 ad 1. See A. Royo-Marín, *Teología de la salvación* (Madrid: Editorial Católica, 1956), 363–67. Francis of Sales has the same thing to say: "The punishments inflicted [in hell] are much inferior to the guilt and crimes for which they are imposed," *Treatise on the Love of God*, 9:1.

110. Catherine said: "Lord, how can I be happy as long as one of those, who were created like me in your image and likeness, be lost or be taken from your hands? I do not wish any of my brothers, who are united with me in nature and grace, to be lost. . . . Should your truth and your justice permit, I would wish that hell be destroyed, or at least that no soul, from now onwards, would descend there," *Vita di S. Caterina scritta dal B. Raimundo di Capua* (Siena: Cantagalli, 1982), 27.

111. *CAA* 209–12.   112. Thomas Aquinas, *S. Th. I*, q. 21, a. 3 ad 2.
113. *DS* 858.

but clearly there are different degrees of *conversio ad creaturas,* of the inordinate attachment to creatures that occasioned separation from God in the first place. Speaking of those who had maltreated widows, for example, Jesus said clearly that "they will receive the greater condemnation" (Lk 20:47).[114] Besides, their situation will neither improve nor get worse, for they are simply confirmed in sin forever.[115]

Justice and Order

Above we saw that whereas temporal punishment makes sense, in that it offers the transgressor the opportunity to rectify and convert, eternal punishment seems to be useless to the sinner. It should be kept in mind, however, that punishment inflicted for crimes of any kind not only involves the possible rectification and purification of the individual criminal, but also the reestablisment of the cosmic and societal order disturbed by sinful actions. As we saw above, sin not only damages those who sin, thus destroying their spiritual relationship with the Divinity, but also damages—and seriously so—the relationship with the entire social fabric and cosmic order. And this is so for the simple reason that humans are social and cosmic to the very core of their being. Their actions influence these spheres directly. Good and bad actions not only leave good and bad tangible effects, but also deeper hidden ones, which society may attempt to rectify by legal means, but which God will certainly take into account in the future reckoning. The condemnation of the sinner, though useless for the one condemned, constitutes in essence God's act of restitution of justice and order in the wider social and cosmic context. "God inflicts punishments, not for his own sake, as though he took pleasure in them, but for the sake of something else: namely on account of the order that must be imposed on creatures, in which order the good of the universe consists."[116] That is, it may be said to be useful for the whole, though not necessarily for the part. This restitution becomes a public event, as it were, when final resurrection makes universal judgment possible. In fact only an individualistic understanding of the human being would allow us to think that hell is useless, that it achieves nothing.

In his autobiographical work, *Crossing the Threshold of Hope,* Pope John Paul II speaks of the reasonableness of eternal punishment in the context of the tremendous crimes, both public and covert, that humans have committed and con-

114. See Mt 16:27; Ws 6:7–9; 2 Cor 5:10; Rv 18:7.

115. Some authors consider that the sufferings of the condemned may be alleviated or varied on a temporal basis: see A. Piolanti, *La comunione dei santi,* 448–49. Yet Thomas says that "it is surer and simpler to say that suffrages are of no use to the damned and that the Church should not pray for them," *S. Th. III, Suppl.,* q. 71, a. 5 c.

116. Thomas Aquinas, *III C. Gent.,* 144.

Hell: Perpetual Retribution 213

tinue to commit. "There is something in man's moral conscience itself that rebels against any loss of this conviction: Is not God who is Love also ultimate Justice? Can he tolerate these terrible crimes, can they go unpunished? Isn't final punishment in some way necessary in order to re-establish equilibrium in the complex history of humanity? Is not hell in a certain sense the ultimate safeguard of man's moral conscience?"[117]

Are Humans Capable of Committing Sins Worthy of Condemnation?

What degree of freedom is required for people to commit sins that may endure forever and destroy their entire life project? Two observations should be made.[118]

First, as has been mentioned above, eternal punishment is not occasioned by sinful action as such, but by *unrepented* sinful action. Perhaps this is what is meant when we speak of the sin against the Holy Spirit: the sin that not only separates one from God, perhaps through weakness or passion, but is, rather, an attitude that hardens with time, in such a way that the one who commits it becomes closed to repentance, and eventually becomes virtually incapable of it. *Second*, many trends in modern psychology have suggested that human actions are often carried out without full willingness.[119] In theological terms, it might be said that sinful inclinations left by original and personal sin reduce responsibility to a greater or lesser degree. Nonetheless, Scripture does speak of the possibility of closing one's heart definitively to God's grace through certain actions, and says that this closure merits perpetual loss of communion with God. Rather than taking for granted that human freedom is incapable of grave crimes, and deducing from that that hell is an absurdity, it is more correct, theologically speaking at least, to consider hell as a real possibility that speaks of a free will with the capacity of closing oneself off from the friendship and love of God. The possibility of eternal punishment reveals, albeit indirectly, the depth and power of human freedom. Nicholas Berdiaev has it that personality, freedom, and the possibility of condemnation are inseparable in human beings. Thus "if we systematically affirm personality and freedom we have to be prepared to accept the possibility of hell. It is easy to pass over the idea of hell, but in doing so both personality and freedom are undone."[120]

---

117. John Paul II, *Crossing the Threshold of Hope*, ed. V. Messori (London: J. Cape, 1994), 186.

118. See the interesting reflections J. L. Ruiz de la Peña, *La pascua de la creación*, 236, nn. 38–39, on the link-up between guilt, responsibility, and freedom, and the tendency to deny the first and later on the other two.

119. See, for example, B. F. Skinner, in his works *Beyond Freedom and Dignity* (New York: Knopf, 1972), passim; *Walden Two* (New York: McMillan, 1976), 286.

120. N. Berdiaev, *Esprit et liberté. Essai de philosophie chrétienne* (Paris: Je Sers, 1933), 342. This author, however, ends up denying the existence of hell: see C. Journet, *Le mal*, 205–6.

Such a possibility might at first suggest a pessimistic view of society, of the world, and of human freedom. It should not do so. Should humans be considered not truly free and responsible for the crimes they commit, the only conclusion we can come to, since humans do commit tremendously grave crimes that have caused untold suffering throughout history, is that evil must be considered an intrinsic part of the structure of reality. The fact that evil originates in the order of the will, however, means on the whole that humans are, at least in principle, in a position to change, and that the world can be redeemed. This is the Gospel, the "good news" of Christian faith.

To conclude this section, we may refer to Jerome's "merciful" understanding of hell:

We should leave this to the knowledge of God alone, who holds on his scales not only mercy but punishment, and who knows whom he should judge, and in what way, and for how long. Let us only say, as befits human fragility, "Lord, do not reproach me in your anger; do not destroy me in your rage" (Ps 6:1). And as we believe that the devil and all apostates and impious sinners, who say in their heart "There is no God," will undergo eternal punishments, so we consider that those who are sinners—even impious ones—and yet Christians, will have their works tried and purged in fire, but will receive from the judge a moderate sentence, mingled with mercy.[121]

How Real Is the Possibility of Some People Being Condemned?

The question should now be asked: given that condemnation is a possibility that does not openly contradict revelation, is it a real possibility, or just a doctrinal hypothesis that expresses, indirectly perhaps, the power of God in Christ and the role of human freedom in salvation? Will many be condemned? Or a few perhaps, or none at all? For obvious reasons, no clear response can be given to these questions. There is no way of demonstrating from a systematic standpoint that all will (necessarily) be saved, as Origen attempted to do, without seriously prejudicing the proper interpretation of Scripture and opposing the traditional teaching of the Church. This does not mean that we are obliged to believe that some will necessarily have to be condemned. If each and every person can be saved, then the whole of humanity, taken one by one, can be saved. That is to say, the salvation of all is not a contradiction in terms. It may be added that whereas the Church through the process of canonization has proclaimed that some Christians have certainly reached heaven, it has never taken the opposite path, declaring that such and such a person has been condemned.[122] However, it would be

---

121. Jerome, *In Is.*, 18,66:24.
122. See A. Royo-Marín, *La teología de la salvación*, 374–77.

incorrect to infer a systematic or theological necessity in respect of the salvation of all from a possible factual a posteriori universality.[123]

What should be kept in mind, as we saw above, is the fact that whereas nowadays most authors would consider hell as an extreme possibility, an exception, many Christian authors throughout the ages—perhaps a majority of theologians, spiritual writers, and saints—took it that most of humanity will be condemned.[124] How can this be accounted for?

Stating and Situating the Maximalist Position

Some points should be kept in mind in respect of the position Thomas Aquinas summed up in the phrase *pauciores sunt qui salvantur*,[125] "only a minor part of humanity will be saved." In the *first* place, that the authors in question are aware that they are not dealing with an article of faith in the strict sense of the word, but rather with a kind of spiritual conviction. *Second*, in the first three centuries, the Fathers of the Church for the most part took a less severe position, and the posterior reaction suggesting condemnation of the majority was conditioned to some degree by Origen's teaching on universal reconciliation. *Third*, a certain confusion may be detected among the Fathers of the Church between eternal condemnation and purgatory.[126] The two came to be fully distinguished only during the Middle Ages. That the majority of humans (including Christian believers) might be submitted to temporary purification in the afterlife, of course, would be quite acceptable, although on the face of things this is not what the Fathers spoke of. *Fourth*, the pastoral challenges stemming from the widespread diffusion and subsequent cooling off of Christian faith and life from the fourth century onward, from the influence of Origen's *apokatastasis*, and from the superficial optimism of Pelagianism, brought many Pastors to insist on the seriousness of the threat of eternal perdition.

It should be kept in mind that a new lease on life for the maximalist position stemmed among Protestants, from the Calvinist doctrine of predestination, and among Catholics, from Jansenist neo-Augustinianism, which taught that many or most humans will be condemned. In spite of material coincidence, this doctrine marks a change in direction in respect of what the Fathers had actually taught,

---

123. See G. Biffi, *Linee*, 61. During Vatican Council II, some Fathers requested that an explicit mention be made to the effect that some have in fact been condemned. The Doctrinal Commission replied that there was no need to do so, for Jesus' own affirmations on the matter were phrased in the future tense, not hypothetically or conditionally. See *Acta Synodalia S. Conc. Œc. Vat. II*, III; 8 (Città del Vaticano: Vaticana, 1976), 144–48.

124. See n. 38 above, and the article of A. Michel, "Elus (Nombre des)."

125. Thomas Aquinas, *S. Th. I*, q. 23, a. 7 ad 3.

126. See pp. 294–95 below.

for the certainty of the condemnation of the majority became in recent centuries a dogmatic position rather than an expression of spiritual conviction and pastoral challenge. It is taken that God creates (some) humans and predestines them to condemnation, and others to salvation. The power of sin and the corruption of the human will only go to confirm this understanding. It is interesting to note, however, that although many saints and spiritual writers over recent centuries (Theresa of Avila, for example)[127] have held that the majority would be lost, others are more optimistic (possibly Francis of Sales).[128] The witness of the saints is of particular value on account of their familiarity with the workings of God's grace in the soul and their deep understanding of the mystery of sin and malice.

The Gospel Message

Jesus "went on his way through towns and villages, teaching, and journeying toward Jerusalem," Luke tells us (13:22). "And someone said to him, 'Lord, will those who are saved be few?' And he said to them, 'Strive to enter by the narrow door; for many, I tell you, will seek to enter and will not be able'" (Lk 13:23–24). Jesus goes on to explain that it is impossible to be saved by one's own strength and that the condemned will hear the following words: "'I do not know where you come from.... And men will come from east and west, and from north and south, and sit at table in the kingdom of God'" (Lk 13:28–29).

Similar texts abound, especially in the Synoptic gospels. "Enter by the narrow gate; for the gate is wide and the way is easy that leads to destruction, and those who enter are many," we read in Matthew. "For the gate is narrow and the way is hard that leads to life, and those who find it are few" (Mt 7:13–14). "For many are called," Jesus says, "but few are chosen" (Mt 22:14).[129]

Four observations may be made on these texts.

First, to the one who asked about salvation Jesus gave the right answer to the wrong question. Salvation does not belong to a group of people as such, but to individuals, taken one by one. As we saw above, the New Testament shifts decisively from an ethnical to an ethical criterion when speaking of salvation and judgment.[130] Belonging to God's people—Israel or the Church—involves a serious responsibility of holiness and apostolate, but not the certainty of being saved. *Second*, Christians are meant to strive perseveringly to do the will of God in order to be saved. "If the righteous man is scarcely saved," Scripture says, "where will the impious and sinner appear?" (1 Pt 4:18). Salvation is the fruit of grace, but it involves an arduous personal correspondence. In the words of M.-J. Lagrange, "Je-

---

127. Theresa of Avila, *Moradas del Castillo Interior V*, 2:14.
128. A. Michel, "Elus (Nombre des)," col. 2370.   129. *CAA* 139–40.
130. See pp. 131–33.

sus does not intend to give a direct reply of a speculative kind. It is more important to know what we must strive after in order to enter the palace."[131] *Third*, the term "many" is not equivalent to "the majority," but rather is opposed to "the few."[132] And for Jesus, who came to "seek and to save the lost" (Lk 19:10), "many" who are condemned may seem few for us, since he was prepared to leave the "ninety-nine in the wilderness, and go after the one which is lost, until [*heōs*] he finds it" (Lk 15:4). In this sense, it may be said that even one person condemned is already too many. In any case, *fourth*, Jesus does not wish to give a statistical solution to a personal problem. The fact that superficial similarities may exist between two people's lives does not ensure that if one is saved, so will the other automatically be. God's gifts of nature and grace are different for each one. God may ask much of one person to whom he gives much, in which case negligence will be severely punished (Mt 25:14–30); yet of one who has received little, much less may be required, and if their response was more generous, their eternal union with God may well be richer.

The Number of the Saved

The book of Revelation speaks on different occasions of a particular number of those who will be saved, 144,000 (Rv 7:4; 14:1,3), the implication being that all the rest will be lost. It should be kept in mind, however, that the number involved refers primarily to perfection and extraordinary abundance: 12 × 12, the number of the tribes of Israel, 4, the number of the elements or the four parts of the world (earth, sea, sky, abyss); 10 × 10 × 10, the perfect quantity.[133] This typology may be found in the book of Revelation itself, which indicates this number as a sign of perfection in the construction of the heavenly Jerusalem (Rv 21:17).

In any case, it is by no means unreasonable to hold that few will be lost and very many will be saved, given the following factors: the abundance of divine *mercy*, God's maximum attribute;[134] divine *justice*, for, as Theresa of Lisieux said, the Christian expects as much from God's justice as from his mercy;[135] the doctrine of the *universal saving will* of God (1 Tm 2:4), who takes "no pleasure in the death of the wicked but that the wicked turn from their ways and live" (Ez 33:11);[136]

---

131. M.-J. Lagrange, *Évangile selon Saint Luc* (Paris: J. Gabalda, 1927), 388.
132. See p. 85, nn. 67–68.
133. See M.-É. Boismard, "L'Apocalypse," in *Introduction à la Bible*, ed. A. Robert and A. Feuillet, vol. 2: *Nouveau Testament* (Paris: Desclée, 1959), 709–42; especially 715.
134. Thomas Aquinas, *S. Th. I*, q. 21, a. 3; John Paul II, Enc. *Dives in Misericordia* (1980); *Dominum et vivificantem* (1986), nn. 53–54; *Redemptoris Missio* (1990), nn. 10 and 28.
135. "J'espère autant de la justice du Bon Dieu que de sa miséricorde," Theresa of Lisieux, Letter to P. Roulland dated 9 May 1897, in *Lettres de sainte Thérèse de l'Enfant-Jésus* (Lisieux: Office central, 1948), 226.
136. See also 2 Cor 5:15; 1 Jn 2:2.

the abundance of *Christ's redeeming work*, for "where sin has increased, grace has abounded all the more" (Rom 5:20; cf. Jn 3:16); the powerful *intercession of Our Lady* for sinners; and lastly the many ways in which sinners can be *purified*, especially in purgatory.

The *Catechism of the Catholic Church* concludes: "The affirmations of Sacred Scripture and the teachings of the Church on the subject of hell are a call to responsibility incumbent upon man to make use of his freedom in view of his eternal destiny. They are at the same time an urgent call to conversion."[137]

Should Christians "Hope" for the Salvation of All?

Even though it is possible at a hypothetical level that all will eventually be saved (if each one can be saved, one and all may be saved), it is clearly unwarranted to believe in the salvation of all, for the doctrine of faith requires us to believe that those who die in the state of mortal sin will be eternally condemned. Any theological construct that systematically involves the salvation of all (Origen's *apokatastasis* comes particularly to mind) must be excluded. In effect, our act of faith is directed to God, who we believe will give all humans the grace they need for conversion. Yet this act of ours cannot include the personal response of each individual that salvation requires.

In fact it has become quite common of late to hold that all humans, without exception, will be saved. This is the position of the Protestants Karl Barth[138] and Wilhelm Michaelis,[139] although many Evangelicals do not share their position, in that it would take away from the seriousness of divine judgment.[140] Although Eastern authors traditionally rejected Origen's *apokatastasis*, some recent Orthodox theologians, such as Sergei Bulgàkov and Pavel Evdokimov, are more open to it.[141] This is so for reasons similar to those put forward by Scotus Eriugena[142] and others to the effect that if God were not to eventually eliminate all evil, the reality

---

137. CCC 1036.

138. The position of Barth is subtle: "*Apokatastasis panton?* No, because a grace that reaches and embraces each and every one would not be free grace, would not be divine grace. But if it is divine grace, how can we impede God from reconciling everyone?" *Die Botschaft von der freien Gnade Gottes* (Zürich: Evangelisches Verlag, 1947), 8. Elsewhere he writes: "Whoever does not believe in the *apokatastasis* is an ox, whoever says he does is an ass," *Dogmatik im Dialog*, vol. 1: *Die Kirche und die Letzten Dinge*, ed. F. Buri, 314 (Gütersloh: Mohn, 1973).

139. W. Michaelis, *Die Versöhnung des Alls* (Bern: Haller, 1950).

140. See, for example, P. Althaus, *Die letzten Dinge*, 9th ed. (Gütersloh: Bertelsmann, 1964), 187–96; E. Brunner, *Das Ewige als Zukunft*, 197–200. P. Maury, *L'eschatologie* (Genève: Labor et Fides, 1959), takes the following position: "we must reject the falsely evangelical doctrine, such as that of Origen, of the reestablishment of all things, which in the last analysis would be the re-establishment of all sin," 85.

141. See M. Bordoni and N. Ciola, *Gesù nostra speranza*, 130–32.

142. Scotus Eriugena, *De divisione naturae* V, 28–29.

Hell: Perpetual Retribution 219

of evil and perversion would eventually constitute an eternal principle, coexisting forever alongside God. A similar position is taken by Charles Péguy.[143]

Other authors are of the opinion that whereas it would be improper to believe in the salvation of all, Christians should on the contrary *hope for the salvation of all*.[144] In the *Catechism of the Catholic Church* we read: "God predestines no one to go to hell; for this, a willful turning away from God (a mortal sin) is necessary, and persistence in it until the end. In the Eucharistic liturgy and in the daily prayers of her faithful, the Church implores the mercy of God, who does not want 'any to perish, but all to come to repentance' (2 Pt 3:9): 'Father, accept this offering from your whole family. Grant us your peace in this life, save us from final damnation, and count us among those who have chosen' (*Roman Canon*)."[145] The text just cited from the *Roman Canon* (or First Eucharistic Prayer) seems to petition God for the salvation of all, in such a way that none would be condemned. And as Thomas Aquinas says, *oratio est interpretativa spei*,[146] "prayer serves as an interpretation of hope." Thus we petition God for what we are entitled to hope for from him. Besides, being a liturgical prayer, the prayer of the whole Church, such a petition should have special value.

The Position of Hans Urs von Balthasar

The author who has most strenuously defended the notion that we must hope for the salvation of all is Hans Urs von Balthasar.[147] He holds that this doctrine is supported by important Christian writers such as Origen, Gregory of Nyssa, Didymus the Blind, and Maximus the Confessor. The basis of their argument is twofold. First, in God's design the end coincides with the beginning, and thus all spiritual beings should eventually be reconciled; second, that evil, being a finite reality, cannot endure forever. From the spiritual and Christological standpoint, von Balthasar adds that the death of Christ on the Cross and his subsequent "descent into hell" (the supreme expression of the *kenosis*, or self-emptying of God in Christ) is so radical that it transforms the very heart of reality, the very depths of hell, the hearts of all sinners.[148]

---

143. Cfr. E. Mounier, *La Pensée de Charles Péguy* (Paris: Plon, 1931), 182–83.

144. Karl Rahner speaks in similar terms: "as a Christian, humanity has the right and the sacred 'duty' to hope that the history of freedom will have, for themselves and for others, a happy ending," G. Mann and K. Rahner, "Weltgeschichte und Heilsgeschichte," in *Christlicher Glaube in moderner Gesellschaft*, 23 (Basel: Herder, 1982), 87–125, here 114. The same idea is to be found in O. González de Cardedal, *Madre y muerte* (Salamanca: Sígueme, 1993), 115.

145. *CCC* 1037.   146. *S. Th.* II-II, q. 17, a. 2 ad 3.

147. See Von Balthasar's principal work on the matter: *Dare We Hope That All Men Will Be Saved?: with a Short Discourse on Hell and Apocatastasis* (San Francisco: Ignatius, 1988). They were published originally as "Was dürfen wir hoffen?" and "Kleiner Diskurs über die Hölle" (Einsiedeln: Johannes, 1986).

148. See H. U. von Balthasar, *Theologie der drei Tage: Mysterium Pasquale* (Zurich: Benzinger, 1969);

From the historical standpoint, however, it should be kept in mind that whereas it is true that Didymus fully assumed Origen's position, von Balthasar is incorrect in seeking support for the doctrine of universal reconciliation in Gregory and Maximus. Gregory, as we have already seen, speaks of the reconciliation of nature as a whole, but not that of each and every individual.[149] Likewise, for Maximus the Confessor God's plan involves the salvation of nature, but not of each person.[150]

As regards the doctrine of *apokatastasis*, the biblical scholar Pierre Grelot says that "no text from Scripture offers the slightest basis."[151] The mistake made by authors who teach this doctrine is one of attempting to extend the universal to the particular, of extending God's will to save all to the effective salvation of all.[152] The fact is that God cannot condemn man without man's consent. And man is capable of making irrevocable decisions.[153] Speaking of the possibility of eternal condemnation, Joseph Ratzinger says that what is peculiar to Christianity "is this conviction of the greatness of man. Human life is fully serious." On the contrary, the notion of universal reconciliation, he says, is "derived from the system rather than from the biblical witness."[154] To hold the contrary would amount to

---

Theodramatik, vol. 5, 277–84. Benedict XVI in the encyclical *Spe salvi* has the following to say: "Christ descended into 'Hell' and is therefore close to those cast into it, transforming their darkness into light. Suffering and torment is still terrible and well-nigh unbearable. Yet the star of hope has risen—the anchor of the heart reaches the very throne of God," SS 37.

149. See n. 28 above.

150. Maximus the Confessor, *Quaest. ad Thal.* 22,59:63. Maximus did hold that the salvation of all was a legitimate hope: *Quaest. et dubia*, 1:13. Von Balthasar, in his work on Maximus, *Kosmische Liturgie. Das Weltbild Maximus' des Bekenners*, 2nd ed. (Einsiedeln: Johannes, 1961), follows the position of E. Michaud, "S. Maxime le confesseur et l'apocatastase," *Revue internationale de théologie* 10 (1902): 257–72, who claims that Maximus indeed teaches the *apokatastasis*. However, later studies have shown conclusively that this was not Maximus's position, especially those of P. Sherwood, *The Earlier Ambigua of Saint Maximus Confessor and His Refutation of Origenism* (Roma: Herder; Pontificium Institutum S. Anselmi, 1955); B. E. Daley, "Apokatastasis and 'Honorable Silence' in the Eschatology of Maximus the Confessor," in *Maximus Confessor. Actes du symposium sur Maxime le Confesseur (1980)*, ed. F. Heinzer and C. Schönborn (Fribourg: Editions Universitaires, 1982), 309–39; and *The Hope*, 202. Von Balthasar remained unconvinced of this critique: *Was dürfen wir hoffen?*, 51–52, n. 38.

151. P. Grelot, *Le monde à venir* (Paris: Le Centurion, 1974), 120.

152. *Inter alia*, see J. L. Ruiz de la Peña, *La pascua de la creación*, 241–44.

153. Authors such as J. R. Sachs, "Current Eschatology: Universal Salvation and the Problem of Hell," *Theological Studies* 52 (1991): 227–54, explain that the irrevocability of man's "no" must derive from human freedom, not from grace. And this, he holds, is not possible. In that sense humans will always be able to turn back to God. Authors such as K. Rahner, "Ewigkeit aus Zeit," in *Schriften zur Theologie*, vol. 14 (Einsiedeln: Benzinger, 1980), 422–34, on whom Sachs bases his discussion, say, however, that freedom is "constitutively habilitated," and capable of opting once and for all. This is so of course because, according to Rahner, at heart freedom is intrinsically bound up with grace, with the "supernatural existential." In any case Rahner, from the purely anthropological standpoint, does hold that definitive exclusion from God is possible.

154. J. Ratzinger, *Eschatology*, 216–17.

a totalitarian view of salvation, what Torres Queiruga calls "theocentric verticalism."[155] Sesboüé holds besides that von Balthasar's understanding, which speaks of Christ assuming the sufferings of the condemned, attempts to comprehend the incomprehensible,[156] and in real terms tends toward the *apokatastasis*.

Hoping for the Salvation of All?

But what may be said of von Balthasar's notion that Christians should hope for the salvation of all? The object of Christian hope is twofold: the glorious *Parousia* of Christ at the end of time and the salvation of each one of the elect. It is clear that the common hope of Christians is constituted, indeed, by the coming of Christ in glory at the end of time, with which the world is renewed, the dead are raised up, humanity is definitively judged, and justice will be done once and for all. It is clear besides that each Christian should hope for his or her own salvation. Loss of hope would involve a culpable mistrust in God who promised in Christ the offer of saving grace to all. In other words, the individual's hope for salvation and his personal response to grace coincide *in re*. However, even though the hope of Christians should include trust in God's benevolence toward every human being, it simply cannot include their response to God's grace, for this is the exclusive right and duty of each Christian believer, of each person. In brief, the believer's act of hope includes ipso facto their own trusting response to God, but not the personal response of others. It is fair to say that Christians can and should desire the salvation of all, in that God seeks it (1 Tm 2:4). Besides, they should strive to achieve salvation under God's grace and attempt to communicate it to the rest of humanity. Yet the salvation of each and every person cannot as such be considered an object of Christian hope in the strict sense of the word. If God himself had no intention of supplanting or suppressing the free will of each Christian, on what basis should other humans be in a position to do so? The collective and individual elements of Christian eschatology are closely linked, doubtless, but cannot be reduced one to the other.

---

155. A. Torres Queiruga, *¿Qué queremos decir cuando decimos 'infierno'?* (Santander: Sal Terrae, 1995), 98.

156. See B. Sesboüé, "Bulletin de Théologie Dogmatique: Christologie," *Recherches de science religieuse* 59 (1971): 88–89.

Part Three. The Stimulus of Hope in the World

8

The Living Presence of the *Parousia*

> My life, I will not let you go except you bless me, but then I will let you go.
> —*Karen Blixen*[1]

> Let us not resist the first coming so that the second may not startle us.
> —*Augustine*[2]

When Will the Parousia Take Place?

As we saw earlier on, the moment when the *Parousia* takes place will depend, to some degree, on humans' correspondence (or lack of it) to God's gifts and inspiration.[3] In Matthew 23:39 we read: "For I tell you, you will not see me again *until you say* 'Blessed is he who comes in the name of the Lord.'" This does not mean, "When the Messiah comes, his people will bless him," but rather the opposite, "When his people bless him, the Messiah will come."[4] This declaration is confirmed by Jesus' admonition: "When the Son of man comes, will he find faith on earth?" (Lk 18:8).

Nonetheless, the return of the Lord Jesus in glory is fundamentally an act of God, an act of divine power. God is the only Sovereign, the only Lord, the only One in a position to decide when humanity is truly prepared, the only One capable of raising up the dead and judging humans. Hence, "of that day or that hour no one knows, not even the angels in heaven, nor the Son, but only the Father" (Mk 13:32; cf. Mt 24:36). As he ascended into heaven, Jesus said to the disciples: "it is not for you to know times and seasons which the Father has fixed by his own authority" (Acts 1:7). And Augustine comments: "Whoever claims that the Lord will come soon, he is speaking in a way that may be dangerously mistaken."[5] "For you yourselves know well that the day of the Lord will come like a thief in the night," Paul writes to the Thessalonians. "When people say, 'There is peace and

---

1. I. Dinesen (ps. Karen Blixen), *Out of Africa—Shadows on the Grass* (New York: Vintage International, 1989), 265.
2. Augustine, *Enn. in Ps.*, 95:14.
3. See pp. 60–61.
4. See ch. 2, nn. 108–10.
5. Augustine, *Ep.* 199, *de fine saeculi*.

security', then sudden destruction will come upon them as travail comes upon a woman with child, and there will be no escape" (1 Thes 5:2–3).

There is much to be said for the position of Bonaventure, who suggested we do not know the hour of final judgment because we do not really need it to ensure our salvation.[6] Schweitzer and the "thoroughgoing" eschatology school took it that the New Testament's vagueness and imprecision regarding the end of the world and the return of the Messiah indicated that Jesus was unaware of his mission and mistaken as regards his identity.[7] It would seem rather that this vagueness, such as it is, underpins an important theological statement: only God knows when the time is ripe for the harvest (Mt 3:12); and he will send his Son from his right hand to judge the world when he sees fit, neither sooner nor later. "Let both [wheat and weeds] grow until the harvest; and at harvest time *I will tell the reapers*, 'Gather the weeds . . .'" (Mt 13:30).

However, it is clear from Scripture and from the experience of Christian life, that the power and presence of the *Parousia* already makes itself felt here on earth before the definitive coming of the Lord Jesus will take place. As we saw earlier, Christian eschatology is not entirely future-bound; it is also, though not exclusively, a "realized" eschatology.[8] Salvation won by Christ is like a living ferment, constantly enlivened by the Holy Spirit, that acts and moves and changes human hearts and lives. For Augustine, a key image for the economy of salvation lies in the pilgrim character of the Church, as it hopes and longs for its full realization. The Church, he says, "like a stranger in a foreign land, presses forward amid the persecutions of the world and the consolations of God."[9] Maximus the Confessor explains that in terms of God's approach to us, the "end of the ages" has already come, but in terms of our approach to God, it is still ahead of us, and so far is present only in "types and patterns" through grace.[10]

In this chapter we shall consider the question of the presence of the *Parousia*, the stimulus of hope in the world, from four points of view. First, we shall consider how, according to the witness of the New Testament, the "Kingdom of God" is present and active during the earthly sojourn of Christ and throughout the whole life of the Church, especially in the latter's sacramental action and in the preaching of the word. Then we shall describe three ways in which the Kingdom of God becomes humanly visible and tangible: in scriptural texts speaking of the visibility of the Kingdom, the "signs" or end-time portents that, according to the New Testament, signal the Lord's presence and indicate the closeness of the *Parousia*; and the different manifestations throughout history of the phenomenon of

---

6. Bonaventure, *In IV Sent.*, D 48, a. 1.
8. See pp. 50–53.
10. Maximus the Confessor, *Quaest. ad Thal.*, 22.

7. See pp. 46–50.
9. Augustine, *De Civ. Dei XVIII*, 51:2.

millennialism, which has important consequences for understanding the degree to which eschatology is already "realized" in the world.[11]

The Presence and Dynamism of the Kingdom of God

Christians do not know how and when God's power will be finally manifested, nor "the times and seasons which the Father has fixed" (Acts 1:7). However, we are told in the Acts of the Apostles, the Apostles "shall receive power when the Holy Spirit has come upon you; and you shall be my witnesses in Jerusalem and in all Judea and Samaria and to the end of the earth" (Acts 1:8). Christian eschatology has a future, a definitive, public, and universal element, but also has a beginning here on the earth with the saving work of Christ, who sent the Holy Spirit, his Apostles and disciples to evangelize the world until he comes again in glory. Of course if God is the Creator of all that exists, his Lordship over the universe may not be understood in purely eschatological terms. God has been, is and always will be, Lord of the universe, even though his dominion may not always be apparent to us. In that sense, the universe and everything it contains is God's kingdom, God's domain, the realm of God's effective sovereignty. And if certain aspects or elements of the created world do not come under God's de facto sovereignty at the present moment, this is principally on account of human sinfulness.[12]

The theme of the "kingdom of God" is absolutely central in Christ's preaching, the term (*basileia tou Theou*) occurring more than 120 times in the New Testament, almost 100 in the Synoptics, and some 90 times on the lips of Jesus himself. Instead of the term "kingdom of God," Matthew's Gospel speaks of the "kingdom of heaven." The two expressions are rigorously equivalent. The latter, however, would have been more to the liking of the Jews, for whom Matthew wrote this gospel, as they employed God's proper name as sparingly as possible. But the heavenly nature of God's kingdom by no means indicates that it belongs or refers to an exclusively spiritual, hidden, or heavenly sphere. God's sovereignty should be as complete on earth as it is in heaven: so Christians pray in the Our Father (Mt 6:10). That is to say, just as the angels and the saints subject themselves freely to God in everything, so also should all humans and the entire universe do so.

---

11. In chapter 1, pp. 33–36, we already considered an essential aspect of the presence and stimulus of hope in the world, which underpins all the rest, the action of the Holy Spirit.

12. On the central role of the Kingdom of God in Christian eschatology, see J. Ratzinger, *Eschatology*, 24–35; W. Pannenberg, *Systematic Theology*, vol. 3, 527–32; J. J. Alviar, *Escatología*, 96–151. On the extensive bibliography available on the topic, see the recent work of L. D. Chrupcala, *The Kingdom of God: A Bibliography of 20th Century Research* (Jerusalem: Franciscan Printing Press, 2007).

Christ as the Definitive Manifestation of God's Kingdom

In the Old Testament the kingdom of God is said to be present on earth, provisionally, as a foreshadow. God exercises this kingship through human instruments (judges, prophets, seers, kings), but above all promises that when the Messiah (the Christ) is sent, his kingdom will be established on earth definitively.

From the very outset of the New Testament the coming about of the kingdom of God is related to repentance from sin, and salvation. Jesus announced that with his coming, "the time is fulfilled and the kingdom of God is at hand; repent and believe in the gospel" (Mk 1:15). In effect, the devil who induces humans to sin had become in a sense "the ruler [*archōn*] of this world" (Jn 12:31), and Jesus had come to "cast him out" (ibid.). However, the most critical element of New Testament teaching on God's kingdom lies not so much in the fact that divine sovereignty is present and active with the coming of Christ. Jesus not only proclaims the kingdom, but is, in person, its prime manifestation.

The constitution *Lumen gentium* sums up this doctrine as follows: "This kingdom shone out before men in the word, in the works and in the presence of Christ."[13] In his *word*, principally through the parables (one thinks, for example, of the seed planted in a field that grows to harvest: Mk 4:14,26–29);[14] in his *works*, and especially in the miracles (for example, the expulsion of demons: "But if it is by the finger of God that I cast out demons, then the kingdom of God has come upon you," Lk 11:20); and in his own *presence*. In fact, *Lumen gentium* specifies that "principally the kingdom is revealed in the person of Christ himself, Son of God and Son of Man, who came to 'serve and to give his life as a ransom for many' (Mk 10:45)."[15] André Feuillet explains that "the presence of the Kingdom of God is to be found not only in the action but in the very person of Jesus; this is insinuated in the Synoptics by the extraordinary significance given to the 'I' of Jesus."[16] Ethelbert Stauffer puts this as follows: "Jesus ends one religious epoch by inaugurating another one entirely dependent on himself."[17]

Joseph Ratzinger draws attention to the fact that whereas in the gospels (especially the Synoptics), the topic of the Kingdom of God is absolutely central, in the other writings (Acts, the letters of Paul, John, etc.), it is almost entirely absent. Could this be so, he asks, because Jesus was mistaken in his preaching, or that early Christians had been unfaithful to his word? Was Alfred Loisy right perhaps when he said at the beginning of the twentieth century that "Jesus preached

---

13. *LG* 5a.
14. See pp. 57–58.
15. *LG* 5a.
16. A. Feuillet, "Règne de Dieu III: Évangiles synoptiques," in *Dictionnaire de la Bible, Supplément*, vol. 10, cols. 61–165, here 67–68.
17. E. Stauffer, "Das christologische ἐγώ" in *TWNT* 2, 243–48.

the kingdom but the Church appeared instead"?[18] On the one hand, it is probably fair to say that among the early Church Fathers the eschatological term "kingdom" was substituted by that of "resurrection."[19] On the other hand, Ratzinger gives another, more convincing and consistent, explanation of the phenomenon: "it is this very change in the Leitmotif of preaching" that provided "the way in which a self-identical theme was preserved under different conditions."[20] In effect, when Jesus spoke in the Synoptics of the coming of God's kingdom, he was speaking fundamentally of himself, which is exactly what the other New Testament writers did.[21] This awareness brought Origen to say that Christ is the *autobasileia*, the "kingdom of God in person,"[22] and Tertullian: *In Evangelio est Dei regnum Christus ipse*,[23] "in the Gospel God's kingdom is Christ himself."

How Does Christ Establish God's Kingdom?

In what way does Christ bring about the kingdom of God on earth, being himself the definitive manifestation of the kingdom? First, we shall examine what Christ achieved through his saving activity, and then how he achieved it.

God's dominion over the created universe is and always will be complete. Besides, all things were created through the Word (Jn 1:3), the Word that would become incarnate in Jesus of Nazareth to save humanity. God's sovereignty is incomplete only in the ambit where sin (and its correlates: death and the devil) obtains. Thus Christ established God's kingdom principally by defeating the triple slavery of the devil, death, and sin. That of the *devil* (Lk 11:20; Heb 2:14–15), by overcoming the temptations that were directed against him;[24] that of the power of *death*, by willingly identifying himself with human mortality and overcoming it through the resurrection, as we shall see in the next chapter;[25] and that of *sin*, by redeeming humans and offering them an extraordinary abundance of filial, reconciling grace (Jn 1:16; Rom 5:20).

And how did Christ achieve the salvation of humanity? To establish the king-

---

18. A. Loisy, *L'Évangile et l'Église*, 3rd ed. (Paris: Bellevue, 1904), 155.
19. Thus, W. Pannenberg, *Systematic Theology*, vol. 3, 527–28, and R. Frick, *Die Geschichte des Reich-Gottes-Gedankens in der alten Kirche bis zu Origenes und Augustinus* (Giessen: Töpelmann, 1928), 40. Pannenberg also notes that with Irenaeus's anti-Gnosticism, the doctrine of creation acquires prominence, in such a way that the Kingdom of God may be considered to be already established. That is to say, the basis of Christ's teaching on the Kingdom is creation, not eschatology. With the Gnostic Marcion, however, the Kingdom of God is considered to begin with Christ's coming: ibid., 528, n. 7. According to John Damascene (*De fide orth.* 4:27), eschatology is derived from resurrection and judgment, and makes no reference to the Kingdom.
20. J. Ratzinger, *Eschatology*, 25.
21. The same notion is developed by J. Ratzinger/Benedict XVI, *Jesus of Nazareth*, 46–63.
22. Origen, *Comm. in Matth.*, 14:7, on Mt 18:28.   23. Tertullian, *Adv. Marc.*, 4:33.
24. *CAA* 200–206.   25. See especially pp. 266–73.

dom of God on earth, Christ, who continually beheld God's face, allowed the power and presence of the Father to penetrate into the very depths of his being, giving God free rein over each and every facet and thought and action of his life. Jesus reveals God's kingdom primarily by doing the Father's will in everything. "My food is to do the will of him who sent me" (Jn 4:34). "His entire life reveals God as Lord," Schmaus says.[26] Above we referred to Jesus' identification with God's kingdom in terms of his "I," for example, when he says "truly, truly, I say to you," or uses similar expressions. It is clear, however, that the power he effortlessly dispenses in his preaching and miracles is divine power, received from his Father, to whom he submitted himself unconditionally (Mt 7:29).

The mystery of Christ's loving obedience peaks, as it were, during his passion and death. In obeying "unto death, even death on a cross" (Phil 2:8), "Jesus renounced all sovereignty over his life, the very human will of being able to control his own life."[27] The one who died on the cross was the Servant of Yahweh (Is 49–55). And through his apparent defeat, Jesus not only manifests the Father's sovereignty over himself and over the universe, but receives, besides, from his Father through the resurrection complete and perpetual power over creation. "Therefore God has highly exalted him and bestowed on him the name which is above every name, that at the name of Jesus every knee should bow, in heaven and on earth and under the earth, and every tongue confess that Jesus Christ is Lord, to the glory of God the Father" (Phil 2:9–11). By the resurrection, we read in Romans, Jesus was constituted Son and Lord over the whole of creation (Rom 1:4).

Jesus will exercise this power in a supreme and definitive way at the time of judgment. However, even now it is operative and tangible in the life of the Church, in and through all those who believe in him.

The Presence and Action of the Risen Lord in the Church's Liturgy

The sacraments are not only signs that commemorate the past, representing the Lord's passion, death, and resurrection, nor simple operative symbols of God's grace in the present moment. Besides, the sacraments constitute a promise of future glory,[28] a prefigurement of the hoped-for *Parousia*. As such they are destined to disappear at the end of time,[29] when Reality will take the place of Figure. For example, Schmaus says that the sacrament of penance "expresses the judgment which the Father has made through the death of Christ over humanity

---

26. M. Schmaus, *Katholische Dogmatik*, vol. 4.2: *Von den letzten Dingen*, 104.
27. Ibid., 105.
28. Thomas Aquinas, *S. Th. III*, q. 60, a. 3. Aquinas speaks of the sacrament as a *signum rememorativum, demonstrativum, prognosticum*. On this, see J. M.-R. Tillard, "La triple dimension du signe sacramentel. A propos de Sum. Theol., III, 60, 3," *Nouvelle Revue Théologique* 83 (1961): 225–54.
29. *LG* 48c.

fallen into sin. . . . But at the same time, the sacrament of penance anticipates the future judgment of the sinner. . . . If future judgment is anticipated in the sacrament of penance, because the sinner requests it be applied to him now, it will not be an occasion of terror in the future."[30] That is to say, the administration of the sacrament is a kind of "coming forward," an anticipation of Christ's definitive presence in the believer.

Of particular importance is the eschatological side of the *Eucharist*. In effect, the Eucharistic celebration not only applies all the power and efficacy of the sacrifice of Christ on the cross, but in a very real way provides us with an anticipation of the *Parousia*, as it invites us to look forward to the Lord's final coming. Paul is acutely aware of this presence when he describes the Eucharistic celebration in the following terms: "For as often as you eat this bread and drink the cup, you proclaim the Lord's death *until he comes*" (1 Cor 11:26). On several occasions Vatican II documents speak of this presence, as do liturgical texts throughout all periods of history.[31] In words attributed to Peter Damian, "the citizens of both cities live on the same Bread."[32]

The Visible and Tangible Quality of God's Kingdom

God's kingdom is active and present in the world, powerfully thrusting toward eschatological fullness. It is a living power, however, that does not impose itself. It urges, invites, and provokes reaction: "The law and the prophets were until John; since then the good news of the kingdom of God is preached, and every one enters it violently" (Lk 16:16). Yet it is a power that respects human freedom fully; more exactly, it awakens human response in the most human way possible.[33] We shall now examine different texts in which Scripture describes how the Kingdom of God becomes visible and tangible to humanity: texts speaking of the visibility of the Kingdom, the "signs" of the *Parousia*. In chapter 1 we already considered the action of the Holy Spirit in arousing hope.[34]

The Visibility of God's Kingdom

It is clear that God is Lord over the universe and that even now Christ exercises divine power over the whole of creation, as universal High King.[35] It is also

---

30. See M. Schmaus, *Katholische Dogmatik*, vol. 4.2, 116. The same idea may be found in A.-M. Roguet, "Les sacrements nous jugent," *Vie spirituelle* 45 (1963): 516–23.

31. See pp. 67–71.

32. "Uno pane vivunt cives utriusque patriae," Peter Damian (attrib.), *Med. 26: Rhythmus de gloria paradisi*.

33. See my study "Is Christianity a Religion?"   34. See pp. 69–71.

35. See the encyclical of Pius XI, *Quas primas* (1925).

clear that God will be seen to reign in a fully visible and public way only when Christ returns in glory to judge the living and the dead, that is, to reveal once and for all the kingdom of God in its full splendor and power. In the meantime, it may be asked, how visible is God's kingdom? Or better, how visible is it meant to be? Christ now reigns in heaven, efficaciously (Rom 8:34; Heb 7:25), yet unseen by humans in their pilgrim state. His authority (*exousia*) is exercised on earth in different, derived ways through the agency of the family, the state, the Church, and so on (Rom 13:1–7). But how tangible is and should his authority be? Or to put it the other way around: to what degree do human authorities partake directly in Christ's authority? When Jesus said to the disciples: "The days are coming when you will desire to see *one of the days of the Son of man*, and you will not see it" (Lk 17:22), he seemed to be suggesting that his power and presence will be absent, at least apparently so, in the life of the Church and the world, in certain periods and places. Let us consider the "visibility" of the Kingdom in a text immediately preceding the one just cited (Lk 17:20–21).

Some Pharisees, considering the coming of the Kingdom of God in terms of a tangible sign that would involve the public defeat of God's enemies, asked Jesus when God's kingdom would arrive. They were seeking visible signs of God's power. And he replied: "The kingdom of God is not coming with signs to be observed; nor will they say, 'Lo, here it is!' or 'There!' for behold, the kingdom of God is in the midst of you [*entos humōn estin*]" (Lk 17:20–21). Jesus makes it clear that the kingdom will not be visibly observable (he uses the term *paratērēseōs*), nor will its dynamism be open to a cut-and dried-diagnostic. Rather it is *entos humōn estin*, translated by the Neo-Vulgate as *intra vos est*, "in the midst of you." Throughout history, the text has been understood in three ways.[36]

First, some have translated the phrase to mean "the kingdom of God will come suddenly among you." This translation, a recent one that is almost impossible to justify linguistically, draws on the theory of "thoroughgoing eschatology," according to which God's kingdom has not appeared yet but is about to do so in any moment.[37]

In the *second* place, it has been traditional, at least since the time of Origen,[38] to translate the text as "the kingdom of God is *within* you."[39] That is to say, the kingdom is not external, to be observed by signs, but interior, present in the

---

36. Following J. Ratzinger, *Eschatology*, 32–35.
37. On this reading, see F. Mussner, *Praesentia salutis. Gesammelte Studien zu Fragen und Themen des Neuen Testamentes* (Düsseldorf: Patmos, 1967), 95; J. Jeremias, *Neutestamentliche Theologie* (Gütersloh: G. Mohn, 1971), vol. 1, 104.
38. Origen, *Or.* 25:1.
39. This reading is quite typical in a monastic context. It may be found for example in Athanasius's *Vita Ant.*, n. 20, where the Kingdom of God represents a life in pursuit of monastic perfection.

heart of the believer. This is the most correct translation of the Greek text, and is fully in keeping with many other aspects of Jesus' teaching, for example, when he exhorts the Pharisees to "first cleanse *the inside* [the only other New Testament usage of *entos*] of the cup and of the plate, that the outside also may be clean" (Mt 23:26).[40] The difficulty with this interpretation, however, is that Jesus' words were directed toward several persons simultaneously, not just to one.

Third, it is common nowadays to translate Luke's phrase *entos humōn estin* as "in the midst of you." It is true that the term "among you," "in the midst of you," is normally translated in the New Testament as *en mesō* (for example, "I am *among* you as one who serves," Lk 22:27). However, keeping in mind that (1) Jesus was speaking to the Pharisees and wished to emphasize the need to avoid pure exteriority, and (2) the phrase is directed to a plurality of persons, it makes sense to translate it as "in the midst of you." This approach does not involve a collective, external rendering of God's action in opposition to an individual, interior one. If we keep in mind that Jesus himself is the kingdom of God in person, then indeed God's kingdom (Christ) is in the midst of believers, it is operative and effective, though not perhaps in a way the Pharisees had expected for the Messiah. In that sense Luke 17:20–21 may be considered as a parallel expression to Luke 11:20: "But if it is by the finger of God that I cast out demons, then the kingdom of God has come upon you."[41] A similar teaching may be found in Matthew 18:20, in which Jesus says: "For where two or three are gathered in my name, there am I in the midst of them."

In sum, the presence of the Kingdom of God that characterizes the period preceding the *Parousia* derives from Christ in person, and is at once both interior and ecclesial, both personal and collective.

John the Baptist, from prison, sent his disciples to Jesus asking: "Are you he who is to come, or shall we look for another?" (Lk 7:19). Perhaps John had been expecting the appearance of unequivocal apocalyptic signs that would vindicate the just (among them, John himself, who had accused Herod of grievous crimes) and punish sinners.[42] Jesus replied by referring to the Messianic signs mentioned in Isaiah 35:5–6. In doing so he showed that the "signs" of God's saving power working through him would not be, at least for the moment, of a spectacular, visible, and incontrovertible kind. They would reveal, rather, the compassionate love of God for his creatures. "Go and tell John what you have seen and heard: the blind receive their sight, the lame walk, lepers are cleansed, and the deaf

---

40. The same position is held by M. Meinertz, *Theologie des Neuen Testaments* (Bonn: Hanstein, 1940), 34–35.
41. Thus R. Otto, *The Kingdom of God and the Son of Man*, 135.
42. *CAA* 193–200.

hear, the dead are raised up, the poor have the good news preached to them" (Lk 7:22).[43]

Those who belong to Christ, those in whom Christ lives (Gal 2:20), live in the world as carriers of their Lord and Savior, as *alter Christus, ipse Christus*, as "other Christs, Christ himself," to use the words of Josemaría Escrivá.[44] Thus through Christian believers, who are *Christ-carriers*, the Kingdom of God is made ever more present, active, and effective in the world.

Signs of the Parousia

Apocalyptic works speak consistently of a series of signs and portents indicating that final consummation is about to take place,[45] as do Old Testament Messianic texts for that matter. Generally speaking, the signs in question show up the sinful decadence of a world destined for destruction and eventual restoration through the power of God.[46] These signs involve every aspect of human and cosmic life: the breakdown of human solidarity, cosmic calamities, human prodigies and abominations, wars and angelic strife. Similar signs are spoken of in the New Testament.[47] While less dramatic and tragic in character than those present in the apocalyptic corpus, the signs the New Testament speaks of serve as indicators that the Kingdom of God is present and growing, that the *Parousia* is near at hand. Perhaps the principal difference between the two lies in the fact that the New Testament signs, situated between the two comings of Jesus, are closely linked with the Church's evangelizing action, that of preaching the Good News throughout the whole world.[48]

The first century *Didachē* presents the end-time signs in the following sequence: the stretching out of a cross in the heavens, a trumpet blast, and the resurrection of the saints joining Jesus in triumphal march into heaven. Origen considers end-time signs in a more spiritual way: the hunger before the coming of Christ refers to the Christian's hunger for a deeper meaning in Scripture;[49] the Antichrist is the symbol of all false interpretations.[50] In his work *De Civitate Dei*, Augustine summed up the signs as follows: "Elias the Thesbite will return, the Jews will believe, the Antichrist will persecute the Church, Christ will be the Judge, the dead will rise, the good will be separated from the wicked, the world will suffer from fire, but will be renewed. Of course, what we believe is the simple fact that all these things are to be; but how and in what sequence the events are

43. On this passage *CAA* 198–99.
44. See my study "The Inseparability of Holiness and Apostolate."
45. *CAA* 79–81. 46. See pp. 239–41.
47. *CAA* 150–54. 48. See J. J. Alviar, *Escatología*, 89–93.
49. Origen, *Comm. in Matth.*, 37. 50. Ibid., 33.

to occur, we must leave to future experience, which alone can teach these truths so much better than human intelligence can at present understand. My own view is that they will occur in the order I have just mentioned."[51] The biblical scholar Franz Mussner presents the following seven signs: the preaching of the gospel throughout the world, the coming of many false Christs and false prophets, the spreading of iniquity and cooling off of love and faith, the great apostasy, disastrous cosmic calamities, the manifestation of the Antichrist, the conversion of the Jews.[52]

It is fair to say that the principal signs may be reduced to three: the universal preaching of the gospel, the conversion of Israel, and the coming of the Antichrist with the general apostasy of believers. To the latter may be added calamities of a cosmic kind, as the following text indicates: "For then there will be great tribulation, such as has not been from the beginning of the world until now, no, and will never be. And if those days had not been shortened no human being would be saved; but for the sake of the elect those days will be shortened" (Mt 24:21–22).

The interpretation of these signs as precursors of the *Parousia* is a highly complicated matter. Clear, neat explanations are inadvisable, even hazardous. On the one hand, it is not clear to what degree the signs must be fulfilled in order to ensure that the coming of the Lord may be said to be imminent. On the other hand, even if it could be demonstrated that the sign had been perfectly fulfilled, it would be impossible to say how much time would have to elapse before the *Parousia* would actually take place. As we saw above, the *Parousia* depends to an important degree on human correspondence and faith, but is primordially a mysterious act of God who reads the human heart.

Universal Preaching of the Gospel

In Matthew's Gospel we read: "This gospel of the kingdom will be preached throughout the whole world, as a testimony to all nations; and *then the end will come*" (24:14). It does not seem necessary to apply this prophecy to each and every individual throughout history, but rather to peoples and nations as a whole, perhaps to culturally identifiable groups (Acts 2:9–11). The text makes it clear, however, that the task of evangelization is the very purpose for which the Church exists, and that only when the task is achieved may the world come to an end. The time that elapses between the incarnation of the Word and his coming in glory constitutes primarily a space and opportunity for evangelization.[53] It is

51. Augustine, *De Civ. Dei XX*, 30:5.
52. See F. Mussner, "Kennzeichen des nahen Endes nach dem Neuen Testament," in *Weisheit Gottes, Weisheit der Welt. Festschrift für Joseph Kardinal Ratzinger zum 60. Geburtstag*, vol. 2 (St. Ottilien: EOS, 1987), 1295–308.
53. *CAA* 144–45, on this motif in Matthew's Gospel.

interesting to note that this "missionary" sign is entirely absent from classical apocalyptic works, for the latter speak of the imminent revelation of the good and the evil, of judgment, but not of the salvation of sinners.[54]

The Conversion of Israel

The evangelization of all peoples is linked closely with the conversion of Israel, which Paul speaks of openly in his letter to the Romans. "I want you to understand this mystery, brothers: a hardening has come upon part of Israel, until the full number of the Gentiles comes in, and so all Israel will be saved" (Rom 11:25–26). The true reason for the eventual salvation of Israel is not a contingent one. It is not directly related to the national, cultural, or political unity of Jesus' own people. In effect, Jesus was not recognized as the Messiah by his own people (Jn 1:11), but was in fact rejected by many of them, although his Father vindicated him for the sake of the elect by raising him from the dead (Acts 2:14–28). The reason why Paul is sure that the conversion of the Jews will eventually take place has deep theological roots: "the gifts and the call of God are irrevocable" (Rom 11:29). The prayer of Jesus, "Father, forgive them for they know not what they do" (Lk 23:34), is more powerful than his being rejected by a "part of Israel" (Rom 11:25): "His blood be on us and on our children!" (Mt 27:25). In this sense, the conversion of Israel is not really a sign, but rather a prophecy.[55]

For both Jesus and Paul the ultimate salvation of their own people was literally a matter of life and death. "O Jerusalem, Jerusalem," Jesus cried out, "killing the prophets and stoning those who are sent to you! [these were actions that deserved eschatological judgment and punishment]. How often would I have gathered your children together as a hen gathers her brood under her wings, and you would not! Behold, your house is forsaken and desolate. For I tell you, you will not see me again, until you say 'Blessed is he who comes in the name of the Lord'" (Mt 23:37–39). And Paul: "My conscience bears me witness in the Holy Spirit that I have great sorrow and unceasing anguish in my heart. For I could wish that I myself were accursed and cut off from Christ for the sake of my brothers, my kinsmen by race. They are Israelites, and to them belong the sonship, the glory, the covenants, the giving of the law, the worship, and the promises; to them belong the patriarchs, and of their race according to the flesh, is the Christ" (Rom 9:3–5).

The *Catechism of the Catholic Church* sums up the question in the following terms: "The glorious Messiah's coming is suspended at every moment of history

---

54. Augustine does take the conversion of sinners as a sign of end of time: *Ep.* 197:4; 199:46–51; *De Civ. Dei XX*, 30.

55. See J. Ratzinger, *Eschatology*, 200.

until his recognition by 'all Israel.' . . . The 'full inclusion' of the Jews in the Messiah's salvation, in the wake of 'the full number of the Gentiles', will enable the People of God to achieve 'the measure of the stature of the fullness of Christ' (Rm 11:12) in which 'God may be all in all' (1 Co 15:28)."[56]

The Antichrist, Persecution, and Apostasy

It is understandable that Christians in their evangelizing task would encounter resistance and opposition when faced with a sinful, hostile world. Jesus himself encountered it, and it brought about his death. He warned his disciples to "beware of men; for they will deliver you up to councils, and flog you in their synagogues, and you will be dragged before governors and kings for my sake, to bear testimony before them and the Gentiles. . . . Brother will deliver up brother to death, and the father his child, and children will rise against parents and have them put to death; and you will be hated by all for my name's sake" (Mt 10:17–18,21–22). Jesus goes on to give the reason for the persecution of Christian believers: "A disciple is not above his teacher, nor a servant above his master" (Mt 10:24). And more openly during the Last Supper: "If they persecuted me, they will persecute you" (Jn 15:20).

These texts make it clear that systematic, recurrent opposition to Christian life and mission is not the simple result of misunderstanding, tactless evangelization, or disturbed comfort. It is a battle against the power of sin and the devil. "For we are not contending against flesh and blood," Paul writes, "but against the principalities, against the powers, against the world rulers of this present darkness, against the spiritual hosts of wickedness in the heavenly places" (Eph 6:12).[57]

The New Testament speaks in fact of the coming of a figure that is openly opposed to the Savior. This figure is called the "Antichrist" in John's writings (1 Jn 2:18,22; 4:3; 2 Jn 7), and is presented in terms of a coming together of a variety of pernicious forces, an aggressive, diabolic, anti-Christian spirit.[58] "The antichrists are many," John says (1 Jn 2:18). Conversely, Paul speaks of the "Man of iniquity," "the son of perdition," or the "Lawless One" (2 Thes 2:3,8), who seems, rather, to be a unique, concrete individual. The Antichrist will fight against Christians and obtain an important though partial victory in terms of a major apostasy of believers.[59]

---

56. *CCC* 674.

57. Among the Fathers of the Church, for example Ambrosiaster, Jerome, and Gregory the Great, the Antichrist is considered to be the incarnation of the devil. On Gregory, see H. Savon, "L'Antéchrist dans l'œuvre de Grégoire le Grand," in *Grégoire le Grand [Chantilly Colloquium, 1982]*, ed. J. Fontaine et al. (Paris: Éditions du CNRS, 1986), 389–404.

58. On the theme of the Antichrist in the context of eschatology, see M. Schmaus, *Katholische Dogmatik*, vol. 4.2: *Von den letzten Dingen*, 170–88.

59. Ibid., 173–74.

238 The Stimulus of Hope

The following extensive text from the second letter to the Thessalonians describes the Pauline figure of the "Man of iniquity."[60] "For that day [the *Parousia*] will not come, unless the rebellion comes first, and the man of iniquity is revealed, the son of perdition, who opposes and exalts himself against every so-called god or object of worship, so that he takes his seat in the temple of God, proclaiming himself to be God.... For the mystery of iniquity is already at work; only he who now restrains it will do so until he is out of the way. And then the Lawless One will be revealed, and the Lord will slay him with the breath of his mouth and destroy him by his appearing and his coming [*parousias*]. The coming of the Lawless One by the activity of Satan will be with all power and with pretended signs and wonders and with all wicked deception for those who are to perish, because they refused to love the truth and so be saved" (2 Thes 2:3–4,7–10).

Likewise in Revelation 13 the action of the Antichrist is vividly described in terms of two beasts rising up out of the sea. The first one is adored by humans, who exclaim: "Who is like the beast, and who can fight against it?" (Rv 13:4). The Antichrist is given three and a half years to exercise its spurious authority until it is defeated by the Lamb. The second beast "works great signs, even making fire come down from heaven to earth in the sight of men" (Rv 13:13).[61]

The Antichrist attempts to provoke apostasy among Christians by means of persecution to the point of martyrdom. "Those who believe in the world must persecute those who believe in Christ, even though they are united to them by bonds of blood," Schmaus writes. "The persecution of those who believe in Christ, at the hands of those who believe in the world, is not based on any kind of misunderstanding or ineptitude or mistaken tactics on the part of Christians, but on the very nature of their faith in Christ and of faith in the world."[62]

Speaking of the Antichrist and the Christ who is to come, Paul wrote in the same letter to the Thessalonians: "And you know what is restraining him [Christ] now so that he may be revealed in his time" (2 Thes 2:6). The persecution of Christians and the prayer of the martyrs will eventually provoke divine anger

60. See E. Ghini, "La parusia di Cristo e dell'anticristo nelle lettere ai Tessalonicesi," *Parola, Spirito e Vita* 8 (1983): 119–32.

61. See the collection of texts by F. Sbaffoni, ed., *Testi sull'anticristo: sec I-II; sec. III*, 2 vols. (Firenze: Nardini, 1992). On the Antichrist in the early centuries of Christianity, see G. C. Jenks, *The Origins and Early Development of the Antichrist Myth* (Berlin: de Gruyter, 1991); B. McGinn, *Antichrist: Two Thousand Years of the Human Fascination with Evil* (San Francisco: HarperSan Francisco, 1994); L. J. L. Peerbolte, *The Antecedents of Antichrist: A Traditio-Historical Study of the Earliest Christian Views on Eschatological Opponents* (Leiden: E. J. Brill, 1996); C. Badilita, *Métamorphoses de l'antéchrist chez les Pères de l'Église* (Paris: Beauchesne, 2005).

62. M. Schmaus, *Katholische Dogmatik*, vol. 4.2: *Von den letzten Dingen*, 162.

(Rv 6:9–10). For the sufferings of Christians are like the travail of a new creation (Rom 8:23). The apologist Aristides said: "Not even I doubt that the fervent prayer of Christians is capable of conserving the world in existence."[63] And Justin Martyr: "The ruin of the universe, the destruction of the whole world, as well as that of condemned angels and men, is delayed on account of the tender seed of Christianity."[64] The history of Christendom until the *Parousia* takes place imitates and reflects the earthly life of Jesus. Hence it makes sense to say that the final stages of history will be accompanied by the greatest expressions of suffering and hate. Yet in the end, when the number of faithful is complete (Rv 6:11), Christ will appear, although Scripture seems to indicate that many believers will have fallen away: "when the Son of man comes, will he find faith on earth?" (Lk 18:8).

The End-Time Signs and Portents: An Invitation to Vigilance

Paul firmly encourages the Thessalonians not to be impatient and credulous in respect of end-time signs and portents. "Concerning the coming of our Lord Jesus Christ and our assembling to meet him, we beg you, brothers, not to be quickly shaken in mind or excited, either by spirit or by word, or by letter purporting to be from us, to the effect that the day of the Lord has come. Let no one deceive you in any way; for that day will not come unless the rebellion [the Antichrist] comes first, and the man of iniquity is revealed, the son of perdition" (2 Thes 2:1–3). Ephrem the Syrian teaches in the same spirit, but is less specific than the Apostle: "Even though the Lord has indicated the signs of his coming, we do not know their final cadence, because they will come with many variations, they will pass and will still be in act."[65]

On many occasions throughout the New Testament the prospect of the glorious return of Jesus Christ is seen as an occasion for Christians to renew their sense of vigilance. "Let your loins be girded and your lamps burning, and be like men who are waiting for their master to come home from the marriage feast, so that they may open to him at once when he comes and knocks. Blessed are those servants whom the master finds awake when he comes; truly, I say to you, he will gird himself and have them sit at table, and he will come and serve them. . . . You also must be ready, for the Son of man is coming at an unexpected hour" (Lk 12:35–37,40).[66] Mark speaks repeatedly of the need for vigilance: "Take heed,

---

63. Aristides, *Apol.*, 16:6.
64. Justin, *II Apol.*, 6.
65. Ephrem, *Comm. in Diatess.*, 18:16. For Ephrem's eschatology, see his *Hymns on Paradise*. See also I. Ortiz de Urbina, "Le paradis eschatologique d'après saint Ephrem," *Orientalia Christiana Periodica* 21 (1955): 467–72; J. Teixidor, "Muerte, cielo y seol en san Efrém," *Orientalia Christiana Periodica* 27 (1961): 82–114.
66. See also Lk 12:42–48; Mt 24:42–51; 25:1–13;14–30.

watch; for you do not know when the time will come.... Watch therefore for you do not know when the master of the house will come.... And what I say to you I say to all: 'Watch'" (Mk 13:33,35,37).[67]

The same message is to be found in the first letter of Peter and other New Testament writings. "The end of all things is at hand; therefore keep sane and sober for your prayers" (1 Pt 4:7). The second letter of Peter (3:9) explains that God has not wished to judge humans immediately after the life of Christ, thus giving them the opportunity to repent. In this way we can see that the patience of God invites believers not to indolence and irresponsibility, but to vigilance and gratitude. The same message is to be found in Paul's letter to the Romans: "Or do you presume on the riches of his kindness and forbearance and patience? Do you not know that God's kindness is meant to lead you to repentance? But by your hard and impenitent heart you are storing up wrath for yourself on the day of wrath when God's righteous judgment will be revealed. For he will render to every man according to his works" (Rom 2:4–6). And in the book of Revelation the following words are written to the church of Sardis: "I know your works, you have the name of being alive and you are dead. Awake and strengthen what remains and is on the point of death.... If you will not awake, I will come like a thief, and *you will not know at what hour* I will come upon you" (Rv 3:1–3).

Ephrem says that Jesus "hid the hour of the *Parousia* so that we would be vigilant and each one would be convinced that it could take place this very day. If the day of his coming had been revealed, it would have little impact, neither would his manifestation be the object of hope for nations and for the world.... In this way the hope of his coming is kept alive for all peoples and times."[68] Hillary of Poitiers says that we do not know when the world will come to an end, yet God in his goodness offers us "an ample space of time for repentance, yet keeps us always vigilant by our fear of the unknown."[69] "We are happy to ignore when the end will come, because God wishes we ignore it," Augustine says,[70] yet he exhorts Christians "not to resist the first coming so that the second one does not startle us."[71] Hence he says we should avoid attempting to calculate the end of time.[72] On the contrary, Gregory the Great considered that the end of time was truly imminent.[73] Nonetheless, there was still time available for preparation and evangelization. The main purpose of Gregory's urgency was not to spread gloom among believers but to move his hearers to fear God and his judgments, and "to

---

67. The vigilance motif is frequent throughout the New Testament: 1 Cor 16:13; Eph 5:15; 6:18; 1 Tm 4:16; 2 Tm 4:5; Heb 12:15; 1 Pt 1:13; 5:8; Rv 3:3; 16:15.

68. Ephrem, *Comm. in Diatess.*, 19:15.   69. Hillary of Poitiers, *In Matth.*, 26:4.

70. Augustine, *Enn. in Ps.*, 6:2.   71. Ibid., 95:14.

72. Augustine, *Sermo* 199 *de fine saeculi*.   73. See texts in B. E. Daley, *The Hope*, 211–12.

lift up their minds in hope of the glory that is to follow."⁷⁴ Thomas Aquinas says that these signs are not meant to satisfy our idle curiosity, but rather to "move our heart to submit ourselves to the Judge who is coming."⁷⁵

The fact that the future coming of Jesus is prefigured in signs that move believers to vigilance and conversion does not mean that such promises are merely symbolic, functional, or performative. Should the promised *Parousia* not eventually take place, then the promises and the signs themselves would be meaningless and deceptive.⁷⁶ Thomas Aquinas in a well-known expression said that "the act of faith does not point so much to the affirmation that is made, but to the very reality to which the affirmation refers."⁷⁷ The same may be said here. The object of Christian hope is not primarily the biblical description of the *Parousia*, the signs that precede it and their immediate relevance, but rather the future promised realities that the description refers to in all their mysterious realism.

Gozzelino sums up the meaning of the signs along with the delay in the *Parousia* as follows: "the possibility of reading faith in history, an invitation to vigilance, the dissolution of all illusions, the support of courage and the increase in the missionary action of the Church."⁷⁸

The Ebb and Flow of Millennialism

In the book of Revelation John recounts the following spectacular vision: "I saw an angel coming down from heaven, holding in his hand the key of the bottomless pit and a great chain. And he seized the dragon, that ancient serpent, who is the Devil and Satan, and bound him for a thousand years, and threw him into the pit, and shut it and sealed it over him, that he should deceive the nations no more, till the thousand years were ended" (Rv 20:1–3). While the devil was bound, John continues, the just (that is, the martyrs and those who had not worshipped the beast), "reigned with Christ for a thousand years," whereas "the rest of the dead did not come to life until the thousand years were ended. This is the first resurrection" (Rv 20:4–5).

The text speaks of a promised one-thousand-year reign of freedom and peace for Christian believers, during which the devil will be enchained. After the thousand years are up, however, the devil "must be loosed for a little while" (Rv 20:3), "and will come out to deceive the nations which are at the four corners of the

---

74. Gregory the Great, *Mor. in Job*, 13, 24:28. See *Hom. in Ev.* 1, 1:1.
75. Thomas Aquinas, *S. Th. III, Suppl.*, q. 73, a. 1c.
76. *CAA* 46–47.
77. Thomas Aquinas, *S. Th. II-II*, q. 1, q. 2 ad 2.
78. G. Gozzelino, *Nell'attesa*, 388.

earth" (Rv 20:8). However, as the devil and his hosts attack the saints, the vision recounts, "fire came down from heaven and consumed them, and the devil who had deceived them was thrown into the lake of fire . . . and will be tormented day and night for ever and ever" (Rv 20:9–10).[79]

Understandably, Revelation 20, along with other important biblical texts with numerical content, such as Genesis 1 (the six days of creation followed by a day of rest), Psalm 90:5 ("A thousand years are to you like a yesterday which has passed") and 2 Peter 3:8 ("with the Lord one day is as a thousand years, and a thousand years as one day"), gave Christian authors ample material to develop a theology of history spanning what many of them considered the chronicle of the cosmos and of salvation: a multi-cycle seven-thousand-year period with a wide variety of modulations.[80]

The theory of the thousand-year reign came to be known as "millennialism" (or "chiliasm," from *chilioi*, the Greek word for "thousand"). Over the centuries it has taken on a wide variety of forms,[81] both secular and spiritual, although on occasions the two have merged with one another. Norman Cohn has suggested that "for long stretches, the history of Christianity has been identical with the struggle for the Thousand Years' empire."[82] Whatever may be said of the details, Christians were convinced that true hope was meant to leave a visible and tangible mark on history, on peoples, on institutions, on the Church, on society, and on political life. Three principal forms of millennialism emerged and consolidated: apocalyptic, worldly, and spiritual.

---

79. From the exegetical standpoint, see, for example, M. Gourgues, "The Thousand-Year Reign (Rev 20:1–6): Terrestrial or Celestial?" *Catholic Biblical Quarterly* 47 (1985): 676–81; U. Vanni, "Apocalisse e interpretazioni millenaristiche," in *Spirito, Eschaton e storia*, ed. N. Ciola (Roma: Mursia, 1998), 189–215; C. H. Giblin, "The Millennium (Rev 20,1–6) as Heaven," *New Testament Studies* 45 (1999): 553–70; R. Lux, "Was sagt die Bibel zur Zukunft des Menschen? Eine biblisch-kerygmatische Besinnung zur Jahrtausendwende," *Kerygma und Dogma* 46 (2000): 2–21; A. Yarbro Collins, "The Apocalypse of John and Its Millennial Themes," in *Apocalyptic and Eschatological Heritage: The Middle East and Celtic Realms*, ed. M. McNamara (Dublin: Four Courts, 2003), 50–60.

80. Especially Irenaeus, *Adv. Haer. V*, 28:3 and 33:2.

81. On the history of millennialism, see L. Gry, *Le millénarisme dans ses origines et son développement* (Paris: Picard, 1904); N. Cohn, *The Pursuit of the Millennium: Revolutionary Millenaria and Mystical Anarchists of the Middle Ages* (Oxford: Oxford University Press, 1970); B. McGinn, "Early Apocalypticism: The Ongoing Debate," in *The Apocalypse in English Renaissance Thought and Literature*, ed. C. A. Patrides and J. Wittreich (Manchester: Manchester University Press, 1984), 2–39; T. Daniels, *Millennialism: An International Bibliography*; C. E. Hill, *Regnum caelorum: Patterns of Future Hope in Early Christianity*, 2nd ed. (Grand Rapids, Mich.: W. B. Eerdmans, 2001); S. Hunt, ed., *Christian Millennarianism: From the Early Church to Waco* (London: Hurst, 2001); R. A. Landes, ed., *Encyclopedia of Millennialism and Millennial Movements* (New York: Routledge, 2000). In the context of eschatology, see J. Moltmann, *The Coming of God: Christian Eschatology* (London: SCM, 1996), 146–202.

82. Cit. by J. Moltmann, *The Coming*, 146.

The Living Presence 243

Apocalyptic Millennialism

Several early Christian authors,[83] such as Cerinthus,[84] Papias,[85] Justin,[86] Irenaeus,[87] Tertullian,[88] and Lactantius,[89] offered a more or less literal interpretation of Revelation 20. They held that for a period of a thousand years the devil will be unable to tempt Christians, who will live in the world under Christ in

---

83. On the question of millennialism among the Fathers of the Church, see B. E. Daley, *The Hope*, passim; C. Nardi, "Il regno millenario nelle attese dei primi cristiani," in *La fine dei tempi. Storia e escatologia*, ed. M. Naldini (Fiesole: Nardini, 1994), 50–75; C. Nardi, ed., *Il millenarismo: testi dei secoli I-II* (Firenze: Nardini, 1995); C. Nardi, "Il millenarismo nel cristianesimo primitivo. Cronografia e scansione del tempo," in *Apocalittica e liturgia del compimento*, ed. A. N. Terrin (Padova: Messaggero; Abbazia di S. Giustina, 2000), 145–83; M. Simonetti, "L'Apocalisse e l'origine del millennio," *Vetera Christianorum* 26 (1989): 337–50; "Il millenarismo cristiano dal I al V secolo," *Annali di Storia dell'esegesi* 15 (1998): 7–20. On the presence of millennialism in the liturgy, see B. Botte, "Prima resurrectio. Un vestige de millénarisme dans les liturgies occidentales," *Recherches de théologie ancienne et médiévale* 15 (1948): 5–17.

84. See L. Gry, *Le Millenarisme*, 65.

85. On Papias, see Irenaeus, *Adv. Haer.* V, 33:3–4, who refers to the former's *Exposition of the Sayings of the Lord*. See B. E. Daley, *The Hope*, 18; G. Pani, "Il millenarismo: Papia, Giustino e Ireneo," *Annali di Storia dell'esegesi* 15 (1998): 53–84.

86. Justin speaks of Christian believers reigning with Christ in the new Jerusalem for a thousand years, in the state of prosperity depicted by Is 65:17–25: *Dial. cum Tryph.*, 80–81. This situation, he says, is a prelude to final resurrection and retribution: "thereafter the general, and, to put it briefly, eternal resurrection and judgment of all will . . . take place," ibid., 81. He also speaks of the eternal possession of Holy Land by the saints "after the holy resurrection," ibid., 113, 139. On Justin's thought, see A. L. W. Barnard, "Justin Martyr's Eschatology," *Vigiliae Christianae* 19 (1965): 94–95; G. Pani, "Il millenarismo."

87. B. E. Daley, *The Hope*, 31, sums up Irenaeus's teaching as follows: "It is fitting for the righteous first to receive the promise of the inheritance which God promised the fathers, and to reign in it, when they rise again to behold God in this creation which is renewed, and that the judgment should take place afterwards (5,32,1)." Irenaeus insists that Old Testament teaching on the reward of the just should not be allegorized: *Adv. Haer.* V, 35:1–2. He says that millennialism is appropriate, for it prepares believers "to partake in the divine nature" *Adv. Haer.* V, 32:1. Still, his "underlying concern seems to be to defend the inclusion of the material side of creation in the unified plan of God's salvation," B. E. Daley, *The Hope*, 31. On Irenaeus's understanding of millennialism, see E. Norelli, "Il duplice rinnovamento del mondo nell'escatologia di San Ireneo," *Augustinianum* 18 (1978): 98–106; M. O. R. Boyle, "Irenaeus' Millennial Hope: A Polemical Weapon," *Recherches de théologie ancienne et médiévale* 36 (1969): 5–16; C. Mazzucco and E. Pietrella, "Il rapporto tra la concezione del millennio dei primi autori cristiani e l'apocalisse di Giovanni," *Augustinianum* 18 (1978): 29–45; C. R. Smith, "Chiliasm and Recapitulation in the Theology of Irenaeus," *Vigiliae Christianae* 48 (1994): 313–31; S. Tanzarella, "Alcuni aspetti antropologici del millenarismo di Ireneo di Lione," in *Cristologia e antropologia. In dialogo con M. Bordoni*, ed. C. Greco (Roma: AVE, 1994), 131–46; "'Ogni acino spremuto darà venticinque metrete di vino' (Adversus haereses V,33,3): il problema delle fonti del millenarismo di Ireneo," *Vetera Christianorum* 34 (1997): 67–85; R. Polanco Fermandois, "El milenarismo de Ireneo o teología antignóstica de la *caro capax Dei*," *Teología y Vida* 41 (2000): 16–29.

88. On Tertullian, see B. E. Daley, *The Hope*, 35–36. Tertullian speaks of a restored heavenly Jerusalem (*Adv. Marc.*, 3:24) in recompense for all that has been lost. At the end of the thousand years, there will be a great destruction and conflagration. In other works, Tertullian takes a more allegorical approach, for example, in *De res.*, 26.

89. Lactantius deals with millennialism in his *Divinae institutiones*. He offers a powerful though

peace and harmony; this is what John calls the "first resurrection." Once this period had elapsed, the devil will be released once more, they said, and his brief but ferocious attack on believers—closely linked with the coming of the Antichrist and the resulting apostasy of many Christians—will eventually end in his total defeat, the return of the Lamb in glory, and the "second resurrection."

Although the literal apocalyptic view was abandoned for the most part later on, many Fathers taught it because they wished to avoid Gnostic speculations involving a spiritualistic anthropology and eschatology. For this reason, among others, they insisted forcefully on the material side of final resurrection.[90] Interestingly, Paul Althaus notes that "the most important justification of chiliasm is that it points to the necessary this-worldly character of Christian hope."[91]

Worldly Millennialism

The Church historian Eusebius of Caesarea considered the Roman Empire as a direct preparation for the coming of Christianity, a true *praeparatio evangelica*, which came to its culmination when Constantine was emperor. The merging of Christianity and Rome occasioned the advent of the so-called Holy Roman Empire. The latter is characterized by the formula *pax romana, pax Christiana*, which may be roughly translated as follows: "peace in the Empire guarantees peace for Christians." He rejected the position of earlier authors such as Papias for their excessively apocalyptic or other-worldly approach to God's presence in the world.[92] "When God's Messiah appeared . . . the fulfillment followed in exact correspondence to the prophecies," he wrote. "For among the Romans every rule by the many was at once abolished, since Augustus assumed the sole rule at the very point in time when our Redeemer appeared [Lk 2:1]."[93] In his Oration at the *Tricennalia*, Eusebius interpreted the enthronement of Constantine as emperor as a literal fulfillment of Daniel 7:18: "the saints of the Most High shall receive the

---

eclectic vision of what is to come. He speaks of the "extreme old age of a tired and crumbling world," *Div. Inst. VII*, 14. Only two hundred years are left: *Div. Instit. VII*, 25. Rome will fall, he says, and the East will rule again. The Antichrist will mete out three and a half years of persecution, but then God will send the great king from heaven to destroy it: *Div. Instit. VII*, 17–19. This will be followed by an age of peace. Lactantius was particularly influential on the thought of the Middle Ages; his doctrine "was to have a life of its own," B. E. Daley, *The Hope*, 68. On his teaching, see V. Fàbrega, "Die chiliastische Lehre des Laktanz," *Jahrbuch für Antike und Christentum* 17 (1974): 126–46; B. E. Daley, *The Hope*, 66–68; M. Simonetti, "Il millenarismo in Occidente: Commodiano e Lattanzio," *Annali di Storia dell'esegesi* 15 (1998): 181–89.

90. In particular Irenaeus and Tertullian: see B. E. Daley, *The Hope*, 31.

91. P. Althaus, *Die letzten Dinge*, 314, cit. in J. Moltmann, *The Coming*, 153.

92. Eusebius, *Hist. Eccl.* 3,39:13; 7,24:1. On Eusebius's thought, see J. Eger, "Kaiser und Kirche in der Geschichtstheologie Eusebius' von Cäsaräa," *Zeitschrift für die neutestamentliche Wissenschaft* 38 (1939): 97–115.

93. Eusebius, *Praep. Evang.* 1:4–5; *Hist. Eccl.* 10,4:53.

kingdom."[94] The Roman Empire, he said, had become irrevocably fused with the universal kingdom of Christ. It is quite understandable that Eusebius came to be known as the "first political theologian in the Christian Church."[95] Christ's kingdom was firmly established on earth, and the emperor was his representative. Hermann Dörries sums up Eusebius's view in the following formula: "One God, one *Logos*, one emperor."[96]

Under Constantine and his successors, Church and State would come to constitute a single, albeit articulated, structure. This position, which counted on precedents among the Ebionites and Montanists,[97] remained common and even prevalent for many centuries in the Christian world, as may be seen in the writings of authors as far apart as Otto von Freising in the twelfth century and Jacques B. Bossuet in the seventeenth.[98] The same principle was commonly to be found in Byzantium and the Oriental Empire.[99] Charles Taylor describes this conviction in the following terms: "The promise of the Parousia, that God will be all in all, can be realized here, albeit in the reduced form which requires constraint."[100]

Spiritual Millennialism

Origen was openly scornful of the apocalyptic understanding of millennialist texts, considering them to be "Jewish" interpretations of Scripture that falsely idealized earthly beatitude.[101] He interpreted Scripture in an allegorical way. Victorinus of Pettau, who died a martyr during the persecution of Diocletian (304), developed Origen's intuition.[102] He speaks of the first resurrection and the thousand years in a spiritual, not a material, sense, and taught that resurrection will free us from eating, drinking, and all kinds of bodily activities.[103]

94. Eusebius, *De laudibus Constantini*; *Hist. Eccl.* 10,4. On this, J. Moltmann, *The Coming*, 161.
95. J. Eger, "Kaiser und Kirche."
96. H. Dörries, *Konstantin der Grosse* (Stuttgart: Kohlhammer, 1958), 146–50.
97. See A. M. Berruto, "Millenarismo e montanismo," *Annali di Storia dell'esegesi* 15 (1998): 85–100; B. E. Daley, *The Hope*, 18.
98. Otto von Freising, *Chronicon sive historia de duabus civitatibus* (written 1143–46). Otto's work is based on Augustine's *De Civitate Dei*, but is more optimistic and simplistic in tone. The author writes: "I attempted to write the history of two cities, that of God and that of man. Looking at the facts, however, I realized that the two come together when kings and peoples are all Christian. Then there is only one city, the *civitas christiana*, the Church of kings and peoples and therefore only one history." The position is to be found, substantially unaltered, in Bossuet's work *Discours sur l'histoire universelle* (1681).
99. W. Brandes, "Endzeiterwartung und Kaiserkritik in Byzanz um 500 n. Chr.," *Byzantinische Zeitschrift* 90 (1997): 24–63.
100. C. Taylor, *A Secular Age* (Cambridge, Mass.: Belknap Press of Harvard University Press), 243.
101. Origen, *De princip. II*, 11:2; *Comm. in Matth.*, 17:35. See G. Moioli, *L'"Escatologico" cristiano*, 62–63.
102. On Victorinus, see C. Curti, "Il regno millenario di Vittorino di Petovio," *Augustinianum* 18 (1978): 419–33; B. E. Daley, *The Hope*, 65–66. See especially his *Commentary on Matthew* 24, and his *Commentary on the Apocalypse of John*. Jerome, *De Vir.*, 3:74, summed up his position.
103. Victorinus, *Comm. in Mt.*, 11.

This reading is also found in Marcellus of Ancira, who speaks of the coming age of the Spirit,[104] when the Incarnation of the Word and the Kingdom of Christ will come to a close, being no longer necessary as soon as redemption has been achieved.[105] It is interesting to note how a spiritualistic view of Christian salvation is associated with a downgrading of the relevance of the mystery of the Incarnation.

Likewise, Jerome holds that literal, apocalyptic millennialism is but a fable.[106] He does not consider the de facto consolidation of Constantinianism as a valid expression of the advent of the kingdom of Christ, among other reasons because it occasioned a falling off in religious fervor among believers. "As the Church gained princes for its cause, it grew in power and riches, but fell away in virtues."[107] To some degree this facilitated the growth of monastic life, considered in many cases as a kind of *fuga mundi*.[108] Nonetheless, as long as materialistic Jewish hopes are avoided, Jerome says, the millennial tradition may be considered a venerable one. Thus Revelation 20 may be looked upon as an allegorical reference to the historical Church.[109] He holds, besides, that there will be a period of "silence" between the defeat of the Antichrist and judgment.[110]

In his earlier writings Augustine was quite open to millennial beliefs. In later ones, however, he presented apocalyptic millennialism as a "grotesque fable."[111] The reason is a simple one: from the moment Christ redeemed the world, the devil has been definitively defeated and enchained.[112] Thus "first resurrection" refers to baptism and "second resurrection" to the human body at the end of time.[113] Augustine does, of course, insist on the powerful though ambivalent influence of Christ's kingdom (what he calls the "City of God") on the world and on secular history.[114] But he clearly distinguishes between one and the other. The critique of

---

104. See A. Grillmeier, *Christ in Christian Tradition*, vol. 1 (London: J. Knox, 1975), 281–82; J. F. Jansen, "I Cor 15:24–28 and the Future of Jesus Christ"; M.-T. Nadeau, "Qu'adviendra-t-il de le souveraineté du Christ à la fin des temps?" *Science et Esprit* 55 (2003): 61–74.

105. Marcellus was forced to retract at a Roman synod in 340, according to Epiphanius, *Panarion*, 72,2:6–7.

106. Jerome, *In Dan.*, 2:7,17–18; *In Is.*, 16,59:14. See B. E. Daley, *The Hope*, 102.

107. Jerome, *Vita Mal. Monach.*, 1.

108. See J. Galot, "Eschatologie," in *Dictionnaire de la Spiritualité*, vol. 4/1 (1960), col. 1047.

109. Jerome, *In Ezek.*, 11:36. He refers to Tertullian, Victorinus, Irenaeus, and Apollinarius.

110. Jerome, *In Dan.*, 4,12:12.

111. Augustine, *De Civ. Dei XXII*, 7:1. On his thought, see W. Kamlah, *Christentum und Geschichtlichkeit: Untersuchungen zur Entstehung des Christentums und zu Augustinus "Bürgerschaft Gottes,"* 2nd ed. (Stuttgart: W. Kohlhammer, 1951); M. G. Mara, "Agostino e il millenarismo," *Annali di Storia dell'esegesi* 15 (1998): 217–30.

112. Augustine, *De Civ. Dei XX*, 7–8.   113. Augustine, *De Civ. Dei XXII*, 6:1–2.

114. Augustine, *De Civ. Dei XIV*, 28.

millennialism given by Ambrose[115] and Tychonius[116] is in line with Augustine's. However, the most influential form of spiritual millennialism during the Middle Ages was developed by the abbot Joachim da Fiori.[117] Joachim spoke of three periods in human history: that of the early stages of the Old Testament, a period personified by God the Father, qualified by slavery and the law, and made visible in the people of Israel; that of the New Testament, of God the Son, marked by freedom from the law and made visible in the Church with its hierarchical priesthood; and finally, that of the Spirit, characterized by perfect and spontaneous freedom in which the saints would truly reign over the world, in which the predominant point of reference would be consecrated Christians. The latter period, he said, would constitute the beginning of the definitive millennium. In fact, Joachim suggested it would begin around the year 1260. The kingdom of the Spirit would take over from the monarchic and Constantinian millennialism sustained by Eusebius and others. Joachim's position constituted a clear break with Augustine's,[118] for the latter did not envisage a tripartite diachronic division of history and a special age of the Spirit divorced from that of the Son. Augustine, on the contrary, held that *inseparabilia sunt opera Trinitatis*, "the works of the Trinity are inseparable" from one another, that is, the three Persons always act in unison.[119] Thus there is no theological reason to speak of three consecutive ages.

Joachim's view arises with surprising frequency during the second millennium in a variety of philosophical, religious, and political forms, those of Lessing and Comte, of Hegel, Kant,[120] and Marx, of Engels and Nietzsche.[121] Strangely enough, what began as a spiritual movement frequently became a highly politicized, extremist, and worldly one. Likewise, millennialism is commonly found in the teachings of some fundamentalist Protestant sects.[122] In Luther's time,

---

115. J. Derambure, "Le millénarisme de S. Ambroise," *Revue des études anciennes* 17 (1910): 545–56. Ambrose sees the period between "first" and "second" resurrection as a time of intermediate purification.

116. Tychonius, *Comm. in Rev.*

117. On Joachim's understanding of millennialism, see R. E. Lerner, *Refrigerio dei santi. Gioacchino da Fiore e l'escatologia medievale*, Opere di Gioacchino da Fiore 5 (Roma: Viella, 1995); for a brief introduction and critique, *CAA* 270–73. A similar position is to be found in Almaricus of Bène, a contemporary of Joachim's, whose teaching on the three epochs was condemned by a Synod in Paris in 1210. See also B. D. Dupuy, "Joachimisme," in *Catholicisme*, vol. 6 (Paris: Letouzey et Ané, 1967), cols. 887–99.

118. See R. E. Lerner, *Refrigerio dei santi*, 194.

119. Augustine, *Sermo* 213, 6; also *CAA* 274–75.

120. Althaus speaks of the philosophical chiliasm of Kant: "The chiliasm of philosophers is clearly a secularization of theological chiliasm, and in general of Christian eschatology," *Die Letze Dinge*, 23.

121. The process has been carefully documented by N. Cohn, *The Pursuit of the Millennium;* H. de Lubac, *La postérité spirituelle de Joachim de Flore*, 2 vols. (Paris: Lethielleux, 1979–81).

122. See T. Daniels, *A Doomsday Reader: Prophets, Predictors, and Hucksters of Salvation* (New York: New York University Press, 1999).

Thomas Müntzer preached the coming millennial kingdom in a revolutionary context. In North America William Miller predicted the proximate coming of the millennial kingdom, giving rise to what is now called the "Seventh-Day Adventists." Similar positions are to be found among religious groups such as the Jehovah's Witnesses and the Church of Jesus Christ of Latter-Day Saints (Mormons).[123]

Reinterpreting the Millennium

From the third century onward, as we saw, literal and apocalyptic forms of millennialism were openly rejected by Origen (on the basis of his spiritual or allegorizing interpretation of scriptural texts), as well as by Jerome, Augustine, and others. On the one hand, Church Fathers wished to avoid Christian teaching being instrumentalized for the purposes of worldly political philosophies or nontranscendent eschatologies. On the other hand, it seemed obvious to them that the number "1000" signified, more than anything else, the perfection of a divine work (10 × 10 × 10), and thus the transcendence of eschatological consummation, as distinct from its tangible manifestations. In this context Augustine, in his work *De Civitate Dei*, presented a theology of history in which evil would not be fully overcome, even temporarily, until the final coming of Christ. Although he tended to identify God's kingdom with the Church,[124] he warned against dreaming of a future earthly and physical kingdom of Christ. The realism and visibility of Christ's definitive kingdom will not be revealed until the end of time, with resurrection from the dead and final judgment, that is, once death, "the last enemy" (1 Cor 15:26), has been defeated.

Doubtless, the promise of the *Parousia* in which God would reign effectively, visibly, and definitively over humanity and every aspect of created reality serves as a stimulus to Christian hope. Yet hope is a theological virtue, which has the possession of God as its object, and the action of God as its agent.[125] The divine promise and presence may not be identified with purely human projects or, much less, with worldly utopias, just as the Kingdom of God may not be identified with political society.[126] "Give to Caesar the things that are of Caesar, and to God the things that are God's" (Mt 22:21). As we saw at the beginning of this chapter, the fact that Scripture does not attempt to specify when the world will come to an end (Mk 13:32) does not mean that Christ or Christians were confused on the matter; rather, it meant that the coming of the Kingdom is a divine work.

---

123. The Holy Office in a decree dated 21 July 1944 considered dangerous the position of the Chilean priest Manuel de Lacunza y Díaz (in a work on the return of Christ written in 1810), according to which Christ would return visibly to the earth to reign before final judgment takes place (*DS* 3839).

124. Augustine *De Civ. Dei*, passim; *Ep.* 199.   125. See pp. 11-12.

126. See pp. 227-31.

John Paul II in his encyclical *Centesimus annus* (1991) warned of the dangers of the utopian spirit among Christians:

> When people think they possess the secret of a perfect social organization which makes evil impossible, they also think that they can use any means, including violence and deceit, in order to bring that organization into being. Politics then becomes a "secular religion" which operates under the illusion of creating paradise in this world. But no political society—which possesses its own autonomy and laws—can ever be confused with the Kingdom of God. The Gospel parable of the weeds among the wheat (Mt 13:24–30,36–43) teaches that it is for God alone to separate the subjects of the Kingdom from the subjects of the Evil One, and that this judgment will take place at the end of time. By presuming to anticipate judgment here and now, man puts himself in the place of God and sets himself against the patience of God.[127]

Likewise Pope Benedict XVI in his 2005 encyclical *Deus caritas est* says that "the Church cannot and must not take upon herself the political battle to bring about the most just society possible. She cannot and must not replace the State. Yet at the same time she cannot and must not remain on the sidelines in the fight for justice. She has to play her part through rational argument and she has to reawaken the spiritual energy without which justice, which always demands sacrifice, cannot prevail and prosper. A just society must be the achievement of politics, not of the Church. Yet the promotion of justice through efforts to bring about openness of mind and will to the demands of the common good is something which concerns the Church deeply."[128]

---

127. John Paul II, Enc. *Centesimus annus*, n. 25c.
128. Benedict XVI, Enc. *Deus caritas est*, n. 28a.

Part Four. Honing and Purifying Christian Hope

9

Death, the End of the Human Pilgrimage

Instability. It is a horrible thing to feel all that we possess slipping away.
—*Blaise Pascal*[1]

Death is a very narrow difficult passage—certainly not constructed for the proud.
—*Georges Bernanos*[2]

I think I understand what death is. At death we will open up to what we have lived during our life.
—*Gabriel Marcel*[3]

With death, our life-choice becomes definitive.
—*Benedict XVI*[4]

Death will come eventually, and it will come for everybody. Seneca confirms this common conviction and declares that there is nothing more certain than death.[5] Yet death, as it presents itself to humans, constitutes a profound enigma. We do not know what it is meant to achieve, other than keeping a limit on world population and ensuring that generations follow on from one another, thus avoiding the cultural stagnation of the world. We are certain that it often involves suffering, pain, and, perhaps more than anything else, an acute sense of loss. Its pervading presence seems to spread a cloud of meaninglessness over life. More optimistic spirits might look upon death as a form of definitive liberation, and envision the human soul soaring above and beyond corruptible matter. But all in all, it makes sense that people would inquire into its meaning, its origin, and its purpose. Not surprisingly, death has been explained, or in some cases explained away, in an enormous variety of ways.[6] A Christian reflection on death should, of course, take into account not only the phenomenon of death in all its anthropological implications, but also the fact that the salvation of humanity

---

1. B. Pascal, *Pensées* (ed. Brunschvig), n. 212.
2. G. Bernanos, *Diary of a Country Priest*, 170.
3. G. Marcel, *La soif* (Paris: Desclée, 1938).
4. *SS* 45.
5. Seneca, *Ep.* 99:9.
6. See J. Pieper, *Tod und Unsterblichkeit*, 43.

was brought about by Jesus Christ, God's own Son, dying on the cross. If death is not a side issue for religion in general, it certainly is not for Christianity.

In this chapter we shall examine the following issues. In the first place, we shall enquire into some aspects of the phenomenology of death and immortality, and the questions they pose. This we shall do under three headings: the presence of death within life; the evil quality and destructive power of death; and death in the light of promised immortality. Then, second, we shall consider the Christian view of death under the same three fundamental headings, though in a slightly different order:

Death as the outer manifestation of human sinfulness, that is, as punishment for sin (death as evil);

Understanding death—and ultimately clarifying its meaning—in terms of the Christian's life and death being incorporated into the death of Christ, in order to rise up with him (death and immortality);

Living out human mortality: death as the end of the human pilgrimage (the presence of death within human life).

A Phenomenology of Death and Immortality

Three aspects of the reality of death may be considered: the presence of death within life itself; death as evil; death in the light of immortality.

Death Is Present in the Midst of Life

Humans share mortality with all living entities. Like all multi-cell beings, humans will certainly die. In fact, humans are already on their way to death, to extinction as individuals. Yet among all living beings, humans are the only ones who are aware of this, who attempt to face up to it and do everything possible to delay or avoid it.[7] For death is perceived as a rupture of all the relationships that give meaning to his life. At death "there is always a sense of loneliness, for even though we may be surrounded by affection, every person dies alone."[8] Death is the "triumph of total irrelationality," in the words of Eberhard Jüngel.[9] "All humans die alone. The loneliness of death seems perfect," said Karl Jaspers.[10] Yet this gradual breakdown takes place day by day, year by year, and reminds us that death approaches inexorably. Max Scheler offers a powerful description of human life as it moves toward death, perceived as an ever-growing constriction of

---

7. M. Scheler, "Tod und Fortleben," in *Gesammelte Werke*, vol. 10 (München: A. Franke, 1957), 9.
8. Josemaría Escrivá, *Furrow*, n. 881.
9. E. Jüngel, *Tod* (Stuttgart: Kreuz-Verlag, 1971), 150.
10. K. Jaspers, *Philosophie*, vol. 2: *Existenzerhellung* (Göttingen: Springer, 1956), 221.

the possibilities that are at the disposal of each person.[11] The philosopher Martin Heidegger explains death in terms of future annihilation that comes forward into the present moment of human life, pressurizing and infecting the latter with its nothingness. He thus defines man as a *being-for-death*, and encourages him to live authentically by opening himself up to the certainty of future annihilation with full freedom and awareness.[12] Likewise, Pope Gregory the Great spoke of the *prolixitas mortis*,[13] the gradual invasion of death into human life. The medieval hymn reads: *media vita in morte sumus*, "in the midst of this life we are already immersed in death."[14] So also the poet George Herbert: "Death is working like a mole, and digs my grave at each remove."[15]

This awareness brought many Christians during the later Middle Ages to develop a literary genre called the *ars moriendi*, the science and art of knowing how to die.[16] Plato had already spoken of the "practice of dying,"[17] as had the Christian Neoplatonist Clement of Alexandria.[18]

Death as Something That Should Not Happen

Death presents itself to human consciousness as something deficient, repugnant, evil, unwanted. It seems to sum up and express all possible evils. Not only those of nature in general, but of each and every person. The English poet Edward Young wrote: "Men think all men mortal but themselves."[19] Many people attempt to trivialize death, by refusing to think about it, or by considering it as something that affects human nature in general, but not themselves personally.[20]

---

11. See M. Scheler, *Tod und Fortleben*.

12. M. Heidegger, *Sein und Zeit*, 266, 384–85.

13. Gregory the Great, *Hom. in Lc.*, 14:25.

14. The original motif is to be found in the *Lamentation* of the Benedictine Notker called "the Stammerer," and it reads: "Media vita in morte sumus, quem quaerimus adiutorem, nisi te, Domine, qui pro peccatis nostris juste irasceris" in J.-P. Migne, ed., *Series Latina*, 87:58b. Likewise, see Gerhoh of Richterberg (ibid., 193:1642c) and Sicardus of Cremona (ibid., 213:272a). The following hymn is of the same period: "et ideo media vita in morte sumus, ego anima inter spiritum et corpus media vita, quae non est aliud quam divina essentia" ibid., 194:970b.

15. G. Herbert, "Grace," in *The Complete English Poems*, ed. J. Tobin (London: Penguin Books, 1991).

16. *Ars moriendi* is the title of a small pious anonymous handbook, dating approximately from the 14th century. Works on the same subject may be found in Henry Suso, Jean Gerson. Robert Bellarmine and then Alphonsus M. de Liguori also wrote on the subject. Of the latter, see *Apparecchio alla morte*, ed. P. A. Orlandi (Torino: Gribaudi, 1995).

17. Plato, *Phaedo*, 81a.

18. Clement of Alexandria, *Strom. II*, 20,109,1.

19. E. Young, "Night Thoughts," in *Works* (London: J. Taylor, 1774), vol. 3, 17.

20. It is common nowadays to speak of death as something "natural" or even banal. Max Scheler and Theodor Adorno have noted the widespread practice of removing death from human consciousness, the tendency to avoid reflecting on one's own death. On this topic, see J. Pieper, *Tod und Unsterblichkeit*, 32–43; G. Scherer, *Das Problem des Todes in der Philosophie* (Darmstadt: Wissenschaftliche Buchgesellschaft, 1979), 33–42; L.-V. Thomas, *Anthropologie de la mort* (Paris: Payot, 1988). On the notion of refusing death, see also D. Clark, ed., *The Sociology of Death* (Oxford: Blackwell, 1993).

Edgar Morin says that the "modern tragedy consists of a flight from tragedy. The very thing that stands in the way of the tragedy of death is the effort to forget it. This becomes the true tragedy."[21] The attempt humans make to forget death only goes to prove that they wish to avoid considering something they find deeply repugnant. For we know instinctively that death is evil; it simply should not take place.

Peter Chrysologus says that death is all ugliness and evil, "the mistress of despair, the mother of disbelief, the sister of decay, the parent of hell, the spouse of the devil, the queen of all evils."[22] "Death is never welcome," he says in the same sermon, "whereas life always delights us."[23] He observes that the undeniable usefulness and value of death has wrongly led some Christians to speak of death as a good thing, as a release from life's troubles,[24] referring perhaps to Ambrose's work *De bono mortis*. Chrysologus continues: "Those who try to write about 'death as good' are wrong, brothers and sisters. There is nothing strange in this: the wise ones of our world think they are great and distinguished if they can persuade simple folk that the greatest evil is really the greatest good. . . . But truth removes these notions, brothers and sisters, the Scripture puts them to flight, faith challenges them, the Apostle marks them down and Christ destroys them, who, while he restores the good that life is, unmasks and condemns the evil that death is, and banishes it from the world."[25] Understandably, Chrysologus concludes that "the whole hope of Christian faith is built upon the resurrection of the dead."[26]

Against this, however, some authors have considered death in a highly positive light. Scripture seems at times to lend its weight to this. "For to me to live is Christ and to die is gain," Paul says to the Philippians (1:21). "Blessed are the dead who die in the Lord," we read in the book of Revelation (14:13).[27] We have already referred to Ambrose's *De bono mortis*.[28] Likewise modern romantic philosophers such as Moses Mendelssohn, Johann W. von Goethe, Friedrich Hölderlin, and Rainer M. Rilke all claim that death is supremely desirable because through it, man attains definitive self-realization.[29] Ludwig Wittgenstein said, "The fear of

21. E. Morin, *Le vif du sujet* (Paris: Seuil, 1969), 321.
22. Peter Chrysologus, *Sermo* 118:3. On his eschatology, see J. Speigl, "Petrus Chrysologus über die Auferstehung der Toten," in *Jenseitsvorstellungen in Antike und Christentum. Gedenkschrift für Alfred Stuiber* (Münster: Aschendorff, 1982), 140–53, and the classic work of F. J. Peters, *Petrus Chrysologus als Homilet* (Köln: 1918), especially 69–75; 83–84.
23. Peter Chrysologus, *Sermo* 118:2.   24. Ibid., 6.
25. Ibid.   26. Ibid., 1.
27. See also 2 Sm 14:14; 1 Kgs 2:2.
28. In *Spe salvi*, n. 10, Benedict XVI refers to death as benefit, citing Ambrose.
29. On this period, see J. Pieper, *Tod und Unsterblichkeit*, 67–119. The question being asked is the following: if both life and death are natural, how can both be good? F. Schiller suggests that "death can-

death is the best sign of a false life, of an evil life."[30] This position has influenced more recent philosophers such as Martin Heidegger, and through him theologians such as Karl Rahner and Ladislao Boros.[31]

However, from a purely phenomenological standpoint it would be dishonest and misleading to speak of death in an unequivocally positive way. Death is not natural, but violent. "There is no such thing as a natural death," says Simone de Beauvoir. "All humans are mortal, but for each one death is a kind of accident that always constitutes a sort of unjustified violence, no matter how much we recognize or accept it."[32] Jean-Paul Sartre also reflected on the absurdity of death, saying: "Everything that exists is born without reason, is prolonged in weakness, and dies by pure chance."[33] He cogently attacked Heidegger's superficially optimistic view of life and death, explaining that death is the very thing, perhaps the only thing, that cannot be neatly "fitted in" to the human picture.[34] Likewise, the

---

not be evil if it is something general," *Zu Karoline von Wolzogen. Schillers Leben* (Tübingen: J.G.Cotta, 1830), 268, cit. by J.Pieper, *Tod und Unsterblichkeit*, 68. A. Schopenhauer says the same thing as Schiller in a pessimistic way: "Do not fear! With death you will no longer be anything. In fact it would have been better had you never begun to be so," *Sämtliche Werke*, vol. 2, 2nd ed. (Leipzig: F.A.Brockhaus, 1916), 1288. "At heart we are something we should not be; for this reason we will cease to be so some day" ibid., 1295. And he adds: "perhaps one's own death will be for us the most wonderful thing in the world" ibid., 1270. According to R.M.Rilke, death is a "familiar and cordial invasion of the earth," cit. by R.Guardini, *The Last Things*, 14. Hölderlin considers death as the consummation of life.

30. L. Wittgenstein, *Notebooks, 1914–1916*, ed. G.H. von Wright and G.E.M. Anscombe (Oxford: B. Blackwell, 1961), annotation of 8.7.1916.

31. See K. Rahner, *On the Theology of Death* (Freiburg i. B.: Herder, 1961); L. Boros, *The Mystery of Death* (New York: Herder and Herder, 1965). Also G. Gozzelino, *Nell'attesa*, 431, speaks of death as a fulfilling, joyful event (transformation) rather than a hidden one (breakage).

32. S. de Beauvoir says: "il n'y a pas de mort naturelle.... Tous les hommes sont mortels: mais pour chaque homme sa mort est un accident et, même s'il la connaît et lui consent, une violence indue," "Une mort si douce," *Les Temps modernes* 20 (1964): 1985.

33. "Tout existant naît sans raison, se prolonge par faiblesse et meurt par rencontre," Roquentin (character), in J.-P. Sartre, *La Nausée* (Paris: Gallimard, 1938), 174. It cannot be said, however, that death is unnatural, says Sartre, for the simple reason that there is no such thing as a definable human nature in respect of which "the absurd character of death could be verified," *L'Être et le Néant*, 671.

34. According to Sartre, *L'Être et le Néant*, 615–38, every experience I have is my experience, which nobody can live for me. "Il n'y a aucune vertu personnalisante qui soit particulière à ma mort. Bien au contraire, elle ne devient ma mort que si je me place déjà dans la perspective de la subjectivité; c'est ma subjectivité, définie par le Cogito préréflexif, qui fait de ma mort un irremplaçable subjectif et non la mort qui donnerait l'ipséité irremplaçable à mon pour-soi," ibid., 618–19. "Nous avons, en effet, toutes les chances de mourir avant d'avoir rempli notre tâche ou, au contraire, de lui survivre.... Cette perpétuelle apparition du hasard au sein de mes projets ne peut être saisie comme *ma* possibilité, mais, au contraire, comme la néantisation de toutes mes possibilités, néantisation qui *elle-même ne fait plus partie de mes possibilités*. Ainsi, la mort n'est pas *ma* possibilité de ne plus réaliser de présence dans le monde, *mais une néantisation toujours possible de mes possibles, qui est hors de mes possibilités*," ibid., 620–21. "Puisque la mort ne paraît pas sur le fondement de notre liberté, elle ne peut qu'*ôter à la vie toute signification*," ibid., 623. "La réalité humaine demeurerait finie, même si elle était immortelle, parce qu'elle se fait finie en se choisissant humaine. Etre fini, en effet, c'est se choisir, c'est-à-dire se faire an-

existentialist philosopher Søren Kierkegaard scornfully rejected the position of those who look upon death as a "night of rest," "a sweet sleep," and so on.[35]

Thomas Aquinas in a lucid and profoundly realistic way insisted that death is an evil, the most terrible evil that exists in the created order,[36] for the simple reason that with it, life comes to an end, and life is God's greatest created gift.[37] Death is the "greatest of human misfortunes,"[38] he concludes. Aquinas does accept the doctrine of the survival of the soul, though not in very positive terms, because the role of the soul is precisely that of "informing" the body and making it human, and it is unable to carry out this task after death.[39] Death as a result is obscurity, the end;[40] it is a *passio maxime involuntaria*,[41] a tendency that is completely contrary to human inclinations.

Of course this opens an important question: if death is something evil, something that should not take place, something improper, then what value does it have? What does it derive from? How can Christ assume death to save humanity? And so, what role does it play in human life? What meaning does it have? We shall return to these issues presently.

The Horizon of Immortality

The content and meaning of death may be understood only in the context of the immortality humans hope for or project beyond death. Humans instinctively withdraw from death not only because it is frequently a painful experience and always an unknown one, but above all out of fear for what awaits them after dying, the "dread of something after death.—The undiscover'd country, from whose bourn no traveller returns," to quote Shakespeare's *Hamlet*.[42] "If I fear death," the philosopher Nicholas Malebranche said, "that is because I know well what I will lose, and I know nothing of what I will gain."[43] The novelist Jorge Luis

---

noncer ce qu'on est en se projetant vers un possible, à l'exclusion des autres. L'acte même de liberté est donc assomption et création de finitude," ibid., 631.

35. S. Kierkegaard, "Christelige Taler," in *Søren Kierkegaards samlede Værker*, vol. 10 (Copenhagen: Gyldendals Forlag, 1928), 260.

36. Thomas Aquinas, *S. Th. I*, q. 72, a. 2c; *II C. Gent.*, 80; *De Anima*, q. 14, arg. 14. On the topic of death in Thomas, see L. F. Mateo-Seco, "El concepto de muerte en la doctrina de S. Tomás de Aquino," *Scripta Theologica* 6 (1974): 173–208; J. I. Murillo Gómez, *El valor revelador de la muerte: estudio desde Santo Tomás de Aquino* (Pamplona: Servicio de Publicaciones de la Universidad de Navarra, 1999).

37. Thomas Aquinas, *De Ver.*, q. 26, a. 6, ad 8.   38. Thomas Aquinas, *Comp. Theol.*, 227.

39. See pp. 24–25 above.

40. See especially B. Collopy, "Theology and the Darkness of Death," *Theological Studies* 39 (1978): 22–54, especially 44, 47–50.

41. Thomas Aquinas, *In II Sent.*, D. 30, q. 1, a. 1, arg 6.

42. W. Shakespeare, *Hamlet* III, 1:78.

43. N. Malebranche, "Entretiens sur la mort," in *Œuvres complètes*, vol. 12–13, 3rd ed. (Paris: J. Vrin, 1984), 436.

Borges explained his own experience when facing the prospect of death, saying: "I have no fear of death. I have seen many people die. But I am afraid of immortality. I am tired of being Borges."[44] The event of death thus presents itself as the beginning of a possible immortal existence that humans desire from the depth of their heart, or perhaps of a perpetual emptiness that they deeply fear.

In any case, the final destiny of humans, their immortality, whatever it consists of, is the ultimate horizon that gives meaning to earthly and mortal life, and hence to death itself. In other words, neither death nor life on earth can give an account of themselves; their meaning will be fully understood only in the light of the immortal life awaiting humans after death, whether this life be of grace or disgrace, of fullness or emptiness, of heroism or mediocrity. Cyprian says: "Do not think of death but of immortality; not of time-bound suffering but of eternal glory."[45]

But what kind of immortality awaits humans after death? What is the true object of our fear (as Plato might say), of our weariness (in Borges's experience), of our boredom (as Unamuno put it), of our hope (for the Christian believer)?

There is a real paradox here. On the one hand death marks the end of human existence; its very essence seems to mock at any promise of immortality. On the other hand, to speak of immortality, on the face of things, is the same thing as to deny death. Immortality would seem to rob death of its power and value, by turning it into a minor passing phase, a mere step toward our final destiny. That is to say, immortality in principle eliminates death. Those who are immortal, by definition, do not die. This is the golden rule of Greek religious philosophy: the gods are immortal, they cannot die; the soul is likewise immortal, and thus humans do not really die. The point is, of course, that the immortal state, whatever shape it may eventually assume, involves a way of living that is clearly distinct from this "mortal life," in that the latter is determined by temporality and impermanence, corruptibility and decay, whereas the former is not. And death is the crossing-over point between the two; it defines a frontier between the transient and the permanent. This is where its importance lies. It is clear nonetheless that immortal life, such as it is, requires some kind of continuity with mortal life; yet to the extent that mortal and immortal life merge with one another, death's power and sway is attenuated.

Although the basic thrust toward immortality is universal in the history of humankind, philosophers, writers, and theologians have considered human immortality in a myriad different ways. In chapter 1,[46] we have considered two fun-

---

44. See J. L. Borges, "El Inmortal," in *El Aleph* (Buenos Aires: Alianza; Emecé, 1981), 7–28. On Borges, see J. Stewart, "Borges on Immortality," *Philosophical Literature* 17 (1993): 295–301.

45. Cyprian, *Epist.* 6, 2:1.   46. See pp. 25–31.

damental forms: the immortality of human life and the immortality of human selfhood. In chapter 3, dealing with final resurrection,[47] we have seen that the two forms are compatible with one another in a Christian perspective: on the basis of the doctrine of final resurrection it is possible to integrate the immortality of human life with that of human selfhood; human individuals will live on forever with the fullness of their own corporality, history, relationships, identity, and individuality.

Yet we still must inquire what Christian revelation says about the origin and meaning of death, and how it can be overcome.

Death as the Outer Manifestation of Human Sinfulness

In order to understand the meaning of death in the light of Christian faith, we must in the first place consider its origin. Two possible explanations may be offered.[48]

Death as the Result of Sin

As we saw above, humans perceive death spontaneously as something undesirable, as something improper, repugnant, and even evil. It is understandable therefore that Christians have held that death is not something the good God wanted in the first place, but something that came into the world for reasons independent of the divine will. Specifically, death would be the result of an unfortunate yet nondefinitive accident within the bounds of created reality itself, that is, the sin of humans, their rebellion against the living God. Thus, death would not belong to God's original design, being simply a punishment for sin. In spite of the appearances, this explanation does not involve a negative evaluation of the world and of creation. Quite the contrary. Oscar Cullmann notes that a positive appreciation of creation tends to involve a negative view of death. "Behind a pessimistic conception of death is hidden an optimistic view of creation," he says. "Conversely, when death is considered as a liberation, for example in Platonism, then the visible world is not recognized as divine creation."[49]

---

47. See pp. 109–12.

48. On death in Scripture, see, for example, P. Hoffmann, *Die Toten in Christus*; L. Wächter, *Der Tod im Alten Testament*; N. J. Tromp, *Primitive Conceptions of Death and the Netherworld in the Old Testament* (Rome: Pontifical Biblical Institute, 1969); P. Grelot, "L'homme devant la mort," in *De la mort à la vie éternelle: études de théologie biblique* (Paris: Cerf, 1971), 51–102; A.-L. Decamps, "La mort selon l'Écriture," in *La mort selon la Bible dans l'antiquité classique et selon le manichéisme*, ed. J. Ries (Louvain-la-Neuve: Centre d'histoire des religions, 1983), 15–89; L. Coenen and W. Schmithals, "Death; Dead," in *NIDNTT* 1, 429–47.

49. O. Cullmann, *Immortalité de l'âme ou résurrection des morts?* (Neuchâtel: Delachaux et Niestlé, 1957), 36.

Scripture, in both Old and New Testaments, openly teaches that death is a punishment for the sin of our first parents.[50] On expelling Adam from the Garden of Eden, God declared: "Cursed is the ground because of you; in toil you shall eat of it all the days of your life. . . . By the sweat of your face you shall eat bread until you return to the ground, for out of it you were taken" (Gn 3:17,19). In the book of Wisdom, it is made quite clear where death took its origin: "God did not make death, nor does he delight in the death of the living. For he created all things so that they might exist. . . . God created us for incorruptibility, and made us in the image of his own eternity, but through the devil's envy death entered the world" (Ws 1:13–14; 2:23–24).[51] In the letter to the Romans, the same message is repeated: "Sin came into the world through one man and death through sin, and so death spread to all men because all men sinned" (Rom 5:12). Later on, Paul sums up this message saying: "the wages of sin is death" (Rom 6:23). And finally the apostle James unequivocally states: "Then desire when it has conceived gives birth to sin; and sin when it is full-grown brings forth death" (Jm 1:15).

The Fathers of the Church for the most part repeated this position, in particular Augustine.[52] Major ecumenical councils taught it.[53] Vatican Council II's constitution *Gaudium et spes* explains that "bodily death, from which man would have been immune had he not sinned, will be overcome when that wholeness which he lost through his own fault will be given once again to him by the almighty and merciful Savior."[54] The *Catechism of the Catholic Church* repeats the same doctrine.[55]

Death as an Integral Element of God's Design

However, it seems to make more sense to argue that death is simply a characteristic of creation itself, a sign of the way things are, of the finitude of created beings, of the perishable quality that marks all multi-cell life. In other words, death would simply be natural, and humans should humbly and realistically accept it as such, rather than fighting against it or trying to explain it away in ethical or mythical terms. For a Christian believer, however, who believes in God as Creator, this would mean that death should be taken, no more and no less, as the will of God, as an integral part of the eternal project God has mapped out for his creatures. The logical consequence would be, therefore, that the passage of

---

50. *Inter alia*, see B. Domergue, "Le péché et la mort," *Christus* 25 (1976): 422–33.
51. See L. Mazzinghi, "'Dio non ha creato la morte' (Sap 1,13). Il tema della morte nel libro della Sapienza," *Parola, Spirito e Vita* 32 (1995): 63–75.
52. Augustine, *De Civ. Dei XIII*, 6.
53. That of Trent for example, when explaining the doctrine of original sin in session 5: *DS* 1512.
54. *GS* 18.
55. *CCC* 1008.

death is simply the condition for our definitive self-realization as human beings. In other words, death as such would have a clearly positive side to it.[56] Karl Barth suggests that "death belongs to the life of the creature and is thus necessary to it."[57] Likewise, Karl Rahner describes death in the following terms: "The end of the human being as a spiritual person is an active immanent consummation, an act of self-completion, a life-synthesizing self-affirmation, an achievement of a person's total self-possession, a creation of himself, the fulfillment of his personal reality."[58]

However, this position has serious drawbacks. If death is an integral aspect of human nature, positively willed by God, then human life on earth may easily be considered as a passing and more or less irrelevant phase, and one would have to accept death with some form of rationalized resignation.

To What Degree Does Death Depend on Sin?

With a considerable dose of common sense, Thomas Aquinas sums up Christian teaching on the origin of death in the following formula: *necessitas moriendi partim ex natura, partim ex peccato*:[59] the need for humans to die derives in part from nature, from the physical, biological condition of humans, in part from sin. It is not of course that sin and nature are equal parts in the process, for the simple reason that they are not commensurate categories, and as such may not be quantitatively compared. Sin is not an "aspect" of nature (equivalent, for example, to its limitedness), as some philosophers have thought;[60] just as material created nature is not a manifestation of sin, as Origen's creation-as-fall theory might suggest.[61] What is original in God's plan is immortality; sin, which stalls human life and potentially destroys it, is an accident, albeit an important one.[62]

Clement of Alexandria, on the basis of a Platonic bipartite anthropology (humans composed of body of soul) and in continuity with Origen,[63] suggested a

---

56. 2 S 14:14; Gn 3:19. On this position, see G. Gozzelino, *Nell'attesa*, 429–30.

57. K. Barth, *Church Dogmatics* III/2, 639.

58. K. Rahner, *On the Theology of Death*, 40. According to Rahner, the positive side of death, the result of a coincidence between death and the present state of life, is required by the configuration of the human spirit as free; thus death is the definitive act of human fulfillment.

59. Thomas Aquinas, *III Sent.*, D. 16, q. 1, arg. 1, c. Elsewhere, he says: "mors est et naturalis ... et est poenalis," *S. Th. II-II*, q. 164, a. 1 ad 1; "mors quodammodo est secundum naturam et quodammodo contra naturam," *De malo*, q. 5, a. 5 ad 17. On this issue, see J. Pieper, *Tod und Unsterblichkeit*, 67–119.

60. The term Aristotle uses for "sin" is *hamartia*, which literally means "missing the target," that is, more or less, making a mistake. It is simply the result of ignorance. In a different context, P. Teilhard de Chardin presents moral evil principally as a limit within the human condition in respect of the future perfection of the Omega Point. See especially his work *Comment je crois*, in *Œuvres*, vol. 11 (Paris: Seuil, 1971).

61. Origen, *De princip. I*.

62. According to Aquinas, immortality in man is originally due to God's action: *S. Th. I-II*, q. 85, a. 6c. See *Comp. Theol.*, 152.

63. Origen, *De princip. I*, 2:4.

somewhat simplistic solution to the problem of the origin of death. He said that death is natural for humans[64] in that it involves only the destruction of the body, whereas sin—which is fruit of our ignorance of the Father[65]—would occasion only the death of the soul.[66] Athanasius argued that death is natural in the sense that the possibility of death is written into nature, whereas the concrete fact of death is due to sin: neither one nor the other suffices for death to take place, for they act concomitantly.[67] This position became quite common among the Fathers of the Church. Athanasius holds that if it were not for original sin, humans would be immortal in body and soul, a position taken up later by Gregory of Nyssa[68] and Augustine.[69] The latter holds that this "death," fruit of original sin, is corporal, and should not be confused with "second death" (that is, personal sin and condemnation) that Scripture speaks of (Rv 2:11, 20:6,14; 21:8). This became the received position in Catholic theology: that death is a punishment for sin.

Given the fact that Protestant theology tends to closely associate creation and fall, sin and nature, at least at an existential level, it is not surprising that the classic explanation of death as a punishment for sin came under close scrutiny and strain.[70] Already in the sixteenth century, Socinians considered the doctrine offensive.[71] As Protestant thought began to take on a more liberal and optimistic tone, and the teaching on original sin was gradually left aside, mortality came to be understood simply as an aspect of the finitude of human nature. Only for sinners can it be taken as a coherent expression of divine punishment. In fact, only the subjective experience of death (fear, anguish, etc.) may be understood as the result of sin.[72] The position was assumed by the philosophers of the Encyclopedia (Diderot, D'Alembert, Voltaire),[73] who taught that death was totally natural and that the proper thing for a mature person to do was to overcome the fear of death through the cultivation of philosophy.

Throughout the twentieth century, however, some Protestant theologians have attempted to recuperate the realism of the bond linking sin and death that Scripture clearly speaks of. Several of them, such as Althaus, Brunner, Barth, and

---

64. Clement of Alexandria, *Strom. IV*, 12:5.
65. Ibid., *II*, 34:2.
66. Ibid., *III*, 64:1.
67. Athanasius, *De inc.*, 4.
68. Gregory of Nyssa, *Orat. Catech.*, 8:1–2.
69. Augustine, *De Civ. Dei XIII*, 6.
70. See W. Pannenberg, *Systematic Theology*, vol. 2, 265–75. In Catholic theology, see H. Köster, *Urstand, Fall und Erbsünde in der katholischen Theologie unseres Jahrhunderts* (Regensburg: F. Pustet, 1983).
71. See W. Pannenberg, *Systematic Theology*, vol. 2, 232, n. 196.
72. See, for example, F. Schleiermacher, *Der christliche Glaube* (orig., 1830; Berlin: W. de Gruyter, 1960), § 76, 2; on this, E. Herms, "Schleiermachers Eschatologie nach der zweiten Auflage der 'Glaubenslehre,'" *Theologische Zeitschrift* 46 (1990): 97–130. See also A. Ritschl, *Die christliche Lehre von der Rechtfertigung und Versöhnung*, vol. 3: *Die positive Entwicklung der Lehre* (Bonn: A. Marcus, 1888), 330, 336–37, 339–40.
73. See D. Hattrup, *Eschatologie* (Paderborn: Bonifatius, 1992), 120–24.

Jüngel, look upon death in terms of divine judgment on sinners, not just as the human sense of guilt but as an expression of God's wrath.[74] Others, such as Oscar Cullmann, insist that death derives directly from sin.[75] The Lutheran Wolfhart Pannenberg explains that death is a consequence of finitude.[76] But he adds: "The distinction between finitude and death may be seen here in the fact that it is precisely the sinners' non-acceptance of their finitude [Gn 3:5] that delivers them up to death."[77]

Indeed, humans recognize death as a sign of their finitude, of their incapacity to save themselves, of being creatures that have received existence and everything they possess from Another. But humans rebelled against their Creator, attempting to live as if God did not exist, as if humans could acquire immortality and plenitude with a power that belonged to them alone. Even though God created humans for immortality, the structure of the human being was such that it would degenerate and decline if humans did not submit themselves willingly to the Creator. It may be said that death, written into human nature as a potentiality, was a kind of safety mechanism to ensure that humans, though made in the image and likeness of God, would not attempt to surpass the limits of their nature, or at least would be corrected in their attempts to do so. Since humans did attempt to thwart God's plans through sin, however, death and ensuing disgrace entered the world.

In What Sense Is Death a Punishment for Sin?

Insofar as sin involves separation from God as well as alienation from other people and from the cosmos itself, it makes sense to consider death, the "triumph of total irrelationality," as the inner and most logical consequence of sin.[78] However, it may be asked: What would have happened if humans had never sinned? Would they have died? If the "death as finitude" argument is correct, humans would have to die sooner or later. Yet if death is, strictly speaking, a punishment for sin, then we would have to conclude that in its absence humans would have lived on forever. But this does not seem to fit in with biblical witness to the fact that Adam's life on earth, even before he sinned, was considered as a trial, a test of faith, finite in time, that was meant to come to a close. The trial would have had to end eventually.

We may conclude that if man had not in fact sinned, death would have been

---

74. See K. Barth, *Church Dogmatics* III/2, 628–33. On the other authors, see W. Pannenberg, *Systematic Theology*, vol. 2, 269, n. 324.
75. See O. Cullmann, *Immortalité de l'âme*, 33–46.
76. See W. Pannenberg, *Systematic Theology*, vol. 3, 556–63.
77. Ibid., 561.
78. On this aspect of death, see G. Gozzelino, *Nell'attesa*, 440–43; J. Ratzinger, *Eschatology*, 80–101.

different than it is now. Instead of the prospect of a dramatic end, or a drawn-out, painful destruction and decay of the human being, humans would have acquired immortality, body and soul, and eternal life, at the conclusion of their earthly lives. There would have been no resurrection of those long dead. Perhaps the situation of humanity would not have been unlike that of Our Lady, who, having been conceived without original sin, and having lived a life of deep faith and untainted holiness, was assumed at the end of her earthly existence into heaven in body and soul, without having to suffer the dissolution of human life in the grave.[79]

This explanation of the relationship between death and sin is confirmed by Leo Scheffczyk, who suggests that human immortality before the fall would consist of "the promise, excluding all fear of death, of an entirely gratuitous transformation, at the end of our earthly existence."[80] A similar position may be found in the 1986 catechesis of John Paul II.[81] Speaking of the state of original justice in which humans were created, the pope teaches that man "possessed and maintained within himself an interior equilibrium, and did not experience anguish at the prospect of decay and death."[82] On the contrary, he says, speaking of fallen human nature, "man has been created by God for immortality: death, which seems to be a kind of tragic jump into the dark, is the consequence of sin, due to a kind of immanent logic, but above all due to divine punishment.... Without sin, the end of the trial would not have been as dramatic."[83] In other words, in the absence of sin, humans would in all probability have reached the end of their earthly existence either by a nondramatic death (like that represented by the *dormitio Mariae*) or by directly entering heaven without dying. On account of sin, however, they die, for the end of human existence on earth has come under a curse.[84]

However, if death is truly a punishment for sin, what meaning does it take on for a Christian? How is it resolved and transformed by Christ? How should it be prepared for?

---

79. Germanus of Constantinople said that Mary was assumed into heaven "ut ex hoc etiam a resolutione in pulverem deinceps sit alienum": from the Roman Breviary, *Officium Lectionis* of August 15th.

80. L. Scheffczyk, "Die Erbschuld zwischen Naturalismus und Existentialismus. Zur Frage nach der Anpassung des Erbsündendogmas an das moderne Denken," *Münchener Theologische Zeitschrift* 15 (1964): 53.

81. John Paul II, Audience "The Sin of Man and the State of Original Justice" (3.9.1986), *Insegnamenti di Giovanni Paolo II* 9/2 (1986): 526.

82. Ibid.

83. John Paul II, Audience "The 'Status' of Fallen Humanity," *Insegnamenti di Giovanni Paolo II* 9/2 (1986): 971.

84. E. Jüngel, *Tod*, 128.

The Death of the Christian as an Incorporation into the Lord's Passover

The central element of Christian preaching, from its very inception, was the resurrection of Jesus Christ. From the anthropological standpoint, resurrection reveals both the unconditional character of God's pardoning love for humanity and the future identity of humanity itself in a risen, immortal state.[85] However, it is clear from the New Testament that for believers the promise of future resurrection is simply inseparable from the need to follow Jesus in life as in death, to "carry the cross of each day," as Luke says (9:23). The passage of death is the *conditio sine qua non* for resurrection, just as it was for Jesus: the eternal rewards God destines for his Son's followers will come after their death and on condition of their death. Paul insists repeatedly on this point. "Do you not know that all of us who have been baptized into Christ Jesus were baptized into his death?" (Rom 6:3).[86] This is the true reason why Christians may cry out: "blessed are the dead who die in the Lord" (Rv 14:13). Only on account of the promised resurrection can Paul exclaim: "For to me to live is Christ, and to die is gain" (Phil 1:21).[87]

In brief, Scripture considers the death of the Christian as a true participation in the death of Christ and, as a result, in his resurrection. What took place in Jesus will be reproduced, to some degree, in those who believe in him.[88] This confirms what we saw above:[89] that the enigma of death may be understood and resolved in the light of the kind of immortality we expect—in this case, the immortality represented by final resurrection.

Christians are incorporated into Christ's death and resurrection in a very real way through baptismal grace and the practice of Christian life.[90] The death of a Christian is as authentic and as painful as the death of anybody else, for it still constitutes the loss of human life. Yet in a mysterious way it is transformed, not only indirectly through the promise of resurrection, but also directly, by the fact that it takes on, at least in part, the meaning and efficacy of Christ's own death. Christ triumphs over death, but he does so on the cross: he triumphs by dying. Knowingly and willingly he embraced a life that brought about a death he did not deserve,[91] identifying himself with the principle of corruption introduced by sin and defeating it definitively. "God ... sent his own Son in the likeness of sinful flesh and for sin, he condemned sin in the flesh" (Rom 8:3). The *Catechism of*

---

85. See pp. 74–114.
86. See Rom 6:4–5; Col 2:12.
87. See also Rom 8:3; Heb 2:14–15; 2 Cor 4:10.
88. In this sense death is a form of "being in Christ" (2 Cor 5:1–8; Phil 1:21–24): see G. Ancona, *Escatologia cristiana*, 104–8. Alviar notes that in this sense, death can take on a positive value: *Escatología*, 298–301. G. Gozzelino, *Nell'attesa*, 193, speaks of death as the *dies natalis*.
89. See pp. 258–60.
90. See pp. 269–71.
91. Jn 10:17. On Christ's assumption of mortality, see Thomas Aquinas, *S. Th. III*, q. 14, a. 1.

the Catholic Church puts it as follows: "For those who die in Christ's grace, [death] is a participation in the death of the Lord, so that they can also share his Resurrection."[92]

Two possible explanations may be given to account for the efficacy of Christ's willing assumption of death: either that dying has an inner power that is in some way released at the moment of his death or that Christ's acceptance of death occasioned the pouring out of the forgiving and transforming power of God, in which believers partake.

Does Death Have an Inner Power That Christ Actualizes?

One possibility is that Jesus assumes death because it contains an inner power for human self-realization, which is perfectly actualized in him, and as a result also in believers. His death would thus constitute for us principally an example of courage, loyalty, and love,[93] much like that of Socrates.[94] Or more, perhaps, the *kenosis* or self-emptying involved in Christ's death (Phil 2:7) would reflect a more profound *kenosis* within the Trinity itself.[95] Christ's very death, in other words, might be considered as a Trinitarian act, directly occasioning the divine outpouring of grace. Some authors have spoken of death in these terms, suggesting besides that each person will enjoy a moment of perfect lucidity at the instant of their demise, and they will be in a position to make their final decision for God or against God. Christ will be present in this moment as an inspiration and comfort.

The theory, inspired in the philosophy of romantic idealism and in Heidegger,[96] has been taught by several Catholic scholars.[97] According to them, death would constitute a single, unrepeatable, moment, in which the pilgrim state and

---

92. *CCC* 1006.
93. See 1 Pt 2:21–25. See also Thomas Aquinas, *S. Th. III*, q. 46.
94. See O. Cullmann, *L'immortalité de l'âme*; J. Bels, "Socrate et la mort individuelle," *Revue des sciences philosophiques et théologiques* 72 (1988): 437–42.
95. See H. U. von Balthasar, *The Christian State of Life* (San Francisco: Ignatius Press, 1983), 186.
96. On the role of death in Heidegger, see R. Jolivet, *Le problème de la mort chez M. Heidegger et J.-P. Sartre*.
97. The theory began with the studies of P. Glorieux, "Endurcissement final et grâces dernières," *Nouvelle Revue Théologique* 59 (1932): 869–92, and "In hora mortis," in *Mélanges de Sciences Religieuses* 6 (1949): 185–216. See also H. Rondet, *Problèmes pour la réflexion chrétienne* (Paris: Spes, 1945), 142–47; É. Mersch, *La théologie du corps mystique*, vol. 1, 3rd ed. (Paris: Desclée de Brouwer, 1954), 313–22. Later on, the theory was popularized by R. W. Gleason, *The World to Come* (New York: Sheed and Ward, 1958), 72–85; A. Winklhofer, "Zur Frage der Endentscheidung im Tode," *Theologie und Glaube* 57 (1967): 191–310; L. Boros, *The Mystery of Death*, passim; K. Rahner, *On the Theology of Death*; J. Pieper, *Tod und Unsterblichkeit*, 120–32; J. Troisfontaines, *Je ne meurs pas* . . . (Paris: Editions universitaires, 1960), 121–49; L. Boff, *Vita oltre la morte*, 3rd ed. (Assisi: Cittadella, 1984), 27–45. See also J. L. Ruiz de la Peña, *L'altra dimensione*, 299–315, who, although he accepts the theory in general terms, also points out significant drawbacks.

the final state come together in an instant of perfect, active lucidity. Karl Rahner, for example, says that "death by nature constitutes personal self-realization."[98] Ladislao Boros explains that "in death the possibility of man's first fully personal decision opens out. Consequently, death is a place where man attains full awareness, where he meets God and decides his eternal lot."[99] Leaving aside for the moment the philosophical roots of this theory,[100] several theological and pastoral reasons have been adduced to justify it.

First, it is said that shortly before death people frequently experience an exceptional level of mental clarity, in which they contemplate their lives and everything they have done; this would permit them to take stock of their true situation and make a final, irrevocable decision for God or against God.[101] *Second*, the Church has always been solicitous for the administration of the last sacraments to the dying. The moment of death would seem therefore to be of paramount importance. *Third*, authors such as Thomas Aquinas and Cajetan cite a text of John Damascene that establishes a parallel between the death of humans and the primordial, instantaneous decision of angels for or against God. *Hoc est hominibus mors quod est angelis casus*,[102] Thomas says, "death is for humans what the fall was for angels." Among other things, this theory would serve to explain the awkward question of the salvation of nonbaptized infants, and the wider one of the salvation of non-Christians.[103] Moreover, it is suggested that the theory provides confirmation of the "fundamental option" theory in moral theology, for at death a definitive decision is made. *Fourth*, theologically, a parallel is established between the death of Christ and that of those who "die in the Lord." Just as Jesus died crying out loud, openly commending his spirit to the Father (Lk 23:46), as the earth shook (Mt 27:51), so also, it is said, humans will obtain perfect self-realization at the moment of death.[104] Some would even argue that death in Christ constitutes a kind of quasi-sacrament, that offers humans *ex opere operato* a privileged moment of grace.[105]

---

98. L. Boros, *The Mystery of Death*, 29.

99. L. Boros, *We Are Future*, 157.

100. Boros bases his reflection on the philosophy of M. Blondel as regards the will, on Maréchal, in respect of knowledge, on Bergson as regards perception and memory, and on Marcel as regards love.

101. Gregory the Great notes that death often a moment of special illumination: *Dial.*, 4, 27:1.

102. John Damascene, *De fide orth.*, 2:4; cit. by Thomas Aquinas, *De Ver.*, q. 24, q. 10, s. c. 4; *S. Th. I*, q. 64, a. 2. Card. Cajetan also quotes John Damascene: *In S. Th. I*, q. 64, a. 2, n. 18; q. 63, a. 6, nn. 4 and 7.

103. The issue, among many others, is considered in the document of the International Theological Commission, *The Hope of Salvation for Children Who Die without Baptism* (19.1.2007).

104. Ruiz de la Peña holds with Rahner that death is an act (*La pascua de la creación*, 269, n. 98), even though this is not sufficiently explained: G. Colzani, *La vita eterna*, 203.

105. See L. Boros, *The Mystery of Death*, 141–65. "Death is an eminently sacramental situation," ibid., 164.

A Critique of the Theory of "Final Decision in the Moment of Death"

The theory we have just considered tends to concentrate the entire eschatological horizon within the very moment of death: judgment, resurrection, *Parousia*, the initiation of eternal life or condemnation, purification. It suggests besides a somewhat Pelagian view of salvation that considers the phenomenon of death anthropologically, in little need of God's gracious intervention. Besides, from the point of view of Christian spirituality, the deep link that binds everyday life and action on the one hand and eternity on the other is severed. After all, eternity is not gained or lost in a single moment, no matter how lucid and important it may be, but on the basis of a lifetime of repeated actions, for we die as we have lived. "Well done, good and faithful servant; you have been faithful over a little, I will set you over much" (Mt 25:21).[106] Besides, theories of this kind tend toward Platonic renderings of anthropology in which death is seen as a liberation from the bonds of matter, time, and the world. In fact the hypothesis of the final decision in the moment of death is seldom held nowadays.[107]

In reply to the four reasons given above in favor of this theory, it should be said, *first*, that the moment of special clarity is not experienced necessarily by everyone who dies, and in any case may be accounted for in terms of the laws of nature without involving those of grace; *second*, the sacrament of the anointing of the sick is a sacrament of the living, to be received—if at all possible—when the sick person is still conscious, not in the actual moment of death; *third*, the historical reason (John Damascene's text) is weak not only on account of its once-off character, but also because it is discordant with other positions of the same authors, particularly in respect of the nonangelic character of human nature; and *fourth*, a possible parallel with the death of Christ is not applicable to humans, for he was our Savior, and did not inherit mortality on account of sin like the rest of humanity, but assumed it willingly (Jn 10:17). Let us examine the latter question in more detail.

The Transformation of Death by Christ

The second way of explaining the incorporation of the believer into Christ at death (and subsequently at resurrection) is to see it in terms of God pouring out his grace and power in resurrection on account of his Son's obediently forfeiting the gift of life as a willing expression of his mission to save humanity. That is to

---

106. On the meaning and difficulties with the fundamental option theory, see John Paul II, Enc. *Veritatis splendor* (1993), nn. 65–70.

107. See the critiques of J. L. Ruiz de la Peña, *L'altra dimensione*, 163–73; G. Gozzelino, *Nell'attesa*, 428, n. 32; G. Lorizio, *Mistero della morte come mistero dell'uomo: un'ipotesi di confronto fra la cultura laica e la teologia contemporanea* (Napoli: Dehoniane, 1982), 163–73.

say, death of itself would have no intrinsic power or value to save, for it constitutes the simple loss of life. In fact, Aquinas teaches that death has neither a formal cause, nor a final cause, nor an efficient cause; at best it may be said to have a "deficient cause."[108] The death of Christ "is utterly different from Socrates' death, which the latter portrays as leaving this condition for a better one."[109]

Yet Christ gives death new value, in such a way that those who are incorporated into him by baptism obtain the benefits of the resurrection. Christ redeems death not only by fully expressing his solidarity with fallen humanity by assuming it, but also by showing himself fully faithful, to the point of renouncing his life, to the will of his Father and to his love for those he was sent to save.

Jesus' death on the cross was shameful in the extreme. It was a death reserved for criminals: "Cursed is everyone who hangs on a tree" (Dt 21:23; cf. Gal 3:13). His death represented to all appearances the failure of his mission, the ruin of an entire life-project.[110] "He had no form or majesty that we should look at him, nothing in his appearance that we should desire him. He was despised and rejected by others; a man of suffering and acquainted with infirmity; and as one from whom others hide their faces he was despised, and we held him of no account" (Is 53:2–3; cf. Ps 22:6–8). Besides, and this is the most surprising aspect, he assumed death willingly (Jn 10:17), carrying the disgrace of humanity on his shoulders, as if he were to blame for the sins of humans, in this way letting his disciples go free (Jn 18:8). "He has borne our infirmities and carried our diseases," we read in the book of Isaiah, "yet we accounted him stricken, struck down by God, and afflicted. But he was wounded for our transgressions, crushed for our iniquities; upon him was the punishment that made us whole, and by his bruises we are healed" (Is 53:4–5; cf. Mt 8:17).

However, Jesus' assumption of the tremendous, destructive power of death was incapable of undoing his filial love for his Father and his unconditional dedication to humanity. Jesus, himself the author of life (Jn 1:4), loved life more than anyone else,[111] and, Thomas says, "exposed it out of charity."[112] By renouncing the most precious gift of human life, he not only dignified it, but demonstrated the greatest possible love. "Greater love has no man than this, that a man lay down his life for his friends" (Jn 15:13). In the Old Testament love and fidelity are shown in maximum grade by one's disposition to die (2 Mc 7). But Jesus does not suffer any kind of death. All the distress, all the indifference, all the pain and anguish, all the weariness and dismay borne by the prophets, the patriarchs, the

---

108. On this, see L. F. Mateo-Seco, "El concepto de muerte en la doctrina de Santo Tomás de Aquino," 182–84.

109. C. Taylor, *A Secular Age*, 17.

110. *CAA* 211–12.

111. Thomas Aquinas, *S. Th. III*, q. 46, a. 6.

112. Ibid., ad 4.

"poor of Yahweh," seem to bear down on Jesus, crushing him. Christ experienced death more than anyone else, not only because of the perfection of his humanity, or because the pain inflicted was exquisite, but also because in a mystical way he suffered the death of all, he encountered the sins of humanity.[113]

It was this willing acceptance, for the love of God and of humanity, of what he did not deserve, of the loss of life, God's greatest created gift, that turned the tide on death, transforming it into a source of grace and redemption. Neither Abraham, nor Job, nor Jeremiah, nor any of the prophets, was asked to confide in God and obey him to the extent Jesus was. All three were reprieved at the last moment (Gn 22:16–17 in respect of Isaac; Jb 41–42; Jer 37–40), but Jesus was not. "He became obedient unto death, death on the Cross" (Phil 2:8). After all, "he considered that God was able to raise men even from the dead" (Heb 11:19). In effect, as a result of Jesus' obedience, "God has highly exalted him and bestowed on him the name which is above every name" (Phil 2:9). Jesus, we read in the *Catechism of the Catholic Church*, "despite his anguish as he faced death, accepted it in an act of complete and free submission to his Father's will. The obedience of Jesus has transformed the curse of death into a blessing."[114]

Three consequences, among others, may be drawn from the foregoing reflection: first, that death as such is not suppressed by baptism but is transformed from curse into blessing; then, union with Christ dispels the believer's fear of death; and finally, Christian mortification, or dying to self, becomes a meaningful, fruitful, indeed necessary practice for the development of Christian life. Let us consider them one by one.

The Transformation of the Curse of Death into a Blessing

Although baptism does forgive sin, it does not suppress death that derives from sin.[115] But it transforms death. For those who are incorporated into Christ, death is no longer a curse, a punishment. It becomes a source of blessing, of grace, of growth, of fruitfulness, an opportunity to demonstrate the radical quality of the Christian's love of God, to "live in Christ." The believer "can transform his own death into an act of obedience and love towards the Father, after the example of Christ," we read in the *Catechism of the Catholic Church*.[116] Of itself, of course, death achieves nothing, for it involves the destruction of the human be-

---

113. See M. Hauke, "La visione beatifica di Cristo durante la Passione."
114. *CCC* 1009.
115. Aquinas holds that baptism does not suppress death. Should it do so, then people would be inclined to seek baptism for the corporal benefit it affords (*IV C. Gent.*, ed. Marietti, 3958b), and would be obliged to believe (ibid., c). Rather baptism turns death from being a punishment into an opportunity of living in conformity with Christ (*S. Th. III*, q. 49, a. 3, ad 3).
116. *CCC* 1011.

ing. Yet the willing acceptance of death, of all that it involves, opens the possibility of Christ establishing his own life fully in believers (Gal 2:20). Believers are invited insistently by Jesus "to leave all things" (Mt 19:27), among other reasons because at the end of their lives they will have to do so anyhow, abandoning life, physical comfort, the company of other people, possessions, fond memories, and other things that go to make life on earth worth living. Life itself, therefore, is meant to become for the Christian a process of gradually dying, dying to self, dying to the world. In this way, death acquires, in union with Christ, a special corredemptive value,[117] for Christians "always carry in the body the death of Jesus, so that the life of Jesus may also be manifested in our bodies" (2 Cor 4:10).

Overcoming the Fear of Death

One specific effect of Christians' incorporation into the death of Christ is that they need no longer fear death, since Christ has entered into its very depths and redeemed it. In the letter to the Hebrews we read that Christ has "destroyed him who has the power of death, that is, the devil, and delivered all those who *through fear of death* were subject to lifelong bondage" (2:14–15). Death induces fear in all humans, fear of the unknown, fear of another life, fear of losing what we possess. The same applies to Christians. However, in faith they obtain the guarantee that the evil of death will lose hold on them definitively once they enter glory and are filled definitively with the love of God. This love is already infused into the lives of believers (Rom 5:5). And as John says, "there is no fear in love, but perfect love casts out fear. For fear has to do with punishment, and he who fears is not perfect in love" (1 Jn 4:18). Thomas Aquinas gives the following explanation: "among the kinds of fear that can be experienced on earth, the worst of all is that of death. If man overcomes this kind of fear, he overcomes all possible kinds.... Now, Christ through his death has broken this bond, and has removed the fear of death.... When man considers that the Son of God, the Lord of death, wished to die, he no longer has any fear of death."[118] And Josemaría Escrivá: "A son of God fears neither life nor death, because his spiritual life is founded on a sense of divine sonship. So he says to himself: God is my Father and he is the Author of all good; he is all Goodness."[119]

Death, Mortification, and the Purification of Hope

The fear of death and lack of familiarity with the afterlife may also be seen in the human tendency to feverishly build up, hold on to, and rely exclusively upon

117. See G. Ancona, *Escatologia cristiana*, 331–32.
118. Thomas Aquinas, *Ad Heb.*, c. 2, on Heb 2:14–15.
119. Josemaría Escrivá, *The Forge*, n. 987. See *The Way*, n. 739; *Furrow*, n. 880.

the good things that this life offers. Scripture speaks of the man who "says to his soul: 'Soul, you have ample goods laid up for many years; take your ease, eat, drink, be merry.' But God said to him, 'Fool! This night your soul will be required of you'" (Lk 12:19). What is asked of Christians, on the contrary, is to "lay up treasure in heaven" (Mt 6:20), to "leave all things" (Mt 19:27) and follow Christ. In freely giving back to God, throughout their lifetime, everything that he has given them, especially their own will, Christ's disciples are promised "a hundred-fold" and the inheritance of "eternal life" (Mt 19:29). As we saw in the chapter on final resurrection,[120] at the end of time God will give back to believers, multiplied, purified, and elevated, all that they have given and renounced without reserve and with a pure heart while on earth. God will do so in the next life, and also, to some degree, in this life. Perhaps this is why those who live the *relictis omnibus*, those who "leave all things," who generously "mortify" what is at their disposal, live joyfully, fruitfully, without experiencing an excessive fear of death.

Death as the End of the Human Pilgrimage

Death is a point of arrival, but it is not the end of human life. It marks the end of mortality, yet the beginning of immortality. It is a crossover point, and a critical one at that. For immortality is not a neutral situation for humans, nor a previously guaranteed one. This is so not only because the afterlife presents humans with an unfamiliar territory, but above all because it will be determined, under God's judgment, by the life one has lived, be it good or bad. Death becomes a critical juncture, a moment of "crisis" in the true sense of the word (*krisis* in Greek, "decision," comes from *krinō*, "to judge"), the end of the earthly pilgrimage, the beginning of eternity. We shall consider several questions concerning death as the end of the time of trial God has offered humans. *First*, the scriptural and patristic evidence for death being the true end of the human pilgrimage. *Second*, we shall consider the teaching of the Church on "full retribution" after death, for those fully purified, in heaven, and for those who die in mortal sin, in hell. *In the next section*, we shall consider the question of "particular judgment," which takes place just after death and makes full retribution possible.

Death as the End of the Earthly Pilgrimage

In the book of Qoheleth we read: "Whatever your hand finds to do, do with your might; for there is no work or thought or knowledge or wisdom in *she'ol*, to which you are going" (Qo 9:10).[121] New Testament teaching points in the same

---

120. See pp. 109–14.
121. For this section, see C. Pozo, *La teología del más allá*, 468–73.

direction: after death there will be no opportunity for repentance. Matthew's judgment discourse (Mt 25:24–46) makes it clear that the outcome will depend on the actions one has carried out in this life: giving the hungry to eat, the thirsty to drink, and the like. In Luke's discourse on the beatitudes (Lk 6:20–6) we read that the future reward relates to the life one has lived on earth. "Blessed are you that hunger now, for you shall be satisfied" (v. 21). Also in the parable of the wheat and the weeds (Mt 13:24–30,36–43) it is clear that the field where the evildoers planted the seed is "the world" (v. 38). John also says: "He who loves life loses it, and he who hates his life *in this world* will keep it for eternal life" (12:25). Perhaps the clearest text is the following one from Paul's letter to the Corinthians: "For we must all appear before the judgment seat of Christ, so that each one may receive good or evil, according to *what he has done in the body*" (2 Cor 5:10).

Clement of Rome writes: "While we are on earth let us repent with all our heart of the sins we have committed, so that the Lord may save us within the time of penance. For when we leave this world we will be unable to do works of penance."[122] Jerome compares the one who dies with a tree trunk that falls and stays where it is.[123] Elsewhere he explains that death marks the moment in which the grain is harvested.[124]

Will Conversion Be Possible after Death?

A passage from Peter's first letter, speaking of Christ's "descent into hell," seems to indicate, however, that repentance will be possible after death. Hence the latter would no longer mark the end of the human pilgrimage. The text reads as follows: "For Christ has died for sins once for all. . . . He went and preached to the spirits in prison, *who formerly did not obey*, when God's patience waited in the days of Noah, during the building of the ark" (1 Pt 3:18–20). Clement of Alexandria[125] and other authors of Origenist sympathies suggested that this text allows for the possibility of repentance after death, such as would lead eventually to some form of universal reconciliation.[126] Some recent authors hold the same position.[127]

Among the Fathers of the Church, however, the most common interpretation of 1 Pt 3:18–20 is that Christ, upon descending into the underworld, communicated salvation to those who were chastised by God in the times of Noah, had repented before dying, and were waiting for salvation in the "bosom of Abra-

---

122. Clement of Rome, *Ep. in Cor.*, 8:2.
123. Jerome, *Comm. in Eccl.*, 11.
124. Jerome, *In Gal.*, 3, 6:10, on Gal 6:9.
125. See C. Pozo, *La teología del más allá*, 471–72.
126. On Augustine, see B. E. Daley, *The Hope*, 139.
127. L. Lochet, *Jésus descendu aux enfers* (Paris: Cerf, 1979), 127–33; 169–70; J. R. Sachs, "Current Eschatology," 233–42.

ham" (Lk 16:22).[128] That is to say, the "prison" in question was not hell, the state of definitive condemnation, but *she'ol*, the underworld.

Full Retribution after Death in Scripture

Besides texts that speak of death as the end of the earthly pilgrimage, Scripture also insists that full retribution can take place immediately after death. As regards eternal condemnation, we have already seen that it is not possible to repent of one's sin after dying.[129] There is no reason why God would put off personal retribution for a later moment. In the parable of Lazarus and the rich man (Lk 16:19–31), the reward for both, it would seem, comes immediately after death: "He died and was buried" (v. 22). It is clear, besides, that the situation of Lazarus and the rich man does not constitute a kind of intermediate waiting stage, that could eventually be modified, for Abraham says to the rich man: "Between us and you a great chasm has been fixed, in order that those who would pass from here to you may not be able, and none may cross from there to us" (v. 26). Although the purpose of the parable is not primarily one of teaching eschatological salvation and condemnation,[130] Jesus speaks in this way to provoke an ethical challenge with real, eschatological consequences. Besides, some Fathers of the Church understand the text as an affirmation of immediate retribution.[131]

However, it is interesting to note that the question of full retribution after death was not a clear-cut issue among Church Fathers.[132]

The Controversy Concerning Full Retribution among the Fathers

The Apostolic Fathers held that full retribution would take place right after death.[133] Cyprian, for example, said that all who live and die in fidelity to Christ will be admitted to the Kingdom of God straight after death.[134] Other authors such as Justin, Irenaeus, and Tertullian, while speaking of the difference between the situations of the just and the unjust, explain that one and all must wait until final judgment has taken place for the definitive separation to occur.[135] Only mar-

---

128. See C. Pozo, *La teología del más allá*, 443–45. 129. See pp. 273–75.
130. See C. Pozo, *La teología del más allá*, 248–51.
131. See, for example, John Chrysostom, *In I Cor. hom.*, 42,3; *In Ep. 6 ad Gal.*, 3; *De Lazaro Conc.* 7:3.
132. Thus C. Pozo, *La teología del más allá*, 473–74, 490–92.
133. Thus Clement of Rome, Ignatius of Antioch, Polycarp, the Shepherd of Hermas.
134. Cyprian, *Ad Fort.*, 13. Immediate retribution is destined for those who "forsook and condemned all their possessions," who "stood in the firmness of the faith and in the fear of God" ibid., 12. Salvation "is a gratuitous gift from God, and it is accessible to all," *Ad Donat.*, 14.
135. Justin says that "the souls of the pious stay in a better place, whereas those of the unjust and evil in worse one, waiting the time of judgment," *Dial. cum Tryph.*, 5:3. This position is probably determined by both Jewish and Gnostic teaching: "if you find some Christians who say that there is no resurrection of the dead, but that at the moment of dying their souls are assumed into heaven, do not

tyrs, who are perfectly united with Christ, will receive an immediate and definitive reward,[136] although some Church Fathers extend this privilege to patriarchs, prophets, and apostles.[137] The period of waiting between death and resurrection for the just was commonly called the *refrigerium interim*.[138] Tertullian, who probably coined this expression,[139] said in his Montanist period that "the soul undergoes punishment and consolation in *hadēs* during the interval [between death and resurrection], while it awaits judgment, with a certain anticipation of gloom and glory."[140] The position of Origen on the matter is not very clear: at times he speaks of immediate retribution, at times of a deferred one.[141]

Most fourth-century Church Fathers, however, defended the doctrine of full retribution after death: Hillary of Poitiers, Gregory of Nazianzen, Gregory of Nyssa, Epiphanius, Cyril of Alexandria, Gregory the Great, Julian of Toledo, and others.[142] Jerome said: "after the resurrection of the Lord the saints are not detained in the underworld at all.... Whoever is with Christ surely does not remain in the underworld."[143] John Chrysostom, likewise.[144]

There were exceptions, however. Ambrose said that "all the dead will remain in *hadēs* until final judgment, some waiting for chastisement, others for glory

---

consider them Christians," *Dial.*, 80:4. The same position may be found in Irenaeus, *Adv. Haer.* V, 31:2; *De anima*, 55.

136. This position is unanimous among the Fathers of the Church. See C. Noce, *Il martirio. Testimonianze e spiritualità nei primi secoli* (Roma: Studium, 1978), 55. Martyrs are all with Christ, according to Ignatius of Antioch, *Ad Rom.*, 6:1–2. On Ignatius, see F. Bergamelli, "Morte e vita in Ignazio d'Antiochia," *Parola, Spirito e Vita* 32 (1995): 273–88. The same position may be found in Clement of Rome, *Ep. in Cor. I*, 5:4–7; *Ad Fort.*, 13; Polycarp, *Ad Phil.*, 9:2. On the latter, see C. Burini, "'. . . Questo giorno e questa ora' (Mart. Polyc. 14,2)," *Parola, Spirito e Vita* 32 (1995): 259–71. See also Tertullian, *De res.*, 43:4, who speaks of the special situation of the martyrs as "a prerogative that derives from their martyrdom." Augustine says: "Iniuria est pro martyre orare, cuius nos debemus orationibus commendari," *Sermo* 159,1:1.

137. See, for example, Ambrose, *In Luc.*, 7:4–5.

138. On the notion of *refrigerium interim*, see A. Stuiber, *Refrigerium interim. Die Vorstellungen vom Zwischenzustand und die frühchristliche Grabeskunst* (Bonn: Hanstein, 1957); L. De Bruyne, "Refrigerium interim," *Rivista di Archeologia cristiana* 34 (1958): 87–118, which offers a critical response to Stuiber.

139. According to J. B. Russell, *A History of Heaven*, 68.

140. Tertullian, *De anima*, 58.

141. In some works (for example *De princip. I*, praef. 5), Origen speaks of immediate retribution, and in others (*In Lev. Hom.*, 7:2), of retribution at the end of time. See H. Crouzel, "Morte e immortalità nel pensiero di Origene," in *Morte e immortalità nella catechesi dei Padri del III–V secolo*, ed. S. Felici (Roma: Las, 1985), 316–57; C. Noce, *Il martirio;* B. E. Daley, *The Hope*, 55–56.

142. Hillary of Poitiers, *Tract. Ps.*, 51:23; Gregory of Nazianzen, *Or.* 7:21; Cyril of Alexandria clearly teaches that reward or punishment is for all immediately after death: *In Joann.*, 12, on Jn 19:30; Gregory the Great, in respect of heaven: *Dial.*, 4:26:1–2; and hell: *Dial.*, 4:29; Julian of Toledo, *Prognost. fut. saec. II*, 37.

143. Jerome, *In Eccl.*, 9:10.

144. Chrysostom says that punishment and reward begin just after death. See his reflection on the parable of Lazarus and the rich man: *In cap. 6 Ep. ad Gal.*, 3; *De Lazaro Conc.*, 7:3. As regards the immediacy of the reward, see *De Beato Philogonio*, 1.

and honor."[145] Likewise, Augustine had it that "between death and final resurrection, souls are to be found in hidden places *(abditis receptaculis)*, whether of rest, or of punishment, according to the merits deriving from their life on earth."[146] In the Liturgy of the Hours the following prayer may be read: *Spem defunctorum adimple, ut in adventu Christi resurrectionem assequantur:*[147] "Fill up the hope of the dead that in the coming of Christ they may obtain the resurrection." This would seem to indicate that final retribution is deferred.

From the eighth century onward, full retribution after death became the generally accepted position among Fathers and theologians. Some exceptions remained: Bernard in the West[148] and Photius of Constantinople and Theofilactus (eleventh century) in the East.[149] In fact, a considerable part of Eastern theology up until the Middle Ages put final eschatological destiny off until the time of final judgment.[150]

The following three reasons were generally adduced to justify a delay in full retribution after death. *First*, the question of doctrinal continuity with the Old Testament doctrine of *she'ol*.[151] All humans descended into *she'ol* after death, awaiting the coming of the Savior. At the saving death of Christ the gates of heaven were opened, and his "descent into hell" put an end to *she'ol* as a substantially undifferentiated state.[152] However, since it is said that Christ's saving work does not change the dynamics of retribution in respect of time, but only in respect of content,[153] it is possible for retribution to be deferred. Against this, it may be added that with the ascension of Christ into heaven there is no reason why God would put off offering man the promised prize.[154]

Second, it is clear from Scripture that resurrection and final judgment occu-

---

145. Ambrose, *De bono mortis*, 10:47. On this work, see R. Iacoangeli, "La catechesi escatologica di S. Ambrogio," *Salesianum* 41 (1979): 403–17.

146. Augustine, *Enchirid.*, 109. On "Abraham's bosom" and paradise, *Ep. 187*, 2:6. The same idea may be found in *In Io. Ev. tr.*, 49:10; *Retract. I*, 14:2 in respect of beatific vision.

147. *Preces, ad II Vesp., Fer. VI, Haeb. VII Paschae*. According to de Lubac, *Catholicism*, 130–33, Christ himself experiences a kind of hope with respect to final retribution.

148. See, for example, Bernard, *Sermo in Nat. S. Victoris Conf.*, 5; *Sermo* 138, 4; *De diligendo Deo*, 30; *Ep.* 374; *In trans. B. Malachiae*, 2. On Bernard's position, see B. De Vrégille, "L'attente des saints d'après saint Bernard," *Nouvelle Revue Théologique* 70 (1948): 225–44.

149. Photius, *De Amphilochium quaest.*, 6:2, and Theofilactus, *Exp. in Ep. ad Heb.*, 11:39–40.

150. See J. Meyendorff, *Byzantine Theology: Historical Trends and Doctrinal Themes* (New York: Fordham University Press, 1974), 218–22; on the journey of the soul after death toward judgment, see J.-C. Larchet, *La vie après la mort selon la Tradition orthodoxe* (Paris: Cerf, 2001), 63–211.

151. See pp. 79–80.

152. *CCC* 635.

153. Thus Justin, *Dial. cum Tryph.*, 5; *I Apol.*, 18:20, and Irenaeus, *Adv. Haer. II*, 34:1.

154. According to J. Ratzinger (*Eschatology*, 138), the position of the Fathers was based on the Jewish idea of *she'ol*, but even more so on the fact that, with the ascension of Christ, the heavens are opened.

py center stage in the Christian economy of salvation. The same may be said of Church Fathers. If the saving work of Christ is not yet complete, and will not be so until the *Parousia*, then a definitive separation between just and unjust after death would not be possible. This was the difficulty Augustine experienced with immediate retribution.[155] Two points should be kept in mind, however: (1) as we saw earlier on,[156] final judgment is not, strictly speaking, a form of salvation from sin, but rather the public manifestation of a saving act that at a substantial level has already taken place, or that has not produced the desired effect; (2) the resurrection of the dead, which is a prelude to the judgment of sinners and saints alike, does not, strictly speaking, change the situation of the person with respect to God, although the just certainly long for it. The book of Revelation (6:9–11) notes that the martyrs—whom all the Fathers consider to have obtained full possession of God in heaven—incessantly cry out to God for justice. So, definitive judgment by right should not take place until the end of time.

In the *third* place, the hesitation of the Fathers in respect of full retribution may have been occasioned by their opposition to Gnostic thought. Gnostics held that the elect were admitted into glory at the very moment of their death, in that death is supposed to break the bonds (world, body, matter) holding them back from being united with the Divinity.[157] They considered death as the definitive stage of their liberation. This would explain why some Fathers would hold the doctrine of deferred retribution.

It is clear of course that immediate retribution, such as it is, is not due to death as such, which in itself is destructive rather than liberating. Rather, with death the human pilgrimage comes to a close, and God has no reason to hold back the definitive offer of eternal communion with him, or perpetual condemnation. In brief terms, we may conclude by saying that death is not the cause but the occasion of full retribution.

Church Teaching on Full Retribution in the Fourteenth Century

During the exile of the papacy in Avignon, the question of full retribution arose again.[158] Pope John XXII, in a series of sermons preached at Paris in 1331,

---

155. Augustine, *Rectrat. I*, 13:3–4; C. Tibiletti, "Le anime dopo la morte: stato intermedio o vicine di Dio? (dalla Patristica al sec. XIV)," *Augustinianum* 28 (1988): 631–59, especially 637.
156. See pp. 135–36.
157. See n. 135 above.
158. On this period, see D. Douie, "John XXII and the Beatific Vision," *Domincan Studies* 3 (1950): 154–74; F. Lakner, "Zur Eschatologie bei Johannes XXII," *Zeitschrift für Katholische Theologie* 72 (1950): 326–32; A. Tabarroni, "Visio beatifica e Regnum Christi nell'escatologia di Giovanni XXII," in *La cattura della fine: variazioni dell'escatologia in regime di cristianità*, ed. G. Ruggieri and A. Gallas (Genova: Marietti, 1992), 123–49; C. Trottmann, *La vision béatifique: des disputes scolastiques à sa définition par Benôit XII*

drawing on the writings of Bernard and others, began to teach that the souls of the saints contemplate the sacred humanity of Christ, while the contemplation of the divine essence will be possible for them only after final resurrection. In another series of sermons, he taught that the souls of sinners, likewise, will not enter hell until after final judgment; in the meantime, they are situated in an intermediate state and are tormented by the devil.[159]

On neither occasion does it seem that the pope intended to speak authoritatively; much less did he wish to define a new dogma. In fact he openly admitted that he was prepared to rectify the position taken. Understandably, however, his declarations gave rise to a spirited polemic,[160] his position being firmly rejected by William of Ockham and others.[161] Shortly before dying, Pope John retracted, and his retraction was made public by his successor Benedict XII.[162] Some time afterward the latter pope promulgated the constitution *Benedictus Deus* (1336) with the express will of defining the doctrine of full retribution as a dogma of the Church. The document speaks also of the nature of beatific vision, but as regards full retribution of the just, has the following to say:

> The souls of all the saints who departed from this world . . . , provided they were not in need of any purification when they died . . . and again the souls of children who have been reborn by the same baptism of Christ . . . if they die before attaining the use of free will: all these souls, immediately after death [*mox post mortem*] and, in the case of those in need of purification, after the purification . . . already before they take up their bodies again and before the general judgment, have been, are and will be with Christ in heaven. . . . Since the passion and death of the Lord Jesus Christ, these souls have seen and see the divine essence with an intuitive vision and even face to face . . . and in this vision they enjoy the divine essence.[163]

As regards sinners, the text concludes: "the souls of those who die in actual mortal sin go down to hell *immediately after death* and there suffer the pains of hell."[164]

It is clear therefore that full retribution will take place right after death, for all humans. The doctrine of *Benedictus Deus* has been confirmed frequently in official Church teaching, for example, in the Council of Florence,[165] which contrasted the position of Photius and Theofilactus. Vatican Council II's *Lumen gen-*

(Roma: École francaise de Rome, 1995); J. Gil-i-Ribas, "El debat medieval sobre la visió beatífica. Noves aportacions," *Revista Catalana de Teología* 27 (2002): 295–351; 28 (2003): 135–96.

159. See M. Dykmans, *Les sermons de Jean XXII sur la vision béatifique* (Roma: Presses de l'université Grégorienne, 1973).

160. See L. Ott and E. Naab, *Eschatologie in der Scholastik* (Handbuch der Dogmengeschichte 4.7.2; Basel: Herder, 1990), 244–51.

161. William of Ockham was a Franciscan, as was John XXII's successor, Pope Benedict XII.

162. *DS* 990–91.   163. *DS* 1000.

164. *DS* 1002.   165. *DS* 1305–6.

tium[166] also repeats this doctrine, as do Paul VI's *Creed*[167] and the *Catechism of the Catholic Church*.[168]

Death and Particular Judgment

The *Catechism of the Catholic Church*, just mentioned, has the following to say: "Every man receives his eternal retribution in his immortal soul at the very moment of his death, in a *particular judgment* that refers his life to Christ: either entrance into the blessedness of heaven—through a purification or immediately—or immediate and everlasting damnation."[169] For there to be full retribution right after death, there must be some kind of judgment (or manifestation) by which sinners are separated from saints. This is normally called "particular judgment," in that it does not involve the judgment of the whole of humanity, but of individual humans, as they die one by one. *Lumen gentium* also teaches the distinction between particular and general judgment: "Before we reign with Christ in glory we must all appear 'before the judgment seat of Christ, so that each one may receive good or evil, according to what he has done in the body' (2 Cor 5:10), and at the end of the world 'they will come forth, those who have done good, to the resurrection of life, and those who have done evil, to the resurrection of judgment' (Jn 5:29)."[170] The interpretation given by the Council document to 2 Corinthians 5 seems to be that Christian believers, before reigning with Christ at the *Parousia*, will be judged one by one.[171]

Objections to the Notion of Particular Judgment

Scripture speaks of judgment frequently,[172] but does so almost always in the context of the general judgment destined for the whole of humanity and taking place at the end of time. It is understandable therefore that some authors would call the existence of "particular judgment" into question. Three objections are commonly made.

First, the doctrine would seem to involve a duplication of judgment. What sense would it make for humans to be judged twice by God, with the possibility of the first judgment being revised? Luther once gave expression to this argument when he said: "When we die each one will have his own final judgment."[173]

---

166. *LG* 49.
167. Paul VI, *Creed of the People of God*, n. 28.
168. *CCC* 1022.
169. Ibid.
170. *LG* 48d.
171. See C. Pozo, *La teología del más allá*, 556–57.
172. See pp. 131–34.
173. Cit. by L. Scheffczyk, *La teoria della "risurrezione nelle morte" come tentativo di identificazione della dualità tra consumazione individuale e consumazione universale*, Lecture given at the Pontifical University of the Holy Cross, 1987, 28.

A *second* argument against the existence of particular judgment suggests that humans are so deeply involved in and conditioned by their social situation and the created world they live in that to speak of grievous individual sin, personal judgment, and definitive retribution would be unsound from an anthropological standpoint. Sin should be understood in primarily social terms, it is said, and can be manifested and judged only in a context of the common humanity that final judgment will make present.[174]

Third, some authors suggest, in quite an opposite direction, that each person at death will undergo (or better, undertake) a form of *self-judgment.* That is to say, judgment will not take place as an encounter between God and man, concluded by a divine sentence. Rather, each one will place himself or herself in the position that corresponds to each one.[175] Each person constructs his or her own eternal identity. Ladislao Boros gives expression to this theory in the following terms: "the encounter takes place in the hidden center of our personal life. . . . [In judgment] Christ . . . is the ultimate ground of our experiences, hope, aspirations, etc."[176] Eternal condemnation, he continues, "is simply a human being who is totally identified with what he is, with what he can forcibly acquire and accomplish of himself. . . . Hell is not a threat; it is the ontological projection of our own pettiness."[177]

Nonetheless, the doctrine of particular judgment does find a sufficient basis in Scripture and in the Fathers of the Church.[178]

The Doctrine of Particular Judgment in Scripture

Two observations may be made as regards the presence of the doctrine of particular judgment in Scripture.[179]

First, several texts speaking of individual judgment are to be found in the New Testament. Luke speaks of the nobleman who, upon returning home, "commanded the servants, to whom he had given the money, to be called to him, that he might know what they had gained by trading" (Lk 19:15). He called them separately, one after another, and each one was judged on his own merits or de-

---

174. According to Hegel, man will be judged by history: see J. Milet, "Le jugement de Dieu, mythe ou réalité? Étude philosophique," *Esprit et vie* 98 (1988): 403–11; 417–25, here 403–4. See also G. Gozzelino, *Nell'attesa,* 374.

175. On the notion of correspondence between sin and punishment, see pp. 205–6 above.

176. L. Boros, *We Are Future,* 170.

177. Ibid., 172.

178. On the basis of Aquinas's *S. Th. III,* q. 69, a. 2c, L. Beaudouin, "Ciel et résurrection," in *Le mystère de la mort et sa célébration* (Paris: Cerf, 1951), 253–74, speaks only of a general awareness on the part of the sinner of merit or demerit, and denies the doctrine of particular judgment.

179. On the notion of gradual judgment in the Old and New Testament, see G. Gozzelino, *Nell'attesa,* 376.

merits, although comparison with others was not excluded. In fact the one who had failed to invest was unable to find an excuse and was condemned "out of his own mouth" (Lk 19:22). The parables of the poor man Lazarus (Lk 16:22) and the good thief (Lk 23:43) may well indicate that the definitive situation of each person before God will be clarified right after death. The following text from the letter to the Hebrews suggests the idea of judgment taking place when the person dies: "And just as it is appointed for men to die once, and after that comes judgment" (Heb 9:27).[180]

Second, almost all New Testament texts speaking of judgment refer to the actions of individuals, without mentioning the precise moment of judgment. We have already cited 2 Corinthians 5:10: "each one may receive good or evil, according to what he has done in the body." At the end of time people will be judged on the basis of their own actions (Mt 25:35–36, 42–43). In other words, they will not be judged as hidden parts of an anonymous whole. On repeated occasions Jesus points out that individual moral rectitude is required for salvation, and that simply belonging to God's People, whether to Israel or to the Church, is not sufficient in order to ensure salvation.[181] A Christian ecclesiology, a Christian anthropology, a new ethics based on faith puts the human person and his or her responsibility at the center. As a result, some kind of particular judgment becomes an essential element of Christian eschatology.

Particular Judgment in the Fathers of the Church

Understandably, doubts among the Church Fathers on the question of full retribution influenced their opinion on the matter of particular judgment. However, several of them speak openly of it, among them Basil, Hillary of Poitiers, Ephrem, John Chrysostom, Cyril of Alexandria, and Jerome.[182] The latter says unhesitatingly that "what will happen to all on the day of judgment, has already taken place for each one on the day of their death."[183] Ambrose says that all those entering Paradise must pass by the cherub's flaming sword, which is the fire of a painful personal judgment.[184] Likewise Augustine, in spite of his doubts in respect of full retribution, said that "we firmly believe . . . that souls are judged when they leave their bodies, before coming to that judgment in which they will have to be judged when they recuperate their bodies."[185] Finally, among the me-

---

180. See also 2 Cor 5:8; Phil 1:23; 2 Tm 1:9–10; Heb 12:23.
181. See pp. 216–17.
182. Basil, *Hom. in Ps.*, 7:2; Hillary of Poitiers, *Tract. Ps.*, 2:49; Ephrem, *Sermo in eos, qui in Christo dormierunt*; John Chrysostom, *Hom. in Matth.*, 14:4; Cyril of Alexandria, *Hom.* 14.
183. Jerome, *In Joel*, 2:1.   184. Ambrose, *In Ps.* 118, 3:16.
185. Augustine, *De anima II*, 4:8.

dieval theologians, Thomas Aquinas says that "there is another divine judgment in which, after death, each one will receive the sentence it deserves. . . . After all, it cannot be supposed that the separation [between just and unjust] be made without divine judgment, or that this judgment not be exercised under the sovereign power of Christ."[186]

The Relationship between Particular and General Judgment

As regards the objections mentioned above (the doubling-up of judgment; judgment in collective or in individual terms), the following may be said.

The foregoing discussion shows that the doctrine of particular judgment need not lead to an ethical individualism that makes no account of the social implications of sin. Rather it refers to an entirely personal encounter with God, who illuminates the practical intellect and manifests to each one the true situation of their own conscience. Thus people are saved or condemned on the basis of their own lives, which are judged by God alone and not by the rest of humanity, the standard being Jesus himself, and those who are fully conformed to him, both angels and saints.[187]

The principal objection, however, is that it seems people will be judged twice, once at the particular judgment, again at the general. Such a duplication seems difficult to justify. It should be kept in mind however, as we have already seen, that divine judgment issues in a manifestation rather than in a verdict. People are not judged twice, for their situation at death is unchangeable. After death, God manifests to them the true situation of their personal lives according to the truth of their conscience. On that basis, and on none other, will they receive their recompense. At the end of time, however, their lives will be manifested openly before God and in front of the whole of humanity, and they will receive just recognition from other humans for the good and evil they carried out, the good perhaps that they thought only God could see (Mt 6:4,6,18), and the evil they hoped nobody would ever see (Jn 3:19). When Jesus tells his followers to invite the poor, the lame, and the blind to the banquet instead of inviting those who can repay the favor (Lk 14:12), he says quite specifically that they will be repaid for their generosity "at the resurrection of the just" (Lk 14:14). The full truth of what he often repeated will be made manifest: "Many that are first will be last, and the last first" (Mk 10:31).

The apparent doubling-up of judgment simply reflects the fact that humans are individual persons and at the same time belong to society. It means besides

---

186. Thomas Aquinas, *Comp. Theol.*, 242; *IV C. Gent.*, 91. See also the explanation given in the *Catechismus Romanus*, I, art. 7.

187. See pp. 144–47.

that these two elements can neither be separated from one another nor fused one with the other.[188] Thomas Aquinas explains that

each one is, at one and the same time, an individual person and part of the whole human race. It makes sense therefore that there be two judgments. One is individual, just after death, and in it each one will receive the sentence corresponding to the works done in the body, not completely however, but only in respect of the soul. Each one stands in need therefore of another judgment in respect of their belonging to the human race of which he is a part. Hence each one will be judged when universal judgment comes . . . by the separation of good and evil. Still, God does not judge the same thing twice, because he does not punish the same sin twice. Rather at final judgment punishment that was not meted out before this judgment will be completed.[189]

Particular Judgment as Self-Judgment?

And what may be said of the third objection to particular judgment, expressed in the idea that people judge themselves? This position seems to count on interesting precedents among the Fathers of the Church. Augustine, for example, when writing about the biblical "book of life" (Rv 3:5; 13:8; 17:8), affirms that the latter refers to "a divine force and power by which humans remember all their works, so that they may be seen by them, accusing them or absolving them."[190] Thomas Aquinas comments on the following text of Paul's letter to the Romans: "They show that what the law requires is written on their hearts, while their conscience also bears witness and their conflicting thoughts accuse or perhaps excuse them" (2:15), and says: "God at judgment uses the conscience of the sinner as an accuser."[191] The soul, he says elsewhere, illuminated by divine light, knows instantaneously if it is worthy of reward or punishment.[192]

Interestingly, Hillary of Poitiers[193] and Zeno of Verona[194] hold that final judgment is meant only for the in-betweens, as it were, because both good and bad have already been judged at death.[195] In the same direction, Ambrose observes that "Christ judges by knowing our hearts, not by questioning us about our deeds";[196] in fact, our very deeds judge us as we perform them.[197]

---

188. See pp. 309–13.
189. Thomas Aquinas, *In IV Sent.*, D. 47, q. 1, a. 1, ql. 1 ad 1.
190. Augustine, *De Civ. Dei XX*, 14.
191. Thomas Aquinas, *S. Th. II-II*, q. 67, a. 3 ad 1.
192. Thomas Aquinas, *De Ver.* q. 19, a. 1c. H. U. von Balthasar also teaches this: *Theodramatik 4/2: Das Endspiel*, 264–67.
193. Hillary of Poitiers, *Tract. Ps.*, 1:17; 57:7.
194. Zeno of Verona, *Tract.*, 2:21. He says that judgment "comes into existence in situations of ambiguity" ibid., 2:21,1.
195. On this question, see B. E. Daley, *The Hope*, 94–97. Ambrose says that only the "sinful believer" is judged: *In Ps.* 51. Paulinus of Nola agrees: *In Carm.*, 7:24–36.
196. Ambrose, *In Luc.*, 10:46.
197. Ambrose, *Ep.* 77:10,14.

The theory of self-judgment intends above all to avoid judgment being considered extrinsic or unjust. Judgment should, rather, correspond to the true situation of the person as they see themselves in conscience. Wishing to avoid divine extrinsicism and arbitrariness, however, the theory may go to the opposite extreme, by turning judgment into nonjudgment. For conscience is not the prime source of individual morality. It is not an expression of the person's ethical autonomy with respect to God. God is the supreme protagonist of the human conscience. Hence only God can judge humans, rewarding the good by bringing them to partake in his own life, or punishing the unjust by banishing them from his presence forever. Sin, judgment, reward, and punishment are all deeply dialogical in nature. If each person judged itself, how can we interpret the surprise experienced by those being judged, whether for good or for ill (Mt 25:37,44)? In the Council of Trent we read that "Neither should anyone pass judgment on himself, even if he is conscious of no wrong, because the entire life of man should be examined and judged, not by human judgment but by the judgment of God 'who will bring to light the things now hidden in darkness and will disclose the purposes of the heart. Then every man will receive his commendation from God' (1 Co 4:5)."[198]

198. *DS* 1549.

10

Purgatory: The Purification of the Elect

> Simon, son of John, do you love me?
> —*John 21:15*
>
> The alternative to hell is purgatory.
> —*T. S. Eliot*[1]
>
> Even their virtues were being burned away.
> —*Flannery O'Connor*[2]

"Purgatory" designates that state of definitive purification, after death, for those who have died in friendship with God but are stained by the remains of sin. "All who die in God's grace and friendship," says the *Catechism of the Catholic Church*, "but still imperfectly purified, are indeed assured of their salvation; but after death they undergo purification, so as to achieve the holiness necessary to enter the joy of heaven."[3] It is commonly held that the doctrine of purgatory is one of the most "human" of Christian doctrines, in that it gives expression (1) to the holiness of God that cannot endure anything blemished in his presence, (2) to a realistic appraisal of the sinful condition many, if not most, people find themselves in at the end of their lives, and (3) to the unity of the Church, Christ's mystical body, which provides the mysterious solidarity that makes the purification of its sinful members possible.[4] In the words of St. Josemaría Escrivá, "Purgatory shows God's great mercy and washes away the defects of those who long to become one with Him."[5]

The doctrine of purgatory is a typically "Catholic" one. Orthodox Christians explain *postmortem* purification in a somewhat different way from Catholics. Traditionally, Protestants deny the existence of purgatory altogether. It is also true

---

1. T. S. Eliot, *The Idea of a Christian Society* (London: Faber and Faber, 1954), 24.
2. F. O'Connor, "Revelation," in *The Complete Stories* (orig. 1971; New York: Farrar, Straus and Giroux, 2007), 508.
3. *CCC* 1030.
4. See E. J. Fortman, *Everlasting Life after Death* (New York: Alba House, 1976).
5. Josemaría Escrivá, *Furrow*, n. 889.

that the latter was not officially defined by the Church until the Middle Ages, and does not seem to occupy a substantial place in Scripture. However, the reason why the Church had not clearly defined the doctrine of *postmortem* purification at that stage is simple enough: in real terms, nobody had ever really denied it. As this doctrine is present at an implicit level in theology and Church practice, it is also deeply present throughout Scripture, albeit at an implicit level.

The Doctrine of Purgatory in Scripture

Scripture provides a solid basis for the doctrine of purgatory at a general level and in concrete texts. We shall consider the former first.

The Scriptural Background for Purgatory

Above we mentioned three fundamental reasons that account for the existence of purgatory. All three are clearly attested in Scripture.

First, God is holy and requires a holy life of his people.[6] "O Lord, who may abide in your tent? Who may dwell on your holy mountain? Those who walk blamelessly, and do what is right, and speak the truth from the heart" (Ps 14:1–2). "Nothing unclean shall enter it [the New Jerusalem], nor any one who practices abomination or falsehood, but only those who are written in the Lamb's book of life" (Rv 21:27). In the Old Testament great importance was given to ritual purity, which is always considered as a manifestation of interior purity.[7] This need was especially applicable to the priests, who on account of their ministry enjoyed an especially close contact with the Lord (Lv 8–9). When John speaks of the eschatological promise of the direct vision of God (1 Jn 3:2), he adds the following exhortation: "And every one who thus hopes in him purifies himself as he is pure" (1 Jn 3:3). The prospect of seeing God face to face requires believers to purify their lives. In effect, during the Sermon on the Mount Jesus said: "Blessed are the pure of heart, for they shall see God" (Mt 5:8).

Second, humans generally are aware of the power and apparently intractable quality of sin in their lives.[8] "For I know my transgressions, and my sin is ever before me. . . . Indeed I was born guilty, a sinner when my mother conceived me" (Ps 51:3,5). Jesus, who had come "to seek and to save the lost" (Lk 19:10), was moved by human weakness: "when he saw the crowds, he had compassion for them, because they were harassed and helpless, like sheep without a shepherd" (Mt 9:36). Paul in the letter to the Romans gave clear expression to the power of sin present

---

6. On the importance of this motif, see J. J. Alviar, *Escatología*, 334–40.
7. See H.-G. Link and J. Schattenmann, "Pure," in *NIDNTT* 3, 100–108.
8. On the presence of sin in the lives of believers, *SS* 46.

in the human heart: "I do not do what I want, but I do the very thing I hate. . . . I delight in the law of God, in my inmost self, but I see in my members another law at war with the law of my mind. . . . Wretched man that I am! Who will deliver me from this body of death?" (Rom 7:15,22–24). Of course, the fact that all humans are sinners speaks in favor of the need for their being purified after death.

Third, not only are Christians saved by Christ in faith, but this takes place in the Church with the assistance of the prayer and penance of other believers. This doctrine is especially present in Paul's teaching on the mystical body of Christ, which later came to be known as the "communion of saints."[9] In the letter to the Ephesians we read, regarding the unity of the Body that is the Church: "We grow up in every way into him who is the head, into Christ, from whom the whole body, joined and knit together by every joint with which it is supplied, when each part is working properly, makes bodily growth and builds itself up in love" (Eph 4:15–16). "God has so composed the body . . . that there may be no discord in the body, but that the members may have the same care for one another. If one member suffers, all suffer together; if one member is honored, all rejoice together. Now you are the body of Christ and individually members of it" (1 Cor 12:24–27). "Now I rejoice in my sufferings for your sake," Paul writes to the Colossians, "and in my flesh I complete what is lacking in Christ's afflictions for the sake of his body, that is the Church" (Col 1:24). Because of this, he can exhort Christians to "bear one another's burdens, and so fulfill the law of Christ" (Gal 6:2). The same doctrine is to be found in apocalyptic writings[10] and also in Augustine, who says, among other things, that "the souls of the faithful defunct are not separated from the Church, which in time is the Kingdom of Christ."[11] In brief, the solidarity of Christ's mystical body makes it possible for Christians to partake in the purification of all its members, dead and alive.

Besides, several scriptural texts speak openly of the existence of purgatory.

Purgatory in the Old Testament

The clearest text speaking about the possibility of *postmortem* purification in the Old Testament is to be found in the second book of Maccabees (12:40–45).[12] The text speaks of the suffrages offered by the leader of the Israelite troops, Judas Maccabeus, in favor of soldiers who had fought bravely against their adversaries in defense of God's chosen nation, but in the hour of battle had sought assistance from pagan divinities through superstitious practices. "Then under the tunic of

---

9. See my study "Comunión de los santos."
10. See Testament of Abraham 12–14; Apoc. Moses 35:2; 36:1; 47; 1 Enoch 13:4; 15:2.
11. Augustine, *De Civ. Dei XXII*, 9:2.
12. See E. O'Brien, "The Scriptural Proof for the Existence of Purgatory from 2 Maccabees 12,43–45," *Sciences Ecclésiastiques* 2 (1949): 80–108.

each one of the dead they found sacred tokens of the idols of Jamnia, which the law forbids the Jews to wear. . . . And they turned to supplication, praying that the sin that had been committed might be wholly blotted out" (2 Mc 12:40–42). Judas then "took up a collection, man by man, to the amount of two thousand drachmas of silver, and sent it to Jerusalem to provide for a sin offering. In doing so he acted very well and honorably, taking account of the resurrection. For if he were not expecting that those who had fallen would rise again, it would have been superfluous and foolish to pray for the dead. . . . It was a holy and pious thought . . . that he made atonement for the dead, so that they might be delivered from their sin" (ibid., 43–45).

On the one hand, it is clear that the soldiers died fighting to defend Israel, God's own People. On the other, they had sinned by not trusting totally in the power of God, but sought supplementary help through idolatrous practices, which were completely prohibited to Jews on account of their faith in Yahweh as the only Lord. It was considered, however, that their sin was not a grave, unpardonable one, but could be forgiven and expiated even after death. For the purpose of obtaining perfect purification, sacrifices were offered in Jerusalem. The text confirms the fact that the practice was a well-established one.[13] The fact that no explicit mention is made of a purgatorial state as such is offset by the naturalness and inner logic of the practice of offering sacrifice for the dead. The text is applied to purgatory by Ephrem in the East, Augustine in the West, and several other Fathers of the Church.[14] Besides, Vatican Council II, the *Catechism of the Catholic Church*, and Benedict XVI cite the text in support of this doctrine.[15]

Purgatory in the New Testament

The New Testament refers to purgatory principally in Paul's first letter to the Corinthians (3:10–15). This is recognized by the *Catechism of the Catholic Church* and by Pope Benedict XVI.[16] The text speaks of the baptized, of those who be-

---

13. For the Jews, the rite of Kippur (Lv 4–5) was used to redeem sins not only of the living but also of the dead. According to the Rabbinic text of the school of Shammai, "in judgment there are three kinds of people: some are destined for eternal life, those completely impious for eternal shame and dishonor; the in-betweens (neither entirely good nor entirely bad, an intermediate place) descend into the gehenna to be pressed and purified; then they rise and are saved," cit. in F. de Fuenterrabía, "El purgatorio en la literatura judía precristiana," in *En torno al problema de la escatología individual del Antiguo Testamento (Semana Bíblica Española 15, 1954)* (Madrid: CSIC, 1955), 115–50, here 145. See also A. Lods, *La croyance à la vie future et le culte des morts dans l'antiquité israélite*.

14. "If the followers of the Maccabees expiated the crimes of the dead with sacrifices, how much more can the priests of the Son do this with holy offerings and the prayers of their lips," Ephrem, *Testamentum*, 78. See Augustine, *De cura pro mortuis gerenda*, 1:3.

15. *LG* 50; *CCC* 1032; *SS* 48.

16. The *Catechism of the Catholic Church* applies 1 Cor 3 to purgatory in *CCC* 1031, n. 605; so does Benedict XVI in *SS* 46.

long to Christ, and live and die in charity. "Let each one take care how he builds upon it [the foundation laid by the Apostle]. For no other foundation can any one lay than that which is laid, which is Jesus Christ" (vv. 10–11). The text continues: "Now if any one builds on the foundation with gold, silver, precious stones, wood, hay, straw, each man's work will become manifest; for the Day will disclose it, because it will be revealed with fire, and the fire will test what sort of work each one has done. If the work which any man has built on the foundation survives, he will receive a reward. If any man's work is burned up, he will suffer loss, though he himself will be saved, but only as through fire" (vv. 12–15).

Some exegetes hold that the text does not refer to purgatory, but simply offers an image of the revelation of God's majesty, of the inaccessibility of the Holy One.[17] Others recognize that the core of the doctrine of purgatory is present in this text.[18] Perhaps it would be correct to say that the passage offers a good description of the general dynamic of Christian purification. But the text has an undeniable eschatological cadence, and the final manifestation will be on "that Day," which is equivalent to the *Parousia*, or end of time. Personal repentance as such is not envisaged, but rather a purification of the sinner is effected. Some Fathers of the Church saw in the text a basis to justify Origen's doctrine of universal reconciliation or *apokatastasis*.[19] Others, such as John Chrysostom, understood it in terms of purification as a characteristic of Christian life as such.[20] Yet several Church Fathers applied it directly to purgatory:[21] Ambrose,[22] Caesarius of Arles,[23] Gregory the Great,[24] and in particular Augustine.[25] Likewise, several

17. For example, J. Gnilka, *Ist I Kor 3,10–15 ein Schriftzeugnis für das Fegfeuer?* (Düsseldorf: Triltsch, 1955). Gnilka holds that the testing "fire" on the "day of the Lord" refers to Christ's return for final judgment. "Fire" would simply be "an image of the majesty of God who reveals himself, of the inaccessibility of the Holy One," ibid., 126.

18. For example C. Spicq, "Purgatoire dans l'Ancien Testament," in *Dictionnaire de la Bible, Supplément*, vol. 9 (1979), cols. 555–57, here col. 557; E. B. Allo, *Première Épitre aux Corinthiens* (Paris: Gabalda; Lecoffre, 1934), 60–63, 66–67; S. Cipriani, "Insegna I Cor 3,10–15 la dottrina del Purgatorio?" *Revue Biblique* 7 (1959): 25–43. Likewise, J. Michl, "Gerichtsfeuer und Purgatorium zu I Kor 3,12–15," in *Studiorum Paulinorum Congressus Internationalis Catholicus* (1961), vol. 1 (Roma: Pontificio Istituto Biblico, 1963), 395–401, holds that at least the core of the doctrine of purgatory may be found here.

19. See H. Crouzel, "L'exégèse origénienne de 1 Co 3,11–25 et la purification eschatologique," here 282.

20. John Chrysostom, *1 in Cor.*, hom. 9,3.

21. See G. Moioli, G., *L'"Escatologico" cristiano*, 185–88.

22. Ambrose, *In Ps.*, 36:25.

23. Caesarius of Arles, *Sermo* 167:6–7; see *Sermo* 179.

24. Gregory the Great speaks of a "cleansing fire before judgment for certain minor faults" *Dial.*, 4, 41:3–4.

25. See J. Ntedika, *L'évolution de la doctrine du purgatoire chez S. Augustin* (Paris: Études augustiniennes, 1966), especially 67–68. In particular Augustine says that "some of the faithful, in accordance with their love for fleeting goods, will be purified, more or less speedily, by means of a purging fire," *Enchirid.*, 109. See *Enn. in Ps.*, 37,3; *De Civ. Dei XXI*, 25–27. See also P. Jay, "Saint Augustin et la doctrine du purgatoire," *Recherches de théologie ancienne et médiévale* 36 (1969): 17–30.

Purgatory 291

contemporary theologians apply the text to purgatory, interpreting the purifying fire in a Christological way. We shall return to this explanation later on.[26]

According to Tertullian[27] and other Fathers, purgatory is also spoken of in Jesus' teaching on the need to be reconciled with one's accuser rather than being sent to jail, "for truly I say to you, you will never get out till you have paid the last penny" (Mt 5:25-26). The term "prison" is often taken as an equivalent to *hadēs* or the underworld.[28] The Old Testament doctrine of permanence in *hadēs* may now be seen as "the purgatory that all are in need of."[29]

The Doctrine of Purgatory in the Fathers and the Liturgy

There are many clear affirmations of the doctrine of purgatory among the Fathers of the Church. Some have just been mentioned. The principal authors include Tertullian,[30] Lactantius,[31] Ephrem,[32] Basil,[33] Gregory of Nyssa,[34] Augustine,[35] Caesarius of Arles,[36] and Gregory the Great.[37] The following text of Pope Gregory should suffice as an example: "we must believe in a cleansing fire before the judgment for certain minor faults."[38]

However, it is particularly interesting to note that this doctrine is powerfully present from the very beginning of the life of the Church in the liturgical practice of praying for the dead.[39] The 1979 Letter of the Congregation for the Doctrine of

---

26. See pp. 307-8.

27. Tertullian, *De anima*, 35; 58:8. Some authors argue that the latter text of Tertullian does not refer to a temporally limited purifying suffering, but rather a temporary anticipation in the sinner's soul of his eternal fate: see B. E. Daley, *The Hope*, 37. See also A. J. Mason, "Tertullian and Purgatory," *Journal of Theological Studies* 3 (1902): 598-601, and H. Finé, *Die Terminologie der Jenseitsvorstellungen bei Tertullian: ein semasiologischer Beitrag zur Dogmengeschichte des Zwischenzustandes* (Bonn: Hanstein, 1958).

28. See J. Ratzinger, *Escathology*, 223, citing E. Stauffer, *Die Theologie des Neuen Testaments*, 4th ed. (Stuttgart: W. Kohlhammer, 1948), 196, 296, n. 697.

29. J. Fischer, *Studien zum Todesgedanken in der alten Kirche. Die Beurteilung des natürlichen Todes in der kirchlichen Literatur der ersten drei Jahrhunderte* (München: H. Hüber, 1954), 258.

30. Tertullian, *De anima*, 58.   31. Lactantius, *Div. Instit. VII*, 21:1-8.
32. Ephrem, *Testamentum*, 72.   33. Basil, *In Ps.*, 7:2.
34. Gregory of Nyssa, *De mortuis or.*

35. Augustine, *Enn. in Ps.*, 37:3. He says: "In hac vita purges me et talem me reddas, cui iam emendatorio igne non opus sit," *De Gen. c. Manich.*, 2,20:30. After this life, sinners will have "vel ignem purgationis vel poenam aeternam," *De Civ. Dei XXI*, 13; 24:2. On prayer for the dead, see *Enchirid.*, 69; 109-110.

36. Caesarius of Arles, *Sermo* 44, 2.

37. Gregory the Great, *Dial.*, 4, 39. On Gregory's teaching on purgatory, see J. Le Goff, *La naissance du Purgatoire* (Paris: Gallimard, 1982), 121-31.

38. Gregory the Great, *Dial.*, 4, 41:3.

39. On prayer for the dead over the patristic period, see H. B. Swete, "Prayer for the Departed in the First Four Centuries," *Journal of Theological Studies* 8 (1907): 500-14; A. M. Triacca, "La commemorazione dei defunti nelle anafore del IV secolo: testimonianza pregata della sopravvivenza," in *Morte e immortalità nella catechesi dei Padri del III-IV secolo*, ed. S. Felici (Roma: LAS, 1985), 161-96. After that, see J. Ntedika, *L'évocation de l'au-delà dans la prière pour les morts: étude de patristique et de liturgie latines*

the Faith on eschatology made reference to the importance of the liturgy in the development of Christian eschatology: the Church's "prayer, funeral rites and cult of the dead constitute, substantially, true theological sources [*loci theologici*]."[40] The *Catechism of the Catholic Church* states that the existence of purgatory "is also based on the practice of prayer for the dead. . . . From the beginning the Church has honored the memory of the dead and offered prayers in suffrage for them, above all the Eucharistic sacrifice, so that, thus purified, they may attain the beatific vision of God."[41]

The logic is straightforward enough: prayers for the dead would be of no use either to those already saved, for they enjoy the presence of God, or to the condemned, because they have forfeited heaven forever. If Christians as a whole do pray for the dead, it means the latter may be assisted in purifying their faults. Many Fathers of the Church are convinced of the value of prayers offered for the dead. Important references to this praxis are to be found, among others, in Tertullian,[42] Cyril of Alexandria,[43] John Chrysostom,[44] Augustine,[45] and Gregory the Great. The latter speaks especially of the thirty Masses to be offered for the monk Justus, who will then be "released from the torments of fire."[46] Thus the so-called

---

(IVᵉ–VIIIᵉ s.) (Louvain: Nauwelaerts, 1971). See also P. A. Février, "Quelques aspects de la prière pour les morts," in *La prière au Moyen Age (littérature et civilisation)* (Aix-en-Provence: Université, 1981), 253–82.

40. See *Recentiores episcoporum Synodi* (1979), n. 4. See also Paul VI, Apost. Const. *Indulgentiarum doctrina* (1968), n. 3.

41. *CCC* 1032.

42. The *Passion of St Perpetua* (often attributed to Tertullian, probably from the Montanist period) recounts the saint's vision of her brother Dinocrates, who had just died, suffering grievously in purgatory. Perpetua understands immediately that this vision constitutes a call to prayer, and shortly afterward she sees her brother again, clean, well-dressed, fully healed, contented. A. Stuiber (*Refrigerium interim*, 61–65.) considers that this work is not Tertullian's, and besides that it refers to neither guilt nor punishment, but to those who die young. J. Fischer, *Studien zum Todesgedanken in der alten Kirche*, 259–60, takes an opposite view.

43. Speaking of the Eucharistic celebration, Cyril said: "Let us offer Christ immolated for our sins, propitiating divine clemency for the living and the dead," *Catech. Mystag.*, 5:9.

44. "How can we alleviate . . . the dead?" Chrysostom asks. "Praying for them, asking others to do the same, frequently giving alms to the poor. For these rules were established by the Apostles themselves, in such a way that in the midst of these tremendous mysteries we can remember those who have died. . . . We know that the dead draw great benefit from this," *In ep. ad Phil., hom.*, 3:4. "Let us have recourse to them and commemorate them. If the sons of Job were purified by the sacrifice of their father, why should we doubt that our offerings for the dead should bring them some consolation? Let us not hesitate to assist those who are dead and offer our prayers for them," *Hom. in I ad Cor.*, 41:5.

45. "The dead should not be denied the comfort of being prayed for by the Church, when the sacrifice [the Eucharist] is offered for them, or alms are given for them," Augustine, *Enchirid.*, 110. See H. Kotila, *Memoria mortuorum: The Commemoration of the Departed in Augustine* (Roma: Institutum Patristicum Augustinianum, 1992).

46. Gregory the Great, *Dial.*, 57:14–15. On the consequences of Gregory's doctrine, see C. Vogel, "Deux conséquences de l'eschatologie grégorienne: la multiplication des messes privées et les moines-prêtres," in *Grégoire le Grand* [*Chantilly Colloquium, 1982*], 267–76.

Gregorian Masses that are commonly celebrated every day for a month after the death of Christian believers. Isidore of Seville offers the following explanation: "The offering of the sacrifice [the Eucharist] for the dead... is a custom observed throughout the whole world. Hence it would seem to be a custom taught by the Apostles themselves. In effect, the Catholic Church observes it everywhere. Now, if the Church did not believe in the forgiveness of sins for the faithful who have died, she would not give alms for their souls, nor would she offer the sacrifice to God for them."[47] The archaeological study of Christian sites and artifacts reveals an enormous number of inscriptions that attest to the custom of praying for the dead.[48]

The doctrine of purgatory is developed theologically by Cyprian (in the context of the reconciliation of the *lapsi*, those Christians who had been unfaithful during the persecution of Diocletian),[49] by Augustine (who insisted, however, that martyrs enter heaven without passing through purgatory),[50] and by Gregory the Great.

Asceticism, Eastern Theology, and the Council of Florence

As we saw above, for Tertullian, in his rigorist Montanist period, purgatory is considered as a kind of jail (Mt 5:25–26) destined for all humans at least until the end of time. In this context, however, Tertullian attenuates the value of the prayer of the Church, for, he says, each one must make amends for his or her own transgressions. What is possible before death ("make friends quickly with your accuser") is not so afterward ("till you have paid the last penny"). With this position Tertullian reverted, at least in part, to the Gnostic doctrines of individualistic purification that left no space for the intervention of the Church's prayer in the purification of humans. For the Gnostic Basilides (second century) for example, *post-mortem* purification constituted a kind of reincarnation,[51] a doctrine that has been followed by neo-Gnostic movements in the Middle Ages and modern times.[52]

---

47. Isidore of Seville, *De eccl. offic.*, 1,18:11.

48. H. Leclercq, in his article "Purgatoire," in *Dictionnaire d'Archéologie chrétienne et de Liturgie* 14/2, col. 1979, mentions the following: "Spiritus tuus bene requiescat," "Accepta sis in Christo," "Vivas in Domino Iesu," "In pace Domini dormias," "Vivas in Deo et roga," "Viva sis cum fratribus tuis," "Solus Deus defendat animam tuam," "In Christo vivas. Deum, te precor ut paradisum lucis possit vivere."

49. See especially Cyprian, *Ep.* 55. On this text, see J. Ratzinger, *Eschatology*, 232–33; P. Jay, "Saint Cyprien et la doctrine du purgatorie."

50. See p. 276, n. 136 above.

51. On the position of Basilides, see Origen, *Comm. in Matth.*, 38.

52. On the connection between purgatory and reincarnation, see Y. M.-J. Congar, "Le Purgatoire," in *Le mystère de la mort et sa célébration* (Paris: Cerf, 1951), 279–336.

Clement of Alexandria's Attempt to Develop a Christian Gnosticism

In this context it is interesting to take note of the effort made by Christian authors such as Clement of Alexandria to dialogue with Gnostic thought.[53] Clement starts out with Paul's doctrine of purification by fire (1 Cor 3:10–15). The Gnostics take it that the elect are spared this fire, being protected by the water of Baptism and the breeze of the Spirit. The rest of humanity is scorched by fire for their education (*paideia*) and to bring about the destruction of evil. Purification is designated as a kind of "wise fire."[54] Clement assumes this system and explains that the life of the Christian consists of a gradual, ascending process of spiritualization, which culminates in the resurrection of the dead.[55] The same idea may be found in Gregory of Nyssa, who says that believers are "either purified in the present life through diligence and 'philosophy' [that is, asceticism], or after leaving this world through being dissolved in the purifying fire."[56] In contrast with the Gnostics, however, Clement includes the critical Christian corrective: that purification is not a process that each one undergoes alone; rather, the whole Church is involved in bringing about purification.[57]

The Meaning of Purgatorial Fire

All in all, and in spite of the variety of explanations given, the doctrine of *postmortem* purification is pacifically accepted in the East. Gregory of Nyssa has it that the impure soul "after having left the body, cannot participate of the life of the Divinity, unless a purifying fire has purged the stains of the soul."[58] John Chrysostom develops the doctrine of purgatory on the basis of 1 Corinthians 3:10–15. Yet he rejects Origen's explanation that leads to the doctrine of univer-

---

53. See K. Schmöle, *Läuterung nach dem Tode und pneumatische Auferstehung bei Klemens von Alexandrien* (Münster: Aschendorff, 1974); J. Ratzinger, *Eschatology*, 233–36; B. E. Daley, *The Hope*, 44–47.

54. See W. C. Van Unnik, "The 'Wise Fire' in a Gnostic Eschatological Vision," in *Kyriakon: Festschrift Johannes Quasten*, ed. P. Granfield and J. A. Jungmann, vol. 1 (Münster: Aschendorff, 1970), 277–88.

55. "Fire sanctifies neither flesh nor sacrifice, but sinful souls—understanding by fire not the all-devouring flame of everyday life, but the discerning kind, that pierces through the soul that walks through fire," *Strom.*, 7,6,34:4. Emphasis on purification as part of the divinization process differentiates Eastern doctrine somewhat from the Latin doctrine of expiation: see Y. M.-J. Congar, "Le Purgatoire," 302–4.

56. Gregory of Nyssa, *De mortuis or.* Maximus the Confessor speaks of the purgative experience after death: *Quaest. et Dub.*, 1:10.

57. On the notion of purification in Clement and Origen, see G. Anrich, "Clemens und Origenes als Begründer der Lehre vom Fegfeuer," in *Theologische Abhandlungen für Heinrich Julius Holtzmann*, ed. W. Nowack (Tübingen: J. C. B. Mohr, 1902), 95–120; T. Spácil, "La dottrina del purgatorio in Clemente Alessandrino ed Origene," *Bessarione* 23 (1919): 131–45; K. Schmöle, *Läuterung nach dem Tode*. Schmöle says that purification after death offers "a kind of metaphysical bridge between the Platonic concept of immortality of the soul and resurrection," ibid., 135. See also R. B. Eno, "The Fathers and the Cleansing Fire," *Irish Theological Quarterly* 53 (1987): 184–202.

58. Gregory of Nyssa, *De mortuis or.*

sal reconciliation (*apokatastasis*) through fire, and proposes instead the idea that all will descend into the underworld (*she'ol*) to be purified. For Eastern authors, purgatory is not generally considered as a place where suffering is inflicted in expiation for sin. Instead, the living, through their prayer, almsgiving, and participation in the Eucharist, can obtain alleviation and comfort for the souls in purgatory. Rather than expiation of one's faults, purification involves alleviation from affliction deserved by those faults.[59]

In Eastern theology the result is twofold. *First*, the existence of purgatory is linked directly to the delay in full retribution after death, which we considered earlier on.[60] This results in a possible confusion between purgatory and what is called the *refrigerium interim*. And *second*, purgatory is clearly dissociated from purifying fire, for the latter is considered to be a necessary correlate of Origen's *apokatastasis*. Let us consider the latter point more closely.

The Definition of Purgatory in the Middle Ages

It should now be clear why the question of the nature (whatever of the existence) of purgatory became relevant in the relationship between Orthodox and Latin Christianity during the Middle Ages.[61] Latin Fathers from the time of Augustine and Gregory the Great accepted the idea of the "fire" of purgatory.[62] Thomas Aquinas not only taught it, but claimed besides that the fire of purgatory is identical with that of hell.[63] On account of the realism of this "fire," it was quite common to consider purgatory as a physical place.[64] However, both the realism of hellfire and its location were contested by the Eastern Church.[65]

The controversy came to a head during the thirteenth century on occasion of an encounter between two bishops, one Greek Orthodox, the other Catholic.[66] The former took it that the insistence among Catholics on the fire of hell signaled a return to Origen's *apokatastasis*, and thus a denial of the perpetuity of hell. Later on, the Orthodox theologian Simon of Thessalonica stated that the Latins, "following Origen, eliminate hell, suggesting a kind of purification instead of that torment; in

---

59. I. N. Karmirês, "Abriss der dogmatischen Lehre der orthodoxen katholischen Kirchen," in *Die Orthodoxe Kirche in griechischer Sicht*, ed. P. I. Bratsiotis, vol. 1 (Stuttgart: Evangelisches Verlag, 1959), 15–120, especially 113–17.

60. See pp. 275–78.   61. See C. Pozo, *La teología del más allá*, 496–97.
62. See pp. 292–93.

63. "Idem est ignis qui damnatos cruciat in inferno, et qui iustos in Purgatorio purgat," Thomas Aquinas, *Qu. de Purgatorio*, a. 2c.

64. This is found in Peter Lombard, *IV Sent.*, D. 43, and Thomas Aquinas, *S. Th. III, Suppl.*, q. 97, a. 7.

65. See the studies of Anrich, Spácil, and Schmöle mentioned in n. 57.

66. The protagonists were the metropolitan of Corfu, George Bardanes, and the Franciscan brother Bartholemew. See M. Roncaglia, *Georges Bardanes métropolite de Corfou et Barthelemy de l'ordre Franciscain* (Roma: Scuola Tipografica Italo-orientale 'San Nilo', 1953); D. Stiernon, "L'escatologia nelle Chiese

this Purgatory sinners enter, and pay their punishment until the last day. This doctrine is not held by the saints, since it denies the Lord's words which clearly state that hell is eternal, just as life is eternal."[67]

When in 1439 an attempt was made at the Council of Florence to reestablish doctrinal unity between Orthodox and Catholics, the theme of purgatory was broached, and a solemn definition given.[68] For those who "are truly penitent and die in God's love before having satisfied by worthy fruits of penance for their sins of commission and omission," the conciliar decree says, "their souls are cleansed after death by purgatorial penalties [*poenis purgatoriis*], the acts of intercession [*suffragia*] of the living faithful benefit them, namely the sacrifice of the Mass, prayers, alms and other works of piety which the faithful are wont to do for the other faithful according to the Church's practice."[69] Interestingly, no mention is made either of the "fire" of purgatory or of the latter's possible location. On two earlier occasions the Church spoke of purgatory and made no mention of purgatorial "fire": the Second Council of Lyons (1274),[70] which like Florence attempted to restore doctrinal unity between East and West; and Benedict XII's constitution *Benedictus Deus* (1336).[71] Some minor Church documents of the Middle Ages, however, do mention the "fire" of purgatory,[72] as do Paul VI's *Creed of the People of God*[73] and the *Catechism of the Catholic Church*.[74]

---

separate d'Oriente," in *L'aldilà*, ed. A. Piolanti (Torino: Marietti, 1956), 283–93, especially 284–85; C. Pozo, *La teología del más allá*, 529–30; J.-C. Larchet, *La vie après la mort selon la Tradition orthodoxe*, 179–211.

67. Simon of Thessalonica, *Dial. c. Haer.*, n. 23.

68. For the controversial texts between Catholics and Orthodox (especially Mark of Ephesus, called Eugenicus) during the Council of Florence, see J. Gill, G. Hofmann, L. Petit, and G. Scholarius, *De purgatorio disputationes in Concilio Florentino habitae* = *Concilium Fiorentinum*, vol. 8/2 (Roma: Pontificium Institutum Orientalium Studiorum, 1969). See also A. D'Ales, "La question du Purgatoire au Concile de Florence 1438," *Gregorianum* 3 (1922): 9–50; J. Gill, *Constance et Bâle-Florence* (Paris: Éditions de l'orante, 1965); J. Jorgenson, "The Debate over the Patristic Texts on Purgatory at the Council of Ferrara-Florence 1438," *St. Vladimir's Theological Quarterly* 30 (1986): 309–34; A. De Halleux, "Problèmes de méthode dans les discussions sur l'eschatologie au concile de Ferrare et de Florence," in *Christian Unity*, ed. G. Alberigo (Leuven: Leuven University Press; Peeters, 1991), 251–99. For a summary of the discussions between Latins and Orthodox at Florence, see J.-C. Larchet, *La vie après la mort*, 186–208, which presents especially the position of Mark of Ephesus and Bessarion of Nicea.

69. Council of Florence, *Decretum pro Graecis: DS* 1304.

70. *DS* 856.   71. *DS* 1000.

72. For example, a letter of Pope Innocent IV sent in 1254 to the Eastern Church, *Sub catholica professione* (*DS* 838), and the letter *Super quibusdam* (1351) of Pope Clement VI (*DS* 1067).

73. "Credimus animas eorum omnium, qui in gratia Christi moriuntur—sive quae adhuc *Purgatorii igne expiandae* sunt, sive quae statim ac corpore separatae . . . a Iesu in Paradisum suscipiuntur—Populum Dei constituere post mortem," Paul VI, *Creed of the People of God*, n. 28, in *AAS* 60 (1968): 445. The Italian translation presented in the *Enchiridion Vaticanum* 3:564 translates the text simply by saying that souls will "be purified still in Purgatory."

74. *CCC* 1031, citing Gregory the Great, *Dial.*, 4:39.

Purgatory, Protestantism, and the Council of Trent

It may be noted that the Church, inspired by the universal custom of praying for the dead, came to solemnly define the existence of purgatory as an attempt to reestablish unity between East and West. The fact that its existence had not been defined previously by the Church is not difficult to account for, since it had never really been denied.

Medieval Development of the Doctrine of Purgatory

The doctrine of purgatory developed considerably during the Middle Ages. In the first place the distinction between grave and light sins (*peccata capitalia et venialia*)[75] played an important role, as did that of the distinction between the *reatus culpae* and the *reatus poenae* (guilt and punishment) at the hands of Peter Lombard.[76] The idea of purgatory being situated physically between heaven and hell also played a role, giving rise to the consolidation of the locative term "purgatory," *purgatorium*, around the year 1180.[77] Purification was not considered simply as a process or a state, but rather as a place where divine justice is meted out, and in which the Church is seen to play a direct role, even beyond the grave. In fact, some contemporary authors have suggested that the doctrine of "purgatory" came into existence at this stage in time for predominantly sociological and political reasons linked with the emergence of a third (middle) class in medieval society, and with the consolidation of jurisprudence.[78] Other authors have shown that these reasons, though indicative, are decidedly tenuous.[79] It is true, however, that the teaching on purgatory became highly developed in theology, and came to be associated with the doctrine of indulgences.[80] These factors, along with the relative absence of an open witness to purgatory in Scripture, account for the fact that the doctrine came to be denied outright during the sixteenth century by Protestant theologians.[81]

---

75. Alan of Lille, *Liber poenitentialis;* Simon of Tournai, *Disputationes*.
76. Peter Lombard, *In Sent. IV*, D. 17, q. 2; D. 18, q. 1, D. 21, D. 45.
77. On the origin of the term "purgatory," see J. Le Goff, *La naissance*, 209–35.
78. This is the thesis of J. Le Goff, *La naissance*, 407–10. See also H. J. Berman, *Law and Revolution: The Formation of the Western Legal Tradition* (Cambridge, Mass.: Harvard University Press, 1983), chapter 3.
79. See, for example, L. Genicot, "L'Occident du Xe au XIIe siècle," *Revue d'Histoire Ecclésiastique* 78 (1983): 397–429, here 421–26; J.-G. Bougerol, "Autour de 'La naissance du Purgatoire,'" *Archives d'Histoire Doctrinale et Littéraire du Moyen-Age* 58 (1983): 7–59; M. P. Ciccarese, "La nascita del purgatorio," *Annali di Storia dell'esegesi* 17 (2000): 133–50.
80. See the extensive historical overview by A. Michel and M. Jugie, "Purgatoire," in *DTC* 13 (1936): 1163–357.
81. See H. Wagner, "Probleme der Eschatologie: ökumenische Perspektiven," *Catholica* 42 (1988): 209–23, especially 214.

The Denial of Purgatory

Luther, in spite of his aversion toward indulgences and similar practices, initially accepted the doctrine of purgatory. Under the insistence of Zwingli,[82] however, he came to teach in 1519 that it is not to be found in Scripture, this affirmation involving, among other things, a rejection of the canonicity of 2 Maccabees.[83] In 1524 he taught that Mass should not be offered for the dead.[84] In his 1530 work *Rectractatio purgatorii*, on the occasion of the Diet of Augsburg,[85] he denied its existence, and in the 1537 *Smalcald Articles* called it *mera diaboli larva*, "a mere larva of the devil."[86] Likewise, Zwingli and Calvin openly denied the existence of purgatory.[87] Two reasons may be suggested for this rejection, one involving fundamental theology (the doctrine of tradition), the other dogma (the teaching of justification).[88]

As regards tradition, Calvin recognized that from earliest times the custom of praying for the dead had existed in the Church: "It has been the practice of thirteen hundred years to offer prayer for the dead." However, he observed, "I admit those who practiced it were also carried away by error, the usual effect of rash credulity being to destroy judgment. . . . We should not imitate them in this."[89] For Calvin, the witness of liturgy and Church life is not fully trustworthy. Traditions come and go, and Scripture alone should be used to determine the doctrine of faith. Understandable human inclinations, such as that of praying to God for loved ones who have died, do not offer a sure guide in matters of faith, and in this case had led believers to accept doctrines of philosophical and pagan provenance that corrupt true Christian teaching.

The denial of purgatory is also closely linked with the Lutheran doctrine of "justification by faith alone," that is, without works.[90] For Protestant thought, either humans are saved, exclusively by God's grace, or they are condemned for the

---

82. See H. Zwingli, "Amica exegesis, id est: expositio eucharistiae negocii, ad Martinum Lutherum," in *Corpus Reformatorum*, vol. 92, 716–18. On Luther's doctrine of purgatory, see L. Cristiani, "I novissimi nella dottrina di Lutero," in *L'aldilà*, ed. A. Piolanti, 297–300; E. Kunz, *Protestantische Eschatologie*, 21–22.

83. From the Leipzig Disputation, condemned later on by Pope Leo X: *DS* 1487–90.

84. M. Luther, *De abroganda Missa*.

85. M. Luther, *Rectractatio purgatorii*, in *WA* 30/2:367–90.

86. M. Luther, *Artic. Smalcald.*, 2:11, in *WA* 50:204–7.

87. J. Calvin, *Instit. christ.*, 3:5. On the position of Protestants in general, see Y. M.-J. Congar, *Le mystère de la mort*, 280–93; T. F. Torrance, "The Eschatology of the Reformation," in *Eschatology: Four Papers Read to the Society for the Study of Theology*, ed. T. F. Torrance and J. K. S. Reid (Edinburgh: Oliver and Boyd, 1953), 36–90. Specifically on Luther's doctrine, see P. Althaus, "Luthers Gedanken über die letzen Dinge," *Luther Jahrbuch* 23 (1941): 22–28, and on Calvin, see H. Schutzeichel, "Calvins Protest gegen das Fegfeuer," *Catholica* 36 (1982): 130–49.

88. L. Cristiani, "I novissimi nella dottrina di Lutero"; E. Kunz, *Protestantische Eschatologie*.

89. J. Calvin, *Instit. christ.*, 3,5:10.

90. See my study *Fides Christi*, passim.

sins they have surely committed. Humans do not contribute as such to their salvation: God sees Christ in those who believe in him, and thus saves them. Classical Lutheranism teaches that justification does not produce primarily an inner renewal of the sinner (that would involve the painful purification of the soul), but principally an extrinsic imputation of the merits of Christ.[91] Zwingli had insisted with Luther that the doctrine of justification by faith was incompatible with that of the *potestas clavium*, or power of the keys, that the Church exercises.[92] In fact, Calvin was of the opinion that the doctrine of purgatory was mainly "a question of feeding priests."[93]

The two reasons are connected with one another. Humans are incapable of good works because they are deeply corrupted by sin. This makes it all the more likely for them to accept flawed human inclinations, such as praying for dead loved ones, instead of trusting the word of God as the only point of reference for their faith. And for the same reason, the justifying power of God must remain extrinsic to humans.

The Council of Trent on Purgatory

The Council of Trent did not deal extensively with the doctrine of purgatory. In the twenty-fifth session (1563) it simply reminded Christians of the pastoral and practical issues purgatory involves, repeating the definitions already given by the Church.[94] However, its teaching both on the role of tradition in Christian doctrine[95] and on the doctrine of justification provides the dogmatic basis for the teaching on purgatory. As regards the latter, the following position is rejected: "after the grace of justification has been received, the guilt is remitted and the debt of eternal punishment blotted out for any repentant sinner, to such a degree that no debt of temporal punishment remains to be paid, either in this world or in the next, in purgatory."[96] Besides, the council attempted to ensure that no abuse be associated with Church teaching on purgatory.[97]

---

91. See J. A. Möhler, *Symbolik*, 9th ed. (München: Nationale Verlagsanstalt Buch, 1894), §§ 52–53. This work clearly shows the connection between the denial of purgatory and the Protestant view of justification.

92. H. Zwingli, "Amica exegesis," 718. He insisted with Luther that the doctrine of purgatory was incompatible with salvation.

93. J. Calvin, *Instit. christ.*, 4,5:9.

94. *DS* 1820. On the XXV session of Trent, see H. Jedin, *Geschichte des Konzils von Trient*, vol. 4/2 (Freiburg i. B.: Herder, 1975). Session XXII on the Mass also made reference to purgatory: *DS* 1753. See also *DS* 1867, 1986, 2534, 2642, etc. See P. Schäfer, *Eschatologie. Trient und Gegenreformation* (Freiburg i. B.: Herder, 1980).

95. Session IV: *DS* 1501–5.

96. *DS* 1580, from Session VI *de Iustificatione*, can. 30.

97. *DS* 1820.

Purgatory and Ecumenism

Catholic theological reflection on purgatory after Trent was ample and detailed.[98] Authors such as Robert Bellarmine[99] and Francisco Suárez[100] considered the doctrine carefully, and attempted to explain a wide variety of issues, such as the location of purgatory, its duration and intensity, and the nature of the pain of purgatory. Devotion to the holy souls in purgatory went beyond the bounds of common liturgical practice; religious orders, sodalities, and prayer groups gave special attention to those who had left this pilgrim world and stood in need of purification.

The existence and role of *postmortem* purification was never really denied by Orthodox theologians, not, that is, until the seventeenth century, possibly under the influence of Protestant theology.[101] One well-known author is Peter Moghila, the metropolitan of Kiev. While accepting the practice of praying for the dead, he rejects the idea of purification after death on account of the danger of confusing it with Origen's *apokatastasis*.[102] Another author, Dosideus, patriarch of Jerusalem, in a letter to other Orthodox patriarchs, insists on the idea of immediate retribution, saying that purgatory would be a form of non-eternal hell, which is unacceptable.[103] Bordoni and Ciola sum up the relationship between Western and Eastern understanding of eschatology in the following terms: "The points of divergence between East and West refer especially to intermediate eschatology. The latter is conceived as a continuation of the drama of salvation characterized not by forms of penal satisfaction but rather as a kind of active waiting in which humans are purified, are freed from some imperfections and, to take up some of the expressions of modern Orthodox theology, also from the past state and damnation."[104]

Surprisingly, perhaps, over the last century or so, some Orthodox authors, in particular Sergei Bulgàkov and Pavel Evdokimov, have returned to a position close to Origen's *apokatastasis*. Bulgàkov states that in real terms "hell is a purga-

---

98. See A. Michel, "Purgatoire" (1936). On the recent history and decline of the doctrine of purgatory, see G. Cuchet, *Le crépuscule du purgatoire* (Paris: A. Colin, 2005).

99. Robert Bellarmine, *Disputationes de controversiis christianae fidei adversus huius temporis haereticos* (Milano: Bellagatta, 1721); "De Ecclesia quae est in purgatorio," in *Opera omnia*, vol. 2 (Naples: 1877), 351–414.

100. See F. Suárez, "De purgatorio," in *De poenitentia*, disp. 47.

101. See G. Panteghini, "Il purgatorio: l'incontro purificatore con Dio," *Credere oggi* 8 (1988): 79–91, here, 86; M. Bordoni and N. Ciola, *Gesù nostra speranza*, 126–34.

102. See P. Moghila, *Great Catechism: Confession of the Orthodox Faith*, cit. by W. Pannenberg, *Systematic Theology*, vol. 3, 620. See also R. Zuzek, "L'escatologia di Pietro Moghila," *Orientalia Christiana Periodica* 54 (1988): 353–85.

103. Dosideus, *Letter to the Patriarchs (Confession)*.

104. M. Bordoni and N. Ciola, *Gesù nostra speranza*, 133–34.

tory."[105] Orthodox theologians attempt to avoid a view of purgatory centered on penal satisfaction. *Postmortem* purification does not involve, they say, "a punishment to be purged but a continuation of one's destiny: purification, liberation, healing,"[106] "a never-ending ascent, into which the entire communion of saints— the Church in heaven and the Church on earth—has been initiated in Christ."[107] One must exclude, John Meyendorff adds, "any legalistic view of the Church's pastoral and sacramental powers over either the living or the dead, or any precise description of the state of the departed souls before final resurrection."[108]

At a substantial level, however, there is no longer any serious disagreement between Catholics and Orthodox on the doctrine of *postmortem* purification.[109] Besides, although the doctrine of purgatory has traditionally been one of the principal areas of controversy between Catholics and Protestants, modern ecumenical dialogue, especially in the area of justification, has taken the rough edges off the debate.[110] Nonetheless, full doctrinal convergence has not yet been established.[111]

The Purpose and Characteristics of *Postmortem* Purification[112]

In the first place, it is essential to distinguish between the punishment of purgatory and that of hell. The former belongs to the ambit of salvation, and is "theologically" closer to eternal life than to condemnation, which simply excludes salvation. The 1979 Letter of the Congregation for the Doctrine of the Faith on eschatology states that "the Church believes in the eventual purification of the elect, prelimi-

105. S. Bulgàkov, *L'orthodoxie* (Paris: F. Alcan, 1932), 255–56.
106. P. Evdokimov, *L'orthodoxie* (Neuchâtel: Delachaux et Niestlé, 1959), 293.
107. J. Meyendorff, *Byzantine Theology*, 221. On orthodox soteriology, see Y. Spiteris, *Salvezza e peccato nella tradizione orientale* (Bologna: EDB, 1999).
108. J. Meyendorff, *Byzantine Theology*, 221. He adds that "the East will never have a doctrine of 'indulgences,'" ibid.
109. On the present-day situation of Orthodox theology, see I. N. Karmirês, "Abriss der dogmatischen Lehre der orthodoxen katholischen Kirchen," 112–20; P. N. Trembelas, *Dogmatique de l'Église orthodoxe catholique*, vol. 3 (Paris: Desclée, 1968), 435–55.
110. See E. Lanne, "The Teaching of the Catholic Church on Purgatory," *One in Christ* 28 (1992): 13–30; D. M. Chapman, *Rest and Light Perpetual: Prayer for the Departed in the Communion of Saints* (Surrey: Ecumenical Society of the Blessed Virgin Mary, 1996); my study *Fides Christi: The Justification Debate*.
111. Protestant authors such as P. Maury (*L'eschatologie* [Genève: Labor et Fides, 1959], 45–46) and P. Althaus (*Die letzen Dinge*, 209–20) for the most part maintain the traditional Protestant teaching for same reasons as before, although the latter does reject it altogether: ibid., 210–11. So also does P. Tillich, who speaks of a gradual incorporation into God through death. On this, see H. Wohlgschaft, *Hoffnung angesichts des Todes: das Todesproblem bei Karl Barth und in der zeitgenössischen Theologie des deutschen Sprachraums* (München: F. Schöningh, 1977), 143, 146. On prayer for the dead among Protestants, see F. Heidler, *Die biblische Lehre von der Unsterblichkeit der Seele, Sterben, Tod, ewiges Leben im Aspekt lutherischer Anthropologie*, 189–90.
112. See G. L. Müller, "'Fegfeuer.' Zur Hermeneutik eines umstrittenen Lehrstückes in der Eschatologie," *Theologische Quartalschrift* 166 (1986): 523–41.

nary to the vision of God, which is, however, completely different from the pains of the damned."[113] The *Catechism of the Catholic Church* says as much: "The Church gives the name *Purgatory* to this final purification of the elect, which is entirely different from the punishment of the damned."[114] Generally, it is hazardous to inquire too closely into the nature of the afterlife; purgatory is no exception to this rule. Nonetheless, in the coming pages we shall examine some positions, solidly backed up by theological reflection and spiritual experience, that explain the purpose and characteristics of purgatory, which Dante describes in the simple formula: *a farsi belli*, to bring humans under God's grace to the fullness of splendor and beauty.[115]

The Doctrine of Purgatory according to Thomas Aquinas

According to Thomas, purgatory is a true punishment, to be understood analogously with eternal punishment. For in purgatory there is a double pain, "one of damnation *(damni)* by the retarding of vision, the other of the senses through corporal fire."[116]

It is clear of course that since the souls in purgatory are united with God in charity they have not actually lost God. They are deprived temporarily of the vision of God, which they deeply yearn to enjoy,[117] whom they wish to praise unreservedly. This is a source of great suffering because the situation is brought about by their personal fault, and also because the loss, though temporary, is particularly painful. Humans are created to rejoice in the presence of God; thus there is great pain in being held back as they are on the very point of obtaining their objective. No longer is this pain mitigated by the distracting consolation and tangible comfort of a created world in which God is perceived as hardly necessary. Rather, they experience the bitter taste of their own emptiness because the only One who is in a position to fill it, the only One they yearn to praise, is absent for them.[118]

Aquinas, in line with most Latin theologians,[119] holds that purgatory also involves a pain inflicted on the senses by "fire." If it is understood that the "fire" by

---

113. Congregation for the Doctrine of the Faith, Doc. *Recentiores episcoporum Synodi*, n. 7.

114. *CCC* 1031. So does the Catechism of the Italian Conference of Bishops: "La purificazione dopo l'esistenza terrena non può che essere opera d'amore, da parte di Dio e da parte dell'uomo. Dio, per donarsi all'uomo in modo totale, rimuove ogni ostacolo per dilatare la capacità di accoglimento dell'uomo," in *Signore, da chi andremo? Il catechismo degli adulti* (Roma: Fondazione di religione, 1988), 467.

115. Dante Alighieri, *Divina Commedia: Purgatorium II*, 75.

116. Thomas Aquinas, *Qu. de Purgatorio*, a. 3c: "in purgatorio erit duplex poena: una damni, inquantum scilicet retardantur a divina visione; alia sensus, secundum quod ab igne corporali punientur."

117. Dante Alighieri, *Divina Commedia: Purgatorium V*, 57: God "che del disìo di sé veder ne accora."

118. Catherine of Genova, *Trattato del Purgatorio* (Genova: Vita francescana, 1954), 17. On this work, see F. Holböck, *Die Theologin des Fegefeuers. Hl. Catharina von Genua*, 2nd ed. (Stein am Rhein: Christiana, 1991).

119. See pp. 295–96 above.

which the senses are afflicted corresponds to the *conversio ad creaturas*, the disorderly turning toward creatures, then his claim to the effect that the "fire" of purgatory is one and the same with the "fire" of hell makes sense.[120] He also teaches that, since no conversion or merit is possible after death, purgatory is not a form of expiation or *satisfactio* (Thomas never applies this term to purgatory) that the creature offers the Creator under grace. Some Orthodox authors mistakenly suggest that Catholic theology accepts "satisfaction" in purgatory.[121] Rather it should be considered a kind of *satispassio*, a purification passively received from Christ through the Church, which takes an active part in the sanctification of departed souls.[122] It is interesting to note that, historically speaking, denial of the doctrine of purgatory (and of indulgences) went side by side with denial of the role of the Church in the justification and purification of sinful humanity.[123]

It is commonly held that *three aspects* of sin are purged after death: the guilt of venial sins remaining at the end of life, the inclination of the will toward sin, and the temporal punishment due to sin. In the *first* place, purification obtains the forgiveness of venial sins, which are truly sinful, although they do not separate humans definitively from God. Aquinas holds that this takes place with the first act of perfect love/contrition made after death, when the soul perceives the deformity of sin and the goodness of God.[124] *Second*, the inclination to sin, often called the *fomes peccati*, or concupiscence, is purified. This of course is not sin in the strict sense of the word, but rather "derives from sin and leads to sin."[125] It corresponds to the deeply seated sinful habits that only exceptionally are fully uprooted in this life.[126] The violent separation of humans from the world and from all it contains, through death, certainly contributes toward this aspect of *postmortem* purification.[127] The soul is obliged to recognize God as the only Lord of the universe, and must learn anew to praise and thank him. *Third*, the tempo-

---

120. See pp. 203–4 above.
121. J. Meyendorff says mistakenly that "legalism, which applied to individual human destiny the Anselmian doctrine of 'satisfaction,' is the *ratio theologica* of the Latin doctrine of purgatory," *Byzantine Theology*, 221.
122. See especially F. Suárez, "De purgatorio," in *De poenitentia*, disp. 47, 2:7.
123. This was the case among heretical movements during the Middle Ages (Albigensians, Cathars, and later on, Luther). J. Le Goff says: "These heretics, who do not love the Church, also take the opportunity of denying her any role after death, to ensure that her power does not extend to humans," *La Naissance*, 189.
124. Thomas Aquinas, *De malo*, q. 7, a. 11. Duns Scotus holds they are pardoned at death in virtue of preceding merits: *IV Sent.*, D. 21, a. 1.
125. *DS* 1515 (Council of Trent).
126. Josemaría Escrivá, *The Forge*, n. 312: "Sanctity consists in struggling, in knowing that we have defects and in heroically trying to overcome them. Sanctity, I insist, consists in overcoming those defects—although we will still have defects when we die; for if not, as I have told you, we would become proud."
127. See pp. 272–73 above.

ral punishment due to sin, that is, the disorder introduced into one's own life, into the lives of other people, and even into the created cosmos, by sin. "Contrition certainly cancels sins," says Thomas Aquinas, "but it does not remove the entire debt of punishment due to them. . . . Divine justice requires the re-establishment of the disturbed order through a proportionate punishment. . . . To deny purgatory is, therefore, to blaspheme against divine justice."[128] Whereas each individual must assume personally the pain of purifying the disordered inclination to sin, the temporal punishment due to sin may be compensated for by the prayers of the faithful and the intercession of the Church. As Benedict XVI says, while reflecting on purgatory, "no one lives alone. No one sins alone. No one is saved alone."[129]

As a result, purgatory brings about in those purified a perfect and definitive union with God, with other people, and with the entire cosmos.[130]

Maturation, Temporal Punishment, and the Teaching of Vatican II

Some authors in recent times have suggested that purgatory should be understood not so much as a punishment that is inflicted, but rather as a form of personal maturation of the individual. One such author writes: "This reduction of man [through death] to his essential disposition is simply purgatory. It is man's meeting up with what he is, the concentration of his whole life, a momentary occurrence of self-realization in the abyss of death."[131] This text certainly stresses the need for personal responsibility and involvement on the part of the believer. However, it expresses the doctrine of purgatory inadequately, for it pays little attention to the fact that holiness in the first place requires God's grace, not personal self-purification. More specifically, the explanation of purgatory as self-maturation renders superfluous the help one may receive from others in the Church in overcoming the "temporal punishment" due to the disorder that sins introduced into the created world. It is interesting to note that the specific contribution to the doctrine of purgatory that Vatican Council II wished to make consists in that of the prayer of the Church in favor of the dead.[132] The council accepts Christian faith "in the living communion which exists between us and our brothers who are in the glory of heaven or who are yet being purified after their death."[133]

128. Thomas Aquinas, *S. Th. III, Suppl.*, q. 71, a. 1.

129. *SS* 48. "The lives of others continually spill over into mine: in what I think, say, do and achieve. And conversely, my life spills over in to that of others: for better or for worse. So my prayer for another is not something extraneous to that person, something external, not even after death. So my prayer in the interconnectedness of being, my gratitude to the other—my prayer for him—can play a small part in his purification," ibid.

130. On the "social" side of purgatory, see Y. M.-J. Congar, "Le Purgatoire," 324; J. Ratzinger, *Eschatology*, 231–32.

131. L. Boros, *We Are Future*, 169. See also O. Betz, "Il purgatorio come maturazione in Dio," in *Il cristiano e la fine del mondo*, ed. O. Betz, F. Mussner, and L. Boros (Roma: Paoline, 1969), 173–89.

132. *LG* 50a.   133. Ibid., 51a.

Of course Christians have no certain knowledge about the efficacy of their prayer for the dead, neither in respect of specific people nor in relation to the degree of assistance they are capable of providing. With the book of Wisdom the Church is content to exclaim: "The souls of the just are in the hand of God" (3:1). It is probably fair to say that the prayers of Christians benefit all those who are being purified. Besides, on the basis of the doctrine of the communion of saints,[134] it is commonly held that the souls in purgatory can assist with their prayers those who are still on their earthly pilgrimage.[135]

Purgatory and Spirituality

Augustine,[136] Isidore of Seville,[137] and Thomas Aquinas[138] are all of the opinion that the intensity of the suffering in purgatory is greater than any possible suffering that can take place on earth. For Aquinas, as we saw, this is due principally to the delay in obtaining the vision of God. Many authors hold, however, that the souls in purgatory experience deep consolation from the fact that their salvation is already guaranteed. In a sense their pain and their joy spring from the same source: the closeness of the love of God, which purifies them, comforts them, and helps them appreciate the value of their suffering. Through the intercession of the saints, besides, it is said that those in purgatory obtain the *solatium purgatorii*, the solace of purgatory. This was the opinion of Bernardine of Siena, François Fénelon, Frederick W. Faber, and especially Cardinal John H. Newman in his work *The Dream of Gerontius*.[139] Catherine of Genova, in her *Treatise* on purgatory, speaks often of the happiness experienced by the souls in purgatory, a joy

---

134. Ibid., 49.

135. Gregory of Nazianzen says: "To the dead let us confide our lives and that of those who, having lived in another time, having gone before us, are already in the eternal abode," *Dissertat.*, 7. Julian of Toledo writes that "the souls in purgatory will not be beaten in generosity, and will pay us back petitioning graces and blessings," *Prognost. fut. saec. II*, 26. The same position is held by F. Suárez, *De purgatorio*, D. 47, a. 2. See also St. Alphonsus Maria di Liguori, "Il gran mezzo della preghiera," in *Opere ascetiche*, vol. 2 (Torino: Marietti, 1846), nn. 42–46. St. Josemaría Escrivá writes: "The holy souls in purgatory. Out of charity, out of justice, and out of excusable selfishness—they have such power with God!—remember them often in your sacrifices and in your prayers," *The Way*, n. 571. That the holy souls can pray for us is a common position among theologians. See the classic work of J. B. Walz, *Die Fürbitte der Armen Seelen und ihre Anrufung durch die Gläubigen auf Erden. Ein Problem des Jenseits dogmatisch untersucht und dargestellt* (Freiburg i. B: Herder, 1932). The same position may be found among Orthodox theologians: see J.-C. Larchet, *La vie après la mort*, 241–42. See also A. Minon, "Peut-on prier les âmes du purgatoire?" *Revue Ecclésiastique de Liège* 35 (1948): 329–35; A. Rudoni, *Escatologia* (Torino: Marietti, 1972), 195–96; M. Huftier, "Purgatoire et prière pour les morts," *Esprit et vie* 44 (1972): 609–17; A. Piolanti, *La communione dei santi e la vita eterna*, 283–89. See also A.-M. Roguet, "Les sacrements nous jugent," *Vie spirituelle* 45 (1963): 516–23, who argues against this position.

136. Augustine, *Enn. in Ps.*, 37:3.   137. Isidore, *De ordine creat.*, 14:12.

138. Thomas Aquinas, *Qu. de Purgatorio*, a. 3c.

139. See F. Holböck, *Fegfeuer: Leiden, Freuden und Freunde der armen Seelen*, 2nd ed. (Stein am Rhein: Christiana, 1978).

that is perfectly compatible with the punishment they suffer.[140] John Paul II in his catechesis on purgatory said: "Even if the soul in that passage to heaven had to undergo purification for the remains of sin in purgatory, it is full of light, of certitude, of joy, because it is sure that it belongs to its God forever."[141]

Several spiritual authors have come to appreciate the reality of purgatory through the purification the saints experience in this life. Francis of Assisi, for example, spoke of the joy of purification here on earth.[142] John of the Cross in his *Dark Night of the Soul* carefully mapped the parallels that exist between purification on earth and in purgatory.[143] Speaking of the mystical experience of Christians, the spiritual author Mary Starkey-Greig suggested that "in purgatory we shall all be mystics."[144] Other authors speak of purgatory as a mystery of mercy,[145] as the place of divine love,[146] or say that we need purgatory "to please the good God,"[147] that its existence speaks of the "thirst for the living God."[148]

Even though some contemporary authors hold that purification is instantaneous and coincides with death itself,[149] Catholic tradition generally teaches that the duration and intensity of purgatory will depend on the situation of each person.[150] Following Thomas Aquinas, we may distinguish between the objective

---

140. "Non credo che ci sia una felicità comparabile con quella di un'anima del Purgatorio, eccetto quella dei santi nel paradiso. E questa felicità cresce ogni giorno per l'azione corrispondente di Dio *(corresponsio)* in quell'anima, azione che consuma giorno dopo giorno tutto quello ch'è ostacolo" *Trattato del Purgatorio*, 5.

141. John Paul II, Audience "The Holy Spirit, guarantee of eschatological hope and of final perseverance" (3.7.1991), *Insegnamenti Giovanni Paolo II*, 14, no. 1 (1991): 27–38.

142. "Tanto è il bene che mi aspetto che ogni pena mi è diletto," Francis of Assisi, *Fioretti*, n. 8.

143. John of the Cross, *Noche oscura del alma II*, 7:7. See also the *Llama de amor viva I*, 24. On the purgatorial aspect of the spiritual life in general and the parallel between purification on earth and after death, see L. F. Mateo-Seco, "Purgación y purgatorio en San Juan de la Cruz," *Scripta Theologica* 8 (1976): 233–77. See also U. Barrientos, *Doctrina de San Juan de la Cruz sobre el Purgatorio a la luz de su sistema místico* (Roma: Angelicum, 1959).

144. M. Starkey-Greig, *The Divine Crucible of Charity* (London: Burns, Oates & Washbourne, 1940), 40. On this question, see the classic work of J. Bautz, *Das Fegfeuer: im Anschluss an die Scholastik, mit Bezugnahme auf Mystik und Ascetik dargestellt* (Mainz: Kirchheim, 1883). See also R. Garrigou-Lagrange, *Perfection chrétienne et contemplation* (Paris: Desclée, 1923), 182–83; Y. M.-J. Congar, "Le purgatoire," 319.

145. See G. Lefebure, "Le purgatoire, mystère de miséricorde," *Vie spirituelle* 45 (1963): 143–52.

146. B. Moriconi, "Il purgatorio soggiorno dell'amore," *Ephemerides Carmeliticae* 31 (1980): 539–78.

147. P. de la Trinité, *Il purgatorio. Che ne pensa S. Teresa di Lisieux* (Roma: Teresianum, 1972).

148. See D. Carnovale Guiducci, *Sete del Dio vivente: il purgatorio, preludio alla gioia piena* (Città del Vaticano: Vaticana, 1992).

149. See L. Boros, *The Mystery of Death*, 129–39; H. Rondet, "Immortalité de l'âme ou résurrection de la chair?" *Bulletin de littérature ecclésiastique* 74 (1973): 53–65; G. Martelet, *L'au-delà retrouvé: christologie des fins dernières* (Paris: Desclée, 1975), 140–53; G. Greshake and G. Lohfink, *Naherwartung. Auferstehung. Unsterblichkeit* (Freiburg i. B.: Herder, 1975), 138; K. Lehmann, "Was bleibt vom Fegfeuer?" *Communio* (Deutsche Ausg.) (1980): 236–43, 239–40. Interesting also the reflection of J. Ratzinger, *Eschatology*, 219–20.

150. See E. Brisbois, "Durée du purgatoire et suffrages pour les défunts," *Nouvelle Revue Théologique* 81 (1959): 838–45.

gravity of sins committed and the degree to which such sins are rooted in the will.[151] The liturgical practice of praying for the dead over an extended period of time seems to suggest that an instantaneous purification through death is not acceptable.[152] However, it would be hazardous to speak of "time" in purgatory in a way that corresponds to the time frame obtaining on earth.[153] Doubtless, the suffering of purgatory would extend the time of purification at least on a subjective plane. After all, "with the Lord one day is as a thousand years, and a thousand years as one day" (2 Pt 3:8).[154]

In any case, the doctrine of purgatory offers Christians a vivid reminder of God's mercy and a strong motive for hope in their path toward holiness.[155]

The Christological Aspect of Purification

We have already considered Paul's teaching to the Corinthians on the purification of the life of Christians (1 Cor 3:10–15). The text is articulated in three stages: it speaks of the saving work of Christ, followed by judgment and then "fire."[156] Purification is presented above all as the work of Christ, which reveals the situation of believers and purifies them from every stain of sin. The work of Christ is the work of God, who is depicted in Scripture as a fire that destroys and purifies (Is 66:15–16). "The fire of divine holiness in Christ will reveal the value of the different 'constructions', to the point of destroying what is perishable but also saving the one who strove to build on the foundation that was Christ."[157] Christ's work is one of judgment (in that he seeks conformity with himself in believers) and of purification by fire (because Christ purifies believers by making them conform to

---

151. "Acerbitas poenae proprie respondet quantitati culpae; sed diuturnitas respondet radicationi culpae in subjecto; unde potest contingere quod aliquis diutius moretur qui minus affligitur, et e converso," *Qu. de Purgatorio*, a. 8 ad 1.

152. See pp. 291–93 above.

153. "There is no need to convert earthly time into God's time: in the communion of souls simple terrestrial time is superseded," *SS* 48.

154. Before the liturgical reform that followed Vatican Council II, partial indulgences were calculated on the basis of days. This does not refer of course to time spent in purgatory, but rather to the number of days of canonical penance the particular devotion corresponds to. That those who wear the scapular of Our Lady of Mount Carmel will be freed from purgatory the Saturday after their death (the so-called Sabbatine privilege) has a long and deeply rooted tradition in the Church. See B. Zimmermann, "De Sacro Scapulario Carmelitano," *Analecta Ordinis Carmelitarum Discalceatorum* 2 (1927–28): 70–80; L. Sassi, "Scapulaire," in *Dictionnaire de la Spiritualité* 14 (1990): cols. 390–96, especially 393–94. This privilege is spoken of in the summary of indulgences drawn up by Pope Innocent XI (1678) and by Pius X (July 1908). See also Josemaría Escrivá, *The Way*, n. 500.

155. The divine mercy that purgatory involves serves as a support for the hope of Christians: see K. Reinhardt, "Das Verständnis des Fegfeuers in der neuern Theologie," *Trierer theologische Zeitschrift* 96 (1987): 111–22, especially 120–22.

156. See W. Pannenberg, *Systematic Theology*, vol. 3, 616–20.

157. G. Moioli, *L'"Escatologico" cristiano*, 183.

his life), and as a result of salvation: he forges our likeness to himself—that is, he saves us—by judging and purifying us.

The Christological aspect of purgatory has been especially emphasized by Yves Congar, Hans Urs von Balthasar, and Giovanni Moioli. Pope Benedict XVI refers to it likewise in the encyclical *Spe salvi*.[158] Congar has it that "the mystery of purgatory should be considered in the overall context of the Christian mystery, which is the mystery of the passage of Christ to the Father, through the 'consummation' of his body. This passage, which is that of humanity and has general resurrection as its goal, continues even after the veil of death has fallen, with the three essential elements: purification, liberation and expiation."[159] The same author goes on to insist that purgatory should be understood soteriologically in connection with the doctrine of Christ's descent into hell.[160] Von Balthasar, following Congar, describes purgatory as a "dimension of judgment, as the encounter of the sinner with the 'eyes . . . like a flame of fire, his feet . . . like burnished bronze' (Rv 1:14–15. = Dn 10:6) of Christ."[161] And Moioli sums up this position by saying: "Purgatory would be the expression of the basic meaning of saved death, a kind of participation in the death of Christ, and hence as the definitive destruction of death, in love-charity and suffering."[162]

On the basis of a Christological understanding of purgatory, it is easy to appreciate that once Christ comes in glory at the *Parousia* there will no longer be any need for purgatory. This is the common position of the Church, taught by both Augustine[163] and Thomas Aquinas.[164]

---

158. "Some recent theologians are of the opinion that the fire which both burns and saves is Christ himself, the Judge and Savior. The encounter with him is the decisive act of judgment. Before his gaze all falsehood melts away. This encounter with him, as it burns us, likewise transforms and frees us, allowing us to become truly ourselves. All that we build during our lives can prove to be mere straw, pure bluster, and it collapses. Yet in the pain of this encounter, when the impurity and sickness of our lives become evident to us, there lies salvation. His gaze, the touch of his heart, heals us through an undeniably painful transformation 'as through fire.' But it is a blessed pain, in which the holy power of his love sears through us like a flame, enabling us to become totally ourselves and thus totally of God. In this way the interrelation between justice and grace also becomes clear: the way we live our lives is not immaterial, but our defilement does not stain us for ever if we have at least continued to reach out towards Christ, towards truth and towards love. Indeed, it has already been burned away through Christ's Passion," *SS* 47.

159. Y. M.-J. Congar, "Le Purgatoire," 335–36.

160. Ibid., 284. In the same direction, also the citations of J. Guitton and B. Sesboüé, in G. Gozzelino, *Nell'attesa*, 457–58.

161. See H. U. von Balthasar, *Theodramatik 4/2: Das Endspiel*, 329–37.

162. G. Moioli, *L'"Escatologico" cristiano*, 194.

163. Augustine, *De Civ. Dei XXI*, 16.

164. Thomas Aquinas, *S. Th. III, Suppl.*, q. 74, a. 8 ad 5, on account of the tremendous sufferings the *Parousia* will involve.

11

The Implications of an "Intermediate Eschatology"

> I am hard pressed between the two. My desire is to depart and be with Christ, for that is far better.
> —*Philippians 1:23*

> It shall rest in the Patriarch's bosom, as did Lazarus, hedged round with flowers.
> —*Aurelius Prudentius*[1]

The Dynamic of Individual and Collective Eschatologies

For an extended period of time, it is fair to say, Catholic eschatology paid more attention to the "last things" of the *individual:* death, personal judgment, heaven or hell, beatific vision, personal purification, and so on.[2] It is not of course that other critical elements were excluded. As we have seen throughout the preceding chapters, the individual aspects of Christian eschatology would be meaningless were they not understood in an interpersonal context. Death, for example, involves separation from others. Judgment is centered on our actions with respect to other people. The agent and standard of these actions is Another, Jesus Christ. Heaven and hell are lived in communion with God and with other people, or in separation from them. Furthermore, the different elements that go to make up the *Parousia* in the strict sense (the coming of Christ in glory, resurrection and renewal of the cosmos, universal judgment) were by no means excluded in traditional Catholic eschatology. But it is probably true to say that these collective elements were considered for the most part as accidental adjuncts within a structure centered on the union of the individual with the Divinity.[3] It was common, for example, to speak of the "accidental glory" that beatified souls obtain through resurrection.[4] Theologically speaking, the expression is

---

1. Aurelius Prudentius, *Hymn for the Burial of the Dead*, 149–53.
2. See p. 41, n. 12.
3. On the modern history of eschatology see P. Müller-Goldkuhle, *Die Eschatologie in der Dogmatik des 19. Jahrhunderts* (Essen: Ludgerus; Wingen, 1966), 8–10; I. Escribano-Alberca, *Eschatologie*.
4. On the Scholastic notion of "accidental glory," see Aa.vv., *Sacrae theologiae summa*, 4th ed. (Madrid: Editorial Católica, 1964), 1014–16.

quite legitimate, but the impression may be given that the end of the world is of secondary importance in the study of eschatology, whereas, as we have seen, it sets the scene for eschatology at a fundamental level, and goes to the very heart of New Testament Christology.

From many points of view this emphasis on individual eschatology may be seen as a blessing in disguise, for it provided the basis for an anthropology that valued the individual human being, that did not allow human persons to be considered as replaceable or dispensable parts of an anonymous aggregate. Christian eschatology should reflect—and has traditionally done so—the fact that each human being, destined by God for immortality, is precious and unique. However, this understanding also tended to facilitate a somewhat other-worldly, spiritualistic, individualistic view of human destiny that seemed incapable of inspiring an incisive social ethics, a spirituality deeply involved in transforming the world.

The fact is that Christian appreciation of the intrinsically social nature of being human gradually brought scholars to attempt to widen the scope of the study of eschatology to the hope of the whole Church: the *Parousia*, the coming of the Lord Jesus in glory at the end of time.[5] A greater awareness of the eschatological character of the entire New Testament, the liturgical movement, the awareness of the role of Christian faith and holiness in society, developments of ecclesiology, the universal call to holiness, the urgent need to evangelize and promote justice and peace, all made their contribution to this shift in emphasis. In effect, Christian eschatology, far from promoting an escapist or pietistic attitude to life and to the world, must be in a position to transform it under the power of Christ.[6] Whereas classical manuals of eschatology, both Protestant and Catholic,[7] dealt primarily with an individual eschatology, the emphasis began to shift toward a collective one, centered primarily on the *Parousia*. Among the first Catholic authors to assume this position were Michael Schmaus[8] in 1948 and Romano Guardini some years earlier.[9]

John Paul II, in an extensive 1982 interview with André Frossard, described this process in the following terms.

---

5. The individual and collective aspects of Christian eschatology are bound together, without separation or confusion: see G. Gozzelino, *Nell'attesa*, 306; G. Pattaro, *La svolta antropologica. Un momento forte della teologia contemporanea* (Bologna: EDB, 1991), 42; A. Rudoni, *Introduzione all'escatologia* (Torino: Marietti, 1988), 78–79.

6. E. Troeltsch suggested that eschatology should be the object of preaching and piety, not of study: *Glaubenslehre III* (München-Leipzig: Dunker and Humbolt, 1925), 36.

7. See p. 41, n. 12. See the manual of the Protestant D. Hollaz, *Examen theologicum acroamaticum* (Stargard: 1707), vol. 2, 370–416; vol. 3, § II, chapters 9–10.

8. See M. Schmaus, *Katholische Dogmatik*, vol. 4.2: *Von den letzten Dingen*.

9. See R. Guardini, *The Last Things*.

An "Intermediate Eschatology" 311

It was the Second Vatican Council [1961–65] that helped me, so to speak, to synthesize my personal faith; in the first place Chapter 7 of the constitution Lumen gentium, the one entitled, "The eschatological character of the pilgrim Church and its relation with the Church in heaven." I was already a bishop when I took part in the Council. Before that, I had obviously studied the treatise of the last things . . . dealing with beatitude and the beatific vision. Nevertheless, I think it was the Conciliar constitution on the Church that enabled me to discover the synthesis of this reality for which we hope. . . . The discovery that I made at that time consists in this: whereas previously I envisaged principally the eschatology of man and my personal future in the after-life, which is in the hands of God, the Council constitution shifted the center of gravity toward the Church and the world, and this gave the doctrine of the final end of man its full dimension.[10]

This change of emphasis from an individual, almost private, eschatology to a collective, public one, was accompanied at times and inspired by an excessively horizontal, this-worldly socialization of Christian spirituality and ethics. Personal spirituality tended to be replaced by social *engagement*. A one-track eschatology of an individual and spiritual kind was replaced by a one-track eschatology of a collective and more material kind. As a result, important elements of individual eschatology came to be neglected: particular judgment (replaced by general judgment), condemnation of the unrepentant sinner (replaced by society as a whole as the object of salvation), beatific vision (replaced by communion with humanity), separation of body and soul (replaced by resurrection in the moment of death). The individual was somehow lost in the collective realization of humanity, absorbed by a would-be perfect society.

Paradoxically, one-track eschatologies of an individualist kind are not as far, theologically speaking, from ones of a collectivist kind as one might suppose. A collectivist monism easily replaces an individualist monism, humanity simply taking the place of the human individual, the species replacing the person. Returning to the question of the collective or cosmic aspect of eschatological salvation in chapter 7 of *Lumen gentium*, John Paul II in his 1994 autobiography *Crossing the Threshold of Hope* wrote: "We can ask ourselves if man, with his individual life, his responsibility, his destiny, with his personal eschatological future, his heaven or hell or purgatory, does not end up getting lost in this cosmic dimension. . . . It is necessary to respond honestly by saying yes: To a certain degree man does get lost; so too do preachers, catechists, teachers; and as a result, they no longer have the courage to preach the threat of hell. And perhaps even those who listen to them have stopped being afraid of hell."[11] Likewise, Benedict XVI

---

10. John Paul II and A. Frossard, *"Be Not Afraid!": Pope John Paul II Speaks Out on His Life, His Beliefs, and His Inspiring Vision for Humanity* (New York: St. Martin's Press, 1984), 71–72. See also John Paul II, *Crossing the Threshold of Hope*, 182–87.

11. John Paul II, *Crossing the Threshold of Hope*, 183.

in his encyclical *Spe salvi* speaks of the need to integrate anew the individual and collective aspects of Christian salvation.[12]

The Need to Integrate Individual and Collective Eschatology

From the point of view of Christian faith, no opposition need be posited between the two aspects of eschatology just mentioned.[13] In effect, the individual person not only receives its being and life from other people, but realizes its own potentialities by giving itself to others—even more, by losing itself for the sake of others, following the lead of Christ, who redeemed the world by dying on the cross: "whoever would save his life will lose it; and whoever loses his life for my sake, he will save it" (Lk 9:24).[14] A seamless integration between the two, however, will not be achieved until the end of time. "As we view the resurrection of the dead as an event at the end of the *aeon* that is common to all individuals," observes Wolfhart Pannenberg, "we bind together individual and universal eschatology."[15]

This delicate articulation between individual and collective eschatology finds an important expression in the proper understanding of what has come to be known in twentieth-century theology as the question of "intermediate eschatology," that space or time that elapses between death (which represents the culmination of the individual's life) and resurrection (the culmination of the life of humanity as a whole). In a one-track eschatology of an individual kind the fact of an intermediate eschatology is taken for granted, but considered practically irrelevant, since the end of time will add little or nothing, anthropologically or theologically speaking, to salvation. A one-track eschatology of a collective kind, conversely, which reduces everything to the *Parousia*, eliminates any kind of intermediate eschatology from the opposite direction, by emptying the role of the individual, whose life culminates at death. The one renders an intermediate eschatology irrelevant; the other virtually abolishes it.

---

12. For Christians, "salvation has always been considered a 'social' reality. . . . This real life, towards which we try to reach out again and again, is linked to a lived union with a 'people,' and for each individual it can only be attained within this 'we.' It presupposes that we escape from the prison of our 'I,' because only in the openness of this universal subject does our gaze open out to the source of joy, to love itself—to God," *SS* 14.

13. The continuity between the individual and collective dimensions of eschatology (and thus between death and resurrection) is at the heart of many recent studies: J. L. Ruiz de la Peña, *Imagen de Dios. Antropología teológica fundamental* (Santander: Sal Terrae, 1988), 149; G. Haeffner, "Jenseits des Todes. Überlegungen zur Struktur der christlichen Hoffnung," *Stimmen der Zeit* 193 (1975): 773–84, especially 777; G. Greshake, "Theologiegeschichtliche und systematische Untersuchungen zum Verständnis der Auferstehung," in *Resurrectio Mortuorum. Zum theologischen Verständnis der leiblichen Auferstehung*, ed. G. Greshake and J. Kremer, 2nd ed. (Darmstadt: Wissenschaftliche Buchgesellschaft, 1992), 252.

14. *CAA* 187–231, especially 227–30.

15. W. Pannenberg, *Systematic Theology*, vol. 3, 578.

An "Intermediate Eschatology" 313

In 1979 the Congregation for the Doctrine of the Faith prepared a document with the express purpose of proposing anew "the Church's teaching in the name of Christ especially in respect of what takes place between the death of the Christian and final resurrection."[16]

We shall consider the question[17] under the following three headings: intermediate eschatology in the context of Protestant theology; the theory of "resurrection in the moment of death" and its drawbacks; the underlying need to affirm the existence of the human soul.

Intermediate Eschatology in Protestant Theology

The possibility of eliminating "intermediate eschatology," understood as a space or time that extends from death to resurrection, began to consolidate in nineteenth-century Protestant biblical theology.

De-Hellenizing Christianity: The Exile of the Soul

With a view to promoting a definitive de-Hellenization of Christian theology, several Protestant authors attempted to put aside the notion of the human "soul." We have considered this in chapter 1.[18] The idea of a spiritual, subsistent, immortal human core surviving death and living on forever came to be considered as an unwarranted import from Platonic thought into Christian theology. Although other Protestant authors had prepared the way,[19] this thesis was defended openly by the Reformed theologian Oscar Cullmann in a famous 1955 conference entitled *Immortality of the Soul or Resurrection of the Dead?*[20] Cullmann claimed that the key Christian eschatological doctrine is not the immortal soul, but rather final resurrection. In the mind of Christians, however, the former had come to occupy the place of the latter. According to Cullmann, Christian understanding of death and resurrection was "determined entirely by the history of salvation . . . and is incompatible with the Greek credence in the immortality of the soul."[21]

However, Protestant authors on the whole did hold to the realism of the *Parousia* as a future, public event in which Christ will return to raise up the dead and judge humanity. That is to say, death of the individual and final resurrection are distinguished in time from one another. If this is the case, then, what situation obtains between the two events? What remains of the human being if there is

---

16. *Recentiores episcoporum Synodi*, praef., *in fine*.
17. On the following section, see my study *La muerte y la esperanza*, 75–96.
18. See pp. 19–22.
19. Especially A. von Harnack, P. Althaus, K. Barth.
20. See O. Cullmann, *Immortalité de l'âme ou résurrection des morts?*
21. Ibid., 18.

no such thing as an immortal separated soul? To these questions, Protestant authors offered three possible solutions.[22]

The *first*, attributable to Carl Stange[23] and Adolf von Schlatter,[24] and to some degree Helmut Thielicke,[25] Werner Elert,[26] and Eberhard Jüngel,[27] suggests that death involves the complete elimination of the individual, that is, "total death" (*Ganztod*).[28] Death is judgment on sin and involves the elimination of the sinner. "With death we are completely taken up," Althaus writes. "Body and soul both disappear. Death is the collapse of man into a bottomless pit. . . . It is an exit into nothingness."[29] Jüngel openly says that "at death man is annihilated."[30] As a result, resurrection can be understood only as a new creation of the whole man. There is no intermediate eschatology because the human being no longer exists between death and resurrection.

Other authors, such as Karl Barth[31] and Emil Brunner,[32] have suggested a *second* solution to the dilemma. Death is indeed distinguished from resurrection, but, they say, the former places humans in the sphere of the divine, and therefore outside time. Objectively, then, there is an intermediate eschatology, but subjectively there is none. Each person experiences resurrection as taking place in the moment of their death. Several Catholic authors likewise follow this "atemporal" understanding of intermediate eschatology.[33]

A *third* position is suggested by Oscar Cullmann[34] and others[35] to the effect

---

22. See C. Pozo, *La teología del más allá*, 167–83; M. Bordoni and N. Ciola, *Gesù nostra speranza*, 111–26.
23. See C. Pozo, *La teología del más allá*, 176–77.
24. Ibid., 170.
25. See H. Thielicke, *Tod und Leben. Studien zur christlichen Anthropologie*, 2nd ed. (Tübingen: Mohr, 1946). On this work, see C. Pozo, *La teología*, 176, n. 45.
26. See W. Elert, *Der christliche Glaube: Grundlinien der lutherischen Dogmatik*, 3rd ed. (Hamburg: Furche, 1956). On his position, see H. Wohlgschaft, *Hoffnung angesichts des Todes*, 131–37.
27. See E. Jüngel, *Tod*.
28. Some Catholic authors seem likewise to hold this position: P. Laín Entralgo, for example, who was horrified by the notion of the separated soul, according to J. L. Ruiz de la Peña, *La pascua de la creación*, 273–74; also X. Zubiri, in ibid., 274. See also J.-M. Pohier, *Concilium* 11 (1975): 352–62.
29. P. Althaus, *Die letzen Dinge*, 83.
30. E. Jüngel, *Tod*, 140.
31. See K. Barth, *Church Dogmatics* III/2, 426–36; *Die Auferstehung der Toten*.
32. See E. Brunner, *Das Ewige als Zukunft und Gegenwart* (Zürich: Zwingli, 1953).
33. For example O. Betz, *Die Eschatologie in der Glaubensunterweisung* (Würzburg: Echter, 1965), 208–10; J. L. Ruiz de la Peña, *L'altra dimensione*, 335–84; G. Biffi, *Linee di escatologia cristiana*, 97–99; K. Rahner, "The Intermediate State," in *Theological Investigations*, vol. 17 (London: Darton, Longman, and Todd, 1981); C. Tresmontant, *Problèmes du christianisme* (Paris: Seuil, 1980), 102; F.-J. Nocke, *Eschatologie*, 70–71; 115–25; H. U. von Balthasar, *Theodramatik* 4/2: *Das Endspiel*, 315–37; J. B. Libânio and M. C. L. Bingemer, *Escatologia cristã* (Petrópolis: Vozes, 1985), 214–24.
34. See O. Cullmann, *L'immortalité de l'âme*.
35. See P. H. Menoud, *Le sort des trépassés d'après le Nouveau Testament*, 2nd ed. (Neuchâtel: Delachaux

that the "interior man" survives between death and resurrection, in a transitory, imperfect state of dormition. This survival is accounted for by a special intervention of the Holy Spirit in the believer. The idea of an intermediate state as an extended period of sleep may be found in Scripture[36] and was openly taught by Luther.[37]

The Theological Underpinnings

Several observations may be made on the positions assumed by Protestant authors.

First, the living reality of intermediate eschatology, the communion of saints, the "throbbing vault" as Gabriel Marcel calls it, which is central to Catholic ecclesiology, liturgy, and spirituality, is virtually eliminated. Little or no space is left for the intercession and protection of Our Lady and the saints, for the heavenly liturgy and the doctrine of purgatory.[38] It may be noted that although some early Christian authors have suggested that the period between death and resurrection is one of sleep, this has not been the common position.[39]

Second, the authors mentioned apply for the most part the principle of *sola Scriptura*.[40] In effect, Scripture speaks much more about resurrection of the dead than it does about immortality, and speaks even less of the soul and its spirituality. It is not difficult to arrive at the conclusion, therefore, that the soul be considered as a Platonic construct artificially grafted onto the Christian substance. However, apart from the fact that the soul and its immortality is spoken of in the book of Wisdom,[41] the Old Testament speaks openly of the survival through death of the shades (*refa'im*) of human beings,[42] well before the doctrine of resurrection begins to occupy its rightful, central place.[43] In the strict sense, immortality of the soul is a Platonic concept and as such belongs to a dualistic vision of things. However, the Christian doctrine of the soul[44] is as different from the Platonic as the Council of Nicea's understanding of the *Logos* is from the Neo-

---

et Niestlé, 1966); J. J. von Allmen, "Mort," in *Vocabulaire biblique* (Neuchâtel: Delachaux et Niestlé, 1954), 187. See also the Catholic A. Hulsbosch, "Die Unsterblichkeit der Seele," *Trierer theologische Zeitschrift* 78 (1966): 296–304.

36. See pp. 84–85, 94–95.

37. M. Luther, *Resolutiones Lutherianae super propositionibus suis Lipsiae disputi*, in WA 2,422. P. Hoffmann, *Die Toten in Christus*, 237–38, does not accept this position.

38. Some Protestant authors are aware of this. See A. Ahlbrecht, *Tod und Unsterblichkeit*, 139–45.

39. Jerome rejected the position of Vigilantius—whom he ironically nicknamed Dormitantius—who had adopted this position: *Ep.* 109:1; *Contra Vigilantium*, 6 and 17. See also DS 3223.

40. See my study "*Sola Scriptura o tota Scriptura?* Una riflessione sul principio formale della teologia protestante," in *La Sacra Scrittura, anima della teologia*, ed. M. Tábet (Città del Vaticano: Vaticana, 1999), 147–68.

41. See pp. 80–81.   42. See pp. 79–80.
43. See pp. 84–86.   44. See my article "Anima."

platonic *Logos* of the Arians. For the Christian, the soul is temporarily separable from the body and will be united with it once more at resurrection; whereas for the Platonist, the soul is destined to be separated forever from the body once its purification is complete. As we have seen above, death, that is, separation of the soul from the body, according to Christian faith, is the result of sin,[45] but for the Platonist it constitutes the supreme moment of liberation and salvation. The fact that the Church assumed Platonic terminology does not mean it a-critically assumed Platonic philosophical content. Israel was the chosen people, but Aramaic was not the chosen language, or Judaism the chosen culture. All in all, therefore, it would be simplistic to distinguish between Jewish monism and Hellenic dualism as some of these authors tend to do.[46]

A *third* factor should be kept in mind to appreciate the Protestant position: the central doctrine of "justification by faith." Human beings, being created, sinful and mortal, are not in a position to contribute anything to their own salvation, because to do so would be to pretentiously deny the transcendence and sovereignty of God, as well as fallen human nature. To hold that humans have an immortal soul, it would seem, would be tantamount to saying they are already saved.[47] For God alone is immortal, Barth argues, citing 1 Timothy 6:16.[48] It should be said, however, that if the soul is incorruptible "by nature," this is entirely due to God's free creating action.[49] Historically speaking, when Protestants denied the existence of the immortal soul in order to be faithful to Scripture, they were reacting for the most part against an autonomous understanding of the soul typical of some modern philosophers.[50] Ratzinger states that "the idea of the soul as found in Catholic liturgy and theology up to the Second Vatican Council

---

45. See pp. 260–65.

46. This is a basic thesis of M. Guerra, *Antropologías y teología* (Pamplona: Eunsa, 1976), 370. G. W. E. Nickelsburg, *Resurrection, Immortality and Eternal Life*, 177–80, does not accept the position of Cullmann that opposes the Hellenic and the Jewish.

47. On this way of focusing the problem, see H. Thielicke, *Tod und Leben*, Annex 4; A. Ahlbrecht, *Tod und Unsterblichkeit*, 112–20; E. Jüngel, *Tod*, chapter 4.

48. See K. Barth, *Die Auferstehung der Toten*.

49. Thomas Aquinas, *II Sent.*, D. 19, q. 1, a. 1 ad 7; *De Anima*, a. 14 ad 19; *S. Th. I*, q. 75, a. 6 ad 2. J. Ratzinger, *Eschatology*, 150–53, speaks of a "dialogical immortality." On this concept in Ratzinger's thought, see the study of G. Nachtwei, *Dialogische Unsterblichkeit*, referred to by J. Ratzinger, *Eschatology*, 267–70.

50. The Platonic and Idealistic notion of the immortality of the soul used by these authors is a far cry from the Christian understanding: see J. Pieper, *Tod und Unsterblichkeit*, 169–88; W. Pannenberg, *Systematic Theology*, vol. 3, 532–33. Kant and others took the resurrection of Jesus as something symbolic, as a figurative way of expressing the notion of immortality: ibid., 533–34. Ratzinger (*Eschatology*, 140) considers the Christian understanding of the soul as antithetical to the "pure" Greek Renaissance understanding of immortality that preceded the modern one, in particular that of P. Pomponazzi, whose doctrine was rejected at Lateran Council V (1513).

An "Intermediate Eschatology" 317

has as little to do with [Greek] antiquity as has the idea of the resurrection."[51] Thus there is no a priori theological reason for denying the soul's existence and immortality, as several Protestant authors nowadays have come to recognize.[52]

From the anthropological standpoint, a *fourth* difficulty may be raised with the Protestant account of intermediate eschatology. The authors in question for the most part hold that humans do survive, temporarily, between death and resurrection, but in God. In the case of the defenders of "total death," *Ganztod*, resurrection is a form of re-creation, for God is thought to create the person anew. Yet if God does this, it can only be on the basis of the essence (or *eidos*) of the person in question, which God in some way retains as living memory. Something of a kind is present in the doctrine of the atemporality of the next life typical of Barth and Brunner. Coincidence of two distinct events—in this case death and resurrection—is possible only in God, for whom time does not exist, but not in humans, in whom finite acts succeed one another. It is traditional to say that spiritual beings (angels, for example) experience some kind of succession in their actions, what is often called *aeviternitas*.[53] Simultaneity of death and resurrection, conversely, could not but involve humans being absorbed in some way into God's own life.[54] Lastly, the position of Cullmann moves in the same direction in that the survival of a human nucleus between death and resurrection is due, he says, to a special intervention of God's Spirit. "The Holy Spirit is a gift which cannot be lost with death," he says.[55] For Cullmann what lives on at death is the Holy Spirit as such; but what is left of the human being itself? The difficulty arises here specifically in respect of the survival and immortality of the damned. If the Holy Spirit is not present in their lives at death, how can they be said to survive? Either

---

51. J. Ratzinger, *Eschatology*, 150.

52. Pannenberg states: "Early Christian theology rightly greeted the Platonic idea of the immortality of the soul with great skepticism. . . . It seemed to be the expression of an arrogant equality with God such as characterizes human sin," *Systematic Theology*, vol. 3, 561; 570. Having at first denied the doctrine of the immortal soul, P. Althaus initiated a certain return to it in his important study: "Retraktationen zur Eschatologie," *Theologische Literaturzeitung* 75 (1950): 253–60. "There is affinity between philosophy and Biblical wisdom as regards immortality," he says. For this reason "Christian theology . . . has no need to combat 'immortality' as such." Besides, "the idea of divine judgment does not require that humans be ontologically annihilated at death," ibid., 256. Likewise the Lutheran author F. Heidler considers that the immortality of the soul may be demonstrated: see *Die biblische Lehre von der Unsterblichkeit der Seele, Sterben, Tod, ewiges Leben*. For a recent study of the topic among Protestants, see C. Hermann, *Unsterblichkeit der Seele durch Auferstehung. Studien zu den anthropologischen Implikationen der Eschatologie* (Göttingen: Vandenhoeck and Ruprecht, 1997).

53. See ch. 6, n. 169.

54. For a critique of atemporalism, see W. Künneth, *Theologie der Auferstehung* (München: Claudius, 1951), 230–35. According to Cullmann (*Immortalité de l'âme*, 66–67) and Ahlbrecht (*Tod und Unsterblichkeit*, 139–45), atemporalism draws not on Scripture but on a doubtful philosophy.

55. O. Cullmann, *Immortalité de l'âme*, 75.

all are saved by the power of the Holy Spirit, a position some authors do countenance,[56] or the condemned are annihilated, a position assumed by other authors who share Cullmann's view,[57] but decidedly problematic, as we already saw.[58]

The position adopted by Protestant authors responds also to the fact that Protestant theology on the whole has tended to refer eschatology entirely to the future, specifically to the end of the world.[59] Besides, the way in which Protestant authors have presented the problem suggests what might be called a "metaphysical deficit," in that they do not give sufficient weight to the human person as such, as a created spiritual being, distinguishable from the immediate workings of grace and sin.[60] In effect, Protestant theology tends to focus on the person exclusively in the context of salvation.[61] Luther himself said that *fides facit personam*,[62] "faith makes the person." Emil Brunner, for example, said that to be a person comes about in the very act of responding to the word of God.[63] Affirmations of this kind tend easily to undervalue the created dignity and originality of the human person, of each and every human being.[64] Other authors, such as Helmut Thielicke, realized the danger of the tendency to reduce the person to a purely interpersonal faith dynamic.[65]

The Theory of "Resurrection in the Moment of Death"

Whereas insistence on the realism of the future *Parousia* is a common characteristic among Protestant authors,[66] others, such as Rudolf Bultmann, take

---

56. See pp. 218–21.

57. For example, P. H. Menoud, *Le sort des trépassés*, 79. See pp. 208–9 above on the possibility of the annihilation of the damned at death.

58. See pp. 209–10.   59. See G. Gozzelino, *Nell'attesa*, 226.

60. The doctrine of total death (*Ganztod*) finds a certain precedent in a theory called "thnetopsiquism," taught by some Arabic authors of the first centuries after Christ, according to Eusebius of Caesarea: *Hist. Eccl.* 6, 37. According to them, Eusebius tells us, with death "the human soul dies in the supreme moment along with the body, and corrupts with it, but it will come back to life, with the body, one day, at the moment of resurrection," ibid.

61. On this issue, see the work of H. Mühlen, *Das Vorverständnis von Person und die evangelisch-katholische Differenz. Zum Problem der theologischen Denkform* (Aschendorff: Münster, 1965) and the studies of C. Morerod, "La philosophie dans le dialogue catholique-luthérien," *Freiburger Zeitschrift für Philosophie und Theologie* 44 (1997): 219–40; *Œcuménisme et philosophie: questions philosophiques pour renouveler le dialogue* (Paris: Parole et silence, 2004).

62. M. Luther, *Zirkulardisputation de veste nuptiali*, in *WA* 39/1,293.

63. See E. Brunner, *Dogmatique*, vol. 2 (Genève: Labor et fides, 1965), 69. Of the same author, see *Wahrheit als Begegnung: sechs Vorlesungen über das christliche Wahrheitsverständnis* (Berlin: Furche, 1938).

64. On the "metaphysical deficit" in Cullmann, see G. Gozzelino, *Nell'attesa*, 257–58.

65. See H. Thielicke, "Die Subjekthälftigkeit des Menschen," in *Der Mensch als Bild Gottes*, ed. L. Scheffczyk (Darmstadt: Wissenschaftliche Buchgesellschaft, 1969), 352–58.

66. This is clear in the works of W. Pannenberg, *Systematic Theology*, vol. 3, 578–80, and also in J. Moltmann, *The Coming of God*, 259–319. On the latter, *CAA* 50–53.

An "Intermediate Eschatology" 319

an different view on the matter.[67] He says quite openly that whenever the New Testament speaks of the *Parousia* or its equivalents, it is not speaking of the end of time, which is of no theological interest, but of *thanatos*, or death of the individual.[68] There is no end to time, in the classic sense of the word, but just an end to individual lives, one after the other. This position is a direct application of Bultmann's understanding of the death of Christ as the moment in which his resurrection took place.

The Development of a Theory

Bultmann's understanding of death and resurrection has left a mark on some Catholic scholars.[69] The exegete Anton Vögtle, for example, was quite content to hold that the New Testament deals not with an end to the world that takes place by the power of God, but rather with the end of each human person.[70] Likewise, according to Gerhard Lohfink, it is quite acceptable to identify the *Parousia* with the encounter that each person will have with God at death.[71] At a dogmatic level, the notion was furthered by Ghisbert Greshake, who in the late 1960s began to speak of resurrection taking place *in the very moment of death*.[72] In a study coauthored with Greshake,[73] Lohfink says that human beings are one with the world and with history, and when they are presented before God at death, the world and history come to an end.[74] In this way, humans when they die experi-

---

67. See pp. 51–53.
68. R. Bultmann, "A Reply to the Theses of J. Schniewind," *Kerygma and Myth*, 114.
69. See, for example, J. M. Hernández Martínez, "La asunción de María como paradigma de escatología cristiana," *Ephemerides Mariologicae* 51 (2000): 249–71; G. Greshake, "Auferstehung im Tod. Ein parteiischer Rückblick auf eine theologische Diskussion," *Theologie und Philosophie* 73 (1998): 538–57; M.-É. Boismard, *Faut-il encore parler de "resurrection"?*; V. M. Fernández, "Inmortalidad, cuerpo y materia. Una esperanza para mi carne," *Aquinas* 78 (2001): 405–37; G. Gozzelino, "'Io sono stato conquistato da Cristo' (Fil 3, 12): il compimento individuale nella realizzazione del disegno di Dio. Dialettica dell'escatologia individuale con l'escatologia collettiva," *Annali di Studi Religiosi* 2 (2001): 313–29; F. Brancato, "Lo stadio *intermedio*—Status quaestionis," *Sacra Doctrina* 47 (2002): 5–80. Other references may be found in G. Gozzelino, *Nell'attesa*, 468, n. 201.
70. A. Vögtle, *Das Neue Testament und die Zukunft des Kosmos* (Düsseldorf: Patmos, 1970).
71. Lohfink holds that the *Parousia* should be considered as an encounter of each one at the moment of death: G. Greshake and G. Lohfink, *Naherwartung. Auferstehung. Unsterblichkeit*. See G. Canobbio, *Fine o compimento?* 213. The message of the New Testament is one of salvation, Greshake and Lohfink hold, and is not scientific in character. Greshake's position is close to Vögtle's.
72. See G. Greshake, *Auferstehung der Toten. Ein Beitrag zur gegenwärtigen theologischen Diskussion über die Zukunft der Geschichte* (Essen: Ludgerus, 1969). Later on, Greshake rectified his position somewhat: "Auferstehung im Tod" (1998). See also L. Boff, *A Ressurreição de Cristo: a nossa ressurreição na morte* (Petrópolis: Vozes, 1975).
73. See G. Greshake and G. Lohfink, *Naherwartung. Auferstehung. Unsterblichkeit*.
74. "Man in fact is a 'piece' of the world and of history, and when faced with God, the world and history reach their fulfillment: at death man experiences not only his own *eschaton*, but also the *eschaton* of history in general," ibid., 72.

ence at one and the same time their own *eschaton* or "end," as well as the *eschaton* of the world and history in general. It would seem that Lohfink's position is related to the theory of "thoroughgoing" eschatology.[75] The fact that Christianity went ahead and prospered in spite of the fact that the promised imminent "end" did not arrive only goes to show that God's sovereignty, made present in the resurrection, stands in no need of being manifested at the end of time, he observes, but rather during history in the dying and rising up of each and every person.[76]

In general terms, it may be said that Protestant theologians pay more attention to what God does for humanity in Christ, and less to what humans do for themselves. Catholic scholars, conversely, tend to pay particular attention to the ontological consistency of creation and human beings, before and after death, to the realism of grace received in and through the "now" of the Church, and not so much to the promised, future, *eschaton*. Given, besides, the traditional Catholic doctrine of the reception of eternal retribution *mox post mortem*, "straight after death,"[77] given the generalized diffidence toward the notion of a separated immortal soul, it is understandable that the theory of "resurrection in the moment of death" came, for a period, to be widely accepted.[78]

The theory was considered, however, in the 1979 document of the Congregation for the Doctrine of the Faith on eschatology, already mentioned. The central text reads as follows: "The Church holds to the survival and subsistence, after death, of a spiritual element with consciousness and will, in such a way that the same human 'I' subsists, even without the complement of one's own body. To designate this element, the Church uses the term 'soul', widely used in Sacred Scripture and Tradition."[79]

Likewise the theory has been criticized by both Protestants such as Wolfhart Pannenberg[80] and Catholics such as Juan Alfaro,[81] Joseph Ratzinger,[82] and others.[83] The following five issues may be considered.

75. See pp. 46–50.
76. See N. Lohfink, "Zur Möglichkeit christlicher Naherwartung," in G. Greshake and G. Lohfink, *Naherwartung. Auferstehung. Unsterblichkeit*, 38–81, here 78–80.
77. See pp. 279–80.
78. See pp. 313–18.
79. *Recentiores episcoporum Synodi*, n. 3. Emphasis added.
80. See W. Pannenberg, *Die Auferstehung Jesu und die Zukunft des Menschen* (München: Minerva, 1978), 14–18; *Systematic Theology*, vol. 3, 577–79.
81. See J. Alfaro, "La resurrección de los muertos en la discusión teológica sobre el porvenir de la historia," *Gregorianum* 52 (1971): 537–54.
82. See J. Ratzinger, *Eschatology*, 241–60, and "Zwischen Tod und Auferstehung," *Communio* (Deutsche Ausg.) 9 (1980): 209–23.
83. For a presentation of the position of Greshake and Lohfink, and a summary of the critique, see G. Canobbio, "Fine o compimento? Considerazioni su un'ipotesi escatologica." See also A. Ziegenaus,

The Meaning of "Resurrection"

From the strictly exegetical, liturgical, and historical standpoint, the Christian notion of "resurrection"[84] may be applied to three moments of life: to baptism, in which humans die with Christ in order to rise up to a life of grace;[85] to the present moment of Christian conversion (Col 3:2; Phil 3:10) and Eucharistic life (1 Cor 11:26); and lastly, to resurrection at the end of time, for the judgment of living and dead.[86] When Paul writes to the Romans, he expressly distinguishes, in temporal terms, between spiritual death and final resurrection. "For if *we have been* united with him in a death like his, *we shall* certainly be united with him in a resurrection like his" (Rom 6:5).[87] From the historical and exegetical standpoint there is no reason to argue that the notion of "resurrection" may be applied precisely to the moment of death.

In this respect Joseph Ratzinger observes "that early Christian proclamation never identified the destiny of those who die before the Parousia with the quite special event of the resurrection of Jesus. The special event depended on Jesus' unique and irreducible position in the history of salvation."[88] Marcello Bordoni points out that if we intend to be coherent with Paul's theology, the "social" character of death excludes "the idea of a process of resurrection which is actuated throughout history through a series of individual resurrections of each one in the moment of their death."[89] Walter Kasper writes: "The perfection of the individual and that of all of mankind cannot be complete until the cosmos, too, is included in that completion."[90] The Anglican exegete J. A. T. Robinson, in a classic study on the human body dated well before the recent controversy, said that "it would be a mistake to consider the writings of Paul with the modern idea that corporal resurrection is in some way related to the moment of death.... In no

---

"Auferstehung im Tod: das geeigneter Denkmodell?" *Münchener Theologische Zeitschrift* 28 (1977): 109–32, and *Katholische Dogmatik*, vol. 8: *Die Zukunft der Schöpfung in Gott: Eschatologie* (Aachen: MM, 1996), 65–135; C. Marucci, "Resurrezione nella morte? Esposizione e critica di una recente proposta," in *Morte e sopravvivenza*, ed. G. Lorizio, 289–316; my study *La muerte y la esperanza*, 75–96; G. Gozzelino, *Nell'attesa*, 469, n. 199.

84. On the meaning of term "resurrection," see G. Greshake and J. Kremer, *Resurrectio Mortuorum*, 8–15; M. J. Harris, *Raised Immortal: Resurrection and Immortality in the New Testament* (London: Marshall, Morgan and Scott, 1986), 269–72.

85. See Rom 6:3–8; 1 Cor 15:29; Col 2:12; 1 Pt 1:3; 3:21; Rv 20:5.

86. See Jn 6; Acts 24:15; 1 Cor 15:12–19.

87. Texts used to justify resurrection in the moment of death include: Lk 23:43; Phil 1:23; 2 Cor 5:8; 1 Thes 5:10; and Col 3:1–4. As they stand, however, these texts simply teach that the just are rewarded after death.

88. J. Ratzinger, *Eschatology*, 111–12.

89. M. Bordoni and N. Ciola, *Gesù nostra speranza*, 251.

90. W. Kasper, "Hope in the Final Coming," 378.

part of the New Testament is there to be found an essential relationship between resurrection and the moment of death. The key moments [of Christian resurrection] . . . are Baptism and the Parousia."[91]

Resurrection "on the Third Day"

Some suggest that when Scripture speaks of Jesus rising from the dead "on the third day" (1 Cor 15:4), this should be taken not in a chronological sense, but in a theological one. The expression "the third day," it is said, provides a plastic way of expressing the power and transcendence of God's saving action, as he establishes his Sovereignty over the whole of creation.[92] However, this interpretation of the scriptural text, though not wholly mistaken,[93] is somewhat one-sided, in that it does not sufficiently reflect Christian faith in the resurrection of the Lord. In effect, the latter is based on the "essential sign" of the empty tomb.[94] "If Jesus had risen on the Cross," Irenaeus noted in his critique of Gnostic soteriology, "without any doubt he would immediately have gone up to heaven abandoning his body on the earth."[95]

Besides, the Lord's resurrection is celebrated every Sunday in commemoration of Easter Day, the third day after the death of Jesus, and not on Good Friday (the day Jesus died) nor on Holy Saturday (an a-liturgical day within the Paschal Triduum that expresses the "silence" of the descent of Jesus into the underworld).[96] The Church in her liturgy celebrates primarily the actions of God on the earth, the *magnalia Dei,* and not so much the faith of the people that these actions give rise to. Faith does not produce the event; rather the event, historically inserted by God within created time, creates the faith that is celebrated by

---

91. J. A. T. Robinson, *The Body,* 88–89. The same position is held by F.-X. Durrwell, *La résurrection de Jésus, mystère de salut. Étude biblique,* 2nd ed. (Le Puy: X. Mappus, 1954), 300–301, and by J. Blenkinsopp, "Theological Synthesis and Hermeneutic Conclusion," *Concilium* (English ed.) 6 (1970/10): 144–60.

92. The position was defended especially by K. Lehmann, *Auferweckt am dritten Tag nach der Schrift: exegetische und fundamentaltheologische Studien zu 1 Kor. 15, 3b–5,* 2nd ed. (Freiburg i. B.: Herder, 1968). G. Greshake, *Auferstehung im Tod,* 549–52, taking his cue from Adolf Kopling and Hans Kessler, holds that the theological basis for resurrection in the moment of death is precisely the dynamic of the death/resurrection of Jesus. The "third day" refers to Jesus showing *us* his glory: ibid., 550. See also G. Greshake and G. Lohfink, *Naherwartung,* 141–46; M. Riebl, *Auferstehung Jesu in der Stunde seines Todes?: zur Botschaft von Mt 27,51b–53* (Stuttgart: Katholisches Bibelwerk, 1978).

93. In the Old Testament, the "third day" often refers to the realization of a decisive and imminent event, although the exact date is unknown: Gn 22:4; 42,17–18; Ex 19:10–11,16; 2 Sm 1:2; 2 Kgs 20:5; Est 5:1; Jon 1:17; Hos 6:2.

94. See the studies of O'Collins and Davis, in S. T. Davis, D. Kendall, and G. O'Collins, eds., *The Resurrection.* Also *CCC* 640, 657, and pp. 89–91 above.

95. Irenaeus, *Adv. Haer. V,* 31:1.

96. In Vatican Council II, we read: "By a tradition handed down from the apostles, which took its origin from the very day of Christ's resurrection, the Church celebrates the paschal mystery every seventh day, which day is appropriately called the Lord's Day or Sunday," *Sacrosanctum Concilium,* n. 106.

the Church. Indeed, the Church's Creed openly professes that Jesus rose "on the third day."

This displacement until the third day after the death of Jesus not only of his apparitions but of the very resurrection event constitutes, in fact, an important theological foundation for the possibility of an intermediate eschatology. For we see that even in the case of Christ, death and resurrection do not coincide in time.[97] Thus "the realism of the Incarnation and the Resurrection of Christ demand the realism of the *Parousia*."[98] Christoph Schönborn explains this as follows: "The first thing we have to infer from the Resurrection of Jesus for our own resurrection is the clear distinction between death and resurrection. . . . It is therefore irreconcilable with faith to assert that the resurrection happens in death. . . . [It] contradicts the fact of Jesus' deposition and the 'Resurrection on the third day.'"[99]

The Anthropological Relevance of End-Time Resurrection

The idea of resurrection at the very moment of death does not fit in with Christian faith and hope in a final resurrection for all humans together at the end of time. As we already saw,[100] hope in the resurrection of the dead, understood as the definitive revelation of the glory of the children of God, universal judgment, the unique and final end of humanity, the very target and purpose of human history, is what underpins an integral Christian anthropology,[101] expressing and defending the freedom, historicity, social condition, and bodily character of humans. Juan Alfaro says that apocalyptic texts demonstrate that "humanity as community and history as totality are under the saving sovereignty of God in Christ."[102] Should there be no absolute end to history, he says, "God would never be Lord of history as a whole, but would ever be on the way towards dominion over history."[103] According to Juan Luis Ruiz de la Peña, the idea of resurrection in the moment of death would simply involve the privatization of the *eschaton*.[104]

---

97. C. Pozo (*La teología del más allá*, 248–65) notes that several manifestations of intermediate eschatology are to be found in the New Testament: for example, Lk 16:19–31 (the rich man and Lazarus); Lk 23:42–43 (the good thief). Also Paul speaks of being "with Christ" after death, especially in 1 Cor 5:1–10.

98. J. L. Ruiz de la Peña, *La pascua de la creación*, 136.

99. C. Schönborn, "Resurrection of the Flesh in the Faith of the Church," *Communio* (English ed.) 17/1 (1990): 8–26, here 19.

100. See pp. 112–14.

101. See pp. 93–100 and C. Ruini, "Immortalità e risurrezione," 191.

102. J. Alfaro, "La resurrección de los muertos," 550.

103. Ibid., 552. The same idea may be found in A. De Giovanni, "Escatologia come termine, o come pienezza? Il problema dell'ultimità della storia," in Aa. vv., *Mondo storico ed escatologia* (Brescia: Morcelliana, 1972), 244–49.

104. See J. L. Ruiz de la Peña, *L'altra dimensione*, 171. G. Canobbio refers to the "privatizzazione

Wolfhart Pannenberg points out that with the theory of resurrection in the moment of death "it is not possible to conceive of the event as bodily, and this means that the individual's completion of salvation is detached and individualized relative to the consummation of the race. But precisely this link between individual and universal fulfillment of salvation is an essential element of biblical hope in the future."[105]

A Return to Platonism

It is interesting to note that the very Platonic and spiritualizing categories that the defenders of this theory wished to exorcise return, in spite of their best intentions, with a vengeance.[106] Greshake says that "matter as such cannot (as atom, molecule, organ) come to perfection. Hence, if at death human freedom comes to a climax, in that very moment the human being is freed forever from the body, from the world, from history."[107] The dead/risen person would now belong to the invisible world, that of the pure spirits; the human body no longer partakes of salvation. With this theory one would have to posit the idea of two human perpetually parallel worlds: that of mortal/earthly humans on their way toward death/resurrection, and that of dead/risen humans, in a duality that will never be fully eliminated, for there will be no end to time. Besides, anthropological duality, if perpetuated, may sooner or later turn into dualism (requiring a double origin to the universe), and motivate a somewhat other-worldly spirituality.[108]

---

dell'*eschaton* e quindi sulla dimenticanza della dimensione cosmica dello stesso. Questo . . . aspetto della critica è apparso predominante negli ultimi anni in coincidenza con la ripresa di interesse per la creazione da parte della teologia e con gli stimoli provenienti dalla recente cosmologia. La considerazione della dimensione cosmica rischia però di appiattire la fine; compimento del mondo con la fine; compimento della storia umana. Allo scopo di evitare tale rischio si è proposto di tener conto del luogo ermeneutico delle asserzioni escatologiche, che è la dinamica della libertà umana il cui esercizio in vista del compimento è reso possibile dall'apparire dell'evento Cristo, che costituisce l'evento escatologico," *Fine o compimento?* 237–38. He adds: "Leggendo il NT si resta colpiti da come, a partire dei frammenti, si sia giunti a pensare a un esito compiuto del tutto. Al fondo del processo del pensiero neotestamentario non sta una proiezione del frammento sull'orizzonte (immaginato) del tutto. Sta piuttosto la lettura della realtà parziale dal versante dell'opera di Dio compiuta in Gesù. L'idea del compimento, che implica una fine anche di *questo* mondo, nasce dalla convinzione che la Signoria di Dio abbraccia il tutto, per il fatto che è di Dio. . . . L'affermazione della fine risulta così un'affermazione *teo*-logica," ibid., 237. He observes that Greshake and Lohfink in fact are opposed to the modern tendency of recuperating the integration of individuals, history, and the cosmos at the *Parousia*. And he concludes: "sullo sfondo delle posizioni qui richiamate sta una vicenda teologica che, accettando la sfida del pensiero moderno, ha 'preteso' di collocare la persona umana come vertice e ricapitolazione del cosmo, e ha pensato si dovesse considerare quest'ultimo solo in relazione all'uomo," ibid., 225.

105. W. Pannenberg, *Systematic Theology*, vol. 3, 578.
106. See J. Ratzinger, *Eschatology*, 143–46.
107. G. Greshake, *Auferstehung der Toten*, 387.
108. The position may be found among the Messalians in the fourth century. According to the

The Singularity of the Assumption of Our Lady

The theory of "resurrection in the moment of death" commonly involves a reinterpretation of the dogma of the Assumption of Our Lady. The Church teaches that, at the end of her earthly sojourn, Mary was assumed body and soul into heaven.[109] Some authors argue that her situation is no different substantially from that of the rest of humanity. For like her, it is said, all will resurrect in the moment of their death.[110] However, this explanation does not take into account the fact that although Mary came to the end of her earthly pilgrimage like all human beings, she did not deserve to suffer the corruption of death,[111] for she was conceived immaculately and never committed sin.[112] Pope Paul VI pointed to the singularity of the Assumption in the following terms: "Mary is the only human creature, along with the Lord Jesus, her Son, who has entered paradise, body and soul, at the end of her earthly life."[113] The 1979 document of the Congregation for the Doctrine of the Faith states that "the Church in her teaching on what awaits humans after death, excludes any explanation that would take away from the Assumption of Mary what it has of unique, that is the fact that the bodily glorification of the Virgin is the anticipation of the glorification reserved for all the other elect."[114]

Toward a Proper Understanding of the Human Soul

It should now be clear that the notion of the human spirit (or soul) surviving after death does not compromise the doctrine of the resurrection of the dead. Quite the contrary. In the *first* place because the doctrine of final resurrection in the absence of a previously subsisting spirit would no longer be a *re-surrectio*, a rising up again "of the dead," "of the flesh," "of the body," but a *re-creatio*, literally a new creation.[115] The reason why the early Church hardly mentioned the immortality of the soul was because it had never really been denied.[116] And *second*,

---

homilies of Ps.-Macarius, resurrection takes place at death, in keeping with the practice of prayer and ascetical life: *Hom.* 32:1–6. See B. E. Daley, *The Hope*, 118.

109. Pius XII, Bull *Munificentissimus Deus* (1951): *DS* 3900–4.

110. The position was defended by D. Flanagan, "Eschatology and the Assumption," *Concilium* (English ed.) 5 (1969/1): 153–65; K. Rahner, "The Intermediate State," in *Theological Investigations*, vol. 17, 114–15. The hypothesis of the assumption for all was also suggested by O. Karrer, "Über unsterbliche Seele und Auferstehung," *Anima* (1953), 332–36, and repeated more recently by J. M. Hernández Martínez, "La asunción de María como paradigma de escatología cristiana."

111. See pp. 260–65.

112. *DS* 1573, 2800–3.

113. Paul VI, Audience "The Light of Christ Is to Be Found in Mystery of the Assumption" (15.8.1975), *Insegnamenti Paolo VI* 13 (1975): 849–53, here 851.

114. *Recentiores episcoporum Synodi*, n. 6.   115. See nn. 48–52. above.

116. J. Ratzinger, *Eschatology*, 133.

the notion of a naturally incorruptible "soul" is perfectly acceptable in a Christian context as long as its capacity to survive perpetually is understood in terms of a gift of God (by creation), and not as a perpetual and native possession (as in Plato), or as a power humans provide for themselves (as in Fichte and Nietzsche). *Third*, the fact that the soul may well remain somewhat inactive when separated from the body does not prejudice its continued existence,[117] among other reasons because in no created being is essence perfectly identified with act.[118] Perhaps, the best explanation given remains that of Thomas: the soul is by its very essence the "form of the body," even though temporarily it may not exercise this function and remains in a diminished, though incorruptible state.[119]

117. Boros suggests that the idea of God keeping the separated soul in existence without the activity of informing the body, is bizarre: L. Boros, "Does Life Have Meaning," *Concilium* (English ed.) 6 (1970/10): 32. To some degree this corresponds to the Aristotelian view of the soul, assumed by Thomas Aquinas. A similar idea is to be found in the Syrian theologian Narsai: see B. E. Daley, *The Hope*, 171–74.

118. See G. Gozzelino, *Nell'attesa*, 474–78.

119. J. Ratzinger (*Eschatology*, 149, 153) cites the study of A. C. Pegis, "Some Reflections on the Summa contra Gentiles II, 56," in *An Etienne Gilson Tribute*, ed. C. J. O'Neil (Milwaukee: Marquette University Press, 1959), 169–88. See also G. Gozzelino, *Nell'attesa*, 475–76. Aquinas's position is likewise substantially assumed by G. Canobbio, "Morte e immortalità. Elementi per una considerazione dell'aspetto dogmatico," *Vivens Homo* 17 (2006): 307–20. Interestingly, P. Masset, "Immortalité de l'âme, Résurrection des corps. Approches philosophiques," *Nouvelle Revue Théologique* 105 (1983): 321–44, argues that diminution really means amputation, and so the separated soul cannot survive. F. Van Steenberghen, "Plaidoyer pour l'âme séparée," *Revue Thomiste* 75 (1987): 630–41, disagrees with Masset's position.

Part Five. The Power and Light of Hope

12

The Central Role of Christian Eschatology in Theology

The Greek word *eschaton* originally meant "end," maybe even "dregs," in the most abject sense of the term, equivalent perhaps in Greek to *peras*. Under the saving power of Christ and the impulse of hope, Christianity radically transformed the term's meaning into "goal" (closer to the Greek *telos*), that is, ultimate purpose, target, summit, or plenitude. So the fact that the study of Christian eschatology has traditionally been situated as the last of the dogmas does not mean that it should be considered simply as an end of the line, where Christian reflection, exhausted, says its last word and peters out. Rather, eschatology serves as the definitive vantage point from which to contemplate the entirety of Christian revelation, theology, spirituality, ethics, and wisdom. In this chapter we shall briefly consider some ways in which eschatology is decisively present in the principal Christian treatises and areas of study.

Many authors are of the opinion that eschatology occupies a pivotal place in Christian theology.[1] The Lutheran Wolfhart Pannenberg speaks of the "constitutive significance of eschatology for Christian theology."[2] The Calvinist theologian Karl Barth, using the somewhat drastic terminology that characterized his early works, says that "a Christianity that is not totally and utterly eschatological has nothing whatever to do with Christ."[3] The Orthodox theologian John Meyendorff has it that "eschatology can never really be considered a separate chapter of Christian theology, for it qualifies the character of theology as a whole."[4] "In our own time," Joseph Ratzinger writes, "eschatology has moved into the very center of the theological stage."[5]

The same idea may be found at the heart of the doctrine of Thomas Aquinas,

---

1. See C. Pozo, *La teología del más allá*, 79–81.
2. W. Pannenberg, *Systematic Theology*, vol. 3, 532. And the Lutheran Emil Brunner said: "A Church that has nothing to teach about future eternity, has nothing to teach at all, but is bankrupt," *Das Ewige als Zukunft und Gegenwart*, 237.
3. K. Barth, *The Epistle to the Romans* (1922 ed.) (London: Oxford University Press, 1963), 314.
4. J. Meyendorff, *Byzantine Theology*, 218.
5. J. Ratzinger, *Eschatology*, 1.

articulated in three key elements. First, the entire structure of his anthropology and ethics, he tells us, is determined by the *finis ultimus*, the last end.[6] That is to say, the "last things" are not a mere appendix to the study of theology, but determine from within each and every aspect of the life and moral action of the human being, in particular of the believer, and of the whole Church. Secondly, according to Aquinas, the "last end" is determined by the saving work of Jesus Christ;[7] it is essentially Christological in content and mode. It is therefore fair to say that eschatology, though implicitly, occupies center stage in his theology. Third and last, theology as a whole is subaltern to the knowledge the blessed have of God.[8] In effect, theology is essentially eschatological in both its apophatic and luminous quality.

Eschatology and Christology

Throughout the text, Christian eschatology has consistently been presented in terms of a working out and culmination of Christ's saving work.[9] Eschatology does not, in a strict sense, deal with the process of Christian salvation. Yet eschatology is determined critically by salvation in that it brings the saving process to a close with judgment and the definitive separation of saints and sinners. In turn, the life and saving work of Christ on earth marks the beginning both of the divine offer of saving mercy to a fallen humanity and of a countdown, as it were, that will come to a definitive close with the *Parousia*.

However, to say that Christ's entire life, words, and actions are responsible for setting in motion the process of salvation that culminates in judgment[10] does not go far enough. Rather, it should be said that Christ in person is our *eschaton*. With the coming of Christ, the incarnation of the Only Son, God has said his

---

6. "Sicut Damascenus dicit, homo factus ad imaginem Dei dicitur, secundum quod per imaginem significatur *intellectuale et arbitrio liberum et per se potestativum;* postquam praedictum est de exemplari, scilicet de Deo, et de his quae processerunt ex divina potestate secundum eius voluntatem; restat ut consideremus de eius imagine, idest de homine, secundum quod et ipse est suorum operum principium, quasi liberum arbitrium habens et suorum operum potestatem.... Ubi primo considerandum occurrit de ultimo fine humanae vitae; et deinde de his per quae homo ad hunc finem pervenire potest, vel ab eo deviare, ex fine enim oportet accipere rationes eorum quae ordinantur ad finem," *S. Th. I-II, prol.* and q. 1; also qq. 1–5.

7. "Quia Salvator noster Dominus Iesus Christus, teste angelo, populum suum salvum faciens a peccatis eorum, viam veritatis nobis in seipso demonstravit, per quam ad beatitudinem immortalis vitae resurgendo pervenire possimus, necesse est ut, ad consummationem totius theologici negotii, post considerationem ultimi finis humanae vitae et virtutum ac vitiorum, de ipso omnium salvatore ac beneficiis eius humano generi praestitis nostra consideratio subsequatur," *S. Th. III, prol.*

8. Thomas Aquinas, *S. Th. I*, q. 1, a. 2, and M. L. Lamb, "The Eschatology of St. Thomas Aquinas," 227.

9. See especially pp. 184–88.

10. See M. Bordoni and N. Ciola, *Gesù nostra speranza*, 44–51.

last Word, and has no reason to "come" anew to humanity until he comes again in glory. In Christ, John tells us, God's eschatological glory has been definitively revealed (Jn 1:14, 18). According to the Synoptics, the coming of Christ is presented as the history of the coming of God's eschatological kingdom (Lk 10:20).[11] Not only do Jesus' words and works have a direct and practical meaning for the present situation of humans, but they also point toward the definitive future of humanity. This is what the so-called anagogical sense of Scripture refers to (the term derives from Augustine of Dacia's *quo tendis, anagogia*).[12] New Testament Christology from the earliest times is deeply eschatological in character, centered on the resurrection of Christ and on his return in glory, the *Parousia* (1 Thes). Likewise, Christ's Lordship is closely linked to his resurrection (Acts 2:33–34).

Nonetheless, it should also be added that in the person and work of Christ, the *eschaton*, the fullness of time, has been anticipated in a very real sense. Whereas the eschatology present in Old Testament prophetic writings is of a future (though this-worldly) kind, in Christ the end of time has already begun in a real way. In technical terms, Christian eschatology is a "realized" one, to an important degree. Thus it is possible to divide the history of salvation into three distinct periods: the time of the promise (Israel, the prophets), the time of fullness and anticipation (Christ and the Church) and the time of perfect fulfillment (*Parousia*, resurrection). Eschatology is "realized," we said, though not entirely so. For the working out of Christian eschatology does not bring about an immediate, tangible, and glorious triumph for Christian believers. The Kingdom of God is not yet fully established. Rather, the working-out of salvation history assumes and follows the temporal rhythm of Christ's own life: his patience, his vigilance, his miracles, his prayer, his words, and especially his death and resurrection. Specifically, the death of Christ on the Cross reveals the provisional character of human life and of the world we live in,[13] whereas the resurrection proclaims in tangible form the truth of God's promise of immortality and glory.

Two further points, extensively considered throughout the text, should also be kept in mind. *First*, Christ, the Incarnate Word, is directly involved in bringing about eternal life and the risen state, the condemnation of the unjust, the purification of sinners, and the resurrection of the dead.[14] And *second*, the action of Christ on believers takes place by the sending of the Holy Spirit, who may be considered as "the cause and power of hope."[15]

---

11. See pp. 228–31.

12. See the document of the Pontifical Biblical Commission, *The Interpretation of the Bible in the Church* (1993), II, B; and my study "La Biblia en la configuración de la teología," 873–74.

13. See M. Bordoni, *Gesù di Nazaret, Signore e Cristo, 1: Problemi di metodo* (Roma: Herder; Pontificia Università Lateranense, 1982), 207–13.

14. See pp. 88–91, 307–8.   15. See ch. 1, n. 147.

To sum up, as Jean Daniélou has cogently argued,[16] should the Church forgo its eschatology, it would likewise be obliged to forgo its Redeemer and Savior, Jesus Christ, and as a result its ecclesiology, sacraments, anthropology, ethics, and spirituality.

Eschatology, Ecclesiology, and Sacraments

The Second Vatican Council's contribution to eschatology, as we have seen, may be found principally in the Constitution on the Church, *Lumen gentium*.[17] It made sense that a document paying special attention to the life of the Church and the variety of vocations and missions present in it would end on a double note: on the one hand, the object of the pilgrimage of God's people, heaven (chapter 7, whose full title is: "The Eschatological Character of the Pilgrim Church and Its Union with the Heavenly Church"), and the supreme living model and goal of Christian faith and holiness, Our Lady (chapter 8: "The Blessed Virgin Mary, Mother of God in the Mystery of Christ and the Church"). The Church is Christ's body, protected infallibly by his Spirit. Nonetheless, it lives as a pilgrim in the world. Thus, *Lumen gentium* says, "the Church on earth is endowed already with a holiness that is real though imperfect."[18] In effect, the Church has not yet reached its final perfection and lives, as Augustine says, "like a stranger in a foreign land, pressing forward amid the persecutions of the world and the consolations of God."[19] Hence, *Lumen gentium* continues, "the Church, to which we are all called in Christ Jesus, and in which by the grace of God we acquire holiness, will receive its perfection only in the glory of heaven, when will come the time for the renewal of all things."[20] Thus it may be said that eschatology is the culmination of ecclesiology,[21] and gives ultimate meaning to the Church and

---

16. See J. Daniélou, "Christologie et eschatologie."

17. The constitution *Gaudium et spes* also considers some eschatological questions, such as death (n. 18) and the fulfillment of human activity through the Paschal Mystery of Christ (nn. 38–39). On the eschatology of *Lumen gentium*, see the study of N. Camilleri, "Natura escatologica della Chiesa," in *La costituzione dogmatica sulla Chiesa*, ed. A. Favale (Leumann [Torino]: Elle di Ci, 1965), 875–93; A. Molinari, "L'indole escatologica della Chiesa," in *La Chiesa del Vaticano II: studi e commenti intorno alla Costituzione dommatica "Lumen gentium,"* ed. G. Baraúna (Firenze: Vallecchi, 1965), 1113–31; G. Philips, *L'Église et son mystère au IIe Concile du Vatican: histoire, texte et commentaire de la constitution Lumen gentium* (Paris: Desclée, 1967–68), vol. 2, 161–205; C. Pozo, *La teología del más allá*, 538–70; L. Sartori, *La 'Lumen gentium': traccia di studio*, 2nd ed. (Padova: Messaggero, 2003), 103–110; M. Bordoni and N. Ciola, *Gesù nostra speranza*, 52–54.

18. *LG* 48c. See my study "The Holiness of the Church in 'Lumen Gentium,'" *Thomist* 52 (1988): 673–701.

19. Augustine, *De Civ. Dei XVIII*, 51:2, cit. in *LG* 8d.

20. *LG* 48a.

21. The classic position in this respect is that of F. A. Staudenmaier, who in his 3-volume work *Die*

its mission. Should the ultimate purpose of Christian salvation not be eternal life and universal resurrection, the mission and action of the Church would be very different from what it is.

The sacramental action of the Church is the action of Christ himself, who in the power of the Spirit prepares the pilgrim people to be with him forever in the glory of the Father. The celebration of each and every sacrament, therefore, should reflect this fact: Christ is their living source, Christ is their end. Not only do the sacraments evoke the saving death and resurrection of Christ, not only do they celebrate the saving action of the One who "always lives to make intercession" for believers (Heb 7:25); they also anticipate Christ's glorious return in glory. This is so especially in respect of the Holy Eucharist, but is true also of the other sacraments.[22] For this reason, Paul tells us, the Church celebrates the Eucharist, culmination of its very existence, proclaiming "the Lord's death until he comes" (1 Cor 11:26).[23] Medieval authors such as Peter of Poitiers and Rupert of Deutz[24] paid particular attention to the eschatological side of sacramental life. Traditionally, in fact, the systematic study of eschatology has followed that of sacraments.[25] Still, *Lumen gentium* tells us, the sacramental life of the Church as we know it will come to a close at the end of time: "the pilgrim Church in its sacraments and institutions, which belong to this present age, carries the mark of this world which will pass and she herself takes her place among the creatures which groan and travail yet and await the revelation of the sons of God."[26]

Eschatology and Anthropology

The question humans ask most persistently, though not always most openly, refers to the kind of immortality, if any, that awaits them after death, that is, their eschatological destiny. As we have seen, God has promised to those who are faithful to him an eternal reward that consists of perpetual union with the Trinity, eternal life, and beatific vision, as well as personal and collective perfection, both bodily and spiritual, through final resurrection. Thus the eschatological promise affects anthropology decisively, on all fronts. It accounts for the spirituality and immortality of human beings, and their desire for the infinite; it

---

christliche Dogmatik (Freiburg i. B.: Herder, 1844–48) holds that eschatology is really a part of ecclesiology, just as ecclesiology is vitally linked to the saving work of Christ, redemption.

22. See pp. 230–31.
23. See pp. 67–71.
24. On Peter of Poitiers, see *In Sent. libri*, V, cap. 1. On Rupert, see W. Kahles, *Geschichte als Liturgie: die Geschichtstheologie des Ruperts von Deutz* (Münster: Aschendorff, 1960), 7–8.
25. See C. Pozo, *La teología del más allá*, 6–16.
26. *LG* 48c.

manifests their irreplaceable quality as human persons (it would be meaningless to speak of the dignity of each human being should they not live on individually forever); it gives significance and depth to their temporality and historicity, and explains why their earthly sojourn may be considered as a time of trial and testing, of fidelity and perseverance; it shows the purpose of their corporeity, for they are destined to live forever in a profound union of body and soul; it reveals the depth and power of their free will, for they can be confronted with choices and possibilities that will shape their eternal destiny; it drives the virtue of hope, in its divine and human aspects. In brief, anthropology is stimulated, renewed, and empowered not only by theological anthropology in the strict sense, that is, by the doctrine of grace, but also, and more fundamentally perhaps, by eschatology, which confronts believers with their promised destiny and offers them the possibility of grasping the meaning of life in the widest and richest possible sense.[27]

Commenting on the theology of Gregory of Nyssa and Maximus the Confessor, the Orthodox theologian John Meyendorff speaks of the powerful influence our knowledge of the last things has over human life: "The ultimate end itself is a dynamic state of man and of the whole of creation: the goal of created existence is not, as Origen thought, a static contemplation of divine 'essence', but a dynamic ascent of love, which never ends, because God's transcendent being is inexhaustible, and always contains new things yet to be discovered *(novissima)* through the union of love."[28]

Eschatology and Ethics

The ethical structure of human existence, according to Thomas Aquinas, is based on the end or purpose of human life, what he calls the *finis ultimus*, the "last end." In fact, his study of moral theology (which corresponds to the second part of the *Summa Theologiae*) situates the question of the "last end" at the very outset. Straight away Aquinas begins to reflect on the *beatitudo*, human happiness and fulfillment, which culminates in the face-to-face vision of God.[29] His principal contribution to eschatology directly relates to Christian ethics. Speaking of eschatology in the context of the immortality of the soul, Blaise Pascal acutely observed: "It is true that the mortality or immortality of the soul must

27. See M. Bordoni and N. Ciola, *Gesù nostra speranza*, 57–63; 82.
28. J. Meyendorff, *Byzantine Theology*, 219.
29. Thomas Aquinas, *S. Th. I-II*, qq. 1–5. On the profound relevance of eschatology for Aquinas, see two studies of P. Künzle, "Thomas von Aquin und die moderne Eschatologie," *Freiburger Zeitschrift für Philosophie und Theologie* 8 (1961): 109–20; "Die Eschatologie im Gesamtaufbau der wissenschaftlichen Theologie," *Anima* 20 (1965): 231–38, as well as M. L. Lamb, "The Eschatology of St Thomas Aquinas."

make a huge difference to morality. And yet philosophers have constructed their ethics independently of this."[30] Ethical endeavor should be directed and determined by the perceived, permanent outcome of the life-project God has designed for humanity as a whole, and for the life-project of each person (vocation). A properly focused Christian eschatology, besides, is in a position to prevent ethical enquiry from slipping into a one-sided, earthbound consequentialism. The ultimate promise of eternal life is, or should be, in a position to direct and coordinate the myriad of "partial ends" that each and every human life is made up of. It is clear, besides, that the reality of the divine promise of eternal salvation, alongside the possibility of eternal damnation, offers an indication of the decisive quality of free human action.

The doctrine of final resurrection means, besides, that the immortal destiny of the human person is strictly corporeal. This provides a solid basis for affirming the dignity of the living human being, as well as the inviolable character of human sexuality.[31] Likewise, the essentially communitarian character of final resurrection and judgment serves as a pressing invitation to live charity and justice with all other human beings.[32] Besides, the eschatological horizon of all Christian teaching imposes a systematic "eschatological reserve" on theories, political philosophies, utopian ideologies, and ethical systems, a reserve that establishes and maintains the distance between tangible created reality on the one hand and the being and action of God, his saving purposes, on the other hand. Indeed, God has promised that in heaven "no eye has seen, nor ear heard" (1 Cor 2:9).

Why Should Christians Pardon the Offenses of Others?

The Gospel clearly teaches that believers should make a point of pardoning offenses and avoiding all forms of vindictiveness and judgment of persons (Mt 7:1–5). The spirit of divine mercy must be assimilated and lived by all those who believe that divine mercy has been revealed definitively in Christ, in particular to themselves (Mt 6:10). The fact that humans should not judge does not mean of course that God may not do so. It means in reality that only God can judge and punish the sinner in full justice and mercy, even to the point of condemning him or her forever. To be faithful to himself, to his transcendence and dominion over the universe, God must assure that all things are brought or restored to the state he planned they would assume, that full justice is done. For God is Lord over the entire universe, and nobody or nothing may disdain his laws and ordi-

---

30. B. Pascal, *Pensées* (ed. Brunschvig), n. 219.
31. See my study "La fórmula 'Resurrección de la carne' y su significado para la moral cristiana."
32. See my work *La muerte y la esperanza*, 97–109, and especially the 2009 encyclical of Benedict XVI, *Caritas in veritate*.

nances. Those who do so are excluded ipso facto from his friendship, and from the warmth and welcome of a created universe that is meant to proclaim always and in everything nothing other than the glory and sovereignty of its Creator.

To pardon one's neighbor involves neither acceptance of their sin nor an indifferent attempt to understate the importance of the offense committed. Neither is the act of forgiveness a sign or act of weakness or cowardice. Rather, to pardon someone constitutes at heart a vibrant, living act of faith—of faith, hope, and trusting petition—so that God will do justice, either in this life by obtaining through his insistent, merciful love the sinner's reception of justifying grace (with the collaboration of Christian witness and apostolate),[33] or in the next by eventually condemning the sinner who obstinately refuses to accept such grace. To pardon the offenses of others means renouncing the desire and pretension to play God's part. But God himself will not renounce that role.

Eschatology and Spirituality

The dynamic of Christian spirituality, like that of ethics, is determined by the ultimate horizon of human life, that is, eternal communion with the Trinity and with the rest of saved humanity.[34] Communion with the Trinity and the contemplation of God, face to face, filled with joyful adoration, is the culmination of an extended process that begins in this life.[35] In this sense all Christian spirituality is clearly eschatological:[36] it points beyond itself; indeed, it points ultimately beyond death.

The essentially eschatological horizon of the believer's existence is critical for the spiritual life in several ways. First, believers must be purified from all disorderly or idolatrous attachment to the passing things of life. Second, they are urged to develop a spirit of persevering prayer that will joyfully flourish as an eternal contemplative dialogue with the Trinity. Third, they should learn to respect the natural dynamics of corporal and psychological life, which will reach consummation at final resurrection. Fourth, they are meant to live in trusting, fraternal communion with their fellow men and women, with whom they are destined to share divine communion forever. And fifth, they must come to understand the passing of time not as a loss or source of despair, but as an opportunity, a spiritual space, to grow in closeness to God and communicate his word and saving power to the rest of humanity.

33. *CCC* 2843.
34. See J. L. Illanes, *Tratado de teología espiritual* (Pamplona: Eunsa, 2007), 305–8.
35. See L. Touze, ed., *La contemplazione cristiana: esperienza e dottrina. Atti del IX Simposio della Facoltà di Teologia della Pontificia Università della S. Croce, Roma* (Città del Vaticano: Vaticana, 2007).
36. See pp. 11–12.

The Central Role of Christian Eschatology

As we saw in the first chapter,[37] the spiritual consistency of the Christian message must be tested in the context of the contrast between what we called the "prize" and the "price" of heaven: that is, eternal life on the one hand, rapt, perpetual communion with the Trinity, and death, the loss of human life, on the other. In order to be able to accept the Church's teaching on eschatology, believers must be in a position to reconcile, within their own living experience, these two extremes, accepting the magnanimity of divine love that promises humans infinitely more than they could dream of obtaining with their own effort, yet trusting in the fidelity of God who requires his children, his disciples, to "leave all things and follow" him (Mt 19:27), to leave all things . . . including life itself, which is God's supreme gift, in the hope of the resurrection.

37. See pp. 31–33.

Selected Bibliography

The following bibliography contains a selection of the principal textbooks and source materials in Christian eschatology cited frequently throughout the text, wherever possible in English original or translation. A list of principal abbreviations has been included following the preface.

Althaus, Paul. *Die letzten Dinge.* 9th ed. Gütersloh: Bertelsmann, 1964.
Alviar, J. José. *Escatología.* Pamplona: Eunsa, 2004.
Ancona, Giovanni. *Escatologia cristiana.* Brescia: Queriniana, 2003.
Biffi, Giacomo. *Linee di escatologia cristiana.* Milano: Jaca Book, 1984.
Bordoni, Marcello, and Nicola Ciola. *Gesù nostra speranza. Saggio di escatologia in prospettiva trinitaria.* 2nd ed. Bologna: Dehoniane, 2000.
Boros, Ladislao. *We Are Future.* New York: Herder and Herder, 1970.
Brunner, Emil. *Das Ewige als Zukunft und Gegenwart.* Zürich: Zwingli, 1953.
Bynum, Caroline W. *The Resurrection of the Body in Western Christianity, 200–1336.* New York: Columbia University Press, 1995.
Colzani, Gianni. *La vita eterna: inferno, purgatorio, paradiso.* Milano: A. Mondadori, 2001.
Daley, Brian E. *The Hope of the Early Church: A Handbook of Patristic Eschatology.* 3rd ed. Cambridge: University Press, 1995.
Daniélou, Jean. "Christologie et eschatologie." In *Das Konzil von Chalkedon. Geschichte und Gegenwart,* edited by A. Grillmeier and H. Bacht, 3:269–86. Würzburg: Echter, 1954.
Escribano-Alberca, Ignacio. "Eschatologie: von der Aufklärung bis zur Gegenwart." In *Handbuch der Dogmengeschichte, 4.4.7.4.* Freiburg i. B.: Herder, 1987.
Gozzelino, Giorgio. *Nell'attesa della beata speranza. Saggio di escatologia cristiana.* Leumann (Torino): Elle di Ci, 1993.
Greshake, Gisbert. *Stärker als der Tod. Zukunft, Tod, Auferstehung, Himmel, Hölle, Fegfeur.* Mainz: M. Grünewald, 1976.
Guardini, Romano. *The Last Things.* 1949. New York: Pantheon, 1954.
Kunz, Erhard. "Protestantische Eschatologie: von der Reformation bis zur Aufklärung." In *Handbuch der Dogmengeschichte, 4.7.3.1.* Freiburg i. B.: Herder, 1980.
Lavatori, Renzo. *Il Signore verrà nella Gloria.* Bologna: Dehoniane, 2007.
Moltmann, Jurgen. *The Coming of God: Christian Eschatology.* London: SCM, 1996.
O'Callaghan, Paul. *The Christological Assimilation of the Apocalypse: An Essay on Fundamental Eschatology.* Dublin: Four Courts, 2004.
———. *La muerte y la esperanza.* Madrid: Palabra, 2004.
O'Connor, James T. *Land of the Living: A Theology of the Last Things.* New York: Catholic Books, 1992.

Pannenberg, Wolfhart. *Systematic Theology*. Vol. 3. Edinburgh: T. & T. Clark, 1998.
Pieper, Joseph. *Tod und Unsterblichkeit*. München: Kösel, 1968.
Pozo, Cándido. *La teología del más allá*. 3rd ed. Madrid: BAC, 1992.
Rahner, Karl. *On the Theology of Death*. Freiburg i. B.: Herder, 1961.
Ratzinger, Joseph. *Eschatology: Death and Eternal Life*. Washington, D.C.: The Catholic University of America Press, 1988.
Ruiz de la Peña, Juan L. *La pascua de la creación*. Madrid: BAC, 1996.
Scheffczyk, Leo, and Anton Ziegenaus. *Katholische Dogmatik*. Vol. 8: *Die Zukunft der Schöpfung in Gott: Eschatologie*. Aachen: MM, 1996.
Schmaus, Michael. *Katholische Dogmatik*. Vol. 4.2: *Von den letzten Dingen*. 1948. München: Hüber, 1959.
Von Balthasar, Hans Urs. "Eschatology." In *Theology Today*. Vol. 1: *Renewal in Theology*, edited by J. Feiner, J. Trütsch, and F. Böckle, 222–44. Milwaukee: Bruce Publishing, 1965.
———. *Theo-drama: Theological Dramatic Theory*. Vol. 4. San Francisco: Ignatius Press, 1994.

General Index

"Accidental glory," 180–81, 309
Aevum, aeviternitas, 180, 317
Alienation, 10, 26–28, 205
Angels, 23, 41, 87, 100–102, 145–47, 159, 165, 170–71, 177–78, 203, 207–8, 227, 268, 317
Annihilation of condemned, 208–10
Anthropology, 40–42; consistency of, ix, 25–31; distinction between God and humans, 122, 162–63, 169, 181–82; eschatology as a catalyst for, 91, 125, 282, 310; human freedom, 170–74; human fulfillment, 157–60, 282; resurrection, 91, 96–98, 323–24
Antichrist, 237–39
Apocalyptic, viii, xi, xiii, 14–17, 43, 45–47, 49, 51, 60, 80, 84–86, 118, 121, 125, 131–34, 137, 194, 233–34, 242–46, 288, 323
Apokatastasis, 134, 171, 195–97, 206, 215, 218–21, 290, 295, 300
Apostasy, 235, 237–39, 244
Apostolate, 56–59, 216, 234–36
Arianism, 68, 165–66
Asceticism, 42, 271–73, 293–95

Beatific vision. *See* Eternal life
"Book of life," 284, 287
Buddhism, 96, 155
Burial, 79, 94–96

Carolingian liturgy, 68–69
Celtic liturgy, 70
Chiliasm. *See* Millennialism
Collective eschatology, ix, 15, 28–29, 41, 43, 83–85, 221, 283–84, 309–13, 333
Coming in glory. *See Parousia*
Communion of saints, 175, 288, 301 305, 315
Conscience, 15, 130, 213, 283–85
Consequentialism, 335
Constantinople, I Council of, 185
Constantinople, II Council of, 116

Constantinople, Synod of, 103, 189, 197
Cosmology, 7, 44–46, 83, 120–25, 99, 116–17, 120–22, 127
Creation, 44–45, 73, 82–85, 87, 115–17, 119–21, 123–25, 131, 144, 152, 167, 172, 176, 188, 204, 229–30, 243, 260–62, 320, 322, 326
Cremation, 94–95

Death, 253–85
Death, characteristics of: aspect of human nature, 261–62; certainty, 253–54; conversion after, 274–75; detachment from life, 32–33, 274–75; end of human pilgrimage, 273–81; evil, improper, unwanted and violent, 255–58; fear of, 255–56, 271–72; final decision in moment of, 267–69; full and deferred retribution, 275–80, 295; *Ganztod* (total), 314, 317–18; horizon of immortality, 258–60; incorporation into Christ's Passover, 266–73, 308; liberation, 253, 256–57, 260, 269, 278; mortification, 271–73; overcoming fear of, 272; as *Parousia*, 52, 267–69, 319; positive quality of, 261–62, 267–68; preparation for, 269–73; present in the midst of life, 254–55; purification of hope, 272–73; purpose of, 264, 271–73; *refa'im* (the dead), 79–80, 315; result of/ punishment for sin, 260–65; "resurrection in moment of death," 318–325; rupture of relationships, 254; sleep, 84–85, 94–95, 159, 315; transformation by Christ, 269–72
Death, context: Church Fathers, 256, 262–64, 275–78; magisterium, 278–80; New Testament, 261, 270–75, 281–83; Old Testament, 29, 261, 273–74; philosophy, 27–29, 254–60; Protestantism, 263–64, 313–19
Death, referred to: anthropology, 254–60, 273–80; individual and collective eschatology, ix, 221, 233, 283–84, 309–13, 333; Jesus Christ, 32, 266–73; particular judg-

341

Death, referred to *(cont.)*
    ment, 280–85; resurrection, 260, 266–67, 269–70, 276–77
De-hellenization, 19–20, 100, 313–14, 316
Delay in end-time. *See* Parousia
Despair. *See* Hope
Destruction of temple, 54–55
Devil, 140, 147, 163, 171, 203, 228–29, 241–42, 237–38, 241–44, 246, 261, 272,
Dreams, xiii, 9
Dualism, 96, 121, 316, 324

Ecclesiology, 282, 310, 332–33
Ecology, 204–5, 264
End of time, xiii, 41, 44, 52, 56–58, 61, 64–65, 116, 135–36, 153, 185–86, 195, 225–27, 240, 248, 273, 283, 290, 312, 331, 333
Entropy, 45, 121
Epistemology: anagogical sense of Scripture, 331; anthropological consistency, ix, 12–13, 19–31; centrality of Scripture, ix–x; content and truth of statements, 14–18; and the Holy Spirit, 33–36; interpretation of Scripture, 14–18, 193–95, 241, 245; liturgical practice, 291–93, 298; metaphor, 72, 83, 194, 202; priority of revelation, ix–x; and risk, 13, 19, 25; spiritual consistency, 31–33, 337; soul's spirituality as knowable, 22–23; theological hermeneutics, ix, 17. *See also* Truth of eschatological statements
Escapism, 121, 153–55, 201, 310
Eschatology, 4; and anthropology, 12–13, 333–34; bibliography, x–xiii, 339–40; and Christology, 330–32; collective, 29, 283–84, 309–13; and conversion, 13, 48, 52, 236–37; and ecclesiology and sacraments, 332–33; "eschatological reserve," ix, 335; and ethics, 5–6, 48–49, 282–84, 310, 334–35; in Europe, xi–xii; future, 3–4, 8–9, 318; and humility, 32–33; importance of, 329–30; individual, 52–53, 60–61, 283–84, 309–13; and joy, 34, 40–41, 69, 103–5, 137, 148, 156–56, 160, 173, 176–77, 181, 305–6; and last end, x, 5, 10, 13, 52, 124–25, 330, 334; and pessimism, 68–69, 214; promise, 3–4, 11–12, 149–50; realized, 46, 50–54, 56, 62, 65, 226–27, 331; as salvation, 330–31; and spirituality, 31–33, 48–49,

80–81, 310, 336–37; structure of treatise, viii; as theology, ix, 11–12; thoroughgoing, 46–50, 53, 56, 59, 226, 232, 320; in United States, x–xiii
Eternal glory. *See* Eternal life
Eternal life, 149–88; as a term, 150, 152–53
Eternal life, characteristics of: beatific vision, 149–50, 161–70; boredom, 154–55, 157, 259; charity and vision, 160, 163, 174–79, 183; Christ's presence and mediation, 163–64, 166, 184–86; communion with God and others, 175–78, 181–88; contemplation of God, 158–59, 164–65, 174, 279; divine energies, 165–66; divinization (*theosis*), 156–57; dynamism and activity, 153–55, 157–59; fixity and repose, 154–55, 157–59; freedom, 170–74; glorification, 186–88; glory (*doxa*), 104–5, 150, 165–66; grades of glory, 181–83; growth, 153–56, 179–81; happiness, 10–12, 31, 117, 150, 153–57, 177, 305, 334–35; immediacy of vision, 165–69; listening to God's word, 169–70; love of God and others, 178–79; *Lumen gloriae*, 168–69; mediation of vision, 185–86; *mox post mortem*, 270–80; paradise, 119–20, 158–59; partaking in divine glory, joy, and happiness, 157; praise of God, 79, 157, 159–60, 174, 186–88; presence of humanity and creation, 175–79; rest, 153–59; sinlessness, 170–73; social aspect, 174–79; time and eternity, 157–58, 160–61, 170–74, 179–80, 314; Trinity, 181–88
Eternal life, context: art, 149–50; Church Fathers on vision of God, 164–66; magisterium, 150–51, 168–69; medieval theology, 171–73; New Testament, 152–53, 163–64; religions, 155–56
Eternal life, referred to: anthropology, 153–55, 170–81; Christology, 184–86; ethics, 164, 171–74; God, 152–53, 156–57, 164–68; heavenly liturgy, 159–60, 186–88; Holy Spirit, 187–88; hope, 153; human desire for eternal happiness, 10–11, 153–61; life, 152–53, 161–62; light, 161–62; resurrection, 104–5, 153, 180–81
Eternal punishment. *See* Perpetual condemnation
Eternal return, myth of, 8–9, 50

Eternity, 157–58, 160–61, 170–74, 179–80, 314; supra-temporalism, 51–53
Evolution, 6–7, 121–22

Final judgment. *See* Judgment
Florence, Council of, 151, 166, 182, 279, 293, 296
Forecasting, 9, 51, 247–48
Forgiveness, 134–36, 335–36
Full and deferred retribution, 275–80, 295
Fundamentalism, fideism, xiii, 22, 44, 247

Gnosticism, 9, 30, 59, 107–9, 118, 168–69, 196, 244, 278; Christian, 294
God: capable of saving humanity, 10, 81–82; determined to save humanity, 10; as fire, 202–3; invisible and transcendent, 167–69; just, 139–40, 208, 210–14, 304; merciful, 29, 72, 85, 118, 136, 138, 140, 145, 162, 190, 196, 202, 207, 210–14, 217, 286, 307, 335–36; source of life, 82, 88, 125, 150, 152–53, 164, 168, 172–73; simple, 166, 182; sovereign, 15, 20, 32, 52, 87, 97, 122, 131, 180, 225, 227–31, 316, 320, 322–23, 336; worthy of trust, 10–11, 32–33, 157, 221, 289, 299, 337; ultimate motive and object of eschatology, 11–12. *See also* Eternal life; Holy Spirit; Jesus Christ
Gregorian Masses, 292–93

Heaven. *See* Eternal life
Hell. *See* Perpetual Condemnation
Hinduism, 75–76, 95, 155
Holiness, 61, 119, 146, 164, 176, 216, 265, 286–87, 304, 307, 310, 332
Holy Spirit: action and presence of, 33–36, 227; and Christ, 11, 13, 33–37, 226, 331; epoch of, 246–48; and eschatology, viii; and eternal life, 157, 186–88, 315; and hope, 34–35, 68, 231, 331; and judgment, 135, 143–44; and the *Parousia*, 59; and perpetual condemnation, 192, 213, 317–18; and resurrection, 88, 91–92, 111; and truth, 14, 18, 33–36
Hope, vii–ix, 8, 3–36; anthropological implications, 4–14, 36, 334; collective and individual, 221, 311–13; and despair, 5–6, 8, 81, 200–201, 256, 336; of early Christians, 63–64; *elpis*, 4, 8; in eternal life, 149–50, 153–54, 157, 174; future, 8; in God, 10; as hermeneutic, vii, ix; and Holy Spirit, 33–36, 331; in judgment, 130, 147–48; and love, 9–10; and memory, 5; in the new heavens and new earth, 129; in other people, 10; in *Parousia*, 40–41, 53, 63, 66–73; as passion, 4–5; and perpetual condemnation, 200–201, 218–21; *praeambula spei*, 18–19, 25; purification of, 253–308, 272–73, 307; in resurrection, 74–75, 85, 112–14; in salvation of all, 218–21; as stimulus, vii, 13, 225–49; as theological virtue, xi, 5–14, 32, 248; truth of, 14; ultimate and penultimate, 13–14
Human involvement in the *Parousia*, 56, 60–61, 239

Idolatry, 81, 117, 191, 289
Immortality: and anthropology, 12–13, 333–34; and death, 254, 258–60; and eschatology, 12–13, 25–31; and ethics, 334–35; integral, ix, 18, 30–33, 36, 112, 260, 312–13; of life, 27–29; and modern philosophy, 21, 26; Old Testament, 78–80, 85–86; philosophical arguments, xi, 18, 22–25; projection of, 26–27; Protestantism, 19–22, 313–18; and resurrection, 102–3; and science, xii, 45–46; of selfhood, 29–31; and sin, 262–65. *See also* Soul
Individual and collective eschatology, ix, 221, 233, 283–84, 309–13, 333
Integrated anthropology, ix, 18, 30–33, 36, 112, 260, 312–13
Interim ethics, 47, 58
Intermediate eschatology, 309–26; and anthropology, 309–13; atemporality, 314, 317; and God, 317–18; exile of the soul, 313–16, 325–26; and "justification by faith," 316–17; Church teaching, 320; modern philosophy, 98–100; Protestant theology, 313–18; and rejection of history, 323–24; "resurrection in moment of death," 318–25; return to Platonism, 324; role of Church, 315; sleep, 63, 84–85, 94–95, 314–15; "total death," 314, 317–18
Israel, xii, 60–61, 78–79, 82–83, 191, 216, 235–36, 289, 316

344 General Index

Jehovah's Witnesses, 248
Jesus Christ: ascension, 69, 72, 277; authority, 140–42, 231–34; basis of eschatology, viii, 17, 330–32; cosmic Christ, 122–23; creation for Christ, 124; creation in Christ, 124–25; cross, 127–28, 312, 331; descent into hell, 69, 219–20, 274–75, 277, 308, 322; *ephapax* (only once), 77; as *eschaton*, 16–17, 36, 330–31; *kenosis* (self-emptying), 91, 59–60, 219, 267; Messiah, 48, 61, 192, 226, 236–37; messianic signs, 233–34; mission of, 49–50; obedience, 32, 34, 230, 270–71; presence and action, 230–31; resurrection, 88–91, 322–23; as savior, vii, 32–33, 51, 229–31, 312, 330–31; as savior/judge, 15, 17, 134–42; son of man, 47–48, 54–55, 60, 72, 133–34, 232; and thoroughgoing eschatology, 46–49. *See also* Holy Spirit; Judgment; Parousia
Judaism. *See* Israel
Judgment, 130–48, 280–85
Judgment, characteristics of: angels and saints, 145–47; charity as measure, 137–38; "Day of Yahweh," 62, 132; end of time, 135–36; humanity of, 144–45; interpersonal, 137–38; location of, 146–47; manifestation of identity, 136, 142–48; particular, 280–85; public and definitive, 138; "self-judgment," 281, 284–85; universal, 133, 135–37
Judgment, contexts: "book of life," 284; from ethnic to ethical, 84, 132–33, 137, 216; full retribution, 278; New Testament, 133–34, 136–42, 281–82; Old Testament, 131–33; from prophetic to apocalyptic, 131–33
Judgment, referred to: anthropology, 138–39; divine praise, 146; God as judge, 138–40, 142–44; Holy Spirit, 143–44; hope, 147–48; Jesus Christ as judge, 140–42; justice, 130–32, 135–36, 144–45; mercy, 144–45; resurrection, 135–36, 145, 148; salvation, 134–42; truth, 135–36, 142
Justice, 78, 80–81, 126–29, 208, 210–14, 304, 310

Kingdom of God, 226–41; Christ as definitive manifestation of, 228–31, 331; church and state, 245; establishment of, 229–30; and eternal life, 159–60, 187–88; kingdom of Christ, 141–42, 185–86, 246, 288, 331; and millennialism, 243–49; and new heavens and new earth, 118–19, 126–28; and political society, xii, 43, 244–49; presence and dynamism of, 53–54, 57–60, 227–31; and realized eschatology, 50–52; and resurrection, 92, 105; and Roman Empire, 244–46; and salvation, 229–30; and thoroughgoing eschatology, 46–49; visibility of, 231–42

Last end, x, 5, 10, 13, 52, 124–25, 330, 334
Lateran, IV Council, 109, 189
Lateran, V Council, 316
Life, 6–7, 18, 21, 24–31, 31–33, 57, 75–76, 78–80, 82–83, 88, 91, 94–95, 106, 113, 120, 125, 141–42, 152–53, 155, 161–62, 168, 254–58, 258–60, 270–73, 294, 312–13, 334–37; eternal, 12–13, 18, 34–35, 50, 71, 84, 92, 101, 150, 150–55, 156–59, 160–62, 170, 175–77, 179–82, 184, 187, 192, 197, 333; once lived, 109–11, 259–60
Liturgy, 66–71, 92–95, 107, 219, 230–31, 291–93, 298, 310, 315, 322–23. *See also* Parousia
Lyons, II Council of, 211, 296

Marriage, 79, 87, 103–4
Martyrs, 64, 84–85, 147, 153, 182; and the Antichrist, 238–39; immediate salvation of, 276, 293
Marxism, 6–7, 26–29, 43, 99, 113–14, 126–27, 247
Matter: and cosmic renewal, 7, 45, 99, 116–17, 120–22, 127; and resurrection, 77–78, 96–100, 106–8, 113–14, 204; trivializing, 28, 30–31, 46, 95–97, 108, 113–14, 253, 278, 324; vocation to eternity, 98, 125, 324
"Merciful Fathers," 196, 214
Metempsychosis. *See* Reincarnation
Millennialism, xiii, 64–66, 241–49; apocalyptic, 243–44; chiliasm, 242; and justice, 248–49; and political society, 244–49; rejection of utopian spirit, 248–49; scriptural issues, 241–42; significance of, 248–49; spiritual, 245–48; three periods of history, 247–48; worldly, 244–45
Monophysitism, 68

Mormonism, 248
Mortification, 271–73

Near death experiences, xiii
Neoplatonism, 30, 40, 94, 97, 123–24, 255
New Age spirituality, xiii, 77
New heavens and new earth, 115–29
New heavens and new earth, characteristics of: continuity and discontinuity, 126–29; destruction, 117–18; justice, 126, 128; new world, 118–20; paradise, 119–20
New heavens and new earth, contexts: New Testament, 116–19; Marxism, 126–27; science, 120–23; Vatican II, 116, 127–29
New heavens and new earth, referred to: Christology, 122–25; cosmology, 44–46, 120–25; creation, 123–25; eschatologism, 126–27; incarnationism, 126–27; matter, 116–17, 120–22; resurrection, 115–16, 121–22; work, 126–29
Nicea, Council of, 124, 185, 315

Original sin, 169, 261, 263, 265
Our Lady: death, 265; intercession, 218, 315; position in heaven, 178, 332; Sabbatine privilege, 307; singularity of assumption, 107, 265, 325

Paradise, 119–20, 149–50, 158, 249
Parapsychology, xiii
Parousia, 3–73
Parousia, characteristics of: coming of Holy Spirit, 59; delay in end-time, 225–27; destruction of temple, 54–55; fear of, 40–41; growth and waiting, 57–58; hope in, 66–73; human involvement in, 56, 60–61, 239; imminence of, 44–50, 52, 54–57, 60, 63–66, 132, 135, 232, 235–36, 240, 320; individual and collective eschatology, 309–13; joyful expectation, 66, 71–72; living presence of, 225–49; *Parousia*, 39–40; public victory, 71–72; realism of, 40–66, 72–73; realized, 50–53; thoroughgoing, 46–50
Parousia, contexts: Church Fathers, 64–66; liturgy, 67–71; Paul and John, 61–63, 67; philosophy, 42–44; physics, 44–46; synoptics, 46–63

General Index 345

Parousia, referred to: Antichrist, 237–39; Christology, 46–66, 72–73; church and evangelization, 48, 56–57, 59, 235–36, 310; creation, 73; judgment, 37–38; new heavens, 37–38; resurrection of Christ, 59; resurrection of the dead, 37–38; transfiguration, 55; vigilance, 67, 239–41
Perpetual condemnation, 189–211
Perpetual condemnation, characteristics of: annihilation, 208–10; *aversio a Deo*, 198–99, 203–5; constriction, 204–5; *conversio ad creaturas*, 198–99, 203–5; despair, 200; disorder, 206, 212–14; eternity, 193, 206–7; existence, 16–17, 189–98; "fire," 202–5; fixity of the will of condemned, 207–8; freedom and responsibility, 189, 205, 207, 213–16, 220; fruit of unrepentant sin, 198–210; frustration, 200; *gēnna*, 79, 189, 191–93, 195, 197, 199, 289; hate, 200, 206; *mox post mortem*, 270–80; number of saved, 217–18; pain of loss, 199–201; pain of sense, 201–5; punishment for sin, 205–6; real possibility of condemnation, 214–18; rejection by Christ, 192, 194–95, 199; *she'ol (hadēs*, underworld), 79–80, 81–82, 191, 277; solitude, 201, 205–6; unpardonable sin, 192; whether of most of humanity, 197–98, 215–16; whether to hope for salvation of all, 218–21
Perpetual condemnation, contexts: Church Fathers, 195–98; interpretation of Scripture, 16–17; literature, 200–201; magisterium, 190–91; Old Testament, 191, 202; New Testament, 16–17, 192–95, 202–3, 216–18; religions, 190
Perpetual condemnation, referred to: anthropology, 189–90, 200–201, 207–8; conversion and repentance, 207–8, 213–14; ethics, 192–93, 212–14; freedom, 213–14; God's justice and mercy, 189, 210–14; hermeneutics of Scripture, 16–17, 193–95; hope, 218–21; justice and order, 212–14, 217; number of saved, 217–18. *See also* Apokatastasis
Persecution, 54, 63, 84, 234, 237–39
Physics, xii, 44–46, 121
Politics, xii, 14, 244–49, 297, 335
Praeambula spei, 18–19, 25
Praise of God. *See* Eternal life

Process philosophy, xi, 43–44
Protestantism: and the soul, 19–21, 313–18; future, 318; justification by faith, 298–99, 316; metaphysical deficit, 318; person, 318; realized eschatology, 50–53; *sola scriptura*, 315–16; thoroughgoing eschatology, 47–50
Purgatory, 286–308
Purgatory, characteristics of: Christological, 307–8; distinction from condemnation, 301–2; duration, 306–7; and earthly purification of the saints, 306; existence, 287–301; fire, 290–91, 294–96, 302–303, 307–8; forgiveness of venial guilt, 303; intensity of pain, 302, 305; joy and consolation, 302, 305–6; pain of loss/delay, 302; pain of sense, 302–3; *purgatorium*, 297; purification of concupiscence, 290, 294, 303; role of Church, 304–5; *satispassio*, 303; temporal punishment, 303–4; time, 306–7
Purgatory, contexts: Church Fathers, 291–93; ecumenism, 293–96, 298–301; Gregorian masses, 292–93; liturgy, 289, 291–93, 296, 298, 307; magisterium, 295–96, 299, 304–5; New Testament, 289–91; Old Testament, 288–89; oriental theology, 293–96, 300–301; Protestantism, 297–99; Thomas Aquinas, 302–4; Vatican II, 304–5
Purgatory, referred to: anthropology, 286–88; Church, 286, 288, 302–3; communion of saints, 301, 305; God's holiness and justice, 286–87, 304, 307; indulgences, 297–98, 301, 303–4, 307; Jesus Christ, 291, 307–8; judgment, 307–8; justification by faith, 298–99; prayer for dead, 289, 291–93, 296, 298, 304–5, 307; prayer of holy souls, 305; salvation, 307–8; spirituality, 305–7

Rapture, xiii
Realized eschatology. *See* Eschatology
Refrigerium interim, 276, 295
Reincarnation, xiii, 6, 25, 31, 76–78
Relics, 107
Resurrection of the dead, 19, 74–114, 256
Resurrection of the dead, characteristics of: agility, 104–5; beauty, 105; of condemned, 87–88, 92–93, 105; first/second resurrection, 243–48; glory and novelty of risen body, 90–91, 100–105; identity of risen and earthly body, 106–9; of the individual, 84–86; of Israel, 78–79, 82–83; of just, 87–88, 92–93, 104–5, 135; of a life once lived, 109–11, 259–60; otherworldly, 84, 86–87; sexual distinction, 103–4; social aspect, 85, 89–91, 112–14; subtlety, 104; suffering, 104; universal, 84–85, 87–88, 108
Resurrection of the dead, referred to: anthropology, 91, 96–98, 323–24; Christian materialism, 96–98, 114; Christology, 88–91, 322–23; cosmic renewal, 83; cremation, 94–95; eternal life, 104–5, 153, 180–81; ethics, 91, 107–12; Eucharist, 92–93; God, 74, 76, 78, 83, 87, 95, 97–98, 106, 113, ; Holy Spirit, 88, 91–92, 111; human body, 107–9, 113–14; immortality, 102–3, 259–60; judgment, 135–36, 145, 148; justice, 78, 80–81, 84–85, 129, 135; life, 78–80, 82–83, 88, 91, 94–95, 106, 113; marriage, 103–104; new heavens and new earth, 115–16, 121–22; philosophical and theological challenge, 91, 96–100, 122, 125; reincarnation, xiii, 6, 25, 31, 76–78; relics, 107; resurrection of Christ, 88–91, 266–67; salvation, 84, 92, 97, 99, 108–9; and soul, 96–98, 325–26
Resurrection of the dead, sources: art, 84, 94, 125; Church Fathers, 93–98; images of sun, phoenix, seeds, and flowers, 97; Judaism, 75–76; liturgy, 94–95; New Testament, 86–93, 101, 322–23; Old Testament, 78–86; Religions, 75–77
Roman liturgy, 68

Sacraments, 332–33; anointing of the sick, 268–69; baptism, 48, 62, 70, 89, 173, 246, 266–67, 270–71, 292–94, 321, 333; Eucharist, 59, 67–71, 91–93, 125, 206, 219, 231, 292–93; penance, 230–31
Salvation. *See* Jesus Christ
Satan. *See* Devil
Science: and cosmic renewal, 120–25; and the *Parousia*, 44–46. *See also* Parapsychology; Thanatology
Second coming. *See* Parousia
Seventh-Day Adventists, 248
Sexual distinction of risen, ix, 103–4

Sexuality, dignity of, 335
Signs of end-time, 117, 233–41; Antichrist, persecution, apostasy, 237–39; conversion of Israel, 236–37; seeking signs, 59–60; significance of, 239–41; universal preaching of the Gospel, 235–36
Sola scriptura, 315–16
Soul, different views of, 315–16; *anima forma corporis*, 98, 258, 326; created nature of, 20–21, 316; existence of, 7, 22–25, 29–30; immortality/incorruptibility of, xi, 19–25, 313–20; and intermediate eschatology, 313–20, 325–26; Platonism, 23–24, 77, 315–16, 324–25; and Protestantism, 19–21, 313–19; and resurrection, 96–98; separated soul, xi, 19–20, 98, 207–8, 314, 326; Thomas Aquinas, 24–25
Spirituality, 31–33, 48–49, 80–81, 310, 324, 336–37; millennialism, 245–49; vigilance, 239–41
Stoicism, 5–6, 28, 65, 77
Supra-temporal eschatology, 51–53
Syro-Malabarese liturgy, 70

Thanatology, xii–xiii, 29
Theodicy, 42

"Third day," 322–23
Thoroughgoing eschatology. *See* Eschatology
Transience of world, 3, 62
Transmigration of souls. *See* Reincarnation
Trent, Council of, 69, 261, 285, 297, 299–300, 303
Truth of eschatological statements, 14–18; apocalyptic interpretation, 14–15; different approaches, 18–19; on eternal life, 153–59; existential interpretation, 15–16; and hope, 14; and judgment, 135–36, 142; on the *Parousia*, 46–66; performative interpretation, 15–16; on perpetual condemnation, 16–17, 193–95; on resurrection, 89–91; revelation by the Spirit, 33–36

Universal call to holiness, 310
Utopian spirit, 22, 28, 248–49, 334

Vatican, II Council, 26, 37, 69, 110, 116, 126–27, 186, 190, 215, 231, 261, 279–80, 289, 304–5, 307, 311, 316, 322, 332
Vienne, Council of, 168
Vigilance, 67, 239–41

Work, 30; and cosmic renewal, 126–29

Index of Names

Achilles, 32
Adam, K., 68, 177
Adorno, T. W., 113, 255
Aeschylus, 27, 75
Aesculapius, 75
Ahern, B. M., 88
Ahlbrecht, A., 20, 315, 316, 317
Aikman, D., xi
Ajax, 27
Alan of Lille, 297
Alberigo, G., 296
Albright, C. R., xii
Albright, W. F., 76
Alcuin of York, 23
Aldwinckle, R. F., 180
Alexander of Hales, 169
Alexander, P. H., ix
Alexandre, M., 102
Alfaro, J., 185, 320, 323
Alfeche, M., 94
Alfonsus Maria di Liguori, 197, 255, 305
Alfrink, B. J., 84
Allen, L. C., 83
Allen, W., 74
Allison, D. C., xi, 46, 54–57, 60, 61, 137
Allo, E. B., 290
Almaricus di Bène, 169, 247
Althaus, P., 92, 218, 244, 247, 263, 298, 301, 313–14, 317, 339
Alviar, J. J., x, xiii, 33, 70, 131, 136, 143, 189, 227, 234, 266, 287, 339
Ambrose, 159, 177, 196–97, 247, 256, 276–77, 282, 284, 290
Ambrosiaster, 196, 237
Ancona, G., x, xiii, 23, 110, 119, 144, 156, 266, 272, 339

Anderson, R. S., xiii
Andrew of Caesarea, 159
Angué, J. L., 95
Anrich, G., 294–95
Anscombe, G. E. M., 257
Anselm, 23
Apollinarius, 246
Arendt, H., 27
Aristides, 135, 239
Aristotle, 4–6, 98, 119–20, 162, 262
Arius, 124, 165
Arnold of Bonneval, 120
Arocena, F. M., 175
Arroniz, J., 135, 156
Athanasius, 23, 232, 263
Athenagoras, 93, 97–98, 106
Aubineau, M., 156
Audet, L., 102
Augustine, x, 5, 9, 19, 23, 35, 55, 65–66, 94, 95–97, 101–3, 105, 112, 115, 120, 138, 142, 145, 148–49, 158–59, 161–62, 164, 167–68, 173–74, 176–77, 181, 186, 197, 208, 211, 225–26, 234–36, 240, 245–48, 261, 263, 274, 277–78, 282, 284, 288–93, 295, 305, 308, 332
Augustine of Dacia, 331
Aune, D. E., 49, 65, 70
Aurelius Prudentius, 309
Austin, J. L., 15–17
Averroes, 162
Avery-Peck, A. J., xii, 29
Ayán-Calvo, J. J., 93

Bacht, H., viii, 339
Badilita, C., 238
Balabanski, V., 51
Baraúna, G., 332

Barbaglio, G., 16
Barbour, I. G., xii
Bardanes, G., 295
Bardy, G., 156
Barlaam of Calabria, 166
Barnard, A. L. W., 243
Barrientos, U., 306
Barth, K., xii, 20, 21, 89, 109, 180, 208, 218, 262, 263–64, 301, 313–14, 316–17, 329
Bartsch, H.-W., 52
Basil, 70, 103, 134, 165, 167, 197, 199, 282, 291
Basilides, 293
Bauckham, H. J., xi
Baumann, M., vii
Baur, F. C., 58
Bautz, J., 306
Beasley-Murray, G. R., xi, 140
Beauchamp, P., 86
Beaudouin, L., 281
Beck, H., 76
Becker, E., xiii
Becker, H., 41
Becker, J., 80
Bede, the Venerable, 59, 177
Beider, W., 100
Bellarmine, R., 144, 255, 300
Bels, J., 267
Benedict XII, 151, 166, 279, 296
Benedict XVI, vii, xv, 10–11, 13, 17, 20, 32, 59, 71, 113, 130, 135, 142, 144, 147, 153, 157, 159, 179, 201, 220, 229, 249, 253, 256, 289, 304, 308, 311, 335
Berdiaev, N., 208, 213
Bergamelli, F., 276
Bergson, H., 121, 268
Berman, H. J., 297

349

350 Index of Names

Bernanos, G., 189, 206, 209, 253
Bernard, 179, 181, 197, 277, 279
Bernardine of Siena, 305
Bernstein, A. E., xi
Berruto, A. M., 245
Bertholet, A., 75
Bertola, E., 24
Bessarion of Nicea, 296
Betz, O., 304, 314
Beyreuther, E., xv
Bianchi, U., 195
Bietenhard, H., xv, 202
Biffi, G., x, 3, 8, 182, 207, 215, 314, 339
Biffi, I., 40
Billerbeck, P., 88
Billot, L., 41, 107
Bingemer, M. C. L., 314
Biran, Maine de, 121
Bjorling, J., xiii
Black, M., 86
Blasich, G., 106
Bleeker, C. J., 49
Blenkinsopp, J., 83, 322
Blixen, K., 225
Bloch, E., xi, 6–7, 12–13, 28, 99, 126–27
Block, D. I., 83
Blomberg, C. L., 56
Blondel, M., 64, 268
Böckle, F., viii, 340
Boethius, 161, 180
Boff, L., 267, 319
Boismard, M.-É., 62, 209, 217, 319
Boliek, L. E., 93
Bonaventure, 174–75, 207, 226
Bonhöffer, D., 13, 33
Bonitz, H., 4
Bonnard, E., 55
Bonsirven, J., 87
Bonwetsch, G. N., 93
Boobyer, G. H., 55
Bordoni, M., x, 33, 101, 115,

207, 218, 243, 300, 314, 321, 330–32, 334, 339
Borges, J. L., 259
Bornkamm, G., 46
Boros, L., 205, 257, 267–68, 281, 304, 306, 326, 339
Börresen, K. E., 94
Bortone, G., 79, 81, 132
Bossuet, J.-B., 245
Botte, B., 243
Bougerol, J.-G., 297
Bouillard, H., 209
Bourgeois, H., 67
Bourke, J., 132
Bouyer, L., 188
Bovet, T., 110
Bovon-Thurneyson, A., 88
Boyle, M. O. R., 243
Braaten, C. E., x, 44
Brancato, F., 319
Brandes, W., 245
Bratsiotis, I., 295
Braun, R., 158
Breuning, W., 110
Brisbois, E., 306
Brown, C., xv, 86
Brown, M., 98, 180
Brown, R. B., 68
Bruaire, C., 121
Bruce, F. F., 68
Brunner, E., 50, 66, 209, 218, 263, 314, 317–18, 329, 339
Buchberger, M., xv
Bucher, G., 89
Bückers, H., 85
Bukovski, L., 76
Bulgàkov, S. N., 35, 218, 300–301
Bultmann, R., 15, 46, 51–53, 54, 99–100, 116, 163, 318–19
Burggraf, J., 175
Buri, F., 46, 218
Burini, C., 276
Burkitt, F. C., 60
Burney, C. F., 29
Bynum, C. W., xi, 40, 93, 339

Caesarius of Arles, 159, 290–91
Cajetan, 22, 169, 268
Calvin, J., 185, 298–99
Camilleri, N., 332
Camus, A., 29
Canobbio, G., 319–20, 323, 326
Capelle, B., 41
Carle, J., 93
Carnovale-Guiducci, D., 306
Carozzi, C., 41
Cassiodorus, 23, 103
Castellucci, E., 46
Castillo-Pino, E., 16
Catherine of Genova, 302, 305
Catherine of Siena, 211
Cavallin, H. C. C., 82
Celsus, 93
Cerinthus, 243
Chadwick, H., 93
Chapman, D. M., 301
Charles, R. H., 76, 84
Charlesworth, J. H., xi, 75
Chilton, B., 86
Chrupcala, L. D., 227
Ciccarese, M., 297
Cicero, 6, 27–28
Cilleruelo, L., 164
Cimosa, M., 132
Ciola, N., x, xiii, 33, 101, 218, 242, 300, 314, 321, 330, 332, 334, 339
Cipriani, S., 290
Clark, D., 255
Clark, R., 59
Claudius Mamertius, 23
Clayton, P., 44
Clement of Alexandria, 20, 23, 55, 255, 262–63, 274, 294
Clement of Rome, 58, 97, 107, 274–76
Clément, O., 65, 122
Cobb, J. B., xi, 43–44
Cocagnac, A. M., 41, 147

Index of Names 351

Coenen, L., xv, 86, 260
Cohn, N., 242, 247
Collins, J. J., xi
Collins, M., x
Collopy, B., 29, 258
Colzani, G., x, 78, 81, 107, 209, 268, 339
Commodianus, 244
Comte, A., 247
Congar, Y. M.-J., 293–94, 298, 304, 306, 308
Conte, N., 67
Copleston, F., 26
Cornehl, P., 42
Cornelis, H., 77
Courtois, S., 29
Cousins, E. W., 44
Couture, A., 76
Cox, D., 81
Craig, W. L., 90
Cristiani, L., 298
Croce, V., 95
Crossan, J. D., 50, 90
Crouse, R. D., 161
Crouzel, H., 93, 171, 195–96, 276, 290
Cruz Cruz, J., 24
Cuchet, G., 300
Cullmann, O., 19, 49, 51, 54, 64, 260, 264, 267, 313–14, 316–18
Cumont, F. V., 30, 95
Curti, C., 245
Cyprian, x, 64, 158, 164, 176–77, 182, 259, 275, 293
Cyril of Alexandria, 55, 92, 276, 282, 292
Cyril of Jerusalem, 55, 93, 97, 101, 135

Dagens, C., 65
Dahl, N. A., 57
Dahood, M., 81
D'Alembert, J., 263
Daley, B. E., x, xi, 9, 23, 57, 64–65, 93–94, 101, 107–8, 134, 158–59, 164, 177, 195–96, 201, 208, 220, 240, 243–46, 274, 276, 284, 291, 294, 325–26, 339
Dalmais, I.-H., 156
Daniélou, J., viii, 14, 94, 146, 173, 196, 332, 339
Daniels, T., 44, 242, 247
Dante Alighieri, 200, 302
Dassmann, E., 83
Daube, D., 39
Dauphinais, M., 145
Dautzenberg, G., 86
David, B., 145
Davies, W. D., 39, 46, 54–57, 137
Davis, S. T., 90, 322
De Beauvoir, S., 154, 257
De Bruyne, L., 276
Decamps, A. L., 260
De Carlo, G., 132
De Fuenterrabía, F., 289
De Georges, A., 76
De Giovanni, A., 323
De Haes, P., 67
De Halleux, A., 296
Deiana, G., 79
De Lacunza y Díaz, M., 248
De Lavalette, H., 196
Del Cura Elena, S., 76
De Lubac, H., 10, 247, 277
Delumeau, J., 41, 149, 209
De Montherlant, P., 154
Denis, F., xiii
Dennis, T. J., 102
Denzinger, J., xv
Derambure, J., 196, 247
Derrida, J., 22
Descartes, R., 22, 99, 154
Des Places, E., 156
De Unamuno, M., 26, 154, 259
Devoti, D., 108
De Vrégille, B., 277
Dhanis, E., 88
Dianich, S., 16
Diderot, D., 263
Didymus the Blind, 167, 196, 219–20
Dillon, J. M., 19
Diocletian, 245, 293
Diogenes Laertius, 28
Disley, E., 183
Dodd, C. H., 46, 50–51, 54, 62
Dölger, F. J., 70
Domergue, B., 261
Donaldson, T. L., 57
Dondeine, H.-F., 169
Donne, J., 112
Dörries, H., 245
Dosideus, 300
Dostoevskij, F., 206
Douie, D., 278
Dreyfus, F. G., 87
Ducay, A., xiii
Duns Scotus, 22, 172, 303
Dupont, J., 63
Dupuy, B.-D., 247
Duquoc, C., 49
Durandus of St. Porcianus, 107
Durrwell, F.-X., 67, 322
Duval, Y.-M., 102, 104
Dykmans, M., 279

Eckhart, 169–70
Eger, J., 244–45
Elert, W., 314
Eliade, M., 8
Eliot, T. S., 39, 286
Elkaisy-Friemuth, M., 19
Ellis, G. F. R., xii, 45
Engels, F., 247
Eno, R. B., 294
Ephrem, 55, 158, 239–40, 282, 289, 291
Epicurus, 28
Epimetheus, 8
Epiphanius of Salamis, 101, 246, 276
Errázuriz, C. J., 169
Escribano-Alberca, I., 21, 42, 309, 339
Eunomius, 165
Euripides, 27
Eusebius of Caesarea, 59, 65, 97, 147, 244–45, 247, 318

Index of Names

Eutychios, 104
Evagrius Ponticus, 185, 196
Evdokimov, P., 218, 300–301

Fabbri, M. V., 86
Faber, F. W., 305
Fàbrega, V., 244
Favale, P., 332
Feder, A., 77
Feine, P., 54
Feiner, J., viii, 110, 340
Feingold, L., 10
Felici, S., 276, 291
Fénelon, F., 305
Fernández, A., 187
Fernández, V. M., 319
Ferrisi, A., 94
Festugière, A.-J., 27
Feuerbach, L., 26
Feuillet, A., 39, 72, 217, 228
Feuling, D., 107
Février, A., 292
Fichte, J.-G., 21, 155, 206, 326
Fierro, A., 93, 100
Filoramo, G., 93, 180
Finé, H., 291
Finkelstein, L., 87
Fischer, J., 291–92
Flanagan, D., 325
Flew, A. N., xiii, 29
Florovsky, G., 50, 195
Flusser, D., 49
Fontaine, J., 104, 237
Forget, J., 120
Fornberg, T., 58
Forte, B., 157
Fortman, E. J., x, 286
Foster, D. R., 24
Francis of Assisi, 306
Francis of Sales, 211, 216
Frick, R., 229
Frossard, A., 154, 310–11

Gaechter, P., 58
Gagliardi, M., 59
Gaine, S., 172
Gallas, A., 278

Galleni, L., 122
Galot, J., 246
Gandavius, 169
Garrigou-Lagrange, R., 306
Genicot, L., 297
Gerhoh of Richterberg, 255
Germanus of Constantin-
   ople, 265
Gerson, J., 255
Gevaert, J., 25
Ghini, E., 238
Giblet, J., 34
Giblin, C. H., 242
Gide, A., 154
Gil-i-Ribas, J., 279
Gilkey, L., 43
Gill, J., 296
Gillespie, J., xiii, 80
Gillet, G., 106
Gillet, R., 104
Gillman, N., xii
Gilson, E., xi, 326
Girardi, M., 134
Giudici, A., 16
Glasson, T. F., 76
Gleason, R. W., 267
Glorieux, P., 267
Gnilka, J., 54, 56, 290
Goethe, J. W., 110, 256
Goñi, P., 94
González de Cardedal, O.,
   219
Gougand, L., 70
Gourgues, M., 242
Gozzelino, G., x, 7, 20–21, 78,
   95, 107, 144, 148, 150, 204,
   241, 257, 262, 264, 266,
   269, 281, 308, 310, 318–19,
   321, 326, 339
Granfield, P., 294
Grässer, E., 46–47, 60
Greco, C., 243
Greenberg, M., 83
Greenspoon, L. J., 84
Gregory of Elvira, 108
Gregory of Nazianzen, 164,
   183, 197, 202, 276, 305

Gregory of Nyssa, x, 23, 94,
   98, 102–3, 105–7, 109, 143,
   146, 174, 177, 179–81, 188,
   196, 210, 219, 263, 276,
   291, 294, 334
Gregory Palamas, 165–66, 173
Gregory the Great, 59, 65,
   96–97, 104, 166, 176, 183,
   203, 237, 240–41, 255, 268,
   276, 290, 291–93, 295–96
Grelot, P., 80, 84, 86, 220,
   260
Grenz, S. J., xii
Greshake, G., x, 80, 87, 89,
   93, 306, 312, 319–22, 324,
   339
Griffin, D. R., 43
Grillmeier, A., viii, 246, 339
Gross, J., 156
Grundmann, W., 55
Gry, L., 242–43
Guardini, R., x, 74, 110–11,
   257, 310, 339
Guerra, M., 316
Guitton, J., 204, 308
Gundry, R. H., 55–56, 90
Guntermann, F., 6
Gutenberg, J., 110

Haag, E., 83
Haeffner, G., 312
Hagner, D. H., 55, 57–58, 60,
   137–38, 183
Halpern, B., 84
Hannam, W., 161
Hanson, P., xi
Harris, M. J., 321
Hasel, G. F., 84
Hattrup, D., 21, 42, 263
Haugen, J., xii
Hauke, M., 185, 271
Hawthorne, G. F., 49
Hayes, Z., x–xii
Hayward, J., 112
Healy, N. J., xii
Hegel, G. W. F., 42–43, 113,
   247, 281

Index of Names 353

Heidegger, M., 29, 51, 53, 255, 257, 267
Heidler, F., 209, 301, 317
Heinzer, F., 220
Heitmann, C., 35
Hellemo, G., 135
Hellholm, D., 58
Hengel, M., 75
Henry, M., 121
Henry, M.-L., 93
Herbert, G., 255
Hermann, C., 21, 317
Hermann, W., 44
Hermas, 57, 108, 275
Herms, E., 263
Hernández Martínez, J. M., 319, 325
Herodotus, 27–28
Hervé, J. M., 203
Hesiod, 8
Hettinger, F., 107
Hick, J., xiii, 77
Hiers, R. H., 46
Hill, C. E., 242
Hillary of Poitiers, x, 55, 91, 101, 105–6, 146, 187, 197, 240, 276, 282, 284
Himmelfarb, M., xi
Hirsch, E., 44
Hjelde, S., 16
Hoffmann, P., 6, 80, 260, 315
Hoffmann, Y., 132
Hofmann, G., 296
Holböck, F., 302, 305
Hölderlin, F., 149, 256–57
Hollaz, D., 310
Holtzmann, H. J., 58, 294
Homer, 27, 75
Honorius of Autun, 105
Hopkins, G. M., 110–11
Horn, H.-J., 201
Huftier, M., 305
Hugh of Saint-Cher, 169
Hugh of St. Victor, 102, 115, 169, 174, 176
Hulsbosch, A., 315
Hunt, S., 242

Iacoangeli, R., 277
Iammarrone, L., 24
Ignatius of Antioch, 64–65, 88, 92, 112, 153, 195, 275–76
Illanes, J. L., 9, 126, 336
Innocent III, 189
Innocent IV, 296
Innocent XI, 307
Introvigne, M., 77
Irenaeus of Lyons, x, 21, 24, 64, 82, 91–93, 105, 108, 116–17, 135, 156, 179, 187, 195, 229, 242–44, 246, 275–77, 322
Irsigler, H., 71, 132
Iserloh, E., 196
Isidore of Seville, 200, 293, 305
Izquierdo, C., 175

Jaeger, W., 30
James, W., 15
Jansen, J. F., 185, 246
Jaspers, K., 254
Jay, P., 290, 293
Jedin, H., 299
Jenks, G. C., 238
Jensen, R. M., 84, 94
Jenson, R. W., xi
Jeremias, J., 50, 57, 67, 85, 232
Jerome, x, 102–3, 106, 120, 147, 195–97, 202, 214, 237, 245–46, 248, 274, 276, 282, 315
Joachim da Fiore, 247
Jodl, F., 26
John Chrysostom, 55, 59, 65–66, 70, 94, 101, 120, 164–65, 181, 197, 199, 207, 275–76, 282, 290, 292, 294
John Damascene, 229, 268–69
John of the Cross, 5, 130, 138, 306
John Paul II, 22, 70–71, 102, 110, 128, 211–13, 217, 249, 265, 269, 306, 310–11

John Philoponus, 107
John the Deacon, 65
Johnson, S., 79
Jolif, J. F., 25
Jolivet, R., 53, 267
Jorgenson, J., 296
Josemaría Escrivá, 113–14, 125, 146, 178–79, 234, 254, 272, 286, 303, 305, 307
Journet, C., 203, 207, 213
Jugie, M., 165–66, 297
Julian of Toledo, 115, 276, 305
Julian Pomerius, 105
Jüngel, E., 20, 109–10, 209, 254, 264–65, 314, 316
Jungmann, J. A., 68, 294
Justin Martyr, 24, 64, 93, 97, 108, 239, 243, 275, 277

Kahles, W., 333
Kamlah, W., 246
Kant, I., 21, 26, 99, 247, 316
Karmirês, I. N., 295, 301
Karrer, O., 325
Käsemann, E., 46, 49
Kasper, W., xv, 39, 117, 321
Kauffer, R., 29
Keating, D. A., x
Kee, H. C., 56
Kehl, M., 76
Keller, E., 70
Kellermann, U., 80, 85
Kelly, A. J., xi
Kendall, D., 90, 322
Kerr, F., 25
Kessler, H., 322
Kierkegaard, S., 210, 258
Kittel, G., xv
Klock, C., 102
Kloppenburg, B., 76
Knoch, O. B., 58
Knox, R. A., 60
Knox, W. L., 93
Kolarcik, M., 21
Komonchak, J. A., x
Konstan, D., 5
Kopling, A., 322

Index of Names

Korosak, B. J., 208–9
Köster, H., 263
Kotila, H., 292
Kramer, K., xiii
Kraner, S. N., 159
Krause, G., 75
Kreeft, P., xi
Kremer, J., 80, 87, 89, 93, 312, 321
Kretschmar, G., 93, 108
Kübler-Ross, E., xiii, 29
Kümmel, W. G., 54
Kundera, M., 27
Künneth, W., 317
Kunz, E., 19, 298, 339
Künzi, M., 55, 58, 60
Künzle, P., 334
Kvanvig, J. L., 209

Lacan, M. F., 209
Lactantius, 23, 64, 97, 243–44, 291
Lagrange, M.-J., 58, 216–17
Laín Entralgo, P., 5, 8–9, 314
Lakner, F., 278
Lamb, M. L., x, 98, 112, 145, 161, 330, 334
Lampe, G. W. H., 94
Landes, R. A., 44, 242
Lane, D. A., x
Lang, B., xi, 149, 154
Lang, U. M., 70
Lanne, E., 156, 301
Larcher, C., 86
Larchet, J.-C., 156, 277, 296, 305
Larrimore, D., 46
Lavatori, R., x, 339
Lawrence, N., 7
Le Boulluec, A., 94
Leclercq, H., 293
Leclercq, J., 70
Lefebure, G., 306
Le Goff, J., 291, 297, 303
Le Guillou, M.-J., 34, 144, 154, 187
Lehaut, A., 208

Lehmann, K., 306, 322
Lengsfeld, P., 89
Lennerz, H., 172
Leo IX, 20
Leo X, 298
Leo the Great, 162, 197
Léon-Dufour, X., 90
Leopardi, G., 8
Lerner, R. E., 247
Le Senne, R., 154
Lessing, G. E., 247
Lessius, L., 206
Levenson, J. D., xii, 80, 83–84
Levering, M. W., 145
Lévy, I., 76
Lewis, C. S., 97, 103–4, 120, 159, 201, 206
Libânio, J.-B., 314
Link, H.-G., 150, 287
Lochet, L., 274
Lods, A., 78, 289
Lohfink, G., 306, 319–20, 322, 324
Löhrer, M., 110
Lohse, E., 88
Loisy, A., 46, 228–29
López, T., 27
Lorizio, G., 269, 321
Lortz, J., 196
Lossky, V., 165
Lotzika, I., 95
Luther, M., xv, 22, 41, 182–83, 247, 280, 298–99, 303, 315, 318
Lux, R., 242
Luz, U., 55–56, 58
Lyons, A., 122

MacIntyre, A., 29
Mackenzie, N. H., 111
MacRae, G. W., 50
Madigan, K., xii, 80
Maggioni, B., 56, 61, 63
Magris, A., 108
Maimonides, 162
Maldamé, J.-M., 122
Mâle, E., 94

Malebranche, N., 121, 258
Malevez, L., 126, 209
Mann, G., 219
Manns, P., 196
Mansi, J. D., 116
Mara, M. G., 246
Marcel, G., xi, 3–4, 6, 7–8, 12, 18, 28, 74, 99, 112, 127, 177, 253, 268, 315
Marcellus of Ancyra, 185, 246
Marcion, 118, 229
Marcovich, M., 93, 98
Marguerat, D. L., 133
Mark of Ephesus (Eugenicus), 296
Marsch, W.-D., 14
Martelet, G., 91, 122, 306
Martin, R., xi
Martin-Achard, R., 79, 81, 85
Martínez y Martínez, E., 67
Martini, C. M., 90
Martini, M., 208
Marucci, C., 81, 321
Marx, K., 6, 26, 28, 113–14, 247
Marxsen, W., 46
Mason, A. J., 291
Maspero, G., 94, 174, 196
Masset, P., 326
Mateo-Seco, L. F., 94, 258, 270, 306
Maurer, A. A., xi
Maury, P., 218, 301
Maximus the Confessor, x, 23, 78, 166, 219, 220, 226, 294, 334
Mazzinghi, L., 261
Mazzucco, C., 243
McDannell, C., xi, 149, 154
McGinn, B., xi, 238, 242
McGrath, A. E., 149
McInerny, R., 162
McNamara, M., 242
Medina, J. J., 3
Meier, J., 46
Meinertz, M. P., 233
Melton, J. G., vii

Index of Names 355

Mendelssohn, M., 21, 256
Menoud, H., 314, 318
Merkel, H., 140
Merklein, H., 47
Merleau-Ponty, M., 121
Mersch, É., 122, 267
Messori, V., 213
Methodius of Olympus, 93,
    101, 107
Metz, J.-B., 53, 117
Meyendorff, J., 165, 277, 301,
    303, 329, 334
Meyer, H. A. W., 58
Michaelis, W., 218
Michaud, E., 197, 220
Michel, A., 107, 195, 197, 202,
    215–16, 297, 300
Michl, J., 290
Migne, J.-P., 255
Milet, J., 281
Millán-Puelles, A., 30
Miller, W., 248
Milton, J., 32
Minois, G., 198
Minon, A., 305
Minucius Felix, 97, 108
Miranda, A., 94
Moghila, P., 300
Möhler, J. A., 299
Moioli, G., 16, 166, 169, 182,
    203–4, 207–8, 245, 290,
    307–8
Molina, L., 197
Molinari, A., 332
Möller, C., 6, 27
Moltmann, J., xii, 6, 13, 242,
    244–45, 318, 339
Monod, J., 8, 29
Moody, R., xiii
Mooney, C. F., 122
Moore, M. S., 84
Moraldi, L., 79, 159, 190
Morales, J., 98
Morerod, C., 318
Moriconi, B., 306
Morin, E., 256
Mühlen, H., 35, 318

Müller, G., 75
Müller, G. L., 301
Müller-Goldkuhle, P., 309
Müntzer, T., 248
Murillo-Gómez, J. I., 258
Mussner, F., 87, 90, 152, 232,
    235, 304

Naab, E., 279
Nachtwei, G., 21, 316
Nadeau, M. T., 246
Naldini, M., 243
Nardi, C., 243
Narsai, 326
Nautin, P., 92
Neale, R. E., xiii
Neiman, D., 195
Nemeshegyi, P., 195
Neubaur, I., 206
Neusner, J., xii, 29, 86
Neville, R. C., 43
Newman, J. H., 305
Newton, I., 120
Nickelsburg, G. W. E., xi,
    86, 316
Nicolas, M.-J., 107
Niebuhr, H. R., xii
Nietzsche, F., 26, 156, 200,
    205–6, 247, 326
Noce, C., 276
Nocke, F. J., 136, 149, 314
Nolland, J., 82
Norelli, E., 243
Notker, 255
Novak, J. A., 24
Novatianus, 196
Nowack, W., 294
Ntedika, J., 67, 290, 291

O'Brien, E., 288
O'Callaghan, P., vii–viii, xi,
    xv, 4, 6–7, 13–14, 17–18, 20,
    22–24, 28–30, 45, 49–50,
    53, 59, 61, 74, 78, 88, 93,
    98–99, 106–9, 121, 123–24,
    134, 139, 146, 151, 169–70,
    175, 231, 234, 288, 298,
    301, 313, 315, 320, 331–32,
    335, 339
O'Collins, G., 90, 322
O'Connor, D., 7
O'Connor, F., 286
O'Connor, J. T., x, 110, 177,
    339
Oepke, A., 39
O'Hagan, A., 116
O'Neil, C. J., xi, 326
Orbe, A., 77, 93, 108
Origen, x, 9, 16, 23, 59, 93, 96,
    100–103, 106–7, 116, 122,
    134, 164, 166, 170–71, 173,
    185, 187, 189, 193, 195–97,
    201–3, 206, 214–15, 218–
    20, 229, 232, 234, 245, 248,
    262, 276, 290, 293–95,
    300, 334
Orlandi, P. A., 255
Orr, W. F., 163
Ortiz de Urbina, I., 239
Ott, L., 279
Otten, W., 161
Otto, R., 43, 51, 57, 233
Otto von Freising, 245

Palazzini, P., 95
Pandit, B., 76
Pani, G., 243
Pannenberg, W., x, xii, 11–12,
    21, 42–44, 77, 81, 102,
    110–11, 123, 131, 136, 140,
    143, 160, 179, 180, 188, 194,
    227, 229, 263–64, 300,
    307, 312, 316–18, 320, 324,
    329, 340
Panteghini, G., 300
Papias, 243–44
Pascal, B., 175, 201, 253,
    334–35
Paterson, R. W. K., 25
Patrides, C. A., 242
Patroclus, 27
Pattaro, G., 310
Paul VI, 37, 74–75, 189, 203,
    280, 292, 296, 325

356 Index of Names

Paulinus of Nola, 284
Pavan, V., 70
Peerbolte, L. J. L., 238
Pegis, A. C., xi, 24, 326
Péguy, C., vii, 111, 115, 219
Pellistrandi, S., 104
Pericles, 28
Perrin, J.-M., 209
Perrot, C., 39
Peter Chrysologus, 111, 256
Peter Damian, 231
Peter Lombard, 102, 143, 160, 295, 297
Peter of Poitiers, 333
Peters, F. J., 256
Petit, L., 296
Petrà, B., 20
Pfleiderer, O., 58
Phan, P. C., xii
Philippe de la Trinité, 306
Philips, G., 332
Philo of Alexandria, 137
Photius, 277, 279
Pieper, J., 21, 253, 255–57, 262, 267, 316, 340
Pietrella, E., 243
Piolanti, A., 202, 212, 296, 298, 305
Pioli, G., 208
Pius X, 307
Pius XI, 128, 231
Pius XII, 123, 168, 325
Plato, 19, 20, 23–25, 30–31, 40, 77, 120, 142, 255, 259, 316, 326
Plotinus, 40, 180
Plummer, A., 55, 163
Pohier, J.-M., 314
Polanco-Fermandois, R., 243
Polkinghorne, J. C., xii
Polycarp, 88, 195, 275–76
Pomponazzi, P., 316
Porphyry, 96–97
Pozo, C., x, 13–14, 20–21, 66–68, 71, 79–81, 86, 90, 96, 107, 126–27, 152, 165, 191, 202, 273–75, 280,

295–96, 314, 323, 329, 332–33, 340
Prat, F., 174
Premm, M., 207
Prestige, G. L., 79
Prigent, P., 93
Prosper of Aquitaine, 158
Pryke, J., 86
Ps.-Denis the Areopagite, 166
Ps.-Macarius, 325
Puech, É., 80
Puig, F., 169
Pythagoras, 77

Quint, J., 170
Quodvultdeus of Carthage, 158

Rädle, F., 41
Rahner, K., xii, 16, 53, 193, 204, 219–20, 257, 262, 267–68, 314, 325, 340
Rahula, W., 155
Ratzinger, J., x, 17, 21, 30, 35, 70, 77–78, 80, 100, 107, 136, 143, 203, 220, 227–29, 232, 235–36, 264, 277, 291, 293–94, 304, 306, 316–17, 320–21, 324–26, 329, 340
Rego, J., xiii
Reichenbach, B. R., 97
Reid, J. K. S., 298
Reimarus, S., 46, 58
Reinhardt, K., 307
Remberger, F.-X., 203, 207
Richardson, C. C., 195
Riebl, M., 322
Ries, J., 260
Riestra, J. A., 186
Rigaux, B., 87
Rilke, R. M., 256–57
Ritschl, A., 44, 263
Rius-Camps, J., 195
Rizzi, A., 209
Robert, A., 217
Robertson, A., 163
Robillard, J. A., 204

Robinson, J. A. T., 89, 321–22
Roguet, A.-M., 231, 305
Rohde, E., 79
Roncaglia, M., 295
Rondeau, M.-J., 187
Rondet, H., 109–10, 204, 207, 267, 306
Rordorf, W., 70
Rouillard, P., 176
Roulland, P., 217
Rousseau, M. F., xi
Rowley, H. H., 75
Royo-Marín, A., 160, 211, 214
Rudoni, A., 305, 310
Ruggieri, G., 278
Ruini, C., 323
Ruiz de la Peña, J. L., x, 13, 26, 28, 47, 76, 84, 89, 92, 101, 118, 135, 180, 203–4, 209, 213, 220, 267–69, 312, 314, 323, 340
Ruiz-Retegui, A., 27–28, 31, 110
Rupert of Deutz, 333
Rusche, H., 89
Russell, J. B., xi, 149, 276

Sabourin, L., 56
Sacchi, P., 21
Sachs, J. R., 171, 209, 220, 274
Sagnard, F. M. M., 108
Salmona, B., 196
Sanders, E. P., 46
Saraiva-Martins, J., 34
Sartori, L., 332
Sartory, G., 209
Sartory, T., 209
Sartre, J.-P., 6, 8, 29, 53, 201, 206, 257, 267
Sassi, L., 307
Savon, H., 237
Sbaffoni, F., 238
Schäfer, P., 299
Schatkin, M., 195
Schattenmann, J., 287
Scheeben, M.-J., 89, 102, 104, 179

Index of Names 357

Scheffczyk, L., 24, 76, 77, 117, 265, 280, 318, 340
Scheler, M., 254–55
Schell, H., 107
Scherer, G., 255
Schiewietz, S., 197
Schillebeeckx, E., 209
Schiller, F., 256–57
Schlatter, A. Von, 314
Schlegel, J. L., 95
Schleiermacher, F., 263
Schlier, H., 62
Schmaus, M., x, 19, 53, 159, 198, 203–4, 230–31, 237–38, 310, 340
Schmemann, A., 113
Schmidt, B. B., 29
Schmied, A., 209
Schmithals, W., 46, 89, 260
Schmitt, A., 90
Schmitz, E. D., 175
Schmöle, K., 294–95
Schnackenburg, R., 47, 53
Schneider, W., 131, 152
Schniewind, J., 52, 319
Scholarius, G., 296
Scholem, G., 46, 81
Schönborn, C., 76–77, 220, 323
Schönmetzer, A., xv
Schopenhauer, A., 257
Schubert, K., 86
Schulz, S., 56–57
Schürer, E., 86
Schutzeichel, H., 298
Schwarz, H., x–xii
Schweitzer, A., 46–51, 53–54, 226
Scotus Eriugena, 169, 205, 218
Segarra, F., 106
Sellin, G., 89
Seneca, 253
Sesboüé, B., 39, 70, 110, 221, 308
Severus of Antioch, 158–59
Shakespeare, W., 258

Shaw, G. B., 205
Sherwood, P., 220
Sicardus of Cremona, 255
Sicari, A. M., 147, 204
Simon of Thessalonica, 295–96
Simon of Tournai, 297
Simonetti, M., 243–44
Siniscalco, P., 93
Skinner, B. F., 213
Smith, C. R., 243
Socinus, F., 208, 263
Socrates (historian), 165
Socrates (philosopher), 31, 267, 270
Söding, T., 47
Solon, 28
Sophocles, 27, 75
Spácil, T., 294–95
Spanneut, M., 65
Speigl, J., 256
Spicq, C., 186, 290
Spinoza, B., 21
Spira, A., 102
Spiteris, Y., 301
St. Hilaire, G., 26
Stange, C., 21, 314
Starkey-Greig, M., 306
Staudenmaier, F. A., 332
Stauffer, E., 228, 291
Stefani, P., 41
Stein, E., 161
Stemberger, G., 86
Stendhal, K., 30
Stewart, J., 259
Stiernon, D., 295
Stoeger, W. G., 120
Stone, M. E., xi
Strack, H. L., 88
Strecker, G., 56, 57
Strumìa, A., 20
Stuiber, A., 256, 276, 292
Suárez, F., 197, 205, 300, 303, 305
Suchecki, Z., 95
Sullivan, C., 46
Suso, H., 255

Sutcliffe, E. F., 85
Swete, H. B., 93, 108, 291

Tabarroni, A., 278
Tábet, M., 315
Talbot, C. H., 58
Tanzarella, S., 243
Tanzella-Nitti, G., 20
Tatian, 24, 77, 106
Taviani-Carozzi, H., 41
Taylor, C., 245, 270
Taylor, R. J., 21
Teilhard de Chardin, P., xii, 110, 122–23, 126, 162, 262
Teixidor, J., 239
Temple, W., 43
Tenney, M. C., 49
Terrin, A. N., 243
Tertullian, x, 23–24, 74, 76, 93–94, 96–97, 101–2, 108, 112, 118, 124, 131, 135, 139, 160, 199, 229, 243–44, 246, 275–76, 291–93
Theodoret of Cyrus, 103, 136, 165–66, 173
Theofilactus, 277, 279
Theophilus of Antioch, 20, 106
Theresa of Avila, 105, 154, 182, 216
Theresa of Lisieux, 33, 149, 217, 306
Thielicke, H., 20, 93, 314, 316, 318
Thomas Aquinas, x, xi, 4–5, 9–10, 19, 24–25, 49, 98, 100–105, 112, 115, 117, 119, 130–31, 143–45, 150, 160, 162, 165, 168–69, 172–74, 177–80, 182–83, 185–86, 197–98, 200, 203–7, 211–12, 215, 217, 219, 230, 241, 258, 262, 266–68, 270–72, 281, 283–84, 295, 302–6, 308, 316, 319, 326, 329–30, 334
Thomas, L.-V., 255

Index of Names

Thomas, P., 76
Thucydides, 28
Tibiletti, C., 278
Tierno Galván, E., 154
Tillard, J. M.-R., 70, 230
Tillich, P., 301
Timmermann, J., 64
Tipler, F. J., xii, 45
Tiso, F., vii
Tobin, J., 255
Tödt, H. E., 13–14
Tornos, A., 209
Torrance, T. F., 298
Torres-Queiruga, A., 99, 221
Tournay, R. J., 81
Touze, L., 336
Trembelas, N., 301
Treschow, M., 161
Tresmontant, C., 314
Triacca, A. M., 291
Troeltsch, E., 310
Troisfontaines, J., 267
Tromp, N. J., 260
Trottmann, C., 278
Trütsch, J., viii, 340
Tsirpanlis, C. N., 196
Tychonius, 247
Tyranius Ruffinus, 108

Ulysses, 27

Vacant, A., xv
Van Bavel, T. J., 103
Van den Brock, R., 97
VanderKam, J. C., xi
Van der Kwaak, H., 60
Vanni, U., 63, 242
Van Steenberghen, F., 326
Van Unnik, W. C., 64, 294

Vernet, M., 154
Victorinus of Pettau, 245–46
Vigilantius, 315
Vigilius I, 103
Virgil, 119
Vogel, C., 292
Vögtle, A., 319
Voltaire (François-Marie Arouet), 263
Volz, P., 87
Von Allmen, J. J., 315
Von Balthasar, H. U., viii, xii, 110, 170, 179, 204, 209, 219–21, 267, 284, 308, 314, 340
Von Eijk, T. H. C., 93, 108
Von Harnack, A., 313
Vonier, A., 109
Von Weizsäcker, E. U., 121
Von Wright, G. H., 257
Vorgrimler, H., 110

Wächter, L., 78–79, 260
Wagner, H., 297
Wainwright, G., 67, 91
Waldenfels, H., 76
Walther, J. A., 163
Walz, J. B., 305
Weber, H. J., 77
Wegscheider, J. A. L., 21
Wehrt, H., 121
Weinandy, T. G., x
Weiss, J., 46–50, 53–54, 64
Weisse, C. H., 58
Wellhausen, J., 46
Wendland, H. D., 68
Wendt, H. H., 44
Werblowsky, R. J. Z., 49
Werner, M., 46–50, 54, 314

White, T. J., 185
Whitehead, A. N., xi, 43–44
Widmer, T., xiii
Wielockx, R., 185
William of Ockham, 22, 279
Williams, A. N., 165
Williams, D. D., 44
Winklhofer, A., 92, 203, 267
Winling, R., 187
Wissmann, H., 75
Wittgenstein, L., 256–57
Wittreich, J., 242
Wohlgschaft, H., 301, 314
Wood, A. S., 93
Wordsworth, W., 117
Wright, C. J. H., 83
Wright, J. H., 117
Wright, N. T., xi, 82
Wust, P., 19
Wuthnow, R., xii

Yarbro-Collins, A., 242
Yocum, J., x
Young, E., 255

Zähner, R. C., 75–76
Zaleski, C., xiii
Zedda, S., 61–63
Zeno of Verona, 284
Ziegenaus, A., x, 320, 340
Zimmerli, W., 83
Zimmermann, B., 307
Zorell, F., 90
Zubiri, X., 314
Zuzek, R., 300
Zwingli, H., 49, 298–99, 314, 339

Christ Our Hope: An Introduction to Eschatology was designed and typeset in StonePrint by Kachergis Book Design of Pittsboro, North Carolina. It was printed on 55-pound Natural Text and bound by Versa Press of East Peoria, Illinois.

www.ingramcontent.com/pod-product-compliance
Lightning Source LLC
Chambersburg PA
CBHW031404290426
44110CB00011B/253